2026
브랜드 만족 1위 수석합격 연속 배출

9급 공무원 영어 시험대비

박문각 공무원

기출문제

New Trend 단기합격 길라잡이

신경향 대비 합격률 4.2배 증가!

최신 기출 및 출제 기조 전환 완벽 반영

9급 기출 빅데이터 분석을 통한 핵심 기출문제 수록

어휘, 문법, 생활영어, 독해 전 영역 기출 단권화

진가영 편저

진가영 영어
반드시 한번에 다 잡는다 기출

PREFACE 머리말

수험생들에게 최고의 기출문제집이 될
합격까지, **반**드시 **한** 번에 **다**잡는다!
진가영 영어 반한다 기출을 펴내며...

안녕하세요, 단기합격의 길라잡이 진가영입니다.

모든 수험생이 알고 있듯이, 공무원 영어 시험에서 기출문제의 중요성은 아무리 강조해도 지나치지 않습니다. 하지만 단순히 기출문제를 풀고 해설을 확인하는 것만으로는 부족합니다. 진짜 실력으로 이어지는 학습을 위해서는 기출문제를 통해 이론을 다시 정리하고 실전 문제에 이론을 적용하는 훈련을 꾸준히 하며 출제 유형과 정답의 패턴, 출제 기조를 분석하는 학습이 반드시 필요합니다. 이러한 기출의 본질에 충실한 학습을 돕기 위해, **진가영 영어 반한다 기출**이 탄생했습니다. 이번 **진가영 영어 반한다 기출**은 모든 영역을 한 권에 담아 출간하게 되었습니다.

✪ 어휘 기출문제는 상세한 해설과 함께, 중요한 핵심 어휘들을 체계적으로 정리하여 기출을 기반으로 출제 가능성이 높은 어휘들을 효율적으로 학습할 수 있도록 구성하였다.

✪ 문법 기출문제를 영역별로 구분하여, 배운 이론들을 기출 문제에 적용해 보는 훈련이 가능하도록 구성하였다.

✪ 각 문법 영역에 대한 핵심 개념 정리와, 문제 풀이에 도움을 주는 실전 꿀팁인 '찐 Tip' 코너를 통해 학습 효과를 높일 수 있도록 구성하였다.

✪ 해설에서는 정답 해설뿐 아니라 오답 해설도 함께 제공하며, 각 선지가 출제된 문법 포인트까지 상세하게 표시하여 약점 파악이 가능하도록 구성하였다.

✪ 생활영어 기출문제는 최근 출제 기조 변화에 맞춰 효율적으로 대비할 수 있도록 구성하였다.

✪ 독해 기출문제를 영역별로 체계적으로 구분하여, 배운 이론을 실제 문제에 적용하는 과정을 훈련할 수 있도록 구성하였다.

✪ 기출 독해 어휘 중 핵심 어휘를 제시하며 어휘 테스트를 제공하여 독해의 기본 토대를 탄탄히 다질 수 있도록 구성하였다.

✪ 해설지에는 지문 속 정답 단서를 표시하여, 감으로 독해를 하는 것이 아니라 정확한 독해가 가능하도록 구성하였다.

이 기출문제집의 강점은 단순한 문제 풀이에 머무르지 않고, 기출문제를 통해 출제 알고리즘을 익히고, 시험장에서 단서를 바탕으로 확신을 가지고 정답을 고르는 실력을 키울 수 있도록 설계되었다는 점입니다. 또한 저자 직강과 함께 이 교재를 꾸준히 활용하신다면, 여러분은 더 이상 감으로 문제를 찍지 않고, 출제 의도를 간파하는 실전형 독해력과 문법·어휘·생활영어 실력을 갖추게 될 것입니다. 결국, 이 교재를 선택하는 순간 여러분은 합격에 최적화된 영어 학습서를 손에 넣은 것입니다. 매일 조금씩, 그러나 꾸준하게 자신의 공부 상태를 점검하고 복습한다면 여러분의 꿈은 반드시 이루어집니다.

진가영 영어 반한다 기출에 진심으로 반하셔서 반드시 빠른 합격을 이루시길 진심으로 응원합니다.

여러분들의 노력이 반드시 합격으로 이어지도록 현명한 길라잡이로서 더 좋은 수업을 통해 뵙도록 하겠습니다. ❀

Dreams come true!
꿈은 반드시 이루어진다!

진심을 다해 가르치는 영어 - 진가영

REVIEW '생생한' 합격 후기

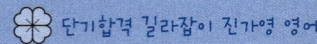
단기합격 길라잡이 진가영 영어

가영쌤과 점수 수직 상승을 만들어 낸 "생생한" 후기

★★★★★ **2025년 국가직 9급 일반행정 합격**　　　　　　　　　　김**

교재와 커리 구성만으로도 탄탄하게 이루어져 있지만 마지막으로 가영쌤만의 장점! 왜 가영쌤이어야 했는지, 그 이유를 꼽자면 바로 진심을 다해 수강생을 도와주시려고 한다는 점입니다! 저의 경우에는 처음 공시를 시작했을 때 어려움을 겪었던 문법 파트와, 공부 기간이 늘어남에도 불구하고 마땅한 해결책을 찾지 못해 힘들어했던 독해 순서 맞추기 유형과 문장 삽입 유형에 대한 고민이 깊을 때마다 가영쌤께 찾아가서 질문을 드리고 도움을 요청하였습니다. 그럴 때마다 항상 진심을 다해 도와주려 하시고, 구체적으로 어떻게 문제인지 정확하게 진단해 주시면서 명확한 솔루션을 주신 덕에 단점을 보완하고 무려 100점이라는 성적으로 합격할 수 있었습니다~!!~!! 항상 너무 감사드립니다 교수님~!!~!! Thank you for everything you've done for me!!

★★★★★ **2025년 국가직 9급 교정직 합격**　　　　　　　　　　한**

제가 공시하러 처음 왔을 때 2024년 4월 월간 모의고사 영어점수가 30점이었어요. 그러다 5월부터 수업을 들어가기 시작했는데 그때 임신 중인 선생님께서 저희를 위해 일요일에도 보강하시는 모습 보고 저는 이 선생님 밑에서 최고득점하고 싶은 마음이 들었습니다. 선생님 커리큘럼 상담 모든 게 다 반영돼서 95점이 나온 거 같아요. 인생에 목표가 있어 행복한 시간이었고 좋은 친구 옆에서 공부한 거에 감사하고 최고의 선생님의 가르침을 받아서 인생에서 가장 기억에 남을 순간일 것 같습니다. 앞으로 저는 더 많은 걸 도전할 거 같아요. 저는 꺾이지 않고 계속 노력하는 선생님이 너무 좋았습니다. 가끔 올라가서 인사 올리겠습니다. 존경하는 선생님.

★★★★★ **2025년 검찰직 합격**　　　　　　　　　　대**

2024년 1월부터 박문각 인강으로 공부해서 1년 3개월 동안 공부했고 검찰직 합격했습니다. 인강 들으면서 전화 상담까지 해주셨던 교수님은 진가영 교수님뿐이셔서, 게다가 영어가 심리적으로 오랫동안 힘든 과목이었기 때문에 감사한 마음뿐입니다. 워낙 영어가 취약 과목이었고 꽤 오랫동안 독해 때문에 힘든 시간을 보냈지만 임신, 출산하시면서도 강의에 영향 없이 최선을 다해 주시는 모습에 감동을 받았고 그만큼 교수님께서 이 일을 얼마나 소중히 하고 계시는지 느껴졌습니다. 교수님이 안보이는 곳에서 얼마나 노력하고 계시는지 너무 잘 알 것 같아서 그저 리스펙이라고 밖에는 표현할 길이 없습니다. 마지막 문법 특강 끝에 기도하시듯 손 모으고 말씀하시는 모습에 뭉클했고 나는 교수님처럼 내 일에 최선을 다한 적이 있었는지 스스로 반성도 하게 되었습니다. 간절한 시간을 보낸 만큼 앞으로 최선을 다해서 공직 생활하도록 하겠습니다.

★★★★★ **2025년 국가직 9급 우정직 합격**　　　　　　　　　　경**

제가 생각하는 가영쌤만의 장점은 첫째로, 미친 반복입니다. 공부가 하기 싫어도, 저절로 하게 되고, 강의를 듣지 않아도 떠오르는 경지가 될 때까지 정말 열심히 가르쳐주십니다. 동형 문제를 풀 때 알아서 개념이 뽑아져 나올 정도로 들었고, 단어강의는 최소 20회독을 했을 정도로 많이 복습하니 이젠 툭 치면 알아서 가영쌤이 가르쳐주신 내용이 나옵니다. 둘째로, 가영쌤의 친절하고 꼼꼼한 학생관리입니다. 현강에서는 학생들 하나하나 잘 챙겨주시고, 질문은 시간이 오래 걸려도 자세하게 받아주시며, 상담 신청했을 때 누구보다도 열정적인 자세로 상담을 받아주십니다. 카페에서도 학생들 질문을 잘 받아주시기도 하니, 현강생 뿐 아니라 인강생도 가영쌤의 정성을 느끼실 수 있습니다. 셋째로, 자신의 실력을 점검하고 보완할 수 있는 다양한 커리큘럼입니다. 구문이 부족하면 구문 강의로, 문법이 부족하면 단판승으로, 독해가 부족하면 독해 끝판왕으로, 신경향이 낯설면 신경향 독해 마스터로 보완할 수 있도록 세분화되어 있습니다. 꼭 모든 강의를 강제로 들을 필요는 없지만, 부족한 부분이 있다면 발췌하시는 것도 좋은 선택입니다.

CURRICULUM — '단기합격' 커리큘럼

진가영 영어
반한다 기출

단계	강의명	학습 내용 및 특징
[0단계] 입문	기초탄탄 입문 이론	**기초부터 탄탄하게, 차근차근 시작!** • 공무원 영어의 기초를 쉽게 이해하고, 탄탄하게 다질 수 있는 입문 강의 • 영어 공부가 처음인 분들도 기초부터 확실히 잡고, 영어에 대한 장벽을 낮춰주는 강의
[1단계] 이론 완성	✮ 단기합격 필수 커리 ✮ 단기합격 All In One (문법/독해/어휘)	**흔들리지 않는 실력을 위한 공무원 영어의 뼈대를 세우는 과정!** • 공무원 영어의 전반적인 이론 및 내용을 한 번에 배우고, 중요한 내용은 집중적으로 학습할 수 있는 강의 • 시험장에서 흔들리지 않는 토대를 만드는 필수 이론 과정을 완성하는 강의
[2단계] 기출 분석	반한다 기출 분석 시리즈 (독해/ 문법·어휘&생활영어)	**출제 경향 및 알고리즘 분석으로 문제를 보는 안목을 키우는 과정!** • 출제 경향과 알고리즘 분석을 통해 시험의 흐름을 완벽히 이해하고 배운 내용을 문제 풀이 실력으로 만드는 강의 • 자주 출제되는 문제 유형을 철저히 분석하며 실력을 쌓아 시험을 꿰뚫어 볼 수 있는 안목을 키우는 강의
[3단계] 문제 풀이	끝판왕 문제 풀이 N제 시리즈 (어휘/문법/독해)	**배운 것들을 문제에 빠르고 정확하게 적용하는 과정!** • 영역별 문제 풀이로 각 부분을 체계적으로 점검하고 약점을 보완해 점수 상승을 이끄는 강의 • 출제 예상 문제를 집중적으로 풀면서 빠르고 정확하게 문제를 풀 수 있는 기술을 배우는 강의
[4단계] 파이널	만점으로 가는 실전 동형 모의고사	**100% 실력 발휘를 위한 실전 모의고사 과정!** • 실제 시험과 유사한 구성의 고퀄리티 모의고사로 전 범위를 점검하고, 실력을 최종 완성하는 강의 • 다양한 난이도의 실전 동형 모의고사로 어떤 시험 상황에서도 굳건한 점수를 얻을 수 있도록 하는 강의
	'진족보' 마무리 합격 특강	**합격의 열쇠, 단 한 권으로 마지막 준비 완료!** • 시험 직전, 전 영역 핵심 내용을 완벽하게 총정리하며 부족한 부분까지 확실히 채우는 합격 특강 • 시험의 마지막 순간에, 쌓아 온 실력을 시험장에서 발휘하도록 돕는 총정리 특강

데일리 학습 [루틴 형성]

단기합격 VOCA
• 객관적 적중률로 검증된 공무원 전용 어휘 학습
• 필수 · 핵심 · 실무 어휘까지 한번에 총정리!

굿모닝 '기출 문장' 구문독해
• 양질의 기출 문장으로 꾸준한 30분 트레이닝
• 감이 아닌 구조로 읽어, 빠르고 정확한 해석 실력 완성!

매일합격[일일] 모의고사
• 하루 10문제로 가볍게 시작하는 영어 루틴
• 영어가 익숙해지고 실력이 쌓이는 가장 확실한 방법!

올타임 레전드 하프 모의고사
• 수업 시간에 배운 핵심 개념을 문제로 복습
• 중간 실력 점검으로 부족한 부분을 파악하고 보완!

ANALYSIS 최신 출제 경향

전반적인 최신 출제 경향

★ 이번 2025년 9급 영어 시험은 **전 영역에 걸쳐 기존 출제 기조를 유지**하면서도 예시문제 범위 내에서 변형된 형태로 출제되었습니다.

★ 기존 기출과 예시문제를 충분히 복습한 수험생이라면 대부분의 문제를 무리 없이 풀 수 있었을 것입니다.

★ 전반적인 **난이도는 무난한 편**이었으며, 크게 어렵다고 느껴질 문제는 많지 않았습니다. 다만, 수험생 간의 점수 차이를 만들어내는 **고난도 문제**가 각 영역마다 한 문제 정도씩 **출제**되었습니다.

★ 특히 **문법** 영역에서는 문맥을 바탕으로 **문장의 구조를 정확히 분석**해야 하는 문제가 눈에 띄었습니다. 단순 암기보다 **실전 문장 속에서 문법을 적용하고 해석하는 능력**이 중요한 시험이었습니다.

영역별 최신 출제 경향

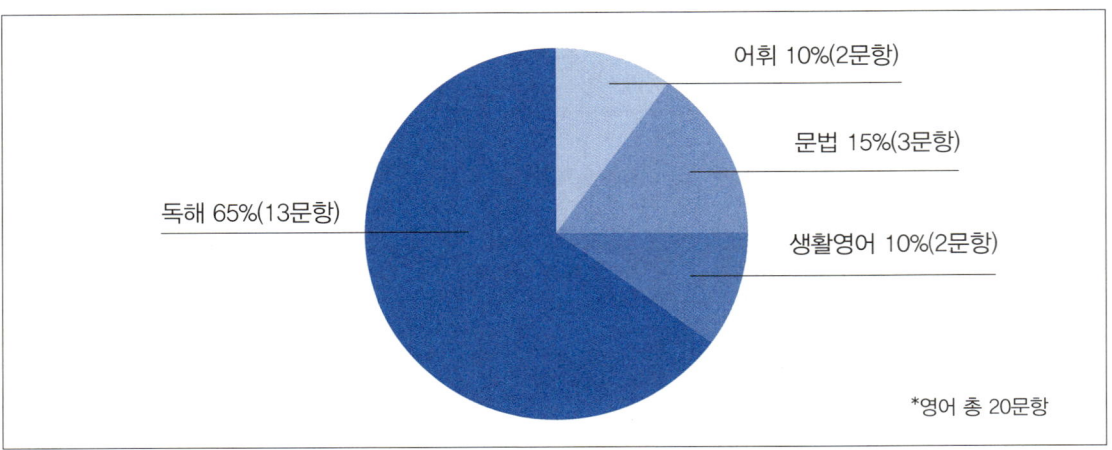

01 어휘 [2문항 출제]

★ 기존 9급 공무원 시험에서 **반복적으로 출제된 기출 어휘**가 다수 포함되었습니다.

★ 고등학교 수준의 익숙한 단어들도 일부 포함되어 있어 전반적인 체감 난이도는 무난하거나 살짝 어려운 수준이었습니다.

★ 빈칸 앞뒤 문장이나 전체 문맥 속에 **정답을 유추할 수 있는 분명한 단서**가 제시되었습니다.

02 문법 [3문항 출제]

★ 기존 9급 시험에서 **자주 출제된 문법 포인트를 기반으로** 문제가 출제되었습니다.

★ 문장은 비교적 길고, 주어·동사·수식어구 등이 **복합적으로 얽힌 구조**로 구성되었습니다.

★ 해석에 의존하기보다는, **문장을 빠르게 문법적으로 분해하여 핵심 요소를 파악하는 능력**이 중요했습니다.

★ 문법 지식뿐만 아니라, 문장 전체의 흐름을 이해하는 능력도 함께 요구되었습니다.

03 생활영어 [2문항 출제]

★ 표면적으로는 자연스러운 대화였지만, 그 속뜻이나 뉘앙스를 파악해야 정답을 도출할 수 있는 문제들이었습니다.

★ 표현이나 어휘를 정확히 외우지 않더라도, **앞뒤 문맥과 화자의 의도를 바탕으로 정답을 유추**할 수 있는 문제가 출제되었습니다.

04 독해 [13문항 출제]

★ 지문 유형, 질문 방식, 정답의 위치 등은 **기출 및 예시문제에서 반복적으로 사용된 구조와 매우 유사하게** 출제되었습니다.

★ 지문의 길이나 난이도는 중간 수준이었으나, 처음부터 끝까지 전부 해석하려 할 경우 **시간 부족이 발생할 수 있었습니다.**

★ 핵심 정보를 중심으로 효율적으로 읽는 능력이 요구되었으며, **구문독해 훈련을 통해 문장을 구조 단위로 끊어 읽는 것이 필요합니다.**

★ 특히 **빈칸 추론, 문장 삽입, 주제 파악, 무관한 문장 찾기** 등의 유형은 **전략적 접근과 풀이 방식 숙지**가 중요했습니다.

★ 정답은 대부분 **지문 속 명확한 단서에 근거해 도출**할 수 있었으며, 전체 지문을 모두 해석하기보다는 **핵심 문장을 정확히 파악하는 전략**이 필요합니다.

ANALYSIS 최신 출제 경향

✧ 2025년 국가직 9급 기출 내용 분석

01 어휘 영역 [총 2문항]

[1번] 빈칸	① currency 통화 ② identification 신원 확인 서류	③ insurance 보험 ④ luggage 수하물
[2번] 빈칸	① depriving 빼앗다(deprive) ② informing 통지하다(inform)	③ accusing 비난하다(accuse) ④ curing 치료하다(cure)

02 문법 영역 [총 3문항] (단판승 적중 포인트100 교재 기준)

[3번] 빈칸	적중 포인트 067 주의해야 할 조동사와 조동사 관용 표현 & 적중 포인트 034 완료시제와 잘 쓰이는 시간 부사
[12번] 밑줄	① 적중 포인트 078 등위접속사와 병렬 구조 ② 적중 포인트 055 감정 분사와 분사형 형용사 ③ 적중 포인트 039 현재시제 동사와 be동사의 수 일치 ④ 적중 포인트 078 등위접속사와 병렬 구조
[13번] 밑줄	① 적중 포인트 089 주의해야 할 전치사 ② 적중 포인트 060 to부정사의 명사적 역할 & 적중 포인트 078 등위접속사와 병렬 구조 ③ 적중 포인트 078 등위접속사와 병렬 구조 ④ 적중 포인트 054 분사 판별법[현재분사 VS 과거분사]

03 생활영어 영역 [총 2문항]

[4번] 빈칸	① Yes, it's an online meeting 네, 온라인 회의예요 ② Yes, be sure to reply to the email 네, 이메일에 꼭 답장하세요 ③ No, I didn't receive your text message 아니요, 문자 메시지를 받지 못했어요 ④ No, I don't have another meeting today 아니요, 오늘 다른 회의는 없어요
[5번] 빈칸	① I have already read it 나 이미 그거 읽었어 ② Lin Lee is the author Lin Lee가 저자야 ③ It originally belongs to me 그건 원래 내 거야 ④ She is one of my relatives in Korea 그녀는 한국에 있는 내 친척 중 한 명이야

04 독해 영역 [총 13문항]

	지문	유형		지문	유형
신유형 (7)	세트형 문항 (홈페이지 게시글)	제목 내용 불일치	기존 유형 (6)	대의 파악	주제
	세트형 문항 (안내문)	유의어 목적		일관성	문장 삽입
	단일형 문항 (전자메일)	목적		일관성	문장 제거
	단일형 문항 (안내문)	내용 불일치		일관성	순서 배열
	단일형 문항 (안내문)	내용 일치		빈칸 추론	빈칸

✧ 2025 지방직 9급 기출 내용 분석

01 어휘 영역 [총 2문항]

[1번] 빈칸	① nourish 영양을 주다, 키우다 ② eradicate 근절하다, 박멸하다	③ proliferate 급증하다, 확산되다 ④ detect 발견하다, 감지하다
[2번] 빈칸	① humility 겸손 ② sincerity 진심, 진실, 정직	③ frugality 절약, 검소 ④ punctuality 시간 엄수, 꼼꼼함

02 문법 영역 [총 3문항] (단판승 적중 포인트100 교재 기준)

[3번] 빈칸	적중 포인트 054 분사 판별법[현재분사 vs 과거분사]
[13번] 밑줄	① 적중 포인트 060 to부정사의 명사적 역할 ② 적중 포인트 088 전치사와 명사 목적어 ③ 적중 포인트 043 혼동하기 쉬운 주어와 동사 수 일치 ④ 적중 포인트 049 5형식 동사의 수동태 구조
[14번] 밑줄	① 적중 포인트 017 어순에 주의해야 할 형용사와 부사 ② 적중 포인트 080 부사절 접속사의 구분과 특징 ③ 적중 포인트 063 to부정사의 동사적 성질 ④ 적중 포인트 082 관계대명사의 선행사와 문장 구조

03 생활영어 영역 [총 2문항]

[4번] 빈칸	① I'm on a tight budget. 나는 예산이 빠듯해. ② I need to get in shape. 나는 몸매를 가꿀 필요가 있어. ③ It should clear up soon. 곧 날씨가 개일 거야. ④ I can pick you up later. 나중에 너를 태우러 갈게.
[5번] 빈칸	① How early do we need to distribute the materials 　자료를 얼마나 일찍 배포해야 하나요? ② Should we also have a digital version for sharing 　공유를 위해 디지털 버전도 준비해야 할까요? ③ Will the materials be printed in color or black and white 　자료는 컬러로 인쇄되나요, 아니면 흑백으로 인쇄되나요? ④ Are there any specific materials we should avoid including 　우리가 포함하지 말아야 할 특정 자료가 있나요?

04 독해 영역 [총 13문항]

	지문	유형		지문	유형
신유형 (7)	세트형 문항 (홈페이지 게시글)	제목 내용 불일치	기존 유형 (6)	대의 파악	주제
	세트형 문항 (홈페이지 게시글)	유의어 목적		일관성	순서 배열
	단일형 문항 (전자메일)	목적		일관성	문장 삽입
	단일형 문항 (홈페이지 게시글)	내용 일치		일관성	문장 제거
	단일형 문항 (안내문)	내용 불일치		빈칸 추론	빈칸

ANALYSIS 최신 출제 경향

◆ 9급 출제기조 전환 1차 예시문제

01 어휘 영역 [총 2문항]

[1번] 빈칸	① irregular 불규칙한, 고르지 못한 ② consistent 한결같은, 일관된	③ predictable 예측[예견]할 수 있는 ④ ineffective 효과[효력] 없는
[2번] 빈칸	① temporary 일시적인, 임시의 ② rational 이성[합리]적인	③ voluntary 자발적인, 임의적인 ④ commercial 상업의, 상업적인

02 문법 영역 [총 3문항] (단판승 적중 포인트100 교재 기준)

[3번] 빈칸	적중 포인트 038 시제 관련 표현
[4번] 밑줄	① 적중 포인트 039 현재시제 동사와 be동사의 수 일치 ② 적중 포인트 032 의미와 구조에 주의해야 할 타동사 ③ 적중 포인트 014 형용사와 부사의 차이 ④ 적중 포인트 053 암기해야 할 동명사 표현
[5번] 밑줄	① 적중 포인트 053 암기해야 할 동명사 표현 ② 적중 포인트 082 관계대명사의 선행사와 문장 구조 ③ 적중 포인트 054 분사 판별법[현재분사 VS 과거분사] ④ 적중 포인트 015 주의해야 할 형용사

03 생활영어 영역 [총 2문항]

[6번] 빈칸	① Yes, I'd like to upgrade to business class. 네, 비즈니스 클래스로 업그레이드하고 싶어요. ② No, I'd like to buy a one-way ticket. 아니요, 편도 티켓을 사고 싶어요. ③ No, I don't have any luggage. 아니요, 짐은 없습니다. ④ Yes, I want an aisle seat. 네, 복도 쪽 좌석을 원해요.
[7번] 빈칸	① You need to bring your own laptop. 개인 노트북을 직접 가져와야 합니다. ② I already have a reservation. 저는 이미 예약했어요. ③ Follow the instructions on the bulletin board. 게시판의 안내를 따르세요. ④ You should call the doctor's office for an appointment. 진료 예약을 하시려면 병원에 전화하셔야 해요.

04 독해 영역 [총 13문항]

	지문	유형		지문	유형
신유형 (6)	세트형 문항 (전자메일)	목적 유의어	기존 유형 (7)	대의 파악	주제
				대의 파악	요지
	세트형 문항 (안내문)	제목 내용 불일치		일관성	문장 제거
	단일형 문항 (홈페이지 게시글)	내용 불일치		일관성	문장 삽입
				일관성	순서 배열
	단일형 문항 (홈페이지 게시글)	내용 일치		빈칸 추론	빈칸

✧ 9급 출제기조 전환 2차 예시문제

01 어휘 영역 [총 2문항]

[1번] 빈칸	① cozy 편한, 아늑한 ② stuffy 답답한, 통풍이 되지 않는	③ ample 충분한, 풍만한 ④ cramped 비좁은
[2번] 빈칸	① secret 비밀, 기밀 ② priority 우선 사항, 우선(권)	③ solution 해결책, 해법 ④ opportunity 기회

02 문법 영역 [총 3문항] (단판승 적중 포인트100 교재 기준)

[3번] 빈칸	적중 포인트 034 완료시제와 잘 쓰이는 시간 부사 & 적중 포인트 045 능동태와 수동태의 차이
[4번] 밑줄	① 적중 포인트 054 분사 판별법[현재분사 VS 과거분사] ② 적중 포인트 078 등위접속사와 병렬 구조 ③ 적중 포인트 029 명사나 형용사를 목적격 보어로 취하는 5형식 동사 ④ 적중 포인트 086 관계부사의 선행사와 완전 구조
[5번] 밑줄	① 적중 포인트 019 주어만 있으면 완전한 1형식 자동사 ② 적중 포인트 045 능동태와 수동태의 차이 ③ 적중 포인트 045 능동태와 수동태의 차이 ④ 적중 포인트 045 능동태와 수동태의 차이 & 054 분사 판별법[현재분사 VS 과거분사]

03 생활영어 영역 [총 2문항]

[6번] 빈칸	① Could I have your contact information? 연락처를 알 수 있을까요? ② Can you tell me the exact date of your meeting? 회의가 정확히 언제인지 알려주실 수 있나요? ③ Do you need a beam projector or a copy machine? 빔프로젝터나 복사기가 필요하신가요? ④ How many people are going to attend the meeting? 회의에 참석할 사람은 몇 명인가요?
[7번] 빈칸	① You can save energy because it's electric 전기식이라 에너지를 절약할 수 있어요 ② Just apply for a permit to park your own bike 자전거를 주차하려면 허가증만 신청하세요 ③ Just download the bike sharing app and pay online 공유 자전거 앱을 다운로드하고 온라인으로 결제하면 됩니다 ④ You must wear a helmet at all times for your safety 안전을 위해 항상 헬멧을 착용해야 합니다

04 독해 영역 [총 13문항]

	지문	유형		지문	유형
신유형 (6)	세트형 문항 (홈페이지 게시글)	내용 일치 유의어	기존 유형 (7)	대의 파악	주제
	세트형 문항 (안내문)	제목 내용 불일치		대의 파악	요지
	단일형 문항 (전자메일)	목적		일관성	문장 제거
	단일형 문항 (안내문)	내용 불일치		일관성	문장 삽입
				일관성	순서 배열
				빈칸 추론	빈칸

GUIDE 구성 및 특징

단기합격 길라잡이 진가영 영어

1 어휘 기출문제는 상세한 해설과 함께, 중요한 핵심 어휘들을 체계적으로 정리하여 기출을 기반으로 출제 가능성이 높은 어휘들을 효율적으로 학습할 수 있도록 구성하였다.

03

정답 ③

지문 해석

분명히, 언어 예술의 어떤 측면도 배움이나 가르침에 있어서 분리되어 있지 않다. 듣기, 말하기, 읽기, 쓰기, 보기, 그리고 시각적 표현은 서로 관계가 있다.

선지 해석

① distinct 뚜렷한, 명백한
② distorted 비뚤어진, 왜곡된
   가 있는

Vol. 2 문법

PART 01 문장과 동사
출제 경향 분석 & 출제 내용 점검 ········· 58
Chapter 01 문장의 이해
반드시 한번에 다잡는 최빈출 개념 정리 ········· 59
실전 기출문제 ········· 60
Chapter 02 단어의 이해
반드시 한번에 다잡는 최빈출 개념 정리 ········· 61
실전 기출문제 ········· 62

PART 03 조동사와 조동사를 활용한 구문
출제 경향 분석 & 출제 내용 점검 ········· 94
Chapter 10 조동사
반드시 한번에 다잡는 최빈출 개념 정리 ········· 95
실전 기출문제 ········· 96
Chapter 11 도치 구문과 강조 구문
반드시 한번에 다잡는 최빈출 개념 정리 ········· 98
실전 기출문제 ········· 99
Chapter 12 가정법
반드시 한번에 다잡는 최빈출 개념 정리 ········· 101
실전 기출문제 ········· 102

2 문법 기출문제를 영역별로 구분하여, 배운 이론들을 기출문제에 적용해 보는 훈련이 가능하도록 구성하였다.

3 각 문법 영역에 대한 핵심 개념 정리와, 문제 풀이에 도움을 주는 실전 꿀팁인 '찐 Tip' 코너를 통해 학습 효과를 높일 수 있도록 구성하였다.

01

정답 ③

정답 해설

③ [적중 포인트 001] 문장의 구성요소
문장에 동사가 2개 존재하기 위해서는 접속사가 필요하다. 밑줄 친 부분인은 be동사와 vary라는 동사가 2개 존재하기 때문에 옳지 않다. 문맥상 be동사를 쓰는 것보다 vary가 더 자연스러우므로 be vary 대신 be를 삭제한 vary로 써야 올바르다.

찐Tip vary는 '다르다, 달라지다'의 뜻의 1형식 자동사로 주로 쓰인다.

오답 해설

① [적중 포인트 054] 분사 판별법[현재분사 VS 과거분사]
& [적중 포인트 039] 현재시제 동사와 be동사의 수 일치
명사 뒤의 현재분사와 과거분사는 명사를 수식하는 형용사적 용법으로서 모두 올 수 있지만 타동사 뒤에 목적어가 있으면 현재분사형으로, 목적어가 없으면 과거분사형으로 쓴다. 따라서 목적어(an earthquake)가 있으므로 현재분사로 올바르게 쓰였다. 또한 주어와 동사 사이에 수식어로 인해 주어와 동사가 멀리 떨어져 있으면 주어 동사 수 일치 확인도 필요하다. 주어는 Fire 단수형이므로 단수동사 is가 올바르게 쓰였다.

찐Tip of + 추상명사(of special interest)는 형용사 역할을 하므로 be

4 해설에서는 정답 해설뿐 아니라 오답 해설도 함께 제공하며, 각 선지가 출제된 문법 포인트까지 상세하게 표시하여 약점 파악이 가능하도록 구성하였다.

⑤ 생활영어 기출문제는 최근 출제 기조 변화에 맞춰 효율적으로 대비할 수 있도록 구성하였다.

생활영어 유형 학습 전략

수험생들은 생활영어 문제에 대비하기 위해 빈칸 유형을 중심으로 학습을 진행해야 에서 쓰이는 표현들을 다루기 때문에, 문맥 속에서 적절한 단어나 표현을 추론하는 훈 단순히 어휘를 알고 있는지 여부만을 묻는 것이 아니라, 실제 상황에서 그 단어가 요구한다. 이에 따라, 기본적인 어휘력 강화는 물론이고, 실용적인 문장 구조와 문 중요하다. 그러므로 수험생들은 다양한 예문과 함께 생활영어 빈칸 문제를 풀어보는 꾸준히 하며, 문맥을 읽고 적합한 답을 추론하는 능력을 키워야 한다. 이와 함께, ⅍ 숙지하고, 다양한 생활 상황에서 쓰이는 중요한 표현을 문제를 통해 체득하는 것이

Vol. 3 독해

PART 01 홈페이지 게시글 유형
- 출제 경향 분석 ········· 124
- 반드시 한번에 다잡는 '홈페이지 게시글' 유형 기출 독해 어휘 ··· 124
- 실전 기출문제 ········· 125
- 홈페이지 게시글 유형 기출 독해 어휘 복습 TEST ····· 130

PART 02 전자메일 유형
- 출제 경향 분석 ········· 132
- 반드시 한번에 다잡는 '전자메일' 유형 기출 독해 어휘 ··· 132

PART 06 문장 삽입 유형
- 출제 경향 분석 ········· 188
- 반드시 한번에 다잡는 '문장 삽입' 유형 기출 독해 어휘 ··· 188
- 실전 기출문제 ········· 189
- 문장 삽입 유형 기출 독해 어휘 복습 TEST ····· 204

PART 07 순서 배열 유형
- 출제 경향 분석 ········· 206
- 반드시 한번에 다잡는 '순서 배열' 유형 기출 독해 어휘 ··· 206
- 실전 기출문제 ········· 207
- 순서 배열 유형 기출 독해 어휘 복습 TEST ····· 225

PART 08 빈칸 추론 유형

⑥ 독해 기출문제를 영역별로 체계적으로 구분하여, 배운 이론을 실제 문제에 적용하는 과정을 훈련할 수 있도록 구성하였다.

⑦ 기출 독해 어휘 중 핵심 어휘를 제시하며 어휘 테스트를 제공하여 독해의 기본 토대를 탄탄히 다질 수 있도록 구성하였다.

01 홈페이지 게시글 유형 기출 독해 어휘 복습 TEST

1	exclude		21	approved
2	common		22	vehicle
3	plastic waste		23	post
4	reusable		24	registered
5	biodegradable		25	prosperous
			26	substantial

04 정답 ④

정답 해설
본문의 여덟 번째 문장에서 '등록된 차량 소유자에게 딱지가 우편으로 발송된다'라고 언급하고 있다. 따라서 글의 내용과 일치하는 것은 ④이다.

오답 해설
① 본문의 세 번째 문장에서 '링크를 클릭하거나 결제 세부 정보를 제공하지 마십시오'라고 언급하고 있으므로 일치하지 않는다.
② 본문의 네 번째 문장에서 '해당 메시지는 휴대폰 서비스 제공업체에 신고한 후 삭제하십시오'라고 언급하고 있으므로 일치하지 않는다.
③ 본문의 다섯 번째 문장에서 '저희는 문자, 미디어, 또는 소셜 미디어를 통해 과태료를 고지하지 않는다'라고 언급하고 있으므로 일치하지 않는다.

지문 해석
경고! 가짜 주차 위반 딱지 결제 문자 메시지
우리는 연체된 주차 위반 딱지 과태료를 납부하라는 문자 메시지를 통해 사람들을 노리는 사기 사건에 대해 통지받았습니다.
• 이러한 문자 메시지는 저희가 보낸 것이 아닙니다.
• 링크를 클릭하거나 결제 세부 정보를 제공하지 마십시오.

06 정답 ③

정답 해설
이 글은 NHC Foundation이라는 기관이 무엇을 하는 곳이며, NHC를 어떻게 지원하고 있는지를 독자에게 알리고 있다. 초반부에서는 건강이 인권의 중요한 요소이며, 사회적 안녕과 경제 성장, 평화에 기여한다고 설명하면서 건강의 중요성을 강조하고 있다. 그러나 건강에 대한 접근이 공평하지 않다는 문제점을 지적하며, 이 문제 해결을 위한 기관으로 NHC와 NHC Foundation을 소개하고 있다. 따라서 글의 목적으로 가장 적절한 것은 ③이다.

지문 해석
사람들을 위한 건강
사람들은 행복하고, 건강하며, 번영하는 삶을 살 수 있어야 합니다. 건강은 인권의 본질적인 요소이며, 사회적 복지, 경제 성장, 그리고 평화에 중요한 기여를 합니다.
하지만 건강에 대한 접근은 공평하지 않습니다.
국립보건센터 재단(NHC 재단)은 국립보건센터(NHC)가 모든 사람들이 최고 수준의 건강을 누리는 나라를 실현하겠다는 비전을 달성할 수 있도록 지원하기 위해 존재합니다. NHC는 건강을 증진하기 위한 계속

⑧ 해설지에는 지문 속 정답 단서를 표시하여, 감으로 독해를 하는 것이 아니라 정확한 독해가 가능하도록 구성하였다.

CONTENTS 차례

Vol. 1 어휘 & 생활영어

PART 01 어휘
출제 경향 분석 & 어휘 유형 문항 수 …………… 18
출제되는 어휘 & 출제되는 유형 ………………… 18
반드시 한번에 다잡는 최빈출 어휘 정리 ………… 19

Chapter 01 국가직 9급 핵심 기출문제
실전 기출문제 ……………………………………… 20

Chapter 02 지방직 9급 핵심 기출문제
실전 기출문제 ……………………………………… 31

Chapter 03 2025년 출제 기조 전환 예시 문제
실전 기출문제 ……………………………………… 40

PART 02 생활영어
출제 경향 분석 & 생활영어 문항 수 ……………… 42
출제되는 유형 & 생활영어 유형 학습 전략 ……… 42
반드시 한번에 다잡는 실전 생활영어 표현 ……… 43

Chapter 01 국가직 및 지방직 최신 4개년 핵심 기출문제
실전 기출문제 ……………………………………… 44

Chapter 02 국가직 및 지방직 기타 핵심 기출문제
실전 기출문제 ……………………………………… 50

Chapter 03 2025년 출제 기조 전환 예시 문제
실전 기출문제 ……………………………………… 54

Vol. 2 문법

PART 01 문장과 동사
출제 경향 분석 & 출제 내용 점검 ………………… 58

Chapter 01 문장의 이해
반드시 한번에 다잡는 최빈출 개념 정리 ………… 59
실전 기출문제 ……………………………………… 60

Chapter 02 단어의 이해
반드시 한번에 다잡는 최빈출 개념 정리 ………… 61
실전 기출문제 ……………………………………… 62

Chapter 03 동사의 유형
반드시 한번에 다잡는 최빈출 개념 정리 ………… 63
실전 기출문제 ……………………………………… 64

Chapter 04 동사의 시제
반드시 한번에 다잡는 최빈출 개념 정리 ………… 68
실전 기출문제 ……………………………………… 69

Chapter 05 주어와 동사 수 일치
반드시 한번에 다잡는 최빈출 개념 정리 ………… 71
실전 기출문제 ……………………………………… 72

Chapter 06 수동태
반드시 한번에 다잡는 최빈출 개념 정리 ………… 76
실전 기출문제 ……………………………………… 77

PART 02 준동사
출제 경향 분석 & 출제 내용 점검 ………………… 82

Chapter 07 동명사
반드시 한번에 다잡는 최빈출 개념 정리 ………… 83
실전 기출문제 ……………………………………… 84

Chapter 08 분사
반드시 한번에 다잡는 최빈출 개념 정리 ………… 85
실전 기출문제 ……………………………………… 86

Chapter 09 부정사
반드시 한번에 다잡는 최빈출 개념 정리 ………… 90
실전 기출문제 ……………………………………… 91

PART 03 조동사와 조동사를 활용한 구문
출제 경향 분석 & 출제 내용 점검 ………………… 94

Chapter 10 조동사
반드시 한번에 다잡는 최빈출 개념 정리 ………… 95
실전 기출문제 ……………………………………… 96

Chapter 11 도치 구문과 강조 구문
반드시 한번에 다잡는 최빈출 개념 정리 ………… 98
실전 기출문제 ……………………………………… 99

Chapter 12 가정법
반드시 한번에 다잡는 최빈출 개념 정리 ………… 101
실전 기출문제 ……………………………………… 102

PART 04 연결어

출제 경향 분석 & 출제 내용 점검 ···················· 104

Chapter 13 접속사
반드시 한번에 다잡는 최빈출 개념 정리 ·············· 105
실전 기출문제 ··· 106

Chapter 14 관계사
반드시 한번에 다잡는 최빈출 개념 정리 ·············· 110
실전 기출문제 ··· 111

Chapter 15 전치사
반드시 한번에 다잡는 최빈출 개념 정리 ·············· 114
실전 기출문제 ··· 115

PART 05 비교 구문

출제 경향 분석 & 출제 내용 점검 ···················· 116

Chapter 16 비교 구문
반드시 한번에 다잡는 최빈출 개념 정리 ·············· 117
실전 기출문제 ··· 118

Vol. 3 독해

PART 01 홈페이지 게시글 유형

출제 경향 분석 ·· 124
반드시 한번에 다잡는 '홈페이지 게시글' 유형 기출 독해 어휘 ··· 124
실전 기출문제 ··· 125
홈페이지 게시글 유형 기출 독해 어휘 복습 TEST ··········· 130

PART 02 전자메일 유형

출제 경향 분석 ·· 132
반드시 한번에 다잡는 '전자메일' 유형 기출 독해 어휘 ······· 132
실전 기출문제 ··· 133
전자메일 유형 기출 독해 어휘 복습 TEST ················ 137

PART 03 안내문 유형

출제 경향 분석 ·· 138
반드시 한번에 다잡는 '안내문' 유형 기출 독해 어휘 ········ 138
실전 기출문제 ··· 139
안내문 유형 기출 독해 어휘 복습 TEST ·················· 145

PART 04 중심 내용 파악 유형

출제 경향 분석 ·· 147
반드시 한번에 다잡는 '중심 내용 파악' 유형 기출 독해 어휘 ··· 147
실전 기출문제 ··· 148
중심 내용 파악 유형 기출 독해 어휘 복습 TEST ············ 168

PART 05 문장 제거 유형

출제 경향 분석 ·· 170
반드시 한번에 다잡는 '문장 제거' 유형 기출 독해 어휘 ······ 170
실전 기출문제 ··· 171
문장 제거 유형 기출 독해 어휘 복습 TEST ················ 186

PART 06 문장 삽입 유형

출제 경향 분석 ·· 188
반드시 한번에 다잡는 '문장 삽입' 유형 기출 독해 어휘 ······ 188
실전 기출문제 ··· 189
문장 삽입 유형 기출 독해 어휘 복습 TEST ················ 204

PART 07 순서 배열 유형

출제 경향 분석 ·· 206
반드시 한번에 다잡는 '순서 배열' 유형 기출 독해 어휘 ······ 206
실전 기출문제 ··· 207
순서 배열 유형 기출 독해 어휘 복습 TEST ················ 225

PART 08 빈칸 추론 유형

출제 경향 분석 ·· 227
반드시 한번에 다잡는 '빈칸 추론' 유형 기출 독해 어휘 ······ 227
실전 기출문제 ··· 228
빈칸 추론 유형 기출 독해 어휘 복습 TEST ················ 254

진가영 영어
반한다 기출

진가영 영어연구소 | cafe.naver.com/easyenglish7

PART 01 어휘
PART 02 생활영어

PART 01 어휘

출제 경향 분석

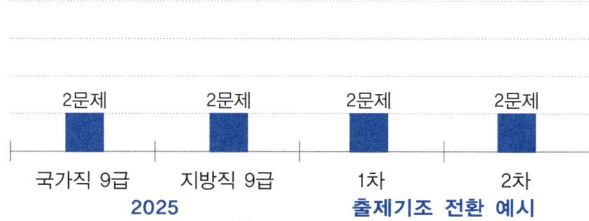

어휘유형 문항수

현재 시행 중인 9급 공무원 영어 시험에서는 총 20문항이 출제되며, 이 중 어휘 문제는 2문항으로 출제되고 있다. 과거 출제 기조 전환 전에는 유의어 추론 문제가 독해 지문 내에서 3~4문항 출제되기도 했으나, 최근 기조에 따르면 유의어 문제는 독해 유형에서 1문항만 등장하고 있으며, 실질적인 어휘 문항은 빈칸 어휘 2문항으로 보는 것이 타당하다. 따라서, 수험생은 직접 어휘력을 측정하는 빈칸 어휘 유형에 초점을 맞추어 기본 어휘력 강화와 문맥 속 의미 추론 훈련에 집중해야 하며, 유의어 추론은 독해 전략의 일부로 병행 학습하는 것이 효율적이다.

출제되는 어휘

어휘의 정확한 범위를 단정 지을 수는 없지만 분명 공무원 시험에 출제되는 어휘의 범위를 예측할 수 있고 그 범위 내에서 크게 벗어나지 않는 선에서 출제되고 있다. 최근 출제되는 경향으로 종합해보면 어휘의 범위는 공무원 시험에서 기출된 어휘들과 중학교 또는 고등학교에서 다뤄지는 다소 평이한 어휘들 위주로 출제되고 있음을 판단할 수 있다. 특히, 「New Trend 단기합격 VOCA」 교재는 이러한 출제 기조 전환 예시문제들의 경향을 반영하여 구성되어있기 때문에 사실상 「New Trend 단기합격 VOCA」를 성실하게 외우고 빈칸 유형 문제 풀이 연습을 꾸준히 해준다면 시험장에서 무난하게 어휘 문제를 맞힐 수 있다.

출제되는 유형

빈칸 유형은 말 그대로 빈칸에 들어갈 적절한 어휘를 고르는 문제이다. 단어 문제를 위한 빈칸 유형은 문장이 짧게 출제되기 때문에 긴 독해 지문에서 주어지는 빈칸 문제보다는 부담이 적은 편이다. 하지만, 유의어 유형보다는 빈칸 유형이 더 어려운 유형에 속하기 때문에 이 유형을 제대로 대비하기 위해서는 반드시 지문 속에 존재하는 단서를 찾아 정확하게 정답을 고르는 연습이 필요하다. 이때 기본이 되는 것은 구문 해석 실력이고 탄탄한 독해 실력을 갖추기 위해 반드시 '굿모닝 기출 문장 구문독해' 강의와 '신독기(신경향 독해 기본 체력 다지기) 구문독해' 강의를 활용하여 구문 실력을 보완한다면 분명 빈칸 유형 문제도 큰 무리 없이 정답을 맞힐 수 있을 것이다.

반드시 한번에 다잡는 최빈출 어휘 정리

- priority 우선(권), 우선 사항
- identify 발견하다, 확인하다, 동일시하다
- facilitate 가능하게[용이하게] 하다, 촉진[조장]하다
- interfere 간섭하다 (in), 방해하다 (with)
- examine 조사하다, 검사하다
- disclose 밝히다, 드러내다
- deprive 빼앗다, 면직[파면]하다
- mandatory 명령의, 의무적인, 강제적인
- discern 식별하다, 분별하다, 알아보다, 인식하다
- underestimate 과소평가하다, 경시하다, 얕보다
- comprehend 이해하다, 포함하다
- intimate 친밀한, 사적인, 개인적인
- abandon 버리다, 포기하다
- transparency 투명성
- exhaust 기진맥진하게 하다, 고갈시키다
- engage 끌다, 사로잡다, 몰두시키다, 고용하다, 약속하다, 약혼시키다
- acquaint 익히다, 숙지하다
- account 설명, 계좌, 간주하다, 여기다
- intimidate 겁을 주다, 위협하다
- imitate 모방하다, 흉내 내다
- provoke 화나게 하다, 유발하다, 선동하다
- reserved 내성적인, 과묵한, 보류된, 예약된
- obsolete 구식의, 쇠퇴한, 쓸모없는

Chapter 01 국가직 9급 핵심 기출문제

01 밑줄 친 부분에 들어갈 말로 가장 적절한 것은?

2025. 국가직 9급

> All international travelers must carry acceptable _____ when entering Canada. For example, a passport is the only reliable and universally accepted document when traveling abroad.

① currency
② identification
③ insurance
④ luggage

02 밑줄 친 부분에 들어갈 말로 가장 적절한 것은?

2025. 국가직 9급

> We are polluting the oceans, killing the fish and thereby _____ ourselves of invaluable food supply.

① depriving
② informing
③ accusing
④ curing

03 밑줄 친 부분에 들어갈 말로 가장 적절한 것은?

2024. 국가직 9급

> Obviously, no aspect of the language arts stands alone either in learning or in teaching. Listening, speaking, reading, writing, viewing, and visually representing are _____.

① distinct
② distorted
③ interrelated
④ independent

04 밑줄 친 부분에 들어갈 말로 가장 적절한 것은?

2024. 국가직 9급

> The money was so cleverly _____ that we were forced to abandon our search for it.

① spent
② hidden
③ invested
④ delivered

05 밑줄 친 부분에 들어갈 말로 가장 적절한 것은?

2024. 국가직 9급 변형

To _____ the anxiety of the citizens, the mayor announced an increase in police patrols in the affected areas.

① soothe
② counter
③ enlighten
④ assimilate

06 밑줄 친 부분에 들어갈 말로 가장 적절한 것은?

2024. 국가직 9급 변형

Many people _____ the dedication and effort required to achieve true mastery in any field, often believing it comes easily to those who succeed.

① discern
② dissatisfy
③ underline
④ underestimate

07 밑줄 친 부분에 들어갈 말로 가장 적절한 것은?

2024. 국가직 9급 변형

Despite having prepared thoroughly for the presentation, she was still _____ about how her ideas would be received by the audience.

① anxious
② fortunate
③ reputable
④ courageous

08 밑줄 친 부분에 들어갈 말로 가장 적절한 것은?

2023. 국가직 9급 변형

Jane wanted to have a small wedding rather than a fancy one. Thus, she planned to invite her family and a few of her _____ friends to eat delicious food and have some pleasant moments.

① nosy
② intimate
③ rigorous
④ considerable

09 밑줄 친 부분에 들어갈 말로 가장 적절한 것은?

2023. 국가직 9급 변형

Due to _____ disruptions in public transportation, the city implemented a plan to provide temporary shuttle services during peak hours.

① virtuous
② reticent
③ ingenious
④ intermittent

10 밑줄 친 부분에 들어갈 말로 가장 적절한 것은?

2023. 국가직 9급 변형

Because of the pandemic, the company had to _____ the plan to provide the workers with various training programs.

① convince
② release
③ mount
④ suspend

11 밑줄 친 부분에 들어갈 말로 가장 적절한 것은?

2023. 국가직 9급 변형

The committee will not _____ any late submissions, so it's important to meet the deadline if you want your proposal to be considered.

① accept
② deteriorate
③ postpone
④ abridge

12 밑줄 친 부분에 들어갈 말로 가장 적절한 것은?

2022. 국가직 9급 변형

For years, detectives have been trying to _____ the mystery of the sudden disappearance of the twin brothers.

① solve
② create
③ imitate
④ meditate

13 밑줄 친 부분에 들어갈 말로 가장 적절한 것은?

2022. 국가직 9급

> Before the couple experienced parenthood, their four-bedroom house seemed unnecessarily _____.

① hidden
② luxurious
③ empty
④ solid

14 밑줄 친 부분에 들어갈 말로 가장 적절한 것은?

2022. 국가직 9급 변형

> The boss hit the _____ when he saw that we had already spent the entire budget in such a short period of time.

① sack
② road
③ book
④ roof

15 밑줄 친 부분에 들어갈 말로 가장 적절한 것은?

2022. 국가직 9급

> A mouse potato is the computer _____ of television's couch potato: someone who tends to spend a great deal of leisure time in front of the computer in much the same way the couch potato does in front of the television.

① technician
② equivalent
③ network
④ simulation

16 밑줄 친 부분에 들어갈 말로 가장 적절한 것은?

2022. 국가직 9급 변형

> Mary decided to _____ her Spanish before going to South America.

① review
② curtail
③ defend
④ dismiss

17 밑줄 친 부분에 들어갈 말로 가장 적절한 것은?

2021. 국가직 9급 변형

> A perfect _____ of flavors made the dish incredibly delicious, leaving everyone at the table amazed.

① combination
② comparison
③ place
④ case

18 밑줄 친 부분에 들어갈 말로 가장 적절한 것은?

2021. 국가직 9급 변형

> The influence of Jazz has been so _____ that most popular music owes its stylistic roots to jazz.

① deceptive
② ubiquitous
③ persuasive
④ disastrous

19 밑줄 친 부분에 들어갈 말로 가장 적절한 것은?

2021. 국가직 9급 변형

> This novel is about the _____ parents of an unruly teenager who quits school to start a business.

① callous
② vexed
③ reputable
④ confident

20 밑줄 친 부분에 들어갈 말로 가장 적절한 것은?

2021. 국가직 9급 변형

> A group of young demonstrators attempted to _____ into the police station.

① bump
② run
③ turn
④ break

21 밑줄 친 부분에 들어갈 말로 가장 적절한 것은?

2020. 국가직 9급 변형

> She was very _____ about her concerns during the meeting, not holding anything back.

① frank
② logical
③ implicit
④ passionate

22 밑줄 친 부분에 들어갈 말로 가장 적절한 것은?

2020. 국가직 9급 변형

> The very bright neon sign was _____ from a mile away, so everyone looked at it.

① passive
② vaporous
③ dangerous
④ conspicuous

23 밑줄 친 부분에 들어갈 말로 가장 적절한 것은?

2020. 국가직 9급

> He's the best person to tell you how to get there because he knows the city _____.

① eventually
② culturally
③ thoroughly
④ tentatively

24 밑줄 친 부분에 들어갈 말로 가장 적절한 것은?

2020. 국가직 9급 변형

> The university decided to _____ Dr. Smith by naming the new research facility after him, recognizing his groundbreaking work in the field of medicine.

① honor
② compose
③ discard
④ join

25 밑줄 친 부분에 들어갈 말로 가장 적절한 것은?

2019. 국가직 9급 변형

> Natural Gas World subscribers will receive accurate and reliable key facts and figures about what is going on in the industry, so they are fully able to _____ what concerns their business.

① discern
② confine
③ undermine
④ abandon

26 밑줄 친 부분에 들어갈 말로 가장 적절한 것은?

2019. 국가직 9급 변형

> The film's special effects were incredibly _____, creating a visually stunning experience that captivated the audience.

① overwhelmed
② impressive
③ depressed
④ neutral

27 밑줄 친 부분에 들어갈 말로 가장 적절한 것은?

2019. 국가직 9급 변형

> Due to the new regulations, it is _____ for businesses to report their financial earnings quarterly to ensure transparency and accountability.

① complimentary
② enticing
③ mandatory
④ innovative

28 밑줄 친 부분에 들어갈 말로 가장 적절한 것은?

2019. 국가직 9급 변형

> The company finally _____ the details of their new product launch during the press conference.

① disclosed
② exploded
③ abated
④ disappointed

29 밑줄 친 부분에 들어갈 말로 가장 적절한 것은?

2018. 국가직 9급 변형

> _____ neighborhoods often face challenges such as limited access to healthcare, poor infrastructure, and high unemployment rates.

① Itinerant
② Impoverished
③ Sensory
④ Indigenous

30 밑줄 친 부분에 들어갈 말로 가장 적절한 것은?

2017. 국가직 9급 변형

> He _____ the constant noise from the construction site next door and complained to the management.

① defended
② detested
③ confirmed
④ abandoned

31 밑줄 친 부분에 들어갈 말로 가장 적절한 것은?

2017. 국가직 9급 변형

> The weather was _____ for this time of year, with snow falling unexpectedly in the middle of spring season.

① odd
② ongoing
③ obvious
④ offensive

32 밑줄 친 부분에 들어갈 말로 가장 적절한 것은?

2017. 국가직 9급 변형

> The plant is able to _____ extreme temperatures, making it suitable for various climates.

① modify
② record
③ tolerate
④ evaluate

33 밑줄 친 부분에 들어갈 말로 가장 적절한 것은?

2016. 국가직 9급

> The campaign to eliminate pollution will prove _____ unless it has the understanding and full cooperation of the public.

① enticing
② enhanced
③ fertile
④ futile

34 밑줄 친 부분에 들어갈 말로 가장 적절한 것은?

2016. 국가직 9급 변형

> It's important not to _____ in matters that don't concern you, especially when it could cause unnecessary conflict.

① hurry
② interfere
③ sniff
④ resign

35 밑줄 친 부분에 들어갈 말로 가장 적절한 것은?

2016. 국가직 9급

> Newton made _____ contributions to mathematics, optics, and mechanical physics.

① mediocre
② suggestive
③ unprecedented
④ provocative

36 밑줄 친 부분에 들어갈 말로 가장 적절한 것은?

2015. 국가직 9급

> The young knight was so _____ at being called a coward that he charged forward with his sword in hand.

① aloof
② incensed
③ unbiased
④ unpretentious

37 밑줄 친 부분에 들어갈 말로 가장 적절한 것은?

2015. 국가직 9급 변형

> Back in the mid-1970s, an American computer scientist called John Holland _____ upon the idea of using the theory of evolution to solve notoriously difficult problems in science.

① look
② depend
③ put
④ hit

38 밑줄 친 부분에 들어갈 말로 가장 적절한 것은?

2015. 국가직 9급 변형

> After the accident, the doctor _____ explained the procedure to the patient to ensure they understood every aspect before agreeing to the treatment plan.

① carefully
② hurriedly
③ decisively
④ delightfully

39 밑줄 친 부분에 들어갈 말로 가장 적절한 것은?

2015. 국가직 9급 변형

> When the fire alarm rang, all the students _____ evacuated the building without hesitation or panic.

① immediately
② punctually
③ hesitantly
④ periodically

40 밑줄 친 부분에 들어갈 말로 가장 적절한 것은?

2014. 국가직 9급

> Before she traveled to Mexico last winter, she needed to _____ her Spanish because she had not practiced it since college.

① make up to
② brush up on
③ shun away from
④ come down with

41 밑줄 친 부분에 들어갈 말로 가장 적절한 것은?

2014. 국가직 9급 변형

> The doctor will _____ the patient thoroughly to determine the cause of their symptoms.

① examine
② distribute
③ discard
④ pursue

42 밑줄 친 부분에 들어갈 말로 가장 적절한 것은?

2014. 국가직 9급 변형

> The gymnast's _____ skills during the Olympics led to a new world record.

① faultless
② unreliable
③ gutless
④ unscientific

43 밑줄 친 부분에 들어갈 말로 가장 적절한 것은?

2013. 국가직 9급

> Visa okay assists the Australian travel industry, corporations and government, and individuals by _____ the entire visa advice and visa issuance process. Visa okay minimizes the complexity and time delays associated with applying for and obtaining travel visas.

① appreciating
② aggravating
③ meditating
④ facilitating

44 밑줄 친 부분에 들어갈 말로 가장 적절한 것은?

2013. 국가직 9급

> Given our awesome capacities for rationalization and self-deception, most of us are going to measure ourselves _____: I was honest with that blind passenger because I'm a wonder person. I cheated the sighted one because she probably has too much money anyway.

① harshly
② leniently
③ honestly
④ thankfully

45 밑줄 친 부분에 들어갈 말로 가장 적절한 것은?
2013. 국가직 9급 변형

In Korea, the eldest son tends to _____ a lot of responsibility.

① take over
② take down
③ take on
④ take off

46 밑줄 친 부분에 들어갈 말로 가장 적절한 것은?
2013. 국가직 9급 변형

In order to _____ the budget shortfall, the company implemented a series of cost-cutting measures.

① conceive
② review
③ solve
④ pose

47 밑줄 친 부분에 들어갈 말로 가장 적절한 것은?
2012. 국가직 9급 변형

His _____ view on his academic performance prevented him from recognizing the need for improvement and achieving better results.

① scornful
② simulated
③ complacent
④ condescending

48 밑줄 친 부분에 들어갈 말로 가장 적절한 것은?
2012. 국가직 9급

The usual way of coping with taboo words and notions is to develop euphemisms and circumlocutions. Hundreds of words and phrases have emerged to express basic biological functions, and talk about _____ has its own linguistics world. English examples include "to pass on," "to snuff the candle," and "to go aloft."

① death
② defeat
③ anxiety
④ frustration

49 밑줄 친 부분에 들어갈 말로 가장 적절한 것은?
2012. 국가직 9급 변형

The enjoyment of life, pleasure, is the natural object of all human efforts. Nature, however, also wants us to help one another to enjoy life. She's equally anxious for the welfare of every member of the species. So she tells us to make quite sure that we don't pursue our own interests at the _____ of other people's.

① discretion
② mercy
③ end
④ expense

50 밑줄 친 부분에 들어갈 말로 가장 적절한 것은?

2011. 국가직 9급 변형

> The new policy introduced by the government was highly _____, sparking heated debates among politicians and the public.

① manageable
② reconcilable
③ augmentative
④ controversial

51 밑줄 친 부분에 들어갈 말로 가장 적절한 것은?

2011. 국가직 9급 변형

> To avoid death duty, the man _____ the greater part of his property to his only son as soon as he retired.

① made up
② made over
③ made out
④ made against

52 밑줄 친 부분에 들어갈 말로 가장 적절한 것은?

2011. 국가직 9급

> In general terms, tablet PC refers to a slate-shaped mobile computer device, equipped with a touchscreen or stylus to operate the computer. Tablet PCs are often used where normal notebooks are impractical or _____, or do not provide the needed functionality.

① unwieldy
② inconclusive
③ exclusive
④ unprecedented

53 다음 밑줄 친 부분에 들어갈 말로 가장 적절한 것은?

2010. 국가직 9급

> Sarah frequently hurts others when she criticizes their work because she is so _____.

① reserved
② wordy
③ retrospective
④ outspoken

54 다음 문장의 빈칸에 들어갈 말로 가장 적절한 것은?

2010. 국가직 9급

> The executives should estimate their debt-to-income ratios to see whether they run the risk of becoming _____.

① insolvent
② inverted
③ distracted
④ decoded

Chapter 02 지방직 9급 핵심 기출문제

01 밑줄 친 부분에 들어갈 말로 가장 적절한 것은?

2025. 지방직 9급

> Some plant diseases are indeed difficult to _____ because they can spread rapidly and easily, impacting multiple plants in a vast area.

① nourish
② eradicate
③ proliferate
④ detect

02 밑줄 친 부분에 들어갈 말로 가장 적절한 것은?

2025. 지방직 9급

> In the business world, _____ is highly valued as it showcases a person's commitment to meeting deadlines and respecting others' time.

① humility
② sincerity
③ frugality
④ punctuality

03 밑줄 친 부분에 들어갈 말로 가장 적절한 것은?

2024. 지방직 9급

> While Shakespeare's comedies share many similarities, they also differ _____ from one another.

① softly
② markedly
③ marginally
④ indiscernibly

04 밑줄 친 부분에 들어갈 말로 가장 적절한 것은?

2024. 지방직 9급

> Jane poured out the strong, dark tea and _____ it with milk.

① washed
② diluted
③ connected
④ fermented

05 밑줄 친 부분에 들어갈 말로 가장 적절한 것은?

2024. 지방직 9급 변형

> The survey results were skewed because some responses were accidentally _____ during data collection.

① excluded
② supported
③ submitted
④ authorized

06 밑줄 친 부분에 들어갈 말로 가장 적절한 것은?

2024. 지방직 9급 변형

> If you _____ that we are planning a surprise party, Dad will never stop asking you questions.

① reveal
② observe
③ believe
④ possess

07 밑줄 친 부분에 들어갈 말로 가장 적절한 것은?

2024. 지방직 9급

> Automatic doors in supermarkets _____ the entry and exit of customers with bags or shopping carts.

① ignore
② forgive
③ facilitate
④ exaggerate

08 밑줄 친 부분에 들어갈 말로 가장 적절한 것은?

2023. 지방직 9급 변형

> After the failure of the first experiment, the team made adjustments and achieved success in the _____ trials.

① required
② subsequent
③ advanced
④ gratuitous

09 밑줄 친 부분에 들어갈 말로 가장 적절한 것은?

2023. 지방직 9급

> Folkways are customs that members of a group are expected to follow to show _____ to others. For example, saying "excuse me" when you sneeze is an American folkway.

① charity
② humility
③ boldness
④ courtesy

10 밑줄 친 부분에 들어갈 말로 가장 적절한 것은?

2023. 지방직 9급

> These children have been _____ on a diet of healthy food.

① raised
② advised
③ observed
④ dumped

11 밑줄 친 부분에 들어갈 말로 가장 적절한 것은?

2023. 지방직 9급 변형

> The company chose to _____ its strict dress code, allowing employees to dress more casually.

① abolish
② consent
③ criticize
④ justify

12 밑줄 친 부분에 들어갈 말로 가장 적절한 것은?

2023. 지방직 9급

> Voters demanded that there should be greater _____ in the election process so that they could see and understand it.

① deception
② flexibility
③ competition
④ transparency

13 밑줄 친 부분에 들어갈 말로 가장 적절한 것은?

2022. 지방직 9급 변형

> The new manager was highly _____, quickly adjusting to the company's culture and leading the team through various challenges.

① strong
② adaptable
③ honest
④ passionate

14 밑줄 친 부분에 들어갈 말로 가장 적절한 것은?

2022. 지방직 9급

> Crop yields _____, improving in some areas and falling in others.

① vary
② decline
③ expand
④ include

15 밑줄 친 부분에 들어갈 말로 가장 적절한 것은?

2021. 지방직 9급 변형

> The _____ he received from helping others was far greater than any financial reward he could have earned.

① liveliness
② confidence
③ tranquility
④ gratification

16 밑줄 친 부분에 들어갈 말로 가장 적절한 것은?

2021. 지방직 9급

> Globalization leads more countries to open their markets, allowing them to trade goods and services freely at a lower cost with greater _____.

① extinction
② depression
③ efficiency
④ caution

17 밑줄 친 부분에 들어갈 말로 가장 적절한 것은?

2021. 지방직 9급

> We're familiar with the costs of burnout: Energy, motivation, productivity, engagement, and commitment can all take a hit, at work and at home. And many of the _____ are fairly intuitive: Regularly unplug. Reduce unnecessary meetings. Exercise. Schedule small breaks during the day. Take vacations even if you think you can't afford to be away from work, because you can't afford not to be away now and then.

① fixes
② damages
③ prizes
④ complications

18 밑줄 친 부분에 들어갈 말로 가장 적절한 것은?

2021. 지방직 9급 변형

> The government is seeking ways to soothe salaried workers over their increased tax burdens arising from a new tax settlement system. During his meeting with the presidential aides last Monday, the President _____ for those present to open up more communication channels with the public.

① accounted
② called
③ compensated
④ applied

19 밑줄 친 부분에 들어갈 말로 가장 적절한 것은?

2021. 지방직 9급 변형

> A student who was struggling with math took some time to _____ complex math concepts.

① encompass
② intrude
③ inspect
④ apprehend

20 밑줄 친 부분에 들어갈 말로 가장 적절한 것은?

2020. 지방직 9급

> The issue with plastic bottles is that they're not _____, so when the temperatures begin to rise, your water will also heat up.

① sanitary
② insulated
③ recyclable
④ waterproof

21 밑줄 친 부분에 들어갈 말로 가장 적절한 것은?

2020. 지방직 9급 변형

> The new green space was designed to _____ the effects of urban heat islands in the city.

① compromise
② accelerate
③ calculate
④ alleviate

22 밑줄 친 부분에 들어갈 말로 가장 적절한 것은?
2020. 지방직 9급 변형

> The cruel sights _____ thoughts that otherwise wouldn't have entered her mind.

① gave off
② touched off
③ made off
④ cut off

23 밑줄 친 부분에 들어갈 말로 가장 적절한 것은?
2020. 지방직 9급 변형

> People with a lot of caution tend to _____ the slightest bit of dangerous behavior.

① shun
② warn
③ punish
④ imitate

24 밑줄 친 부분에 들어갈 말로 가장 적절한 것은?
2019. 지방직 9급 변형

> Archaeologists used special tools to carefully _____ fossils embedded in rocks to study.

① excavate
② pack
③ erase
④ celebrate

25 밑줄 친 부분에 들어갈 말로 가장 적절한 것은?
2019. 지방직 9급 변형

> The new medication helped make her symptoms more _____, allowing her to resume daily activities.

① utter
② scary
③ occasional
④ manageable

26 밑줄 친 부분에 들어갈 말로 가장 적절한 것은?
2019. 지방직 9급 변형

> Time does seem to slow to a trickle during a boring afternoon lecture and race when the brain is _____ in something highly entertaining.

① engaged
② stuck
③ located
④ engrossed

27 밑줄 친 부분에 들어갈 말로 가장 적절한 것은?
2019. 지방직 9급 변형

> During the orientation, new employees watched the company's internal video to _____ themselves with the office layout.

① acquaint
② inspire
③ endow
④ avoid

28 밑줄 친 부분에 들어갈 말로 가장 적절한 것은?

2018. 지방직 9급

> The _____ duty of the physician is to do no harm. Everything else — even healing — must take second place.

① paramount
② sworn
③ successful
④ mysterious

29 밑줄 친 부분에 들어갈 말로 가장 적절한 것은?

2018. 지방직 9급 변형

> After completing the marathon, she was completely _____ and could hardly even stand.

① ambitious
② afraid
③ exhausted
④ inherent

30 밑줄 친 부분에 들어갈 말로 가장 적절한 것은?

2018. 지방직 9급

> The student who finds the state-of-the-art approach _____ learns less than he or she might have learned by the old methods.

① humorous
② friendly
③ convenient
④ intimidating

31 밑줄 친 부분에 들어갈 말로 가장 적절한 것은?

2017. 지방직 9급

> Our main dish did not have much flavor, but I made it more _____ by adding condiments.

① palatable
② dissolvable
③ potable
④ susceptible

32 밑줄 친 부분에 들어갈 말로 가장 적절한 것은?

2016. 지방직 9급

> The two cultures were so utterly _____ that she found it hard to adapt from one to the other.

① overlapped
② equivalent
③ associative
④ disparate

33 밑줄 친 부분에 들어갈 말로 가장 적절한 것은?

2016. 지방직 9급

> Penicillin can have an _____ effect on a person who is allergic to it.

① affirmative
② aloof
③ adverse
④ allusive

34 밑줄 친 부분에 들어갈 말로 가장 적절한 것은?

2016. 지방직 9급

> Last year, I had a great opportunity to do this performance with the staff responsible for _____ art events at the theater.

① turning into
② doing without
③ putting on
④ giving up

35 밑줄 친 부분에 공통으로 들어갈 말로 가장 적절한 것은?

2016. 지방직 9급 변형

> • The psychologist used a new test to _____ overall personality development of students.
> • Snacks _____ 25% to 30% of daily energy intake among adolescents.

① stand for
② allow for
③ account for
④ apologize for

36 밑줄 친 부분에 들어갈 말로 가장 적절한 것은?

2015. 지방직 9급 변형

> You should _____ personal information from the report to protect privacy.

① trace
② exclude
③ instruct
④ examine

37 밑줄 친 부분에 들어갈 말로 가장 적절한 것은?

2015. 지방직 9급 변형

> The government introduced tax cuts to _____ the economic pressure on citizens.

① relieve
② accumulate
③ provoke
④ accelerate

38 밑줄 친 부분에 들어갈 말로 가장 적절한 것은?

2015. 지방직 9급 변형

> She has always been _____, choosing to save money rather than spend it on unnecessary items.

① stray
② thrifty
③ wealthy
④ stingy

39 밑줄 친 부분에 들어갈 말로 가장 적절한 것은?

2015. 지방직 9급 변형

> The _____ parents forced their children to participate in all activities, giving them no freedom to choose.

① thrilled
② brave
③ timid
④ pushy

40 밑줄 친 부분에 들어갈 말로 가장 적절한 것은?

2014. 지방직 9급 변형

> The company often tries exaggerated marketing strategies because of its _____ greed for profits.

① infallible
② aesthetic
③ adolescent
④ insatiable

41 밑줄 친 부분에 들어갈 말로 가장 적절한 것은?

2014. 지방직 9급 변형

> If you are someone who is _____, you tend to keep your feelings hidden and do not like to show other people what you really think.

① reserved
② loquacious
③ eloquent
④ analogous

42 밑줄 친 부분에 들어갈 말로 가장 적절한 것은?

2014. 지방직 9급 변형

> A preliminary meeting will _____ the official conference to finalize the agenda.

① pacify
② precede
③ presume
④ provoke

43 밑줄 친 부분에 들어갈 말로 가장 적절한 것은?

2013. 지방직 9급

> Every street or every store is now filled with cell phone users, ranging in age from eight to eighty. However, if we consider rapidly developing technology, an alternative apparatus might replace the cell phone soon and make it _____.

① obsolete
② extensive
③ prevalent
④ competent

44 밑줄 친 부분에 들어갈 말로 가장 적절한 것은?

2012. 지방직 9급

> A _____ gene is one that produces a particular characteristic regardless of whether a person has only one of these genes from one parent, or two of them.

① offensive
② dominant
③ proficient
④ turbulent

45 밑줄 친 부분에 들어갈 말로 가장 적절한 것은?

2012. 지방직 9급 변형

> She showed remarkable _____ during the heated debate, always staying calm and composed.

① concern
② anguish
③ solicitude
④ temperance

46 밑줄 친 부분에 들어갈 말로 가장 적절한 것은?

2011. 지방직 9급 변형

> The whistle-blower chose _____ to protect themselves from potential retaliation for exposing the corruption.

① hospitality
② sightseeing
③ disrespect
④ anonymity

47 밑줄 친 부분에 들어갈 말로 가장 적절한 것은?

2011. 지방직 9급 변형

> The monument was decided to be restored and _____ protected to preserve its historical value and continue to show it to future generations.

① permanently
② temporarily
③ comparatively
④ tentatively

48 밑줄 친 부분에 들어갈 말로 가장 적절한 것은?

2010. 지방직 9급 변형

> Fast-food franchises have been very successful in the U.S. Part of the appeal is the _____. At the major hamburger or chicken franchises, people know what the food is going to taste like, wherever they buy it.

① profitability
② predictability
③ feasibility
④ sustainability

Chapter 03 2025년 출제 기조 전환 예시 문제

01 밑줄 친 부분에 들어갈 말로 가장 적절한 것은?

2025. 출제 기조 전환 2차

> In order to exhibit a large mural, the museum curators had to make sure they had _____ space.

① cozy
② stuffy
③ ample
④ cramped

02 밑줄 친 부분에 들어갈 말로 가장 적절한 것은?

2025. 출제 기조 전환 2차

> Even though there are many problems that have to be solved, I want to emphasize that the safety of our citizens is our top _____.

① secret
② priority
③ solution
④ opportunity

03 밑줄 친 부분에 들어갈 말로 가장 적절한 것은?

2025. 출제 기조 전환 1차

> Recently, increasingly _____ weather patterns, often referred to as "abnormal climate," have been observed around the world.

① irregular
② consistent
③ predictable
④ ineffective

04 밑줄 친 부분에 들어갈 말로 가장 적절한 것은?

2025. 출제 기조 전환 1차

> Most economic theories assume that people act on a _____ basis; however, this doesn't account for the fact that they often rely on their emotions instead.

① temporary
② rational
③ voluntary
④ commercial

생활영어

출제 경향 분석

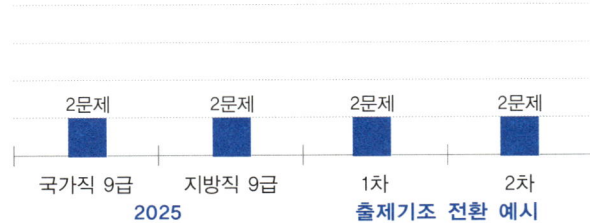

생활영어 유형 문항 수

현재 시행 중인 9급 공무원 영어 시험에서 출제되는 총 20문항 중, 생활영어 문제는 2문항으로 출제되고 있다. 과거에는 생활영어 문제가 빈칸 생활영어 2문제 또는 1문제와 짧은 대화형 1문제의 형태로 출제되어, 최소 2문항에서 최대 3문항까지 출제되기도 했으나 최근 기조 변화에 따라 짧은 대화형 문제는 더 이상 출제되지 않고 있다. 따라서 현재는 빈칸 유형의 생활영어 문제 2문항만 출제되는 것으로 보는 것이 타당하다.

출제되는 유형

9급 공무원 영어 시험에서 출제되는 생활영어 문제는 모두 빈칸 유형으로 출제되며 두 가지 형식으로 구분된다. 첫 번째는 그림 이미지가 포함된 빈칸 문제이고, 두 번째는 일반적인 대화문 형식의 빈칸 문제이다. 두 유형 모두 일상적인 상황을 다루고 있으며, 문맥을 정확히 파악하고 상황에 맞는 답을 선택하는 능력을 평가하기 때문에 생활영어 문제를 모두 맞히기 위해서는 상황을 정확히 이해하고 그에 맞는 자연스러운 답을 선택하는 것이 중요하다.

생활영어 유형 학습 전략

수험생들은 생활영어 문제에 대비하기 위해 빈칸 유형을 중심으로 학습을 진행해야 한다. 빈칸 유형은 주로 일상적인 상황에서 쓰이는 표현들을 다루기 때문에, 문맥 속에서 적절한 단어나 표현을 추론하는 훈련이 필요하다. 또한, 생활영어 문제는 단순히 어휘를 알고 있는지 여부만을 묻는 것이 아니라, 실제 상황에서 그 단어가 어떻게 사용되는지를 파악하는 능력을 요구한다. 이에 따라, 기본적인 어휘력 강화는 물론이고, 실용적인 문장 구조와 문맥에 맞는 단어 선택을 훈련하는 것이 중요하다. 그러므로 수험생들은 다양한 예문과 함께 생활영어 빈칸 문제를 풀어보는 연습을 '매일 합격 모의고사' 등을 통해 꾸준히 하며, 문맥을 읽고 적합한 답을 추론하는 능력을 키워야 한다. 이와 함께, 실전 문제에서 자주 등장하는 표현들을 숙지하고, 다양한 생활 상황에서 쓰이는 중요한 표현을 문제를 통해 체득하는 것이 중요하다.

반드시 한번에 다잡는 실전 생활영어 표현

01 예약 및 일정 관련 표현
- Do you have a meeting room available for that day? (그날 회의실이 있나요?)
- I'd like to book a flight from Seoul to Oakland. (서울에서 오클랜드로 가는 비행기 예약을 하고 싶습니다.)
- Could I have your contact information? (연락처를 알려주시겠어요?)
- What class would you like to book? (어떤 클래스 예약을 원하시나요?, 어떤 좌석 등급으로 예약 원하시나요?)

02 구매 및 상품 관련 표현
- I'd like to get a refund. (환불을 원합니다.)
- Can you help me set up an email account? (이메일 계정을 설정하는 데 도움을 주실 수 있나요?)
- What's the exchange rate? (환율이 어떻게 되나요?)
- Can you send the goods by air freight? (물품을 항공 화물로 보낼 수 있나요?)
- I'll send you the payment information shortly. (잠시 후 결제 정보를 보내드릴게요.)
- I will see you at the Customs office. (세관 사무소에서 뵙겠습니다.)

03 회의 및 업무 관련 표현
- How many copies of the presentation materials do you think we'll need? (발표 자료 몇 부가 필요할 것 같나요?)
- We can accommodate groups of 5 to 20 people. (5명에서 20명까지 수용할 수 있습니다.)

04 건강 및 음식 관련 표현
- Have you taken anything for your cold? (감기에 대해 약을 복용하셨나요?)
- I'll give it a try. (한번 시도해 볼게요.)

05 위치 및 방향 관련 표현
- How can I get up there? (거기까지 어떻게 가나요?)
- Could you tell me how to get to the Personnel Department? (인사부서로 어떻게 가는지 알려주시겠어요?)
- Take the elevator around the corner. (모퉁이를 돌아서 엘리베이터를 타세요.)

06 추천 및 제안 관련 표현
- Why don't you visit the national park, then? (그럼 국립공원을 방문하는 건 어때요?)
- You should check it out as soon as possible. (가능한 한 빨리 그것을 확인해보세요.)
- Let's look for another ride. (다른 놀이기구를 찾아보자.)

07 상태 및 상황 관련 표현
- My computer just shut down for no reason. (제 컴퓨터가 이유 없이 꺼졌어요.)
- The kitchen was a mess this morning. (오늘 아침 부엌이 엉망이었어요.)
- I'm just glad it's over. (그저 끝나서 다행이에요.)

Chapter 01 국가직 및 지방직 최신 4개년 핵심 기출문제

01 밑줄 친 부분에 들어갈 말로 가장 적절한 것은?

2025. 국가직 9급

① Yes, it's an online meeting
② Yes, be sure to reply to the email
③ No, I didn't receive your text message
④ No, I don't have another meeting today

02 밑줄 친 부분에 들어갈 말로 가장 적절한 것은?

2025. 국가직 9급

A: Aren't you going to have lunch?
B: No, I'm not hungry. I'd rather read my book. I'm reading *The Lucky Club*.
A: *The Lucky Club*? What's it about?
B: Well, it's about a group of Korean women who live in Los Angeles. The main character is a woman born in America whose mother came from Korea.
A: It sounds interesting. Who's it by?
B: _____.
A: She wrote *The Heroine Generation*, too, didn't she?
B: No, that was written by May Lee.
A: Oh, I see.

① I have already read it
② Lin Lee is the author
③ It originally belongs to me
④ She is one of my relatives in Korea

03 밑줄 친 부분에 들어갈 말로 가장 적절한 것은?

2025. 지방직 9급

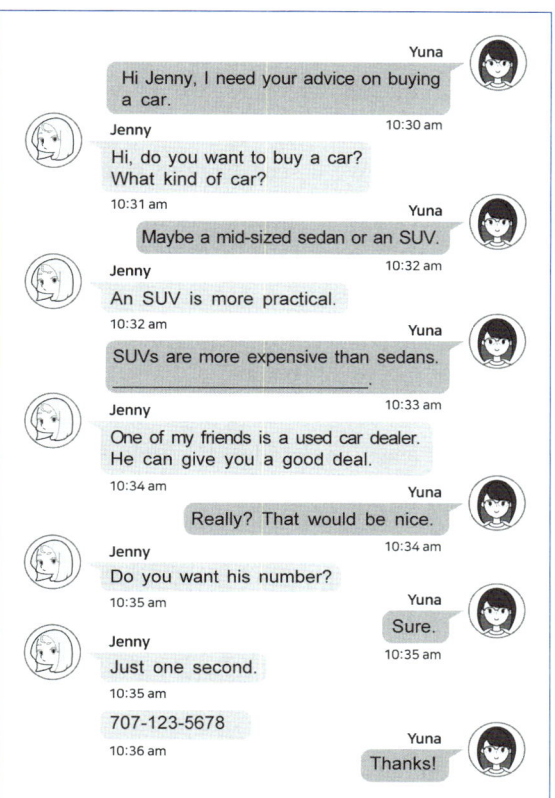

① I'm on a tight budget
② I need to get in shape
③ It should clear up soon
④ I can pick you up later

04 밑줄 친 부분에 들어갈 말로 가장 적절한 것은?

2025. 지방직 9급

A: How many copies of the presentation materials do you think we'll need?
B: 60 should be enough, but it's always good to have extras.
A: True. Better safe than sorry. How many would you recommend then?
B: Let's make it 75 just in case we have more attendees than expected like last time.
A: Good idea. _____?
B: Absolutely. We are going to have people asking for the presentation materials after the presentation.
A: Sure, that way everyone can easily have it whenever needed.

① How early do we need to distribute the materials
② Should we also have a digital version for sharing
③ Will the materials be printed in color or black and white
④ Are there any specific materials we should avoid including

05 밑줄 친 부분에 들어갈 말로 적절한 것은?

2024. 국가직 9급

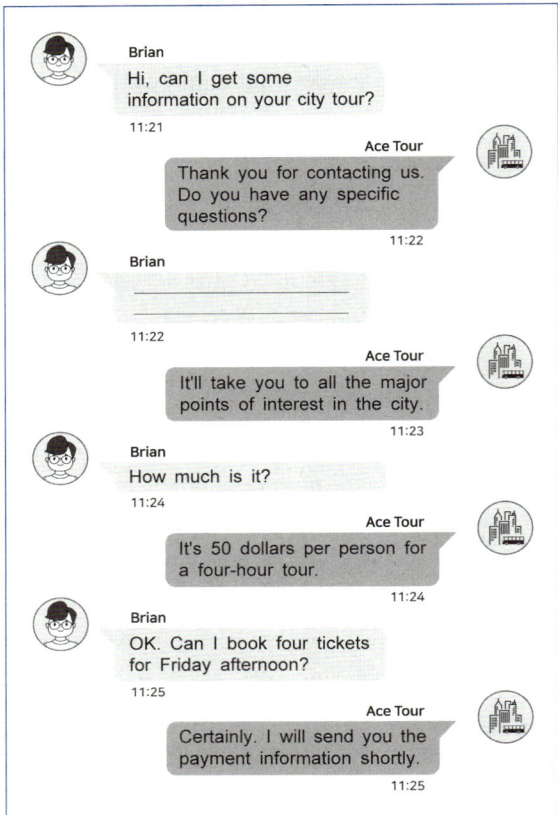

① How long is the tour?
② What does the city tour include?
③ Do you have a list of tour packages?
④ Can you recommend a good tour guide book?

06 밑줄 친 부분에 들어갈 말로 적절한 것은?

2024. 국가직 9급

A: Thank you. We appreciate your order.
B: You are welcome. Could you send the goods by air freight? We need them fast.
A: Sure. We'll send them to your department right away.
B: Okay. I hope we can get the goods early next week.
A: If everything goes as planned, you'll get them by Monday.
B: Monday sounds good.
A: Please pay within 2 weeks. Air freight costs will be added on the invoice.
B: _____
A: I am afraid the free delivery service is no longer available

① I see. When will we be getting the invoice from you?
② Our department may not be able to pay within two weeks.
③ Can we send the payment to your business account on Monday?
④ Wait a minute. I thought the delivery costs were at your expense.

07 밑줄 친 부분에 들어갈 말로 적절한 것은?

2024. 국가직 9급

A: Have you found your phone?
B: Unfortunately, no. I'm still looking for it.
A: Have you contacted the subway's lost and found office?
B: _____.
A: If I were you, I would do that first.
B: Yeah, you are right. I'll check with the lost and found before buying a new phone.

① I went there to ask about the phone
② I stopped by the office this morning
③ I haven't done that yet, actually
④ I tried searching everywhere

08 밑줄 친 부분에 들어갈 말로 적절한 것은?

2024. 지방직 9급

A: Charles, I think we need more chairs for our upcoming event.
B: Really? I thought we already had enough chairs.
A: My manager told me that more than 350 people are coming.
B: _____
A: I agree. I am also a bit surprised.
B: Looks like I'll have to order more then. Thanks.

① I wonder if the manager is going to attend the event.
② I thought more than 350 people would be coming.
③ That's actually not a large number.
④ That's a lot more than I expected.

09 밑줄 친 부분에 들어갈 말로 적절한 것은?

2024. 지방직 9급

A: Can I get the document you referred to at the meeting yesterday?
B: Sure. What's the title of the document?
A: I can't remember its title, but it was about the community festival.
B: Oh, I know what you're talking about.
A: Great. Can you send it to me via email?
B: I don't have it with me. Mr. Park is in charge of the project, so he should have it.
A: _____
B: Good luck. Hope you get the document you want.

① Can you check if he is in the office?
② Mr. Park has sent the email to you again.
③ Are you coming to the community festival?
④ Thank you for letting me know. I'll contact him.

10 밑줄 친 부분에 들어갈 말로 적절한 것은?

2024. 지방직 9급

A: Hello, can I ask you a question about the presentation next Tuesday?
B: Do you mean the presentation about promoting the volunteer program?
A: Yes. Where is the presentation going to be?
B: Let me check. It is room 201.
A: I see. Can I use my laptop in the room?
B: Sure. We have a PC in the room, but you can use yours if you want.
A: _____
B: We can meet in the room two hours before the presentation. Would that work for you?
A: Yes. Thank you very much!

① A computer technician was here an hour ago.
② When can I have a rehearsal for my presentation?
③ Should we recruit more volunteers for our program?
④ I don't feel comfortable leaving my laptop in the room.

11 밑줄 친 부분에 들어갈 말로 알맞은 것은?

2023. 국가직 9급

A: I'd like to go sightseeing downtown. Where do you think I should go?
B: I strongly suggest you visit the national art gallery.
A: Oh, that's a great idea. What else should I check out?
B: _____
A: I don't have time for that. I need to meet a client at three.
B: Oh, I see. Why don't you visit the national park, then?
A: That sounds good. Thank you!

① This is the map that your client needs. Here you go.
② A guided tour to the river park. It takes all afternoon.
③ You should check it out as soon as possible.
④ The checkout time is three o'clock.

12 밑줄 친 부분에 들어갈 말로 가장 적절한 것은?

2023. 지방직 9급

A: Pardon me, but could you give me a hand, please?
B: _____
A: I'm trying to find the Personnel Department. I have an appointment at 10.
B: It's on the third floor.
A: How can I get up there?
B: Take the elevator around the corner.

① We have no idea how to handle this situation.
② Would you mind telling us who is in charge?
③ Yes. I could use some help around here.
④ Sure. Can I help you with anything?

13 밑줄 친 부분에 들어갈 말로 가장 적절한 것은?

2023. 지방직 9급

A: You were the last one who left the office, weren't you?
B: Yes. Is there any problem?
A: I found the office lights and air conditioners on this morning.
B: Really? Oh, no. Maybe I forgot to turn them off last night.
A: Probably they were on all night.
B: _____

① Don't worry. This machine is working fine.
② That's right. Everyone likes to work with you.
③ I'm sorry. I promise I'll be more careful from now on.
④ Too bad. You must be tired because you get off work too late.

14 밑줄 친 부분에 들어갈 말로 가장 적절한 것은?

2022. 국가직 9급

A: Hi there. May I help you?
B: Yes, I'm looking for a sweater.
A: Well, this one is the latest style from the fall collection. What do you think?
B: It's gorgeous. How much is it?
A: Let me check the price for you. It's $120.
B: _____
A: Then how about this sweater? It's from the last season, but it's on sale for $50.
B: Perfect! Let me try it on.

① I also need a pair of pants to go with it
② That jacket is the perfect gift for me
③ It's a little out of my price range
④ We are open until 7 p.m. on Saturdays

15 밑줄 친 부분에 들어갈 말로 가장 적절한 것은?

2022. 지방직 9급

A: Hey! How did your geography test go?
B: Not bad, thanks. I'm just glad that it's over! How about you? How did your science exam go?
A: Oh, it went really well. _____. I owe you a treat for that.
B: It's my pleasure. So, do you feel like preparing for the math exam scheduled for next week?
A: Sure. Let's study together.
B: It sounds good. See you later.

① There's no sense in beating yourself up over this
② I never thought I would see you here
③ Actually, we were very disappointed
④ I can't thank you enough for helping me with it

Chapter 02 국가직 및 지방직 기타 핵심 기출문제

01 밑줄 친 부분에 들어갈 말로 가장 적절한 것은?

2021. 국가직 9급

> A: Were you here last night?
> B: Yes. I worked the closing shift. Why?
> A: The kitchen was a mess this morning. There was food spattered on the stove, and the ice trays were not in the freezer.
> B: I guess I forgot to go over the cleaning checklist.
> A: You know how important a clean kitchen is.
> B: I'm sorry. _____

① I won't let it happen again.
② Would you like your bill now?
③ That's why I forgot it yesterday.
④ I'll make sure you get the right order.

02 밑줄 친 부분에 들어갈 말로 가장 적절한 것은?

2021. 국가직 9급

> A: Have you taken anything for your cold?
> B: No, I just blow my nose a lot.
> A: Have you tried nose spray?
> B: _____
> A: It works great.
> B: No, thanks. I don't like to put anything in my nose, so I've never used it.

① Yes, but it didn't help.
② No, I don't like nose spray.
③ No, the pharmacy was closed.
④ Yeah, how much should I use?

03 밑줄 친 부분에 들어갈 말로 가장 적절한 것은?

2021. 지방직 9급

> A: Did you have a nice weekend?
> B: Yes, it was pretty good. We went to the movies.
> A: Oh! What did you see?
> B: Interstellar. It was really good.
> A: Really? _____
> B: The special effects. They were fantastic. I wouldn't mind seeing it again.

① What did you like the most about it?
② What's your favorite movie genre?
③ Was the film promoted internationally?
④ Was the movie very costly?

04 밑줄 친 부분에 들어갈 말로 가장 적절한 것은?

2020. 국가직 9급

> A: Thank you for calling the Royal Point Hotel Reservations Department. My name is Sam. How may I help you?
> B: Hello, I'd like to book a room.
> A: We offer two room types: the deluxe room and the luxury suite.
> B: _____?
> A: For one, the suite is very large. In addition to a bedroom, it has a kitchen, living room and dining room.
> B: It sounds expensive.
> A: Well, it's $ 200 more per night.
> B: In that case, I'll go with the deluxe room.

① Do you need anything else
② May I have the room number
③ What's the difference between them
④ Are pets allowed in the rooms

05 밑줄 친 부분에 들어갈 말로 가장 적절한 것은?

2020. 지방직 9급

A: Oh, another one! So many junk emails!
B: I know. I receive more than ten junk emails a day.
A: Can we stop them from coming in?
B: I don't think it's possible to block them completely.
A: _____?
B: Well, you can set up a filter on the settings.
A: A filter?
B: Yeah. The filter can weed out some of the spam emails.

① Do you write emails often
② Isn't there anything we can do
③ How did you make this great filter
④ Can you help me set up an email account

06 밑줄 친 부분에 들어갈 말로 가장 적절한 것은?

2019. 국가직 9급

A: Would you like to try some dim sum?
B: Yes, thank you. They look delicious. What's inside?
A: These have pork and chopped vegetables, and those have shrimps.
B: And, um, _____?
A: You pick one up with your chopsticks like this and dip it into the sauce. It's easy.
B: Okay. I'll give it a try.

① how much are they
② how do I eat them
③ how spicy are they
④ how do you cook them

07 밑줄 친 부분에 들어갈 말로 가장 적절한 것은?

2019. 지방직 9급

A: Hello. I need to exchange some money.
B: Okay. What currency do you need?
A: I need to convert dollars into pounds. What's the exchange rate?
B: The exchange rate is 0.73 pounds for every dollar.
A: Fine. Do you take a commission?
B: Yes, we take a small commission of 4 dollars.
A: _____?
B: We convert your currency back for free. Just bring your receipt with you.

① How much does this cost
② How should I pay for that
③ What's your buy-back policy
④ Do you take credit cards

08 밑줄 친 부분에 들어갈 말로 가장 적절한 것은?

2018. 지방직 9급

A: My computer just shut down for no reason. I can't even turn it back on again.
B: Did you try charging it? It might just be out of battery.
A: Of course, I tried charging it.
B: _____
A: I should do that, but I'm so lazy.

① I don't know how to fix your computer.
② Try visiting the nearest service center then.
③ Well, stop thinking about your problems and go to sleep.
④ My brother will try to fix your computer because he's a technician.

09 밑줄 친 부분에 들어갈 말로 가장 적절한 것은?

2018. 지방직 9급

A: Where do you want to go for our honeymoon?
B: Let's go to a place that neither of us has been to.
A: Then, why don't we go to Hawaii?
B: _____

① I've always wanted to go there.
② Isn't Korea a great place to live?
③ Great! My last trip there was amazing!
④ Oh, you must've been to Hawaii already.

10 밑줄 친 부분에 들어갈 말로 가장 적절한 것은?

2017. 국가직 9급

A: May I help you?
B: I bought this dress two days ago, but it's a bit big for me.
A: _____
B: Then I'd like to get a refund.
A: May I see your receipt, please?
B: Here you are.

① I'm sorry, but there's no smaller size.
② I feel like it fits you perfectly, though.
③ That dress sells really well in our store.
④ I'm sorry, but this purchase can't be refunded.

11 밑줄 친 부분에 들어갈 말로 가장 적절한 것은?

2017. 국가직 9급

A: Every time I use this home blood pressure monitor, I get a different reading. I think I'm doing it wrong. Can you show me how to use it correctly?
B: Yes, of course. First, you have to put the strap around your arm.
A: Like this? Am I doing this correctly?
B: That looks a little too tight.
A: Oh, how about now?
B: Now it looks a bit too loose. If it's too tight or too loose, you'll get an incorrect reading.
A: _____
B: Press the button now. You shouldn't move or speak.
A: I get it.
B: You should see your blood pressure on the screen in a few moments.

① I didn't see anything today.
② Oh, okay. What do I do next?
③ Right, I need to read the book.
④ Should I check out their website?

12 밑줄 친 부분에 들어갈 말로 가장 적절한 것은?

2017. 국가직 9급 하반기

> Mary: Hi, James. How's it going?
> James: Hello, Mary. What can I do for you today?
> Mary: How can I arrange for this package to be delivered?
> James: Why don't you talk to Bob in Customer Service?
> Mary: _____

① Sure. I will deliver this package for you.
② OK. Let me take care of Bob's customers.
③ I will see you at the Customs office.
④ I tried calling his number, but no one is answering.

13 밑줄 친 부분에 들어갈 말로 가장 적절한 것은?

2017. 국가직 9급 하반기

> A: Wow! Look at the long line. I'm sure we have to wait at least 30 minutes.
> B: You're right. _____
> A: That's a good idea. I want to ride the roller coaster.
> B: It's not my cup of tea.
> A: How about the Flume Ride then? It's fun and the line is not so long.
> B: That sounds great! Let's go!

① Let's find seats for the magic show.
② Let's look for another ride.
③ Let's buy costumes for the parade.
④ Let's go to the lost and found.

14 밑줄 친 부분에 들어갈 말로 가장 적절한 것은?

2017. 지방직 9급

> A: I just received a letter from one of my old high school buddies.
> B: That's nice!
> A: Well, actually it's been a long time since I heard from him.
> B: To be honest, I've been out of touch with most of my old friends.
> A: I know. It's really hard to maintain contact when people move around so much.
> B: You're right. _____.
> But you're lucky to be back in touch with your buddy again.

① The days are getting longer
② People just drift apart
③ That's the funniest thing I've ever heard of
④ I start fuming whenever I hear his name

15 밑줄 친 부분에 들어갈 말로 가장 적절한 것은?

2017. 지방직 9급 하반기

> A: How do you like your new neighborhood?
> B: It's great for the most part. I love the clean air and the green environment.
> A: Sounds like a lovely place to live.
> B: Yes, but it's not without its drawbacks.
> A: Like what?
> B: For one, it doesn't have many different stores. For example, there's only one supermarket, so food is very expensive.
> A: _____
> B: You're telling me. But thank goodness. The city is building a new shopping center now. Next year, we'll have more options.

① How many supermarkets are there?
② Are there a lot of places to shop there?
③ It looks like you have a problem.
④ I want to move to your neighborhood.

Chapter 03 2025년 출제 기조 전환 예시 문제

01 밑줄 친 부분에 들어갈 말로 가장 적절한 것은?

2025. 출제 기조 전환 2차

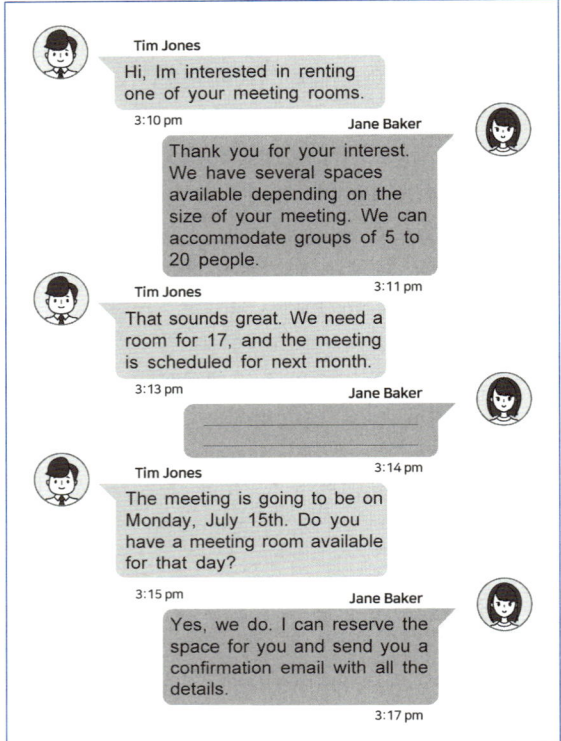

① Could I have your contact information?
② Can you tell me the exact date of your meeting?
③ Do you need a beam projector or a copy machine?
④ How many people are going to attend the meeting?

02 밑줄 친 부분에 들어갈 말로 가장 적절한 것은?

2025. 출제 기조 전환 2차

A: What do you think of this bicycle?
B: Wow, it looks very nice! Did you just get it?
A: No, this is a shared bike. The city launched a bike sharing service.
B: Really? How does it work? I mean, how do I use that service?
A: It's easy. _____
B: It doesn't sound complicated. Maybe I'll try it this weekend.
A: By the way, it's an electric bicycle.
B: Yes, I can tell. It looks cool.

① You can save energy because it's electric
② Just apply for a permit to park your own bike
③ Just download the bike sharing app and pay online
④ You must wear a helmet at all times for your safety

03 밑줄 친 부분에 들어갈 말로 가장 적절한 것은?

2025. 출제 기조 전환 1차

A: Hello. I'd like to book a flight from Seoul to Oakland.
B: Okay. Do you have any specific dates in mind?
A: Yes. I am planning to leave on May 2nd and return on May 14th.
B: Okay, I found one that fits your schedule. What class would you like to book?
A: Economy class is good enough for me.
B: Any preference on your seating?
A: _____
B: Great. Your flight is now booked.

① Yes. I'd like to upgrade to business class.
② No. I'd like to buy a one-way ticket.
③ No. I don't have any luggage.
④ Yes. I want an aisle seat.

04 밑줄 친 부분에 들어갈 말로 가장 적절한 것은?

2025. 출제 기조 전환 1차

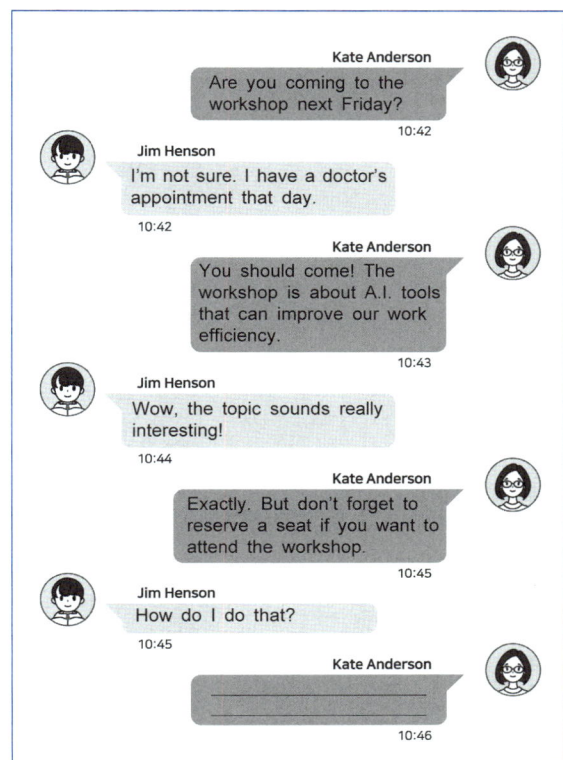

① You need to bring your own laptop.
② I already have a reservation.
③ Follow the instructions on the bulletin board.
④ You should call the doctor's office for an appointment.

진가영 영어
반한다 기출

진가영 영어연구소 | cafe.naver.com/easyenglish7

Vol.2
문법

PART 01 문장과 동사
PART 02 준동사
PART 03 조동사와 조동사를 활용한 구문
PART 04 연결어
PART 05 비교 구문

PART 01 문장과 동사

출제 경향 분석

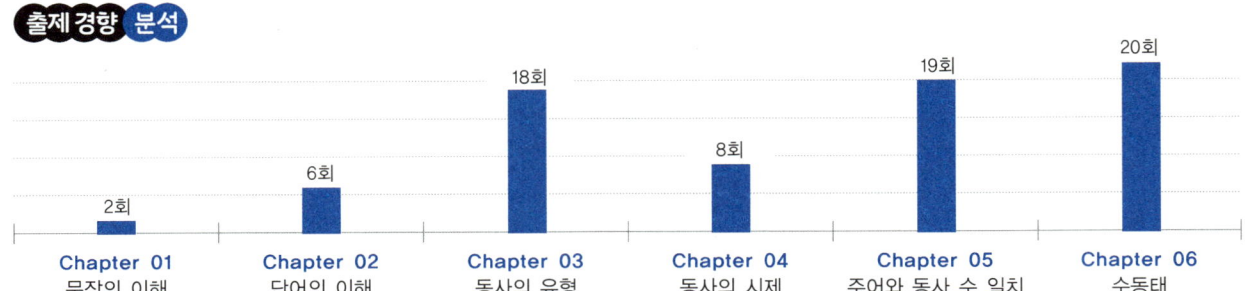

Chapter 01 문장의 이해	Chapter 02 단어의 이해	Chapter 03 동사의 유형	Chapter 04 동사의 시제	Chapter 05 주어와 동사 수 일치	Chapter 06 수동태
2회	6회	18회	8회	19회	20회

출제 내용 점검

Chapter 01 문장의 이해
① 문장의 구성요소와 8품사
② 구와 절, 문장이 길어지는 이유
③ 어순이 중요한 간접의문문
④ 주절의 주어 동사가 중요한 부가의문문

Chapter 02 단어의 이해
⑤ 단어의 8품사
⑥ 가산 명사의 종류와 특징
⑦ 불가산 명사의 종류와 특징
⑧ 주의해야 할 명사의 복수형
⑨ 관사의 종류와 생략
⑩ 격에 따른 인칭대명사
⑪ 재귀대명사의 2가지 용법
⑫ 지시대명사 this와 that
⑬ 부정대명사의 활용
⑭ 형용사와 부사의 차이
⑮ 주의해야 할 형용사
⑯ 수량 형용사와 명사의 수 일치
⑰ 어순에 주의해야 할 형용사와 부사
⑱ 혼동하기 쉬운 부사

Chapter 03 동사의 유형
⑲ 주어만 있으면 완전한 1형식 자동사
⑳ 주격 보어가 필요한 2형식 자동사
㉑ 전치사가 필요 없는 대표 3형식 타동사
㉒ 4형식으로 착각하기 쉬운 3형식 타동사
㉓ 목적어 뒤에 특정 전치사를 수반하는 3형식 타동사
㉔ 목적어를 두 개 취하는 4형식 수여동사
㉕ to부정사를 목적보어로 취하는 대표 5형식 타동사
㉖ 5형식 사역동사의 목적격 보어
㉗ 5형식 지각동사의 목적격 보어
㉘ 분사를 목적격 보어로 취하는 5형식 동사
㉙ 명사나 형용사를 목적격 보어로 취하는 5형식 동사
㉚ '말하다' 동사의 구분
㉛ 혼동하기 쉬운 자동사와 타동사
㉜ 의미와 구조에 주의해야 할 타동사

Chapter 04 동사의 시제
㉝ 과거 시간을 나타내는 부사와 과거시제
㉞ 완료시제와 잘 쓰이는 시간 부사
㉟ 미래를 대신하는 현재시제
㊱ 진행형 불가 동사
㊲ 시제의 일치와 예외
㊳ 시제 관련 표현

Chapter 05 주어와 동사의 수 일치
㊴ 현재시제 동사와 be동사의 수 일치
㊵ 상관접속사와 수 일치
㊶ 부분을 나타내는 명사와 수 일치
㊷ A and B와 수 일치
㊸ 혼동하기 쉬운 주어와 동사 수 일치
㊹ 주어 자리에서 반드시 단수 취급 또는 복수 취급하는 특징 표현

Chapter 06 수동태
㊺ 능동태와 수동태의 차이
㊻ 수동태 불가 동사
㊼ 다양한 3형식 동사와 수동태 구조
㊽ 4형식 수여동사와 수동태 구조
㊾ 5형식 동사와 수동태 구조
㊿ 전치사에 유의해야 할 수동태

Chapter 01 문장의 이해

반드시 한번에 다잡는 최빈출 개념 정리

01 동사 자리에는 _____가 아닌 수, 시제, 태를 표시한 동사를 쓴다.

개념 적용 Young ladies dancing(→ _____) all evening with them.
젊은 여자들은 그들과 함께 저녁 내내 춤을 추었다.

02 명사를 제외한 모든 품사는 형용사가 아닌 _____의 수식을 받는다.

개념 적용 Each officer must perform their duties efficient(→ _____)
각 장교는 그들의 임무를 효율적으로 수행해야 한다.

03 주어, 목적어, 보어 자리에는 동사가 아닌 적절한 _____로 쓴다.

개념 적용 We shared warmth by help(→ _____) the neighbors in need.
우리는 어려운 이웃들을 도우며 온정을 나눴다.

04 간접의문문은 도치 구조의 어순인 '조동사 + 주어'가 아닌 평서문의 어순인 '_____'로 쓴다.

개념 적용 They wondered who should they(→ _____) go and talk to.
그들은 누구에게 가서 이야기해야 할지 궁금했다.

05 부가의문문은 '평서문(긍정문 또는 부정문) + _____의 의문문' 구조로 만든다.

개념 적용 You don't like it, don't(→ _____) you?
너는 그것을 좋아하지 않아, 그렇지?

06 부가의문문을 만들 때 평서문의 _____을 활용하여 만든다.

개념 적용 It's not surprising that book stores don't carry newspapers any more, doesn't(→ _____) it?
서점에서 더 이상 신문을 취급하지 않는 것은 놀라운 일이 아니야, 그렇지?

정답 01 준동사, danced 02 부사, efficiently 03 준동사, helping
04 (주어) + 동사, they should 05 반대 상황, do 06 주절, is

01 밑줄 친 부분 중 어법상 옳지 않은 것은?

2021. 지방직 9급 변형

① Fire <u>following an earthquake is</u> of special interest to the insurance industry.
② Word processors <u>were considered</u> to be the ultimate tool for a typist in the past.
③ Elements of income in a cash forecast will <u>be vary</u> according to the company's circumstances.
④ The world's first digital camera <u>was created</u> by Steve Sasson at Eastman Kodak in 1975.

02 밑줄 친 부분 중 어법상 옳은 것은?

2020. 국가직 9급 변형

① The traffic of a big city is busier than <u>those</u> of a small city.
② I'll think of you when <u>I'll be lying on</u> the beach next week.
③ Raisins were once an expensive food, and only <u>the wealth</u> ate them.
④ The intensity of a color is related to <u>how much gray the color contains</u>.

Chapter 02 단어의 이해

반드시 한번에 다잡는 최빈출 개념 정리

01 형용사가 나오면 부사 자리인지 확인하고 완전한 문장 구조가 나온 후에는 _____가 아닌 _____로 수식한다.

개념 적용 She speaks three languages fluent(→   ).
그녀는 3개 국어를 유창하게 구사한다.

02 서술적 용법으로만 쓰이는 형용사는 asleep, _____, _____, _____은 명사 앞에 쓸 수 없다.

개념 적용 Her voice awoke the asleep(→   ) child.
그녀의 목소리에 자고 있던 아이가 잠이 깼다.

03 부정부사와 전체를 의미하는 표현이 쓰일 때 _____을 의미하므로 해석에 주의한다.

개념 적용 Wealth is not(→   ) synonymous with happiness.
부가 행복과 반드시 아주 밀접한 것은 아니다.

04 혼동하기 쉬운 부사는 형태와 _____를 확인한다.

개념 적용 We hard(→   ) know each other.
우리는 서로 거의 잘 모른다.

05 불가산 명사는 부정관사나 수사와 함께 쓰이지 않고 _____형을 만들 수 없다. 불가산 명사는 _____ 취급하고 _____ 동사로 일치시킨다.

개념 적용 New equipments(→   ) were(→   ) installed at the third floor of our building.
새로운 장비는 빌딩 3층에 설치되었다.

06 _____는 앞에 나온 명사와 성과 수 일치를 확인하고 격에 따라 올바른 형태로 써야한다.

개념 적용 The Earth will not be able to satisfy the food needs of all their(→   ) inhabitants.
지구는 모든 주민들의 식량 수요를 충족시킬 수 없을 것이다.

정답
01 형용사, 부사, fluently
02 alike, afraid, alive, sleeping
03 부분 부정, not necessarily
04 의미, hardly
05 복수, 단수, 단수, equipment, was
06 인칭대명사, its

01 밑줄 친 부분 중 어법상 옳지 않은 것은?

2024. 국가직 9급

① Despite the belief that the quality of older houses is superior to ② those of modern houses, the foundations of most pre-20th-century houses are dramatically shallow ③ compared to today's, and have only stood the test of time due to the flexibility of ④ their timber framework or the lime mortar between bricks and stones.

02 밑줄 친 부분이 어법상 옳지 않은 것은?

2023. 지방직 9급

① I should have gone this morning, but I was feeling a bit ill.
② These days we do not save as much money as we used to.
③ The rescue squad was happy to discover an alive man.
④ The picture was looked at carefully by the art critic.

03 밑줄 친 부분 중 어법상 옳지 않은 것은?

2017. 지방직 9급 변형

① It was not her refusal but her rudeness that perplexed him.
② Parents cannot be too careful about their words and actions before their children.
③ More doctors were required to tend sick and wounded.
④ To make matters worse, there is a report that another typhoon will arrive soon.

04 밑줄 친 부분 중 어법상 옳지 않은 것은?

2013. 지방직 9급 변형

① George has not completed the assignment yet, and Mark hasn't either.
② My sister was upset last night because she had to do too many homeworks.
③ If he had taken more money out of the bank, he could have bought the shoes.
④ It was so quiet in the room that I could hear the leaves being blown off the trees outside.

05 밑줄 친 부분 중 어법상 옳지 않은 것은?

2019. 국가직 9급 변형

① The country with the most person computers changes from time to time.
② What happened to my lovely grandson last summer was amazing.
③ Wooden spoons are excellent toys for children, and so are plastic bottles.
④ I have been doing this work ever since I retired.

06 밑줄 친 부분 중 어법상 옳지 않은 것은?

2019. 국가직 9급 변형

① The new teacher I told you about is originally from Peru.
② I called him five minutes shy of midnight on an urgent matter.
③ What appeared to be a shark was lurking behind the coral reef.
④ She reached the mountain summit with her 16-years-old friend on Sunday.

Chapter 03 동사의 유형

반드시 한번에 다잡는 최빈출 개념 정리

01 1형식 자동사는 _____를 취하지 않으며 _____구조로 쓸 수 없다.

> 개념 적용 He wants to go the documents through(→).
> 그는 서류를 검토하기를 원한다.

> 개념 적용 The meeting will be taken place(→) next week.
> 회의는 다음 주에 열릴 것이다.

02 감각 동사를 포함한 2형식 자동사의 주격 보어로 _____는 쓸 수 없다.

> 개념 적용 Your baby looks lovely and happily(→).
> 당신의 아기는 사랑스럽고 행복해 보인다.

03 대표 3형식 타동사는 _____ 없이 바로 목적어를 수반할 수 있다.

> 개념 적용 You must obey to your parents(→).
> 당신은 부모님 말씀에 순종해야 한다.

04 4형식 수여동사를 3형식으로 전환할 때 간접목적어 앞에 쓰이는 _____에 주의한다.

> 개념 적용 The service will offer many programs about(→) children.
> 이 서비스는 어린이들에게 많은 프로그램을 제공할 것입니다.

05 5형식 지각동사와 사역동사는 목적어와 목적격 보어가 능동의 의미 관계인 경우 목적격 보어 자리에 _____를 쓴다.

> 개념 적용 This dress makes me to look(→) fat.
> 이 원피스는 나를 뚱뚱해 보이게 한다.

06 5형식 타동사는 목적어와 목적격 보어가 수동의 의미 관계인 경우에는 목적보어 자리에 _____를 쓴다. 단 let은 _____를 쓴다.

> 개념 적용 I want this car to fix(→) without delay.
> 나는 이 차를 지체 없이 수리하고 싶다.

정답 01 목적어, 수동태, go through the documents, take place 02 부사, happy
03 전치사, your parents 04 전치사, to 05 원형부정사, look 06 과거분사, be p.p., fixed

01 밑줄 친 부분 중 어법상 옳지 않은 것은?

2025. 출제 기조 전환 2차

We have already ① arrived in a digitized world. Digitization affects not only traditional IT companies, but companies across the board, in all sectors. New and changed business models ② are emerged: cars ③ are being shared via apps, languages learned online, and music streamed. But industry is changing too: 3D printers make parts for machines, robots assemble them, and entire factories are intelligently ④ connected with one another.

02 밑줄 친 부분 중 어법상 옳지 않은 것은?

2024. 지방직 9급 변형

① He found it exciting to work here.
② She mentioned me that she would be leaving early.
③ I didn't want him to come.
④ A more skillful and experienced teacher would have treated him otherwise.

03 밑줄 친 부분 중 어법상 옳지 않은 것은?

2023. 국가직 9급 변형

① All assignments are expected to be turned in on time.
② Hardly had I closed my eyes when I began to think of her.
③ The broker recommended that she buy the stocks immediately.
④ A woman with the tip of a pencil stuck in her head has finally had it remove.

04 밑줄 친 부분 중 어법상 옳지 않은 것은?

2012. 국가직 9급 변형

① We had much snow yesterday, which caused lots of people slip on the road.
② The arrangements were agreed on at the meeting last year.
③ I got scared when I saw the truck closing up on me.
④ I walked out of the front door without looking back.

05 밑줄 친 부분 중 어법상 옳지 않은 것은?

2019. 지방직 7급

Yawning is ① catching. One person's yawn can trigger yawning among an entire group. People who are more empathic are believed to be more ② easily influenced to yawn by others' yawns; brain imaging studies have shown that ③ when humans watch other people yawn, brain areas known to be involved in social function are activated. Even dogs yawn in response to seeing their owners or even strangers ④ to yawn, and contagious yawning has been noted in other animals as well.

06 밑줄 친 부분 중 어법상 옳은 것은?

2017. 지방직 9급 하반기

Last week I was sick with the flu. When my father ① heard me sneezing and coughing, he opened my bedroom door to ask me ② that I needed anything. I was really happy to see his kind and caring face, but there wasn't ③ anything he could do it to ④ make the flu to go away.

07 밑줄 친 부분 중 어법상 옳지 않은 것은?

2018. 지방직 7급

According to a recent report, three quarters of Airbnb listings in New York City were illegal. It also ① founded that commercial operators — not the middle-class New Yorkers in the ads — were making millions renting spaces exclusively to Airbnb guests. In a letter sent to ② elected officials last week, Airbnb said that most of its local ③ hosts — 87 percent — were residents who rented their spaces infrequently "to pay their bills and ④ stay in their homes."

08 밑줄 친 부분 중 어법상 옳지 않은 것은?

2017. 서울시 사회복지직 9급 변형

① We asked to him to do this job.
② They stole everything but the television.
③ Is drinking water while eating good for you?
④ That said, it is still a religious festival.

09 밑줄 친 부분 중 어법상 옳지 않은 것은?

2021. 지방직 9급 변형

① The police authorities had the woman arrested for attacking her neighbor.
② Don't let me distracted by the noise you make.
③ Please let me know the result as soon as possible.
④ He had the students phone strangers and ask them to donate money.

10 밑줄 친 부분 중 어법상 옳지 않은 것은?

2021. 지방직 9급 변형

① His novels are hard to read.
② It is no use trying to persuade the students.
③ My house is painted every five years.
④ As I went out for work, I saw a family moved in upstairs.

11 밑줄 친 부분 중 어법상 옳은 것은?

2016. 국가직 9급

① As the old saying go, you are what you eat. The foods you eat ② obvious affect your body's performance. They may also influence how your brain handles tasks. If your brain handles them well, you think more clearly, and you are more emotionally stable. The right food can ③ help you being concentrated, keep you motivated, sharpen your memory, speed your reaction time, reduce stress, and perhaps ④ even prevent your brain from aging.

12 밑줄 친 부분 중 어법상 옳지 않은 것은?

2020. 국가직 9급 변형

① Human beings quickly adapt themselves to the environment.
② She had no choice but to give up her goal because of the accident.
③ The company prohibited him from promoting to vice-president.
④ It is easy to assemble and take apart the toy car.

13 밑줄 친 부분 중 어법상 옳은 것은?

2013. 국가직 9급 변형

① Few living things are linked together as intimately than bees and flowers.
② My father would not company us to the place where they were staying, but insisted on me going.
③ The situation in Iraq looked so serious that it seemed as if the Third World War might break out at any time.
④ According to a recent report, the number of sugar that Americans consume does not vary significantly from year to year.

14 밑줄 친 부분 중 어법상 옳지 않은 것은?

2019. 지방직 9급 변형

① This is my number just in case you would like to call me.
② I am busy preparing for a trip to Europe.
③ She has married to her husband for more than two decades.
④ I should buy a book for my son to read.

15 밑줄 친 부분 중 어법상 가장 옳지 않은 것은?

2019. 서울시 9급 6월

Inventor Elias Howe attributed the discovery of the sewing machine ① for a dream ② in which he was captured by cannibals. He noticed as they danced around him ③ that there were holes at the tips of spears, and he realized this was the design feature he needed ④ to solve his problem.

16 밑줄 친 부분 중 어법상 옳지 않은 것은?

2017. 서울시 9급 변형

① John promised Mary that he would clean his room.
② John told Mary that he would leave early.
③ John believed Mary that she would be happy.
④ John reminded Mary that she should get there early.

17 밑줄 친 부분 중 어법상 가장 옳지 않은 것은?

2018. 서울시 9급 6월

Blue Planet II, a nature documentary ① produced by the BBC, left viewers ② heartbroken after showing the extent ③ to which plastic ④ affects on the ocean.

18 다음 문장에서 어법상 가장 적절한 것은?

2018. 경찰 1차

- The police officer approached ㉠ to the suspected murderer.
- Your baby looks ㉡ lovely.
- He will explain ㉢ us how he could pass the test.
- He was ㉣ disappointing with the result of the test.

① ㉠   ② ㉡
③ ㉢   ④ ㉣

Chapter 04 동사의 시제

반드시 한번에 다잡는 최빈출 개념 정리

01 명백한 과거를 나타내는 과거 시간 부사가 나오면 _____를 확인한다.

  개념 적용 My mother has undergone(→ _____) major surgery last year.
  우리 어머니께서는 작년에 대수술을 받으셨다.

02 완료 시제와 잘 쓰이는 시간 부사는 _____ 시제 동사를 확인한다.

  개념 적용 I have waited(→ _____) for an hour before he appeared.
  나는 그가 나타나기 전에 한 시간을 기다렸다.

03 시간과 조건 부사절에서는 _____의 내용을 _____시제로 대신한다.

  개념 적용 She will be waiting for me when my flight will arrive(→ _____) this evening.
  오늘 저녁에 내가 탄 비행기가 도착하면 그녀가 나를 기다리고 있을 것이다.

04 상태, 인식, 감각, 소유 동사는 _____으로 쓸 수 없다.

  개념 적용 The contents of shipwrecks are belonging to(→ _____) the state.
  난파선의 내용물은 국가 소유이다.

05 '~하자마자 …했다'라는 시제 관련 표현에서 주절은 _____시제, 종속절은 _____시제를 확인한다.

  개념 적용 She had hardly come home when she starts(→ _____) to complain.
  그녀는 집에 돌아오자마자 불평을 늘어놓기 시작했다.

06 '~한 지 시간이 …지났다'라는 시제 관용 표현은 _____시제 또는 _____시제를 쓴다.

  개념 적용 It was(→ _____) three years since I moved to this house.
  내가 이 집으로 이사 온 지 3년이 되었다.

정답 01 과거시제 동사, underwent   02 완료, had waited   03 미래, 현재, arrives
04 진행형, belong to   05 과거 완료, 과거, started   06 현재, 현재 완료, is / has been

01 밑줄 친 부분에 들어갈 말로 가장 적절한 것은?

2025. 출제 기조 전환 1차

> By the time she _____ her degree, she will have acquired valuable knowledge on her field of study.

① will have finished
② is finishing
③ will finish
④ finishes

02 밑줄 친 부분 중 어법상 옳은 것은?

2021. 국가직 9급 변형

① This guide book tells you where should you visit in Hong Kong.
② I was born in Taiwan, but I have lived in Korea since I started work.
③ The novel was so excited that I lost track of time and missed the bus.
④ It's not surprising that book stores don't carry newspapers any more, doesn't it?

03 밑줄 친 부분 중 어법상 옳지 않은 것은?

2015. 국가직 9급 변형

① He had his political enemies imprisoned.
② There can be no true liberty unless there is economic liberty.
③ I look forward to doing business with you as soon as possible.
④ When he left his hometown thirty years ago, little does he dream that he could never see it again.

04 다음 글의 ㉠, ㉡에서 어법에 맞는 표현을 골라 가장 올바르게 짝지은 것은?

2014. 경찰 2차

> For the last fifty years, advances in chemistry ㉠ brought / have brought many positive changes to the American lifestyle. ㉡ Most / Almost people have simply trusted the government and corporations to ensure the safety of the new product.

	㉠	㉡
①	brought	Almost
②	brought	Most
③	have brought	Almost
④	have brought	Most

05 밑줄 친 부분 중 어법상 옳은 것은?

2013. 국가직 9급 변형

① The house which they have lived for 10 years was badly damaged by the storm.
② It was not until when he failed the math test that he decided to study hard.
③ We had nothing left to eat in the refrigerator, we had to eat out last night.
④ We were enough fortunate to visit the Grand Canyon, which has much beautiful landscape.

06 다음 빈칸에 들어갈 표현으로 가장 적절한 것은?

2018. 경찰 2차

> Maggie will be waiting for me when my flight _____ this evening.

① will arrive
② is arrived
③ arrives
④ will have arrived

07 다음 밑줄 친 부분 중 어법상 가장 적절한 것은?

2018. 경찰 3차

① The game was watching outside the stadium on a huge screen.
② We will never get to the meeting unless the train leaves within five minutes.
③ With sunshine streamed through the window, Hugh found it impossible to sleep.
④ The water which she fell was freezing cold.

08 밑줄 친 부분 중 어법상 옳은 것은?

2018. 지방직 9급 변형

① He went to the station a few days ago to see off his friend.
② The spoiled boy made it believe he didn't hear his father calling.
③ I have never been to Buffalo, so I am looking forward to go there.
④ I have not read today's newspaper yet. Is there anything interested in it?

Chapter 05 주어와 동사 수 일치

반드시 한번에 다잡는 최빈출 개념 정리

01 _____시제 동사 또는 _____가 나오고 주어와 동사가 멀리 떨어져 있는 경우에는 수 일치에 주의한다.

개념 적용 Another way to speed up the process are(→   ) to make the shift to a new system.
그 과정의 속도를 올리는 또 다른 방법은 새로운 시스템으로 전환하는 것이다.

02 주어 자리에 both A and B를 제외한 상관 접속사는 _____에 수 일치한다.

개념 적용 Neither she nor I has(→   ) any plan for the weekend.
그녀도 나도 주말에 아무런 계획이 없다.

03 부분이나 전체를 나타내는 명사가 나오면 _____ 뒤에 명사를 확인해서 동사와 수 일치한다.

개념 적용 Most of the houses is(→   ) out of our price bracket.
그 집들은 대부분이 우리의 가격대를 넘어선다.

04 단일 개념을 의미하는 A and B는 _____ 동사와 수 일치를 확인한다.

개념 적용 Trial and error are(→   ) a fundamental method of problem solving.
시행착오는 문제 해결의 근본적인 방법이다.

05 주어 자리에 _____와 many가 쓰인다면 동사의 수 일치를 주의한다.

개념 적용 The number of accidents are(→   ) proportionate to the increased volume of traffic.
사고 건수는 늘어나는 교통량에 비례한다.

06 _____와 _____은 단수 동사와 수 일치를 확인한다.

개념 적용 Whether it is a good plan or not are(→   ) a matter for argument.
그것이 좋은 계획인지 아닌지는 논쟁의 여지가 있다.

정답 **01** 현재, be동사, is **02** B, have **03** of, are **04** 단수, is **05** number, is **06** 명사구, 명사절, is

01 밑줄 친 부분 중 어법상 옳지 않은 것은?

2025. 지방직 9급

We tend ① to imagine Robin Hood and outlaws in general as fugitives because they defied the king's officials and operated ② outside the law in the great forests of the kingdom. What we forget is that there ③ were an established process behind the creation of outlaws. On the whole, men did not choose to become outlaws; they ④ were made outlaws.

02 밑줄 친 부분 중 어법상 옳지 않은 것은?

2025. 출제 기조 전환 1차

You may conclude that knowledge of the sound systems, word patterns, and sentence structures ① are sufficient to help a student ② become competent in a language. Yet we have ③ all worked with language learners who understand English structurally but still have difficulty ④ communicating.

03 밑줄 친 부분 중 어법상 옳은 것은?

2024. 국가직 9급 변형

① We are glad that the number of applicants is increasing.
② I have received the last e-mail from him two years ago.
③ The bed which he slept last night was quite comfortable.
④ They exchanged New Year's greetings each other on screen.

04 밑줄 친 부분 중 어법상 옳지 않은 것은?

2023. 국가직 9급

While advances in transplant technology have made ① it possible to extend the life of individuals with end-stage organ disease, it is argued ② that the biomedical view of organ transplantation as a bounded event, which ends once a heart or kidney is successfully replaced, ③ conceal the complex and dynamic process that more ④ accurately represents the experience of receiving an organ.

05 밑줄 친 부분 중 어법상 가장 적절하지 않은 것은?

2020. 경찰 1차 변형

① I'm feeling sick. I <u>shouldn't have eaten</u> so much.
② Most of the suggestions made at the meeting <u>was</u> not very practical.
③ <u>Providing</u> the room is clean, I don't mind which hotel we stay at.
④ <u>We'd been</u> playing tennis for about half an hour when it started to rain heavily.

06 밑줄 친 부분에 들어갈 가장 적절한 것은?

2014. 지방직 9급

> A tenth of the automobiles in this district _____ alone stolen last year.

① was
② had been
③ were
④ have been

07 밑줄 친 부분 중 어법상 가장 옳지 않은 것은?

2017. 경찰 2차

> ① <u>Creating</u> the electrical energy also creates environmental problems. We can't give up electricity, but we can control the ways we use ② <u>it</u>. We can use alternative sources of energy that ③ <u>is</u> not as harmful to the environment as those which we are presently ④ <u>using</u>.

08 밑줄 친 부분 중 어법상 옳은 것은?

2014. 지방직 9급 변형

① Many a careless walker <u>was killed</u> in the street.
② Each officer must perform their duties <u>efficient</u>.
③ <u>However you may try hard</u>, you cannot carry it out.
④ German shepherd dogs are smart, alert, and <u>loyalty</u>.

09 밑줄 친 부분 중 어법상 옳은 것은?

2012. 지방직 9급 변형

① Without plants to eat, animals must <u>leave from</u> their habitat.
② He arrived with Owen, who was weak and <u>exhaust</u>.
③ This team usually <u>work</u> late on Fridays.
④ <u>Beside</u> literature, we have to study history and philosophy.

10 밑줄 친 부분 중 어법상 옳지 않은 것은?

2012. 지방직 7급

> The number of people ① <u>taking</u> cruises ② <u>continue to</u> rise and ③ <u>so does</u> the number of complaints about cruise lines. Sufficient ④ <u>information</u> is still missing.

11 밑줄 친 부분 중 어법상 옳지 않은 것은?

2015. 지방직 7급

The immune system in our bodies ① fights the bacteria and viruses which cause diseases. Therefore, whether or not we are likely to get various diseases ② depend on how well our immune system works. Biologists used to ③ think that the immune system was a separate, independent part of our body, but recently they ④ have found that our brain can affect our immune system. This discovery indicates that there may be a connection between emotional factors and illness.

12 다음 밑줄 친 부분 중 어법상 옳지 않은 것은?

2022. 국가직 9급

To find a good starting point, one must return to the year 1800 during ① which the first modern electric battery was developed. Italian Alessandro Volta found that a combination of silver, copper, and zinc ② were ideal for producing an electrical current. The enhanced design, ③ called a Voltaic pile, was made by stacking some discs made from these metals between discs made of cardboard soaked in sea water. There was ④ such talk about Volta's work that he was requested to conduct a demonstration before the Emperor Napoleon himself.

13 밑줄 친 부분 중 어법상 가장 옳지 않은 것은?

2017. 서울시 9급 변형

The idea that justice ① in allocating access to a university has ② something to do with the goods that ③ universities properly pursue ④ explain why selling admission is unjust.

14 밑줄 친 부분 중 어법상 가장 적절하지 않은 것은?

2018. 경찰 3차

If properly stored, broccoli will stay ① fresh for up to four days. The best way to store fresh bunches is to refrigerate them in an open plastic bag in the vegetable compartment, ② which will give them the right balance of humidity and air, and help preserve the vitamin C content. Don't wash the broccoli before ③ storing it since moisture on its surface ④ encourage the growth of mold.

15 밑줄 친 부분 중 어법상 가장 옳지 않은 것은?

2016. 서울시 9급

He acknowledged that ① the number of Koreans were forced ② into labor ③ under harsh conditions in some of the locations ④ during the 1940's.

16 밑줄 친 부분 중 어법상 가장 옳지 않은 것은?

2019. 서울시 9급 6월

Squid, octopuses, and cuttlefish are all ① types of cephalopods. ② Each of these animals has special cells under its skin that ③ contains pigment, a colored liquid. A cephalopod can move these cells toward or away from its skin. This allows it ④ to change the pattern and color of its appearance.

17 밑줄 친 부분 중 어법상 가장 옳지 않은 것은?

2018. 서울시 9급 6월

I'm ① pleased that I have enough clothes with me. American men are generally bigger than Japanese men so ② it's very difficult to find clothes in Chicago that ③ fits me. ④ What is a medium size in Japan is a small size here.

18 밑줄 친 부분 중 어법상 옳지 않은 것은?

2013. 지방직 9급 변형

① They are the largest animals ever to evolve on Earth, larger by far than the dinosaurs.
② She didn't like the term Native American any more than my mother did.
③ Three-quarters of what we absorb in the way of information about nature comes into our brains via our eyes.
④ The number of doctors study hard in order that they can keep abreast of all the latest developments in medicine.

19 밑줄 친 부분 중 어법상 옳지 않은 것은?

2020. 지방직 9급

Elizabeth Taylor had an eye for beautiful jewels and over the years amassed some amazing pieces, once ① declaring "a girl can always have more diamonds." In 2011, her finest jewels were sold by Christie's at an evening auction ② that brought in $115.9 million. Among her most prized possessions sold during the evening sale ③ were a 1961 bejeweled timepiece by Bulgari. Designed as a serpent to coil around the wrist, with its head and tail ④ covered with diamonds and having two hypnotic emerald eyes, a discreet mechanism opens its fierce jaws to reveal a tiny quartz watch.

Chapter 06 수동태

반드시 한번에 다잡는 최빈출 개념 정리

01 사물이 주어 자리에 나오는 경우 _____ 구조로 잘 쓰인다.

  개념 적용 This conference holds(→ _____) to stimulate student's interests in global warming.
  이 학회는 지구온난화에 대한 학생들의 관심을 고취시키기 위해 열린다.

02 _____, _____ 자동사는 능동의 의미만 가능하고 수동태 구조는 불가능하므로 능동태 구조로 쓰였는지 확인한다.

  개념 적용 The plane was disappeared(→ _____) behind a cloud.
  비행기는 구름 뒤로 사라졌다.

03 3형식 타동사구의 수동태 구조에서는 _____ 에 주의한다.

  개념 적용 She was run(→ _____) and killed by a truck.
  그녀는 트럭에 치여 숨졌다.

04 5형식 타동사의 수동태 구조 be p.p. 뒤에는 _____ 가 올바른 형태로 남아있는지 확인한다.

  개념 적용 All children should be encouraged realizing(→ _____) their full potential.
  모든 아동들이 자신의 잠재력을 충분히 발휘할 수 있도록 격려해야 한다.

05 지각동사와 사역동사가 수동태가 될 때 목적보어였던 원형부정사를 _____ 로 쓴다.

  개념 적용 He was seen enter(→ _____) the building.
  그가 그 건물에 들어가는 것이 목격되었다.

06 _____ 에 주의할 수동태 표현들이 있으므로 _____ 를 확인한다.

  개념 적용 She was known as(→ _____) the quickness of her wit.
  그녀는 두뇌 회전이 빠른 것으로 유명했다.

정답 01 수동태(be + p.p.), is held   02 1형식, 2형식, disappeared   03 전치사, was run over
         04 목적보어, to realize   05 to부정사, to enter   06 전치사, 전치사, for

01 밑줄 친 부분에 들어갈 말로 가장 적절한 것은?

2025. 출제 기조 전환 2차

Overpopulation may have played a key role: too much exploitation of the rain-forest ecosystem, on which the Maya depended for food, as well as water shortages, seems to _____ the collapse.

① contribute to
② be contributed to
③ have contributed to
④ have been contributed to

02 밑줄 친 부분 중 어법상 옳지 않은 것은?

2022. 지방직 9급 변형

① He asked me why I kept coming back day after day.
② Toys children wanted all year long has recently discarded.
③ She is someone who is always ready to lend a helping hand.
④ Insects are often attracted by scents that aren't obvious to us.

03 밑줄 친 부분 중 어법상 옳지 않은 것은?

2019. 지방직 9급

Each year, more than 270,000 pedestrians ① lose their lives on the world's roads. Many leave their homes as they would on any given day never ② to return. Globally, pedestrians constitute 22% of all road traffic fatalities, and in some countries this proportion is ③ as high as two thirds of all road traffic deaths. Millions of pedestrians are non-fatally ④ injuring — some of whom are left with permanent disabilities. These incidents cause much suffering and grief as well as economic hardship.

04 밑줄 친 부분 중 어법상 옳지 않은 것은?

2018. 국가직 9급

It would be difficult ① to imagine life without the beauty and richness of forests. But scientists warn we cannot take our forest for ② granted. By some estimates, deforestation ③ has been resulted in the loss of as much as eighty percent of the natural forests of the world. Currently, deforestation is a global problem, ④ affecting wilderness regions such as the temperate rainforests of the Pacific.

05 밑줄 친 부분 중 어법상 옳은 것은?

2022. 국가직 9급 변형

① A horse should be fed according to its individual needs and the nature of its work.
② My hat was blown off by the wind while walking down a narrow street.
③ She has known primarily as a political cartoonist throughout her career.
④ Even young children like to be complimented for a job done good.

06 밑줄 친 부분 중 어법상 옳지 않은 것은?

2015. 국가직 9급 변형

① Despite searching for every job opening possible, he could not find a suitable job.
② The best way to find out if you can trust somebody is to trust that person.
③ Taste sensitivity largely influences on food intake and body weight of individuals.
④ Parents are responsible for providing the right environment for their children to grow and learn in.

07 밑줄 친 부분 중 어법상 옳지 않은 것은?

2011. 지방직 9급 변형

① I will go out if the rain stops.
② I will be finished it if you come home.
③ I had waited for an hour before he appeared.
④ He will graduate from college in three years.

08 밑줄 친 부분 중 어법상 옳지 않은 것은?

2015. 서울시 7급

Innovation, business is now learning, is likely ① to find ② wherever bright and eager ③ people think ④ they can find it.

09 밑줄 친 부분 중 어법상 옳지 않은 것은?

2015. 국가직 9급 변형

① The main reason I stopped smoking was that all my friends had already stopped smoking.
② That a husband understands a wife does not mean they are necessarily compatible.
③ The package, having been wrong addressed, reached him late and damaged.
④ She wants her husband to buy two dozen eggs on his way home.

10 밑줄 친 부분 중 어법상 옳지 않은 것은?

2010. 지방직 9급 변형

① This handbag is fake. It can't be expensive.
② In Korea, a presidential election held every five years.
③ This surface cleans easily.
④ I think it impossible to hand in the paper by tomorrow.

11 밑줄 친 부분 중 어법상 옳은 것은?

2017. 지방직 9급 하반기 변형

① Top software companies are finding increasingly challenging to stay ahead.
② A small town seems to be preferable than a big city for raising children.
③ She destined to live a life of serving others.
④ A week's holiday has been promised to all the office workers.

12 밑줄 친 부분 중 어법상 옳지 않은 것은?

2017. 지방직 7급

In countries where religion ① has been closely identified with ② a people's culture, as in Hinduism and Islam, religious education has been essential ③ to be maintained the society and ④ its traditions.

13 밑줄 친 부분 중 어법상 옳지 않은 것은?

2017. 지방직 7급

A graph of monthly climatological data ① <u>shows</u> the warmest, coolest, wettest and driest times. Also, weekends are ② <u>highlighting</u> on the graph to help you quickly locate the weekend weather ③ <u>should</u> you have activities ④ <u>planned</u>.

14 밑줄 친 부분 중 어법상 가장 옳지 않은 것은?

2017. 서울시 7급 6월

Plastics ① <u>are</u> artificial, or human-made materials ② <u>that</u> consist of polymers — long molecules ③ <u>made</u> of smaller molecules joined in chains. Not all polymers are artificial — wood and cotton are types of a natural polymer called cellulose, but they are not considered plastics because they cannot ④ <u>melt and mold</u>.

15 밑줄 친 부분 중 어법상 옳지 않은 것은?

2014. 국가직 7급

The Netherlands now ① <u>becomes</u> the only country in the world to allow the mercy killing of patients, though there are some strict conditions. ② <u>Those who want</u> medical assistance to die ③ <u>must be undergone</u> unbearable suffering. Doctor and patient must also agree there is no hope of remission. And ④ <u>a second physician</u> must be consulted.

16 밑줄 친 부분 중 어법상 옳지 않은 것은?

2014. 지방직 7급 변형

① This law shall <u>be come</u> into force on the 1st of June.
② I <u>thought too much of</u> his talent.
③ They all <u>looked up to</u> him as their leader.
④ I must work harder to <u>make up for</u> the results of my last term examination.

17 다음 빈칸에 들어갈 표현으로 가장 적절한 것은?

2018. 경찰 2차

> Usually, people who have been adopted _____ have access to their files.

① do not allow
② are not allowed to
③ has not been allowed
④ is not allowed to

18 밑줄 친 부분 중 어법상 옳지 않은 것은?

2013. 서울시 7급 변형

① <u>Maria</u> was awarded <u>first prize</u>.
② <u>250 dollars</u> was fined <u>to him</u>.
③ <u>English</u> wasn't taught <u>there</u>.
④ <u>Our solutions</u> were explained <u>to him</u>.
⑤ <u>Nash</u> was considered <u>a genius</u>.

19 밑줄 친 부분 중 어법상 옳지 않은 것은?

2014. 국가직 7급

> ① <u>Unable to do anything</u> or go anywhere while my car ② <u>was repairing</u> at my mechanic's garage, I suddenly ③ <u>came to the realization</u> that I had become ④ <u>overly dependent</u> on machines and gadgets.

20 밑줄 친 부분 중 어법상 옳지 않은 것은?

2019. 국가직 9급

> A myth is a narrative that embodies — and in some cases ① <u>helps to explain</u> — the religious, philosophical, moral, and political values of a culture. Through tales of gods and supernatural beings, myths ② <u>try to make</u> sense of occurrences in the natural world. Contrary to popular usage, myth does not mean "falsehood." In the broadest sense, myths are stories — usually whole groups of stories — ③ <u>that can be</u> true or partly true as well as false; regardless of their degree of accuracy, however, myths frequently express the deepest beliefs of a culture. According to this definition, the Iliad and the Odyssey, the Koran, and the Old and New Testaments can all ④ <u>refer to</u> as myths.

PART 02 준동사

출제 경향 분석

출제 내용 점검

Chapter 07 동명사
51 동명사의 명사 역할
52 동명사의 동사적 성질
53 암기해야 할 동명사 표현

Chapter 08 분사
54 분사 판별법[현재분사 VS 과거분사]
55 감정 분사와 분사형 형용사
56 여러 가지 분사구문
57 분사의 동사적 성질
58 분사를 활용한 표현 및 구문

Chapter 09 부정사
59 원형부정사의 용법과 관용 표현
60 to부정사의 명사적 역할
61 to부정사의 형용사적 역할
62 to부정사의 부사적 역할
63 to부정사의 동사적 성질
64 to부정사의 관용 구문

Chapter 07 동명사

반드시 한번에 다잡는 최빈출 개념 정리

01 동명사 주어는 _____ 취급하므로 _____ 동사와 수 일치한다.

　개념 적용　Creating the electrical energy create(→ _____) environmental problems.
　　　　　　전기 에너지를 만드는 것은 환경 문제를 야기한다.

02 동명사는 특정 타동사 뒤에서 _____ 역할을 한다.

　개념 적용　I successfully completed to write(→ _____) the book.
　　　　　　나는 성공적으로 그 책을 쓰는 것을 끝마쳤다.

03 _____ 뒤에는 to부정사가 아닌 동명사가 목적어 역할을 한다.

　개념 적용　We shared warmth by to help(→ _____) the neighbors in need.
　　　　　　우리는 불우이웃을 도우며 훈훈한 정을 나눴다.

04 동명사의 주어는 _____ 또는 _____으로 동명사 앞에 쓴다.

　개념 적용　She(→ _____) being honest is known to everybody.
　　　　　　그녀의 솔직함은 모든 사람들에게 알려져 있다.

05 본동사의 시제보다 동명사의 시제가 더 앞설 때는 단순형 동명사가 아닌 _____ 동명사로 쓴다.

　개념 적용　I'm sure of her being(→ _____) honest when young.
　　　　　　나는 그녀가 젊었을 때 정직했다고 확신한다.

06 _____ 표현은 해석이 중요한 영작 문제로 자주 출제되므로 반드시 암기한다.

　개념 적용　They are on the verge to sign(→ _____) a new contract.
　　　　　　그들은 새로운 계약서에 서명을 하기 직전에 있다.

정답　01 단수, 단수, creates　02 목적어, writing　03 전치사, helping　04 소유격, 목적격, Her
　　　　05 완료형, having been　06 동명사 관용, of signing

01 밑줄 친 부분 중 어법상 옳지 않은 것은?

2025. 출제 기조 전환 1차

Beyond the cars and traffic jams, she said it took a while to ① get used to have so many people in one place, ② all of whom were moving so fast. "There are only 18 million people in Australia ③ spread out over an entire country," she said, "compared to more than six million people in ④ the state of Massachusetts alone.

02 밑줄 친 부분 중 어법상 옳은 것은?

2016. 지방직 9급 변형

① That place is fantastic whether you like swimming or to walk.
② She suggested going out for dinner after the meeting.
③ The dancer that I told you about her is coming to town.
④ If she had taken the medicine last night, she would have been better today.

03 밑줄 친 부분 중 어법상 옳지 않은 것은?

2012. 지방직 9급

A mutual aid group is a place ① where an individual brings a problem and asks for assistance. As the group members offer help to the individual with the problem, they are also helping ② themselves. Each group member can make associations to a similar ③ concern. This is one of the important ways in which ④ give help in a mutual aid group is a form of self-help.

04 밑줄 친 부분 중 어법상 옳은 것은?

2018. 경찰 3차 변형

① Yusoo is considering applying for the company.
② The police station provided commodities with refugees.
③ The judge ordered that the prisoner was remanded.
④ He dived deeply into the water.

05 밑줄 친 부분 중 어법상 가장 적절한 것은?

2021. 경찰 2차 변형

① All the vehicles need repairing.
② The immediate security threat has been disappeared.
③ You must enter the password to gain an access to the network.
④ Seohee agreed to accompany with her father on a trip to France.

Chapter 08 분사

반드시 한번에 다잡는 최빈출 개념 정리

01 _____나 _____ 역할을 하는 현재분사 또는 과거분사가 나오면 어떤 분사가 적절한지 분사 판별법을 통해 확인한다.

개념 적용 The man run(→ _____) with a dog is my uncle.
개와 함께 달리고 있는 남자는 나의 삼촌이다.

02 분사의 수식을 받는 명사가 _____ 현재분사로 수식하고, 분사의 수식을 받는 명사가 _____ 과거분사로 수식한다.

개념 적용 Seeing(→ _____) from a distance, it is indistinguishable from its environment.
먼 거리에서 보여질 때, 그것은 주변환경과 구별이 안 된다.

03 _____는 현재분사로 쓸지 과거분사로 쓸지 판단한다.

개념 적용 In summary, this was a disappointed(→ _____) performance.
요컨대 이것은 실망스러운 공연이었다.

04 분사구문이 나오면 분사의 _____를 올바르게 썼는지 먼저 확인한다.

개념 적용 Being(→ _____) out of order, we sent for a mechanic.
기계가 고장 나서 우리는 기계공을 부르러 보냈다.

05 '시간·조건·양보 접속사 + 분사구문'에서는 _____가 올바르게 쓰였는지 확인한다.

개념 적용 Although made(→ _____) a mistake, he could be respected as a good teacher.
비록 실수했지만, 그는 좋은 선생님으로 존경받을 수 있었다.

06 _____의 다양한 표현을 암기하고 올바르게 썼는지 판단한다.

개념 적용 We'll have the party outside, weather permitted(→ _____)
날씨가 괜찮으면, 우리는 밖에서 파티할 것이다.

정답 01 형용사, 부사, running   02 행동하면, 행동을 당하면, Seen   03 감정동사, disappointing
04 의미상 주어, The machine being   05 분사, making   06 분사구문, permitting

01 밑줄 친 부분 중 어법상 옳지 않은 것은?

2025. 국가직 9급

Fire served humans in many ways besides ① cooking. With it they could begin ② rearranging environments to suit themselves, clearing land to stimulate the growth of wild foods and ③ opening landscapes to encourage the proliferation of food animals that could be later driven by fire to a place ④ choosing to harvest them.

02 밑줄 친 부분에 들어갈 말로 가장 적절한 것은?

2025. 지방직 9급

Preliminary investigations indicate that some, if not all, of the clients' money, _____ to be $6 million in total, has found its way into unquoted companies and property purchases.

① believe ② believing
③ believed ④ believes

03 밑줄 친 부분 중 어법상 옳지 않은 것은?

2023. 지방직 9급 변형

① We were made touching with his speech.
② Apart from its cost, the plan was a good one.
③ They watched the sunset while drinking hot tea.
④ His past experience made him suited for the project.

04 밑줄 친 부분 중 어법상 옳지 않은 것은?

2011. 국가직 9급

The Aztecs believed that chocolate ① made people intelligent. Today, we do not believe this. But chocolate has a special chemical ② calling phenylethylamine. This is the same chemical ③ the body makes when a person is in love. Which do you prefer — ④ eating chocolate or being in love?

05 밑줄 친 부분 중 어법상 옳지 않은 것은?

2022. 국가직 9급 변형

① Having drunk three cups of coffee, she can't fall asleep.
② Being a kind person, she is loved by everyone.
③ All things considered, she is the best-qualified person for the position.
④ Sitting with the legs crossing for a long period can raise blood pressure.

06 밑줄 친 부분 중 어법상 옳지 않은 것은?

2014. 국가직 9급 변형

① She does not like going outdoor, not to mention mountain climbing.
② She is more beautiful than any other girl in the class.
③ The country is a small one with the three quarters of the land surrounding by the sea.
④ A number of students are studying very hard to get a job after their graduation.

07 밑줄 친 부분 중 어법상 옳지 않은 것은?

2018. 지방직 9급 변형

① All of the information was false.
② Thomas should have apologized earlier.
③ The movie had already started when we arrived.
④ Being cold outside, I boiled some water to have tea.

08 밑줄 친 부분 중 어법상 옳지 않은 것은?

2012. 국가직 9급

A man who ① shoplifted from the Woolworth's store in Shanton in 1952 recently sent the shop an anonymous letter of apology. In it, he said, "I ② have been guilt-ridden all these days." The item he ③ stole was a two dollar toy. He enclosed a money order ④ paid back the two dollars with interest.

09 밑줄 친 부분 중 어법상 옳지 않은 것은?

2015. 지방직 7급 변형

① <u>Covering</u> with confusion, he left the conference room.
② <u>Walking</u> along the road, he tripped over the root of a tree.
③ <u>With her eyes wide open</u>, she stared at the man.
④ <u>Waving</u> goodbye, she got on the train.

10 밑줄 친 부분 중 어법상 옳지 않은 것은?

2019. 국가직 9급

Domesticated animals are the earliest and most effective 'machines' ① <u>available</u> to humans. They take the strain off the human back and arms. ② <u>Utilizing</u> with other techniques, animals can raise human living standards very considerably, both as supplementary foodstuffs (protein in meat and milk) and as machines ③ <u>to carry</u> burdens, lift water, and grind grain. Since they are so obviously ④ <u>of great benefit</u>, we might expect to find that over the centuries humans would increase the number and quality of the animals they kept. Surprisingly, this has not usually been the case.

11 밑줄 친 부분 중 어법상 옳지 않은 것은?

2020. 지방직 7급 변형

Sports utility vehicles are ① <u>more expensive</u> and use more gas than most cars. But TV ② <u>commercials</u> show them climbing rocky mountain roads ③ <u>and</u> crossing rivers, which seems ④ <u>excited</u> to many people.

12 밑줄 친 부분 중 어법상 옳지 않은 것은?

2010. 국가직 9급

I ① <u>looked forward to</u> this visit more than one ② <u>would think</u>, ③ <u>considered</u> I was flying seven hundred miles to sit alongside a ④ <u>dying man</u>. But I seemed to slip into a time warp when I visited Morrie, and I liked myself better when I was there.

13 밑줄 친 부분 중 어법상 옳은 것은?

2014. 국가직 9급

Compared to newspapers, magazines are not necessarily up-to-the-minute, since they do not appear every day, but weekly, monthly, or even less frequently. Even externally they are different from newspapers, mainly because magazines ① resemble like a book. The paper is thicker, photos are more colorful, and most of the articles are relatively long. The reader experiences much more background information and greater detail. There are also weekly news magazines, ② which reports on a number of topics, but most of the magazines are specialized to attract various consumers. For example, there are ③ women's magazines cover fashion, cosmetics, and recipes as well as youth magazines about celebrities. Other magazines are directed toward, for example, computer users, sports fans, ④ those interested in the arts, and many other small groups.

14 밑줄 친 부분 중 어법상 옳지 않은 것은?

2018. 국가직 9급

Focus means ① getting stuff done. A lot of people have great ideas but don't act on them. For me, the definition of an entrepreneur, for instance, is someone who can combine innovation and ingenuity with the ability to execute that new idea. Some people think that the central dichotomy in life is whether you're positive or negative about the issues ② that interest or concern you. There's a lot of attention ③ paying to this question of whether it's better to have an optimistic or pessimistic lens. I think the better question to ask is whether you are going to do something about it or just ④ let life pass you by.

Chapter 09 부정사

반드시 한번에 다잡는 최빈출 개념 정리

01 to부정사는 특정 타동사 뒤에서 _____ 역할을 한다.

　개념 적용 He managed finishing(→ 　　　　　) the book before the library closed.
　　　　　그는 도서관이 문을 닫기 전에 가까스로 책을 다 읽었다.

02 to부정사가 형용사 역할을 할 때 _____에 주의할 표현이 있으므로 확인한다.

　개념 적용 Have you purchased a house to live(→ 　　　　　) after you get married?
　　　　　결혼해서 살 집은 마련했어요?

03 to부정사의 의미상 주어는 for 목적격으로 쓰지만 인성 형용사를 포함한 구문에서는 의미상 주어를 _____으로 쓴다.

　개념 적용 It was careless for her(→ 　　　　　) to take the wrong bus.
　　　　　그녀가 버스를 잘못 탄 것은 부주의했다.

04 본동사의 시제보다 to부정사의 시제가 더 앞설 때는 단순형 to부정사를 _____으로 쓴다.

　개념 적용 He claims to be(→ 　　　　　) robbed yesterday.
　　　　　그는 어제 도둑을 맞았다고 주장한다.

05 'too 형용사/부사 to부정사' 구문에서 to부정사의 목적어와 그 절의 주어가 같을 때 to부정사 뒤의 목적어는 _____.

　개념 적용 This opportunity is too good for me to miss it(→ 　　　　　).
　　　　　이 기회는 놓치기에는 나에게 너무 좋은 것이다.

06 'enough to부정사'는 형용사와 부사를 _____ 수식한다.

　개념 적용 He's enough old(→ 　　　　　) to take care of himself.
　　　　　그는 스스로를 돌볼 만큼 나이가 들었다.

정답 01 목적어, to finish　　02 전치사, to live in　　03 of 목적격, of her　　04 완료형, to have been
　　　 05 생략한다, to miss　　06 후치, old enough

01 밑줄 친 부분 중 어법상 옳지 않은 것은?

2022. 지방직 9급 변형

① I cannot afford wasting even one cent.
② The smile soon faded from her face.
③ She had no alternative but to resign.
④ I'm aiming to start my own business in five years.

02 밑줄 친 부분 중 어법상 옳지 않은 것은?

2020. 지방직 9급 변형

① I regret to tell you that I lost your key.
② His experience at the hospital was worse than hers.
③ It reminds me of the memories of the past 24 years.
④ I like people who look me in the eye when I have a conversation.

03 밑줄 친 부분 중 어법상 옳은 것은?

2016. 지방직 9급 변형

① The poor woman couldn't afford to get a smartphone.
② I am used to get up early everyday.
③ The number of fires that occur in the city are growing every year.
④ Bill supposes that Mary is married, isn't he?

04 밑줄 친 부분 중 어법상 옳지 않은 것은?

2017. 국가직 9급 변형

① Only after the meeting did he recognize the seriousness of the financial crisis.
② The minister insisted that a bridge be constructed over the river to solve the traffic problem.
③ As difficult a task as it was, Linda did her best to complete it.
④ He was so distracted by a text message to know that he was going over the speed limit.

05 밑줄 친 부분 중 어법상 옳지 않은 것은?

2013. 지방직 7급

> Wisdom enables us to take information and knowledge and ① use them to make good decisions. On a personal level, my mother finished only the fifth grade, ② was widowed in the heart of the depression and had six children ③ very young to work. Obviously she needed wisdom to use the knowledge she had ④ to make the right decisions to raise her family successfully.

07 다음 빈칸에 들어갈 말로 가장 적절한 것은?

2011. 경찰 2차

> Living in the buildings on his construction site, over 1000 workers _____ in one basement.

① used to sleep
② are used to sleep
③ to be sleeping
④ sleeping

06 밑줄 친 부분 중 어법상 옳지 않은 것은?

2014. 지방직 7급 변형

① The bag was too heavy for me to lift it.
② So ridiculous did she look that everybody burst out laughing.
③ He was seen to come out of the house.
④ I can't get that child to go to bed.

08 밑줄 친 부분 중 어법상 옳은 것은?

2016. 국가직 7급 변형

① Time always takes a little to tune in on a professor's style.
② I'm used to waiting until the last minute and staying up all night.
③ The math question was too tough for the student to answer it.
④ Too many hours of hard work really tired of me.

09 밑줄 친 부분 중 어법상 옳지 않은 것은?

2011. 국가직 9급 변형

① He is the last person to deceive you.
② He would much rather make a compromise than fight with his fists.
③ Frescoes are so familiar a feature of Italian churches that they are easy to take it for granted.
④ Even though he didn't go to college, he is a very knowledgeable man.

10 밑줄 친 부분 중 어법상 옳지 않은 것은?

2011. 국가직 9급 변형

① I couldn't finish the exam because I ran out of time.
② It is much more difficult than you'd expect to break a habit.
③ Most people have a strong dislike to excessive violence on TV.
④ Blessed is the man who is too busy to worry in the day and too tired of lying awake at night.

11 밑줄 친 부분 중 어법상 옳지 않은 것은?

2013. 국가직 7급

A final way to organize an essay is to ① proceeding from relatively simple concepts to more complex ones. By starting with generally ② accepted evidence, you establish rapport with your readers and assure them that the essay is ③ firmly grounded in shared experience. In contrast, if you open with difficult material, you risk ④ confusing your audience.

PART 03 조동사와 조동사를 활용한 구문

출제 경향 분석

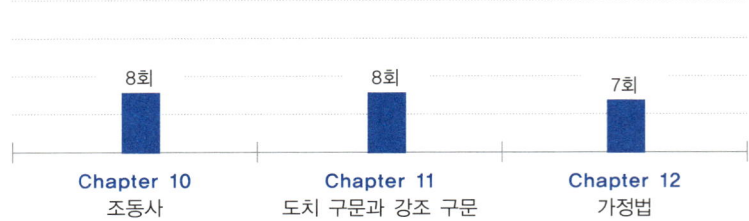

Chapter 10	Chapter 11	Chapter 12
조동사	도치 구문과 강조 구문	가정법
8회	8회	7회

출제 내용 점검

Chapter 10 조동사
⑥⑤ 조동사 뒤의 동사원형과 조동사의 부정형
⑥⑥ 조동사 should의 3가지 용법과 생략 구조
⑥⑦ 주의해야 할 조동사와 조동사 관용 표현

Chapter 11 도치 구문과 강조 구문
⑥⑧ 부정부사와 도치 구문
⑥⑨ 다양한 도치 구문
⑦⓪ 양보 도치 구문과 장소 방향 도치 구문
⑦① 강조 구문과 강조를 위한 표현

Chapter 12 가정법
⑦② 가정법 미래 공식
⑦③ 가정법 과거 공식
⑦④ 가정법 과거완료 공식
⑦⑤ 혼합 가정법 공식
⑦⑥ if 생략 후 도치된 가정법
⑦⑦ 기타 가정법

Chapter 10 조동사

반드시 한번에 다잡는 최빈출 개념 정리

01 주장·요구·명령·제안·충고 동사의 목적어로 that절이 쓰일 때 that절의 동사는 '_____'으로 쓴다.

개념 적용 He ordered that the work was(→ _____) done.
그는 그 일을 해내라고 명령했다.

02 It be 이성적 판단 형용사 that절 구조에서는 that절의 동사는 '_____'으로 쓴다.

개념 적용 It is important that he attends(→ _____) every day.
그가 매일 출석하는 것이 중요하다.

03 「조동사 have p.p.」 구조는 _____ 을 올바르게 썼는지 확인해야 한다.

개념 적용 It should(→ _____) have rained last night.
어젯밤에 틀림없이 비가 왔을 것이다.

04 'need not'에서 need는 조동사이므로 'need not' 뒤에는 _____ 을 쓴다.

개념 적용 Business letters need not to be(→ _____) formal and impersonal.
사업상의 편지라고 해서 딱딱하고 인간미 없게 쓸 필요는 없다.

05 'cannot ~ too 형용사/부사'는 '_____'라는 의미이다.

개념 적용 We cannot be careful(→ _____) in the choice of books.
우리는 책을 선택하는 데는 아무리 주의해도 지나치지 않다.

06 'cannot (help/choose) but 동사원형'은 '_____'라는 의미이다.

개념 적용 In the age of globalization, we cannot but to study(→ _____) foreign languages.
세계화 시대에 우리는 외국어를 공부하지 않을 수 없다.

정답 01 (should) 동사원형, should be / be 02 (should) 동사원형, should attend / attend 03 해석, must
04 동사원형, be 05 아무리 ~해도 지나치지 않다, too careful
06 ~할 수밖에 없다, ~하지 않을 수 없다, study

01 밑줄 친 부분에 들어갈 말로 가장 적절한 것은?

2025. 국가직 9급

> Whitworths, a retailer offering online grocery shopping, says it has discovered that some staff members who are paid a salary _____ paid enough in recent years.

① may not have been
② should not have
③ would not be
④ will not be

02 다음 빈칸에 들어갈 말로 가장 적절한 것은?

2013. 경찰 1차

> Because Oriental ideas of woman's subordination to man prevailed in those days, she _____ meet with men on an equal basis.

① did dare not
② dared not
③ dared not to
④ did dare not to

03 밑줄 친 부분 중 어법상 옳은 것은?

2016. 국가직 9급 변형

① Jessica is a much careless person who makes little effort to improve her knowledge.
② But he will come or not is not certain.
③ The police demanded that she not leave the country for the time being.
④ The more a hotel is expensiver, the better its service is.

04 밑줄 친 부분 중 어법상 옳은 것은?

2012. 국가직 9급 변형

① She felt that she was good swimmer as he was, if not better.
② This phenomenon has described so often as to need no further clichés on the subject.
③ What surprised us most was the fact that he said that he had hardly never arrived at work late.
④ Even before Mr. Kay announced his movement to another company, the manager insisted that we begin advertising for a new accountant.

05 밑줄 친 부분 중 어법상 옳은 것은?

2020. 국가직 9급 변형

① Several problems have raised due to the new members.
② The committee commanded that construction of the building cease.
③ They had to fight against winds that will blow over 40 miles an hour.
④ The seeds of most plants are survived by harsh weather.

06 밑줄 친 부분 중 어법상 옳지 않은 것은?

2016. 지방직 9급 변형

① I'd rather relax at home than going to the movies tonight.
② The police are very unwilling to interfere in family problems.
③ It's no use worrying about past events over which you have no control.
④ I misplace my keys so often that my secretary carries spare ones for me.

07 밑줄 친 부분 중 어법상 옳지 않은 것은?

2017. 국가직 9급 변형

① Please come to the headquarters as soon as you receive this letter.
② I ought to have formed a habit of reading in my boyhood.
③ Having been abroad for ten years, he can speak English very fluently.
④ Had I given up the project at that time, I should have achieved such a splendid.

08 밑줄 친 부분 중 어법상 옳은 것은?

2021. 경찰 2차 변형

① It is essential that every employee wear protective gear.
② No one would ask him to work late, much more force him to do that.
③ As discussing in the meeting, the new policies will bring significant benefits.
④ A CEO visited the factory which most of the company's products are manufactured.

Chapter 11 도치 구문과 강조 구문

반드시 한번에 다잡는 최빈출 개념 정리

01 부정부사가 _____ 처음이나 절 처음에 위치하면 「조동사 + 주어」 도치 구조를 확인한다.

　개념 적용　No longer he could(→　　　　　) distinguish between illusion and reality.
　　　　　　그는 더 이상 착각과 현실을 구별할 수가 없었다.

02 부정부사는 다른 _____와 겹쳐 쓰지 않는다.

　개념 적용　I can't hardly(→　　　　　) make myself understood in English.
　　　　　　나는 영어로 의사소통할 수 없다.

03 so와 neither를 포함한 도치 구문에서 so는 _____과 호응, neither는 부정문과 호응한다. 이때, 조동사는 앞에 나온 동사의 종류와 시제에 따라 결정되고 뒤에 나온 주어와 수 일치한다.

　개념 적용　Prices have gone up, and so does(→　　　　　) the price of education.
　　　　　　가격은 올라가고 그로 인해 교육비도 올라가고 있다.

04 'Only+부사(부사구, 부사절)'가 문장 처음이나 절 처음에 위치하면 _____ 도치 구조를 확인한다.

　개념 적용　Only when he needs something he looks(→　　　　　) for me.
　　　　　　그는 아쉬울 때만 나를 찾는다.

05 _____ 양보 도치 구문은 여러 가지로 쓰일 수 있으므로 주의한다.

　개념 적용　A woman(→　　　　　) as she was, she was brave.
　　　　　　그녀는 여자이지만 용감했다.

06 장소와 방향 부사구가 문장 처음에 쓰일 경우 '1형식 자동사+주어'로 도치되고 _____를 확인한다.

　개념 적용　On the map is(→　　　　　) many symbols that show national boundaries.
　　　　　　지도에는 국경선을 보여주는 많은 기호들이 있다.

정답　**01** 문장, could he　**02** 부정부사, can't　**03** 긍정문, has　**04** '조동사+주어', does he look
　　　　05 As, Woman　**06** 수 일치, are

01 밑줄 친 부분 중 어법상 옳지 않은 것은?
2022. 지방직 9급 변형

① No sooner I have finishing the meal than I started feeling hungry again.
② She will have to pay the bill sooner or later.
③ Reading is to the mind what exercise is to the body.
④ He studied medicine at university but ended up working for an accounting firm.

02 밑줄 친 부분 중 어법상 가장 적절하지 않은 것은?
2020. 경찰 1차 변형

① No sooner had he seen me than he ran away.
② Little I dreamed that he had told me a lie.
③ Written in plain English, the book has been read by many people.
④ When I met her for the first time, I couldn't help but fall in love with her.

03 밑줄 친 부분 중 어법상 옳은 것은?
2017. 지방직 9급 변형

① The oceans contain many forms of life that has not yet been discovered.
② The rings of Saturn are so distant to be seen from Earth without a telescope.
③ The Aswan High Dam has been protected Egypt from the famines of its neighboring countries.
④ Included in this series is "The Enchanted Horse," among other famous children's stories.

04 밑줄 친 부분 중 어법상 옳은 것은?
2017. 국가직 9급 변형

① They didn't believe his story, and neither did I.
② The sport in that I am most interested is soccer.
③ Jamie learned from the book that World War I had broken out in 1914.
④ Two factors have made scientists difficult to determine the number of species on Earth.

05 밑줄 친 부분 중 어법상 옳지 않은 것은?

2015. 지방직 9급 변형

① She regrets not having worked harder in her youth.
② He is a man of both experience and knowledge.
③ Anger is a normal and healthy emotion.
④ Under no circumstances you should not leave here.

06 밑줄 친 부분 중 어법상 옳은 것은?

2021. 국가직 9급 변형

① I look forward to receive your reply as soon as possible.
② He said he would rise my salary because I worked hard.
③ His plan for the smart city was worth considered.
④ Cindy loved playing the piano, and so did her son.

07 밑줄 친 부분 중 어법상 옳지 않은 것은?

2017. 국가직 9급 변형

① A few words caught in passing set me thinking.
② Hardly did she enter the house when someone turned on the light.
③ We drove on to the hotel, from whose balcony we could look down at the town.
④ The homeless usually have great difficulty getting a job, so they are losing their hope.

08 밑줄 친 부분 중 어법상 옳지 않은 것은?

2011. 국가직 7급

A few weeks earlier I had awoken just after dawn to find the bed beside me ① empty. I got up and found Jenny sitting in her bathrobe at the glass table on the screened porch of our little bungalow, bent over the newspaper with a pen in her hand. There was ② nothing unusual about the scene. Not only ③ were the Palm Beach Post our local paper, it was also the source of half of our household income. We were a two-newspaper-career couple. Jenny worked as a feature writer in the Post's "Accent" section; I was a news reporter at the ④ competing paper in the area, the South Florida Sun-Sentinel, based an hour south in Fort Lauderdale.

Chapter 12 가정법

반드시 한번에 다잡는 최빈출 개념 정리

01 「if + 주어 + should 동사원형」 또는 「if + 주어 + were to부정사」가 나오면 가정법 _____를 의미하므로 주절의 동사가 올바르게 쓰였는지 확인해야 한다.

 개념 적용 If you were to ever see it, you will(→ _____) think you were in heaven.
 만일 여러분이 그것을 언젠가 보시게 되면, 아마 천국에 와있는 느낌일 거예요.

02 「if + 주어 + 과거 동사」가 나오면 가정법 _____를 의미하고 「주어 + would/should/could/might 동사원형」이 올바르게 쓰였는지 확인해야 한다.

 개념 적용 If I were in your shoes, I would have resigned(→ _____) immediately.
 내가 당신이라면, 즉시 사임하겠어요.

03 「if + 주어 + had p.p.」가 나오면 가정법 _____를 의미하고 「주어 + would/should/could/might have p.p.」가 올바르게 쓰였는지 확인해야 한다.

 개념 적용 If I have(→ _____) the advertisement in time, I would have applied for the job.
 만약에 내가 그 광고를 제때 봤더라면, 그 직장에 지원을 했을 것이다.

04 if절에 과거 시간 부사와 주절에 _____ 부사가 쓰였다면 혼합 가정법 공식을 확인해야 한다

 개념 적용 If she had started earlier, he would have been(→ _____) here now.
 만약 그녀가 더 일찍 출발했더라면, 지금 여기에 있을 텐데.

05 「_____ 주어 ~」, 「_____ + 주어」, 「_____ + 주어」로 시작한다면 if가 생략된 가정법이므로 가정법 공식을 확인해야 한다.

 개념 적용 Had education focus(→ _____) on creativity, they could have become great artists.
 교육이 창의력에 초점을 맞추었더라면, 그들은 훌륭한 예술가가 될 수도 있었을 것이다.

06 _____를 사용하지 않는 여러 가지 가정법 표현의 형태가 올바르게 쓰였는지 확인한다.

 개념 적용 It is high time that we start(→ _____) a campaign for the environment.
 이제는 우리가 환경 운동을 시작해야 할 때입니다.

정답 01 미래, would 02 과거, resign 03 과거 완료, had seen 04 현재 시간, be
05 Were, Should, Had, focused 06 if, started / should start

01 밑줄 친 부분 중 어법상 옳은 것은?

2018. 지방직 9급 변형

① Please contact to me at the email address I gave you last week.
② Were it not for water, all living creatures on earth would be extinct.
③ The laptop allows people who is away from their offices to continue to work.
④ The more they attempted to explain their mistakes, the worst their story sounded.

02 밑줄 친 부분 중 어법상 옳은 것은?

2011. 국가직 9급 변형

① She objects to be asked out by people at work.
② I have no idea where is the nearest bank around here.
③ Tom, one of my best friends, were born in April 4th, 1985.
④ Had they followed my order, they would not have been punished.

03 밑줄 친 부분 중 어법상 옳지 않은 것은?

2012. 지방직 9급 변형

① He speaks English fluently as if he were an American.
② What if we should fail?
③ If it rains tomorrow, I'll just stay at home.
④ If it had not been for Newton, the law of gravitation would not be discovered.

04 밑줄 친 부분 중 어법상 옳은 것은?

2021. 경찰 1차 변형

① Should you have any questions, please feel free to contact me.
② You would rather stay at home than to go with her.
③ The team manager didn't like the plan, so did the rest of the staff.
④ He met many people during his trip, some of them became his friends.

05 밑줄 친 부분 중 어법상 옳지 않은 것은?

2010. 지방직 9급

Many studies ① have shown the life-saving value of safety belts. When accidents ② occur, most serious injuries and deaths are ③ caused by people being thrown from their seats. About 40 percent of those killed in bygone accidents ④ would be saved if wearing safety belts.

06 밑줄 친 부분 중 어법상 가장 옳은 것은?

2018. 서울시 9급 3월 변형

① If the item should not be delivered tomorrow, they would complain about it.
② He was more skillful than any other baseball players in his class.
③ Hardly has the violinist finished his performance before the audience stood up and applauded.
④ Bakers have been made come out, asking for promoting wheat consumption.

07 밑줄 친 부분 중 어법상 옳은 것은?

2015. 지방직 9급 변형

① She supposed to phone me last night, but she didn't.
② I have been knowing Jose since I was seven.
③ You'd better to go now or you'll be late.
④ Sarah would be offended if I didn't go to her party.

PART 04 연결어

출제 경향 분석

출제 내용 점검

Chapter 13 접속사
- ⑱ 등위접속사와 병치 구조
- ⑲ 명사절 접속사의 구분과 특징
- ⑳ 부사절 접속사의 구분과 특징
- ㉑ 주의해야 할 부사절 접속사

Chapter 14 관계사
- ㉒ 관계대명사의 선행사와 문장 구조
- ㉓ 「전치사 + 관계대명사」 완전 구조
- ㉔ 관계대명사 주의 사항
- ㉕ 유사관계대명사 as, but, than
- ㉖ 관계부사의 선행사와 완전 구조
- ㉗ 관계사, 의문사, 복합관계사의 구분

Chapter 15 전치사
- ㉘ 전치사와 명사 목적어
- ㉙ 주의해야 할 전치사

Chapter 13 접속사

반드시 한번에 다잡는 최빈출 개념 정리

01 등위접속사(and, but, or)가 나오면 _____ 구조를 확인해야 한다.

  개념 적용 He packed up their possessions slowly and deliberate(→ _____).
  그는 그들의 소지품들을 천천히 신중하게 꾸렸다.

02 명사절 접속사 _____ 은 완전 구조를 취하고 명사절 접속사 _____ 은 불완전 구조를 취한다.

  개념 적용 That(→ _____) you say doesn't make any sense to me.
  네가 하는 말을 나는 이해할 수가 없다.

03 주의해야 할 _____ 접속사가 나오면 올바르게 쓰였는지 확인한다.

  개념 적용 He was on full alert lest similar problems are(→ _____) posed again.
  그는 또 다시 비슷한 문제가 생기지 않도록 촉각을 곤두세웠다.

04 _____ 는 동사를 포함한 절을 이끌고 _____ 는 명사를 추가한다.

  개념 적용 Her voice was shaking though(→ _____) all her efforts to control it.
  목소리가 떨리지 않게 하려고 무진 애를 썼는데도 불구하고 그녀는 목소리가 떨렸다.

05 명사절 접속사 _____ 는 '~인지, ~일지'라는 의미로 쓰이며 _____ 자리에 모두 쓰인다.

  개념 적용 If(→ _____) it is a good plan or not is a matter for argument.
  그것이 좋은 계획인지 아닌지는 논쟁의 여지가 있다.

06 명사절 접속사 _____ 는 '~인지, ~일지'라는 의미로 쓰이며 _____ 의 목적어 자리에만 쓰일 수 있다.

  개념 적용 We didn't know what(→ _____) we should write or phone.
  우리는 전화를 해야 할지 편지를 써야 할지 몰랐다.

정답 **01** 병치, deliberately **02** that, what, What **03** 부사절, should be / be **04** 접속사, 전치사, despite
05 Whether, 주어, 목적어, 보어, Whether **06** If, 타동사, if

01 밑줄 친 부분 중 어법상 옳지 않은 것은?

2025. 국가직 9급

The city opened the Smart Senior Citizens' Center, a leisure facility that offers ① customized programs for the elderly. It ② features virtual activities such as silver aerobics and ③ laughter therapy, monitors health metrics in collaboration with public health centers, and ④ including indoor gardening activities.

02 밑줄 친 부분 중 어법상 옳지 않은 것은?

2024. 지방직 9급

One of the many ① virtues of the book you are reading ② is that it provides an entry point into Maps of Meaning, ③ which is a highly complex work ④ because of the author was working out his approach to psychology as he wrote it.

03 밑줄 친 부분 중 어법상 옳지 않은 것은?

2014. 국가직 7급 변형

① He lowered his voice for fear he should not be overheard.
② She would be the last person to go along with the plan.
③ Top executives are entitled to first class travel.
④ To work is one thing, and to make money is another.

04 밑줄 친 부분 중 어법상 옳지 않은 것은?

2021. 국가직 9급

Urban agriculture (UA) has long been dismissed as a fringe activity that has no place in cities; however, its potential is beginning to ① be realized. In fact, UA is about food self-reliance: it involves ② creating work and is a reaction to food insecurity, particularly for the poor. Contrary to ③ which many believe, UA is found in every city, where it is sometimes hidden, sometimes obvious. If one looks carefully, few spaces in a major city are unused. Valuable vacant land rarely sits idle and is often taken over — either formally, or informally — and made ④ productive.

05 밑줄 친 부분 중 어법상 옳지 않은 것은?

2015. 국가직 7급 변형

① It is important that <u>you do</u> it yourself rather than rely on others.
② My car, <u>parked</u> in front of the bank, was towed away for illegal parking.
③ I'll lend you with money provided you <u>will pay</u> me back by Saturday.
④ The game <u>might have been played</u> if the typhoon had not been approaching.

06 밑줄 친 부분 중 어법상 옳은 것은?

2020. 지방직 9급 변형

① Of the billions of stars in the galaxy, how <u>much</u> are able to hatch life?
② The Christmas party was really <u>excited</u> and I totally lost track of time.
③ I must leave right now <u>because</u> I am starting work at noon today.
④ They used <u>to loving</u> books much more when they were younger.

07 밑줄 친 부분 중 어법상 옳지 않은 것은?

2010. 지방직 9급 변형

① Everything changed <u>afterwards</u> we left home.
② At the moment, <u>she's working</u> as an assistant in a bookstore.
③ I'm going to train hard <u>until</u> the marathon and then I'll relax.
④ This beautiful photo album is the perfect gift for <u>a newly-married couple</u>.

08 밑줄 친 부분 중 어법상 가장 옳지 않은 것은?

2017. 서울시 7급 변형

① What personality studies have shown <u>is that</u> openness to change declines with age.
② A collaborative space program could build greater understanding, promote world peace, and <u>improving</u> scientific knowledge.
③ More people may start <u>buying</u> reusable tote bags if they become cheaper.
④ Today, more people <u>are using</u> smart phones and tablet computers for business.

09 밑줄 친 부분 중 어법상 옳지 않은 것은?

2023. 지방직 9급

One reason for upsets in sports — ① <u>in which</u> the team ② <u>predicted</u> to win and supposedly superior to their opponents surprisingly loses the contest — is ③ <u>what</u> the superior team may not have perceived their opponents as ④ <u>threatening</u> to their continued success.

10 밑줄 친 부분 중 어법상 옳은 것은?

2019. 지방직 9급 변형

① The paper charged her <u>with use</u> the company's money for her own purposes.
② The investigation had to be handled with the utmost care lest suspicion <u>be aroused</u>.
③ Another way to speed up the process would <u>be made</u> the shift to a new system.
④ Burning fossil fuels is one of the <u>lead</u> causes of climate change.

11 밑줄 친 부분 중 어법상 옳지 않은 것은?

2013. 국가직 9급

Noise pollution ① is different from other forms of pollution in ② a number of ways. Noise is transient: once the pollution stops, the environment is free of it. This is not the case with air pollution, for example. We can measure the amount of chemicals ③ introduced into the air, ④ whereas is extremely difficult to monitor cumulative exposure to noise.

12 밑줄 친 부분 중 어법상 옳지 않은 것은?

2016. 지방직 7급 변형

① I made a chart so that you can understand it better.
② In case I'm not in my office, I'll let you know my mobile phone number.
③ Speaking of the election, I haven't decided who I'll vote for yet.
④ It's the same that you come here or I go there.

13 밑줄 친 부분 중 어법상 옳지 않은 것은?

2017. 지방직 9급 변형

① You might think that just eating a lot of vegetables will keep you perfectly healthy.
② Academic knowledge isn't always that leads you to make right decisions.
③ The fear of getting hurt didn't prevent him from engaging in reckless behaviors.
④ Julie's doctor told her to stop eating so many processed foods.

14 밑줄 친 부분 중 어법상 옳은 것은?

2021. 국가직 9급 변형

① Rich as if you may be, you can't buy sincere friends.
② It was such a beautiful meteor storm that we watched it all night.
③ Her lack of a degree kept her advancing.
④ He has to write an essay on if or not the death penalty should be abolished.

15 밑줄 친 부분 중 어법상 옳은 것은?

2021. 지방직 9급 변형

① My sweet-natured daughter suddenly became <u>unpredictably</u>.
② She attempted a new method, and needless to say <u>had different results</u>.
③ <u>Upon arrived</u>, he took full advantage of the new environment.
④ He felt <u>enough comfortable to tell</u> me about something he wanted to do.

16 밑줄 친 부분 중 어법상 옳지 않은 것은?

2022. 지방직 9급 변형

① You can write on <u>both sides</u> of the paper.
② My home offers me a feeling of security, <u>warm</u>, and love.
③ <u>The number</u> of car accidents is on the rise.
④ Had I realized what you were intending to do, I <u>would have stopped</u> you.

17 밑줄 친 부분 중 어법상 옳지 않은 것은?

2016. 국가직 9급 변형

① My aunt didn't remember <u>meeting</u> her at the party.
② It took <u>me 40 years to write</u> my first book.
③ A strong wind blew my umbrella inside out <u>as I was walking home</u> from school.
④ It is not the strongest of the species, nor the most intelligent, <u>or</u> the one most responsive to change that survives to the end.

18 밑줄 친 부분 중 어법상 옳지 않은 것은?

2011. 지방직 9급

Yesterday at the swimming pool everything seemed ① <u>to go</u> wrong. Soon after I arrived, I sat on my sunglasses and broke them. But my worst moment came when I decided to climb up to the high diving tower to see ② <u>how</u> the view was like. ③ <u>Once</u> I was up there, I realized that my friends were looking at me because they thought I was going to dive. I decided I was too afraid to dive from that height. So I climbed down the ladder, feeling very ④ <u>embarrassed</u>.

Chapter 14 관계사

반드시 한번에 다잡는 최빈출 개념 정리

01 관계대명사는 _____가 올바르게 쓰였는지 그리고 뒤의 문장 구조가 _____한지 확인해야 한다. 단, 소유격 관계대명사 whose는 _____ 절을 이끌기 때문에 주의해야 한다.

개념 적용 I don't like to speak ill of friends whom you are close to them(→   ).
당신이 가까이 하고 있는 친구들을 나쁘게 말하고 싶지 않다.

02 관계대명사 that은 _____ 용법으로 쓰일 수 없고 _____ 뒤에 쓸 수 없으므로 주의해야 한다.

개념 적용 My sister, that(→   ) lives in Chicago, has two sons.
누이는 시카고에서 사는데, 아들이 둘 있다.

03 「전치사 + 관계대명사」가 나오면 _____에 유의하고 뒤에 _____ 구조인지 확인해야 한다.

개념 적용 The position in which(→   ) you have applied has already been filled.
당신이 지원한 자리는 이미 채용되었다.

04 _____ 관계대명사 뒤에 동사는 선행사와 _____ 한다.

개념 적용 These planets are found near stars that is(→   ) similar to our Sun.
이 행성들은 우리의 태양과 유사한 별 가까이에서 발견된다.

05 유사관계대명사 but은 _____의 의미를 포함하고 있으므로 뒤에 _____ 표현을 쓰지 않는다.

개념 적용 There is no one but doesn't have(→   ) some faults.
실수를 하지 않는 사람은 아무도 없다.

06 관계부사는 _____에 따라 다르고 뒤에 _____ 구조를 이끈다.

개념 적용 We visited the house which(→   ) Shakespeare was born.
우리는 셰익스피어의 생가를 방문했다.

정답 01 선행사, 불완전, 완전한, to 02 계속적, 전치사, who 03 전치사, 완전, for which 04 주격, 수 일치, are
05 부정, 부정, has 06 선행사, 완전, where

01 밑줄 친 부분 중 어법상 옳지 않은 것은?

2025. 지방직 9급

The olive tree was ① such a driving force in the economies of the Ancient Greek city-states ② that it was believed ③ to have been a gift of gods—namely from Athena, the goddess of wisdom, ④ whom Athens took its name.

02 밑줄 친 부분 중 어법상 옳지 않은 것은?

2025. 출제 기조 전환 2차

It seems to me that any international organization ① designed to keep the peace must have the power not merely to talk ② but also to act. Indeed, I see this ③ as the central theme of any progress towards an international community ④ which war is avoided not by chance but by design.

03 밑줄 친 부분이 어법상 옳지 않은 것은?

2024. 지방직 9급

① You must plan not to spend too much on the project.
② My dog disappeared last month and hasn't been seen since.
③ I'm sad that the people who daughter I look after are moving away.
④ I bought a book on my trip, and it was twice as expensive as it was at home.

04 밑줄 친 부분 중 어법상 옳지 않은 것은?

2020. 지방직 9급 변형

① Since the warranty had expired, the repairs were not free of charge.
② A gift card will be given to whomever completes the questionnaire.
③ If I had asked for a vacation last month, I would be in Hawaii now.
④ His father suddenly passed away last year, and, what was worse, his mother became sick.

05 밑줄 친 부분 중 어법상 옳지 않은 것은?

2019. 지방직 7급 변형

① The woman who lives next door is a doctor.
② Have you ever been to London?
③ Please just do which I ordered.
④ The woman he fell in love with left him after a month.

06 밑줄 친 부분 중 어법상 옳지 않은 것은?

2011. 지방직 9급

Chile is a Latin American country ① where throughout most of the twentieth century ② was marked by a relatively advanced liberal democracy on the one hand and only moderate economic growth, ③ which forced it to become a food importer, ④ on the other.

07 밑줄 친 부분 중 어법상 옳지 않은 것은?

2018. 지방직 7급

Officials in the UAE, responding to an incident ① which an Emirati tourist was arrested in Ohio, cautioned Sunday that travelers from the Arab country should "refrain from ② wearing the national dress" in public places ③ while visiting the West "to ensure their safety" and said that women should abide by bans ④ on face veils in European countries, according to news reports from Dubai.

08 밑줄 친 부분 중 어법상 옳은 것은?

2014. 국가직 9급 변형

① While worked at a hospital, she saw her first air show.
② However weary you may be, you must do the project.
③ One of the exciting games I saw were the World Cup final in 2010.
④ It was the main entrance for that she was looking.

09 밑줄 친 부분 중 어법상 옳지 않은 것은?

2014. 지방직 7급

The United States national debt was relatively small ① until the Second World War, during ② when it grew ③ from $43 billion to $259 billion ④ in just five years.

10 밑줄 친 부분 중 어법상 가장 적절하지 않은 것은?

2021. 경찰 1차 변형

① They saw a house which windows were all broken.
② What do you say to playing basketball on Sunday morning?
③ Despite her poor health, she tries to live a happy life every day.
④ If it had not rained last night, the road wouldn't be muddy now.

11 밑줄 친 부분 중 어법상 옳지 않은 것은?

2018. 지방직 9급

I am writing in response to your request for a reference for Mrs. Ferrer. She has worked as my secretary ① for the last three years and has been an excellent employee. I believe that she meets all the requirements ② mentioned in your job description and indeed exceeds them in many ways. I have never had reason ③ to doubt her complete integrity. I would, therefore, recommend Mrs. Ferrer for the post ④ what you advertise.

12 다음 글의 (A), (B), (C)에서 어법상 옳은 것을 모두 고른 것은?

2015. 지방직 9급

Pattern books contain stories that make use of repeated phrases, refrains, and sometimes rhymes. In addition, pattern books frequently contain pictures (A) that/what may facilitate story comprehension. The predictable patterns allow beginning second language readers to become involved (B) immediate/immediately in a literacy event in their second language. Moreover, the use of pattern books (C) meet/meets the criteria for literacy scaffolds by modeling reading, by challenging students' current level of linguistic competence, and by assisting comprehension through the repetition of a simple sentence pattern.

	(A)	(B)	(C)
①	that	immediate	meet
②	what	immediately	meets
③	that	immediately	meets
④	what	immediate	meet

Chapter 15 전치사

반드시 한번에 다잡는 최빈출 개념 정리

01 전치사는 _____ 또는 _____를 목적어로 취하며 동사나 형용사는 전치사의 목적어가 될 수 없다.

개념 적용 The bank violated its policy by giving loans to unemployed(→ _____).
그 은행은 실업자들에게 대출을 해줌으로써 정책을 위반했다.

02 주의해야 할 _____가 나오면 올바르게 쓰였는지 확인한다.

개념 적용 Beside(→ _____) working as a doctor, he also writes novels in his spare time.
그는 의사로 일하는 외에 여가 시간에 소설도 쓴다.

03 '~동안'이라는 의미를 갖는 의미가 있는 전치사인 _____은 숫자 기간을 목적어로 취하고 _____은 어떠한 행동을 한 시점 명사를 목적어로 취한다.

개념 적용 My father was in the hospital during(→ _____) six weeks.
나의 아버지께서는 6주 동안 병원에 계셨다.

04 '_____'라는 의미를 갖는 전치사에는 'regardless of, _____, without regard to'가 있다.

개념 적용 Everyone is treated equally, irrespective(→ _____) race.
인종과 상관없이 모든 사람들이 동등한 대우를 받는다.

05 '_____'라는 의미를 갖는 전치사인 by와 until은 함께 쓰인 동사에 주의한다. 특히, finish, complete, submit, hand in과 쓰이는 전치사는 _____이다.

개념 적용 Please complete the presentation slides until(→ _____) Monday morning
월요일 아침까지 프리젠테이션 슬라이드를 완성해주세요.

06 _____는 전치사 또는 접속사로 쓰일 수 있지만 비슷한 의미가 있는 _____는 부사이므로 명사 또는 절을 이끌 수 없다.

개념 적용 I was delighted to see my mother afterwards(→ _____) such a long time.
나는 참으로 오랜만에 어머니를 만나서 기뻤다.

정답
01 명사, 동명사, the unemployed
02 전치사, Besides
03 for, during, for
04 ~와 관계없이, irrespective of, irrespective of
05 ~까지, by, by
06 after, afterwards, after

01 밑줄 친 부분 중 어법상 옳지 않은 것은?
2023. 국가직 9급 변형

① My cat is three times as old as his.
② We have to finish the work until the end of this month.
③ She washes her hair every other day.
④ You had better take an umbrella in case it rains.

02 밑줄 친 부분 중 어법상 옳은 것은?
2015. 국가직 9급 변형

① China's imports of Russian oil skyrocketed by 36 percent in 2014.
② Sleeping has long been tied to improve memory among humans.
③ Last night, she nearly escaped from running over by a car.
④ The failure is reminiscent of the problems surrounded the causes of the fatal space shuttle disasters.

03 밑줄 친 부분 중 어법상 옳지 않은 것은?
2010. 국가직 9급

New York's Christmas is featured in many movies ① while this time of year, ② which means that this holiday is the most romantic and special in the Big Apple. ③ The colder it gets, the brighter the city becomes ④ with colorful lights and decorations.

04 밑줄 친 부분 중 어법상 옳지 않은 것은?
2012. 국가직 9급 변형

① I am on a tight budget so that I have only fifteen dollars to spend.
② His latest film is far more boring than his previous ones.
③ It's thoughtful of him to remember the names of every member in our firm.
④ I'd lost my front door key, and I had to smash a window by a brick to get in.

PART 05 비교

출제 경향 분석

Chapter 16
비교 구문

출제 내용 점검

Chapter 16 비교 구문
- ⑨⓪ 원급 비교 구문
- ⑨① 비교급 비교 구문
- ⑨② 비교 대상 일치
- ⑨③ 원급, 비교급, 최상급 강조 부사
- ⑨④ 「The 비교급 ~, the 비교급 …」 구문
- ⑨⑤ 라틴어 비교 구문과 전치사 to
- ⑨⑥ 배수 비교 구문에서 배수사의 위치
- ⑨⑦ 원급을 이용한 표현
- ⑨⑧ 비교급을 이용한 표현
- ⑨⑨ 최상급 구문
- ⑩⓪ 원급과 비교급을 이용한 최상급 대용 표현

Chapter 16　비교 구문

반드시 한번에 다잡는 최빈출 개념 정리

01 원급 비교 구문은 '_____'로 쓰고 비교급 비교 구문은 '_____'으로 쓴다.

　개념 적용　She was not as beautiful than(→ 　　　　　) I had imagined.
　　　　　　그녀는 내가 상상했던 것만큼 아름답지는 않았다.

02 비교 표현 뒤에 that과 those가 나오면 앞에 나온 비교 대상의 수에 따라 _____ 명사면 that을 쓰고, _____ 명사면 those를 쓴다.

　개념 적용　The lives of dogs are much shorter than that(→ 　　　　　) of humans.
　　　　　　개의 삶은 인간의 삶보다 훨씬 더 짧다.

03 원급, 비교급, 최상급을 강조하는 _____가 올바르게 쓰였는지 확인한다.

　개념 적용　Jobs nowadays are very(→ 　　　　　) more insecure than they were ten years ago.
　　　　　　오늘날에는 일자리가 십년 전보다 훨씬 더 불안정하다.

04 _____로 끝나는 라틴어 비교 표현은 접속사 than 대신 전치사 to를 쓴다.

　개념 적용　Modern music is often considered inferior than(→ 　　　　　) that of the past.
　　　　　　현대 음악은 흔히 과거의 음악보다 못한 것으로 여겨진다.

05 「The 비교급 ~, the 비교급」 구문에서는 양쪽에 _____와 어순 그리고 최상급이나 원급이 아닌 비교급이 올바르게 쓰였는지 확인한다.

　개념 적용　The more she thought about it, more(→ 　　　　　) depressed she became.
　　　　　　그녀는 그것에 대해 생각을 할수록 점점 더 우울해졌다.

06 최상급 표현은 _____해서 쓰지 않는다.

　개념 적용　The most easiest(→ 　　　　　) way to prevent a cold is washing your hands often.
　　　　　　감기를 예방하는 가장 쉬운 방법은 손을 자주 씻는 것입니다.

정답　01 as 형용사/부사 원급 as, 비교급 than, as　　02 단수, 복수, those　　03 부사, much　　04 -or, to
　　　　05 the, the more　　06 중복, easiest

01 밑줄 친 부분이 어법상 옳지 않은 것은?

2024. 국가직 9급

① They are not interested in reading poetry, <u>still more</u> in writing.
② <u>Once confirmed</u>, the order will be sent for delivery to your address.
③ <u>Provided that</u> the ferry leaves on time, we should arrive at the harbor by morning.
④ Foreign journalists hope to cover as <u>much news</u> as possible during their short stay in the capital.

02 밑줄 친 부분 중 어법상 옳지 않은 것은?

2022. 국가직 9급 변형

① It is by no means easy for us <u>to learn</u> English in a short time.
② Nothing is more precious <u>as time</u> in our life.
③ Children cannot be <u>too careful</u> when crossing the street.
④ She easily believes <u>what</u> others say.

03 밑줄 친 부분 중 어법상 옳지 않은 것은?

2014. 서울시 9급

My ①<u>art history professors</u> prefer Michelangelo's painting ②<u>to viewing his sculpture</u>, although Michelangelo ③<u>himself</u> was ④<u>more proud</u> of the ⑤<u>latter</u>.

04 밑줄 친 부분 중 어법상 옳지 않은 것은?

2016. 국가직 7급 변형

① <u>With many people ill</u>, the meeting was cancelled.
② It is not <u>so straightforward a problem</u> as we expected.
③ <u>How many bags are</u> the students carrying on board with them?
④ No explanation was offered, <u>still more</u> an apology.

05 밑줄 친 부분 중 어법상 옳지 않은 것은?

2017. 지방직 9급 변형

① I made it a rule to call him two or three times a month.
② He grabbed me by the arm and asked for help.
③ Owing to the heavy rain, the river has risen by 120cm.
④ I prefer to stay home than to going out on a snowy day.

06 밑줄 친 부분 중 어법상 옳지 않은 것은?

2016. 지방직 9급 변형

① Can you talk her out of her foolish plan?
② I know no more than you don't about her mother.
③ His army was outnumbered almost two to one.
④ Two girls of an age are not always of a mind.

07 밑줄 친 부분 중 어법상 가장 옳지 않은 것은?

2019. 서울시 9급 6월

There is a more serious problem than ① maintaining the cities. As people become more comfortable working alone, they may become ② less social. It's ③ easier to stay home in comfortable exercise clothes or a bathrobe than ④ getting dressed for yet another business meeting!

08 밑줄 친 부분 중 어법상 옳지 않은 것은?

2015. 지방직 9급 변형

① Jane is not as young as she looks.
② It's easier to make a phone call than to write a letter.
③ You have more money than I.
④ Your son's hair is the same color as you.

09 밑줄 친 부분 중 어법상 가장 적절하지 않은 것은?

2021. 경찰 1차 변형

① She didn't turn on the light lest she should wake up her baby.
② Convinced that he made a mistake, he apologized to his customers.
③ We hope Mr. Park will run his department as efficient as he can.
④ Statistics show that about 50% of new businesses fail in their first year.

10 밑줄 친 부분 중 어법상 옳지 않은 것은?

2018. 국가직 9급 변형

① The speaker was not good at getting his ideas across to the audience.
② The traffic jams in Seoul are more serious than those in any other city in the world.
③ Making eye contact with the person you are speaking to is important in western countries.
④ It turns out that he was not so stingier as he was thought to be.

11 밑줄 친 부분 중 어법상 옳지 않은 것은?

2017. 지방직 9급 하반기 변형

① The budget is about 25% higher than originally expecting.
② There is a lot of work to be done for the system upgrade.
③ It will take at least a month, maybe longer to complete the project.
④ The head of the department, who receives twice the salary, has to take responsibility.

12 밑줄 친 부분 중 어법상 옳은 것은?

2017. 국가직 9급 하반기 변형

① My father was in the hospital during six weeks.
② The whole family is suffered from the flu.
③ She never so much as mentioned it.
④ She would like to be financial independent

진가영 영어
반한다 기출

진가영 영어연구소 | cafe.naver.com/easyenglish7

Vol. 3
독해

PART 01 홈페이지 게시글 유형
PART 02 전자메일 유형
PART 03 안내문 유형
PART 04 중심 내용 파악 유형
PART 05 문장 제거 유형
PART 06 문장 삽입 유형
PART 07 순서 배열 유형
PART 08 빈칸 추론 유형

PART 01 홈페이지 게시글 유형

출제 경향 분석

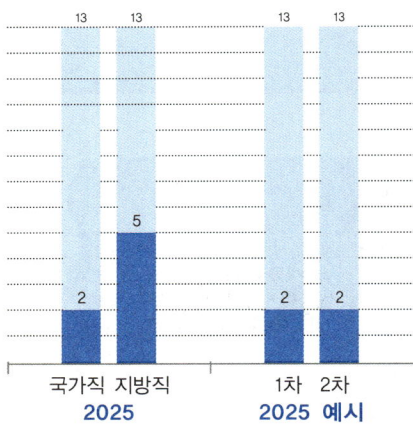

반드시 한번에 다잡는 '홈페이지 게시글' 유형 기출 독해 어휘

- exclude 제외하다, 배제하다
- biodegradable 생분해성의
- material 재료
- dispose of 버리다, 처리하다
- from now on 지금부터 계속
- notify 통지하다, 알리다
- overdue (지불·반납 등의) 기한이 지난, 연체된
- fine 과태료, 벌금
- approved 승인된, 공인된, 입증된
- registered 등록[등기]한, 기명의
- prosperous 번영한, 번창한
- substantial 본질적인, 실체의, 상당한
- attain 달성하다, 이루다
- vulnerable 취약한, 연약한
- administer 운영하다, 관리하다
- domestic 국내의, 가정의
- international 국외의, 국제적인
- wholesome 건강에 좋은, 건전한

- facilitate 촉진하다, 용이하게 하다
- practice 관행, 관례, 실행, 실천
- integrity 진정(성), 진실(성)
- independence 독립, 자립
- objectivity 객관성
- enduring 지속적인, 오래가는
- dedicated 전념하는, 헌신적인
- identity 정체성, 독자성, 유사성
- customs 세관, 관세
- declaration (세관·세무서에의) 신고(서), 선언, 발표
- notable 주목할 만한, 눈에 띄는, 중요한, 유명한
- submit 제출하다, 항복[굴복]하다
- enable ~할 수 있게 하다, 가능하게 하다
- principal 주요한, 주된, 학장, 총장
- regulatory 규제의, 규정의, 조절의
- resolve 해결하다, 결심하다, 분해[용해]하다
- enforcement 집행, 시행, 실시
- compensate for 보상하다, 보충하다

[01~02] 다음 글을 읽고 물음에 답하시오. 2025. 국가직 9급

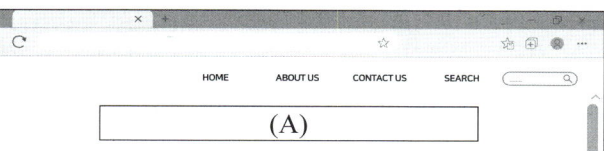

Each year in July people all over the world aim to exclude common plastic waste items from their daily life, opting instead for reusable containers or those made from biodegradable materials. We think this is a great idea and why not make it a year-round effort at home and in the workplace.

The vision started in Western Australia in 2011 and has since moved across the world to help promote the vision and stop the earth becoming further saturated with plastic materials which are part of our convenience lifestyle.

Lots of items are designed to be used once and disposed of. They fill up bins in homes, schools, at work and on streets across the world.

You can assist in achieving the goal of having a world without plastic waste.

Choose what you will do
☐ Avoid single-use plastic packaging
☐ Target the takeaway items that could end up in the ocean
☐ Go completely plastic free

I will participate
☐ for 1 day   ☐ for 1 week
☐ for 1 month   ☐ from now on

01 (A)에 들어갈 윗글의 제목으로 가장 적절한 것은?

① Development of Single-Use Items
② Join the Plastic-Free Challenge
③ How to Dispose of Plastic Items
④ Simple Ways to Save Energy

02 윗글에서 캠페인에 관한 내용과 일치하지 않는 것은?

① 2011년 서호주에서 시작되었다.
② 플라스틱 과다 사용을 줄이기 위해 전 세계로 확산되었다.
③ 실천할 활동을 선택하여 참여할 수 있다.
④ 최대 한 달까지 참여할 수 있다.

[03~04] 다음 글을 읽고 물음에 답하시오. 2025. 지방직 9급

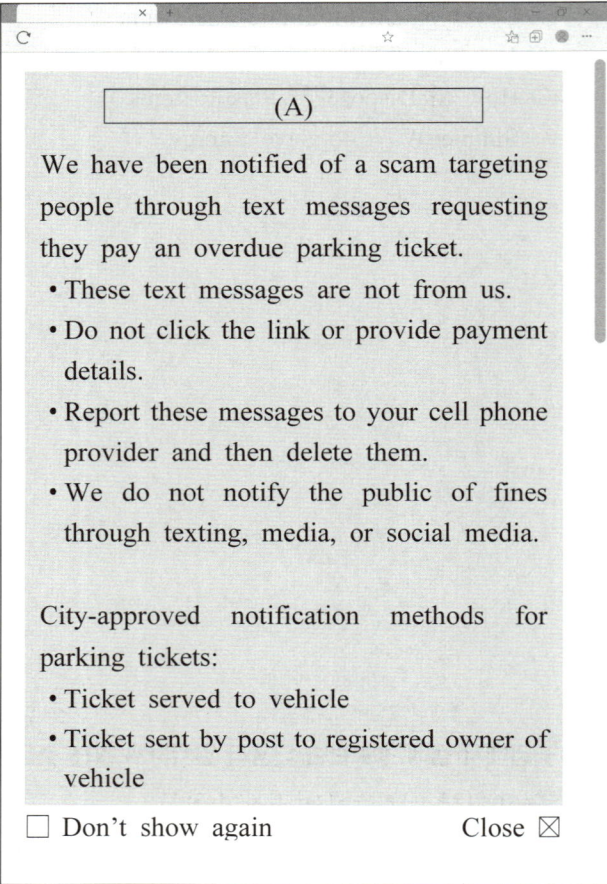

[05~06] 다음 글을 읽고 물음에 답하시오. 2025. 지방직 9급

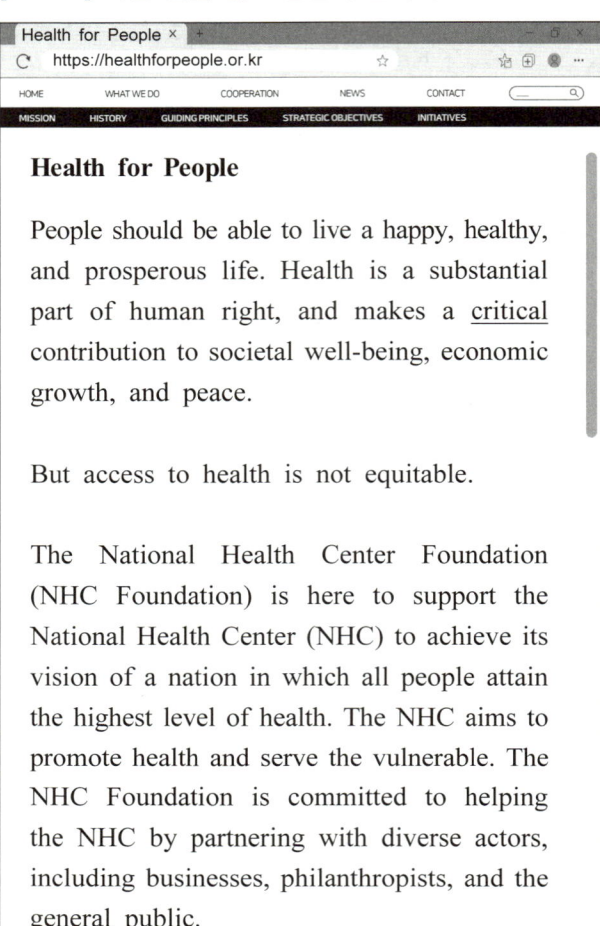

03 (A)에 들어갈 윗글의 제목으로 가장 적절한 것은?

① City Parking Ticket Payment Methods
② How to Avoid Getting Parking Tickets
③ Save Time and Money! Helpful Parking Tips
④ Alert! Fake Parking Ticket Payment Text Messages

04 윗글의 내용과 일치하는 것은?

① 전달된 링크에 결제 세부 정보를 입력해야 한다.
② 수신한 문자는 삭제하면 안 된다.
③ 시에서는 벌금을 문자로 통보한다.
④ 고지서는 등록된 차량 소유주에게 우편으로 발송된다.

05 밑줄 친 critical의 의미와 가장 가까운 것은?

① pivotal
② perilous
③ analytical
④ judgmental

06 윗글의 목적으로 가장 적절한 것은?

① 의료비 지원이 필요한 사람들을 위한 기부를 독려하려고
② 행복하고 건강한 삶을 위한 캠페인을 제안하려고
③ NHC를 지원하는 기관을 소개하려고
④ NHC의 파트너를 선정하려고

[07-08] 다음 글을 읽고 물음에 답하시오.

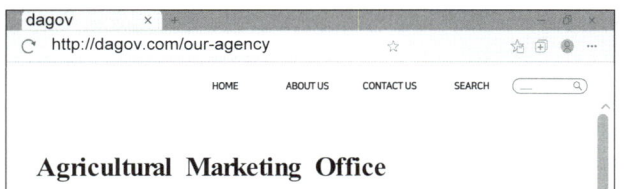

Agricultural Marketing Office

Mission
We administer programs that create domestic and international marketing opportunities for national producers of food, fiber, and specialty crops. We also provide the agriculture industry with valuable services to ensure the quality and availability of wholesome food for consumers across the country and around the world.

Vision
We facilitate the strategic marketing of national agricultural products in domestic and international markets while ensuring <u>fair</u> trading practices and promoting a competitive and efficient marketplace to the benefit of producers, traders, and consumers of national food, fiber, and specialty crops.

Core Values
- Honesty & Integrity: We expect and require complete honesty and integrity in all we do.
- Independence & Objectivity: We act independently and objectively to create trust in our programs and services.

07 윗글에서 Agricultural Marketing Office에 관한 내용과 일치하는 것은?

① It creates marketing opportunities for domestic producers.
② It limits wholesome food consumption around the world.
③ It is committed to benefiting consumers over producers.
④ It receives mandates from other agencies before making decisions.

08 밑줄 친 fair의 의미와 가장 가까운 것은?

① free
② mutual
③ profitable
④ impartial

09 다음 글에서 The National Independence Museum 에 대한 내용과 일치하는 것은? 2025. 지방직 9급

The National Independence Museum

The National Independence Museum preserves the national history through exhibitions, research, and educational programs, while fostering national pride. We invite you to experience this legacy and hear the enduring calls for peace in a scenic rural setting.

Major Projects
- **Exhibitions & Collection Management**: A total of 150,000 relics of the independence movement are displayed in eight exhibition halls.
- **Research**: Dedicated to the study of the independence movement, the Museum supports scholarly work on related historical topics.
- **Education**: Through educational programs, the Museum promotes the national identity and deepens historical understanding among citizens.
- **Cultural Events**: Regular cultural events are held to provide visitors with insights into the national history and culture.

① It is located in an urban environment surrounded by many skyscrapers.
② It displays more than a million artifacts related to the independence movement.
③ It supports educational activities instead of scholarly projects.
④ It offers visitors cultural events on a regular basis.

10 Enter-K 앱에 관한 다음 글의 내용과 일치하지 않는 것은? 2025. 출제 기조 전환 1차

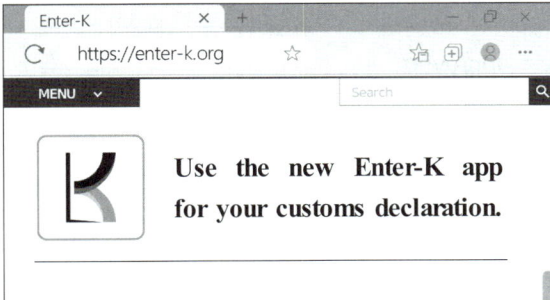

Use the new Enter-K app upon your arrival at the airport. One notable feature offered by Enter-K is the Advance Declaration, which allows travellers the option to submit their customs declaration in advance, enabling them to save time at all our international airports. As part of the ongoing Traveller Modernization initiative, Enter-K will continue to introduce additional border-related features in the future, further improving the overall border experience. Simply download the latest version of the app from the online store before your arrival. There is also a web version of the app for those who are not comfortable using mobile devices.

① It allows travellers to declare customs in advance.
② More features will be added later.
③ Travellers can download it from the online store.
④ It only works on personal mobile devices.

11 Office of the Labor Commissioner에 관한 다음 글의 내용과 일치하는 것은? 2025. 출제 기조 전환 1차

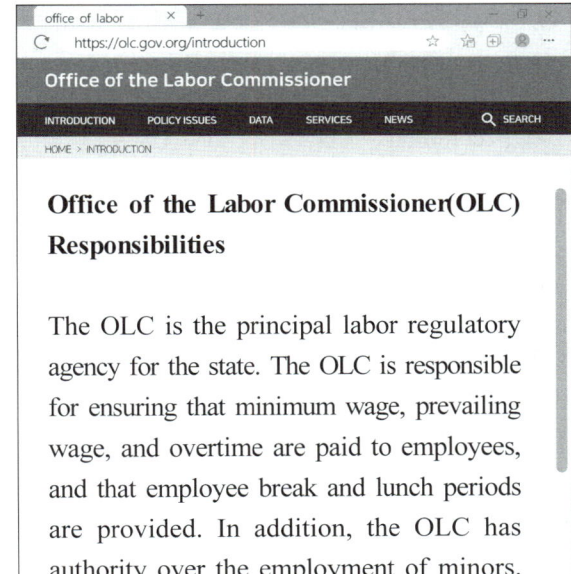

Office of the Labor Commissioner(OLC) Responsibilities

The OLC is the principal labor regulatory agency for the state. The OLC is responsible for ensuring that minimum wage, prevailing wage, and overtime are paid to employees, and that employee break and lunch periods are provided. In addition, the OLC has authority over the employment of minors. It is the vision and mission of this office to resolve labor-related problems in an efficient, professional, and effective manner. This includes educating employers and employees regarding their rights and responsibilities under the law. The OLC takes enforcement action when necessary to ensure that workers are treated fairly and compensated for all time worked.

① It ensures that employees pay taxes properly.
② It has authority over employment of adult workers only.
③ It promotes employers' business opportunities.
④ It takes action when employees are unfairly treated.

01 홈페이지 게시글 유형 기출 독해 어휘 복습 TEST

#	단어		#	단어	
1	exclude		21	approved	
2	common		22	vehicle	
3	plastic waste		23	post	
4	reusable		24	registered	
5	biodegradable		25	prosperous	
6	material		26	substantial	
7	promote		27	contribution	
8	saturated		28	equitable	
9	convenience		29	foundation	
10	dispose of		30	attain	
11	fill up		31	vulnerable	
12	bin		32	philanthropist	
13	across the world		33	administer	
14	single-use		34	domestic	
15	from now on		35	international	
16	notify		36	fiber	
17	overdue		37	specialty crop	
18	report		38	agriculture	
19	delete		39	availability	
20	fine		40	wholesome	

41	facilitate		61	submit	
42	practice		62	enable	
43	integrity		63	ongoing	
44	expect		64	introduce	
45	independence		65	border	
46	objectivity		66	related	
47	exhibition		67	latest	
48	enduring		68	commissioner	
49	relic		69	principal	
50	movement		70	regulatory	
51	dedicated		71	ensure	
52	scholarly		72	minimum wage	
53	identity		73	prevailing wage	
54	deepen		74	overtime	
55	insight		75	minor	
56	skyscraper		76	resolve	
57	customs		77	enforcement	
58	declaration		78	treat	
59	notable		79	fairly	
60	allow		80	compensate for	

PART 02 전자메일 유형

출제 경향 분석

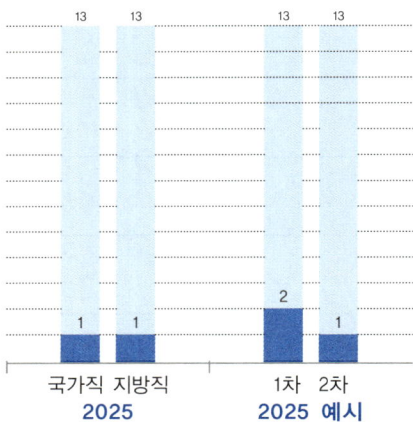

반드시 한번에 다잡는 '전자메일' 유형 기출 독해 어휘

- regarding ~에 대하여, ~에 관하여
- excessive 과도한, 지나친
- district 지역, 지방
- matter 문제, 물질, 재료, 중요하다, 문제가 되다
- take steps 조치를 취하다
- address 해결하다, 다루다, 처리하다, 주소를 쓰다, 연설하다
- tranquility 평온, 고요, 차분함
- council 의회, 자문 위원회
- inform 알리다, 통지하다
- issue 문제, 주제, 쟁점, 사안
- pothole (도로에) 움푹 패인 곳
- crack 균열, 금
- worsen 악화되다, 악화시키다
- disruption 혼잡, 혼란, 분열, 붕괴
- temporary 일시적인, 임시의
- minor 경미한, 가벼운, 작은
- property 부동산, 재산, 소유물, 건물 (구내)
- request 요청[요구/신청]하다

- address 해결하다, 고심하다
- resolve 해결하다, 다짐하다
- conversation 대화
- valuable 매우 유익한, 소중한
- follow up 더 알아보다, ~을 덧붙이다, 후속 조치하다
- status 상황, 신분, 지위
- timeline 일정, 연대표
- additional 추가의
- protect 보호하다, 지키다
- personal 개인의, 사적인
- threat 위협, 협박
- frequently 자주, 흔히
- up to date 최신의, 최근의
- wary of ~을 조심하는
- suspicious 의심스러운, 수상쩍은
- authentication 인증, 증명
- verify 확인하다, 입증하다
- regularly 정기[규칙]적으로

[01~02] 다음 글을 읽고 물음에 답하시오.

2025. 출제 기조 전환 1차

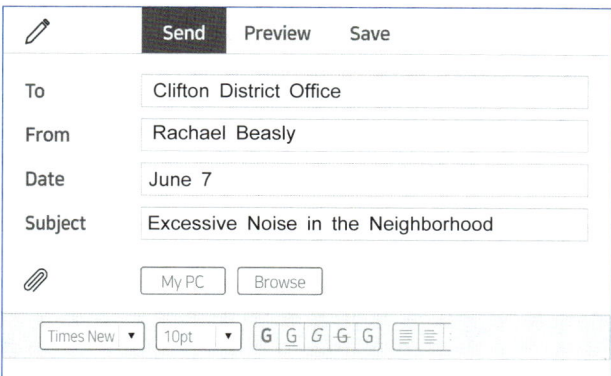

To: Clifton District Office
From: Rachael Beasly
Date: June 7
Subject: Excessive Noise in the Neighborhood

To whom it may concern,

I hope this email finds you well. I am writing to express my concern and frustration regarding the excessive noise levels in our neighborhood, specifically coming from the new sports field.

As a resident of Clifton district, I have always appreciated the peace of our community. However, the ongoing noise disturbances have significantly impacted my family's well-being and our overall quality of life. The sources of the noise include crowds cheering, players shouting, whistles, and ball impacts.

I kindly request that you look into this matter and take appropriate steps to address the noise disturbances. Thank you for your attention to this matter, and I appreciate your prompt response to help restore the tranquility in our neighborhood.

Sincerely,
Rachael Beasley

01 윗글의 목적으로 가장 적절한 것은?

① 체육대회 소음에 대해 주민들의 양해를 구하려고
② 새로 이사 온 이웃 주민의 소음에 대해 항의하려고
③ 인근 스포츠 시설의 소음에 대한 조치를 요청하려고
④ 늦은 시간 악기 연주와 같은 소음의 차단을 부탁하려고

02 밑줄 친 "steps"의 의미와 가장 가까운 것은?

① movements
② actions
③ levels
④ stairs

03 다음 글의 목적으로 가장 적절한 것은? 2025. 국가직 9급

Dear Members of the Woodville City Council,

I am writing to inform you of several issues in our community that need attention. A resident, John Smith, of 123 Elm Street, has reported problems with the road conditions on Elm Street, especially between Maple Avenue and Oak Street. There are many potholes and cracks that have worsened after recent heavy rain, causing traffic disruptions and safety hazards. Even though temporary repairs have been made, the problems continue.

The resident is also concerned about poor lighting in Central Park, especially along Park Lane, because broken or missing streetlights have led to minor accidents and lowered property values. He requests that the Council repair Elm Street and improve the lighting in the park.

I urge the Council to address these issues for the safety and well-being of our community. Thank you for your attention to these matters. I trust we will work together to resolve these issues effectively.

Sincerely,

Stephen James
Head of Woodville City Council

① to express gratitude to the Council for their efforts
② to invite the Council to visit Central Park
③ to solicit the Council to deal with the community problems
④ to update the Council on recent repairs made in the area

04 다음 글의 목적으로 가장 적절한 것은? 2025. 지방직 9급

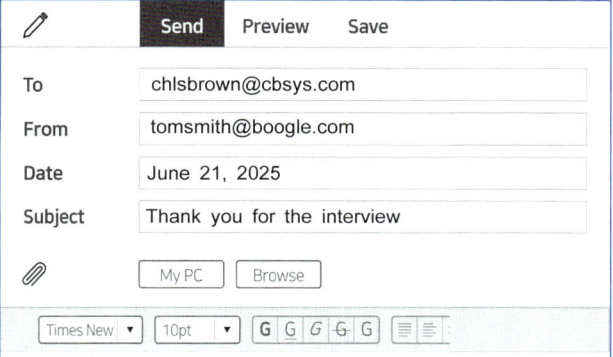

Dear Mr. Charles Brown,

I am writing to thank you for the interview last week. I truly enjoyed our conversation. The information you shared about your new Account Management System was very valuable.

I would like to follow up now to see if there are any updates regarding the status of my application.

This position looks like a great fit for me and my career goals. Anything you can share about your decision timeline or any next steps would be greatly appreciated.

I would gladly provide any additional information if needed. Thank you again.

Sincerely,

Tom Smith

① to submit an application form
② to set up an interview appointment
③ to inquire about updates on the decision process
④ to request more information about the company's business

05 다음 글의 목적으로 가장 적절한 것은?

2025. 출제 기조 전환 2차

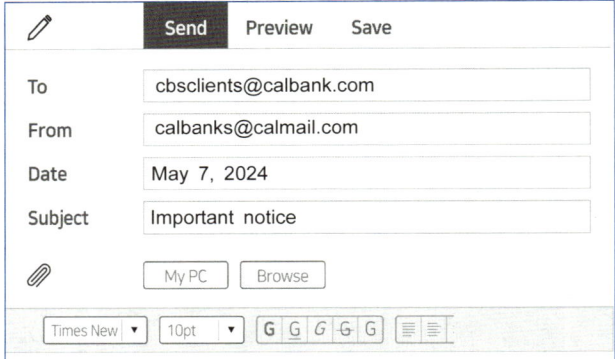

Dear Valued Clients,

In today's world, cybercrime poses a serious threat to your security. As your trusted partner, we want to help you protect your personal and business information. Here are five easy ways to safeguard yourself from cyber threats:

1. Use strong passwords and change them frequently.
2. Keep your software and devices up to date.
3. Be wary of suspicious emails, links, or telephone calls that pressure you to act quickly or give out sensitive information.
4. Enable Two Factor authentication and use it whenever possible. When contacting California Bank & Savings, you will be asked to use a One Time Passcode (OTP) to verify your identity.
5. Back up your data regularly.

Visit our Security Center to learn more about how you can stay safe online. Remember, cybersecurity is a team effort. By working together, we can build a safer online environment for ourselves and the world.

Sincerely,

California Bank & Savings

① to inform clients of how to keep themselves safe from cyber threats
② to inform clients of how to update their software and devices
③ to inform clients of how to make their passwords stronger
④ to inform clients of how to safeguard their OTPs

02 전자메일 유형 기출 독해 어휘 복습 TEST

1	concern		21	address	
2	regarding		22	resolve	
3	excessive		23	conversation	
4	district		24	valuable	
5	look into		25	follow up	
6	matter		26	status	
7	take steps		27	timeline	
8	address		28	additional	
9	tranquility		29	protect	
10	council		30	personal	
11	inform		31	threat	
12	issue		32	frequently	
13	pothole		33	up to date	
14	crack		34	wary of	
15	worsen		35	suspicious	
16	disruption		36	sensitive	
17	temporary		37	authentication	
18	minor		38	verify	
19	property		39	back up	
20	request		40	regularly	

PART 03 안내문 유형

출제 경향 분석

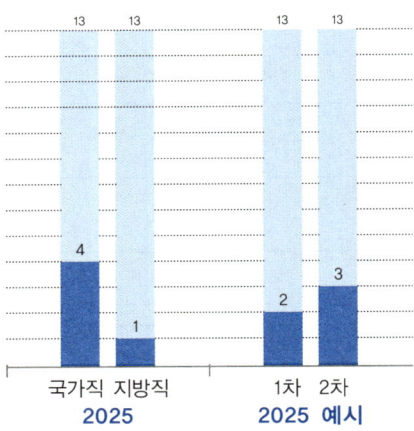

반드시 한번에 다잡는 '안내문' 유형 기출 독해 어휘

- embassy 대사관
- abroad 해외에(서), 해외로
- on behalf of ~을 대신하여, 대표하여
- consent 동의(서), 승낙, 합의
- record 기록하다, 녹음하다
- examine 검토하다, 조사하다
- vibrant 활기찬, 생기가 넘치는, 강렬한, 선명한
- heritage 유산, 전승, 전통
- a variety of 다양한, 여러 가지의
- feast 잔치, 연회, 축제일, 포식하다
- cuisine 요리, 요리법
- pay respect to ~에 경의를 표하다
- dedicated 헌신적인, 전념하는
- property 재산, 소유물, 부동산, 건물 (구내)
- access 접근하다, 들어가다, 이용하다
- show off 자랑하다, 과시하다
- exploration 탐구, 탐사
- experienced 경험[경력]이 있는, 능숙한

- interpretive 해석 중심의, 해석을 제공하는
- enhance 높이다, 향상시키다
- foster 촉진하다, 조성하다
- sustained 지속된, 일관된
- underlying 기초가 되는, 근본적인
- accomplish 달성하다, 성취하다, 해내다
- fulfill 완수하다, 성취하다
- outcome 성과, 결과
- cross-cutting 공통의
- admission 입장료
- free 무료의
- door prize 참가자에게 추첨으로 주는 상품
- sensational 아주 멋진, 선풍적인
- confirmation 확인(서)
- proof 증명(서), 증거(물)
- separate 각각의, 별개의, 분리된
- on-site 현장의
- charge 비용, 요금

[01~02] 다음 글을 읽고 물음에 답하시오.

2025. 국가직 9급

Consular services

We welcome all feedback about our consular services, whether you receive them in the UK or from one of our embassies, high commissions or consulates abroad. Tell us when we get things wrong so that we can <u>assess</u> and improve our services.

If you want to make a complaint about a consular service you have received, we want to help you resolve it as quickly as possible. If you are complaining on behalf of someone else, we must have written, signed consent from that person allowing us to share their personal information with you before we can reply.

Send details of your complaint to our feedback contact form. We will record and examine your complaint, and use the information you provide to help make sure that we offer the best possible help and support to our customers. The relevant embassy, high commission or consulate will reply to you.

01 밑줄 친 assess의 의미와 가장 가까운 것은?

① upgrade
② prolong
③ evaluate
④ render

02 윗글의 목적으로 가장 적절한 것은?

① to give directions to the consulate
② to explain how to file complaints
③ to lay out the employment process
④ to announce the opening hours

[03~04] 다음 글을 읽고 물음에 답하시오.

2025. 출제 기조 전환 1차

(A)

We're pleased to announce the upcoming City Harbour Festival, an annual event that brings our diverse community together to celebrate our shared heritage, culture, and local talent. Mark your calendars and join us for an exciting weekend!

Details
- **Dates** : Friday, June 16 — Sunday, June 18
- **Times** : 10 : 00 a.m. — 8 : 00 p.m. (Friday & Saturday)
  10 : 00 a.m. — 6 : 00 p.m. (Sunday)
- **Location** : City Harbour Park, Main Street, and surrounding areas

Highlights
- **Live Performances**
  Enjoy a variety of live music, dance, and theatrical performances on multiple stages throughout the festival grounds.
- **Food Trucks**
  Have a feast with a wide selection of food trucks offering diverse and delicious cuisines, as well as free sample tastings.

For the full schedule of events and activities, please visit our website at www.cityharbourfestival.org or contact the Festival Office at (552) 234-5678.

---

03 (A)에 들어갈 윗글의 제목으로 가장 적절한 것은?

① Make Safety Regulations for Your Community
② Celebrate Our Vibrant Community Events
③ Plan Your Exciting Maritime Experience
④ Recreate Our City's Heritage

04 City Harbour Festival에 관한 윗글의 내용과 일치하지 않는 것은?

① 일 년에 한 번 개최된다.
② 일요일에는 오후 6시까지 열린다.
③ 주요 행사로 무료 요리 강습이 진행된다.
④ 웹사이트나 전화 문의를 통해 행사 일정을 알 수 있다.

[05~06] 다음 글을 읽고 물음에 답하시오.

2025. 출제 기조 전환 2차

(A)

As a close neighbor, you will want to learn how to save your lake.

While it isn't dead yet, Lake Dimmesdale is heading toward this end. So pay your respects to this beautiful body of water while it is still alive.

Some dedicated people are working to save it now. They are having a special meeting to tell you about it. Come learn what is being done and how you can help. This affects your property value as well.

Who wants to live near a dead lake?

Sponsored by Central State Regional Planning Council

- Location: Green City Park Opposite Southern State College
  (in case of rain: College Library Room 203)
- Date: Saturday, July 6, 2024
- Time: 2:00 p.m.

For any questions about the meeting, please visit our website at www.planningcouncilsavelake.org or contact our office at (432) 345-6789.

05 (A)에 들어갈 윗글의 제목으로 가장 적절한 것은?

① Lake Dimmesdale Is Dying
② Praise to the Lake's Beauty
③ Cultural Value of Lake Dimmesdale
④ Significance of the Lake to the College

06 위 안내문의 내용과 일치하지 않는 것은?

① 호수를 살리기 위해 노력하는 사람들이 있다.
② 호수를 위한 활동이 주민들의 재산에 영향을 미친다.
③ 우천 시에는 대학의 구내식당에서 회의가 열린다.
④ 웹사이트 방문이나 전화로 회의에 관해 질문할 수 있다.

07 다음 글의 내용과 일치하지 않는 것은?

KIDS SUMMER ART CAMP 2025

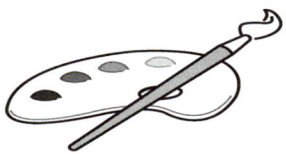

Join the Stan José Art Museum (SJAM) for a week of fun!
Campers get behind-the-scenes access to exhibitions, experiment with the artistic process, and show off their own work in a student exhibition.

WHO

For children ages 6 - 14
Each camper will receive individual artistic support, encouragement, and creative challenges unique to their learning style and skill level.

WHAT

Join SJAM for a summer art camp that pairs creative exploration of art materials and processes led by our experienced gallery teachers and studio art educators. In addition, campers will engage in interpretive art and science lessons created by Eddie Brown, a STEM consultant.

ART CAMP EXHIBITION

We invite families and caregivers to attend a weekly exhibition reception of campers' artwork to celebrate the artistic achievements of each participant.

WHEN

All camps run 9 am - 3 pm, Monday - Friday. Monday, June 9 - Friday, July 25 (no camp the week of June 30)

① Campers will have opportunities to display their work in a student exhibition.
② The camp includes individual artistic support for children ages 6 - 14.
③ A STEM consultant developed interpretive art and science lessons.
④ The camp runs with no break between June 9 and July 25.

08 다음 글의 내용과 일치하는 것은?

2025. 국가직 9급

Department of Health and Human Services

Mission Statement

The mission of the Department of Health and Human Services (HHS) is to enhance the health and well-being of all individuals in the nation, by providing for effective health and human services and by fostering sound, sustained advances in the sciences underlying medicine, public health, and social services.

Organizational Structure

HHS accomplishes its mission through programs and initiatives that cover a wide spectrum of activities. Eleven operating divisions, including eight agencies in the Public Health Service and three human services agencies, administer HHS's programs. While HHS is a domestic agency working to protect and promote the health and well-being of the American people, the interconnectedness of our world requires that HHS engage globally to fulfill its mission.

Cross-Agency Collaborations

Improving health and human services outcomes cannot be achieved by the Department on its own; collaborations are critical to achieve our goals and objectives. HHS collaborates closely with other federal departments and agencies on cross-cutting topics.

① HHS aims to improve the health and well-being of low-income families only.
② HHS's programs are administered by the eleven operating divisions.
③ HHS does not work with foreign countries to complete its mission.
④ HHS acts independently from other federal departments and agencies to achieve its goals.

09 다음 글의 내용과 일치하지 않는 것은?

2025. 지방직 9급

① The East Coast's biggest aviation collectibles show will take place in September.
② Door prizes are exclusively for children under 12.
③ Rare airline and transportation collectibles will be displayed at the show.
④ Visitors can see both national and international collectibles.

10 다음 글의 내용과 일치하지 않는 것은?

2025. 출제 기조 전환 2차

The David Williams Library and Museum is open 7 days a week, from 9:00 a.m. to 5:00 p.m. (NOV−MAR) and 9:00 a.m. to 6:00 p.m. (APR−OCT). Online tickets may be purchased at the link below. You will receive an email confirmation after making a purchase (be sure to check your SPAM folder). Bring this confirmation—printed or on smart device —as proof of purchase.

• **Online tickets**: buy.davidwilliams.com/events

The David Williams Library and Museum and the Home of David Williams (operated by the National Heritage Service) offer separate $10.00 adult admission tickets. Tickets for tours of the Home may be purchased on-site during normal business hours.

• **CLOSED**: Thanksgiving, Christmas and New Year's Day

There is no charge for conducting research in the David Williams Library research room.

For additional information, call 1 (800) 333-7777.

① The Library and Museum closes at 5:00 p.m. in December.
② Visitors can buy tour tickets for the Home on-site.
③ The Home of David Williams is open all year round.
④ One can do research in the Library research room for free.

03 안내문 유형 기출 독해 어휘 복습 TEST

1	consular		21	feast	
2	receive		22	cuisine	
3	embassy		23	form	
4	high commission		24	lake	
5	consulate		25	close	
6	abroad		26	head toward	
7	make a complaint		27	pay respect to	
8	resolve		28	dedicated	
9	on behalf of		29	affect	
10	consent		30	property	
11	reply		31	sponsor	
12	record		32	opposite	
13	examine		33	in case of	
14	form		34	access	
15	vibrant		35	experiment	
16	upcoming		36	show off	
17	bring together		37	exhibition	
18	heritage		38	artistic	
19	a variety of		39	encouragement	
20	throughout		40	exploration	

41	material		61	fulfill	
42	process		62	outcome	
43	experienced		63	objective	
44	interpretive		64	department	
45	invite		65	cross-cutting	
46	caregiver		66	avenue	
47	reception		67	admission	
48	celebrate		68	free	
49	achievement		69	door prize	
50	participant		70	collectible	
51	mission statement		71	sensational	
52	enhance		72	domestic	
53	foster		73	foreign	
54	sustained		74	purchase	
55	underlying		75	below	
56	medicine		76	confirmation	
57	accomplish		77	proof	
58	division		78	separate	
59	domestic		79	on-site	
60	interconnectedness		80	charge	

PART 04 중심 내용 파악 유형

출제 경향 분석

반드시 한번에 다잡는 '중심 내용 파악' 유형 기출 독해 어휘

- artificial 인공의, 인조의
- mimic 흉내내다, 모방하다
- disrupt 방해하다, 지장을 주다
- counteract 상쇄하다, 대응하다
- contagious 전염되는, 전염성의
- eliminate 없애다, 제거하다
- ministry (정부의 각) 부처, 목사, 성직자
- infection 감염, 전염병
- disparity 격차, 차이
- emphasize 강조하다, 두드러지게 하다
- excavate 발굴하다
- exploit 이용하다, 착취하다
- dilute 희석하다, 약화시키다
- replenish 보충하다, 채우다
- means 수단, 방법, 수입
- relieve 수단, 방법, 수입
- competence 능력, 능숙함
- attribute ~의 탓으로 보다, 속성, 특성, 자질

- equate 동일시하다
- crave 갈망하다, 열망하다
- deliberate 고의의, 의도적인, 신중한, 사려 깊은
- resistance 저항력, 내성
- excessive 과도한, 지나친
- overuse 남용, 남용하다
- emit 방출하다, 내뿜다
- meet halfway 타협하다, 절충하다
- shrink 줄어들게 하다, 감소하다
- diffuse 분산되다, 확산되다
- merit 받을 만하다[자격/가치가 있다], 가치, 장점
- incumbent 의무적인, 재임 중인
- intervene 개입하다, 간섭하다
- intact 그대로의, 온전한, 손상되지 않은
- anonymity 익명성
- obsession 강박, 집착, 사로잡힘
- leveling 평준화, 평등화, 단순화
- sanction 제재, 허가, 제재를 가하다, 허가하다

01 다음 글의 주제로 가장 적절한 것은? 2025. 국가직 9급

Young people are fast learners. They are energetic, active and have a 'can-do' mentality. Given the support and right opportunities, they can take the lead in their own development as well as the development of their communities. In many developing countries, agriculture is still the largest employer and young farmers play an important role in ensuring food security for future generations. They face many challenges, however. For example, it is very difficult to own land or get a loan if you do not have a house — which, if you are young and only just starting your career, is often not yet possible. Working in agriculture requires substantial and long-term investments. It is also quite risky and uncertain, because it relies heavily on the climate: flooding, drought and storms can damage and destroy farmers' crops and affect livestock.

① the economic advantages of working in the agricultural sector
② the importance of technology in modern farming practices
③ the roles of young farmers and the challenges they face
④ young people's efforts for urban development

02 다음 글의 주제로 가장 적절한 것은? 2025. 지방직 9급

The reason artificial blue light in devices can be so harmful in the evening is that it mimics the sun's natural blue light—which confuses the body's circadian clock. A study showed that viewing artificial blue light in the evening will push sleep-inducing melatonin hormones down drastically, disrupting bedtimes and affecting daytime behavior. But getting that same blue light from the sun, which contains a health-boosting full spectrum of light, does the opposite. According to the study, the more daytime blue light a person gets, the better defense they have against the harms of evening blue light from screens. Thus, packing the day with sunshine creates a blue-light build-up that helps counteract the consequences of that artificial light at night. In other words, the more sunlight exposure a child gets during the day, the better their brain can build a wall against the harms of artificial blue light later.

① Sunlight's help in fighting artificial blue light effects
② The dangers of using devices during the day
③ How screens affect children's sleep cycles
④ Why melatonin levels drop in the evening

03 다음 글의 주제로 가장 적절한 것은?

2025. 출제 기조 전환 2차

The International Space Station, orbiting some 240 miles above the planet, is about to join the effort to monitor the world's wildlife — and to revolutionize the science of animal tracking. A large antenna and other equipment aboard the orbiting outpost, installed by spacewalking Russian astronauts in 2018, are being tested and will become fully operational this summer. The system will relay a much wider range of data than previous tracking technologies, logging not just an animal's location but also its physiology and environment. This will assist scientists, conservationists and others whose work requires close monitoring of wildlife on the move and provide much more detailed information on the health of the world's ecosystems.

① evaluation of sustainability of global ecosystems
② successful training projects of Russian astronauts
③ animal experiments conducted in the orbiting outpost
④ innovative wildlife monitoring from the space station

04 다음 글의 요지로 가장 적절한 것은?

2025. 출제 기조 전환 2차

Animal Health Emergencies
Preparedness for animal disease outbreaks has been a top priority for the Board of Animal Health (BOAH) for decades. A highly contagious animal disease event may have economically devastating effects as well as public health or food safety and security consequences.

Foreign Animal Diseases
A foreign animal disease (FAD) is a disease that is not currently found in the country, and could cause significant illness or death in animals or cause extensive economic harm by eliminating trading opportunities with other countries and states.

Several BOAH veterinarians who are trained in diagnosing FADs are available 24 hours a day to investigate suspected cases of a FAD. An investigation is triggered when report of animals with clinical signs indicative of a FAD is received or when diagnostic laboratory identifies a suspicious test result.

① BOAH focuses on training veterinarians for FADs.
② BOAH's main goal is to repsond to animal disease epidemic.
③ BOAH actively promotes international trade opportunities.
④ BOAH aims to lead laboratory research on the causes of FADs.

05 다음 글의 주제로 가장 적절한 것은?

2025. 출제 기조 전환 1차

The Ministry of Food and Drug Safety warned that cases of food poisoning have occurred as a result of cross-contamination, where people touch eggs and neglect to wash their hands before preparing food or using utensils. To mitigate such risks, the ministry advised refrigerating eggs and ensuring they are thoroughly cooked until both the yolk and white are firm. Over the past five years, a staggering 7,400 people experienced food poisoning caused by Salmonella bacteria. Salmonella thrives in warm temperatures, with approximately 37 degrees Celsius being the optimal growth condition. Consuming raw or undercooked eggs and failing to separate raw and cooked foods were identified as the most common causes of Salmonella infection. It is crucial to prioritize food safety measures and adhere to proper cooking practices to minimize the risk of Salmonella-related illnesses.

① Benefits of consuming eggs to the immune system
② Different types of treatments for Salmonella infection
③ Life span of Salmonella bacteria in warm temperatures
④ Safe handling of eggs for the prevention of Salmonella infection

06 다음 글의 요지로 가장 적절한 것은?

2025. 출제 기조 전환 1차

Despite ongoing efforts to address educational disparities, the persistent achievement gap among students continues to highlight significant inequities in the education system. Recent data reveal that marginalized students, including those from low-income back grounds and vulnerable groups, continue to lag behind their peers in academic performance. The gap poses a challenge to achieving educational equity and social mobility. Experts emphasize the need for targeted interventions, equitable resource allocation, and inclusive policies to bridge this gap and ensure equal opportunities for all students, irrespective of their socioeconomic status or background. The issue of continued educational divide should be addressed at all levels of education system in an effort to find a solution.

① We should deal with persistent educational inequities.
② Educational experts need to focus on new school policies.
③ New teaching methods are necessary to bridge the achievement gap.
④ Family income should not be considered in the discussion of education.

07 다음 글의 주제로 적절한 것은?

2024. 국가직 9급

It seems incredible that one man could be responsible for opening our eyes to an entire culture, but until British archaeologist Arthur Evans successfully excavated the ruins of the palace of Knossos on the island of Crete, the great Minoan culture of the Mediterranean was more legend than fact. Indeed its most famed resident was a creature of mythology: the half-man, half-bull Minotaur, said to have lived under the palace of mythical King Minos. But as Evans proved, this realm was no myth. In a series of excavations in the early years of the 20th century, Evans found a trove of artifacts from the Minoan age, which reached its height from 1900 to 1450 B.C.: jewelry, carvings, pottery, altars shaped like bull's horns, and wall paintings showing Minoan life.

① King Minos' successful excavations
② Appreciating artifacts from the Minoan age
③ Magnificence of the palace on the island of Crete
④ Bringing the Minoan culture to the realm of reality

08 다음 글의 제목으로 적절한 것은?

2024. 국가직 9급

Currency debasement of a good money by a bad money version occurred via coins of a high percentage of precious metal, reissued at lower percentages of gold or silver diluted with a lower value metal. This adulteration drove out the good coin for the bad coin. No one spent the good coin, they kept it, hence the good coin was driven out of circulation and into a hoard. Meanwhile the issuer, normally a king who had lost his treasure on interminable warfare and other such dissolute living, was behind the move. They collected all the good old coins they could, melted them down and reissued them at lower purity and pocketed the balance. It was often illegal to keep the old stuff back but people did, while the king replenished his treasury, at least for a time.

① How Bad Money Replaces Good
② Elements of Good Coins
③ Why Not Melt Coins?
④ What Is Bad Money?

09 다음 글의 주제로 적절한 것은?
2024. 지방직 9급

In recent years Latin America has made huge strides in exploiting its incredible wind, solar, geothermal and biofuel energy resources. Latin America's electricity sector has already begun to gradually decrease its dependence on oil. Latin America is expected to almost double its electricity output between 2015 and 2040. Practically none of Latin America's new large-scale power plants will be oil-fueled, which opens up the field for different technologies. Countries in Central America and the Caribbean, which traditionally imported oil, were the first to move away from oil-based power plants, after suffering a decade of high and volatile prices at the start of the century.

① booming oil industry in Latin America
② declining electricity business in Latin America
③ advancement of renewable energy in Latin America
④ aggressive exploitation of oil-based resources in Latin America

10 다음 글의 제목으로 적절한 것은?
2024. 지방직 9급

Every organization has resources that it can use to perform its mission. How well your organization does its job is partly a function of how many of those resources you have, but mostly it is a function of how well you use the resources you have, such as people and money. You as the organization's leader can always make the use of those resources more efficient and effective, provided that you have control of the organization's personnel and agenda, a condition that does not occur automatically. By managing your people and your money carefully, by treating the most important things as the most important, by making good decisions, and by solving the problems that you encounter, you can get the most out of what you have available to you.

① Exchanging Resources in an Organization
② Leaders' Ability to Set up External Control
③ Making the Most of the Resources: A Leader's Way
④ Technical Capacity of an Organization: A Barrier to Its Success

11 다음 글의 제목으로 알맞은 것은? 2023. 국가직 9급

The feeling of being loved and the biological response it stimulates is triggered by nonverbal cues: the tone in a voice, the expression on a face, or the touch that feels just right. Nonverbal cues — rather than spoken words — make us feel that the person we are with is interested in, understands, and values us. When we're with them, we feel safe. We even see the power of nonverbal cues in the wild. After evading the chase of predators, animals often nuzzle each other as a means of stress relief. This bodily contact provides reassurance of safety and relieves stress.

① How Do Wild Animals Think and Feel?
② Communicating Effectively Is the Secret to Success
③ Nonverbal Communication Speaks Louder than Words
④ Verbal Cues: The Primary Tools for Expressing Feelings

12 다음 글의 주제로 알맞은 것은? 2023. 국가직 9급

There are times, like holidays and birthdays, when toys and gifts accumulate in a child's life. You can use these times to teach a healthy nondependency on things. Don't surround your child with toys. Instead, arrange them in baskets, have one basket out at a time, and rotate baskets occasionally. If a cherished object is put away for a time, bringing it out creates a delightful remembering and freshness of outlook. Suppose your child asks for a toy that has been put away for a while. You can direct attention toward an object or experience that is already in the environment. If you lose or break a possession, try to model a good attitude ("I appreciated it while I had it!") so that your child can begin to develop an attitude of nonattachment. If a toy of hers is broken or lost, help her to say, "I had fun with that."

① building a healthy attitude toward possessions
② learning the value of sharing toys with others
③ teaching how to arrange toys in an orderly manner
④ accepting responsibility for behaving in undesirable ways

13 다음 글의 요지로 알맞은 것은?   2023. 국가직 9급

Many parents have been misguided by the "self-esteem movement," which has told them that the way to build their children's self-esteem is to tell them how good they are at things. Unfortunately, trying to convince your children of their competence will likely fail because life has a way of telling them unequivocally how capable or incapable they really are through success and failure. Research has shown that how you praise your children has a powerful influence on their development. Some researchers found that children who were praised for their intelligence, as compared to their effort, became overly focused on results. Following a failure, these same children persisted less, showed less enjoyment, attributed their failure to a lack of ability, and performed poorly in future achievement efforts. Praising children for intelligence made them fear difficulty because they began to equate failure with stupidity.

① Frequent praises increase self-esteem of children.
② Compliments on intelligence bring about negative effect.
③ A child should overcome fear of failure through success.
④ Parents should focus on the outcome rather than the process.

14 다음 글의 제목으로 가장 적절한 것은?   2023. 지방직 9급

Well-known author Daniel Goleman has dedicated his life to the science of human relationships. In his book *Social Intelligence* he discusses results from neuro-sociology to explain how sociable our brains are. According to Goleman, we are drawn to other people's brains whenever we engage with another person. The human need for meaningful connectivity with others, in order to deepen out relationships, is what we all crave, and yet there are countless articles and studies suggesting that we are lonelier than we ever have been and loneliness is now a world health epidemic. Specifically, in Australia, according to a national Lifeline survey, more than 80% of those surveyed believe our society is becoming a lonelier place. Yet, our brains crave human interaction.

① Lonely People
② Sociable Brains
③ Need for Mental Health Survey
④ Dangers of Human Connectivity

15 다음 글의 주제로 가장 적절한 것은?

2023. 지방직 9급

Certainly some people are born with advantages (e.g., physical size for jockeys, height for basketball players, an "ear" for music for musicians). Yet only dedication to mindful, deliberate practice over many years can turn those advantages into talents and those talents into successes. Through the same kind of dedicated practice, people who are not born with such advantages can develop talents that nature put a little farther from their reach. For example, even though you may feel that you weren't born with a talent for math, you can significantly increase your mathematical abilities through mindful, deliberate practice. Or, if you consider yourself "naturally" shy, putting in the time and effort to develop your social skills can enable you to interact with people at social occasions with energy, grace, and ease.

① advantages some people have over others
② importance of constant efforts to cultivate talents
③ difficulties shy people have in social interactions
④ need to understand own strengths and weaknesses

16 다음 글의 요지로 가장 적절한 것은?

2023. 지방직 9급

Dr. Roossinck and her colleagues found by chance that a virus increased resistance to drought on a plant that is widely used in botanical experiments. Their further experiments with a related virus showed that was true of 15 other plant species, too. Dr. Roossinck is now doing experiments to study another type of virus that increases heat tolerance in a range of plants. She hopes to extend her research to have a deeper understanding of the advantages that different sorts of viruses give to their hosts. That would help to support a view which is held by an increasing number of biologists, that many creatures rely on symbiosis, rather than being self-sufficient.

① Viruses demonstrate self-sufficiency of biological beings.
② Biologists should do everything to keep plants virus-free.
③ The principle of symbiosis cannot be applied to infected plants.
④ Viruses sometimes do their hosts good, rather than harming them.

17 다음 글의 주제로 가장 적절한 것은?

2023. 법원직 9급

Do you want to be a successful anchor? If so, keep this in mind. As an anchor, the individual will be called upon to communicate news and information to viewer during newscasts, special reports and other types of news programs. This will include interpreting news events, adlibbing, and communicating breaking news effectively when scripts are not available. Anchoring duties also involve gathering and writing stories. The anchor must be able to deliver scripts clearly and effectively. Strong writing skills, solid news judgement and a strong sense of visual storytelling are essential skills. This individual must be a self-starter who cultivates sources and finds new information as a regular part of job. Live reporting skills are important, as well as the ability to adlib and describe breaking news as it takes place.

① difficulties of producing live news
② qualifications to become a news anchor
③ the importance of the social role of journalists
④ the importance of forming the right public opinion

18 다음 글의 주제로 가장 적절한 것은?

2023. 법원직 9급

Cosmetics became so closely associated with portraiture that some photography handbooks included recipes for them. American photographers also, at times, used cosmetics to retouch negatives and prints, enlivening women's faces with traces of rouge. Some customers with dark skin requested photographs that would make them look lighter. A skin lightener advertisement that appeared in an African American newspaper in 1935 referenced this practice by promising that its product could achieve the same look produced by photographers: a lighter skin Cop free of blemishes. By drawing attention to the face and encouraging cosmetics use, portrait photography heightened the aesthetic valuation of smooth and often light-colored skin.

* blemish (피부 등의) 티

① side effects of excessive use of cosmetics
② overuse of cosmetics promoted by photographers
③ active use of cosmetics to make the face look better
④ decreased use of cosmetics due to advances in photography

19 다음 글의 제목으로 가장 적절한 것은?

2022. 국가직 9급

Lasers are possible because of the way light interacts with electrons. Electrons exist at specific energy levels or states characteristic of that particular atom or molecule. The energy levels can be imagined as rings or orbits around a nucleus. Electrons in outer rings are at higher energy levels than those in inner rings. Electrons can be bumped up to higher energy levels by the injection of energy — for example, by a flash of light. When an electron drops from an outer to an inner level, "excess" energy is given off as light. The wavelength or color of the emitted light is precisely related to the amount of energy released. Depending on the particular lasing material being used, specific wavelengths of light are absorbed (to energize or excite the electrons) and specific wavelengths are emitted (when the electrons fall back to their initial level).

① How Is Laser Produced?
② When Was Laser Invented?
③ What Electrons Does Laser Emit?
④ Why Do Electrons Reflect Light?

20 다음 글의 제목으로 가장 적절한 것은?

2022. 국가직 9급

Do people from different cultures view the world differently? A psychologist presented realistic animated scenes of fish and other underwater objects to Japanese and American students and asked them to report what they had seen. Americans and Japanese made about an equal number of references to the focal fish, but the Japanese made more than 60 percent more references to background elements, including the water, rocks, bubbles, and inert plants and animals. In addition, whereas Japanese and American participants made about equal numbers of references to movement involving active animals, the Japanese participants made almost twice as many references to relationships involving inert, background objects. Perhaps most tellingly, the very first sentence from the Japanese participants was likely to be one referring to the environment, whereas the first sentence from Americans was three times as likely to be one referring to the focal fish.

① Language Barrier Between Japanese and Americans
② Associations of Objects and Backgrounds in the Brain
③ Cultural Differences in Perception
④ Superiority of Detail-oriented People

21 다음 글의 요지로 가장 적절한 것은?

2022. 국가직 9급

If someone makes you an offer and you're legitimately concerned about parts of it, you're usually better off proposing all your changes at once. Don't say, "The salary is a bit low. Could you do something about it?" and then, once she's worked on it, come back with "Thanks. Now here are two other things I'd like..." If you ask for only one thing initially, she may assume that getting it will make you ready to accept the offer (or at least to make a decision). If you keep saying "and one more thing...," she is unlikely to remain in a generous or understanding mood. Furthermore, if you have more than one request, don't simply mention all the things you want — A, B, C, and D; also signal the relative importance of each to you. Otherwise, she may pick the two things you value least, because they're pretty easy to give you, and feel she's met you halfway.

① Negotiate multiple issues simultaneously, not serially.
② Avoid sensitive topics for a successful negotiation.
③ Choose the right time for your negotiation.
④ Don't be too direct when negotiating salary.

22 다음 글의 제목으로 가장 적절한 것은?

2022. 지방직 9급

One of the areas where efficiency can be optimized is the work force, through increasing individual productivity — defined as the amount of work (products produced, customers served) an employee handles in a given time. In addition to making sure you have invested in the right equipment, environment, and training to ensure optimal performance, you can increase productivity by encouraging staffers to put an end to a modern-day energy drain: multitasking. Studies show it takes 25 to 40 percent longer to get a job done when you're simultaneously trying to work on other projects. To be more productive, says Andrew Deutscher, vice president of business development at consulting firm The Energy Project, "do one thing, uninterrupted, for a sustained period of time."

① How to Create More Options in Life
② How to Enhance Daily Physical Performance
③ Multitasking is the Answer for Better Efficiency
④ Do One Thing at a Time for Greater Efficiency

23 다음 글의 요지로 가장 적절한 것은?

2022. 지방직 9급

In one study, done in the early 1970s when young people tended to dress in either "hippie" or "straight" fashion, experimenters donned hippie or straight attire and asked college students on campus for a dime to make a phone call. When the experimenter was dressed in the same way as the student, the request was granted in more than two-thirds of the instances; when the student and requester were dissimilarly dressed, the dime was provided less than half the time. Another experiment showed how automatic our positive response to similar others can be. Marchers in an antiwar demonstration were found to be more likely to sign the petition of a similarly dressed requester and to do so without bothering to read it first.

① People are more likely to help those who dress like themselves.
② Dressing up formally increases the chance of signing the petition.
③ Making a phone call is an efficient way to socialize with other students.
④ Some college students in the early 1970s were admired for their unique fashion.

24 다음 글의 주제로 가장 적절한 것은?

2022. 법원직 9급

Daily training creates special nutritional needs for an athlete, particularly the elite athlete whose training commitment is almost a fulltime job. But even recreational sport will create nutritional challenges. And whatever your level of involvement in sport, you must meet these challenges if you're to achieve the maximum return from training. Without sound eating, much of the purpose of your training might be lost. In the worst-case scenario, dietary problems and deficiencies may directly impair training performance. In other situations, you might improve, but at a rate that is below your potential or slower than your competitors. However, on the positive side, with the right everyday eating plan your commitment to training will be fully rewarded.

① how to improve body flexibility
② importance of eating well in exercise
③ health problems caused by excessive diet
④ improving skills through continuous training

25 다음 글의 제목으로 가장 적절한 것은?

2021. 국가직 9급

Warming temperatures and loss of oxygen in the sea will shrink hundreds of fish species — from tunas and groupers to salmon, thresher sharks, haddock and cod — even more than previously thought, a new study concludes. Because warmer seas speed up their metabolisms, fish, squid and other water-breathing creatures will need to draw more oxygen from the ocean. At the same time, warming seas are already reducing the availability of oxygen in many parts of the sea. A pair of University of British Columbia scientists argue that since the bodies of fish grow faster than their gills, these animals eventually will reach a point where they can't get enough oxygen to sustain normal growth. "What we found was that the body size of fish decreases by 20 to 30 percent for every 1 degree Celsius increase in water temperature," says author William Cheung.

① Fish Now Grow Faster than Ever
② Oxygen's Impact on Ocean Temperatures
③ Climate Change May Shrink the World's Fish
④ How Sea Creatures Survive with Low Metabolism

26 다음 글의 주제로 가장 적절한 것은?

2021. 국가직 9급

During the late twentieth century socialism was on the retreat both in the West and in large areas of the developing world. During this new phase in the evolution of market capitalism, global trading patterns became increasingly interlinked, and advances in information technology meant that deregulated financial markets could shift massive flows of capital across national boundaries within seconds. 'Globalization' boosted trade, encouraged productivity gains and lowered prices, but critics alleged that it exploited the low-paid, was indifferent to environmental concerns and subjected the Third World to a monopolistic form of capitalism. Many radicals within Western societies who wished to protest against this process joined voluntary bodies, charities and other non-governmental organizations, rather than the marginalized political parties of the left. The environmental movement itself grew out of the recognition that the world was interconnected, and an angry, if diffuse, international coalition of interests emerged.

① The affirmative phenomena of globalization in the developing world in the past
② The decline of socialism and the emergence of capitalism in the twentieth century
③ The conflict between the global capital market and the political organizations of the left
④ The exploitative characteristics of global capitalism and diverse social reactions against it

27 다음 글의 제목으로 가장 적절한 것은?

2021. 지방직 9급

The definition of 'turn' casts the digital turn as an analytical strategy which enables us to focus on the role of digitalization within social reality. As an analytical perspective, the digital turn makes it possible to analyze and discuss the societal meaning of digitalization. The term 'digital turn' thus signifies an analytical approach which centers on the role of digitalization within a society. If the linguistic turn is defined by the epistemological assumption that reality is constructed through language, the digital turn is based on the assumption that social reality is increasingly defined by digitalization. Social media symbolize the digitalization of social relations. Individuals increasingly engage in identity management on social networking sites(SNS). SNS are polydirectional, meaning that users can connect to each other and share information.

※ epistemological 인식론의

① Remaking Identities on SNS
② Linguistic Turn Versus Digital Turn
③ How to Share Information in the Digital Age
④ Digitalization Within the Context of Social Reality

28 다음 글의 요지로 가장 적절한 것은?

2021. 지방직 9급

"In Judaism, we're largely defined by our actions," says Lisa Grushcow, the senior rabbi at Temple Emanu-El-Beth Sholom in Montreal. "You can't really be an armchair do-gooder." This concept relates to the Jewish notion of tikkun olam, which translates as "to repair the world." Our job as human beings, she says, "is to mend what's been broken. It's incumbent on us to not only take care of ourselves and each other but also to build a better world around us." This philosophy conceptualizes goodness as something based in service. Instead of asking "Am I a good person?" you may want to ask "What good do I do in the world?" Grushcow's temple puts these beliefs into action inside and outside their community. For instance, they sponsored two refugee families from Vietnam to come to Canada in the 1970s.

① We should work to heal the world.
② Community should function as a shelter.
③ We should conceptualize goodness as beliefs.
④ Temples should contribute to the community.

29 다음 글의 요지로 가장 알맞은 것은?

2021. 법원직 9급

If your kids fight every time they play video games, make sure you're close enough to be able to hear them when they sit down to play. Listen for the particular words or tones of voice they are using that are aggressive, and try to intervene before it develops. Once tempers have settled, try to sit your kids down and discuss the problem without blaming or accusing. Give each kid a chance to talk, uninterrupted, and have them try to come up with solutions to the problem themselves. By the time kids are elementary-school age, they can evaluate which of those solutions are win-win solutions and which ones are most likely to work and satisfy each other over time. They should also learn to revisit problems when solutions are no longer working.

① Ask your kids to evaluate their test.
② Make your kids compete each other.
③ Help your kids learn to resolve conflict.
④ Teach your kids how to win an argument.

30 다음 글의 요지로 가장 적절한 것은?

2020. 국가직 9급

Listening to somebody else's ideas is the one way to know whether the story you believe about the world—as well as about yourself and your place in it—remains intact. We all need to examine our beliefs, air them out and let them breathe. Hearing what other people have to say, especially about concepts we regard as foundational, is like opening a window in our minds and in our hearts. Speaking up is important. Yet to speak up without listening is like banging pots and pans together: even if it gets you attention, it's not going to get you respect. There are three prerequisites for conversation to be meaningful: 1. You have to know what you're talking about, meaning that you have an original point and are not echoing a worn-out, hand-me-down or pre-fab argument; 2. You respect the people with whom you're speaking and are authentically willing to treat them courteously even if you disagree with their positions; 3. You have to be both smart and informed enough to listen to what the opposition says while handling your own perspective on the topic with uninterrupted good humor and discernment.

① We should be more determined to persuade others.
② We need to listen and speak up in order to communicate well.
③ We are reluctant to change our beliefs about the world we see.
④ We hear only what we choose and attempt to ignore different opinions.

31 다음 글의 제목으로 가장 적절한 것은?

2020. 국가직 9급

The future may be uncertain, but some things are undeniable: climate change, shifting demographics, geopolitics. The only guarantee is that there will be changes, both wonderful and terrible. It's worth considering how artists will respond to these changes, as well as what purpose art serves, now and in the future. Reports suggest that by 2040 the impacts of human-caused climate change will be inescapable, making it the big issue at the centre of art and life in 20 years' time. Artists in the future will wrestle with the possibilities of the post-human and post-Anthropocene — artificial intelligence, human colonies in outer space and potential doom. The identity politics seen in art around the #MeToo and Black Lives Matter movements will grow as environmentalism, border politics and migration come even more sharply into focus. Art will become increasingly diverse and might not 'look like art' as we expect. In the future, once we've become weary of our lives being visible online for all to see and our privacy has been all but lost, anonymity may be more desirable than fame. Instead of thousands, or millions, of likes and followers, we will be starved for authenticity and connection. Art could, in turn, become more collective and experiential, rather than individual.

① What will art look like in the future?
② How will global warming affect our lives?
③ How will artificial intelligence influence the environment?
④ What changes will be made because of political movements?

32 다음 글의 주제로 가장 적절한 것은?

2020. 국가직 9급

For many people, work has become an obsession. It has caused burnout, unhappiness and gender inequity, as people struggle to find time for children or passions or pets or any sort of life besides what they do for a paycheck. But increasingly, younger workers are pushing back. More of them expect and demand flexibility — paid leave for a new baby, say, and generous vacation time, along with daily things, like the ability to work remotely, come in late or leave early, or make time for exercise or meditation. The rest of their lives happens on their phones, not tied to a certain place or time — why should work be any different?

① ways to increase your paycheck
② obsession for reducing inequity
③ increasing call for flexibility at work
④ advantages of a life with long vacations

33 다음 글의 주제로 가장 적절한 것은?

2020. 지방직 9급

The e-book applications available on tablet computers employ touchscreen technology. Some touchscreens feature a glass panel covering two electronically-charged metallic surfaces lying face-to-face. When the screen is touched, the two metallic surfaces feel the pressure and make contact. This pressure sends an electrical signal to the computer, which translates the touch into a command. This version of the touchscreen is known as a resistive screen because the screen reacts to pressure from the finger. Other tablet computers feature a single electrified metallic layer under the glass panel. When the user touches the screen, some of the current passes through the glass into the user's finger. When the charge is transferred, the computer interprets the loss in power as a command and carries out the function the user desires. This type of screen is known as a capacitive screen.

① how users learn new technology
② how e-books work on tablet computers
③ how touchscreen technology works
④ how touchscreens have evolved

34 다음 글의 제목으로 가장 적절한 것은?

2020. 지방직 9급

Louis XIV needed a palace worthy of his greatness, so he decided to build a huge new house at Versailles, where a tiny hunting lodge stood. After almost fifty years of labor, this tiny hunting lodge had been transformed into an enormous palace, a quarter of a mile long. Canals were dug to bring water from the river and to drain the marshland. Versailles was full of elaborate rooms like the famous Hall of Mirrors, where seventeen huge mirrors stood across from seventeen large windows, and the Salon of Apollo, where a solid silver throne stood. Hundreds of statues of Greek gods such as Apollo, Jupiter, and Neptune stood in the gardens; each god had Louis's face!

① True Face of Greek Gods
② The Hall of Mirrors vs. the Salon of Apollo
③ Did the Canal Bring More Than Just Water to Versailles?
④ Versailles: From a Humble Lodge to a Great Palace

35 다음 글의 요지로 가장 적절한 것은?

2020. 지방직 9급

Evolutionarily, any species that hopes to stay alive has to manage its resources carefully. That means that first call on food and other goodies goes to the breeders and warriors and hunters and planters and builders and, certainly, the children, with not much left over for the seniors, who may be seen as consuming more than they're contributing. But even before modern medicine extended life expectancies, ordinary families were including grandparents and even great-grandparents. That's because what old folk consume materially, they give back behaviorally—providing a leveling, reasoning center to the tumult that often swirls around them.

① Seniors have been making contributions to the family.
② Modern medicine has brought focus to the role of old folk.
③ Allocating resources well in a family determines its prosperity.
④ The extended family comes at a cost of limited resources.

36 다음 글의 제목으로 가장 적절한 것은?

2019. 국가직 9급

Mapping technologies are being used in many new applications. Biological researchers are exploring the molecular structure of DNA ("mapping the genome"), geophysicists are mapping the structure of the Earth's core, and oceanographers are mapping the ocean floor. Computer games have various imaginary "lands" or levels where rules, hazards, and rewards change. Computerization now challenges reality with "virtual reality," artificial environments that stimulate special situations, which may be useful in training and entertainment. Mapping techniques are being used also in the realm of ideas. For example, relationships between ideas can be shown using what are called concept maps. Starting from a general or "central" idea, related ideas can be connected, building a web around the main concept. This is not a map by any traditional definition, but the tools and techniques of cartography are employed to produce it, and in some ways it resembles a map.

① Computerized Maps vs. Traditional Maps
② Where Does Cartography Begin?
③ Finding Ways to DNA Secrets
④ Mapping New Frontiers

37 다음 글의 요지로 가장 적절한 것은?

2019. 국가직 9급

When giving performance feedback, you should consider the recipient's past performance and your estimate of his or her future potential in designing its frequency, amount, and content. For high performers with potential for growth, feedback should be frequent enough to prod them into taking corrective action, but not so frequent that it is experienced as controlling and saps their initiative. For adequate performers who have settled into their jobs and have limited potential for advancement, very little feedback is needed because they have displayed reliable and steady behavior in the past, knowing their tasks and realizing what needs to be done. For poor performers — that is, people who will need to be removed from their jobs if their performance doesn't improve — feedback should be frequent and very specific, and the connection between acting on the feedback and negative sanctions such as being laid off or fired should be made explicit.

① Time your feedback well.
② Customize negative feedback.
③ Tailor feedback to the person.
④ Avoid goal-oriented feedback.

38 다음 글의 주제로 가장 적절한 것은?

2019. 국가직 9급

Imagine that two people are starting work at a law firm on the same day. One person has a very simple name. The other person has a very complex name. We've got pretty good evidence that over the course of their next 16 plus years of their career, the person with the simpler name will rise up the legal hierarchy more quickly. They will attain partnership more quickly in the middle parts of their career. And by about the eighth or ninth year after graduating from law school the people with simpler names are about seven to ten percent more likely to be partners — which is a striking effect. We try to eliminate all sorts of other alternative explanations. For example, we try to show that it's not about foreignness because foreign names tend to be harder to pronounce. But even if you look at just white males with Anglo-American names. so really the true in-group, you find that among those white males with Anglo names they are more likely to rise up if their names happen to be simpler. So simplicity is one key feature in names that determines various outcomes.

① the development of legal names
② the concept of attractive names
③ the benefit of simple names
④ the roots of foreign names

39 다음 글의 주제로 가장 적절한 것은?

2019. 지방직 9급

As the digital revolution upends newsrooms across the country, here's my advice for all the reporters. I've been a reporter for more than 25 years, so I have lived through a half dozen technological life cycles. The most dramatic transformations have come in the last half dozen years. That means I am, with increasing frequency, making stuff up as I go along. Much of the time in the news business, we have no idea what we are doing. We show up in the morning and someone says, "Can you write a story about (pick one) tax policy/immigration/climate change?" When newspapers had once-a-day deadlines, we said a reporter would learn in the morning and teach at night — write a story that could inform tomorrow's readers on a topic the reporter knew nothing about 24 hours earlier. Now it is more like learning at the top of the hour and teaching at the bottom of the same hour. I'm also running a political podcast, for example, and during the presidential conventions, we should be able to use it to do real-time interviews anywhere. I am just increasingly working without a script.

① a reporter as a teacher
② a reporter and improvisation
③ technology in politics
④ fields of journalism and technology

04 중심 내용 파악 유형 기출 독해 어휘 복습 TEST

#	Word		#	Word	
1	mentality		21	organization	
2	employer		22	means	
3	face		23	relieve	
4	loan		24	cherish	
5	artificial		25	competence	
6	mimic		26	attribute	
7	drastically		27	equate	
8	disrupt		28	dedicate	
9	counteract		29	discuss	
10	contagious		30	crave	
11	eliminate		31	countless	
12	ministry		32	deliberate	
13	infection		33	resistance	
14	install		34	extend	
15	disparity		35	solid	
16	emphasize		36	cultivate	
17	excavate		37	negative	
18	exploit		38	excessive	
19	dilute		39	overuse	
20	replenish		40	give off	

41	emit		61	incumbent	
42	excite		62	intervene	
43	focal		63	uninterrupted	
44	inert		64	intact	
45	concerned		65	courteously	
46	meet halfway		66	discernment	
47	optimize		67	migration	
48	simultaneously		68	anonymity	
49	sustain		69	obsession	
50	petition		70	generous	
51	flexibility		71	meditation	
52	shrink		72	pressure	
53	allege		73	leveling	
54	subject		74	tumult	
55	diffuse		75	prosperity	
56	merit		76	frequency	
57	assumption		77	sanction	
58	construct		78	striking	
59	signify		79	transformation	
60	mend		80	inform	

PART 05 문장 제거 유형

출제 경향 분석

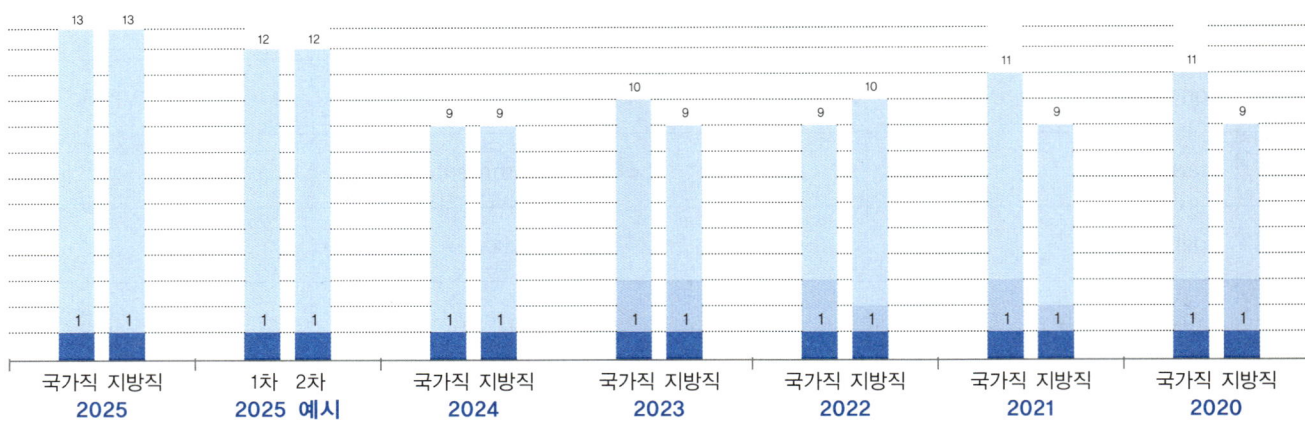

국가직	지방직	1차	2차	국가직	지방직	국가직	지방직	국가직	지방직	국가직	지방직	국가직	지방직
2025		2025 예시		2024		2023		2022		2021		2020	
13/1	13/1	12/1	12/1	9/1	9/1	10/1	9/1	9/1	10/1	11/1	9/1	11/1	9/1

반드시 한번에 다잡는 '문장 제거' 유형 기출 독해 어휘

- paramount 가장 중요한
- replace 대체하다, 대신하다
- quote 인용문, 인용하다
- summarize 요약하다
- deficiency 결핍, 부족
- desperate 필사적인, 절망적인
- urge 충동, 욕구, 충고하다, 권고하다
- conspiracy 음모
- contradict 모순되다, 부정하다
- renowned 유명한, 명성 있는
- reckless 무분별한, 무모한, 신중하지 못한
- insult 모욕, 모욕하다
- fatigued 피로한, 지친
- incapable 무능한, ~을 할 수 없는
- empathy 감정 이입, 공감
- transmission 전염, 전파, 전달
- initiate 시작하다, 착수시키다
- contemporary 현대의, 동시대의

- illustrate 설명하다, 실증하다
- spontaneous 자발적인, 즉흥적인
- sedentary 정적인, 주로 앉아서 하는
- metaphor 은유, 비유
- register 나타내다, 기록하다, 등록하다
- remarkable 놀라운, 주목할 만한
- irritate 자극하다, 짜증나게 하다
- submerge 물속에 잠기다, 잠수하다
- deprive 빼앗다, 박탈하다
- prolong 연장시키다, 늘이다
- urbanization 도시화
- inclined ~을 하고 싶은, ~할 것 같은
- tolerate 용인하다, 참다, 견디다
- hierarchy 계급, 계층
- supervise 감독하다, 지휘하다
- outstanding 뛰어난, 두드러진
- put on hold 보류하다, 연기하다
- dwindle 줄어들다, 감소하다

01 다음 글의 흐름상 어색한 문장은? 2025. 국가직 9급

As OECD countries prepare for an AI revolution, underscored by rapid advancements in generative AI and an increased availability of AI-skilled workers, the landscape of employment is poised for significant change. ① To navigate this shift, it's critical to prioritise training and education to equip both current and future workers with the necessary skills, and to support displaced workers with adequate social protection. ② Additionally, safeguarding workers' rights in the face of AI integration and ensuring inclusive labour markets become paramount. ③ Social dialogue will also be key to success in this new era. ④ Many experts believe that AI will completely replace all human jobs within the next decade. Together, these actions will ensure that the AI revolution benefits all, transforming potential risks into opportunities for growth and innovation.

02 다음 글의 흐름상 어색한 문장은? 2025. 지방직 9급

Scientists in the UK grew special tomatoes with extra vitamin D, which is important for people's health. Vitamin D deficiency affects about one billion people worldwide. ① Tomatoes naturally contain a substance that gets converted into vitamin D. ② The team altered the genes of the tomato plants, breeding them to have more of this substance than usual. ③ Each tomato came to have about as much vitamin D as two medium-sized eggs. ④ Moreover, tomatoes are commonly eaten raw in salads and served as a cooked vegetable. The scientists think the technique could be used with other foods, too.

03 다음 글의 흐름상 어색한 문장은?

2025. 출제 기조 전환 2차

A very common type of writing task — one that appears in every academic discipline — is a reaction or response. ① In a reaction essay, the writer is usually given a "prompt" — a visual or written stimulus — to think about and then respond to. ② It is very important to gather reliable facts so that you can defend your argument effectively. ③ Common prompts or stimuli for this type of writing include quotes, pieces of literature, photos, paintings, multimedia presentations, and news events. ④ A reaction focuses on the writer's feelings, opinions, and personal observations about the particular prompt. Your task in writing a reaction essay is twofold: to briefly summarize the prompt and to give your personal reaction to it.

04 다음 글의 흐름상 어색한 문장은?

2025. 출제 기조 전환 1차

Every parent or guardian of small children will have experienced the desperate urge to get out of the house and the magical restorative effect of even a short trip to the local park. ① There is probably more going on here than just letting off steam. ② The benefits for kids of getting into nature are huge, ranging from better academic performance to improved mood and focus. ③ Outdoor activities make it difficult for them to spend quality time with their family. ④ Childhood experiences of nature can also boost environmentalism in adulthood. Having access to urban green spaces can play a role in children's social networks and friendships.

05 다음 글의 흐름상 어색한 문장은? 2024. 국가직 9급

In spite of all evidence to the contrary, there are people who seriously believe that NASA's Apollo space program never really landed men on the moon. These people claim that the moon landings were nothing more than a huge conspiracy, perpetuated by a government desperately in competition with the Russians and fearful of losing face. ① These conspiracy theorists claim that the United States knew it couldn't compete with the Russians in the space race and was therefore forced to fake a series of successful moon landings. ② Advocates of a conspiracy cite several pieces of what they consider evidence. ③ Crucial to their case is the claim that astronauts never could have safely passed through the Van Allen belt, a region of radiation trapped in Earth's magnetic field. ④ They also point to the fact that the metal coverings of the spaceship were designed to block radiation. If the astronauts had truly gone through the belt, say conspiracy theorists, they would have died.

06 다음 글의 흐름상 어색한 문장은? 2024. 지방직 9급

Critical thinking sounds like an unemotional process but it can engage emotions and even passionate responses. In particular, we may not like evidence that contradicts our own opinions or beliefs. ① If the evidence points in a direction that is challenging, that can rouse unexpected feelings of anger, frustration or anxiety. ② The academic world traditionally likes to consider itself as logical and free of emotions, so if feelings do emerge, this can be especially difficult. ③ For example, looking at the same information from several points of view is not important. ④ Being able to manage your emotions under such circumstances is a useful skill. If you can remain calm, and present your reasons logically, you will be better able to argue your point of view in a convincing way.

07 다음 글의 흐름상 어색한 문장은? 2023. 국가직 9급

In our monthly surveys of 5,000 American workers and 500 U.S. employers, a huge shift to hybrid work is abundantly clear for office and knowledge workers. ① An emerging norm is three days a week in the office and two at home, cutting days on site by 30% or more. You might think this cutback would bring a huge drop in the demand for office space. ② But our survey data suggests cuts in office space of 1% to 2% on average, implying big reductions in density not space. We can understand why. High density at the office is uncomfortable and many workers dislike crowds around their desks. ③ Most employees want to work from home on Mondays and Fridays. Discomfort with density extends to lobbies, kitchens, and especially elevators. ④ The only sure-fire way to reduce density is to cut days on site without cutting square footage as much. Discomfort with density is here to stay according to our survey evidence.

08 다음 글의 흐름상 어색한 문장은? 2023. 지방직 9급

I once took a course in short-story writing and during that course a renowned editor of a leading magazine talked to our class. ① He said he could pick up any one of the dozens of stories that came to his desk every day and after reading a few paragraphs he could feel whether or not the author liked people. ② "If the author doesn't like people," he said, "people won't like his or her stories." ③ The editor kept stressing the importance of being interested in people during his talk on fiction writing. ④ Thurston, a great magician, said that every time he went on stage he said to himself, "I am grateful because I'm successful." At the end of the talk, he concluded, "Let me tell you again. You have to be interested in people if you want to be successful writer of stories."

09 다음 글에서 전체 흐름과 가장 관계 없는 문장은?

2023. 법원직 9급

One of the most interesting discoveries in the field of new sources of sustainable energy is bio-solar energy from jellyfish. Scientists have discovered that the fluorescent protein in this animal can be used to generate solar energy in a more sustainable way than current photovoltaic energy. How is this energy generated? ① The process involves converting the jellyfish's fluorescent protein into a solar cell that is capable of generating energy and transferring it to small devices. ② There has been constant criticism that the natural environment is being damaged by reckless solar power generation. ③ The main advantage of using these living beings as a natural energy source is that they are a clean alternative that does not use fossil fuels or require the use of limited resources. ④ Although this project is still currently in the trial phase, the expectation is that this source of energy will be able to be expanded and become a green alternative for powering the type of small electronic devices that are becoming more and more common.

* photovoltaic 광전기성의

10 다음 글에서 전체 흐름과 가장 관계 없는 문장은?

2023. 법원직 9급

Fast fashion is a method of producing inexpensive clothing at a rapid pace to respond to the latest fashion trends. With shopping evolving into a form of entertainment in the age of fast fashion, customers are contributing to what sustainability experts refer to as a throwaway culture. This means customers simply discard products once they are deemed useless rather than recycling or donating them. ① The consumers are generally satisfied with the quality of fast fashion brand clothing. ② As a result, these discarded items add a huge burden to the environment. ③ To resolve the throwaway culture and fast fashion crisis, the concept of sustainability in fashion is brought to the spotlight. ④ Sustainable fashion involves apparel, footwear, and accessories that are produced, distributed, and utilized as sustainably as possible while taking into account socio-economic and environmental concerns.

11 글의 흐름상 가장 어색한 문장은? 2022. 지방직 9급

The skill to have a good argument is critical in life. But it's one that few parents teach to their children. ① We want to give kids a stable home, so we stop siblings from quarreling and we have our own arguments behind closed doors. ② Yet if kids never get exposed to disagreement, we may eventually limit their creativity. ③ Children are most creative when they are free to brainstorm with lots of praise and encouragement in a peaceful environment. ④ It turns out that highly creative people often grow up in families full of tension. They are not surrounded by fistfights or personal insults, but real disagreements. When adults in their early 30s were asked to write imaginative stories, the most creative ones came from those whose parents had the most conflict a quarter-century earlier.

12 다음 글의 흐름상 가장 어색한 문장은? 2021. 국가직 9급

The term burnout refers to a "wearing out" from the pressures of work. Burnout is a chronic condition that results as daily work stressors take their toll on employees. ① The most widely adopted conceptualization of burnout has been developed by Maslach and her colleagues in their studies of human service workers. Maslach sees burnout as consisting of three interrelated dimensions. The first dimension—emotional exhaustion—is really the core of the burnout phenomenon. ② Workers suffer from emotional exhaustion when they feel fatigued, frustrated, used up, or unable to face another day on the job. The second dimension of burnout is a lack of personal accomplishment. ③ This aspect of the burnout phenomenon refers to workers who see themselves as failures, incapable of effectively accomplishing job requirements. ④ Emotional labor workers enter their occupation highly motivated although they are physically exhausted. The third dimension of burnout is depersonalization. This dimension is relevant only to workers who must communicate interpersonally with others (e.g. clients, patients, students) as part of the job.

13 다음 글의 흐름상 적절하지 않은 문장은?

2021. 지방직 9급

There was no divide between science, philosophy, and magic in the 15th century. All three came under the general heading of 'natural philosophy'. ①Central to the development of natural philosophy was the recovery of classical authors, most importantly the work of Aristotle. ②Humanists quickly realized the power of the printing press for spreading their knowledge. ③At the beginning of the 15th century Aristotle remained the basis for all scholastic speculation on philosophy and science. ④Kept alive in the Arabic translations and commentaries of Averroes and Avicenna, Aristotle provided a systematic perspective on mankind's relationship with the natural world. Surviving texts like his *Physics*, *Metaphysics*, and *Meteorology* provided scholars with the logical tools to understand the forces that created the natural world.

14 글의 흐름상 가장 어색한 문장은?

2021. 법원직 9급

Fiction has many uses and one of them is to build empathy. When you watch TV or see a film, you are looking at things happening to other people. Prose fiction is something you build up from 26 letters and a handful of punctuation marks, and you, and you alone, using your imagination, create a world and live there and look out through other eyes. ①You get to feel things, and visit places and worlds you would never otherwise know. ②Fortunately, in the last decade, many of the world's most beautiful and unknown places have been put in the spotlight. ③You learn that everyone else out there is a me, as well. ④You're being someone else, and when youreturn to your own world, you're going to be slightly changed.

15 다음 글에서 전체 흐름과 관계없는 문장은?

2021. 법원직 9급

Medical anthropologists with extensive training in human biology and physiology study disease transmission patterns and how particular groups adapt to the presence of diseases like malaria and sleeping sickness. ① Because the transmission of viruses and bacteria is strongly influenced by people's diets, sanitation, and other behaviors, many medical anthropologists work as a team with epidemiologists to identify cultural practices that affect the spread of disease. ② Though it may be a commonly held belief that most students enter medicine for humanitarian reasons rather than for the financial rewards of a successful medical career, in developed nations the prospect of status and rewards is probably one incentive. ③ Different cultures have different ideas about the causes and symptoms of disease, how best to treat illnesses, the abilities of traditional healers and doctors, and the importance of community involvement in the healing process. ④ By studying how a human communityperceives such things, medical anthropologists help hospitals and other agencies deliver health care services more effectively.

* epidemiologist 유행[전염]병학자

16 다음 글의 흐름상 가장 어색한 문장은?

2020. 국가직 9급

When the brain perceives a threat in the immediate surroundings, it initiates a complex string of events in the body. It sends electrical messages to various glands, organs that release chemical hormones into the bloodstream. Blood quickly carries these hormones to other organs that are then prompted o do various things. ① The adrenal glands above the kidneys, for example, pump out adrenaline, the body's stress hormone. ② Adrenaline travels all over the body doing things such as widening the eyes to be on the lookout for signs of danger, pumping the heart faster to keep blood and extra hormones flowing, and tensing the skeletal muscles so they are ready to lash out at or run from the threat. ③ The whole process is called the fight-or-flight response, because it prepares the body to either battle or run for its life. ④ Humans consciously control their glands to regulate the release of various hormones. Once the response is initiated, ignoring it is impossible, because hormones cannot be reasoned with.

17 글의 흐름상 가장 어색한 문장은? 2020. 지방직 9급

Philosophers have not been as concerned with anthropology as anthropologists have with philosophy. ① Few influential contemporary philosophers take anthropological studies into account in their work. ② Those who specialize in philosophy of social science may consider or analyze examples from anthropological research, but do this mostly to illustrate conceptual points or epistemological distinctions or to criticize epistemological or ethical implications. ③ In fact, the great philosophers of our time often drew inspiration from other fields such as anthropology and psychology. ④ Philosophy students seldom study or show serious interest in anthropology. They may learn about experimental methods in science, but rarely about anthropological fieldwork.

18 밑줄 친 부분 중 글의 흐름상 가장 어색한 것은? 2019. 국가직 9급

In 2007, our biggest concern was "too big to fail." Wall Street banks had grown to such staggering sizes, and had become so central to the health of the financial system, that no rational government could ever let them fail. ① Aware of their protected status, banks made excessively risky bets on housing markets and invented ever more complicated erivatives. ② New virtual currencies such as bitcoin and ethereum have radically changed our understanding of how money can and should work. ③ The result was the worst financial crisis since the breakdown of our economy in 1929. ④ In the years since 2007, we have made great progress in addressing the too-big-to-fail dilemma. Our banks are better capitalized than ever. Our regulators conduct regular stress tests of large institutions.

19 글의 흐름상 가장 어색한 문장은? 2019. 지방직 9급

Children's playgrounds throughout history were the wilderness, fields, streams, and hills of the country and the roads, streets, and vacant places of villages, towns, and cities. ① The term playground refers to all those places where children gather to play their free, spontaneous games. ② Only during the past few decades have children vacated these natural playgrounds for their growing love affair with video games, texting, and social networking. ③ Even in rural America few children are still roaming in a free-ranging manner, unaccompanied by adults. ④ When out of school, they are commonly found in neighborhoods digging in sand, building forts, playing traditional games, climbing, or playing ball games. They are rapidly disappearing from the natural terrain of creeks, hills, and fields, and like their urban counterparts, are turning to their indoor, sedentary cyber toys for entertainment.

20 글의 흐름상 가장 적절하지 않은 문장은? 2019. 서울시 9급

It seems to me possible to name four kinds of reading, each with a characteristic manner and purpose. The first is reading for information — reading to learn about a trade, or politics, or how to accomplish something. ① We read a newspaper this way, or most textbooks, or directions on how to assemble a bicycle. ② With most of this material, the reader can learn to scan the page quickly, coming up with what he needs and ignoring what is irrelevant to him, like the rhythm of the sentence, or the play of metaphor. ③ We also register a track of feeling through the metaphors and associations of words. ④ Courses in speed reading can help us read for this purpose, training the eye to jump quickly across the page.

21 다음 글에서 전체의 흐름과 가장 관계없는 문장은?

2019. 법원직 9급

The immortal operatically styled single Bohemian Rhapsody by Queen was released in 1975 and proceeded to the top of the UK charts for 9 weeks. ① A song that was nearly never released due to its length and unusual style but which Freddie insisted would be played became the instantly recognizable hit. ② By this time Freddie's unique talents were becoming clear, a voice with a remarkable range and a stage presence that gave Queen its colorful, unpredictable and flamboyant personality. ③ The son of Bomi and Jer Bulsara, Freddie spent the bulk of his childhood in India where he attended St. Peter's boarding school. ④ Very soon Queen's popularity extended beyond the shores of the UK as they charted and triumphed around Europe, Japan and the USA where in 1979 they topped the charts with Freddie's song Crazy Little thing Called Love.

22 다음 글에서 전체 흐름과 관계없는 문장은?

2019. 소방직 9급

Gum disease is frequently to blame for bad breath. In fact, bad breath is a warning sign for gum disease. ① This issue occurs initially as a result of plaque buildup on the teeth. ② Bacteria in the plaque irritate the gums and cause them to become tender, swollen and prone to bleeding. ③ Foul-smelling gases emitted by the bacteria can also cause bad breath. ④ Smoking damages your gum tissue by affecting the attachment of bone and soft tissue to your teeth. If you pay attention when you notice that bacteria-induced bad breath, though, you could catch gum disease before it gets to its more advanced stages.

23 다음 글의 흐름상 가장 어색한 문장은?

2018. 국가직 9급

Biologists have identified a gene that will allow rice plants to survive being submerged in water for up to two weeks — over a week longer than at present. Plants under water for longer than a week are deprived of oxygen and wither and perish. ① The scientists hope their discovery will prolong the harvests of crops in regions that are susceptible to flooding. ② Rice growers in these flood-prone areas of Asia lose an estimated one billion dollars annually to excessively waterlogged rice paddies. ③ They hope the new gene will lead to a hardier rice strain that will reduce the financial damage incurred in typhoon and monsoon seasons and lead to bumper harvests. ④ This is dreadful news for people in these vulnerable regions, who are victims of urbanization and have a shortage of crops. Rice yields must increase by 30 percent over the next 20 years to ensure a billion people can receive their staple diet.

24 밑줄 친 부분 중 글의 흐름상 가장 어색한 것은?

2018. 국가직 9급

Most people like to talk, but few people like to listen, yet listening well is a ① rare talent that everyone should treasure. Because they hear more, good listeners tend to know more and to be more sensitive to what is going on around them than most people. In addition, good listeners are inclined to accept or tolerate rather than to judge and criticize. Therefore, they have ② fewer enemies than most people. In fact, they are probably the most beloved of people. However, there are ③ exceptions to that generality. For example, John Steinbeck is said to have been an excellent listener, yet he was hated by some of the people he wrote about. No doubt his ability to listen contributed to his capacity to write. Nevertheless, the result of his listening didn't make him ④ unpopular.

25 다음 글의 흐름상 가장 어색한 문장은?

2018. 지방직 9급

The Renaissance kitchen had a definite hierarchy of help who worked together to produce the elaborate banquets. ① At the top, as we have seen, was the scalco, or steward, who was in charge of not only the kitchen, but also the dining room. ② The dining room was supervised by the butler, who was in charge of the silverware and linen and also served the dishes that began and ended the banquet — the cold dishes, salads, cheeses, and fruit at the beginning and the sweets and confections at the end of the meal. ③ This elaborate decoration and serving was what in restaurants is called "the front of the house." ④ The kitchen was supervised by the head cook, who directed the undercooks, pastry cooks, and kitchen help.

26 글의 흐름상 가장 어색한 문장은?

2017. 국가직 9급

Children's book awards have proliferated in recent years; today, there are well over 100 different awards and prizes by a variety of organizations. ① The awards may be given for books of a specific genre or simply for the best of all children's books published within a given time period. An award may honor a particular book or an author for a lifetime contribution to the world of children's literature. ② Most children's book awards are chosen by adults, but now a growing number of children's choice book awards exist. The larger national awards given in most countries are the most influential and have helped considerably to raise public awareness about the fine books being published for young readers. ③ An award ceremony for outstanding services to the publishing industry is put on hold. ④ Of course, readers are wise not to put too much faith in award-winning books. An award doesn't necessarily mean a good reading experience, but it does provide a starting place when choosing books.

27 다음 글의 흐름상 가장 어색한 문장은?

2017. 국가직 9급 하반기

Researchers have developed a new model that they said will provide better estimates about the North Atlantic right whale population, and the news isn't good. ① The model could be critically important to efforts to save the endangered species, which is in the midst of a year of high mortality, said Peter Corkeron, who leads the large whale team for the National Oceanic and Atmospheric Administration's Northeast Fisheries Science Center. ② The agency said the analysis shows the probability the population has declined since 2010 is nearly 100 percent. ③ "One problem was, are they really going down or are we not seeing them? They really have gone down, and that's the bottom line," Corkeron said. ④ The new research model has successfully demonstrated that the number of right whales has remained intact despite the worrisome, widening population gap between whale males and females.

28 다음 글의 흐름상 가장 어색한 문장은?

2017. 지방직 9급

Whether you've been traveling, focusing on your family, or going through a busy season at work, 14 days out of the gym takes its toll — not just on your muscles, but your performance, brain, and sleep, too. ① Most experts agree that after two weeks, you're in trouble if you don't get back in the gym. "At the two week point without exercising, there are a multitude of physiological markers that naturally reveal a reduction of fitness level," says Scott Weiss, a New York-based exercise physiologist and trainer who works with elite athletes. ② After all, despite all of its abilities, the human body (even the fit human body) is a very sensitive system and physiological changes (muscle strength or a greater aerobic base) that come about through training will simply disappear if your training load dwindles, he notes. Since the demand of training isn't present, your body simply slinks back toward baseline. ③ More protein is required to build more muscles at a rapid pace in your body. ④ Of course, how much and how quickly you'll decondition depends on a slew of factors like how fit you are, your age, and how long sweating has been a habit. "Two to eight months of not exercising at all will reduce your fitness level to as if you never exercised before," Weiss notes.

29 글의 흐름상 가장 어색한 것은?

2017. 지방직 9급 하반기

A story that is on the cutting edge of modern science began in an isolated part of northern Sweden in the 19th century. ① This area of the country had unpredictable harvests through the first half of the century. In years that the harvest failed, the population went hungry. However, the good years were very good. ② The same people who went hungry during bad harvests overate significantly during the good years. A Swedish scientist wondered about the long-term effects of these eating patterns. He studied the harvest and health records of the area. He was astonished by what he found. ③ Boys who overate during the good years produced children and grandchildren who died about six years earlier than the children and grandchildren of those who had very little to eat. Other scientists found the same result for girls. ④ Both boys and girls benefited greatly from the harvests of the good years. The scientists were forced to conclude that just one reason of overeating could have a negative impact that continued for generations.

30 글의 흐름상 가장 어색한 문장은?

2016. 국가직 9급

One of the largest celebrations of the passage of young girls into womanhood occurs in Latin American and Hispanic cultures. This event is called La Quinceañera, or the fifteenth year. ① It acknowledges that a young woman is now of marriageable age. The day usually begins with a Mass of Thanksgiving. ② By comparing the rites of passage of one culture with those of another, we can assess differences in class status. The young woman wears a full-length white or pastel-colored dress and is attended by fourteen friends and relatives who serve as maids of honor and male escorts. ③ Her parents and godparents surround her at the foot of the altar. When the Mass ends, other young relatives give small gifts to those who attended, while the Quinceañera herself places a bouquet of flowers on the altar of the Virgin. ④ Following the Mass is an elaborate party, with dancing, cake, and toasts. Finally, to end the evening, the young woman dances a waltz with her favorite escort.

05 문장 제거 유형 기출 독해 어휘 복습 TEST

1	rapid		21	reduce	
2	poise		22	renowned	
3	inclusive		23	paragraph	
4	paramount		24	conclude	
5	replace		25	reckless	
6	discipline		26	limited	
7	quote		27	argument	
8	summarize		28	quarrel	
9	extra		29	insult	
10	deficiency		30	exposure	
11	desperate		31	toll	
12	urge		32	fatigued	
13	get out of		33	incapable	
14	let off steam		34	depersonalization	
15	conspiracy		35	speculation	
16	advocate		36	empathy	
17	contradict		37	slightly	
18	rouse		38	transmission	
19	anxiety		39	practice	
20	density		40	involvement	

41	initiate		61	triumph	
42	a string of		62	irritate	
43	chemical		63	tender	
44	widen		64	submerge	
45	lash out		65	deprive of	
46	anthropology		66	prolong	
47	contemporary		67	incur	
48	illustrate		68	urbanization	
49	implication		69	inclined	
50	progress		70	tolerate	
51	spontaneous		71	no doubt	
52	sedentary		72	hierarchy	
53	direction		73	supervise	
54	irrelevant		74	proliferate	
55	metaphor		75	outstanding	
56	register		76	put on hold	
57	association		77	intact	
58	remarkable		78	dwindle	
59	presence		79	isolated	
60	flamboyant		80	astonish	

PART 06 문장 삽입 유형

출제 경향 분석

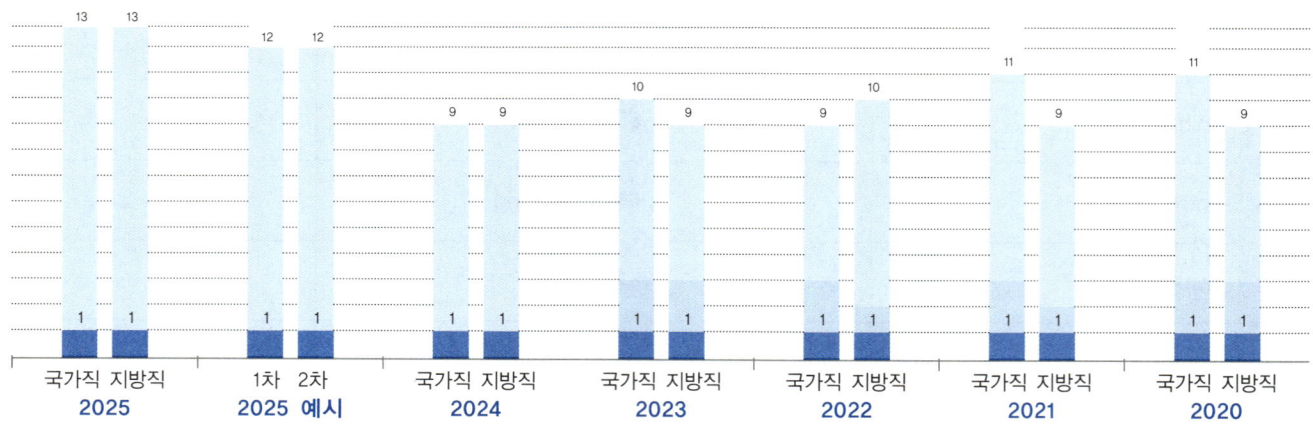

반드시 한번에 다잡는 '문장 삽입' 유형 기출 독해 어휘

- prescribed 미리 정해진, 규정된
- recommend 권하다, 추천하다
- extraneous 관련 없는
- extract 빼다, 뽑다, 추출하다
- controversial 논란이 많은
- strenuous 격렬한, 몹시 힘든, 완강한, 불굴의
- commitment 헌신, 약속, 전념
- inhabit 거주하다, 살다
- reveal 드러내다, 밝히다
- reform 개혁, 개선, 개혁하다, 개선하다
- deputy 대리인, 의원, 보안관
- unverified 검증되지 않은
- escalate 확대되다, 증가되다
- outlook 전망, 관점
- circulate 순환하다, 유포하다
- momentary 순간적인, 잠깐의
- analogy 비유, 유추
- dissimilar 같지 않은, 다른

- reverse (정)반대, 뒤바꾸다
- lay off 해고하다
- indispensable 없어서는 안 될, 필수적인
- addiction 중독
- retain 유지하다, 보유하다
- residue 나머지, 잔여물
- staggering 충격적인, 믿기 어려운
- integral 필수적인, 완전한
- lasting 영속적인, 지속적인
- obligation 의무, 책임, 책무
- persuasion 설득, 신념
- be open to ~의 여지가 있다
- superiority 우월성
- distribution 분배, 분포, 유통
- beneath 아래에, 밑에
- afterward 나중에
- brief 간단한, 간결한, 짧은
- sincerity 진심, 진실성

01 주어진 문장이 들어갈 위치로 가장 적절한 것은?

2025. 국가직 9급

Schedule your time in a way that relegates distracting activities, such as news consumption and social-media scanning, to prescribed times.

When you learn to drive, you are taught to maintain a level of situational awareness that is wide enough to help you anticipate problems but not so wide that it distracts you. The same goes for your project. (①) You need to know what's going on around you that might affect your life and work, but not what is irrelevant to these things. (②) I am not advocating a "full ostrich" model of ignoring the outside world entirely. (③) Rather, I mean to recommend ordering your information intake so that extraneous stuff doesn't eat up your attention. (④) Perhaps you could decide to read the news for 30 minutes in the morning and vegetate* on social media for 30 minutes at the end of the day.

* vegetate: 하는 일 없이 지내다

02 주어진 문장이 들어갈 위치로 가장 적절한 것은?

2025. 지방직 9급

However, according to Mike Tipton, a professor at University of Portsmouth, this is far from the quickest way of lowering your body temperature.

There are plenty of simple, scientifically supported techniques that will help you handle the heat. (①) If you're feeling the heat and somebody offers you a fan, it's likely that you'll try and cool your face first. (②) Certainly, all that breeze on your face will stimulate cold receptors there, which will give you a very powerful sensation of comfort. But actually, it's not going to extract the heat from your body. Instead, a better cooling strategy is to immerse your hands in cold water for 15 to 20 minutes. (③) Your hands have a high surface area to mass area—they have lots of blood flowing in them when you're hot. (④) If your core temperature is hot, your body will send blood to the extremities in order to lose heat.

03 주어진 문장이 들어갈 위치로 가장 적절한 것은?

2025. 출제 기조 전환 2차

> For others, activism is controversial and disruptive; after all, it often manifests as confrontational activity that directly challenges the order of things.

Activism is frequently defined as intentional, vigorous or energetic action that individuals and groups practice to bring about a desired goal. (①) For some, activism is a theoretically or ideologically focused project intended to effect a perceived need for political or social change. (②) Activism is uncomfortable, sometimes messy, and almost always strenuous. (③) In addition, it does not occur without the presence and commitment of activists, that is, folks who develop workable strategies, focus a collective spotlight onto particular issues, and ultimately move people into action. (④) As a noted scholar suggests, effective activists also make noise, sometimes loudly.

04 주어진 문장이 들어갈 위치로 가장 적절한 것은?

2025. 출제 기조 전환 1차

> In particular, in many urban counties, air pollution, as measured by the amount of total suspended particles, had reached dangerous levels.

Economists Chay and Greenstone evaluated the value of cleaning up of air pollution after the Clean Air Act of 1970. (①) Before 1970, there was little federal regulation of air pollution, and the issue was not high on the agenda of state legislators. (②) As a result, many counties allowed factories to operate without any regulation on their pollution, and in several heavily industrialized counties, pollution had reached very high levels. (③) The Clean Air Act established guidelines for what constituted excessively high levels of five particularly dangerous pollutants. (④) Following the Act in 1970 and the 1977 amendment, there were improvements in air quality.

05 주어진 문장이 들어갈 위치로 적절한 것은?

2024. 국가직 9급

Tribal oral history and archaeological evidence suggest that sometime between 1500 and 1700 a mudslide destroyed part of the village, covering several longhouses and sealing in their contents.

From the village of Ozette on the westernmost point of Washington's Olympic Peninsula, members of the Makah tribe hunted whales. (①) They smoked their catch on racks and in smokehouses and traded with neighboring groups from around the Puget Sound and nearby Vancouver Island. (②) Ozette was one of five main villages inhabited by the Makah, an Indigenous people who have been based in the region for millennia. (③) Thousands of artifacts that would not otherwise have survived, including baskets, clothing, sleeping mats, and whaling tools, were preserved under the mud. (④) In 1970, a storm caused coastal erosion that revealed the remains of these longhouses and artifacts.

06 주어진 문장이 들어갈 위치로 적절한 것은?

2024. 지방직 9급

But she quickly popped her head out again.

The little mermaid swam right up to the small window of the cabin, and every time a wave lifted her up, she could see a crowd of well-dressed people through the clear glass. Among them was a young prince, the handsomest person there, with large dark eyes. (①) It was his birthday, and that's why there was so much excitement. (②) When the young prince came out on the deck, where the sailors were dancing, more than a hundred rockets went up into the sky and broke into a glitter, making the sky as bright as day. (③) The little mermaid was so startled that she dove down under the water. (④) And look! It was just as if all the stars up in heaven were falling down on her. Never had she seen such fireworks.

07 주어진 문장이 들어갈 위치로 알맞은 것은?

2023. 국가직 9급

> They installed video cameras at places known for illegal crossings, and put live video feeds from the cameras on a Web site.

Immigration reform is a political minefield. (①) About the only aspect of immigration policy that commands broad political support is the resolve to secure the U. S. border with Mexico to limit the flow of illegal immigrants. (②) Texas sheriffs recently developed a novel use of the Internet to help them keep watch on the border. (③) Citizens who want to help monitor the border can go online and serve as "virtual Texas deputies." (④) If they see anyone trying to cross the border, they send a report to the sheriff's office, which follows up, sometimes with the help of the U. S. Border Patrol.

08 주어진 문장이 들어갈 위치로 가장 적절한 것은?

2023. 지방직 9급

> Yet, requests for such self-assessments are pervasive throughout one's Career.

The fiscal quarter just ended. Your boss comes by to ask you how well you performed in terms of sales this quarter. How do you describe your performance? As excellent? Good? Terrible? (①) Unlike when someone asks you about an objective performance metric (e.g., how many dollars in sales you brought in this quarter), how to subjectively describe your performance is often unclear. There is no right answer. (②) you are asked to subjectively describe your own performance in school applications, in job applications, in interviews, in performance reviews, in meetings—the list goes on. (③) How you describe your performance is what we call your level of self-promotion. (④) Since self-promotion is a pervasive part of work, people who do more self-promotion may have better chances of being hired, being promoted, and getting a raise or a bonus.

09 글의 흐름으로 보아, 주어진 문장이 들어가기에 가장 적절한 곳은?

2023. 법원직 9급

Healthcare chatbots have been purposed to solve this problem and ensure proper diagnosis and advice for people from the comfort of their homes.

People have grown hesitant to approach hospitals or health centers due to the fear of contracting a disease or the heavy sum of consultation fees. (①) This leads them to self-diagnose themselves based upon unverified information sources on the Internet. (②) This often proves harmful effects on the person's mental and physical health if misdiagnosed and improper medicines are consumed. (③) Based upon the severity of the diagnosis, the chatbot prescribes over the counter treatment or escalates the diagnosis to a verified healthcare professional. (④) Interactive chatbots that have been trained on a large and wide variety of symptoms, risk factors, and treatment can handle user health queries with ease, especially in the case of COVID-19.

10 글의 흐름으로 보아, 주어진 문장이 들어가기에 가장 적절한 곳은?

2023. 법원직 9급

But here it's worth noting that more than half the workforce has little or no opportunity for remote work.

COVID-19's spread flattened the cultural and technological barriers standing in the way of remote work. One analysis of the potential for remote work to persist showed that 20 to 25 percent of workforces in advanced economies could work from home in the range of three to five days a week. (①) This is four to five times more remote work than pre-COVID-19. (②) Moreover, not all work that can be done remotely should be; for example, negotiations, brainstorming, and providing sensitive feedback are activities that may be less effective when done remotely. (③) The outlook for remote work, then, depends on the work environment, job, and the tasks at hand, so *hybrid work setups, where some work happens on-site and some remotely, are likely to persist. (④) To unlock sustainable performance and well-being in a hybrid world, the leading driver of performance and productivity should be the sense of purpose work provides to employees, not compensation.

* hybrid 혼합체

11 글의 흐름으로 보아, 주어진 문장이 들어가기에 가장 적절한 곳은?
2023. 법원직 9급

These may appear as challenges which may be impossible to address because of the uncertainty in our ability to predict future climate.

Global warming is a reality man has to live with. (①) This is a very important issue to recognize, because, of all the parameters that affect human existence, on planet earth, it is the food security that is of paramount importance to life on earth and which is most threatened by global warming. (②) Future food security will be dependent on a combination of the stresses, both biotic and *abiotic, imposed by climate change, variability of weather within the growing season, development of **cultivars more suited to different ***ambient conditions, and, the ability to develop effective adaptation strategies which allow these cultivars to express their genetic potential under the changing climate conditions. (③) However, these challenges also provide us the opportunities to enhance our understanding of soil-plant-atmosphere interaction and how one could utilize this knowledge to enable us achieve the ultimate goal of enhanced food security across all areas of the globe. (④)

* abiotic 비생물적인
** cultivar 품종
*** ambient 주변의

12 주어진 문장이 들어갈 위치로 가장 적절한 곳은?
2022. 국가직 9급

Thus, blood, and life-giving oxygen, are easier for the heart to circulate to the brain.

People can be exposed to gravitational force, or g-force, in different ways. It can be localized, affecting only a portion of the body, as in getting slapped on the back. It can also be momentary, such as hard forces endured in a car crash. A third type of g-force is sustained, or lasting for at least several seconds. (①) Sustained, body-wide g-forces are the most dangerous to people. (②) The body usually withstands localized or momentary g-force better than sustained g-force, which can be deadly because blood is forced into the legs, depriving the rest of the body of oxygen. (③) Sustained g-force applied while the body is horizontal, or lying down, instead of sitting or standing tends to be more tolerable to people, because blood pools in the back and not the legs. (④) Some people, such as astronauts and fighter jet pilots, undergo special training exercises to increase their bodies' resistance to g-force.

13 주어진 문장이 들어갈 위치로 가장 적절한 곳은?

2022. 지방직 9급

> The comparison of the heart to a pump, however, is a genuine analogy.

An analogy is a figure of speech in which two things are asserted to be alike in many respects that are quite fundamental. Their structure, the relationships of their parts, or the essential purposes they serve are similar, although the two things are also greatly dissimilar. Roses and carnations are not analogous. (①) They both have stems and leaves and may both be red in color. (②) But they exhibit these qualities in the same way; they are of the same genus. (③) These are disparate things, but they share important qualities: mechanical apparatus, possession of valves, ability to increase and decrease pressures, and capacity to move fluids. (④) And the heart and the pump exhibit these qualities in different ways and in different contexts.

14 글의 흐름으로 보아, 주어진 문장이 들어가기에 가장 적절한 곳은?

2022. 법원직 9급

> The effect, however, was just the reverse.

How we dress for work has taken on a new element of choice, and with it, new anxieties. (①) The practice of having a "dress-down day" or "casual day," which began to emerge a decade or so ago, was intended to make life easier for employees, to enable them to save money and feel more relaxed at the office. (②) In addition to the normal workplace wardrobe, employees had to create a "workplace casual" wardrobe. (③) It couldn't really be the sweats and T-shirts you wore around the house on the weekend. (④) It had to be a selection of clothing that sustained a certain image — relaxed, but also serious.

* wardrobe 옷, 의류

15 글의 흐름으로 보아, 주어진 문장이 들어가기에 가장 적절한 곳은?

2022. 법원직 9급

But the demand for food isn't *elastic; people don't eat more just because food is cheap.

The free market has never worked in agriculture and it never will. (①) The economics of a family farm are very different than a firm's: When prices fall, the firm can lay off people and idle factories. (②) Eventually the market finds a new balance between supply and demand. (③) And laying off farmers doesn't help to reduce supply. (④) You can fire me, but you can't fire my land, because some other farmer who needs more cash flow or thinks he's more efficient than I am will come in and farm it.

* elastic 탄력성 있는

16 주어진 문장이 들어갈 위치로 가장 적절한 것은?

2021. 국가직 9급

For example, the state archives of New Jersey hold more than 30,000 cubic feet of paper and 25,000 reels of microfilm.

Archives are a treasure trove of material: from audio to video to newspapers, magazines and printed material — which makes them indispensable to any History Detective investigation. While libraries and archives may appear the same, the differences are important. (①) An archive collection is almost always made up of primary sources, while a library contains secondary sources. (②) To learn more about the Korean War, you'd go to a library for a history book. If you wanted to read the government papers, or letters written by Korean War soldiers, you'd go to an archive. (③) If you're searching for information, chances are there's an archive out there for you. Many state and local archives store public records — which are an amazing, diverse resource. (④) An online search of your state's archives will quickly show you they contain much more than just the minutes of the legislature — there are detailed land grant information to be found, old town maps, criminal records and oddities such as peddler license applications.

* treasure trove 귀중한 발굴물(수집물)
* land grant (대학·철도 등을 위해) 정부가 주는

17 주어진 문장이 들어갈 위치로 가장 적절한 것은?
2021. 지방직 9급

> And working offers more than financial security.

Why do workaholics enjoy their jobs so much? Mostly because working offers some important advantages. (①) It provides people with paychecks — a way to earn a living. (②) It provides people with self-confidence; they have a feeling of satisfaction when they've produced a challenging piece of work and are able to say, "I made that". (③) Psychologists claim that work also gives people an identity; they work so that they can get a sense of self and individualism. (④) In addition, most jobs provide people with a socially acceptable way to meet others. It could be said that working is a positive addiction; maybe workaholics are compulsive about their work, but their addiction seems to be a safe — even an advantageous — one.

18 주어진 문장이 들어갈 위치로 가장 적절한 것은?
2020. 국가직 9급

> It was then he remembered his experience with the glass flask, and just as quickly, he imagined that a special coating might be applied to a glass windshield to keep it from shattering.

In 1903 the French chemist, Edouard Benedictus, dropped a glass flask one day on a hard floor and broke it. (①) However, to the astonishment of the chemist, the flask did not shatter, but still retained most of its original shape. (②) When he examined the flask he found that it contained a film coating inside, a residue remaining from a solution of collodion that the flask had contained. (③) He made a note of this unusual phenomenon, but thought no more of it until several weeks later when he read stories in the newspapers about people in automobile accidents who were badly hurt by flying windshield glass. (④) Not long thereafter, he succeeded in producing the world's first sheet of safety glass.

19 주어진 문장이 들어갈 위치로 가장 적절한 것은?
2020. 지방직 9급

But there is also clear evidence that millennials, born between 1981 and 1996, are saving more aggressively for retirement than Generation X did at the same ages, 22 ~37.

Millennials are often labeled the poorest, most financially burdened generation in modern times. Many of them graduated from college into one of the worst labor markets the United States has ever seen, with a staggering load of student debt to boot. (①) Not surprisingly, millennials have accumulated less wealth than Generation X did at a similar stage in life, primarily because fewer of them own homes. (②) But newly available data providing the most detailed picture to date about what Americans of different generations save complicates that assessment. (③) Yes, Gen Xers, those born between 1965 and 1980, have a higher net worth. (④) And that might put them in better financial shape than many assume.

20 글의 흐름으로 보아 아래 문장이 들어가기에 가장 적절한 곳은?
2020. 법원직 9급

The great news is that this is true whether or not we remember our dreams.

Some believe there is no value to dreams, but it is wrong to dismiss these nocturnal dramas as irrelevant. There is something to be gained in remembering. (①) We can feel more connected, more complete, and more on track. We can receive inspiration, information, and comfort. Albert Einstein stated that his theory of relativity was inspired by a dream. (②) In fact, he claimed that dreams were responsible for many of his discoveries. (③) Asking why we dream makes as much sense as questioning why we breathe. Dreaming is an integral part of a healthy life. (④) Many people report being inspired with a new approach for a problem upon awakening, even though they don't remember the specific dream.

21 주어진 문장이 들어갈 위치로 가장 적절한 것은?

2019. 국가직 9급

Some of these ailments are short-lived; others may be long-lasting.

For centuries, humans have looked up at the sky and wondered what exists beyond the realm of our planet. (①) Ancient astronomers examined the night sky hoping to learn more about the universe. More recently, some movies explored the possibility of sustaining human life in outer space, while other films have questioned whether extraterrestrial life forms may have visited our planet. (②) Since astronaut Yuri Gagarin became the first man to travel in space in 1961, scientists have researched what conditions are like beyond the Earth's atmosphere, and what effects space travel has on the human body. (③) Although most astronauts do not spend more than a few months in space, many experience physiological and psychological problems when they return to the Earth. (④) More than two-thirds of all astronauts suffer from motion sickness while traveling in space. In the gravity-free environment, the body cannot differentiate up from down. The body's internal balance system sends confusing signals to the brain, which can result in nausea lasting as long as a few days.

22 주어진 문장이 들어갈 위치로 가장 적절한 것은?

2019. 지방직 9급

The same thinking can be applied to any number of goals, like improving performance at work.

The happy brain tends to focus on the short term. (①) That being the case, it's a good idea to consider what short-term goals we can accomplish that will eventually lead to accomplishing long-term goals. (②) For instance, if you want to lose thirty pounds in six months, what short-term goals can you associate with losing the smaller increments of weight that will get you there? (③) Maybe it's something as simple as rewarding yourself each week that you lose two pounds. (④) By breaking the overall goal into smaller, shorter-term parts, we can focus on incremental accomplishments instead of being overwhelmed by the enormity of the goal in our profession.

23 〈보기〉의 문장이 들어갈 위치로 가장 적절한 것은?
2019. 서울시 9급

> 보기
>
> In this situation, we would expect to find less movement of individuals from one job to another because of the individual's social obligations toward the work organization to which he or she belongs and to the people comprising that organization.

Cultural differences in the meaning of work can manifest themselves in other aspects as well. (①) For example, in American culture, it is easy to think of work simply as a means to accumulate money and make a living. (②) In other cultures, especially collectivistic ones, work may be seen more as fulfilling an obligation to a larger group. (③) In individualistic cultures, it is easier to consider leaving one job and going to another because it is easier to separate jobs from the self. (④) A different job will just as easily accomplish the same goals.

24 글의 흐름으로 보아, 주어진 문장이 들어가기에 가장 적절한 곳은?
2019. 법원직 9급

> "Soft power" on the contrary is "the ability to achieve goals through attraction and persuasion, rather than coercion or fee."

The concept of "soft power" was formed in the early 1990s by the American political scientist, deputy defense of the Clinton's administration, Joseph Nye, Jr. The ideas of the American Professor J. Nye allowed to take a fresh look at the interpretation of the concept of "power," provoked scientific debate and stimulated the practical side of international politics. (①) In his works he identifies two types of power: "hard power" and "soft power." (②) He defines "hard power" as "the ability to get others to act in ways that contradict their initial preferences and strategies." (③) The "soft power" of the state is its ability to "charm" other participants in the world political process, to demonstrate the attractiveness of its own culture (in a context it is attractive to others), political values and foreign policy (if considered legitimate and morally justified). (④) The main components of "soft power" are culture, political values and foreign policy.

* contradict 부인하다, 모순되다

25 주어진 문장이 들어갈 위치로 가장 적절한 것은?

2018. 국가직 9급

Some remain intensely proud of their original accent and dialect words, phrases and gestures, while others accommodate rapidly to a new environment by changing their speech habits, so that they no longer "stand out in the crowd."

Our perceptions and production of speech change with time. (①) If we were to leave our native place for an extended period, our perception that the new accents around us were strange would only be temporary. (②) Gradually, we will lose the sense that others have an accent and we will begin to fit in to accommodate our speech patterns to the new norm. (③) Not all people do this to the same degree. (④) Whether they do this consciously or not is open to debate and may differ from individual to individual, but like most processes that have to do with language, the change probably happens before we are aware of it and probably couldn't happen if we were.

26 주어진 문장이 들어갈 위치로 가장 적절한 것은?

2018. 지방직 9급

If neither surrendered, the two exchanged blows until one was knocked out.

The ancient Olympics provided athletes an opportunity to prove their fitness and superiority, just like our modern games. (①) The ancient Olympic events were designed to eliminate the weak and glorify the strong. Winners were pushed to the brink. (②) Just as in modern times, people loved extreme sports. One of the favorite events was added in the 33rd Olympiad. This was the pankration, or an extreme mix of wrestling and boxing. The Greek word pankration means "total power." The men wore leather straps with metal studs, which could make a terrible mess of their opponents. (③) The dangerous form of wrestling had no time or weight limits. In this event, only two rules applied. First, wrestlers were not allowed to gouge eyes with their thumbs. Secondly, they could not bite. Anything else was considered fair play. The contest was decided in the same manner as a boxing match. Contenders continued until one of the two collapsed. (④) Only the strongest and most determined athletes attempted this event. Imagine wrestling "Mr. Fingertips," who earned his nickname by breaking his opponents' fingers!

27 주어진 문장이 들어갈 위치로 가장 적절한 곳은?

2017. 국가직 9급

This inequality is corrected by their getting in their turn better portions from kills by other people.

Let us examine a situation of simple distribution such as occurs when an animal is killed in a hunt. One might expect to find the animal portioned out according to the amount of work done by each hunter to obtain it. (①) To some extent this principle is followed, but other people have their rights as well. (②) Each person in the camp gets a share depending upon his or her relation to the hunters. (③) When a kangaroo is killed, for example, the hunters have to give its main parts to their kinfolk and the worst parts may even be kept by the hunters themselves. (④) The net result in the long run is substantially the same to each person, but through this system the principles of kinship obligation and the morality of sharing food have been emphasized.

28 주어진 문장이 들어갈 위치로 가장 적절한 곳은?

2017. 국가직 9급 하반기

Only New Zealand, New Caledonia and a few small islands peek above the waves.

Lurking beneath New Zealand is a long-hidden continent called Zealandia, geologists say. But since nobody is in charge of officially designating a new continent, individual scientists will ultimately have to judge for themselves. (①) A team of geologists pitches the scientific case for the new continent, arguing that Zealandia is a continuous expanse of continental crust covering around 4.9 million square kilometers. (②) That's about the size of the Indian subcontinent. Unlike the other mostly dry continents, around 94 percent of Zealandia hides beneath the ocean. (③) Except those tiny areas, all parts of Zealandia submerge under the ocean. "If we could pull the plug on the world's oceans, it would be quite clear that Zealandia stands out about 3,000 meters above the surrounding ocean crust," says a geologist. (④) "If it wasn't for the ocean level, long ago we'd have recognized Zealandia for what it was—a continent."

29 주어진 문장이 들어갈 위치로 가장 적절한 것은?

2017. 지방직 9급

> Fortunately, however, the heavy supper she had eaten caused her to become tired and ready to fall asleep.

Various duties awaited me on my arrival. I had to sit with the girls during their hour of study. (①) Then it was my turn to read prayers; to see them to bed. Afterwards I ate with the other teachers. (②) Even when we finally retired for the night, the inevitable Miss Gryce was still my companion. We had only a short end of candle in our candlestick, and I dreaded lest she should talk till it was all burnt out. (③) She was already snoring before I had finished undressing. There still remained an inch of candle. (④) I now took out my letter; the seal was an initial F. I broke it; the contents were brief.

30 주어진 문장이 들어갈 위치로 가장 적절한 곳은?

2017. 지방직 9급 하반기

> However, should understanding not occur, you will find yourself soon becoming drowsy.

Dictionaries are your most reliable resources for the study of words. Yet the habit of using them needs to be cultivated. Of course, it can feel like an annoying interruption to stop your reading and look up a word. You might tell yourself that if you keep going, you would eventually understand it from the context. (①) Indeed, reading study guides often advise just that. (②) Often it's not the need for sleep that is occurring but a gradual loss of consciousness. (③) The knack here is to recognize the early signs of word confusion before drowsiness takes over when it is easier to exert sufficient willpower to grab a dictionary for word study. (④) Although this special effort is needed, once the meaning is clarified, the perceptible sense of relief makes the effort worthwhile.

06 문장 삽입 유형 기출 독해 어휘 복습 TEST

#			#		
1	distracting		21	come by	
2	prescribed		22	subjectively	
3	recommend		23	unverified	
4	extraneous		24	escalate	
5	handle		25	negotiation	
6	extract		26	outlook	
7	controversial		27	variability	
8	messy		28	ultimate	
9	strenuous		29	circulate	
10	commitment		30	localized	
11	federal		31	momentary	
12	suspend		32	horizontal	
13	inhabit		33	analogy	
14	preserve		34	structure	
15	reveal		35	dissimilar	
16	cabin		36	reverse	
17	startle		37	relaxed	
18	reform		38	lay off	
19	resolve		39	application	
20	deputy		40	indispensable	

#	Word		#	Word	
41	financial		61	coercion	
42	satisfaction		62	dialect	
43	addiction		63	fit in	
44	compulsive		64	be open to	
45	advantageous		65	debate	
46	shatter		66	superiority	
47	retain		67	glorify	
48	residue		68	contender	
49	retirement		69	distribution	
50	staggering		70	portion	
51	inspiration		71	kinfolk	
52	integral		72	beneath	
53	realm		73	continent	
54	astronomer		74	stand out	
55	result in		75	afterward	
56	lasting		76	companion	
57	incremental		77	brief	
58	obligation		78	drowsy	
59	on the contrary		79	willpower	
60	persuasion		80	worthwhile	

PART 07 순서 배열 유형

출제 경향 분석

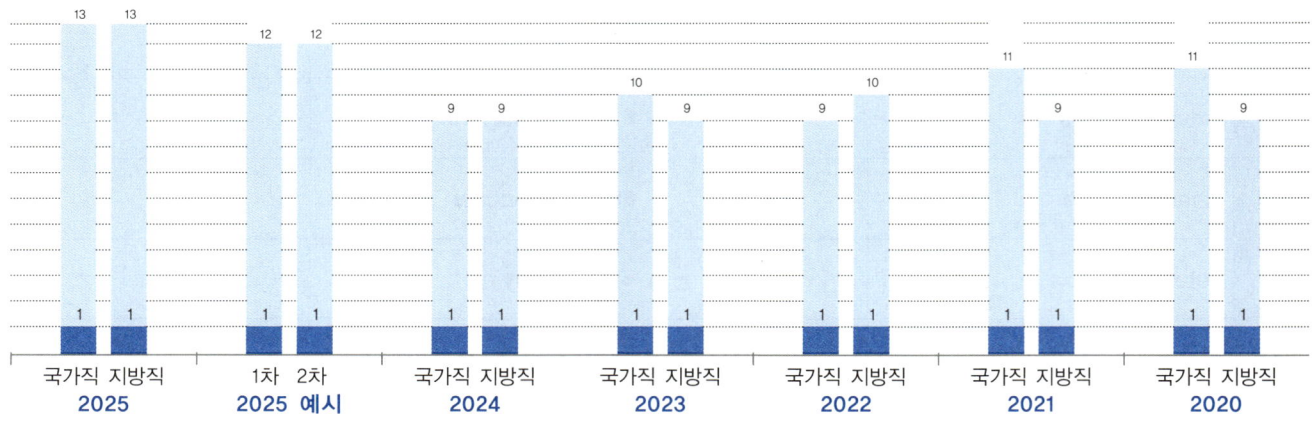

반드시 한번에 다잡는 '순서 배열' 유형 기출 독해 어휘

- reward 보상
- appeal 매력적이다, 관심[흥미]을 끌다
- favoritism 편애, 편파
- discriminate 차별하다, 식별하다
- certificate 증서, 자격증
- witness 목격하다, 목격자, 증인
- expand 확장하다, 넓히다
- authentic 진정한, 진짜의
- renew 갱신하다, 재개하다
- exemplify 전형적인 예가 되다, 예를 들다
- prediction 예측, 예견
- depression 우울증, 불경기
- scrutiny 정밀 조사, 철저한 검토
- mitigate 완화시키다, 경감시키다
- indulge 충족시키다, 채우다
- inheritance 유전, 상속
- offspring 자손, 자식
- mistaken 잘못된, 틀린

- adopt 채택하다, 입양하다
- reconcile 조화시키다, 받아들이다
- diplomat 외교관
- weird 이상한, 기이한, 기괴한
- fall short 부족해지다
- rudimentary 기본적인, 기초적인
- abundance 풍부, 충만, 다수, 대량
- humble 겸손한, 낮은
- deplete 고갈시키다, 대폭 감소시키다
- prestigious 훌륭한, 명성 있는
- province 주, 지방, 분야
- surrender 항복하다, 포기하다
- cease 그치다, 중단되다
- evaporate 증발하다, 사라지다
- exhaustion 피로, 고갈
- obsessed 빠져있는, 집착하는
- variable 변수, 변동이 심한
- pretend ~인 체하다, 가장하다

01 주어진 글 다음에 이어질 글의 순서로 가장 적절한 것은? 2025. 국가직 9급

> The idea that society should allocate economic rewards and positions of responsibility according to merit is appealing for several reasons.

(A) An economic system that rewards effort, initiative, and talent is likely to be more productive than one that pays everyone the same, regardless of contribution, or that hands out desirable social positions based on favoritism.

(B) Rewarding people strictly on their merits also has the virtue of fairness; it does not discriminate on any basis other than achievement.

(C) Two of these reasons are generalized versions of the case for merit in hiring —efficiency and fairness.

① (A)-(C)-(B)
② (B)-(C)-(A)
③ (C)-(A)-(B)
④ (C)-(B)-(A)

02 주어진 글 다음에 이어질 글의 순서로 가장 적절한 것은? 2025. 지방직 9급

> Usually toddlers picking things up from the ground means trouble.

(A) The family reported the find to the Israel Antiquities Authority, which determined it is a beetle-shaped seal from the Middle Bronze Age.

(B) But as 3-year-old Ziv Nitzan of Israel brushed away the sand on what seemed to be a rock, she revealed a nearly 4,000-year-old Egyptian artifact.

(C) Ziv was awarded a certificate for good citizenship, and the Heritage Minister of Israel said the seal "connects us to a grand story," and that "even children can be a part of discovering history."

① (A)-(C)-(B)
② (B)-(A)-(C)
③ (B)-(C)-(A)
④ (C)-(B)-(A)

03 주어진 글 다음에 이어질 글의 순서로 가장 적절한 것은?
2025. 출제 기조 전환 2차

Nick started a fire with some chunks of pine he got with the ax from a stump. Over the fire he stuck a wire grill, pushing the four legs down into the ground with his boot.

(A) They began to bubble, making little bubbles that rose with difficulty to the surface. There was a good smell. Nick got out a bottle of tomato ketchup and cut four slices of bread.

(B) The little bubbles were coming faster now. Nick sat down beside the fire and lifted the frying pan off.

(C) Nick put the frying pan on the grill over the flames. He was hungrier. The beans and spaghetti warmed. He stirred them and mixed them together.

① (B) − (A) − (C)
② (B) − (C) − (A)
③ (C) − (A) − (B)
④ (C) − (B) − (A)

04 주어진 글 다음에 이어질 글의 순서로 가장 적절한 것은?
2025. 출제 기조 전환 1차

Before anyone could witness what had happened, I shoved the loaves of bread up under my shirt, wrapped the hunting jacket tightly about me, and walked swiftly away.

(A) When I dropped them on the table, my sister's hands reached to tear off a chunk, but I made her sit, forced my mother to join us at the table, and poured warm tea.

(B) The heat of the bread burned into my skin, but I clutched it tighter, clinging to life. By the time I reached home, the loaves had cooled somewhat, but the insides were still warm.

(C) I sliced the bread. We ate an entire loaf, slice by slice. It was good hearty bread, filled with raisins and nuts.

① (A) − (B) − (C)
② (B) − (A) − (C)
③ (B) − (C) − (A)
④ (C) − (A) − (B)

05 주어진 글 다음에 이어질 글의 순서로 적절한 것은?

2024. 국가직 9급

Interest in movie and sports stars goes beyond their performances on the screen and in the arena.

(A) The doings of skilled baseball, football, and basketball players out of uniform similarly attract public attention.

(B) Newspaper columns, specialized magazines, television programs, and Web sites record the personal lives of celebrated Hollywood actors, sometimes accurately.

(C) Both industries actively promote such attention, which expands audiences and thus increases revenues. But a fundamental difference divides them: What sports stars do for a living is authentic in a way that what movie stars do is not.

① (A) − (C) − (B)
② (B) − (A) − (C)
③ (B) − (C) − (A)
④ (C) − (A) − (B)

06 주어진 글 다음에 이어질 글의 순서로 적절한 것은?

2024. 지방직 9급

Computer assisted language learning (CALL) is both exciting and frustrating as a field of research and practice.

(A) Yet the technology changes so rapidly that CALL knowledge and skills must be constantly renewed to stay apace of the field.

(B) It is exciting because it is complex, dynamic and quickly changing — and it is frustrating for the same reasons.

(C) Technology adds dimensions to the domain of language learning, requiring new knowledge and skills for those who wish to apply it into their professional practice.

① (A) − (C) − (B)
② (B) − (A) − (C)
③ (B) − (C) − (A)
④ (C) − (B) − (A)

07 주어진 글 다음에 이어질 글의 순서로 알맞은 것은?

2023. 국가직 9급

All civilizations rely on government administration. Perhaps no civilization better exemplifies this than ancient Rome.

(A) To rule an area that large, the Romans, based in what is now central Italy, needed an effective system of government administration.

(B) Actually, the word "civilization" itself comes from the Latin word civis, meaning "citizen."

(C) Latin was the language of ancient Rome, whose territory stretched from the Mediterranean basin all the way to parts of Great Britain in the north and the Black Sea to the east.

① (A) − (B) − (C)
② (B) − (A) − (C)
③ (B) − (C) − (A)
④ (C) − (A) − (B)

08 주어진 글 다음에 이어질 글의 순서로 가장 적절한 것은?

2023. 지방직 9급

Just a few years ago, every conversation about artificial intelligence (AI) seemed to end with an apocalyptic prediction.

(A) More recently, however, Things have begun to change. AI has gone from being a scary black box to something people can use for a variety of use cases.

(B) In 2014, an expert in the field said that, with AI, we are summoning the demon, while a Nobel Prize winning physicist said that AI could spell the end of the human race.

(C) This shift is because these technologies are finally being explored at scale in the industry, particularly for market opportunities.

① (A) − (B) − (C)
② (B) − (A) − (C)
③ (B) − (C) − (A)
④ (C) − (A) − (B)

09 주어진 글 다음에 이어질 글의 순서로 가장 적절한 것은?

2023. 법원직 9급

Sports fan depression is a real phenomenon that affects many avid sports fans, especially during times of disappointment or defeat.

(A) Fans may experience a decrease in mood, appetite, and sleep quality, as well as an increase in stress levels and a heightened risk of developing anxiety or depression. There are many factors that can contribute to sports fan depression, including personal investment in a team's success, social pressures to support a particular team, and the intense media coverage and scrutiny that often accompanies high-profile sports events.

(B) For many fans, their emotional investment in their favorite teams or athletes can be so intense that losing or failing to meet expectations can lead to feelings of sadness, frustration, and even depression. Research has shown that sports fan depression can have a range of negative effects on both mental and physical health.

(C) To mitigate the negative effects of sports fan depression, it's important for fans to maintain a healthy perspective on sports and remember that they are ultimately just games. Engaging in self-care activities such as exercise, spending time with loved ones, and seeking support from a mental health professional can also be helpful.

* avid 열심인

① (A) − (C) − (B) ② (B) − (A) − (C)
③ (B) − (C) − (A) ④ (C) − (B) − (A)

10 주어진 글 다음에 이어질 글의 순서로 가장 적절한 것은?

2023. 법원직 9급

On the human level, a cow seems simple. You feed it grass, and it pays you back with milk. It's a trick whose secret is limited to cows and a few other mammals (most can't digest grass).

(A) A cow's complexity is even greater. In particular, a cow (plus a bull) can make a new generation of baby cows. This is a simple thing on a human level, but inexpressibly complex on a microscopic level.

(B) Seen through a microscope, though, it all gets more complicated. And the closer you look, the more complicated it gets. Milk is not a single substance, but a mixture of many. Grass is so complex that we still don't fully understand it.

(C) You don't need to understand the details to exploit the process: it's a straightforward transformation from grass into milk, more like chemistry — or alchemy — than biology. It is, in its way, magic, but it's rational magic that works reliably. All you need is some grass, a cow and several generations of practical knowhow.

* alchemy 연금술

① (B) − (A) − (C)
② (B) − (C) − (A)
③ (C) − (A) − (B)
④ (C) − (B) − (A)

11. 주어진 글 다음에 이어질 글의 순서로 가장 적절한 것은?

2023. 법원직 9급

At the level of lawmaking, there is no reason why tech giants should have such an ironclad grip on technological resources and innovation.

(A) As the Daily Wire's Matt Walsh has pointed out, for example, if you don't buy your kid a smartphone, he won't have one. There is no need to put in his hand a device that enables him to indulge his every impulse without supervision.

(B) At the private and personal level, there's no reason why they should have control of your life, either. In policy, politics, and our personal lives, it should not be taken as "inevitable" that our data will be sold to the highest bidder, our children will be addicted to online games, and our lives will be lived in the metaverse.

(C) As a free people, we are entitled to exert absolute control over which kinds of digital products we consume, and in what quantities. Most especially, parents should control what tech products go to their kids.

① (B) − (A) − (C)
② (B) − (C) − (A)
③ (C) − (A) − (B)
④ (C) − (B) − (A)

12. 주어진 글 다음에 이어질 글의 순서로 가장 적절한 것은?

2022. 국가직 9급

Today, Lamarck is unfairly remembered in large part for his mistaken explanation of how adaptations evolve. He proposed that by using or not using certain body parts, an organism develops certain characteristics.

(A) There is no evidence that this happens. Still, it is important to note that Lamarck proposed that evolution occurs when organisms adapt to their environments. This idea helped set the stage for Darwin.

(B) Lamarck thought that these characteristics would be passed on to the offspring. Lamarck called this idea *inheritance of acquired characteristics*.

(C) For example, Lamarck might explain that a kangaroo's powerful hind legs were the result of ancestors strengthening their legs by jumping and then passing that acquired leg strength on to the offspring. However, an acquired characteristic would have to somehow modify the DNA of specific genes in order to be inherited.

① (A) − (C) − (B)
② (B) − (A) − (C)
③ (B) − (C) − (A)
④ (C) − (A) − (B)

13 주어진 글 다음에 이어질 글의 순서로 가장 적절한 것은?
2022. 지방직 9급

For people who are blind, everyday tasks such as sorting through the mail or doing a load of laundry present a challenge.

(A) That's the thinking behind Aira, a new service that enables its thousands of users to stream live video of their surroundings to an on-demand agent, using either a smartphone or Aira's proprietary glasses.
(B) But what if they could "borrow" the eyes of someone who could see?
(C) The Aira agents, who are available 24/7, can then answer questions, describe objects or guide users through a location.

① (A) − (B) − (C)
② (A) − (C) − (B)
③ (B) − (A) − (C)
④ (C) − (A) − (B)

14 주어진 글 다음에 이어질 글의 순서로 가장 적절한 것은?
2022. 법원직 9급

Once they leave their mother, primates have to keep on making decisions about whether new foods they encounter are safe and worth collecting.

(A) By the same token, if the sampler feels fine, it will reenter the tree in a few days, eat a little more, then wait again, building up to a large dose slowly. Finally, if the monkey remains healthy, the other members figure this is OK, and they adopt the new food.
(B) If the plant harbors a particularly strong toxin, the sampler's system will try to break it down, usually making the monkey sick in the process. "I've seen this happen," says Glander. "The other members of the troop are watching with great interest — if the animal gets sick, no other animal will go into that tree. There's a cue being given — a social cue."
(C) Using themselves as experiment tools is one option, but social primates have found a better way. Kenneth Glander calls it "sampling." When howler monkeys move into a new habitat, one member of the troop will go to a tree, eat a few leaves, then wait a day.

① (A) − (B) − (C)
② (B) − (A) − (C)
③ (C) − (B) − (A)
④ (C) − (A) − (B)

15 주어진 글 다음에 이어질 글의 순서로 가장 적절한 것은?
2022. 법원직 9급

The historical evolution of Conflict Resolution gained momentum in the 1950s and 1960s, at the height of the Cold War, when the development of nuclear weapons and conflict between the superpowers seemed to threaten human survival.

(A) The combination of analysis and practice implicit in the new ideas was not easy to reconcile with traditional scholarly institutions or the traditions of practitioners such as diplomats and politicians.

(B) However, they were not taken seriously by some. The international relations profession had its own understanding of international conflict and did not see value in the new approaches as proposed.

(C) A group of pioneers from different disciplines saw the value of studying conflict as a general phenomenon, with similar properties, whether it occurs in international relations, domestic politics, industrial relations, communities, or between individuals.

① (B) − (A) − (C)
② (B) − (C) − (A)
③ (C) − (A) − (B)
④ (C) − (B) − (A)

16 주어진 글 다음에 이어질 글의 순서로 가장 적절한 것은?
2022. 법원직 9급

Ambiguity is so uncomfortable that it can even turn good news into bad. You go to your doctor with a persistent stomachache. Your doctor can't figure out what the reason is, so she sends you to the lab for tests.

(A) And what happens? Your immediate relief may be replaced by a weird sense of discomfort. You still don't know what the pain was! There's got to be an explanation somewhere.

(B) A week later you're called back to hear the results. When you finally get into her office, your doctor smiles and tells you the tests were all negative.

(C) Maybe it is cancer and they've just missed it. Maybe it's worse. Surely they should be able to find a cause. You feel frustrated by the lack of a definitive answer.

① (B) − (A) − (C)
② (B) − (C) − (A)
③ (C) − (A) − (B)
④ (C) − (B) − (A)

17 주어진 글 다음에 이어질 글의 순서로 가장 적절한 것은?
2021. 국가직 9급

To be sure, human language stands out from the decidedly restricted vocalizations of monkeys and apes. Moreover, it exhibits a degree of sophistication that far exceeds any other form of animal communication.

(A) That said, many species, while falling far short of human language, do nevertheless exhibit impressively complex communication systems in natural settings.

(B) And they can be taught far more complex systems in artificial contexts, as when raised alongside humans.

(C) Even our closest primate cousins seem incapable of acquiring anything more than a rudimentary communicative system, even after intensive training over several years. The complexity that is language is surely a species-specific trait.

① (A) − (B) − (C)
② (B) − (C) − (A)
③ (C) − (A) − (B)
④ (C) − (B) − (A)

18 주어진 글 다음에 이어질 글의 순서로 가장 적절한 것은?
2021. 지방직 9급

Growing concern about global climate change has motivated activists to organize not only campaigns against fossil fuel extraction consumption, but also campaigns to support renewable energy.

(A) This solar cooperative produces enough energy to power 1,400 homes, making it the first large-scale solar farm cooperative in the country and, in the words of its members, a visible reminder that solar power represents "a new era of sustainable and 'democratic' energy supply that enables ordinary people to produce clean power, not only on their rooftops, but also at utility scale."

(B) Similarly, renewable energy enthusiasts from the United States have founded the Clean Energy Collective, a company that has pioneered "the model of delivering clean power-generation through medium-scale facilities that are collectively owned by participating utility customers."

(C) Environmental activists frustrated with the UK government's inability to rapidly accelerate the growth of renewable energy industries have formed the Westmill Wind Farm Co-operative, a community-owned organization with more than 2,000 members who own an onshore wind farm estimated to produce as much electricity in a year as that used by 2,500 homes. The Westmill Wind Farm Co-operative has inspired local citizens to form the Westmill Solar Co-operative.

① (C) − (A) − (B)   ② (A) − (C) − (B)
③ (B) − (C) − (A)   ④ (C) − (B) − (A)

19 주어진 글 다음에 이어질 글의 순서로 가장 적절한 것은?
2021. 법원직 9급

Religion can certainly bring out the best in a person, but it is not the only phenomenon with that property.

(A) People who would otherwise be self-absorbed or shallow or crude or simply quitters are often ennobled by their religion, given a perspective on life that helps them make the hard decisions that we all would be proud to make.

(B) Having a child often has a wonderfully maturing effect on a person. Wartime, famously, gives people an abundance of occasions to rise to, as do natural disasters like floods and hurricanes.

(C) But for day-in, day-out lifelong bracing, there is probably nothing so effective as religion: it makes powerful and talented people more humble and patient, it makes average people rise above themselves, it provides sturdy support for many people who desperately need help staying away from drink or drugs or crime.

① (B) − (A) − (C)
② (B) − (C) − (A)
③ (C) − (A) − (B)
④ (C) − (B) − (A)

20 주어진 글 다음에 이어질 글의 순서로 가장 적절한 것은?
2021. 법원직 9급

More people require more resources, which means that as the population increases, the Earth's resources deplete more rapidly.

(A) Population growth also results in increased greenhouse gases, mostly from CO_2 emissions. For visualization, during that same 20th century that saw fourfold population growth, CO_2 emissions increased twelvefold.

(B) The result of this depletion is deforestation and loss of biodiversity as humans strip the Earth of resources to accommodate rising population numbers.

(C) As greenhouse gases increase, so do climate patterns, ultimately resulting in the long-term pattern called climate change.

* deplete 고갈시키다, 대폭 감소시키다

① (A) − (B) − (C)
② (B) − (A) − (C)
③ (B) − (C) − (A)
④ (C) − (A) − (B)

21 주어진 글 다음에 이어질 글의 순서로 가장 적절한 것은?

2021. 법원직 9급

Sequoya (1760?-1843) was born in eastern Tennessee, into a prestigious family that was highly regarded for its knowledge of Cherokee tribal traditions and religion.

(A) Recognizing the possibilities writing had for his people, Sequoya invented a Cherokee alphabet in 1821. With this system of writing, Sequoya was able to record ancient tribal customs.

(B) More important, his alphabet helped the Cherokee nation develop a publishing industry so that newspapers and books could be printed. School-age children were thus able to learn about Cherokee culture and traditions in their own language.

(C) As a child, Sequoya learned the Cherokee oral tradition; then, as an adult, he was introduced to Euro-American culture. In his letters, Sequoya mentions how he became fascinated with the writing methods European Americans used to communicate.

① (B) − (A) − (C)
② (B) − (C) − (A)
③ (C) − (A) − (B)
④ (C) − (B) − (A)

22 주어진 글 다음에 이어질 글의 순서로 가장 적절한 것은?

2021. 소방직 9급

There are hundreds of gas stations around San Francisco in the California Bay Area. One might think that gas stations would spread out to serve local neighborhoods.

(A) The phenomenon is partly due to population clustering. Gas stations will be more common where demand is high, like in a city, rather than in sparsely populated areas like cornfields.

(B) But this idea is contradicted by a common observation. Whenever you visit a gas station, there is almost always another in the vicinity, often just across the street. In general, gas stations are highly clustered.

(C) Moreover, there are many factors at play. Locating a gas station is an optimization problem involving demand, real estate prices, estimates of population growth, and supply considerations such as the ease of refueling.

① (A) − (C) − (B)
② (B) − (A) − (C)
③ (C) − (A) − (B)
④ (C) − (B) − (A)

23 주어진 글 다음에 이어질 글의 순서로 가장 적절한 것은?

2020. 국가직 9급

Past research has shown that experiencing frequent psychological stress can be a significant risk factor for cardiovascular disease, a condition that affects almost half of those aged 20 years and older in the United States.

(A) Does this mean, though, that people who drive on a daily basis are set to develop heart problems, or is there a simple way of easing the stress of driving?

(B) According to a new study, there is. The researchers noted that listening to music while driving helps relieve the stress that affects heart health.

(C) One source of frequent stress is driving, either due to the stressors associated with heavy traffic or the anxiety that often accompanies inexperienced drivers.

① (A) − (C) − (B)
② (B) − (A) − (C)
③ (C) − (A) − (B)
④ (C) − (B) − (A)

24 주어진 글 다음에 이어질 글의 순서로 가장 적절한 것은?

2020. 지방직 9급

Nowadays the clock dominates our lives so much that it is hard to imagine life without it. Before industrialization, most societies used the sun or the moon to tell the time.

(A) For the growing network of railroads, the fact that there were no time standards was a disaster. Often, stations just some miles apart set their clocks at different times. There was a lot of confusion for travelers.

(B) When mechanical clocks first appeared, they were immediately popular. It was fashionable to have a clock or a watch. People invented the expression "of the clock" or "o'clock" to refer to this new way to tell the time.

(C) These clocks were decorative, but not always useful. This was because towns, provinces, and even neighboring villages had different ways to tell the time. Travelers had to reset their clocks repeatedly when they moved from one place to another. In the United States, there were about 70 different time zones in the 1860s.

① (A) − (B) − (C)
② (B) − (A) − (C)
③ (B) − (C) − (A)
④ (C) − (A) − (B)

25 주어진 글 다음에 이어질 글의 순서로 가장 적절한 것은?
2020. 법원직 9급

As cars are becoming less dependent on people, the means and circumstances in which the product is used by consumers are also likely to undergo significant changes, with higher rates of participation in car sharing and short-term leasing programs.

(A) In the not-too-distant future, a driverless car could come to you when you need it, and when you are done with it, it could then drive away without any need for a parking space. Increases in car sharing and short-term leasing are also likely to be associated with a corresponding decrease in the importance of exterior car design.

(B) As a result, the symbolic meanings derived from cars and their relationship to consumer self-identity and status are likely to change in turn.

(C) Rather than serving as a medium for personalization and self-identity, car exteriors might increasingly come to represent a channel for advertising and other promotional activities, including brand ambassador programs, such as those offered by Free Car Media.

① (A) − (C) − (B)
② (B) − (C) − (A)
③ (C) − (A) − (B)
④ (C) − (B) − (A)

26 주어진 글 다음에 이어질 글의 순서로 가장 적절한 것은?
2020. 법원직 9급

There is a wonderful story of a group of American car executives who went to Japan to see a Japanese assembly line. At the end of the line, the doors were put on the hinges, the same as in America.

(A) But something was missing. In the United States, a line worker would take a rubber mallet and tap the edges of the door to ensure that it fit perfectly. In Japan, that job didn't seem to exist.

(B) Confused, the American auto executives asked at what point they made sure the door fit perfectly. Their Japanese guide looked at them and smiled sheepishly. "We make sure it fits when we design it."

(C) In the Japanese auto plant, they didn't examine the problem and accumulate data to figure out the best solution—they engineered the outcome they wanted from the beginning. If they didn't achieve their desired outcome, they understood it was because of a decision they made at the start of the process.

① (A) − (B) − (C)
② (A) − (C) − (B)
③ (B) − (A) − (C)
④ (B) − (C) − (A)

27 주어진 글 다음에 이어질 글의 순서로 가장 적절한 것은?
2020. 소방직 9급

In World War II, Japan joined forces with Germany and Italy. So there were now two fronts, the European battle zone and the islands in the Pacific Ocean.

(A) Three days later, the United States dropped bombs on another city of Nagasaki. Japan soon surrendered, and World War II finally ended.

(B) In late 1941, the United States, Britain and France participated in a fight against Germany and Japan; the U.S. troops were sent to both battlefronts.

(C) At 8:15 a.m. on August 6, 1945, a U.S. military plane dropped an atomic bomb over Hiroshima, Japan. In an instant, 80,000 people were killed. Hiroshima simply ceased to exist. The people at the center of the explosion evaporated. All that remained was their charred shadows on the walls of buildings.

① (A) – (B) – (C)
② (B) – (A) – (C)
③ (B) – (C) – (A)
④ (C) – (A) – (B)

28 주어진 글 다음에 이어질 글의 순서로 가장 적절한 것은?
2020. 소방직 9급

Trivial things such as air conditioners or coolers with fresh water, flexible schedules and good relationships with colleagues, as well as many other factors, impact employees' productivity and quality of work.

(A) At the same time, there are many bosses who not only manage to maintain their staff's productivity at high levels, but also treat them nicely and are pleasant to work with.

(B) In this regard, one of the most important factors is the manager, or the boss, who directs the working process.

(C) It is not a secret that bosses are often a category of people difficult to deal with: many of them are unfairly demanding, prone to shifting their responsibilities to other workers, and so on.

① (A) – (B) – (C)
② (B) – (A) – (C)
③ (B) – (C) – (A)
④ (C) – (B) – (A)

29 주어진 문장 다음에 이어질 글의 순서로 가장 적절한 것은?

2019. 국가직 9급

> South Korea boasts of being the most wired nation on earth.

> (A) This addiction has become a national issue in Korea in recent years, as users started dropping dead from exhaustion after playing online games for days on end. A growing number of students have skipped school to stay online, shockingly self-destructive behavior in this intensely competitive society.
>
> (B) In fact, perhaps no other country has so fully embraced the Internet.
>
> (C) But such ready access to the Web has come at a price as legions of obsessed users find that they cannot tear themselves away from their computer screens.

① (A) - (B) - (C)
② (A) - (C) - (B)
③ (B) - (A) - (C)
④ (B) - (C) - (A)

30 주어진 글 다음에 이어질 글의 순서로 가장 적절한 것은?

2019. 지방직 9급

> There is a thought that can haunt us: since everything probably affects everything else, how can we ever make sense of the social world? If we are weighed down by that worry, though, we won't ever make progress.

> (A) Every discipline that I am familiar with draws caricatures of the world in order to make sense of it. The modern economist does this by building models, which are deliberately stripped down representations of the phenomena out there.
>
> (B) The economist John Maynard Keynes described our subject thus: "Economics is a science of thinking in terms of models joined to the art of choosing models which are relevant to the contemporary world."
>
> (C) When I say "stripped down," I really mean stripped down. It isn't uncommon among us economists to focus on one or two causal factors, exclude everything else, hoping that this will enable us to understand how just those aspects of reality work and interact.

① (A) - (B) - (C)
② (A) - (C) - (B)
③ (B) - (C) - (A)
④ (B) - (A) - (C)

31 주어진 문장 다음에 이어질 글의 순서로 가장 적절한 것은?
2018. 국가직 9급

A technique that enables an individual to gain some voluntary control over autonomic, or involuntary, body functions by observing electronic measurements of those functions is known as biofeedback.

(A) When such a variable moves in the desired direction (for example, blood pressure down), it triggers visual or audible displays feedback on equipment such as television sets, gauges, or lights.

(B) Electronic sensors are attached to various parts of the body to measure such variables as heart rate, blood pressure, and skin temperature.

(C) Biofeedback training teaches one to produce a desired response by reproducing thought patterns or actions that triggered the displays.

① (A) − (B) − (C)
② (B) − (C) − (A)
③ (B) − (A) − (C)
④ (C) − (A) − (B)

32 주어진 문장 다음에 이어질 글의 순서로 가장 적절한 것은?
2018. 지방직 9급

Devices that monitor and track your health are becoming more popular among all age populations.

(A) For example, falls are a leading cause of death for adults 65 and older. Fall alerts are a popular gerotechnology that has been around for many years but have now improved.

(B) However, for seniors aging in place, especially those without a caretaker in the home, these technologies can be lifesaving.

(C) This simple technology can automatically alert 911 of a close family member the moment a senior has fallen.

① (B) − (C) − (A)
② (B) − (A) − (C)
③ (C) − (A) − (B)
④ (C) − (B) − (A)

33 주어진 글 다음에 이어질 글의 순서로 가장 적절한 것은?
2017. 국가직 9급

The most innovative of the group therapy approaches was psychodrama, the brainchild of Jacob L. Moreno. Psychodrama as a form of group therapy started with premises that were quite alien to the Freudian worldview that mental illness essentially occurs within the psyche or mind.

(A) But he also believed that creativity is rarely a solitary process but something brought out by social interactions. He relied heavily on theatrical techniques, including role-playing and improvisation, as a means to promote creativity and general social trust.

(B) Despite his theoretical difference from the mainstream viewpoint, Moreno's influence in shaping psychological consciousness in the twentieth century was considerable. He believed that the nature of human beings is to be creative and that living a creative life is the key to human health and well-being.

(C) His most important theatrical tool was what he called role reversal—asking participants to take on another's persona. The act of pretending "as if" one were in another's skin was designed to help bring out the empathic impulse and to develop it to higher levels of expression.

① (A) - (C) - (B)
② (B) - (A) - (C)
③ (B) - (C) - (A)
④ (C) - (B) - (A)

34 주어진 글 다음에 이어질 글의 순서로 가장 적절한 것은?
2017. 국가직 9급 하반기

Through the ages, industrious individuals have continuously created conveniences to make life easier. From the invention of the wheel to the lightbulb, inventions have propelled society forward.

(A) In addition, interactive media can be used to question a lecturer or exchange opinions with other students via e-mail. Such computerized lectures give students access to knowledge that was previously unavailable.

(B) One recent modern invention is the computer, which has improved many aspects of people's lives. This is especially true in the field of education. One important effect of computer technology on higher education is the availability of lectures.

(C) As a result of the development of computer networks, students can obtain lectures from many universities in real time. They are now able to sit down in front of a digital screen and listen to a lecture being given at another university.

① (A) - (B) - (C)
② (B) - (C) - (A)
③ (C) - (A) - (B)
④ (C) - (B) - (A)

35 주어진 글 다음에 이어질 글의 순서로 가장 적절한 것은?

2017. 지방직 9급

I remember the day Lewis discovered the falls. They left their camp at sunrise and a few hours later they came upon a beautiful plain and on the plain were more buffalo than they had ever seen before in one place.

(A) A nice thing happened that afternoon, they went fishing below the falls and caught half a dozen trout, good ones, too, from sixteen to twenty-three inches long.

(B) After a while the sound was tremendous and they were at the great falls of the Missouri River. It was about noon when they got there.

(C) They kept on going until they heard the faraway sound of a waterfall and saw a distant column of spray rising and disappearing. They followed the sound as it got louder and louder.

① (A) − (B) − (C)
② (B) − (C) − (A)
③ (C) − (A) − (B)
④ (C) − (B) − (A)

36 주어진 글 다음에 이어질 글의 순서로 가장 적절한 것은?

2016. 국가직 9급

All animals have the same kind of brain activation during sleep as humans. Whether or not they dream is another question, which can be answered only by posing another one: Do animals have consciousness?

(A) These are three of the key aspects of consciousness, and they could be experienced whether or not an animal had verbal language as we do. When the animal's brain is activated during sleep, why not assume that the animal has some sort of perceptual, emotional, and memory experience?

(B) Many scientists today feel that animals probably do have a limited form of consciousness, quite different from ours in that it lacks language and the capacity for propositional or symbolic thought.

(C) Animals certainly can't report dreams even if they do have them. But which pet owner would doubt that his or her favourite animal friend has perception, memory, and emotion

① (A) − (B) − (C)
② (A) − (C) − (B)
③ (B) − (C) − (A)
④ (C) − (B) − (A)

07 순서 배열 유형 기출 독해 어휘 복습 TEST

1	reward		21	scrutiny	
2	appeal		22	mitigate	
3	regardless of		23	mammal	
4	favoritism		24	rational	
5	discriminate		25	practical	
6	certificate		26	indulge	
7	surface		27	exert	
8	beside		28	evolve	
9	stir		29	inheritance	
10	witness		30	offspring	
11	tear off		31	mistaken	
12	hearty		32	surroundings	
13	expand		33	proprietary	
14	authentic		34	breakdown	
15	renew		35	adopt	
16	dimension		36	harbor	
17	exemplify		37	reconcile	
18	prediction		38	institution	
19	summon		39	diplomat	
20	depression		40	property	

41	immediate		61	represent	
42	weird		62	promotional	
43	definitive		63	executive	
44	fall short		64	assembly	
45	rudimentary		65	surrender	
46	intensive		66	cease	
47	utility		67	evaporate	
48	medium		68	flexible	
49	abundance		69	demanding	
50	humble		70	prone to	
51	sturdy		71	exhaustion	
52	deplete		72	days on end	
53	accommodate		73	obsessed	
54	prestigious		74	make sense of	
55	sparsely		75	representation	
56	cardiovascular		76	attach	
57	confusion		77	variable	
58	refer to		78	solitary	
59	province		79	pretend	
60	exterior		80	tremendous	

PART 08 빈칸 추론 유형

출제 경향 분석

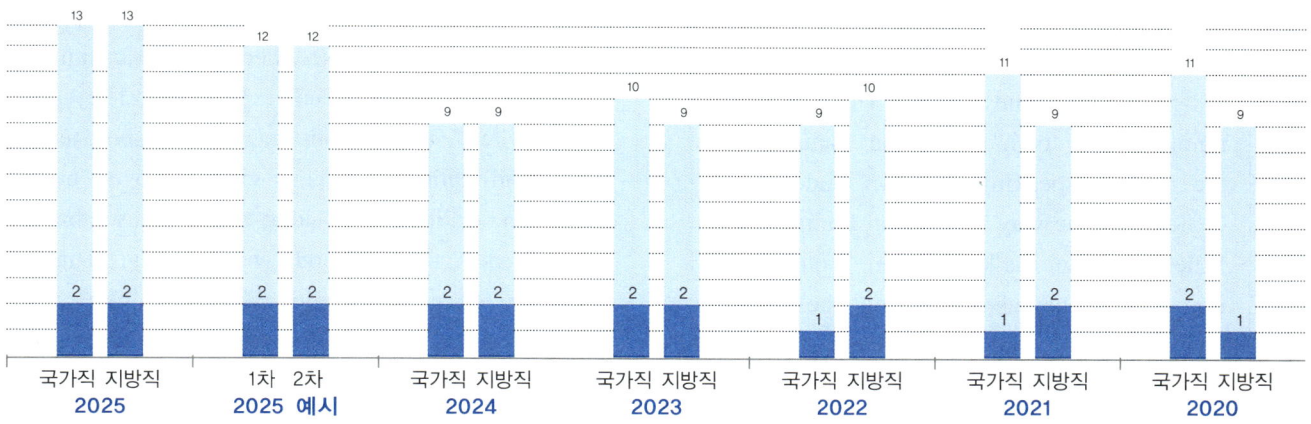

반드시 한번에 다잡는 '빈칸 추론' 유형 기출 독해 어휘

- perceived 인식된, 인지된
- vigilant 주의를 기울이는, 경계하는
- reflect 깊이 생각하다, 심사숙고하다
- innate 선천적인, 타고난
- escape 피하다, 달아나다
- wonder 궁금해하다
- unemployment 실업(률)
- income 소득, 수입
- disastrous 처참한, 재앙의, 불길한
- project 예상하다, 추정하다, 계획하다, 계획, 과제
- population 인구, 주민
- elderly 노인, 어르신들, 나이가 지긋한
- inattention 부주의, 태만, 무관심
- persuasion 설득, 강요
- mortgage 대출(금), 융자(금), 저당 잡히다
- existing 기존의, 현재 사용되는
- paradoxical 역설적인
- disparate 서로 전혀 다른, 이질적인

- distraction 주의 산만, 방해
- massive 거대한, 심각한
- misperception 오해
- unoccupied 비어있는, 점령되지 않은
- decay 부패, 부식, 부패하다, 썩다
- approximate 대략적인, 근사치인
- extinct 멸종된, 사라진
- concrete 구체적인, 사실에 의거한
- modify 수정하다, 변경하다
- bother 신경 쓰다, 귀찮게 하다
- coherent 일관성 있는, 논리 정연한
- conscientious 양심적인, 성실한
- underpin 뒷받침하다, 근거를 대다
- plummet 급락하다, 곤두박질치다
- hypothesis 가설, 추정, 추측
- impede 방해하다, 지연시키다
- trivial 사소한, 하찮은
- altruism 이타주의, 이타심

01 밑줄 친 부분에 들어갈 말로 가장 적절한 것은?

2025. 국가직 9급

Active listening is an art, a skill and a discipline that takes _____.
To develop good listening skills, you need to understand what is involved in effective communication and develop the techniques to sit quietly and listen. This involves ignoring your own needs and focusing on the person speaking—a task made more difficult by the way the human brain works. When someone talks to you, your brain immediately begins processing the words, body language, tone, inflection and perceived meanings coming from the other person. Instead of hearing one noise, you hear two: the noise the other person is making and the noise in your own head. Unless you train yourself to remain vigilant, the brain usually ends up paying attention to the noise in your own head. That's where active listening techniques come into play. Hearing becomes listening only when you pay attention to what the person is saying and follow it very closely.

① a sense of autonomy
② a creative mindset
③ a high degree of self-control
④ an extroverted personality

02 밑줄 친 부분에 들어갈 말로 가장 적절한 것은?

2025. 국가직 9급

The holiday season is a time to give thanks, reflect on the past year, and spend time with family and friends. However, if you're not careful, it can also be a time you overspend on holiday purchases. People have an innate impulse to overspend, experts say. They are "wired" to be consumers. The short-term gratification of giving gifts to loved ones can eclipse the long-term focus that's needed to be good with money. That's where many people fall short. We can overspend because our long-term goals are much more abstract, and it actually requires us to do extra levels of cognitive processing to delay instant gratification. Additionally, consumers may feel _____ _____ because they don't want to appear "cheap." Many companies also promote deals during the holidays that can encourage people to spend more than usual.

① a desire to work at overseas companies
② responsible for establishing their long-term goals
③ like limiting their spending during the holiday season
④ the social pressure to spend more than they might like

03 밑줄 친 부분에 들어갈 말로 가장 적절한 것은?

2025. 지방직 9급

A hunter-gatherer in the Stone Age knew how to make her own clothes, how to start a fire, how to hunt rabbits and how to escape lions. We think we know far more today, but as individuals, we actually know far less. We rely on the expertise of others for almost all our needs. In one humbling experiment, people were asked to evaluate how well they understood the workings of an ordinary zipper. Most people confidently replied that they understood zippers very well—after all, they use them all the time. They were then asked to describe in as much detail as possible all the steps involved in the zipper's operation. Most people had no idea. This is what Steven Sloman and Philip Fernbach have termed 'the knowledge illusion'. We think we know a lot, even though individually we know very little, because we treat knowledge _____ _____ as if it were our own.

① from hands-on experiences
② in the minds of others
③ gained during education
④ learned through trial and error

04 밑줄 친 부분에 들어갈 말로 가장 적절한 것은?

2025. 지방직 9급

A gazelle on the African savanna is trying not to be eaten by cheetahs, but it is also trying to outrun other gazelles when a cheetah attacks. What matters to the gazelle is being faster than other gazelles, not being faster than cheetahs. In the same way, psychologists sometimes wonder why people are endowed with the ability to learn the part of Hamlet or understand calculus when neither skill was of much use to mankind in the primitive conditions where his intellect was shaped. Einstein would probably have been as hopeless as anybody in working out how to catch a woolly rhinoceros. Nicholas Humphrey, a Cambridge psychologist, was the first to see clearly the solution to this puzzle. We use our intellects not to solve practical problems but to outwit each other. Deceiving people, detecting deceit, understanding people's motives, manipulating people—these are what intellect is used for. So what matters is _____ _____.

① not how clever and crafty you are but how much more clever and craftier you are than other people
② that individuals act according to their collective interest rather than their own personal interest
③ to design a society where members cooperate to find optimal solutions to benefit themselves
④ coming up with the best solution to practical problems in a given condition

05 밑줄 친 부분에 들어갈 말로 가장 적절한 것은?

2025. 출제 기조 전환 2차

Technological progress can destroy jobs in a single industry such as textiles. However, historical evidence shows that technological progress does not produce unemployment in a country as a whole. Technological progress increases productivity and incomes in the overall economy, and higher incomes lead to higher demand for goods and thus _____. As a result, workers who lose jobs in one industry will be able to find jobs in others, although for many of them this might take time and some of them, like the Luddites, will end up with lower wages in their new jobs.

① increased job losses
② delayed promotion at work
③ greater work satisfaction
④ higher demand for labor

06 밑줄 친 부분에 들어갈 말로 가장 적절한 것은?

2025. 출제 기조 전환 2차

There is no substitute for oil, which is one reason _____, taking the global economy along with it. While we can generate electricity through coal or natural gas, nuclear or renewables—switching from source to source, according to price—oil remains by far the predominant fuel for transportation. When the global economy heats up, demand for oil rises, boosting the price and encouraging producers to pump more. Inevitably, those high prices eat into economic growth and reduce demand just as suppliers are overproducing. Prices crash, and the cycle starts all over again. That's bad for producers, who can be left holding the bag when prices plummet, and it hurts consumers and industries uncertain about future energy prices. Low oil prices in the 1990s lulled U.S. auto companies into disastrous complacency; they had few efficient models available when oil turned expensive.

① the automobile industry thrives
② it creates disruptions between borders
③ it is prone to big booms and deep busts
④ the research on renewable energy is limited

07 밑줄 친 부분에 들어갈 말로 가장 적절한 것은?

2025. 출제 기조 전환 1차

Falling fertility rates are projected to result in shrinking populations for nearly every country by the end of the century. The global fertility rate was 4.7 in 1950, but it dropped by nearly half to 2.4 in 2017. It is expected to fall below 1.7 by 2100. As a result, some researchers predict that the number of people on the planet would peak at 9.7 billion around 2064 before falling down to 8.8 billion by the century's end. This transition will also lead to a significant aging of populations, with as many people reaching 80 years old as there are being born. Such a demographic shift _____ _____, including taxation, healthcare for the elderly, caregiving responsibilities, and retirement. To ensure a "soft landing" into a new demographic landscape, researchers emphasize the need for careful management of the transition.

① raises concerns about future challenges
② mitigates the inverted age structure phenomenon
③ compensates for the reduced marriage rate issue
④ provides immediate solutions to resolve the problems

08 밑줄 친 부분에 들어갈 말로 가장 적절한 것은?

2025. 출제 기조 전환 1차

Many listeners blame a speaker for their inattention by thinking to themselves: "Who could listen to such a character? Will he ever stop reading from his notes?" The good listener reacts differently. He may well look at the speaker and think, "This man is incompetent. Seems like almost anyone would be able to talk better than that." But from this initial similarity he moves on to a different conclusion, thinking "But wait a minute. I'm not interested in his personality or delivery. I want to find out what he knows. Does this man know some things that I need to know?" Essentially, we "listen with our own experience." Is the speaker to be held responsible because we are poorly equipped to comprehend his message? We cannot understand everything we hear, but one sure way to raise the level of our understanding is to _____.

① ignore what the speaker knows
② analyze the character of a speaker
③ assume the responsibility which is inherently ours
④ focus on the speaker's competency of speech delivery

09 밑줄 친 부분에 들어갈 말로 적절한 것은?
2024. 국가직 9급

_____
_____. Nearly every major politician hires media consultants and political experts to provide advice on how to appeal to the public. Virtually every major business and special-interest group has hired a lobbyist to take its concerns to Congress or to state and local governments. In nearly every community, activists try to persuade their fellow citizens on important policy issues. The workplace, too, has always been fertile ground for office politics and persuasion. One study estimates that general managers spend upwards of 80 % of their time in verbal communication — most of it with the intent of persuading their fellow employees. With the advent of the photocopying machine, a whole new medium for office persuasion was invented — the photocopied memo. The Pentagon alone copies an average of 350,000 pages a day, the equivalent of 1,000 novels.

① Business people should have good persuasion skills
② Persuasion shows up in almost every walk of life
③ You will encounter countless billboards and posters
④ Mass media campaigns are useful for the government

10 밑줄 친 부분에 들어갈 말로 적절한 것은?
2024. 국가직 9급

It is important to note that for adults, social interaction mainly occurs through the medium of language. Few native-speaker adults are willing to devote time to interacting with someone who does not speak the language, with the result that the adult foreigner will have little opportunity to engage in meaningful and extended language exchanges. In contrast, the young child is often readily accepted by other children, and even adults. For young children, language is not as essential to social interaction. So-called 'parallel play', for example, is common among young children. They can be content just to sit in each other's company speaking only occasionally and playing on their own. Adults rarely find themselves in situations where _____ _____.

① language does not play a crucial role in social interaction
② their opinions are readily accepted by their colleagues
③ they are asked to speak another language
④ communication skills are highly required

11 밑줄 친 부분에 들어갈 말로 적절한 것은?

2024. 지방직 9급

Javelin Research noticed that not all Millennials are currently in the same stage of life. While all Millennials were born around the turn of the century, some of them are still in early adulthood, wrestling with new careers and settling down. On the other hand, the older Millennials have a home and are building a family. You can imagine how having a child might change your interests and priorities, so for marketing purposes, it's useful to split this generation into Gen Y.1 and Gen Y.2. Not only are the two groups culturally different, but they're in vastly different phases of their financial life. The younger group is financial beginners, just starting to show their buying power. The latter group has a credit history, may have their first mortgage and is raising young children. The _____ in priorities and needs between Gen Y.1 and Gen Y.2 is vast.

① contrast
② reduction
③ repetition
④ ability

12 밑줄 친 부분에 들어갈 말로 적절한 것은?

2024. 지방직 9급

Cost pressures in liberalized markets have different effects on existing and future hydropower schemes. Because of the cost structure, existing hydropower plants will always be able to earn a profit. Because the planning and construction of future hydropower schemes is not a short-term process, it is not a popular investment, in spite of low electricity generation costs. Most private investors would prefer to finance _____, leading to the paradoxical situation that although an existing hydropower plant seems to be a cash cow, nobody wants to invest in a new one. Where public shareholders/owners (states, cities, municipalities) are involved, the situation looks very different because they can see the importance of the security of supply and also appreciate long-term investments.

① more short-term technologies
② all high technology industries
③ the promotion of the public interest
④ the enhancement of electricity supply

13 밑줄 친 부분에 들어갈 말로 알맞은 것은?

2023. 국가직 9급

In recent years, the increased popularity of online marketing and social media sharing has boosted the need for advertising standardization for global brands. Most big marketing and advertising campaigns include a large online presence. Connected consumers can now zip easily across borders via the internet and social media, making it difficult for advertisers to roll out adapted campaigns in a controlled, orderly fashion. As a result, most global consumer brands coordinate their digital sites internationally. For example, Coca-Cola web and social media sites around the world, from Australia and Argentina to France, Romania, and Russia, are surprisingly _____. All feature splashes of familiar Coke red, iconic Coke bottle shapes, and Coca-Cola's music and "Taste the Feeling" themes.

① experimental
② uniform
③ localized
④ diverse

14 밑줄 친 부분에 들어갈 말로 알맞은 것은?

2023. 국가직 9급

Over the last fifty years, all major subdisciplines in psychology have become more and more isolated from each other as training becomes increasingly specialized and narrow in focus. As some psychologists have long argued, if the field of psychology is to mature and advance scientifically, its disparate parts (for example, neuroscience, developmental, cognitive, personality, and social) must become whole and integrated again. Science advances when distinct topics become theoretically and empirically integrated under simplifying theoretical frameworks. Psychology of science will encourage collaboration among psychologists from various sub-areas, helping the field achieve coherence rather than continued fragmentation. In this way, psychology of science might act as a template for psychology as a whole by integrating under one discipline all of the major fractions/ factions within the field. It would be no small feat and of no small import if the psychology of science could become a model for the parent discipline on how to combine resources and study science _____.

① from a unified perspective
② in dynamic aspects
③ throughout history
④ with accurate evidence

15 밑줄 친 부분에 들어갈 말로 가장 적절한 것은?

2023. 지방직 9급

We live in the age of anxiety. Because being anxious can be an uncomfortable and scary experience, we resort to conscious or unconscious strategies that help reduce anxiety in the moment — watching a movie or TV show, eating, video-game playing, and overworking. In addition, smartphones also provide a distraction any time of the day or night. Psychological research has shown that distractions serve as a common anxiety avoidance strategy. _____, however, these avoidance strategies make anxiety worse in the long run. Being anxious is like getting into quicksand — the more you fight it, the deeper you sink. Indeed, research strongly supports a well-known phase that "what you resist, persists."

① Paradoxically
② Fortunately
③ Neutrally
④ Creatively

16 밑줄 친 부분에 들어갈 말로 가장 적절한 것은?

2023. 지방직 9급

How many different ways do you get information? Some people might have six different kinds of communications to answer — test messages, voice mails, paper documents, regular mail, blog posts, messages on different online services. Each of these is type of in-box, and each must be processed on a continuous basis. It's an endless process, but it doesn't have to be exhausting or stressful. Getting your information management down to a more manageable level and into a productive zone starts by _____.

Every place you have to go to check your messages or to read your incoming information is an in-box, and the more you have, the harder it is to manage everything. Cut the number of in-boxes you have down to the smallest number possible for you still to function in the ways you need to.

① setting several goals at once
② immersing yourself in incoming information
③ minimizing the number of in-boxes you have
④ choosing information you are passionate about

17 다음 빈칸에 들어갈 말로 가장 적절한 것은?

2023. 법원직 9급

As global temperatures rise, so do sea levels, threatening coastal communities around the world. Surprisingly, even small organisms like oysters _____.
Oysters are keystone species with *ripple effects on the health of their ecosystems and its inhabitants. Just one adult oyster can filter up to fifty gallons of water in a single day, making waterways cleaner. Healthy oyster reefs also provide a home for hundreds of other marine organisms, promoting biodiversity and ecosystem balance. As rising sea levels lead to pervasive flooding, oyster reefs act as walls to buffer storms and protect against further coastal erosion.

* ripple effect 파급효과

① can come to our defense
② can be the food for emergency
③ may be contaminated by microplastics
④ can increase the income of local residents

18 다음 빈칸에 들어갈 말로 가장 적절한 것은?

2023. 법원직 9급

Lewis Pugh is a British endurance swimmer, who is best known for his long-distance swims in cold and open waters. He swims in cold places as a way to draw attention to the urgent need to protect the world's oceans and waterways from the effects of climate change and pollution. In 2019, Pugh decided to swim in Lake Imja, which is located in the Khumbu region of Nepal, near Mount Everest. After a failed first attempt, Lewis had a *debrief to discuss the best way to swim at 5,300 meters above sea level. He is usually very aggressive when he swims because he wants to finish quickly and get out of the cold water. But this time he showed _____ and swam slowly.

* debrief 평가회의

① grief
② anger
③ humility
④ confidence

19 밑줄 친 부분에 들어갈 말로 가장 적절한 것은?

2022. 국가직 9급

Scientists have long known that higher air temperatures are contributing to the surface melting on Greenland's ice sheet. But a new study has found another threat that has begun attacking the ice from below: Warm ocean water moving underneath the vast glaciers is causing them to melt even more quickly. The findings were published in the journal Nature Geoscience by researchers who studied one of the many "ice tongues" of the Nioghalvfjerdsfjorden Glacier in northeast Greenland. An ice tongue is a strip of ice that floats on the water without breaking off from the ice on land. The massive one these scientists studied is nearly 50 miles long. The survey revealed an underwater current more than a mile wide where warm water from the Atlantic Ocean is able to flow directly towards the glacier, bringing large amounts of heat into contact with the ice and _____ the glacier's melting.

① separating
② delaying
③ preventing
④ accelerating

20 밑줄 친 부분에 들어갈 말로 가장 적절한 것은?

2022. 지방직 9급

One of the most frequently used propaganda techniques is to convince the public that the propagandist's views reflect those of the common person and that he or she is working in their best interests. A politician speaking to a blue-collar audience may roll up his sleeves, undo his tie, and attempt to use the specific idioms of the crowd. He may even use language incorrectly on purpose to give the impression that he is "just one of the folks." This technique usually also employs the use of glittering generalities to give the impression that the politician's views are the same as those of the crowd being addressed. Labor leaders, businesspeople, ministers, educators, and advertisers have used this technique to win our confidence by appearing to be _____.

① beyond glittering generalities
② just plain folks like ourselves
③ something different from others
④ better educated than the crowd

21 밑줄 친 부분에 들어갈 말로 가장 적절한 것은?

2022. 지방직 9급

As a roller coaster climbs the first lift hill of its track, it is building potential energy—the higher it gets above the earth, the stronger the pull of gravity will be. When the coaster crests the lift hill and begins its descent, its potential energy becomes kinetic energy, or the energy of movement. A common misperception is that a coaster loses energy along the track. An important law of physics, however, called the law of conservation of energy, is that energy can never be created nor destroyed. It simply changes from one form to another. Whenever a track rises back uphill, the cars' momentum—their kinetic energy—will carry them upward, which builds potential energy, and roller coasters repeatedly convert potential energy to kinetic energy and back again. At the end of a ride, coaster cars are slowed down by brake mechanisms that create _____ between two surfaces. This motion makes them hot, meaning kinetic energy is changed to heat energy during braking. Riders may mistakenly think coasters lose energy at the end of the track, but the energy just changes to and from different forms.

① gravity
② friction
③ vacuum
④ acceleration

22 다음 빈칸에 들어갈 말로 가장 적절한 것은?

2022. 법원직 9급

There are a few jobs where people have had to _____. We see referees and umpires using their arms and hands to signal directions to the players—as in cricket, where a single finger upwards means that the batsman is out and has to leave the wicket. Orchestra conductors control the musicians through their movements. People working at a distance from each other have to invent special signals if they want to communicate. So do people working in a noisy environment, such as in a factory where the machines are very loud, or lifeguards around a swimming pool full of school children.

* wicket (크리켓에서) 삼주문

① support their parents and children
② adapt to an entirely new work style
③ fight in court for basic human rights
④ develop their signing a bit more fully

23 다음 빈칸에 들어갈 말로 가장 적절한 것은?

2022. 법원직 9급

Water and civilization go hand-in-hand. The idea of a "*hydraulic civilization" argues that water is the unifying context and justification for many large-scale civilizations throughout history. For example, the various multi-century Chinese empires survived as long as they did in part by controlling floods along the Yellow River. One interpretation of the hydraulic theory is that the justification for gathering populations into large cities is to manage water. Another interpretation suggests that large water projects enable the rise of big cities. The Romans understood the connections between water and power, as the Roman Empire built a vast network of **aqueducts throughout land they controlled, many of which remain intact. For example, Pont du Gard in southern France stands today as a testament to humanity's investment in its water infrastructure. Roman governors built roads, bridges, and water systems as a way of _____.

* hydraulic: 수력학의
** aqueduct: 송수로

① focusing on educating young people
② prohibiting free trade in local markets
③ concentrating and strengthening their authority
④ giving up their properties to other countries

24 밑줄 친 부분에 들어갈 말로 가장 적절한 것은?

2021. 국가직 9급

Social media, magazines and shop windows bombard people daily with things to buy, and British consumers are buying more clothes and shoes than ever before. Online shopping means it is easy for customers to buy without thinking, while major brands offer such cheap clothes that they can be treated like disposable items — worn two or three times and then thrown away. In Britain, the average person spends more than £1,000 on new clothes a year, which is around four percent of their income. That might not sound like much, but that figure hides two far more worrying trends for society and for the environment. First, a lot of that consumer spending is via credit cards. British people currently owe approximately £670 per adult to credit card companies. That's 66 percent of the average wardrobe budget. Also, not only are people spending money they don't have, they're using it to buy things _____. Britain throws away 300,000 tons of clothing a year, most of which goes into landfill sites.

① they don't need
② that are daily necessities
③ that will be soon recycled
④ they can hand down to others

25 밑줄 친 부분에 들어갈 말로 가장 적절한 것은?

2021. 국가직 9급

Excellence is the absolute prerequisite in fine dining because the prices charged are necessarily high. An operator may do everything possible to make the restaurant efficient, but the guests still expect careful, personal service: food prepared to order by highly skilled chefs and delivered by expert servers. Because this service is, quite literally, manual labor, only marginal improvements in productivity are possible. For example, a cook, server, or bartender can move only so much faster before she or he reaches the limits of human performance. Thus, only moderate savings are possible through improved efficiency, which makes an escalation of prices _____. (It is an axiom of economics that as prices rise, consumers become more discriminating.) Thus, the clientele of the fine-dining restaurant expects, demands, and is willing to pay for excellence.

① ludicrous
② inevitable
③ preposterous
④ inconceivable

26 밑줄 친 부분에 들어갈 말로 가장 적절한 것은?

2021. 지방직 9급

As more and more leaders work remotely or with teams scattered around the nation or the globe, as well as with consultants and freelancers, you'll have to give them more _____. The more trust you bestow, the more others trust you. I am convinced that there is a direct correlation between job satisfaction and how empowered people are to fully execute their job without someone shadowing them every step of the way. Giving away responsibility to those you trust can not only make your organization run more smoothly but also free up more of your time so you can focus on larger issues.

① work
② rewards
③ restrictions
④ autonomy

27 다음 빈칸에 들어갈 말로 가장 적절한 것은?

2021. 법원직 9급

Beeches, oaks, spruce and pines produce new growth all the time, and have to get rid of the old. The most obvious change happens every autumn. The leaves have served their purpose: they are now worn out and riddled with insect damage. Before the trees bid them adieu, they pump waste products into them. You could say they are taking this opportunity to relieve themselves. Then they grow a layer of weak tissue to separate each leaf from the twig it's growing on, and the leaves tumble to the ground in the next breeze. The rustling leaves that now blanket the ground — and make such a satisfying scrunching sound when you scuffle through them — are basically _____.

① tree toilet paper
② the plant kitchen
③ lungs of the tree
④ parents of insect

28 다음 빈칸에 들어갈 말로 가장 적절한 것은?

2021. 법원직 9급

The seeds of willows and poplars are so minuscule that you can just make out two tiny dark dots in the fluffy flight hairs. One of these seeds weighs a mere 0.0001 grams. With such a meagre energy reserve, a seedling can grow only 1-2 millimetres before it runs out of steam and has to rely on food it makes for itself using its young leaves. But that only works in places where there's no competition to threaten the tiny sprouts. Other plants casting shade on it would extinguish the new life immediately. And so, if a fluffy little seed package like this falls in a spruce or beech forest, the seed's life is over before it's even begun. That's why willows and poplars _____.

* minuscule 아주 작은

① prefer settling in unoccupied territory
② have been chosen as food for herbivores
③ have evolved to avoid human intervention
④ wear their dead leaves far into the winter

29 밑줄 친 (A), (B)에 들어갈 말로 가장 적절한 것은?

2020. 국가직 9급

When an organism is alive, it takes in carbon dioxide from the air around it. Most of that carbon dioxide is made of carbon-12, but a tiny portion consists of carbon-14. So the living organism always contains a very small amount of radioactive carbon, carbon-14. A detector next to the living organism would record radiation given off by the carbon-14 in the organism. When the organism dies, it no longer takes in carbon dioxide. No new carbon-14 is added, and the old carbon-14 slowly decays into nitrogen. The amount of carbon-14 slowly ____(A)____ as time goes on. Over time, less and less radiation from carbon-14 is produced. The amount of carbon-14 radiation detected for an organism is a measure, therefore, of how long the organism has been ____(B)____. This method of determining the age of an organism is called carbon-14 dating. The decay of carbon-14 allows archaeologists to find the age of once-living materials. Measuring the amount of radiation remaining indicates the approximate age.

  (A)   (B)
① decreases ······ dead
② increases ······ alive
③ decreases ······ productive
④ increases ······ inactive

30 밑줄 친 부분에 들어갈 말로 가장 적절한 것은?

2020. 국가직 9급

All creatures, past and present, either have gone or will go extinct. Yet, as each species vanished over the past 3.8-billion-year history of life on Earth, new ones inevitably appeared to replace them or to exploit newly emerging resources. From only a few very simple organisms, a great number of complex, multicellular forms evolved over this immense period. The origin of new species, which the nineteenth-century English naturalist Charles Darwin once referred to as "the mystery of mysteries," is the natural process of speciation responsible for generating this remarkable _____ with whom humans share the planet. Although taxonomists presently recognize some 1.5 million living species, the actual number is possibly closer to 10 million. Recognizing the biological status of this multitude requires a clear understanding of what constitutes a species, which is no easy task given that evolutionary biologists have yet to agree on a universally acceptable definition.

① technique of biologists
② diversity of living creatures
③ inventory of extinct organisms
④ collection of endangered species

31 밑줄 친 부분에 들어갈 말로 가장 적절한 것은?

2020. 지방직 9급

All of us inherit something: in some cases, it may be money, property or some object — a family heirloom such as a grandmother's wedding dress or a father's set of tools. But beyond that, all of us inherit something else, something _____, something we may not even be fully aware of. It may be a way of doing a daily task, or the way we solve a particular problem or decide a moral issue for ourselves. It may be a special way of keeping a holiday or a tradition to have a picnic on a certain date. It may be something important or central to our thinking, or something minor that we have long accepted quite casually.

① quite unrelated to our everyday life
② against our moral standards
③ much less concrete and tangible
④ of great monetary value

32 다음 빈칸에 들어갈 말로 가장 적절한 것은?

2020. 법원직 9급

Impressionable youth are not the only ones subject to _____. Most of us have probably had an experience of being pressured by a salesman. Have you ever had a sales rep try to sell you some "office solution" by telling you that 70 percent of your competitors are using their service, so why aren't you? But what if 70 percent of your competitors are idiots? Or what if that 70 percent were given so much value added or offered such a low price that they couldn't resist the opportunity? The practice is designed to do one thing and one thing only — to pressure you to buy. To make you feel you might be missing out on something or that everyone else knows but you.

① peer pressure
② impulse buying
③ bullying tactics
④ keen competition

33 다음 빈칸에 들어갈 말로 가장 적절한 것은?

2020. 법원직 9급

Much is now known about natural hazards and the negative impacts they have on people and their property. It would seem obvious that any logical person would avoid such potential impacts or at least modify their behavior or their property to minimize such impacts. However, humans are not always rational. Until someone has a personal experience or knows someone who has such an experience, most people subconsciously believe "It won't happen here" or "It won't happen to me." Even knowledgeable scientists who are aware of the hazards, the odds of their occurrence, and the costs of an event _____.

① refuse to remain silent
② do not always act appropriately
③ put the genetic factor at the top end
④ have difficulty in defining natural hazards

34 밑줄 친 부분에 들어갈 말로 가장 적절한 것은?

2019. 국가직 9급

Why bother with the history of everything? _____.
In literature classes you don't learn about genes; in physics classes you don't learn about human evolution. So you get a partial view of the world. That makes it hard to find meaning in education. The French sociologist Emile Durkheim called this sense of disorientation and meaninglessness anomie, and he argued that it could lead to despair and even suicide. The German sociologist Max Weber talked of the "disenchantment" of the world. In the past, people had a unified vision of their world, a vision usually provided by the origin stories of their own religious traditions. That unified vision gave a sense of purpose, of meaning, even of enchantment to the world and to life. Today, though, many writers have argued that a sense of meaninglessness is inevitable in a world of science and rationality. Modernity, it seems, means meaninglessness.

① In the past, the study of history required disenchantment from science
② Recently, science has given us lots of clever tricks and meanings
③ Today, we teach and learn about our world in fragments
④ Lately, history has been divided into several categories

35 밑줄 친 (A), (B)에 들어갈 말로 가장 적절한 것은?

2019. 지방직 9급

In the 1840s, the island of Ireland suffered famine. Because Ireland could not produce enough food to feed its population, about a million people died of ___(A)___; they simply didn't have enough to eat to stay alive. The famine caused another 1.25 million people to ___(B)___; many left their island home for the United States; the rest went to Canada, Australia, Chile, and other countries. Before the famine, the population of Ireland was approximately 6 million. After the great food shortage, it was about 4 million.

   (A)   (B)
① dehydration ⋯⋯ be deported
② trauma   ⋯⋯ immigrate
③ starvation ⋯⋯ emigrate
④ fatigue   ⋯⋯ be detained

36 밑줄 친 부분에 들어갈 말로 가장 적절한 것은?

2019. 지방직 9급

Language proper is itself double-layered. Single noises are only occasionally meaningful: mostly, the various speech sounds convey coherent messages only when combined into an overlapping chain, like different colors of ice-cream melting into one another. In birdsong also, _____: the sequence is what matters. In both humans and birds, control of this specialized sound-system is exercised by one half of the brain, normally the left half, and the system is learned relatively early in life. And just as many human languages have dialects, so do some bird species: in California, the white-crowned sparrow has songs so different from area to area that Californians can supposedly tell where they are in the state by listening to these sparrows.

① individual notes are often of little value
② rhythmic sounds are important
③ dialects play a critical role
④ no sound-system exists

37 밑줄 친 부분에 들어갈 말로 가장 적절한 것은?

2019. 지방직 9급

Nobel Prize-winning psychologist Daniel Kahneman changed the way the world thinks about economics, upending the notion that human beings are rational decision-makers. Along the way, his discipline-crossing influence has altered the way physicians make medical decisions and investors evaluate risk on Wall Street. In a paper, Kahneman and his colleagues outline a process for making big strategic decisions. Their suggested approach, labeled as "Mediating Assessments Protocol," or MAP, has a simple goal: To put off gut-based decision-making until a choice can be informed by a number of separate factors. "One of the essential purposes of MAP is basically to _____ intuition," Kahneman said in a recent interview with The Post. The structured process calls for analyzing a decision based on six to seven previously chosen attributes, discussing each of them separately and assigning them a relative percentile score, and finally, using those scores to make a holistic judgment.

① improve
② delay
③ possess
④ facilitate

38 글의 흐름상 빈칸에 들어갈 말로 가장 적절한 것은?

2019. 서울시 9급

"Highly conscientious employees do a series of things better than the rest of us," says University of Illinois psychologist Brent Roberts, who studies conscientiousness. Roberts owes their success to "hygiene" factors. Conscientious people have a tendency to organize their lives well. A disorganized, unconscientious person might lose 20 or 30 minutes rooting through their files to find the right document, an inefficient experience conscientious folks tend to avoid. Basically, by being conscientious, people _____ they'd otherwise create for themselves.

① deal with setbacks
② do thorough work
③ follow norms
④ sidestep stress

39 글의 흐름상 빈칸에 들어갈 말로 가장 적절한 것은?

2019. 서울시 9급

Climate change, deforestation, widespread pollution and the sixth mass extinction of biodiversity all define living in our world today—an era that has come to be known as "the Anthropocene". These crises are underpinned by production and consumption which greatly exceeds global ecological limits, but blame is far from evenly shared. The world's 42 wealthiest people own as much as the poorest 3.7 billion, and they generate far greater environmental impacts. Some have therefore proposed using the term "Capitalocene" to describe this era of ecological devastation and growing inequality, reflecting capitalism's logic of endless growth and _____.

① the better world that is still within our reach
② the accumulation of wealth in fewer pockets
③ an effective response to climate change
④ a burning desire for a more viable future

40 다음 빈칸에 들어갈 말로 가장 적절한 것은?

2019. 법원직 9급

With the present plummeting demand market for office buildings, resulting in many vacant properties, we need to develop plans that will enable some future exchange between residential and commercial or office functions. This vacancy has reached a historic level; at present the major towns in the Netherlands have some five million square metres of unoccupied office space, while there is a shortage of 160,000 homes. At least a million of those square metres can be expected to stay vacant, according to the association of Dutch property developers. There is a real threat of 'ghost towns' of empty office buildings springing up around the major cities. In spite of this forecast, office building activities are continuing at full tilt, as these were planned during a period of high returns. Therefore, it is now essential that _____.

① a new design be adopted to reduce costs for the maintenance of buildings
② a number of plans for office buildings be redeveloped for housing
③ residential buildings be converted into commercial buildings
④ we design and deliver as many shops as possible

41 다음 빈칸에 들어갈 말로 가장 적절한 것은?

2019. 법원직 9급

Although we all possess the same physical organs for sensing the world—eyes for seeing, ears for hearing, noses for smelling, skin for feeling, and mouths for tasting—our perception of the world depends to a great extent on the language we speak, according to a famous hypothesis proposed by linguists Edward Sapir and Benjamin Lee Whorf. They hypothesized that language is like a pair of eyeglasses through which we "see" the world in a particular way. A classic example of the relationship between language and perception is the word snow. Eskimo languages have as many as 32 different words for snow. For instance, the Eskimos have different words for falling snow, snow on the ground, snow packed as hard as ice, slushy snow, wind-driven snow, and what we might call "cornmeal" snow. The ancient Aztec languages of Mexico, in contrast, used only one word to mean snow, cold, and ice. Thus, if the Sapir-Whorf hypothesis is correct and we can perceive only things that we have words for, the Aztecs perceived snow, cold, and ice as _____.

① one and the same phenomenon
② being distinct from one another
③ separate things with unique features
④ something sensed by a specific physical organ

42 밑줄 친 부분에 들어갈 말로 가장 적절한 것은?

2018. 국가직 9급

Kisha Padbhan, founder of Everonn Education, in Mumbai, looks at his business as nation-building. India's student-age population of 230 million (kindergarten to college) is one of the largest in the world. The government spends $83 billion on instruction, but there are serious gaps. "There aren't enough teachers and enough teacher-training institutes," says Kisha. "What children in remote parts of India lack is access to good teachers and exposure to good-quality content." Everonn's solution? The company uses a satellite network, with two-way video and audio _____.

It reaches 1,800 colleges and 7,800 schools across 24 of India's 28 states. It offers everything from digitized school lessons to entrance exam prep for aspiring engineers and has training for job-seekers, too.

① to improve the quality of teacher training facilities
② to bridge the gap through virtual classrooms
③ to get students familiarized with digital technology
④ to locate qualified instructors across the nation

43 밑줄 친 부분에 들어갈 말로 가장 적절한 것은?

2018. 지방직 9급

In our time it is not only the law of the market which has its own life and rules over man, but also the development of science and technique. For a number of reasons, the problems and organization of science today are such that a scientist does not choose his problems; the problems force themselves upon the scientist. He solves one problem, and the result is not that he is more secure or certain, but that ten other new problems open up in place of the single solved one. They force him to solve them; he has to go ahead at an ever-quickening pace. The same holds true for industrial techniques. The pace of science forces the pace of technique. Theoretical physics forces atomic energy on us; the successful production of the fission bomb forces upon us the manufacture of the hydrogen bomb. We do not choose our problems, we do not choose our products; we are pushed, we are forced—by what? By a system which has no purpose and goal transcending it, and which _____.

① makes man its appendix
② creates a false sense of security
③ inspires man with creative challenges
④ empowers scientists to control the market laws

44 밑줄 친 부분에 들어갈 말로 가장 적절한 것은?

2018. 지방직 9급

The secret of successful people is usually that they are able to concentrate totally on one thing. Even if they have a lot in their head, they have found a method that the many commitments don't impede each other, but instead they are brought into a good inner order. And this order is quite simple: _____. In theory, it seems to be quite clear, but in everyday life it seems rather different. You might have tried to decide on priorities, but you have failed because of everyday trivial matters and all the unforeseen distractions. Separate off disturbances, for example, by escaping into another office, and not allowing any distractions to get in the way. When you concentrate on the one task of your priorities, you will find you have energy that you didn't even know you had.

① the sooner, the better
② better late than never
③ out of sight, out of mind
④ the most important thing first

45 다음 글의 빈칸에 들어갈 말로 가장 적절한 것은?

2018. 법원직 9급

A great ad is a wonderful thing; it's why you love advertising. But what you're looking at is only half of what's there, and the part you can't see has more to do with that ad's success than the part you can. Before those surface features (the terrific headline or visual or storyline or characters or voiceover or whatever) can work their wonders, the ad has to have something to say, something that matters. Either it addresses real consumer motives and real consumer problems, or it speaks to no one. To make great ads, then, you have to start where they start: with _____.

① the effective tool
② the invisible part
③ the corporate needs
④ the surface features

46 빈칸 (A), (B)에 들어갈 말로 가장 적절한 것은?

2017. 국가직 9급

The amount of information gathered by the eyes as contrasted with the ears has not been precisely calculated. Such a calculation not only involves a translation process, but scientists have been handicapped by lack of knowledge of what to count. A general notion, however, of the relative complexities of the two systems can be obtained by ___(A)___ the size of the nerves connecting the eyes and the ears to the centers of the brain. Since the optic nerve contains roughly eighteen times as many neurons as the cochlear nerve, we assume it transmits at least that much more information. Actually, in normally alert subjects, it is probable that the eyes may be as much as a thousand times as effective as the ears in ___(B)___ information.

　　　　　　　　　　　　　　* cochlear: 달팽이관의

　　　　(A)　　　　　　(B)
① comparing ······ sweeping up
② comparing ······ reducing
③ adding ······ disseminating
④ adding ······ clearing up

47 밑줄 친 부분에 들어갈 말로 가장 적절한 것은?

2017. 국가직 9급

Why might people hovering near the poverty line be more likely to help their fellow humans? Part of it, Keltner thinks, is that poor people must often band together to make it through tough times — a process that probably makes them more socially astute. He says, "When you face uncertainty, it makes you orient to other people. You build up these strong social networks." When a poor young mother has a new baby, for instance, she may need help securing food, supplies, and childcare, and if she has healthy social times, members of her community will pitch in. But limited income is hardly a prerequisite for developing this kind of empathy and social responsiveness. Regardless of the size of our bank accounts, suffering becomes a conduit to altruism or heroism when our own pain compels us to be _____ _____ other people's needs and to intervene when we see someone in the clutches of the kind of suffering we know so well.

① more indifferent to
② more attentive to
③ less preoccupied with
④ less involved in

48 밑줄 친 부분에 들어갈 말로 가장 적절한 것은?

2017. 국가직 9급

The Soleil department store outlet in Shanghai would seem to have all the amenities necessary to succeed in modern Chinese retail: luxury brands and an exclusive location. Despite these advantages, however, the store's management thought it was still missing something to attract customers. So next week they're unveiling a gigantic, twisting, dragon-shaped slide that shoppers can use to drop from fifth-floor luxury boutiques to first-floor luxury boutiques in death-defying seconds. Social media users are wondering, half-jokingly, whether the slide will kill anyone. But Soleil has a different concern that Chinese shopping malls will go away completely. Chinese shoppers, once seemingly in endless supply, are no longer turning up at brick-and-mortar outlets because of the growing online shopping, and they still go abroad to buy luxury goods. So, repurposing these massive spaces for consumers who have other ways to spend their time and money is likely to require a lot of creativity. _____.

① Luxury brands are thriving at Soleil
② Soleil has decided against making bold moves
③ Increasing the online customer base may be the last hope
④ A five-story dragon slide may not be a bad place to start

49 밑줄 친 부분에 들어갈 말로 가장 적절한 것은?

2017. 국가직 9급

It is easy to devise numerous possible scenarios of future developments, each one, on the face of it, equally likely. The difficult task is to know which will actually take place. In hindsight, it usually seems obvious. When we look back in time, each event seems clearly and logically to follow from previous events. Before the event occurs, however, the number of possibilities seems endless. There are no methods for successful prediction, especially in areas involving complex social and technological changes, where many of the determining factors are not known and, in any event, are certainly not under any single group's control. Nonetheless, it is essential to _____.

We do know that new technologies will bring both dividends and problems, especially human, social problems. The more we try to anticipate these problems, the better we can control them.

① work out reasonable scenarios for the future
② legitimize possible dividends from future changes
③ leave out various aspects of technological problems
④ consider what it would be like to focus on the present

50 밑줄 친 부분에 들어갈 말로 가장 적절한 것은?

2017. 지방직 9급

One of the tricks our mind plays is to highlight evidence which confirms what we already believe. If we hear gossip about a rival, we tend to think "I knew he was a nasty piece of work"; if we hear the same about our best friend, we're more likely to say "that's just a rumour." Once you learn about this mental habit—called confirmation bias—you start seeing it everywhere. This matters when we want to make better decisions. Confirmation bias is OK as long as we're right, but all too often we're wrong, and we only pay attention to the deciding evidence when it's too late. How _____ depends on our awareness of why, psychologically, confirmation bias happens. There are two possible reasons. One is that we have a blind spot in our imagination and the other is we fail to ask questions about new information.

① we make our rivals believe us
② our blind spot helps us make better decisions
③ we can protect our decisions from confirmation bias
④ we develop exactly the same bias

51 밑줄 친 부분에 들어갈 말로 가장 적절한 것은?

2017. 지방직 9급

For many big names in consumer product brands, exporting and producing overseas with local labor and for local tastes have been the right thing to do. In doing so, the companies found a way to improve their cost structure, to grow in the rapidly expanding consumer markets in emerging countries. But, Sweets Co. remains stuck in the domestic market. Even though its products are loaded with preservatives, which means they can endure long travel to distant markets, Sweets Co. _____, let alone produce overseas. The unwillingness or inability to update its business strategy and products for a changing world is clearly damaging to the company.

① is intent on importing
② does very little exporting
③ has decided to streamline operations
④ is expanding into emerging markets

52 밑줄 친 부분에 들어갈 말로 가장 적절한 것은?

2017. 지방직 9급

London taxi drivers have to undertake years of intense training known as "the knowledge" to gain their operating license, including learning the layout of over twenty-five thousand of the city's streets. A researcher and her team investigated the taxi drivers and the ordinary people. The two groups were asked to watch videos of routes unfamiliar to them through a town in Ireland. They were then asked to take a test about the video that included sketching out routes, identifying landmarks, and estimating distances between places. Both groups did well on much of the test, but the taxi drivers did significantly better on identifying new routes. This result suggests that the taxi drivers' mastery can be _____ to new and unknown areas. Their years of training and learning through deliberate practice prepare them to take on similar challenges even in places they do not know well or at all.

① confined
② devoted
③ generalized
④ contributed

08 빈칸 추론 유형 기출 독해 어휘 복습 TEST

1	involve		21	elderly	
2	perceived		22	inattention	
3	vigilant		23	comprehend	
4	reflect		24	persuasion	
5	innate		25	devote	
6	eclipse		26	settle down	
7	fall short		27	mortgage	
8	escape		28	existing	
9	ordinary		29	paradoxical	
10	wonder		30	standardization	
11	unemployment		31	roll out	
12	income		32	uniform	
13	substitute		33	disparate	
14	predominant		34	empirical	
15	inevitably		35	distraction	
16	disastrous		36	persist	
17	project		37	immerse	
18	population		38	buffer	
19	aging		39	break off	
20	demographic		40	massive	

41	plain		61	coherent	
42	misperception		62	sequence	
43	interpretation		63	outline	
44	throw away		64	intuition	
45	budget		65	conscientious	
46	hand down		66	setback	
47	prerequisite		67	underpin	
48	unoccupied		68	plummet	
49	determine		69	hypothesis	
50	decay		70	entrance	
51	measure		71	manufacture	
52	approximate		72	transcend	
53	extinct		73	impede	
54	concrete		74	trivial	
55	subject to		75	alert	
56	keen		76	astute	
57	modify		77	altruism	
58	subconscious		78	legitimize	
59	odds		79	nasty	
60	bother		80	streamline	

진가영

주요 약력
現) 박문각 공무원 영어 온라인, 오프라인 대표교수
서강대학교 우수 졸업
서강대학교 영미어문 심화 전공
중등학교 정교사 2급 자격증
단기 공무원 영어 전문 강의(개인 운영)

주요 저서
박문각 공무원 진가영 영어 단판승 문법 적중 포인트 100
박문각 공무원 진가영 영어 단기합격 VOCA
박문각 공무원 진가영 영어 유형별 독해 전략서
박문각 공무원 진가영 영어 기초탄탄 입문서
박문각 공무원 진가영 영어 반한다 기출
박문각 공무원 New Trend 진가영 영어 어휘끝판왕[어판왕]
박문각 공무원 New Trend 진가영 영어 독해끝판왕[독판왕]
박문각 공무원 New Trend 진가영 영어 문법끝판왕[문판왕]
박문각 공무원 New Trend 진가영 영어 진족보 마무리 합격노트
박문각 공무원 진가영 영어 적중동형 국가직·지방직 봉투모의고사 Vol.1
박문각 공무원 진가영 영어 적중동형 봉투모의고사 Vol.2
박문각 공무원 진가영 영어 신독기 구문독해
박문각 공무원 진가영 영어 신경향 어휘 마스터
박문각 공무원 진가영 영어 신경향 독해 마스터 시즌1
박문각 공무원 진가영 영어 신경향 독해 마스터 시즌2
박문각 공무원 진가영 영어 단판승 생활영어 적중 70

진가영 영어 ✧✦ 반한다 기출

초판 인쇄 2025. 9. 5. | **초판 발행** 2025. 9. 10. | **편저자** 진가영
발행인 박 용 | **발행처** (주)박문각출판 | **등록** 2015년 4월 29일 제2019-000137호
주소 06654 서울시 서초구 효령로 283 서경 B/D 4층 | **팩스** (02)584-2927
전화 교재 문의 (02)6466-7202

저자와의
협의하에
인지생략

이 책의 무단 전재 또는 복제 행위를 금합니다.

정가 32,000원
ISBN 979-11-7519-114-3

진가영 영어

New Trend 단기합격 길라잡이

기본서

단판승 문법 적중 포인트 100

유형별 독해 전략서

단기합격 VOCA

기출문제집

반한다 기출

'단기합격' 커리큘럼

단계	강의명	학습 내용 및 특징
[0단계] 입문	기초탄탄 입문 이론	**기초부터 탄탄하게, 차근차근 시작!** • 공무원 영어의 기초를 쉽게 이해하고, 탄탄하게 다질 수 있는 입문 강의 • 영어 공부가 처음인 분들도 기초부터 확실히 잡고, 영어에 대한 장벽을 낮춰주는 강의
[1단계] 이론 완성	단기합격 All In One (문법/독해/어휘)	**흔들리지 않는 실력을 위한 공무원 영어의 뼈대를 세우는 과정!** • 공무원 영어의 전반적인 이론 및 내용을 한 번에 배우고, 중요한 내용은 집중적으로 학습할 수 있는 강의 • 시험장에서 흔들리지 않는 토대를 만드는 필수 이론 과정을 완성하는 강의
[2단계] 기출 분석	반한다 기출 분석 시리즈 (독해/ 문법·어휘&생활영어)	**출제 경향 및 알고리즘 분석으로 문제를 보는 안목을 키우는 과정!** • 출제 경향과 알고리즘 분석을 통해 시험의 흐름을 완벽히 이해하고 배운 내용을 문제 풀이 실력으로 만드는 강의 • 자주 출제되는 문제 유형을 철저히 분석하며 실력을 쌓아 시험을 꿰뚫어 볼 수 있는 안목을 키우는 강의
[3단계] 문제 풀이	끝판왕 문제 풀이 N제 시리즈 (어휘/문법/독해)	**배운 것들을 문제에 빠르고 정확하게 적용하는 과정!** • 영역별 문제 풀이로 각 부분을 체계적으로 점검하고 약점을 보완해 점수 상승을 이끄는 강의 • 출제 예상 문제를 집중적으로 풀면서 빠르고 정확하게 문제를 풀 수 있는 기술을 배우는 강의
[4단계] 파이널	만점으로 가는 실전 동형 모의고사	**100% 실력 발휘를 위한 실전 모의고사 과정!** • 실제 시험과 유사한 구성의 고퀄리티 모의고사로 전 범위를 점검하고, 실력을 최종 완성하는 강의 • 다양한 난이도의 실전 동형 모의고사로 어떤 시험 상황에서도 굳건한 점수를 얻을 수 있도록 하는 강의
	'진족보' 마무리 합격 특강	**합격의 열쇠, 단 한 권으로 마지막 준비 완료!** • 시험 직전, 전 영역 핵심 내용을 완벽하게 총정리하며 부족한 부분까지 확실히 채우는 합격 특강 • 시험의 마지막 순간에, 쌓아 온 실력을 시험장에서 발휘하도록 돕는 총정리 특강

☆ 단기합격 필수 커리 ☆

2026

브랜드 만족 1위

수석합격 연속 배출

9급 공무원 영어 시험대비

박문각 공무원
기출문제

New Trend 단기합격 길라잡이

- 신경향 대비 합격률 4.12배 증가!
- 최신 기출 및 출제 기조 전환 완벽 반영
- 9급 기출 빅데이터 분석을 통한 핵심 기출문제 수록
- 어휘, 문법, 생활영어, 독해 전 영역 기출 단권화

진가영 편저

진가영 영어 [정답 및 해설]
반드시 한번에 다 잡는다 기출

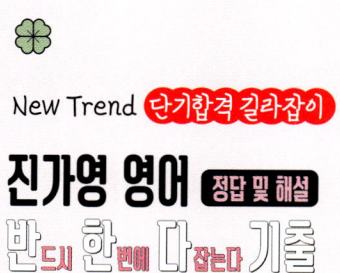

2026

브랜드 만족 1위

수석합격 연속 배출

9급 공무원 영어 시험대비

박문각 공무원

기출문제

New Trend 단기합격 길라잡이

신경향 대비 합격률 4.12배 증가!

최신 기출 및 출제 기조 전환 완벽 반영

9급 기출 빅데이터 분석을 통한 핵심 기출문제 수록

어휘, 문법, 생활영어, 독해 전 영역 기출 단권화

진가영 편저

진가영 영어 정답 및 해설
반드시 한번에 다 잡는다 기출

CONTENTS 차례

단기합격 길라잡이 진가영 영어

정답 및 해설

Vol. 1 어휘 & 생활영어

PART 01 어휘

Chapter 01 국가직 9급 핵심 기출문제 ········· 4
Chapter 02 지방직 9급 핵심 기출문제 ········· 16
Chapter 03 2025년 출제 기조 전환 예시 문제 ········· 27

PART 02 생활영어

Chapter 01 국가직 및 지방직 최신 4개년 핵심 기출문제 ····· 28
Chapter 02 국가직 및 지방직 기타 핵심 기출문제 ········· 33
Chapter 03 2025년 출제 기조 전환 예시 문제 ········· 37

Vol. 2 문법

PART 01 문장과 동사

Chapter 01 문장의 이해 ········· 40
Chapter 02 단어의 이해 ········· 41
Chapter 03 동사의 유형 ········· 43
Chapter 04 동사의 시제 ········· 48
Chapter 05 주어와 동사 수 일치 ········· 50
Chapter 06 수동태 ········· 54

PART 02 준동사

Chapter 07 동명사 ········· 60
Chapter 08 분사 ········· 61
Chapter 09 부정사 ········· 65

PART 03 조동사와 조동사를 활용한 구문

Chapter 10 조동사 ········· 69
Chapter 11 도치 구문과 강조 구문 ········· 71
Chapter 12 가정법 ········· 73

PART 04 연결어

Chapter 13 접속사 ········· 76
Chapter 14 관계사 ········· 81
Chapter 15 전치사 ········· 85

PART 05 비교 구문

Chapter 16 비교 구문 ········· 87

Vol. 3 독해

PART 01 홈페이지 게시글 유형 ········· 92
홈페이지 게시글 유형 기출 독해 어휘 복습 TEST ········· 96

PART 02 전자메일 유형 ········· 98
전자메일 유형 기출 독해 어휘 복습 TEST ········· 101

PART 03 안내문 유형 ········· 102
안내문 유형 기출 독해 어휘 복습 TEST ········· 106

PART 04 중심 내용 파악 유형 ········· 108
중심 내용 파악 유형 기출 독해 어휘 복습 TEST ········· 124

PART 05 문장 제거 유형 ········· 126
문장 제거 유형 기출 독해 어휘 복습 TEST ········· 137

PART 06 문장 삽입 유형 ········· 139
문장 삽입 유형 기출 독해 어휘 복습 TEST ········· 150

PART 07 순서 배열 유형 ········· 152
순서 배열 유형 기출 독해 어휘 복습 TEST ········· 165

PART 08 빈칸 추론 유형 ········· 167
빈칸 추론 유형 기출 독해 어휘 복습 TEST ········· 188

진가영 영어
반한다 기출

어휘 & 생활영어
정답 및 해설
Vol. 1

PART 01 어휘
PART 02 생활영어

진가영 영어연구소 | cafe.naver.com/easyenglish7

PART 01 어휘

Chapter 01 국가직 9급 핵심 기출문제

ANSWER

01 ②	02 ①	03 ③	04 ②	05 ①
06 ④	07 ①	08 ②	09 ④	10 ④
11 ①	12 ①	13 ②	14 ④	15 ②
16 ①	17 ①	18 ②	19 ②	20 ④
21 ①	22 ④	23 ③	24 ①	25 ①
26 ②	27 ③	28 ①	29 ③	30 ②
31 ①	32 ③	33 ④	34 ②	35 ③
36 ②	37 ④	38 ①	39 ③	40 ②
41 ①	42 ①	43 ④	44 ②	45 ③
46 ③	47 ③	48 ①	49 ④	50 ④
51 ②	52 ①	53 ④	54 ①	

01

정답 ②

지문 해석
모든 국제 여행자는 캐나다에 입국할 때 용인할 수 있는 신분 증명서를 소지해야 한다. 예를 들어, 여권은 해외 여행 시 유일하게 신뢰할 수 있고 보편적으로 인정받는 문서이다.

선지 해석
① currency 통화
② identification 신분 증명서, 신원 확인
③ insurance 보험
④ luggage 짐, 수하물

정답 해설
여권이 해외 여행 시 보편적으로 인정받는 유일한 문서라는 예시를 통해, 다른 국가에 입국할 때 여권과 같은 신분증을 소지해야 한다는 문맥이 자연스러우므로 빈칸에는 ②가 적절하다.

지문 어휘
☐ acceptable 용인할 수 있는, 받아들일 수 있는
☐ passport 여권
☐ reliable 신뢰할 수 있는
☐ universally 보편적으로, 일반적으로
☐ abroad 해외로, 해외에(서)

02

정답 ①

지문 해석
우리는 바다를 오염시키고, 물고기를 죽이며, 그것 때문에 소중한 식량 공급원을 스스로 빼앗고 있다.

선지 해석
① depriving 빼앗고, 박탈하고
② informing 알리고, 통지하고
③ accusing 고발하고, 비난하고
④ curing 치료하고

정답 해설
바다를 오염시키고 물고기를 죽이는 행동을 함으로써 결국 스스로 소중한 식량 공급원을 빼앗는다는 문맥이 자연스러우므로 빈칸에는 ①이 적절하다.

지문 어휘
☐ pollute 오염시키다
☐ invaluable 소중한, 매우 유용한, 귀중한

03

정답 ③

지문 해석
분명히, 언어 예술의 어떤 측면도 배움이나 가르침에 있어서 분리되어 있지 않다. 듣기, 말하기, 읽기, 쓰기, 보기, 그리고 시각적 표현은 서로 관계가 있다.

선지 해석
① distinct 뚜렷한, 명백한
② distorted 비뚤어진, 왜곡된
③ interrelated 서로 관계가 있는
④ independent 독립적인

정답 해설
앞부분에 '언어 예술의 측면에서 분리되어 있지 않다'고 하는 것으로 보아 빈칸에는 ③이 적절하다.

지문 어휘
☐ aspect 측면, 양상, 면
☐ stand alone 분리되다, 독립하다
☐ representing 표현

핵심 어휘
✈ distinct
= clear, obvious, conspicuous, apparent, evident, manifest, plain, palpable

04 정답 ②

지문 해석
그 돈은 너무 교묘하게 숨겨져 있어 우리는 그것을 찾는 것을 포기할 수밖에 없었다.

선지 해석
① spent 이미 쓴, 이용한
② hidden 숨겨진, 숨은, 잠재하는
③ invested 투자된, 부여된
④ delivered 배달된, 전달된

정답 해설
뒷 부분에 '찾는 것을 포기할 수 밖에 없었다'라고 하는 것으로 보아 빈칸에는 ②가 적절하다.

지문 어휘
□ cleverly 교묘하게, 영리하게
□ abandon 포기하다, 버리다

핵심 어휘
✱ hidden 잠재하는 = latent

05 정답 ①

지문 해석
시민들의 불안을 진정시키기 위해 시장은 해당 지역에서 경찰 순찰을 강화하겠다고 발표했다.

선지 해석
① soothe 진정시키다, 달래다
② counter 반대하다, 거스르다, 대응하다, 계산대, 판매대
③ enlighten 계몽하다, 가르치다, 이해시키다, 깨우치다
④ assimilate 동화되다, 완전히 이해하다[소화하다]

정답 해설
해당 지역의 순찰을 강화하는 이유는 시민들의 불안을 해소하기 위한 것으로 빈칸에는 ①이 적절하다.

지문 어휘
□ anxiety 불안, 염려, 열망
□ mayor 시장, 군수
□ patrol 순찰(대), 순찰을 돌다

핵심 어휘
✱ soothe
= allay, appease, assuage, calm (down), conciliate, pacify, placate, mollify, tranquilize

06 정답 ④

지문 해석
많은 사람들이 어떤 분야에서 진정한 숙달을 이루기 위해 필요한 헌신과 노력을 과소평가하며, 성공한 사람들에게는 그것이 쉽게 온다고 종종 믿는다.

선지 해석
① discern 식별하다, 분별하다, 알아보다, 인식하다
② dissatisfy 불만을 느끼게 하다, 불평을 갖게 하다
③ underline 강조하다, 밑줄을 긋다
④ underestimate 과소평가하다, 경시하다, 얕보다

정답 해설
많은 사람들이 성공은 쉽게 온다고 믿는다는 내용으로 보아 헌신과 노력들을 과소평가한다는 내용이 자연스우우므로 빈칸에는 ④가 적절하다.

지문 어휘
□ dedication 헌신, 전념
□ mastery 숙달, 통달

07 정답 ①

지문 해석
발표를 철저히 준비했음에도 불구하고, 그녀는 여전히 청중이 자신의 아이디어를 어떻게 받아들일지에 대해 불안해했다.

선지 해석
① anxious 불안해하는, 염려하는(about), 열망하는(for)
② fortunate 운 좋은, 다행한
③ reputable 평판이 좋은, 존경할 만한
④ courageous 용기 있는, 두려움을 모르는

정답 해설
역접(despite)의 단서로 철저하게 발표를 준비한 것의 의미의 상반된 내용이 뒤에 나와야 하므로 빈칸에는 ①이 적절하다.

지문 어휘
□ thoroughly 철저히, 완전히
□ presentation 발표, 제출
□ audience 청중, 관중, 시청자

핵심 어휘
✱ courageous
= intrepid, brave, bold, daring, fearless, audacious, valiant, gallant, plucky

08 정답 ②

지문 해석
Jane은 화려한 결혼식보다는 작은 결혼식을 하고 싶었다. 그래서, 그녀는 자신의 가족과 친한 친구 몇 명을 초대해서 맛있는 음식을 먹고 즐거운 시간을 보내려고 계획했다.

선지 해석
① nosy 참견하기 좋아하는, 꼬치꼬치 캐묻는
② intimate 가까운, 친한
③ rigorous 철저한, 엄격한
④ considerable 상당한, 많은

정답 해설
인과(thus)의 단서로 앞부분에 Jane은 작은 결혼식을 하고 싶다고 하고 있으므로 적은 수의 친한 친구들만 초대하고자 하는 표현이 자연스러우므로 빈칸에는 ②가 적절하다.

지문 어휘
- fancy 화려한
- pleasant 즐거운, 기분 좋은

핵심 어휘
★ outgoing = extrovert, sociable, gregarious
★ nosy = prying, inquisitive, curious
★ considerate = thoughtful

09   정답 ④

지문 해석
대중교통의 <u>간헐적인</u> 혼란으로 인해, 도시는 혼잡 시간대에 임시 셔틀 서비스를 제공하는 계획을 시행했다.

선지 해석
① virtuous 덕이 있는, 덕이 높은, 고결한
② reticent 말이 없는, 과묵한
③ ingenious 기발한, 독창적인
④ intermittent 간헐적인, 간간이 일어나는

정답 해설
인과(due to)의 단서로 혼잡 시간대에 셔틀 서비스가 임시로 시행된다고 하는 것으로 보아 대중교통의 혼란이 간헐적으로 발생했다는 내용이 자연스러우므로 빈칸에는 ④가 적절하다.

지문 어휘
- disruption 혼란, 분열, 붕괴
- temporary 임시의, 일시적인

핵심 어휘
★ intermittent = sporadic, scattered, occasional, irregular

10   정답 ④

지문 해석
전국적인 유행병으로 인해 회사는 직원들에게 다양한 교육 프로그램을 제공하는 계획을 <u>연기해야</u> 했다.

선지 해석
① convince 납득시키다, 확신시키다
② release 풀어 주다, 방출하다, 개봉하다, 석방, 개봉
③ mount 오르다, 증가하다
④ suspend 매달다, 유예[중단]하다, 연기하다

정답 해설
인과(because of)의 단서로 전국적인 유행병의 발병에 따라 교육 프로그램을 연기해야 했다는 표현이 자연스러우므로 빈칸에는 ④가 적절하다.

지문 어휘
- pandemic 전국적인 유행병

핵심 어휘
★ suspend = delay, postpone, defer, shelve, put off, hold over

11   정답 ①

지문 해석
위원회는 늦게 제출된 것은 <u>받아들이지</u> 않으므로, 제안서가 검토되기를 원한다면 기한을 지키는 것이 중요하다.

선지 해석
① accept 받아들이다, 수락하다
② deteriorate 악화되다, 더 나빠지다
③ postpone 연기하다, 미루다
④ abridge 요약[축약]하다

정답 해설
인과(so)의 단서로 제안서가 검토되려면 기한을 지키는 것이 중요하다고 하는 것으로 보아 기한을 지키지 않으면 위원회는 제안서를 받아들이지 않는다는 표현이 자연스러우므로 빈칸에는 ①이 적절하다.

지문 어휘
- submission 제출, 항복
- deadline 기한, 마감 시간

핵심 어휘
★ accept
  = obey, observe, stick to, cling to, adhere to, conform to, comply with, abide by
★ announce
  = publicize, broadcast, advertise, inform, notify

12   정답 ①

지문 해석
수년 동안 형사들은 쌍둥이 형제의 갑작스러운 실종에 대한 미스터리를 <u>해결하려고</u> 노력해 왔다.

선지 해석
① solve 풀다, 해결하다
② create 창조하다, 만들다
③ imitate 모방하다, 흉내내다
④ meditate 명상하다, 숙고하다

정답 해설
형사들은 실종 사건을 해결하려고 노력하는 것이 문맥상 자연스러우므로 빈칸에는 ①이 적절하다.

지문 어휘
- detective 형사
- sudden 갑작스러운
- disappearance 실종

핵심 어휘
★ solve
  = resolve, settle, unravel, hammer out, work out, iron out

13
정답 ②

지문 해석
> 부부가 부모가 되기 전에는, 침실 4개짜리 집은 불필요하게 <u>사치스러워</u> 보였다.

선지 해석
① hidden 숨겨진
② luxurious 사치스러운, 호화로운
③ empty 비어있는
④ solid 단단한, 고체의

정답 해설
부부 단 둘이서는 침실 4개 짜리의 불필요하게 큰 집이 사치스러워 보인다는 것이 문맥상 자연스러우므로 빈칸에는 ②가 적절하다.

지문 어휘
□ parenthood 부모임
□ unnecessarily 불필요하게, 쓸데없이

핵심 어휘
✱ luxurious
  = rich, wealthy, affluent, opulent, prosperous, well-to-do, made of money

14
정답 ④

지문 해석
> 사장님은 우리가 이미 그렇게 짧은 기간에 예산을 다 써버린 것을 보고 <u>화를 냈다</u>.

선지 해석
① hit the sack 잠자리에 들다, 잠을 자다
② hit the road 먼 길을 나서다, 여행 길에 오르다
③ hit the book 열심히 공부하다, 벼락치기 공부하다
④ hit the roof 몹시 화를 내다, 격노하다

정답 해설
짧은 기간에 예산을 다 써버린 것에 화를 냈다는 표현이 문맥상 자연스러우므로 빈칸에는 ④가 적절하다.

지문 어휘
□ entire 전체의, 전부의
□ budget 예산

핵심 어휘
✱ hit the roof = hit the ceiling, go through the roof

15
정답 ②

지문 해석
> 마우스 포테이토는 텔레비전의 카우치 포테이토와 컴퓨터에서 <u>상응하는 것</u>으로, 텔레비전 앞에서 카우치 포테이토가 하는 것과 같은 식으로 컴퓨터 앞에서 많은 여가 시간을 보내는 경향이 있는 사람을 말한다.

선지 해석
① technician 기술자, 전문가
② equivalent 대응물, 동등한 것, 상응하는 것
③ network 망, 네트워크
④ simulation 시뮬레이션, 모의실험

정답 해설
텔레비전 앞에서 카우치 포테이토가 하는 것과 같은 방식으로 컴퓨터 앞에서 많은 여가 시간을 보내는 경향이 있는 사람을 마우스 포테이토라고 한다는 내용을 미루어볼 때 빈칸에는 ②가 적절하다.

지문 어휘
□ mouse potato (일·오락을 위해) 컴퓨터 앞에서 시간을 많이 보내는 사람
□ couch potato 소파에 앉아 TV만 보며 많은 시간을 보내는 사람

핵심 어휘
✱ equivalent 대응물 = counterpart

16
정답 ①

지문 해석
> Mary는 남미에 가기 전에 스페인어를 <u>복습하기로</u> 결심했다.

① review 복습하다
② curtail 줄이다, 축소하다, 삭감하다
③ defend 옹호하다, 변호하다
④ dismiss 해고하다

정답 해설
남미에 가기 전에 스페인어를 복습했다는 내용이 자연스러우므로 빈칸에 ①이 적절하다.

지문 어휘
□ Spanish 스페인어

핵심 어휘
✱ dismiss = lay off, discharge, fire, sack

17
정답 ①

지문 해석
> 양념이 완벽하게 <u>조합되어</u> 요리가 엄청나게 맛있었고, 식탁에 앉아 있던 모두가 감탄했다.

선지 해석
① combination 조합, 결합, 연합
② comparison 비교, 비유
③ place 장소, 곳, 놓다, 배치하다
④ case 경우, 사례, 사실

정답 해설
요리가 엄청 맛있었고 모두가 감탄했다는 것으로 보아 양념이 완벽하게 조합되었다는 내용이 자연스러우므로 빈칸에는 ①이 적절하다.

지문 어휘
□ flavor 양념, 조미료, 풍미, 맛
□ incredibly 엄청나게, 믿을 수 없을 정도로

18

정답 ②

지문 해석

재즈의 영향력은 매우 어디에나 존재해서 대부분의 대중 음악은 그 양식적인 기원을 재즈에 두고 있다.

선지 해석

① deceptive 현혹시키는, 사기의
② ubiquitous 어디에나 존재하는, 도처에 있는
③ persuasive 설득력 있는
④ disastrous 비참한, 처참한

정답 해설

재즈가 대중 음악의 기원을 둔다고 하고 있으므로 재즈의 영향력은 넓게 퍼져있다는 내용이 자연스러우므로 빈칸에는 ②가 적절하다.

지문 어휘

☐ owe A to B A는 B 덕분이다, A를 B에게 빚지다, A를 B에 돌리다
☐ stylistic 양식의
☐ root 뿌리, 기초

핵심 어휘

✱ disastrous
= terrible, tragic, fatal, ruinous, devastating, calamitous, catastrophic

19

정답 ②

지문 해석

이 소설은 사업을 시작하기 위해 학교를 그만 두려고 하는 다루기 힘든 한 십대의 화가 난 부모에 대한 것이다.

선지 해석

① callous 냉담한, 무감각한
② vexed 화가 난, 곤란한
③ reputable 평판이 좋은, 존경할 만한
④ confident 확신하는, 자신감 있는

정답 해설

학교를 그만두려고 하고 또 다루기 힘들다는 표현으로 보아 부모님이 화가 났다는 내용이 자연스러우므로 빈칸에는 ②가 적절하다.

지문 어휘

☐ unruly 다루기 힘든, 제멋대로 구는

핵심 어휘

✱ callous = indifferent, uninterested, aloof, apathetic, nonchalant

20

정답 ④

지문 해석

한 그룹의 젊은 시위대들이 경찰서에 침입하려고 시도했다.

선지 해석

① bump into (우연히) ~와 마주치다
② run into ~와 우연히 만나다
③ turn into ~으로 변하다, 바뀌다
④ break into 침입하다, ~하기 시작하다

정답 해설

시위자와 경찰서라는 단어로 미루어 보아 빈칸에는 ④가 적절하다.

지문 어휘

☐ demonstrator 시위자, 시위[데모] 참가[가담]자

핵심 어휘

✱ turn into = convert into, transform into

21

정답 ①

지문 해석

그녀는 회의 중에 자신의 우려를 매우 솔직하게 표현했으며, 아무것도 비밀로 하지 않았다.

선지 해석

① frank 솔직한
② logical 타당한, 논리적인
③ implicit 암시된, 내포된
④ passionate 열정적인, 열렬한

정답 해설

뒷 부분에 아무것도 비밀로 하지 않았다고 하는 것으로 보아 표현을 숨기지 않고 솔직하게 했다는 내용이 자연스러우므로 빈칸에는 ①이 적절하다.

지문 어휘

☐ concerns 걱정, 염려, 관심사
☐ hold back ~을 비밀로 하다, 저지하다, 방해하다

핵심 어휘

✱ passionate = enthusiastic, eager, ardent, zealous, fervent

22

정답 ④

지문 해석

아주 밝은 네온 사인이 1마일 떨어진 곳에서 눈에 잘 띄어서 모두들 쳐다보았다.

선지 해석

① passive 수동적인, 소극적인
② vaporous 수증기 같은, 수증기가 가득한
③ dangerous 위험한
④ conspicuous 눈에 잘 띄는, 뚜렷한

정답 해설

문맥상 멀리 떨어진 곳에서도 모두가 쳐다보았다는 하는 것으로 보아 네온 사인이 눈에 잘 띈다는 내용이 자연스러우므로 빈칸에는 ④가 적절하다.

지문 어휘

☐ bright 밝은, 눈부신, 선명한, 명랑한, 쾌활한

핵심 어휘

✱ conspicuous
= obvious, clear, evident, apparent, noticeable, outstanding, salient, striking, remarkable, manifest

23

정답 ③

지문 해석

그는 도시를 <u>속속들이</u> 알고 있어서 너에게 어떻게 그곳에 가는지 알려 줄 수 있는 가장 좋은 사람이다.

선지 해석

① eventually 결국, 마침내
② culturally 문화적으로, 교양으로서
③ thoroughly 속속들이, 철저하게
④ tentatively 잠정적으로, 시험적으로

정답 해설

그가 도시의 어디든 어떻게 가는지 알려줄 수 있다는 것으로 보아 도시들을 속속들이 알고 있다는 내용이 자연스러우므로 빈칸에는 ③이 적절하다.

핵심 어휘

✱ eventually = finally, ultimately, after all, in the end, at last

24

정답 ①

지문 해석

대학은 그가 의학 분야에서 획기적인 업적을 이룬 것을 인정하여, 새로운 연구 시설의 이름을 그의 이름을 따서 Smith 박사를 <u>공경하기로</u> 결정했다.

선지 해석

① honor 공경하다, 존경하다, 명예
② compose 구성하다, 작곡하다
③ discard 버리다, 폐기하다
④ join 가입하다, 연결하다

정답 해설

문맥상 획기적인 업적을 이룬 것을 인정하여 연구 시설의 이름을 그의 이름으로 한다는 것으로 보아 그를 기린다는 내용이 자연스러우므로 빈칸에는 ①이 적절하다.

지문 어휘

☐ research facility 연구 시설, 연구소
☐ groundbreaking 획기적인

핵심 어휘

✱ discard
= abandon, relinquish, dispose of, dispense with, do away with, throw away, get rid of

25

정답 ①

지문 해석

Natural Gas World 구독자는 업계에서 어떤 일이 벌어지고 있는지에 대한 정확하고 신뢰할 수 있는 주요 사실과 수치를 제공받게 될 것이므로, 그들은 그들의 사업에 영향을 미치는 사항을 완전히 <u>식별할</u> 수 있다.

선지 해석

① discern 식별하다, 분별하다, 알아보다, 인식하다
② confine 한정하다, 제한하다
③ undermine 약화시키다, 손상시키다
④ abandon 버리다, 포기하다

정답 해설

앞 부분에 정확하고 신뢰할 수 있는 사실과 수치를 제공받는 것으로 보아 사업에 영향을 미치는 사항들을 완전히 파악할 수 있다는 내용이 자연스러우므로 빈칸에는 ①이 적절하다.

지문 어휘

☐ subscriber 구독자
☐ accurate 정확한
☐ reliable 신뢰할 수 있는
☐ figure 수치

핵심 어휘

✱ strengthen
= reinforce, consolidate, fortify, intensify, beef up, shore up

26

정답 ②

지문 해석

그 영화의 특수 효과는 매우 <u>인상적이었으며</u>, 시각적으로 멋진 경험을 만들어 관객을 사로잡았다.

선지 해석

① overwhelmed 압도된
② impressive 인상적인, 인상 깊은
③ depressed 침체된, 낙담한
④ neutral 중립적인

정답 해설

뒷부분에 영화가 시각적으로 관객을 사로잡았다고 하는 것으로 보아 영화의 특수 효과가 인상적으로 보인다는 내용이 자연스러우므로 빈칸에는 ②가 적절하다.

지문 어휘

☐ special effect 특수 효과
☐ stunning 멋진, 굉장한, 깜짝 놀랄
☐ captivate ~의 마음을 사로잡다[매혹하다]

핵심 어휘

✱ depressed = dismal, despondent, dejected, discouraged

27

정답 ③

지문 해석

새로운 규정에 따라, 기업들은 투명성과 책임성을 확보하기 위해 분기마다 재무 실적을 보고하는 것이 <u>의무적이다</u>.

선지 해석

① complimentary 무료의, 칭찬하는
② enticing 유혹적인, 마음을 끄는
③ mandatory 명령의, 의무적인, 강제적인
④ innovative 혁신적인

정답 해설

기업들은 투명성과 책임성을 확보하기 위해 재무 실적을 보고하는 것이 새로운 규정에 따라 의무화되었다는 내용이 자연스러우므로 빈칸에는 ③이 적절하다.

지문 어휘
- regulation 규정, 규제, 단속
- financial 재무의, 재정의
- transparency 투명성

핵심 어휘
✱ complementary = reciprocal, interdependent
✱ mandatory
  = compulsory, obligatory, required, requisite, imperative, incumbent, necessary, essential

28   정답 ①

지문 해석
그 회사는 기자 회견에서 마침내 신제품 출시와 관련된 세부 사항을 공개했다.

선지 해석
① disclosed 공개했다, 발표했다, (비밀을) 폭로했다, 누설했다
② exploded 폭발했다, 터졌다
③ abated 약화시켰다, 완화시켰다
④ disappointed 실망시켰다

정답 해설
회사가 기자 회견을 통해 신제품 출시와 관련된 사항들을 공개했다는 내용이 자연스러우므로 빈칸에는 ①이 적절하다.

지문 어휘
- launch 출시, 개시, 출시하다, 시작하다
- press conference 기자 회견

핵심 어휘
✱ disclose = reveal, divulge, unveil, let on

29   정답 ②

지문 해석
빈곤한 지역 사회는 종종 의료 접근 제한, 열악한 인프라, 높은 실업률 등의 문제에 직면한다.

선지 해석
① Itinerant 떠돌아다니는, 순회하는
② Impoverished 빈곤한, 가난해진
③ Sensory 감각의, 지각의
④ Indigenous 원산의, 토착의

정답 해설
문맥상 의료 접근 제한, 열악한 인프라, 높은 실업률의 문제에 직면한다는 것으로 보아 지역 사회가 빈곤하다는 내용이 자연스러우므로 빈칸에는 ②가 적절하다.

지문 어휘
- face 직면하다, 마주보다, 얼굴
- unemployment rate 실업률

핵심 어휘
✱ impoverished
  = poor, penniless, needy, destitute, indigent, impecunious

30   정답 ②

지문 해석
그는 옆 공사장에서 나는 끊임없는 소음을 몹시 싫어하며 관리자에게 불평했다.

선지 해석
① defended 방어했다, 수비했다
② detested 몹시 싫어했다, 혐오했다
③ confirmed 확인했다, 확증했다
④ abandoned 버렸다, 포기했다

정답 해설
끊임없는 공사장 소음 때문에 관리자를 찾아가 불평했다는 점에서, 소음을 몹시 싫어했다는 내용이 자연스러우므로 빈칸에는 ②가 적절하다.

지문 어휘
- constant 끊임없는, 거듭되는
- construction 공사, 건설

핵심 어휘
✱ abandon
  = renounce, relinquish, discard, dispense with, do away with, forgo, give up
✱ confirm = corroborate, validate, verify, affirm

31   정답 ①

지문 해석
봄 계절 중반에 예기치 못한 눈이 내리는 등 이맘때 날씨가 이상했다.

선지 해석
① odd 이상한, 특이한
② ongoing 계속 진행 중인
③ obvious 분명한[명백한], 확실한
④ offensive 모욕적인, 불쾌한, 공격적인

정답 해설
봄철에 내린 눈이 전혀 예기치 못했다는 것으로 보아 이맘때 눈이 내리는 것은 이상하다는 내용이 자연스러우므로 빈칸에는 ①이 적절하다.

지문 어휘
- weather 날씨, 기상
- unexpectedly 예기치 못한, 갑자기
- spring 봄

핵심 어휘
✱ odd
  = uncanny, strange, weird, bizarre, peculiar, eerie, out in left field

32   정답 ③

지문 해석
그 식물은 극한의 온도를 견딜 수 있어 다양한 기후에 적합하다.

선지 해석
① modify 수정[변경]하다, 바꾸다
② record 기록하다, 기록
③ tolerate 참다, 견디다
④ evaluate 평가하다, 감정하다

정답 해설
문맥상 다양한 기후에 적합하다는 것으로 보아 그 식물은 극한의 온도에서도 버틸 수 있다는 내용이 자연스러우므로 빈칸에는 ③이 적절하다.

지문 어휘
☐ extreme 극한의, 심각한
☐ temperature 온도, 기온

핵심 어휘
✤ tolerate = put up with, endure, bear, stand
✤ modify = change, alter, adjust, adapt, amend, revise

33   정답 ④

지문 해석
공해를 제거하고자 하는 캠페인은 그것이 대중의 이해와 전적인 협력을 얻지 못한다면 소용없음이 드러날 것이다.

선지 해석
① enticing 유혹적인, 마음을 끄는
② enhanced 높인, 강화한
③ fertile 비옥한, 생산력 있는
④ futile 헛된, 소용없는, 쓸모없는

정답 해설
unless는 주절과 종속절의 내용을 역접 관계로 만드는 접속사이다. unless 뒤에 나온 내용이 '대중의 이해와 전적인 협력'이라는 긍정적인 내용이므로 주절에는 부정적인 내용이 나와야 하므로 빈칸에는 ④가 적절하다.

지문 어휘
☐ eliminate 제거하다, 배제하다
☐ pollution 공해
☐ unless ~하지 않으면, ~하지 않는 한
☐ cooperation 협력

핵심 어휘
✤ enticing
= attractive, seductive, tempting, alluring, appealing, fascinating

34   정답 ②

지문 해석
자신과 상관없는 일에 간섭하지 않는 것이 중요하며, 특히 그것이 불필요한 갈등을 초래할 수 있을 때 더욱 그렇다.

선지 해석
① hurry 서두르다, 급히 하다
② interfere 간섭하다(in), 방해하다(with)
③ sniff 코를 훌쩍이다, 냄새를 맡다(at)
④ resign 사직[사임]하다, 체념하다

정답 해설
불필요한 갈등을 초래할 수 있는 상황에서는 특히 조심해야 한다는 점에서, 자신과 상관없는 일에 간섭하지 않아야 한다는 내용이 자연스러우므로 빈칸에는 ②가 적절하다.

지문 어휘
☐ concern 관련되다, 영향을 미치다

핵심 어휘
✤ resign 사직하다 = step down, quit

35   정답 ③

지문 해석
Newton은 수학, 광학, 그리고 기계 물리학에 전례 없는 기여를 했다.

선지 해석
① mediocre 보통의, 평범한
② suggestive 암시[시사]하는, ~을 생각나게 하는(of)
③ unprecedented 전례 없는, 비길 데 없는
④ provocative 도발적인, 화나게 하는

정답 해설
문맥상 Newton이 여러 분야에 기여를 했다는 것으로 보아 출중난 기여를 했다는 내용이 자연스러우므로 빈칸에는 ③이 적절하다.

지문 어휘
☐ contribution 기여, 공헌, 기부
☐ mathematics 수학
☐ optics 광학

핵심 어휘
✤ unprecedented
= unsurpassed, unmatched, matchless, unrivalled, unparalleled

36   정답 ②

지문 해석
그 젊은 기사는 겁쟁이라고 불린 것에 너무 격분해서 그는 손에 검을 쥐고 앞으로 돌진했다.

선지 해석
① aloof 냉담한, 무관심한
② incensed 몹시 화난, 격분한
③ unbiased 선입견이 없는, 편파적이지 않은
④ unpretentious 가식 없는, 잘난 체하지 않는

정답 해설
'so 형용사/부사 that절' 구문은 원인과 결과를 나타내므로 뒤에 that절의 내용에서 손에 칼을 잡고 돌진했다는 내용을 미루어 볼 때 빈칸에는 ②가 적절하다.

지문 어휘
☐ knight (중세의) 기사
☐ coward 겁쟁이
☐ charge 돌진하다
☐ sword 검

핵심 어휘
★ unbiased = equitable, impartial, fair

37
정답 ④

지문 해석
1970년대 중반에 John Holland라고 불리는 미국인 컴퓨터 과학자는 과학계에서 악명높게 어려운 문제들을 해결하기 위해 진화론을 이용하는 아이디어를 생각해내다.

선지 해석
① look upon ~로 간주하다, 고려하다
② depend upon ~에 의존하다
③ put upon ~을 속이다, 학대하다
④ hit upon ~을 (우연히) 생각해내다

정답 해설
빈칸 뒤에 the idea의 내용이 나오고, 문맥상 '생각하다'라는 내용이 자연스러우므로 빈칸에는 ④가 적절하다.

지문 어휘
☐ theory 이론
☐ evolution 진화
☐ notoriously 악명높게

핵심 어휘
★ depend on(upon)
= rely on, count on, hinge on, lean on, rest on, fall back on, turn to, look to, resort to

38
정답 ①

지문 해석
사고 후, 의사는 환자가 치료 계획에 동의하기 전에 모든 절차를 완벽히 이해할 수 있도록 신중히 설명했다.

선지 해석
① carefully 조심스럽게, 신중히
② hurriedly 다급하게, 허둥지둥
③ decisively 결정적으로, 단호히
④ delightfully 기뻐서, 기꺼이

정답 해설
사고가 발생하고 의사가 치료 동의를 받아야 하는 상황이므로, 환자가 모든 절차를 이해할 수 있도록 신중하게 설명했다는 내용이 자연스러우므로 빈칸에는 ①이 적절하다.

지문 어휘
☐ explain 설명하다
☐ procedure 절차, 방법

핵심 어휘
★ hurriedly = hastily

39
정답 ①

지문 해석
화재 경보가 울리자 모든 학생이 주저하거나 당황하지 않고 즉시 건물을 대피했다.

선지 해석
① immediately 즉시
② punctually 시간대로, 정각에
③ hesitantly 머뭇거리며
④ periodically 정기[주기]적으로

정답 해설
화재 경보가 울렸을 때 학생들이 주저하거나 당황하지 않았다는 점에서, 즉시 건물을 대피했다는 내용이 자연스러우므로 빈칸에는 ①이 적절하다.

지문 어휘
☐ fire alarm 화재 경보(기)
☐ evacuate 대피시키다, 떠나다

핵심 어휘
★ immediately = at the drop of a hat, instantly, at once
★ punctually = on time

40
정답 ②

지문 해석
그녀는 지난겨울 멕시코로 여행을 가기 전에, 대학 이후부터 스페인어를 연습하지 않았기 때문에 스페인어를 복습할 필요가 있었다.

선지 해석
① make up to ~에게 아첨하다
② brush up on ~을 복습하다
③ shun away from ~로부터 피하다
④ come down with (병에) 걸리다

정답 해설
문맥상 멕시코로 여행을 가기 전에 스페인어를 복습해야 한다는 내용이 자연스러우므로 빈칸에는 ②가 적절하다.

지문 어휘
☐ practice 연습하다
☐ college 대학

핵심 어휘
★ brush up on = review, go over

41
정답 ①

지문 해석
의사는 증상의 원인을 밝히기 위해 환자를 철저히 검사할 것이다.

선지 해석
① examine 조사하다, 검사하다
② distribute 나눠주다, 분배하다
③ discard 버리다, 폐기하다
④ pursue 추구하다, 뒤쫓다

정답 해설
문맥상 환자의 증상의 원인을 밝히기 위해 환자의 상태를 검사한다는 내용이 자연스러우므로 빈칸에는 ①이 적절하다.

지문 어휘
☐ determine 알아내다, 밝히다, 결정하다

핵심 어휘
✈ examine
= inspect, investigate, scrutinize, go over, pore over, look into, delve into, probe into

42 정답 ①

지문 해석
그 체조 선수의 올림픽 대회 중 흠잡을 데 없는 기술은 새로운 세계 기록으로 이어졌다.

선지 해석
① faultless 흠잡을 데 없는, 완벽한, 무결점의
② unreliable 믿을[신뢰할] 수 없는
③ gutless 배짱[용기] 없는
④ unscientific 비과학적인

정답 해설
문맥상 새로운 세계 기록이 나왔다는 내용으로 보아 체조 선수의 기술이 완벽했다는 내용이 자연스러우므로 빈칸에는 ①이 적절하다.

지문 어휘
☐ gymnast 체조 선수

핵심 어휘
✈ faultless = impeccable, flawless, unblemished, immaculate

43 정답 ④

지문 해석
Visa okay는 전체 비자 자문 및 비자 발급 과정을 용이하게 함으로써 호주의 여행 산업, 기업 및 정부 그리고 개인들을 돕는다. Visa okay는 여행 비자를 신청하고 발급하는 데 따른 복잡함과 시간 지연을 최소화한다.

선지 해석
① appreciating 평가하게 함
② aggravating 악화시키게 함
③ meditating 명상하게 함
④ facilitating 용이하게 함

정답 해설
빈칸 다음 문장에서 Visa okay는 복잡함과 시간 지연을 최소화해 준다는 긍정적인 내용이 언급되었으므로 빈칸에는 ④가 적절하다.

지문 어휘
☐ assist 원조하다, 돕다
☐ corporation 기업
☐ entire 전체의
☐ visa issuance 비자 발급
☐ minimize 최소화하다
☐ complexity 복잡함
☐ delay 지연
☐ obtain 얻다, 획득하다

핵심 어휘
✈ meditate = contemplate, ponder

44 정답 ②

지문 해석
우리의 합리화와 자기기만의 굉장한 능력을 고려해 볼 때, 우리 대부분은 우리 자신을 관대하게 평가할 것이다: 나는 훌륭한 사람이기 때문에 그 눈이 먼 승객에게 정직했다. 그녀는 아마 어차피 너무 많은 돈을 가지고 있기 때문에 나는 그 눈이 보이는 사람을 속였다.

선지 해석
① harshly 엄격히, 가혹하게
② leniently 관대하게
③ honestly 솔직히, 정직하게
④ thankfully 고맙게도, 감사하게, 다행스럽게도

정답 해설
빈칸 앞부분에서 합리화와 자기기만의 굉장한 능력을 고려해 본다는 내용과 콜론(:) 뒤에 설명에서도 자신을 wonder person이라며 긍정적으로 평가하고 있으므로 빈칸에는 ②가 적절하다.

지문 어휘
☐ awesome 경탄할 만한, 굉장한
☐ rationalization 합리화
☐ self-deception 자기기만
☐ blind 눈이 먼
☐ cheat 기만하다, 속이다

핵심 어휘
✈ lenient = generous, merciful, magnanimous

45 정답 ③

지문 해석
한국에서는 장남이 많은 책임을 떠맡는 경향이 있다.

선지 해석
① take over ~을 인계받다, 인수하다, 이어 받다
② take down 적어두다, (구조물 등을) 치우다
③ take on 떠맡다, 고용하다, 띠다
④ take off 이륙하다, 벗다, 쉬다, 빼다

정답 해설
책임의 단어와 어울리는 동사로 떠맡다는 내용이 자연스러우므로 빈칸에는 ③이 적절하다.

지문 어휘
☐ eldest son 장남
☐ responsibility 책임

핵심 어휘
✈ take over = assume

46

정답 ③

지문 해석

예산 부족을 <u>해결하기</u> 위해 회사는 일련의 비용 절감 조치를 시행했다.

선지 해석

① conceive 상상하다, 생각하다, 임신하다
② review 재검토하다, 복습하다
③ solve 해결하다
④ pose (문제 등을) 제기하다, 자세

정답 해설

문맥상 회사가 비용 절감 조치를 한 이유로는 예산 부족을 해결하기 위해 시행했다는 내용이 자연스러우므로 빈칸에는 ③이 적절하다.

지문 어휘

☐ shortfall 부족(분)
☐ implement 시행하다, 도구[기구]
☐ cost-cutting 비용[경비] 절감

핵심 어휘

✱ solve = iron out, resolve, settle, unravel, hammer out, work out

47

정답 ③

지문 해석

자신의 학업 성적에 대한 <u>현실에 안주하는</u> 시각은 개선의 필요성을 인식하지 못하게 하고 더 나은 결과를 얻지 못하게 했다.

선지 해석

① scornful 경멸[멸시]하는
② simulated 흉내 내는, ~인 체하는
③ complacent 현실에 안주하는, 자기만족적인, 만족한
④ condescending 거만한, 거들먹거리는, 잘난 체하는

정답 해설

뒷부분에 개선의 필요성을 인식하지 못하고 더 나은 결과를 얻지 못했다는 내용으로 보아 자신의 성적에 안주하는 시각을 가졌다는 내용이 자연스러우므로 빈칸에는 ③이 적절하다.

지문 어휘

☐ recognize 인식하다, 인정하다, 알아보다
☐ improvement 개선, 호전, 향상

핵심 어휘

✱ condescending
= pompous, arrogant, pretentious, patronizing, presumptuous, supercilious, haughty

48

정답 ①

지문 해석

금기어들과 그 단어의 개념을 대응하는 일상적인 방법은 완곡어법이나 에둘러 말하기를 만들어 내는 것이다. 수백 개의 단어와 관용구는 기초적인 생물학적 기능을 표현하기 위해 등장했고, <u>죽음</u>에 대한 말은 그 자체의 언어 세계를 가지고 있다. 영어의 예로는 "돌아가시다", "촛불을 끄다" 그리고 "높은 곳으로 가다(천당에 가다)" 등이 있다.

선지 해석

① death 죽음, 사망
② defeat 타파, 패배
③ anxiety 불안, 염려
④ frustration 좌절, 불만

정답 해설

빈칸 다음 문장에 나오는 'pass on(사망하다), to snuff the candle(촛불을 끄다), go aloft(천당에 가다)'라는 죽음과 관련되는 예시들로 미루어 보아 빈칸에는 ①이 적절하다.

지문 어휘

☐ cope with ~에 대처[대응]하다, ~에 대항하다
☐ euphemism 완곡어법, 완곡 어구
☐ circumlocution 에둘러[우회적으로] 말하기
☐ linguistic 언어(학)의
☐ pass on 세상을 떠나다(돌아가시다)
☐ snuff the candle (초의) 심지를 끊다
☐ go aloft 천당에 가다, 죽다

핵심 어휘

✱ anxiety = uneasiness, misgiving, apprehension

49

정답 ④

지문 해석

삶의 즐거움, 즉 기쁨은 모든 인간 노력의 자연스러운 목표이다. 그러나 자연은 또한 우리가 삶을 즐길 수 있도록 서로 돕기를 원한다. 그녀는 모든 종들의 행복을 똑같이 갈망하고 있다. 그래서 그녀는 우리가 다른 사람들의 이익을 <u>희생하여</u> 자신의 이익을 추구하지 않는 것을 확실히 하라고 말한다.

선지 해석

① at the discretion of ~의 재량대로
② at the mercy of ~에 좌우되는, ~에 휘둘리는
③ at the end of ~의 말에
④ at the expense of ~을 희생하여, ~을 잃어가며

정답 해설

빈칸 문장 앞의 모든 인간들은 행복을 똑같이 갈망한다는 내용으로 보아 빈칸에도 다른 사람의 이익을 희생하여 자신의 이익을 추구하지 말라는 내용이 되어야 하므로 빈칸에는 ④가 적절하다.

지문 어휘

☐ one another 서로서로
☐ be anxious for ~을 열망하다
☐ welfare 행복, 복지
☐ make sure 확실하게 하다

핵심 어휘

✱ at the expense of = at the cost of

50
정답 ④

지문 해석

정부가 도입한 새로운 정책은 매우 <u>논쟁의 여지가 있었으며</u>, 정치인들과 대중 사이에 격렬한 논쟁을 일으켰다.

선지 해석

① manageable 관리할 수 있는
② reconcilable 화해[조정]할 수 있는
③ augmentative 증가[확대]하는
④ controversial 논란이 많은, 논란[논쟁]의 여지가 있는

정답 해설

뒷부분에 격렬한 논쟁을 일으켰다는 내용으로 보아 새로운 정책이 논쟁이 있었다는 내용이 자연스러우므로 빈칸에는 ④가 적절하다.

지문 어휘

☐ debate 논쟁, 토론, 논의[논쟁]하다
☐ politician 정치인

핵심 어휘

✱ reconcilable = compatible, consistent, congruous, congruent

51
정답 ②

지문 해석

상속세를 피하기 위해, 그 남자는 은퇴하자마자 그의 재산의 많은 부분을 그의 외아들에게 <u>양도했다</u>.

선지 해석

① made up 화장했다, 꾸며냈다, 구성했다, 화해했다
② made over 양도했다, 고쳤다
③ made out 이해했다, 알아봤다
④ made against 불리하게 작용했다

정답 해설

상속세를 피하기 위해서라는 내용으로 미루어 보아 재산을 아들에게 양도했다는 것이 문맥상 자연스러우므로 빈칸에는 ②가 적절하다.

지문 어휘

☐ death duty 상속세
☐ property 재산, 자산
☐ retire 은퇴하다

핵심 어휘

✱ make up 구성하다 = compose, comprise, constitute

52
정답 ①

지문 해석

일상적인 말로 태블릿 PC는 컴퓨터를 조작하기 위한 터치스크린이나 스타일러스를 갖춘 석판 같은 모양을 한 이동식 컴퓨터 장치를 지칭한다. 태블릿 PC는 일반 노트북이 실용적이지 않거나 <u>다루기 힘들거나</u> 필요한 기능을 제공하지 않는 경우에 자주 사용된다.

선지 해석

① unwieldy 다루기 힘든, 부피가 큰
② inconclusive 결론에 이르지 못하는
③ exclusive 독점적인, 배타적인
④ unprecedented 전례 없는, 비길 데 없는

정답 해설

빈칸 앞의 실용적이지 않다는 말과 빈칸 뒤의 필요한 기능을 제공하지 않는다는 말로 미루어 보아 빈칸에는 ①이 적절하다.

지문 어휘

☐ refer to 언급하다, 가리키다, 지칭하다
☐ slate-shaped 석판 같은 모양을 한
☐ mobile 이동식의, 휴대용의
☐ touch screen 터치스크린(손으로 누르면 작동이 되는 컴퓨터 화면)
☐ stylus 스타일러스(특수 컴퓨터 화면에 글을 쓰거나 그림을 그리는 등의 표시를 할 때 쓰는 펜)
☐ impractical 비실용적인
☐ functionality 기능

핵심 어휘

✱ unprecedented = unsurpassed, unparalleled

53
정답 ④

지문 해석

Sarah는 너무 <u>솔직해서</u> 다른 사람의 작품을 비평할 때 종종 그들의 마음에 상처를 준다.

선지 해석

① reserved 내성적인, 과묵한, 보류된, 예약된
② wordy 말이 많은, 장황한
③ retrospective 회고[회상]하는, 소급 적용되는
④ outspoken 솔직한

정답 해설

앞부분에 작품을 비평하면서 그녀의 마음에 상처를 준다고 한 것으로 보아 비평할 때 솔직했다는 내용이 자연스러우므로 빈칸에는 ④가 적절하다.

지문 어휘

☐ frequently 자주, 종종
☐ criticize 비평하다

핵심 어휘

✱ wordy = talkative, verbose, loquacious, garrulous

54
정답 ①

지문 해석

경영진은 <u>파산할 위험에 처할 수 있는지</u> 아닌지를 알기 위해서 총부채 상환 비율을 평가해야 한다.

선지 해석

① insolvent 파산한, 지급불능의
② inverted 역의, 반대의
③ distracted (정신이) 산만해진
④ decoded 해독된

정답 해설

경영진이 총부채 상환 비율을 평가한다는 내용으로 미루어 보아 빈칸에는 ①이 적절하다.

지문 어휘

☐ executive 경영진, 임원, 간부
☐ estimate 평가하다, 추정[추산]하다
☐ ratio 비율
☐ run the risk of ~할 위험에 처하다
☐ debt-to-income 총부채 상환 비율(금융부채 상환능력을 소득으로 따져서 대출한도를 정하는 계산 비율)

핵심 어휘

✻ insolvent = broke, bankrupt

Chapter 02 지방직 9급 핵심 기출문제

ANSWER

01 ②	02 ④	03 ②	04 ②	05 ①
06 ①	07 ③	08 ②	09 ④	10 ①
11 ①	12 ④	13 ②	14 ①	15 ④
16 ③	17 ①	18 ②	19 ④	20 ②
21 ④	22 ②	23 ①	24 ①	25 ④
26 ④	27 ①	28 ①	29 ③	30 ④
31 ①	32 ④	33 ③	34 ②	35 ③
36 ②	37 ①	38 ②	39 ④	40 ④
41 ①	42 ②	43 ①	44 ②	45 ④
46 ④	47 ①	48 ②		

01

정답 ②

지문 해석

일부 식물 질병은 실제로 근절하기 어려운데 왜냐하면 그것들은 매우 빠르고 쉽게 퍼져 넓은 지역의 여러 식물에 영향을 미칠 수 있기 때문이다.

선지 해석

① nourish 영양을 주다, 키우다
② eradicate 근절하다, 박멸하다
③ proliferate 급증하다, 확산되다
④ detect 발견하다, 감지하다

정답 해설

식물 질병이 매우 빠르고 쉽게 퍼지기 때문에, 실제로 이러한 질병을 근절하기 어렵다는 문맥이 자연스러우므로 빈칸에는 ②가 적절하다.

지문 어휘

☐ indeed 실제로, 참으로, 정말로
☐ spread 퍼지다, 확산되다, 퍼뜨리다, 펼쳐지다
☐ vast 넓은, 방대한

02

정답 ④

지문 해석

비즈니스 세계에서는 시간 엄수가 매우 중요하게 여겨지는데 왜냐하면 그것이 마감 기한을 지키고 다른 사람들의 시간을 존중하려는 개인의 책무를 보여주기 때문이다.

선지 해석

① humility 겸손
② sincerity 진심, 진실, 정직
③ frugality 절약, 검소
④ punctuality 시간 엄수, 꼼꼼함

정답 해설

비즈니스 세계에서 마감 기한을 지키고 다른 사람의 시간을 존중하려는 개인의 책임감을 보여주기 때문에 중요하다는 것으로 보아, 시간의 소중함을 강조하는 문맥이 자연스러우므로 빈칸에는 ④가 적절하다.

지문 어휘

☐ highly 매우, 대단히
☐ showcase 보여주다, 전시하다
☐ commitment 책무, 헌신, 약속
☐ deadline 마감 기한

03

정답 ②

지문 해석

셰익스피어의 희극은 많은 유사점을 가지고 있지만, 그것들은 또한 서로 현저하게 다르다.

선지 해석

① softly 부드럽게
② markedly 현저하게, 뚜렷하게
③ marginally 아주 조금, 미미하게
④ indiscernibly 분간하기 어렵게

정답 해설

역접(while)의 단서로 많은 유사점을 가지고 있다는 상반된 내용이 들어가야 하므로 다르다를 수식할 수 있는 부사의 표현이 필요하므로 빈칸에는 ②가 적절하다.

지문 어휘

☐ similarity 유사점, 닮은 점

04
정답 ②

지문 해석

Jane은 진한 흑차를 부었고 그것을 우유로 희석시켰다.

선지 해석

① washed 씻었다
② diluted 희석시켰다, 약화시켰다
③ connected 연결했다, 접속했다
④ fermented 발효시켰다

정답 해설

문맥상 진한 흑차를 우유와 희석시켜서 중화했다는 내용이 자연스러우므로 빈칸에는 ②가 적절하다.

지문 어휘

□ pour out 붓다, 따르다, 쏟다

핵심 어휘

✱ dilute = water down, weaken

05
정답 ①

지문 해석

데이터 수집 중 일부 응답이 뜻하지 않게 제외되어 설문 결과가 왜곡되었다.

선지 해석

① excluded 배제했다, 제외했다
② supported 지원했다, 지지했다
③ submitted 제출했다, 진술했다, 항복했다
④ authorized 승인했다, 권한을 주었다

정답 해설

인과(because)의 단서로 설문 결과가 왜곡되었다고 하는 것으로 보아 일부 응답이 제외되었다는 내용이 자연스러우므로 빈칸에는 ①이 적절하다.

지문 어휘

□ skew 왜곡하다
□ accidentally 뜻하지 않게, 잘못하여, 우연히

핵심 어휘

✱ exclude = preclude, rule out, factor out

06
정답 ①

지문 해석

만약 당신이 우리가 깜짝 파티를 계획하고 있는 것을 드러낸다면, 아버지는 결코 당신에게 질문을 멈추지 않을 것이다.

선지 해석

① reveal 드러내다, 폭로하다, 말하다
② observe 관찰하다, 지키다, 준수하다
③ believe 믿다
④ possess 소유하다, 지니다

정답 해설

뒷부분에 아버지가 질문을 계속 한다는 것으로 보아 어떠한 사실(파티 계획)을 드러냈다는 내용이 자연스러우므로 빈칸에는 ①이 적절하다.

지문 어휘

□ question 질문, 문제, 질문하다, 의문을 갖다

핵심 어휘

✱ reveal
= let on, divulge, expose, reveal, disclose, uncover, betray

07
정답 ③

지문 해석

슈퍼마켓의 자동문은 봉투나 쇼핑 카트를 가지고 있는 고객의 출입을 용이하게 한다.

선지 해석

① ignore 무시하다
② forgive 용서하다
③ facilitate 용이하게[가능하게] 하다, 촉진[조장]하다
④ exaggerate 과장하다

정답 해설

문맥상 슈퍼마켓의 자동문이 있어서 손을 못 쓰는 상황에서 고객들이 출입하는 데 도움이 되고 있다는 내용이 자연스러우므로 빈칸에는 ③이 적절하다.

지문 어휘

□ entry and exit 출입

핵심 어휘

✱ facilitate = expedite, accelerate, precipitate

08
정답 ②

지문 해석

첫 번째 실험의 실패 후, 팀은 조정을 하고 그 다음의 실험에서 성공을 거두었다.

선지 해석

① required 필수의
② subsequent 그 다음의, 이후의
③ advanced 선진의, 진보적인, 고급의
④ gratuitous 불필요한, 쓸데없는

정답 해설

실패한 첫 번째 실험이 끝나고 조정을 거친 후에 성공을 했다라는 내용으로 보아 그 다음의 실험에서 성공을 했다는 내용이 자연스러우므로 빈칸에는 ②가 적절하다.

지문 어휘

□ failure 실패
□ adjustment 조정, 수정, 적응

핵심 어휘

✱ supplementary = additional, extra
✱ subsequent = following, ensuing, succeeding, successive

09   정답 ④

지문 해석
풍속은 한 집단의 구성원들이 다른 사람들에게 공손함을 보이기 위해 따를 것이라고 기대되는 관습이다. 예를 들어, 당신이 재채기할 때 "실례합니다"라고 말하는 것은 미국의 풍속이다.

선지 해석
① charity 자선, 구호 단체
② humility 겸손
③ boldness 대담함, 무모함
④ courtesy 공손[정중]함, 우아[고상]함

정답 해설
예시(for example)의 단서로 재채기 하기 전에 "실례합니다"라고 말하는 것이 풍속이라고 하고 있으므로 다른 사람들에게 예의를 표한다는 내용이 자연스러우므로 빈칸에는 ④가 적절하다.

지문 어휘
☐ folkway 풍습, 사회적 관행
☐ custom 관습, 풍습
☐ sneeze 재채기하다

핵심 어휘
✱ humility = modesty

10   정답 ①

지문 해석
이 아이들은 건강에 좋은 음식을 주식으로 하여 길러져 왔다.

선지 해석
① raised 길렀다, 자랐다, 일으켰다
② advised 권고했다
③ observed 관찰했다, 준수했다
④ dumped 버렸다

정답 해설
문맥상 건강한 음식을 먹으면서 자랐다는 내용이 자연스러우므로 빈칸에는 ①이 적절하다.

지문 어휘
☐ on a diet of ~을 주식으로
☐ healthy 건강한, 건강에 좋은

핵심 어휘
✱ observe 준수하다
  = obey, abide by, stick to, cling to, adhere to, conform to

11   정답 ①

지문 해석
회사는 엄격한 복장 규정을 폐지하기로 선택했고, 직원들이 더 캐주얼하게 옷을 입을 수 있도록 허용했다.

선지 해석
① abolish 폐지하다
② consent 동의하다, 승낙하다, 동의, 일치
③ criticize 비난하다, 책망하다
④ justify 정당화하다

정답 해설
뒷부분에 복장을 더 자유롭게 입을 수 있도록 허용했다고 하는 것으로 보아 엄격한 복장 규정은 없어졌다는 내용이 자연스러우므로 빈칸에는 ①이 적절하다.

지문 어휘
☐ strict 엄격한, 엄한
☐ employee 직원, 종업원, 고용인

핵심 어휘
✱ consent = agree, aseent
✱ criticize
  = condemn, blame, denounce, rebuke, reprimand, reproach

12   정답 ④

지문 해석
유권자들은 그들이 그것을 더 분명히 보고 이해할 수 있도록 선거 과정에서 투명성이 있어야 한다고 요구했다.

선지 해석
① deception 속임, 기만, 사기
② flexibility 유연성, 적응성, 융통성
③ competition 경쟁, 경기
④ transparency 투명성

정답 해설
문맥상 더 분명히 보고 이해할 수 있기 위해서는 투명성이 필요하므로 빈칸에는 ④가 적절하다.

지문 어휘
☐ voter 유권자, 투표자
☐ election 선거

핵심 어휘
✱ deception = deceit, trickery, fraud
✱ flexibility = pliability

13   정답 ②

지문 해석
신임 관리자는 적응력이 뛰어나 회사 문화에 빠르게 적응하고, 여러 도전을 극복하며 팀을 이끌었다.

선지 해석
① strong 강한
② adaptable 적응할 수 있는, 융통성 있는
③ honest 정직한, 솔직한
④ passionate 열정적인

정답 해설

신임 관리자가 적응력이 뛰어나 여러 도전을 극복하며 팀을 이끌었다는 점에서, 회사 문화에 빠르게 적응했다는 내용이 자연스러우므로 빈칸에는 ②가 적절하다.

지문 어휘
☐ adjust 적응하다, 조정[조절]하다

핵심 어휘
✦ strong = sturdy, robust

14
정답 ①

지문 해석
농작물 수확량은 달라지며, 일부 지역에서는 향상되고 다른 지역에서는 감소한다.

선지 해석
① vary 다르다, 변하다, 변화를 주다
② decline 줄어들다, 감소하다, 거절하다
③ expand 확장하다, 팽창하다
④ include 포함하다

정답 해설
뒷부분에 일부 지역에서는 향상되고 또 다른 지역에서는 감소한다는 내용으로 보아 수확량은 조금씩 다르다는 내용이 자연스러우므로 빈칸에는 ①이 적절하다.

지문 어휘
☐ crop 농작물

핵심 어휘
✦ decline = refuse, reject, turn down, brush aside

15
정답 ④

지문 해석
다른 사람들을 돕는 데서 얻은 만족감은 그가 벌 수 있었던 금전적 보상보다 훨씬 컸다.

선지 해석
① liveliness 원기, 활기
② confidence 자신감
③ tranquility 고요, 평온, 침착
④ gratification 만족(감)

정답 해설
문맥상 다른 사람들을 돕는 것이 금전적 보상보다 크다고 한 것으로 보아 사람들을 도우면서 얻는 만족감이 있다는 내용이 자연스러우므로 빈칸에는 ④가 적절하다.

지문 어휘
☐ financial reward 금전적[재정적] 보상
☐ earn 벌다, 얻다

핵심 어휘
✦ liveliness = energy, vigor, vitality

16
정답 ③

지문 해석
세계화는 더 많은 국가들이 그들의 시장을 개방하도록 이끌며, 그들이 더 큰 효율성의 더 낮은 비용으로 상품과 서비스를 자유롭게 거래할 수 있게 한다.

선지 해석
① extinction 멸종, 소화(消火)
② depression 우울함, 불경기
③ efficiency 효율(성), 능률
④ caution 조심, 주의, 경고

정답 해설
문맥상 세계화의 긍정적인 영향에 관한 내용이므로 빈칸에는 ③이 적절하다.

지문 어휘
☐ globalization 세계화
☐ goods 상품
☐ trade 거래[교역/무역]하다

핵심 어휘
✦ extinction 멸종 = extermination, annihilation

17
정답 ①

지문 해석
우리는 번아웃의 대가에 익숙하다: 에너지, 동기, 생산성, 참여 그리고 헌신이 직장과 가정에서 모두 타격을 입을 수 있다. 그리고 많은 해결책은 상당히 직관적이다: 정기적으로 플러그를 뽑아라. 불필요한 회의를 줄여라. 운동해라. 낮 동안 짧은 휴식 시간을 잡아라. 당신이 이따금씩 멀리 떠날 여유가 없기 때문에, 당신이 생각하기로 당신이 일에서 벗어날 여유가 없다고 하더라도 휴가를 내라.

선지 해석
① fixes 해결책
② damages 손해 배상금
③ prizes 상
④ complications 문제, 합병증

정답 해설
뒷부분에 번아웃을 예방할 수 있는 예시들이 나오므로 빈칸에는 ①이 적절하다.

지문 어휘
☐ burnout 번아웃, 극도의 피로
☐ engagement 참여, 개입
☐ take a hit 타격을 입다
☐ intuitive 직관적인
☐ afford ~할 여유가 있다
☐ now and then 가끔, 때때로

핵심 어휘
✦ complication 문제 = problem, issue

18
정답 ②

지문 해석

정부는 새로운 세금 정산 제도에서 발생하는 증가되는 세금 부담에 대해 봉급생활자들을 달래기 위한 방법을 찾고 있다. 지난 월요일 대통령의 보좌관들과의 회의 동안, 대통령은 참석한 사람들에게 더 많은 대중과의 소통의 창구를 열 것을 <u>요구했다</u>.

선지 해석

① accounted 설명했다, 차지했다
② called 요구했다
③ compensated 보상했다, 보충했다
④ applied 지원했다, 신청했다

정답 해설

정부가 봉급생활자들을 달래기 위한 방안을 찾고 있다는 내용을 미루어 보아 대통령이 더 많은 소통 채널을 개설할 것을 요구한 것이 문맥상 자연스러우므로 빈칸에는 ②가 적절하다.

지문 어휘

☐ government 정부
☐ seek 찾다, 추구하다
☐ soothe 달래다, 완화시키다, 진정시키다
☐ burden 부담, 짐
☐ tax settlement 세금 정산
☐ presidential 대통령의
☐ aide 보좌관
☐ present 출석한, 현재의

핵심 어휘

✷ call for = require, request, demand

19
정답 ④

지문 해석

수학으로 고심하는 한 학생은 복잡한 수학 개념을 <u>이해하는</u> 데 시간을 좀 걸렸다.

선지 해석

① encompass 포함하다, 에워싸다
② intrude 침입하다, 끼어들다, 방해하다
③ inspect 점검하다, 조사하다
④ apprehend 이해하다, 체포하다, 염려하다

정답 해설

문맥상 수학 때문에 고심하고 있다는 것으로 보아 복잡한 개념을 이해하는 데 시간이 걸렸다는 내용이 자연스러우므로 빈칸에는 ④가 적절하다.

지문 어휘

☐ struggle with ~로 고심하다

핵심 어휘

✷ encompass 포함하다 = include, involve
       에워싸다 = surround, enclose
✷ intrude = encroach, invade, trespass

20
정답 ②

지문 해석

플라스틱 병의 문제는 그것들이 <u>단열되지</u> 않는다는 것이고 그래서 온도가 상승하기 시작하면, 당신의 물도 뜨거워질 것이다.

선지 해석

① sanitary 위생의
② insulated 단열된
③ recyclable 재활용할 수 있는
④ waterproof 방수의

정답 해설

온도가 올라가기 시작하면 물도 뜨거워진다는 내용을 미루어보아 빈칸에는 ②가 적절하다.

지문 어휘

☐ bottle 병
☐ temperature 온도
☐ heat up 뜨거워지다, 데우다

핵심 어휘

✷ sanitary = hygienic

21
정답 ④

지문 해석

새로운 녹지 공간은 도시의 열섬 현상의 영향을 <u>완화하기</u> 위해 설계되었다.

선지 해석

① compromise 타협하다, 굽히다[양보하다], ~을 위태롭게 하다
② accelerate 가속화하다, 속도를 높이다
③ calculate 계산하다, 산출하다
④ alleviate 완화시키다, 경감하다

정답 해설

문맥상 녹지 공간은 도시의 열섬 현상의 영향을 줄이는 데 도움이 된다는 내용이 자연스러우므로 빈칸에는 ④가 적절하다.

지문 어휘

☐ green space 녹지 공간
☐ heat island 열섬

핵심 어휘

✷ alleviate
  = reduce, ease, relieve, soothe, allay, assuage, pacify, placate, mitigate, mollify

22
정답 ②

지문 해석

그 잔인한 장면들은 그렇지 않았더라면 그녀의 마음속에 떠오르지 않았을 생각들을 <u>유발했다</u>.

선지 해석
① gave off (냄새, 열, 빛 등을) 냈다, 발했다
② touched off 촉발했다, 유발했다
③ made off 급히 떠났다[달아났다]
④ cut off 잘라냈다, 차단했다, 중단했다

정답 해설
문맥상 생각하지도 않았던 생각들이 잔인한 장면들 때문에 생겼다는 내용이 자연스러우므로 빈칸에는 ②가 적절하다.

지문 어휘
☐ cruel 잔인한, 혹독한
☐ sight 장면, 광경, 시력, 시야
☐ otherwise (만약) 그렇지 않으면[않았다면]

핵심 어휘
✱ touch off = cause, trigger, bring about, lead to, give rise to

23 정답 ①

지문 해석
조심성이 많은 사람들은 조금이라도 위험한 행동은 피하는 경향이 있다.

선지 해석
① shun 피하다
② warn 경고하다
③ punish 처벌하다
④ imitate 모방하다, 흉내 내다

정답 해설
문맥상 조심성 많은 사람들은 위험한 행동을 하지 않는다는 내용이 자연스러우므로 빈칸에는 ①이 적절하다.

지문 어휘
☐ caution 조심, 경고, 주의를 주다

핵심 어휘
✱ shun
  = avoid, avert, evade, eschew, dodge, stave off, head off, ward off, steer clear of

24 정답 ①

지문 해석
고고학자들은 연구하기 위해 암석에 박힌 화석을 조심스럽게 발굴하려고 특수 도구를 사용했다.

선지 해석
① excavate 발굴하다, 파다
② pack (짐을) 싸다, 포장하다
③ erase 지우다
④ celebrate 축하하다

정답 해설
문맥상 연구를 하기 위해 특수 도구를 사용하여 화석을 발굴한다는 내용이 자연스러우므로 빈칸에는 ①이 적절하다.

지문 어휘
☐ archaeologist 고고학자
☐ embed 박다, 끼워 넣다, 파견하다

핵심 어휘
✱ excavate = exhume, unearth, burrow, dig up, dig out
✱ erase
  = delete, remove, obliterate, efface, expunge, eliminate, wipe out, cross out, scratch out

25 정답 ④

지문 해석
새로운 약물이 그녀의 증상을 더 관리할 수 있게 도와주어, 그녀가 일상 활동을 재개할 수 있게 되었다.

선지 해석
① utter 완전한, 순전한, 소리를 내다, 말을 하다
② scary 무서운, 겁많은
③ occasional 가끔의, 때때로의
④ manageable 관리할 수 있는

정답 해설
뒷 부분에 일상 활동을 재개했다는 것으로 보아 그녀의 증상을 약물을 통해 관리할 수 있다는 내용이 자연스러우므로 빈칸에는 ④가 적절하다.

지문 어휘
☐ medication 약[약물]
☐ symptom 증상, 징후, 조짐
☐ resume 재개하다, 다시 시작하다

핵심 어휘
✱ utter = sheer, pure, downright

26 정답 ④

지문 해석
지루한 오후 수업 동안 시간은 아주 조금씩 천천히 흐르는 것처럼 느껴지고 뇌가 매우 재밌는 어떤 것에 몰두할 때는 쏜살같이 간다.

선지 해석
① be engaged in ~을 하다, ~에 종사하다
② be stuck in ~에 꼼짝 못하게 되다
③ be located in ~에 위치하다
④ be engrossed in ~에 몰두하다, 열중하다

정답 해설
지루한 것을 할 때는 시간이 느리게 간다는 내용과 대조적으로 재밌는 것에 집중할 때는 시간이 빠르게 흘러간다는 내용이 자연스러우므로 빈칸에는 ④가 적절하다.

지문 어휘
☐ slow to a trickle 아주 조금씩 천천히 흐르다
☐ race 쏜살같이 가다
☐ entertaining 재미있는
☐ apathetic 냉담한, 무관심한
☐ stabilize 안정[고정]시키다

핵심 어휘

✱ be engrossed in
= be preoccupied with, be absorbed in, be immersed in, be up to one's eyes in

27

정답 ①

지문 해석

오리엔테이션 동안, 신입 직원들은 사무실 배치를 숙지하기 위해 회사의 내부 영상을 시청했다.

선지 해석

① acquaint 익히다, 숙지하다
② inspire 고무하다, 영감을 주다
③ endow 부여하다, 주다
④ avoid 피하다

정답 해설

문맥상 처음 온 신입 직원들에게 사무실 배치를 숙지시켜주기 위해 사무실 배치 영상을 보여 주었다는 내용이 자연스러우므로 빈칸에는 ①이 적절하다.

지문 어휘

☐ internal 내부의, 체내의
☐ layout (책·정원·건물 등의) 배치

핵심 어휘

✱ inspire = stimulate, motivate

28

정답 ①

지문 해석

내과 의사의 가장 중요한 의무는 어떠한 해로움도 끼치지 않는 것이다. 그 밖의 모든 것은 — 심지어 치료조차도 — 2순위이어야 한다.

선지 해석

① paramount 가장 중요한, 최고의
② sworn 맹세한, 욕을 한
③ successful 성공한, 성공적인
④ mysterious 신비한, 이해하기 힘든

정답 해설

뒷부분에 2순위라는 표현이 나온 것으로 보아 앞 부분에는 가장 중요한 의무에 대한 내용이 자연스러우므로 빈칸에는 ①이 적절하다.

지문 어휘

☐ duty 책임, 의무, 책무
☐ physician 내과 의사
☐ do(be)no harm 아무런 해가 되지 않다, 아무런 손해를 입히지 않다

핵심 어휘

✱ paramount = chief, supreme, prime, principal, foremost

29

정답 ③

지문 해석

마라톤을 완주한 후, 그녀는 완전히 지쳐서 거의 서 있을 수조차 없었다.

선지 해석

① ambitious 대망을 품은, 야심[야망]을 가진
② afraid 두려워하는, 겁내는, 걱정하는
③ exhausted 지친, 기진맥진한, 고갈된
④ inherent 내재하는, 본래의, 타고난

정답 해설

문맥상 마라톤을 완주하고 거의 서 있을 수조차 없다고 하는 것으로 보아 그녀는 완전히 지쳤다는 내용이 자연스러우므로 빈칸에는 ③이 적절하다.

지문 어휘

☐ complete 완료하다, 끝마치다, 완벽한, 완전한
☐ stand 서다, 일어서다, 태도, 저항

핵심 어휘

✱ exhausted = weary

30

정답 ④

지문 해석

최신의 접근법이 위협적이라고 생각하는 학생은 오래된 방법으로 배웠을지도 모르는 학생들보다 더 적게 배운다.

선지 해석

① humorous 재미있는, 유머러스한
② friendly 친절한, 상냥한
③ convenient 편리한, 간편한
④ intimidating 위협적인, 겁을 주는

정답 해설

비교(less than)의 단서로 오래된 방법보다 최신의 접근법에서 더 적게 배운다고 한 것으로 보아 오래된 방법보다는 최신의 접근법이 더 부정적이라는 내용이 자연스러우므로 빈칸에는 ④가 적절하다.

지문 어휘

☐ state-of-the-art 최신의
☐ approach 접근(법)
☐ might have pp ~했을지도 모른다

핵심 어휘

✱ frightening = scary, terrifying, alarming
✱ friendly = amiable, affable, genial, congenial, cordial

31

정답 ①

지문 해석

우리의 메인 요리는 맛이 별로 없었지만, 내가 조미료를 더해 그 요리를 더 맛있게 만들었다.

선지 해석
① palatable 맛이 좋은, 입에 맞는
② dissolvable 분해할 수 있는
③ potable 마셔도 되는, 음료로 적합한
④ susceptible 민감한, ~의 영향을 받기 쉬운

정답 해설
역접(but)의 단서로 빈칸 앞에 '별로 맛이 없다'라는 내용과 반대의 의미가 필요하므로 빈칸에는 ①이 적절하다.

지문 어휘
□ lavor 맛, 풍미
□ condiment 조미료

핵심 어휘
★ potable = drinkable

32 정답 ④

지문 해석
그 두 문화는 완전히 달랐기 때문에 그녀는 한 문화에서 다른 문화로 적응하는 것이 어렵다는 것을 알았다.

선지 해석
① overlapped 겹치는
② equivalent 동등한, 상응하는
③ associative 연합의, 조합하는
④ disparate 다른, 이질적인

정답 해설
'so 형용사/부사 that절' 구문에서 결과인 that절 내용을 미루어 보아 원인의 내용에도 부정적인 내용이 필요하므로 빈칸에는 ④가 적절하다.

지문 어휘
□ utterly 아주, 전혀, 완전히
□ adapt 적응시키다, 순응하다, 개조하다

핵심 어휘
★ disparate = different, dissimilar, unlike, heterogeneous

33 정답 ③

지문 해석
페니실린은 그것에 알레르기가 있는 사람에게는 부정적인 효과를 줄 수 있다.

선지 해석
① affirmative 긍정적인, 확언적인
② aloof 냉담한, 무관심한
③ adverse 해로운, 부정적인, 불리한
④ allusive 암시적인

정답 해설
빈칸 뒤에 '그것에 알레르기가 있다'는 내용을 미루어 볼 때 빈칸에는 ③이 적절하다.

지문 어휘
□ penicillin 페니실린
□ allergic 알레르기(체질)의

핵심 어휘
★ adverse
= harmful, unfavorable, detrimental, deleterious, pernicious

34 정답 ③

지문 해석
지난해 나는 그 극장에서 예술 행사를 무대에 올리는 데 책임이 있는 스태프들과 이 공연을 할 수 있는 좋은 기회가 있었다.

선지 해석
① turning into ~로 바뀌는
② doing without ~없이 지내는
③ putting on 무대에 올리는
④ giving up 포기하는

정답 해설
목적어로 art event(예술 행사)가 있으므로 문맥상 예술 행사를 무대에 올리는 것이 자연스러우므로 빈칸에는 ③이 적절하다.

지문 어휘
□ opportunity 기회
□ performance 공연, 수행
□ responsible for ~에 책임이 있는

핵심 어휘
★ turn into = convert into, transform into

35 정답 ③

지문 해석
· 그 심리학자는 학생들의 종합적인 성격 발달을 설명하기 위해서 새로운 테스트를 사용했다.
· 간식은 청소년들의 하루 에너지 섭취량의 25~30%를 차지한다.

선지 해석
① stand for 상징하다, 나타내다, 옹호하다
② allow for 고려하다
③ account for 설명하다, 차지하다
④ apologize for ~에 대해 사과하다

정답 해설
해석상 두 가지 빈칸에 '설명하다, 차지하다'의 내용이 자연스러우므로 빈칸에는 ③이 적절하다.

지문 어휘
□ psychologist 심리학자
□ overall 종합적인, 전반적인
□ personality 개성, 성격
□ intake 섭취(량)

핵심 어휘
★ account for 설명하다 = explain
　　　　　　　차지하다 = take up, occupy

36

정답 ②

지문 해석

사생활 보호를 위해 보고서에서 개인 정보를 제외해야 한다.

선지 해석

① trace 따라가다, 추적하다
② exclude 배제하다, 제외하다
③ instruct 지시하다, 가르치다
④ examine 조사[검토]하다, 진찰하다, 시험하다

정답 해설

문맥상 사생활 보호를 하기 위해서는 개인 정보를 빼야 한다는 내용이 자연스러우므로 빈칸에는 ②가 적절하다.

지문 어휘

☐ protect 보호하다, 지키다
☐ privacy 사생활

핵심 어휘

✱ exclude = preclude, rule out, factor out
✱ trace = track down

37

정답 ①

지문 해석

정부는 시민들의 경제적 압박을 완화하기 위해 세금 감면을 도입했다.

선지 해석

① relieve 완화하다, 줄이다, 덜어 주다
② accumulate 모으다, 축적하다
③ provoke 화나게 하다, 유발하다, 선동하다
④ accelerate 가속화하다, 속도를 높이다

정답 해설

문맥상 정부가 세금 감면을 도입했다는 것으로 보아 시민들의 경제적 압박을 줄이고자 하는 내용이 자연스러우므로 빈칸에는 ①이 적절하다.

지문 어휘

☐ tax cut 세금 감면, 감세
☐ pressure 압박, 압력

핵심 어휘

✱ relieve
 = alleviate, reduce, ease, soothe, allay, assuage, pacify, placate, mitigate, mollify

38

정답 ②

지문 해석

그녀는 항상 절약하면서, 불필요한 물건에 돈을 쓰기보다는 저축하는 것을 선택했다.

선지 해석

① stray 길 잃은, 길을 잃다
② thrifty 절약[검약]하는
③ wealthy 부유한
④ stingy (특히 돈에 대해) 인색한

정답 해설

문맥상 불필요한 물건을 사기보다는 저축한다는 것으로 보아 그녀는 절약한다는 내용이 자연스러우므로 빈칸에는 ②가 적절하다.

지문 어휘

☐ unnecessary 불필요한, 쓸데없는

핵심 어휘

✱ wealthy
 = rich, affluent, opulent, luxurious, prosperous, well-to-do, made of money
✱ thrifty = frugal, economical

39

정답 ④

지문 해석

강요하려 드는 부모들은 자녀들이 모든 활동에 참여하도록 강요하여, 그들에게 선택의 자유를 주지 않았다.

선지 해석

① thrilled 흥분한, 감격한
② brave 용감한
③ timid 소심한, 용기가 없는
④ pushy 지나치게 밀어붙이는, 강요하려 드는

정답 해설

뒷부분에 자녀들에게 선택의 자유를 주지 않았다는 것으로 보아 부모가 강압적이고 강요한다는 내용이 자연스러우므로 빈칸에는 ④가 적절하다.

지문 어휘

☐ force ~를 강요하다, 억지[강제]로 ~하다, 힘

핵심 어휘

✱ brave
 = courageous, plucky, intrepid, bold, fearless, daring, audacious, valiant, gallant, confident, undaunted, dauntless, unflinching

40

정답 ④

지문 해석

그 회사는 이익에 대한 만족할 줄 모르는 탐욕 때문에 종종 과장된 마케팅 전략을 시도한다.

선지 해석

① infallible 절대 틀리지[실수하지] 않는
② aesthetic 심미적인, 미학의, 미적인
③ adolescent 사춘[청년]기의, 청춘의
④ insatiable 채울[만족시킬] 수 없는, 만족할 줄 모르는

정답 해설

앞부분에 과장된 마케팅 전략을 시도한다는 것으로 보아 지금의 이익에 만족하지를 못한다는 내용이 자연스러우므로 빈칸에는 ④가 적절하다.

지문 어휘
- exaggerated 과장된, 지나친
- greed 탐욕, 욕심

핵심 어휘
✱ adolescent = juvenile, teenager

41
정답 ①

지문 해석

만약 당신이 내성적인 사람이라면, 당신은 자신의 감정을 숨기는 경향이 있고 다른 사람들에게 당신이 실제로 무엇을 생각하는지 드러내는 것을 좋아하지 않는다.

선지 해석
① reserved 내성적인, 말이 없는
② loquacious 말이 많은, 수다스러운
③ eloquent 웅변의, 유창한
④ analogous 유사한

정답 해설

빈칸 뒤에 자신의 감정을 숨기고, 생각을 드러내는 것을 좋아하지 않는다고 했으므로 빈칸에는 ①이 적절하다.

지문 어휘
- feeling 감정
- hidden 숨은, 숨겨진
- show 드러내다, 보여주다

핵심 어휘
✱ reserved = uncommunicative, mute, taciturn, reticent

42
정답 ②

지문 해석

공식 회의에 앞서 의제를 마무리하기 위해 예비 회의가 선행될 것이다.

선지 해석
① pacify 달래다, 진정시키다
② precede ~에 앞서다, 선행하다, 우선하다
③ presume 추정하다, 간주하다
④ provoke 화나게 하다, 유발하다, 선동하다

정답 해설

문맥상 공식 회의 전에 의제를 마무리하기 위해 그 전에 예비 회의를 진행한다는 내용이 자연스러우므로 빈칸에는 ②가 적절하다.

지문 어휘
- preliminary 예비의
- conference 회의, 학회, 회담
- finalize 마무리짓다

핵심 어휘
✱ provoke 화나게 하다 = irritate, infuriate, incense, enrage

43
정답 ①

지문 해석

요즘은 모든 거리 혹은 모든 가게가 나이가 8세에서 80세에 이르는 휴대 전화 사용자로 가득차 있다. 하지만 우리가 빠르게 발전하는 기술을 고려한다면, 조만간 대체 장비가 휴대 전화기를 대신해서 그것을 쓸모없는 물건으로 만들지도 모른다.

선지 해석
① obsolete 쓸모없는, 구식의
② extensive 넓은, 광범위한
③ prevalent 널리 퍼져 있는, 유행하는
④ competent 유능한, 적임의

정답 해설

문맥상 대체 장비가 휴대 전화기를 대신한다는 말을 미루어 보아 빈칸에는 ①이 적절하다.

지문 어휘
- be filled with ~로 가득하다
- range from A to B A에서 B에 이르다
- apparatus 장치, 기계, 기구

핵심 어휘
✱ obsolete
  = outdated, outmoded, old-fashioned, out of fashion, out of date

44
정답 ②

지문 해석

우성의 유전자는 사람이 유전자를 한쪽 부모로부터 받든, 양쪽 부모로부터 받든지와 상관없이 하나의 특정한 형질을 만들어내는 유전자이다.

선지 해석
① offensive 모욕적인, 불쾌한, 공격적인
② dominant 우성의, 우세한, 지배적인
③ proficient 능숙한, 숙달된
④ turbulent 사나운, 소란스러운

정답 해설

빈칸 뒤에 나온 한쪽 부모 유전자든 양쪽 부모 유전자든 상관없이 특정한 형질을 만들어 낸다는 내용으로 미루어 볼 때 빈칸에는 ②가 적절하다.

지문 어휘
- gene 유전자
- regardless of ~와는 상관없이

핵심 어휘
✱ turbulent = wild, violent, vehement

45
정답 ④

지문 해석
그녀는 열띤 토론 중에도 뛰어난 절제력을 발휘하며 항상 침착하고 차분하게 행동했다.

선지 해석
① concern 관계, 관심, 걱정, 우려
② anguish (극심한) 괴로움, 비통
③ solicitude 불안, 염려, 의혹
④ temperance 절제, 자제, 금주

정답 해설
열띤 토론이 진행되는 동안에도 항상 침착하고 차분하게 행동했다는 점에서 그녀가 뛰어난 절제력을 지녔다는 내용이 자연스러우므로 빈칸에는 ④가 적절하다.

지문 어휘
☐ heated 열띤, 열을 올리는
☐ composed 차분한, 침착한

핵심 어휘
✱ anguish = agony, pain, torment

46
정답 ④

지문 해석
그 내부 고발자는 부패를 폭로한 것에 대한 잠재적인 보복으로부터 자신을 보호하기 위해 익명성을 선택했다.

선지 해석
① hospitality 환대, 후한 대접
② sightseeing 관광
③ disrespect 무례, 결례
④ anonymity 익명(성), 무명

정답 해설
부패를 폭로한 것에 대한 보복으로부터 내부 고발자 자신을 보호한다는 점에서, 내부 고발자가 폭로할 당시 익명성을 선택했다는 내용이 자연스러우므로 빈칸에는 ④가 적절하다.

지문 어휘
☐ whistle-blower 내부 고발자
☐ retaliation 보복, 앙갚음
☐ corruption 부패, 타락

핵심 어휘
✱ disrespect = contempt, disregard, disdain
✱ anonymity = namelessness

47
정답 ①

지문 해석
그 기념물은 역사적 가치를 보존하고 후손에게 계속 보여주기 위해 복원되고 영구히 보호하기로 결정되었다.

선지 해석
① permanently 영구히, 불변으로
② temporarily 일시적으로, 임시로
③ comparatively 비교적, 비교하여
④ tentatively 시험[실험]적으로, 망설이며

정답 해설
문맥상 기념물을 후손에게 계속 보여주기 위해서 복원하여 영구히 보호하기로 했다는 내용이 자연스러우므로 빈칸에는 ①이 적절하다.

지문 어휘
☐ monument 기념물, 역사적인 건축물
☐ preserve 보존하다, 보호하다, 지키다
☐ future generation 후손, 미래 세대

핵심 어휘
✱ permanently
= for good, everlastingly, endlessly, eternally, forever

48
정답 ②

지문 해석
패스트푸드 체인점들은 미국에서 큰 성공을 거두고 있다. 그 매력 중 하나는 예측 가능성이다. 주요 햄버거나 치킨 체인점에서, 사람들은 어디에서 구입을 하든 그 음식 맛이 어떠할지 안다는 것이다.

선지 해석
① profitability 수익성
② predictability 예측 가능성
③ feasibility (실행) 가능성
④ sustainability 지속 가능성

정답 해설
문맥상 사람들은 그들이 무엇을 사든지 간에 그 음식이 어떤 맛이 날지 안다고 하였으므로 빈칸에는 ②가 적절하다.

지문 어휘
☐ major 주요한, 중요한
☐ franchise 체인점, 가맹점

Chapter 03 — 2025년 출제 기조 전환 예시 문제

ANSWER

01 ③   02 ②   03 ①   04 ②

01 　　　　　　　　　　　　　　　　　정답 ③

지문 해석

큰 벽화를 전시하기 위해, 박물관 큐레이터들은 <u>충분한</u> 공간을 확인해야 했다.

선지 해석

① cozy 편안한, 아늑한, 기분 좋은
② stuffy 답답한, 통풍이 되지 않는
③ ample 충분한, 풍만한
④ cramped 비좁은, 갑갑한

정답 해설

대형 벽화를 전시하기 위해서는 충분한 공간이 필요하다는 문맥이 자연스러우므로 빈칸에는 ③이 적절하다.

지문 어휘

☐ exhibit 전시하다, 보이다, 전시(품)
☐ mural 벽화

02 　　　　　　　　　　　　　　　　　정답 ②

지문 해석

해결해야 할 문제가 많음에도 불구하고, 우리 시민들의 안전이 <u>우선순위</u>임을 강조하고 싶다.

선지 해석

① secret 비밀, 비결, 비밀의
② priority 우선 순위, 우선 사항
③ solution 해결(책), 해법, 용액
④ opportunity 기회

정답 해설

시민의 안전이 가장 중요한 문제라는 문맥이 자연스러우므로 빈칸에는 ②가 적절하다.

지문 어휘

☐ solve 해결하다, 풀다
☐ emphasize 강조하다, 역설하다
☐ citizen 시민, 주민

03 　　　　　　　　　　　　　　　　　정답 ①

지문 해석

최근, 종종 "이상 기후"라고 불리는 점점 더 <u>불규칙해지는</u> 날씨 패턴이 전 세계에서 관찰되고 있다.

선지 해석

① irregular 불규칙한, 고르지 못한
② consistent 일관된, ~와 일치하는
③ predictable 예측[예견]할 수 있는
④ ineffective 효과 없는, 쓸모없는

정답 해설

문맥에 있는 'abnormal(이상한, 비정상적인)'을 통해 날씨 패턴이 정상적이지 못하다는 내용이 자연스러우므로 빈칸에는 ①이 적절하다.

지문 어휘

☐ refer to A as B A를 B라고 부르다
☐ abnormal 이상한, 비정상적인

핵심 어휘

★ irregular 고르지 못한 = uneven

04 　　　　　　　　　　　　　　　　　정답 ②

지문 해석

대부분의 경제 이론은 사람들이 <u>이성적으로</u> 행동한다고 가정하지만, 이것은 그들이 종종 감정에 의존한다는 사실을 설명하지 못한다.

선지 해석

① temporary 임시의, 일시적인
② rational 이성적인, 합리적인
③ voluntary 자발적인
④ commercial 상업의, 상업적인

정답 해설

역접(instead)의 단서로 'emotion(감정, 정서)'과 상반된 의미가 자연스러우므로 빈칸에는 ②가 적절하다.

지문 어휘

☐ assume 가정하다, 추정하다, 맡다
☐ account for 설명하다, 차지하다
☐ emotion 감정, 정서

PART 02 생활영어

Chapter 01 국가직 및 지방직 최신 4개년 핵심 기출문제

ANSWER
01 ①   02 ②   03 ①   04 ②   05 ②
06 ④   07 ③   08 ④   09 ④   10 ②
11 ②   12 ④   13 ③   14 ③   15 ④

01 〈정답 ①〉

지문 해석

Alex Brown: 안녕하세요. 오늘 오후에 시청 직원들과 회의 있는 거 기억하시나요?
Cathy Miller: 오늘인가요? 내일 아니었어요?
Alex Brown: 달력을 확인해볼게요. 죄송해요, 제가 잘못 알았네요. 회의는 내일 오후 2시예요.
Cathy Miller: 네, 맞아요.
Alex Brown: 시청까지 가지 않아도 회의할 수 있다는 거 알고 계시죠?
Cathy Miller: <u>네, 화상 회의예요.</u> 그게 때로는 더 편리하더라고요.
Alex Brown: 저도 동의해요. 회의 링크 좀 공유해 주세요. 그리고 ID랑 비밀번호도 같이 보내주실 수 있을까요?
Cathy Miller: 네, 이메일이랑 문자로 보내드릴게요.

선지 해석
① 네, 화상 회의예요
② 네, 이메일에 꼭 답장하세요
③ 아니요, 문자 메시지를 받지 못했어요
④ 아니요, 오늘 다른 회의는 없어요

정답 해설
Brown이 회의 날짜를 착각한 상황에서, 시청까지 직접 가지 않아도 회의에 참석할 수 있다는 점을 Miller에게 물어본다. Miller는 이에 대해 대답하며, 때로는 그 방법이 더 편리하다고 말한다. Brown도 이에 동의하며, 화상 회의에 참석할 수 있는 온라인 링크를 공유해 달라고 요청한다. 이러한 문맥으로 보아 이번 회의는 온라인으로 진행되고 있음을 알 수 있다. 따라서 밑줄 친 부분에 들어갈 말로 가장 적절한 것은 ①이다.

지문 어휘
☐ cityhall 시청
☐ mistaken 잘못 알고 있는
☐ convenient 편리한, 간편한
☐ online meeting 화상 회의

02 〈정답 ②〉

지문 해석

A: 점심 안 먹을 거야?
B: 아니, 배 안 고파. 차라리 책을 읽고 싶어. 'The Lucky Club'을 읽고 있어.
A: 'The Lucky Club'은 무슨 내용이야?
B: 음, 로스앤젤레스에 사는 한국 여성들에 대한 이야기야. 주인공은 미국에서 태어난 여자인데, 그녀의 어머니는 한국에서 오셨어.
A: 재밌겠는데. 누가 쓴 책이야?
B: <u>Lin Lee가 저자야.</u>
A: 그 사람 'The Heroine Generation'도 썼지, 그렇지?
B: 아니, 그건 May Lee가 쓴 책이야.
A: 아, 그렇구나.

선지 해석
① 나 이미 그거 읽었어
② Lin Lee가 저자야
③ 그건 원래 내 거야
④ 그녀는 한국에 있는 내 친척 중 한 명이야

정답 해설
A와 B가 일상적인 대화를 나누는 상황에서, B는 점심을 먹지 않고 대신 책을 읽고 있다고 말한다. 이에 A가 관심을 보이자, B는 책의 내용에 대해 설명한다. 그 후 A는 책의 저자가 누구인지 묻고 있고, 문맥상 B가 자연스럽게 그 책의 저자를 말했음을 알 수 있다. 따라서 밑줄 친 부분에 들어갈 말로 가장 적절한 것은 ②이다.

지문 어휘
☐ born 태어나다
☐ author 저자, 작가

03 〈정답 ①〉

지문 해석

Yuna: 안녕 Jenny, 차를 사는 것에 대해 조언이 필요해.
Jenny: 안녕, 너 차를 사고 싶은 거야? 어떤 종류의 차야?
Yuna: 중형 세단이나 SUV 정도 생각 중이야.
Jenny: SUV가 더 실용적이야.
Yuna: SUV는 세단보다 더 비싸. <u>나는 예산이 빠듯해.</u>
Jenny: 내 친구 중에 중고차 딜러가 있어. 그 친구가 좋은 가격에 해줄 수 있을 거야.
Yuna: 정말? 그거 좋겠다.
Jenny: 그 사람 번호 알려줄까?
Yuna: 응, 좋아.
Jenny: 잠깐만. 707-123-5678
Yuna: 고마워!

선지 해석
① 나는 예산이 빠듯해
② 나는 몸매를 가꿀 필요가 있어
③ 곧 날씨가 갤 거야
④ 나중에 너를 태우러 갈게

정답 해설
Yuna는 차를 구매하기 전에 Jenny에게 조언을 구하며 중형 세단이나 SUV 중에서 고민하고 있는 상황이다. Jenny는 SUV가 더 실용적이라고 추천했지만, Yuna는 SUV가 더 비싸다며 무언가를 말한다. 이에 Jenny가 중고차 딜러인 친구를 소개하며 좋은 가격에 차를 구해줄 수 있다고 한 것으로 보아, Yuna가 차가 비싸 예산이 조금 부족하다고 말했음을 짐작할 수 있다. 따라서 밑줄 친 부분에 들어갈 말로 가장 적절한 것은 ①이다.

지문 어휘
□ practical 실용적인, 타당한
□ expensive 비싼, 돈이 많이 드는
□ get in shape 좋은 몸 상태(몸매)를 유지하다
□ clear up (날씨가) 개다
□ pick up ~를 (차에) 태우러 가다

04 정답 ②

지문 해석
A: 발표 자료는 복사본 몇 부 정도 준비하면 될 것 같아요?
B: 60부면 충분할 것 같은데, 여유분이 있으면 좋죠.
A: 맞아요. 나중에 후회하는 것보단 낫죠. 그럼 몇 부 정도를 추천하시나요?
B: 지난번처럼 예상보다 참석자가 많을 수도 있으니까, 75부로 하죠.
A: 좋은 생각이에요. 공유를 위해 디지털 버전도 준비해야 할까요?
B: 당연하죠. 발표가 끝난 뒤에 발표 자료를 요청하는 사람들도 있을 거예요.
A: 그래요, 그렇게 하면 모두가 필요할 때 쉽게 자료를 볼 수 있겠네요.

선지 해석
① 자료를 얼마나 일찍 배부해야 하나요?
② 공유를 위해 디지털 버전도 준비해야 할까요?
③ 자료는 컬러로 인쇄하나요, 아니면 흑백으로 인쇄하나요?
④ 우리가 포함하지 말아야 할 특정 자료가 있나요?

정답 해설
발표 준비 과정에서 자료를 추가로 준비하자는 의견을 나눈 후, A가 추가로 무언가를 묻자 B는 발표가 끝난 후에도 자료를 요청하는 사람들이 있을 것이라며 당연하다는 듯 동의하고 있다. 이어서 A도 누구나 필요할 때 쉽게 자료를 받을 수 있을 것이라며 응답하고 있는 것으로 보아, A는 자료를 공유하기 위해 디지털 버전도 준비할지 여부를 물었음을 짐작할 수 있다. 따라서 밑줄 친 부분에 들어갈 말로 가장 적절한 것은 ②이다.

지문 어휘
□ copy 복사[복제](본)
□ material 자료
□ attendee 참석자
□ distribute 배부하다, 분배하다

05 정답 ②

지문 해석
A: 안녕하세요. 당신의 도시 투어에 관한 정보를 얻을 수 있을까요?
B: 저희에게 문의해 주셔서 감사합니다. 구체적인 질문이 있으신가요?
A: 도시 투어에는 무엇이 포함되어 있나요?
B: 그것은 도시의 모든 주요 관광지로 데려다 줄 것입니다.
A: 가격은 얼마인가요?
B: 4시간짜리 투어로 한 사람당 50달러입니다.
A: 알겠습니다. 금요일 오후에 4장의 티켓을 예약할 수 있을까요?
B: 물론이죠. 곧 지불 정보를 보내드리겠습니다.

선지 해석
① 여행은 얼마나 오래 걸리나요?
② 도시 투어에는 무엇이 포함되어 있나요?
③ 여행 상품 목록이 있나요?
④ 좋은 여행 가이드북을 추천해주실 수 있나요?

정답 해설
도시 투어 정보를 얻고자 하고 내용으로, 빈칸 앞에 투어에 관한 질문이 있는지 물어보고 빈칸 뒤에 도시 투어 중 하나로 모든 주요 관광지로 데려다 준다고 대답하고 있다. 따라서 밑줄 친 부분에 들어갈 말로 가장 적절한 것은 ②이다.

지문 어휘
□ per person 한 사람당
□ payment 지불, 지급, 납입
□ include 포함하다
□ tour package (여행사의) 일괄 알선 여행
□ recommend 추천하다, 권고하다

06 정답 ④

지문 해석
A: 감사합니다. 귀하의 주문에 감사드립니다.
B: 천만에요. 제품을 항공화물로 보내주실 수 있을까요? 우리는 그것이 빨리 필요해요.
A: 물론이죠. 제품을 귀하의 부서로 바로 보내드리겠습니다.
B: 알겠습니다. 다음 주 초에 제품을 받을 수 있기를 바랍니다.
A: 모든 게 계획대로 진행되면, 월요일에 받으실 수 있습니다.
B: 월요일이라고 하니 좋습니다.
A: 2주 안에 지불해 주시기 바랍니다. 항공화물 비용은 송장에 추가될 것입니다.
B: 잠깐만요. 배송 비용은 그쪽에서 부담하는 거라고 생각했습니다.
A: 유감스럽지만, 더 이상 무료 배송 서비스는 제공하지 않습니다.

선지 해석
① 알겠습니다. 당신으로부터 송장을 언제 받게 될까요?
② 저희 부서는 2주 안에 지불하지 못할 수도 있습니다.
③ 월요일에 당신의 사업 계좌로 보내면 될까요?
④ 잠깐만요. 배송 비용은 그쪽에서 부담하는 거라고 생각했습니다.

정답 해설
항공화물의 배송 서비스에 관한 내용으로, 빈칸 앞에 항공화물 비용은 송장에 추가될 것이라고 안내하고 있고, 빈칸 뒤에 유감스럽다고 말하면서 더 이상 무료 배송 서비스는 제공되지 않는다고 안내하고 있다. 따라서 밑줄 친 부분에 들어갈 말로 가장 적절한 것은 ④이다.

지문 어휘
☐ department 부서, 부처, 학과
☐ goods 상품, 제품, 재산, 소유물
☐ invoice 송장, 청구서

07   정답 ③

지문 해석
A: 전화기를 찾으셨나요?
B: 아쉽게도, 아직 찾지 못했어요. 여전히 찾고 있어요.
A: 지하철의 분실물 보관소에 연락해보셨나요?
B: <u>사실은 그것을 아직 안 해봤어요.</u>
A: 저라면 그걸 먼저 해보겠어요.
B: 네, 당신 말이 맞아요. 새로운 전화기를 사기 전에 분실물 센터에 확인해볼게요.

선지 해석
① 전화기에 관해 물어보러 거기에 갔어요.
② 오늘 아침에 사무실에 잠시 들렀어요.
③ 사실은 그것을 아직 안 해봤어요.
④ 모든 곳을 찾아보려고 노력했어요.

정답 해설
지하철을 이용하다가 전화기를 잃어버린 상황으로, 빈칸 앞에 지하철의 분실소 보관소에 연락했는지 물어보고 있고, 빈칸 뒤에 본인이라면 연락을 먼저 해보겠다고 말하고 있다. 따라서 밑줄 친 부분에 들어갈 말로 가장 적절한 것은 ③이다.

지문 어휘
☐ lost and found office 분실물 보관소
☐ stop by 가는 길에 들르다, 잠시 들르다

08   정답 ④

지문 해석
A: Charles, 우리 다가오는 행사에 더 많은 의자가 필요할 것 같아요.
B: 정말요? 저는 이미 의자들이 충분히 있다고 생각했어요.
A: 제 매니저가 350명 이상의 사람들이 온다고 하더라고요.
B: <u>그건 제가 예상했던 것보다 훨씬 많네요.</u>
A: 저도 동의해요. 저도 조금 놀랐어요.
B: 그럼 의자를 더 주문해야 할 것 같네요. 감사합니다.

선지 해석
① 매니저가 그 행사에 참석할지 궁금하네요.
② 350명 이상이 올 것이라고 생각했어요.
③ 그건 실제로 많은 숫자가 아니에요.
④ 그건 제가 예상했던 것보다 훨씬 많네요.

정답 해설
행사에 필요한 의자 준비와 관련된 대화로, 빈칸 앞에 350명 이상의 사람들이 올 거라고 하고 있고 빈칸 뒤에 B의 말에 공감하며 놀랐다고 말하고 있으므로 예상보다 많았다고 말했음을 짐작할 수 있다. 따라서 밑줄 친 부분에 들어갈 말로 가장 적절한 것은 ④이다.

지문 어휘
☐ upcoming 다가오는
☐ a bit 약간

09   정답 ④

지문 해석
A: 어제 회의에서 언급하신 문서를 받을 수 있을까요?
B: 물론이죠. 그 문서의 제목이 뭐죠?
A: 제목이 기억나지 않지만, 커뮤니티 축제에 관한 것이었습니다.
B: 아, 무슨 말씀하시는지 알겠습니다.
A: 좋습니다. 이메일로 보내주실 수 있을까요?
B: 제가 그것을 가지고 있지 않습니다. 박 씨가 그 프로젝트를 담당하고 있으니, 아마 그가 그것을 가지고 있을 겁니다.
A: <u>알려주셔서 감사합니다. 제가 그에게 연락하겠습니다.</u>
B: 행운을 빕니다. 원하는 문서를 받으시길 바랍니다.

선지 해석
① 그가 사무실에 있는지 확인해 주시겠어요?
② 박 씨가 이메일을 다시 보내셨습니다.
③ 커뮤니티 축제에 오실 건가요?
④ 알려주셔서 감사합니다. 제가 그에게 연락하겠습니다.

정답 해설
회의에서 언급한 문서 요청과 관련된 대화로, 빈칸 앞에 필요한 문서는 본인이 가지고 있지 않고 담당했던 박 씨를 알려주고 있다. 빈칸 뒤에 원하는 문서를 받기를 바란다고 말하고 있으므로 담당했던 박 씨에게 직접 연락하겠다고 말했음을 짐작할 수 있다. 따라서 밑줄 친 부분에 들어갈 말로 가장 적절한 것은 ④이다.

지문 어휘
☐ document 서류, 문서
☐ refer to 지칭하다, 언급하다
☐ festival 축제
☐ via 통해
☐ in charge of 책임을 지는, 담당하고 있는

10

정답 ②

지문 해석

A: 안녕하세요, 다음 주 화요일 발표에 대해 질문 하나 해도 될까요?
B: 자원봉사 프로그램 홍보 발표를 말씀하시는 건가요?
A: 네. 발표는 어디서 진행되나요?
B: 확인해 보겠습니다. 201호입니다.
A: 알겠습니다. 그 방에서 제 노트북을 사용할 수 있나요?
B: 네, 물론입니다. 방에 PC가 있지만, 원하시면 본인 노트북을 사용하셔도 됩니다.
A: 제 발표 리허설은 언제 할 수 있나요?
B: 발표 두 시간 전에 그 방에서 만날 수 있습니다. 괜찮으신가요?
A: 네, 정말 감사합니다!

선지 해석

① 한 시간 전에 컴퓨터 기술자가 여기에 있었습니다.
② 제 발표 리허설은 언제 할 수 있나요?
③ 우리 프로그램에 자원봉사자를 더 모집해야 할까요?
④ 제 노트북을 방에 두고 가는 것이 불안합니다.

정답 해설

홍보 발표의 준비 사항에 대해 질문하는 내용으로, 빈칸 뒤에 발표 두 시간 전에 그 방에서 할 수 있다고 대답하고 있으므로 발표 리허설 시간에 대해 물어봤음을 짐작할 수 있다. 따라서 밑줄 친 부분에 들어갈 말로 가장 적절한 것은 ②이다.

지문 어휘

☐ presentation 발표
☐ volunteer 자원봉사
☐ promoting 홍보, 선전

11

정답 ②

지문 해석

A: 시내 관광여행을 하고 싶어요. 제가 어디로 가야 할까요?
B: 국립 미술관에 가보시기를 강력히 추천드려요.
A: 오, 좋은 생각이네요. 또 어떤 곳을 봐야 할까요?
B: 강 공원 안내 투어요. 오후 내내 걸릴 거예요.
A: 저는 그럴 시간이 없어요. 3시에 고객을 만나야 하거든요.
B: 아, 그렇군요. 그럼 국립 공원에 가보시는 건 어때요?
A: 좋네요. 고마워요!

선지 해석

① 이것이 당신의 고객이 필요로 하는 지도예요. 자 여기 있어요.
② 강 공원 안내 투어요. 오후 내내 걸릴 거예요.
③ 가능한 한 빨리 확인해 보셔야 해요.
④ 체크아웃 시간은 3시예요.

정답 해설

시내 관광여행 추천을 받고 있는 상황이다. 빈칸 앞에 국립 미술관 외에 또 어떤 곳을 봐야 하는지 물어보고 있다. 빈칸 뒤에 그럴 시간이 충분하지 않다고 말하고 있으므로 시간 소요가 있는 새로운 투어를 알려줬음을 짐작할 수 있다. 따라서 밑줄 친 부분에 들어갈 말로 가장 적절한 것은 ②이다.

지문 어휘

☐ go sightseeing downtown 시내 관광여행을 하다
☐ Why don't you ~? ~하는 게 어때요?
☐ I see. 알겠어요., 그렇군요.
☐ Here you go. (상대방에게 무엇을 주면서) 여기 있어요
☐ national art gallery 국립 미술관
☐ check out ~을 확인[조사]하다, (흥미로운 것을) 살펴보다[보다], (호텔 등에서 비용을 지불하고) 나가다[체크아웃하다]
☐ guided tour 안내 투어
☐ it takes 시간 시간이 걸리다
☐ as soon as possible 가능한 한 빨리

12

정답 ④

지문 해석

A: 실례합니다, 혹시 저를 도와주실 수 있으세요?
B: 물론이죠. 무엇을 도와드릴까요?
A: 인사과를 찾고 있는데요. 10시에 약속이 있어서요.
B: 3층에 있습니다.
A: 그곳에는 어떻게 올라가야 하나요?
B: 모퉁이를 돌아 엘리베이터를 타세요.

선지 해석

① 우리는 이 상황을 어떻게 처리해야 할지 전혀 모르겠습니다.
② 누가 담당자인지 우리에게 말해주시겠습니까?
③ 네, 저는 이 근처에서 도움이 좀 필요합니다.
④ 물론이죠. 무엇을 도와드릴까요?

정답 해설

빈칸 앞에 A가 본인을 도와 줄 수 있냐고 물어보고 있다. 빈칸 뒤에 필요한 도움이 무엇인지 설명하고 있으므로 도와주겠다고 말했음을 짐작할 수 있다. 따라서 밑줄 친 부분에 들어갈 말로 가장 적절한 것은 ④이다.

지문 어휘

☐ pardon me 뭐라고요(상대방의 말을 알아듣지 못했을 때 다시 말해 달라는 뜻으로 하는 말) 실례합니다, 죄송합니다
☐ give a hand 도와주다, 거들어주다
☐ personnel department 인사과, 인사 담당 부서
☐ appointment 약속, 임명, 직책
☐ around the corner 모퉁이를 돌아서, 코앞에, 임박하여, 위기를 넘겨
☐ handle 다루다, 처리하다
☐ have no idea 전혀[하나도] 모르다
☐ Would you mind ~ing? ~해도 괜찮으세요?
☐ be in charge 담당하다, 맡다
☐ Can I help you with anything? 무엇을 도와드릴까요?

13

정답 ③

지문 해석

A: 당신이 마지막으로 퇴근하셨죠, 그렇죠?
B: 네. 무슨 문제라도 있으신가요?
A: 오늘 아침 사무실 전등과 에어컨이 켜져 있는 것을 발견했어요.
B: 정말요? 이런. 아마도 제가 어젯밤에 전원 끄는 것을 깜빡한 것 같아요.
A: 아마 밤새 켜져 있었을 거예요.
B: 죄송합니다. 앞으로는 더 조심할게요.

선지 해석

① 걱정하지 마세요. 이 기계는 잘 작동해요.
② 맞아요. 다들 당신과 같이 일하는 걸 좋아해요.
③ 죄송합니다. 앞으로는 더 조심할게요.
④ 안타깝네요. 퇴근이 너무 늦게 퇴근해서 피곤하겠어요.

정답 해설

퇴근할 때 사무실 수칙을 지키지 못한 상황에 B가 실수한 부분을 A가 언급하고 있다. 빈칸 앞에 사무실 에어컨이 밤새 켜져 있었음을 말하고 있으므로 앞으로 주의하겠다고 말하면서 사과했음을 짐작할 수 있다. 따라서 밑줄 친 부분에 들어갈 말로 가장 적절한 것은 ③이다.

지문 어휘

☐ be on 켜져 있다
☐ get off work 퇴근하다
☐ air conditioner 에어컨
☐ turn off (전기·가스·수도 등을) 끄다
☐ work 일하다, 작동하다, 효과가 있다
☐ from now on 앞으로는, 이제부터

14

정답 ③

지문 해석

A: 안녕하세요. 무엇을 도와드릴까요?
B: 네, 스웨터를 찾는 중이에요.
A: 음, 이것은 이번 가을 컬렉션으로 나온 최신 스타일이에요. 어떠세요?
B: 아주 멋진데요. 얼마예요?
A: 가격을 확인해드릴게요. 120달러예요.
B: 제 가격대를 좀 벗어났어요.
A: 그럼 이 스웨터는 어떠세요? 지난 시즌에 나온 건데, 50달러로 할인 중이에요.
B: 완벽해요! 한 번 입어볼게요.

선지 해석

① 나는 그것에 어울리는 바지도 필요해요
② 그 자켓은 나에게 완벽한 선물이에요
③ 제 가격대를 좀 벗어났어요
④ 토요일은 저녁 7시까지 영업합니다

정답 해설

옷 가게에서 스웨터를 구매하는 상황이다. 빈칸 앞에 120달러의 옷을 보여주고 있고, 빈칸 뒤에 50달러로 할인하고 있는 옷을 다시 보여주고 있는 것으로 보아 B는 120달러의 가격의 옷은 사기 힘들다고 말했음을 짐작할 수 있다. 따라서 밑줄 친 부분에 들어갈 말로 가장 적절한 것은 ③이다.

지문 어휘

☐ Let me try it on. 한 번 입어볼게요.
☐ look for 찾다
☐ latest 최신의
☐ on sale 할인 중인
☐ try on 옷 따위를 입어[신어] 보다
☐ go with 어울리다
☐ a little 다소의, 약간의, 조금 있는
☐ price range 가격대, 가격폭

15

정답 ④

지문 해석

A: 이봐! 지리학 시험은 어땠어?
B: 나쁘지 않았어, 고마워. 난 그냥 끝났다는 게 기뻐! 너는 어때? 과학 시험은 어땠어?
A: 오, 그건 정말 잘 됐어. 그것을 도와줘서 너에게 정말 고마워. 그것 때문에 너한테 신세를 졌어.
B: 도움이 되어 나도 기뻐. 그래서 다음 주에 있을 수학 시험을 준비하고 싶어?
A: 물론이지. 같이 공부하자.
B: 좋아. 나중에 봐.

선지 해석

① 이 일에 자책하는 건 의미가 없어
② 너를 여기서 보게 될 줄은 꿈에도 몰랐어
③ 사실, 우리가 매우 실망했어
④ 그것을 도와줘서 너에게 정말 고마워

정답 해설

지리학 시험과 관련된 대화로, 빈칸 뒤에 시험과 관련하여 신세를 졌다고 말하고 있으므로 시험 준비하는 데 도움을 줘서 고맙다고 감사를 표했음을 짐작할 수 있다. 따라서 밑줄 친 부분에 들어갈 말로 가장 적절한 것은 ④이다.

지문 어휘

☐ owe you a treat for ~에 대해 신세를 지다
☐ (It's) my pleasure. (감사의 말에 대하여) 도움이 되어[도와드릴 수 있어서] 저도 기뻐요.
☐ beat oneself up 자책하다
☐ can't thank you enough 대단히 감사합니다, 뭐라 감사의 말씀을 드려야 할지 모르겠어요
☐ go well 잘 되다
☐ feel like ~ing ~하고 싶다

Chapter 02 국가직 및 지방직 기타 핵심 기출문제

ANSWER

01 ①	02 ②	03 ①	04 ③	05 ②
06 ②	07 ③	08 ②	09 ①	10 ①
11 ②	12 ④	13 ②	14 ②	15 ③

01 　정답 ①

지문 해석

A: 당신이 어젯밤에 여기에 있었나요?
B: 네, 마감 교대조로 일했어요. 왜요?
A: 오늘 아침에 주방이 엉망이었어요. 음식이 가스레인지 위에 튀어 있었고, 제빙 그릇도 냉동실 안에 없었습니다.
B: 제가 청소 체크리스트 점검하는 것을 잊은 거 같아요.
A: 깨끗한 주방이 얼마나 중요한지 알잖아요.
B: 죄송해요. 다시는 이런 일이 일어나지 않도록 할게요.

선지 해석

① 다시는 이런 일이 일어나지 않도록 할게요.
② 지금 당신의 계산서를 원하시나요?
③ 그것이 내가 그것을 어제 깜빡한 이유입니다.
④ 당신의 주문 내용이 맞는지 확인해드리겠습니다.

정답 해설

식당에서 같이 일하는 동료들과의 대화로, B가 마감하면서 청소 체크리스트대로 점검을 하지 않아서 A가 그 부분에 대해 지적하고 있다. 빈칸 앞에 B는 사과하고 있으므로 앞으로 주의하겠다고 반성했음을 짐작할 수 있다. 따라서 밑줄 친 부분에 들어갈 말로 가장 적절한 것은 ①이다.

지문 어휘

☐ closing shift 마감 교대조
☐ mess 엉망(진창)인 상태
☐ spatter 튀기다, 흩뿌리다
☐ ice tray 제빙 그릇
☐ go over 점검[검토]하다
☐ make sure (~임을) 확인하다, 확실하게 하다
☐ that's why 그래서 ~하다, 그것이 ~하는 이유이다

02 　정답 ②

지문 해석

A: 감기에 대한 약을 먹은 게 있나요?
B: 아니요, 그냥 코만 많이 풀었어요.
A: 혹시 비강 스프레이를 사용해봤나요?
B: 아니요, 저는 비강 스프레이를 좋아하지 않아요.
A: 그거 정말 효과가 좋아요.
B: 아니요, 괜찮아요. 난 코에 무언가를 넣는 것을 좋아하지 않아서 그것을 한 번도 사용해 본 적이 없어요.

선지 해석

① 네, 하지만 그것은 도움이 되지 않았어요.
② 아니요, 저는 비강 스프레이를 좋아하지 않아요.
③ 아니요, 약국이 문을 닫았어요.
④ 네, 얼마나 많이 사용해야 하나요?

정답 해설

감기 걸린 친구와의 대화로, 빈칸 앞에 비강 스프레이를 사용해봤는지 물어보고 있다. 빈칸 뒤에 B는 코에 무언가를 넣는 것이 싫고 한 번도 사용해 본 적이 없다고 말하고 있으므로 비강 스프레이를 사용하지 않는다거나 싫어한다고 말했음을 짐작할 수 있다. 따라서 밑줄 친 부분에 들어갈 말로 가장 적절한 것은 ②이다.

지문 어휘

☐ blow one's nose 코를 풀다
☐ work great 효과가 좋다
☐ cold 감기
☐ nose spray 비강 스프레이
☐ pharmacy 약국

03 　정답 ①

지문 해석

A: 주말 잘 보냈어?
B: 응, 정말 좋았어. 우리는 영화 보러 갔었어.
A: 오! 뭐 봤어?
B: 인터스텔라. 그건 매우 좋았어.
A: 정말? 어떤 점이 가장 좋았어?
B: 특수 효과야. 정말 환상적이었어. 난 그걸 다시 봐도 괜찮을 것 같아.

선지 해석

① 어떤 점이 가장 좋았어?
② 네가 가장 좋아하는 영화 장르가 뭐야?
③ 그 영화가 국제적으로 홍보되었어?
④ 그 영화가 매우 비쌌어?

정답 해설

친구와의 가벼운 대화로, 빈칸 앞에 주말에 본 인터스텔라 영화가 매우 좋았다고 말하고 있다. 빈칸 뒤에 영화에 대한 좋았던 부분을 말하고 있으므로 어떤 점이 좋았는지 물어봤음을 짐작할 수 있다. 따라서 밑줄 친 부분에 들어갈 말로 가장 적절한 것은 ①이다.

지문 어휘

☐ go to the movies 영화 보러 가다
☐ What did you like the most about it? 어떤 점이 가장 좋았어?
☐ wouldn't mind ~ing ~하면 좋겠다, 상관없다
☐ special effect 특수 효과
☐ fantastic 환상적인, 굉장한
☐ promote 홍보하다, 촉진하다
☐ internationally 국제적으로
☐ costly 값이 비싼

04
정답 ③

지문 해석

A: Royal Point 호텔 예약부에 전화해주셔서 감사합니다. 제 이름은 Sam입니다. 무엇을 도와드릴까요?
B: 안녕하세요, 방을 예약하고 싶습니다.
A: 저희는 두 종류의 방을 제공합니다: 디럭스 룸과 럭셔리 스위트룸이 있습니다.
B: 둘의 차이점이 무엇인가요?
A: 우선, 스위트룸은 매우 큽니다. 침실 외에도, 부엌, 거실 그리고 식당이 있습니다.
B: 그거 비싸겠네요.
A: 음, 하룻밤에 200달러가 더 비쌉니다.
B: 그렇다면 저는 디럭스 룸으로 하겠습니다.

선지 해석

① 다른 거 필요한 게 있으신가요
② 방 번호를 알려 주시겠어요
③ 둘의 차이점이 무엇인가요
④ 애완동물이 방에 들어올 수 있나요

정답 해설

호텔 예약과 관련된 대화로, 빈칸 앞에 두 종류의 방을 설명하고 있다. 빈칸 뒤에 두 종류의 방들의 차이점을 설명하고 있으므로 두 종류의 방의 차이점이 무엇인지 물어봤음을 짐작할 수 있다. 따라서 밑줄 친 부분에 들어갈 말로 가장 적절한 것은 ③이다.

지문 어휘

☐ book 예약하다

05
정답 ②

지문 해석

A: 아, 또 왔어! 스팸 메일이 너무 많이 와!
B: 나도 알아. 하루에 열 통 이상은 받아.
A: 우리가 그것(스팸 메일)들이 오는 것을 막을 수 있을까?
B: 그것들을 완전히 차단하는 것은 가능하지 않을 것 같아.
A: 우리가 할 수 있는 다른 방법이 없을까?
B: 음, 설정에서 차단 프로그램을 설치할 수 있어.
A: 차단 프로그램?
B: 응, 차단 프로그램이 스팸 메일 일부를 제거할 수 있어.

선지 해석

① 이메일을 자주 쓰니
② 우리가 할 수 있는 다른 방법이 없을까
③ 이 훌륭한 차단 프로그램을 어떻게 만들었어
④ 이메일 계정 만드는 것 좀 도와줄래

정답 해설

스팸 메일에 대한 불평을 토로하는 상황이다. 빈칸 앞에 완전히 차단하는 것은 불가능할 거라고 말하고 있다. 빈칸 뒤에 차단하는 방법 중 하나를 말하고 있으므로 차단하는 방법에 대해 물어봤음을 짐작할 수 있다. 따라서 밑줄 친 부분에 들어갈 말로 가장 적절한 것은 ②이다.

지문 어휘

☐ junk email 스팸 메일
☐ weed out 제거하다, 뽑아버리다

06
정답 ②

지문 해석

A: 딤섬 좀 드셔보시겠어요?
B: 네, 감사합니다. 맛있어 보이네요. 안에 뭐가 들었죠?
A: 이것에는 돼지고기와 다진 야채들이 들어 있고, 새우들도 들어 있어요.
B: 그리고, 음, 그것들은 어떻게 먹나요?
A: 젓가락으로 이렇게 한 개를 집어서 소스에 찍어 먹으면 돼요. 쉬워요.
B: 알겠습니다. 한번 해 볼게요.

선지 해석

① 그것들은 얼마죠
② 그것들을 어떻게 먹나요
③ 그것들은 얼마나 맵죠
④ 그것들을 어떻게 만드나요

정답 해설

딤섬을 먹으면서 나누는 대화로, 빈칸 뒤에 딤섬을 먹는 방법을 설명하고 있으므로 딤섬을 어떻게 먹는지 물어봤음을 짐작할 수 있다. 따라서 밑줄 친 부분에 들어갈 말로 가장 적절한 것은 ②이다.

지문 어휘

☐ chop 썰다(다지다), (장작 같은 것을)패다
☐ pick up ~을 집다(들어 올리다)
☐ dip into ~에 담갔다 꺼내다, 적시다

07
정답 ③

지문 해석

A: 안녕하세요. 제가 환전을 좀 해야 합니다.
B: 네. 어떤 통화가 필요하신가요?
A: 달러를 파운드로 환산해야 해요. 환율이 어떻게 되죠?
B: 환율은 달러 당 0.73 파운드입니다.
A: 좋아요. 수수료를 받습니까?
B: 네, 우리는 4달러 정도의 소액의 수수료를 받습니다.
A: 재판매 방침은 어떻게 되나요?
B: 우리는 당신의 통화를 무료로 다시 바꿔드립니다. 그냥 영수증만 가져오세요.

선지 해석

① 이것의 가격은 얼마입니까
② 제가 어떻게 결제하면 됩니까
③ 재판매 방침은 어떻게 되나요
④ 당신은 신용카드를 받습니까

정답 해설

환전을 하고 있는 상황이다. 빈칸 뒤에 영수증만 있다면 무료로 다시 바꿔드린다고 말하고 있으므로 재환전하게 될 경우는 어떻게 되는지 물어봤음을 짐작할 수 있다. 따라서 밑줄 친 부분에 들어갈 말로 가장 적절한 것은 ③이다.

지문 어휘

☐ exchange 환전하다, 교환하다
☐ currency 통화, 통용
☐ take a commission 수수료를 떼다
☐ for free 무료로, 공짜로
☐ receipt 영수증

08
정답 ②

지문 해석
A: 내 컴퓨터가 이유 없이 그냥 꺼져. 난 다시 켤 수도 없어.
B: 너 충전은 해봤어? 그냥 배터리가 나간 것일지도 몰라.
A: 당연하지, 충전해봤어.
B: 그러면 가장 가까운 서비스 센터를 찾아가봐.
A: 그래야 하는데 내가 너무 게을러.

선지 해석
① 난 네 컴퓨터를 고치는 법을 몰라.
② 그러면 가장 가까운 서비스 센터를 찾아가봐.
③ 음, 네 문제에 대해 그만 생각하고 잠이나 자.
④ 우리 오빠가 네 컴퓨터를 고쳐주려고 할거야, 왜냐하면 오빠는 기술자거든.

정답 해설
컴퓨터 켜지지 않는 상황이다. 빈칸 앞에 켜지지 않는 이유가 배터리 부족은 아님을 언급하고 있다. 빈칸 뒤에 수긍하면서 자기가 게을러서 귀찮다고 말하고 있으므로 A에게 약간은 귀찮은 새로운 해결 방법을 말했음을 짐작할 수 있다. 따라서 밑줄 친 부분에 들어갈 말로 가장 적절한 것은 ②이다.

지문 어휘
□ charge 충전하다
□ be out of ~을 다 써서 없다, 바닥나다
□ lazy 게으른, 느긋한
□ fix 수리하다, 바로잡다

09
정답 ①

지문 해석
A: 우리 신혼여행은 어디로 가고 싶어?
B: 우리 둘 다 가보지 않은 곳으로 가보자.
A: 그러면 하와이로 가는 거 어때?
B: 난 늘 그곳에 가고 싶었어.

선지 해석
① 난 늘 그곳에 가고 싶었어.
② 한국은 살기 좋은 곳 아니니?
③ 잘됐어! 그곳에서의 내 마지막 여행은 좋았어.
④ 오, 넌 하와이에 벌써 가본 게 틀림없구나.

정답 해설
신혼여행을 어디로 갈 것인지 의의하고 있는 상황이다. 둘 다 가지 않는 곳으로 가고 싶어하고 있고 빈칸 앞에 하와이가 어떤지 물어보고 있으므로 하와이로 선택하는 것에 동의했음을 짐작할 수 있다. 따라서 밑줄 친 부분에 들어갈 말로 가장 적절한 것은 ①이다.

지문 어휘
□ honeymoon 신혼여행
□ have been to ~에 가본 적이 있다
□ why don't you ~? ~하는 게 어때?, ~하지 않겠니?

10
정답 ①

지문 해석
A: 제가 도와 드릴까요?
B: 제가 이틀 전에 이 옷을 샀는데, 이게 저에게 약간 커서요.
A: 죄송합니다만 더 작은 사이즈는 없습니다.
B: 그러면 환불을 받고 싶어요.
A: 영수증 좀 보여주시겠습니까?
B: 여기 있어요.

선지 해석
① 죄송합니다만 더 작은 사이즈는 없습니다.
② 제 생각엔 손님에게 완벽하게 맞는 것 같은데요.
③ 그 옷은 우리 매장에서 엄청 잘 팔려요.
④ 죄송합니다만, 이 상품은 환불 받으실 수 없습니다.

정답 해설
구매한 옷의 환불을 원하는 상황이다. 빈칸 앞에 구매한 옷이 본인에게 좀 크다고 말하고 있다. 빈칸 뒤에 그렇다면 환불을 받고 싶다고 말하고 있으므로 구매한 옷보다 작은 사이즈는 없다고 알려줬음을 짐작할 수 있다. 따라서 밑줄 친 부분에 들어갈 말로 가장 적절한 것은 ①이다.

지문 어휘
□ refund 환불하다
□ receipt 영수증
□ purchase 구입(품), 구매(품), 매입(품)

11
정답 ②

지문 해석
A: 제가 이 가정용 혈압계를 사용할 때마다 다른 수치가 나옵니다. 제 생각엔 제가 뭔가 잘못하고 있는 것 같아요. 정확하게 그것을 사용하는 방법을 알려주시겠어요?
B: 네, 물론이죠. 먼저 이 조절 끈을 팔에 둘러야 합니다.
A: 이렇게요? 제가 정확하게 하고 있는 건가요?
B: 그건 좀 너무 꽉 조이는 것 같아요.
A: 아, 지금은 어떤가요?
B: 지금은 너무 헐렁해 보여요. 너무 꽉 조이거나 너무 헐렁하면, 부정확한 수치가 나올 겁니다.
A: 오, 알겠습니다. 다음엔 뭘 해야 하나요?
B: 이제 그 버튼을 누르세요. 움직이거나 말씀하시면 안 됩니다.
A: 알겠습니다.
B: 잠시 후 화면에서 혈압(수치)을 보실 수 있을 겁니다.

선지 해석
① 저는 오늘 아무것도 못 봤어요.
② 오, 알겠습니다. 다음에 뭘 해야 하나요?
③ 맞아요, 저는 책을 읽어야 해요.
④ 제가 그 웹사이트를 확인해야 합니까?

정답 해설
가정용 혈압계 사용 방법 안내와 관련된 대화로, 빈칸 앞에 사용하는 절차를 안내해 주고 있다. 빈칸 뒤에 그 다음 과정의 절차를 알려주고 있으므로 그 다음은 무엇을 해야 하는지 물어봤음을 짐작할 수 있다. 따라서 밑줄 친 부분에 들어갈 말로 가장 적절한 것은 ②이다.

지문 어휘
- blood pressure 혈압
- reading 수치, 표시 눈금값[측정값]
- correctly 정확하게, 올바르게

12
정답 ④

지문 해석

Mary: 안녕하세요, James. 어떻게 지내세요?
James: 안녕하세요, Mary. 오늘은 무엇을 도와드릴까요?
Mary: 이 소포를 배송하려면 어떻게 해야 하나요?
James: 고객 서비스 센터에 있는 Bob과 이야기해 보는 게 어때요?
Mary: 그의 번호로 전화를 해봤지만, 아무도 받지 않았어요.

선지 해석
① 물론이죠. 내일 당신을 위해 이 소포를 전달할 거예요.
② 알겠습니다. 제가 Bob의 고객을 상대하겠습니다.
③ 내일 세관 사무소에서 뵐게요.
④ 그의 번호로 전화를 해봤지만, 아무도 받지 않았어요.

정답 해설
소포 배송하는 방법을 물어보는 상황이다. 빈칸 앞에 고객 서비스 센터의 Bob에게 물어 보는 방법을 제안하고 있으므로 Bob과의 연결 방법이 어떻게 됐는지를 말했음을 짐작할 수 있다. 따라서 밑줄 친 부분에 들어갈 말로 가장 적절한 것은 ④이다.

지문 어휘
- package 소포, 꾸러미, (포장용) 상자, 포장물
- Custom office 세관 (사무소)

13
정답 ②

지문 해석

A: 우와! 저 긴 줄을 봐. 우린 적어도 30분은 기다려야 할 거야.
B: 네 말이 맞아. 다른 놀이 기구를 찾아보자.
A: 그거 좋은 생각이다. 나는 롤러코스터를 타고 싶어.
B: 그건 내 취향이 아니야.
A: 그럼 후룸라이드는 어때? 재미도 있고 줄도 별로 안 길어.
B: 그거 괜찮다! 가자!

선지 해석
① 마술쇼 자리를 찾아보자.
② 다른 놀이 기구를 찾아보자.
③ 퍼레이드 의상을 사자.
④ 분실물 보관소로 가보자.

정답 해설
놀이공원에 놀러 간 상황이다. 빈칸 앞에 지금 기다리고 있는 놀이 기구를 타려면 적어도 30분은 기다려야 할 거 같다고 말하고 있다. 빈칸 뒤에 동의하면서 다른 놀이 기구를 타자고 제안하고 있으므로 다른 놀이 기구를 찾아보자고 말했음을 짐작할 수 있다. 따라서 밑줄 친 부분에 들어갈 말로 가장 적절한 것은 ②이다.

지문 어휘
- at least 적어도, 최소한
- ride 타다, 놀이 기구
- not my cup of tea 내 취향이 아닌
- the lost and found 분실물 보관소

14
정답 ②

지문 해석

A: 나는 방금 오랜 고등학교 친구들 중 한 명에게 편지를 한 통 받았어.
B: 잘 됐네!
A: 글쎄, 사실 그 친구 소식을 못 들은 지 오래 됐어.
B: 솔직히, 나도 오랜 친구들 대부분과 더이상 연락하지 않고 지내.
A: 나도 알아. 사람들이 돌아다닐 때 연락을 계속하기가 참 어렵지.
B: 맞아. 사람들은 그냥 멀어지는 거야. 그런데도 넌 친구와 다시 연락이 되다니 참 행운이야.

선지 해석
① 해가 길어지고 있어
② 사람들은 그냥 멀어지는 거야
③ 내가 들은 것 중에 가장 웃긴 일이야
④ 그의 이름을 들을 때마다 화가 나기 시작해

정답 해설
오랫동안 연락이 끊긴 친구에게 편지를 받은 상황이다. 빈칸 앞에 A가 사람들이 돌아다니게 되면서 연락을 계속 유지하기가 힘들다고 하고 B가 수긍하고 있으므로 연락을 계속 유지하기 어렵다거나 사람들이랑 자연스레 멀어질 수밖에 없다고 말했음을 짐작할 수 있다. 따라서 밑줄 친 부분에 들어갈 말로 가장 적절한 것은 ②이다.

지문 어휘
- be out of touch with ~와 더 이상 연락하지 않다
- move around 돌아다니다
- drift apart 사이가 멀어지다
- fume 화내다, (화가 나서) 씩씩대다

15
정답 ③

지문 해석

A: 새로 이사한 곳 근처는 어때요?
B: 대부분 좋아요. 저는 깨끗한 공기와 녹지 환경이 좋아요.
A: 살기 좋은 곳인 것 같네요.
B: 네, 하지만 문제점이 없는 건 아니에요.
A: 어떤 것들이요?
B: 하나는, 다양한 가게들이 많이 없어요. 예를 들어, 슈퍼마켓이 하나밖에 없어서 식료품이 매우 비싸요.
A: 문제가 좀 있는 것 같아 보여요.
B: 내 말이 바로 그 말이에요. 하지만, 정말 다행이에요. 도시에 지금 새로운 쇼핑센터를 짓고 있어요. 내년에는 더 많은 선택지가 생길 거예요.

선지 해석
① 마트가 몇 개 있어요?
② 거기 쇼핑할 데 많아요?
③ 문제가 좀 있는 것 같아 보여요.
④ 저는 당신 동네로 이사 가고 싶어요.

정답 해설
새로 이사 간 곳이 어떤지 물어보고 있다. 빈칸 앞에 이사 온 곳의 주변의 단점들을 말하고 있다. 빈칸 뒤에 A의 말을 동조하고 있으므로 A가 말한 단점들이 문제가 있다고 언급했음을 짐작할 수 있다. 따라서 밑줄 친 부분에 들어갈 말로 가장 적절한 것은 ③이다.

지문 어휘
- neighborhood 근처, 이웃, 인근
- drawback 결점, 문제점
- thank goodness 정말 다행이다

Chapter 03 2025년 출제 기조 전환 예시 문제

ANSWER

01 ②   02 ③   03 ④   04 ③

01   정답 ②

지문 해석

Tim Jones: 안녕하세요, 회의실 중 하나를 임대하고 싶습니다.
Jane Baker: 관심 가져주셔서 감사합니다. 회의 규모에 따라 이용할 수 있는 여러 공간들이 있습니다. 저희는 5명에서 20명까지 수용이 가능합니다.
Tim Jones: 좋습니다. 17명을 위한 방이 필요하며, 회의는 다음 달에 예정되어 있습니다.
Jane Baker: 회의의 정확한 날짜를 말씀해 주실 수 있나요?
Tim Jones: 회의는 7월 15일 월요일에 열릴 예정입니다. 그날에 회의실이 있나요?
Jane Baker: 네, 있습니다. 당신을 위한 장소를 예약해 드리고 모든 세부 사항이 포함된 확인 전자 우편을 보내드리겠습니다.

선지 해석
① 연락처 정보를 알려주실 수 있나요?
② 회의의 정확한 날짜를 말씀해 주실 수 있나요?
③ 빔 프로젝터나 복사기가 필요하신가요?
④ 몇 명이 회의에 참석할 예정이신가요?

정답 해설
회의실 임대 문의와 관련된 대화로, 빈칸 앞에 회의는 다음 달에 예정되어 있다고 말하고 있고, 빈칸 뒤에는 회의의 날짜를 구체적으로 답하고 있으므로 회의 날짜를 물어봤음을 짐작할 수 있다. 따라서 밑줄 친 부분에 들어갈 말로 가장 적절한 것은 ②이다.

지문 어휘
- rent 임대하다, 임차하다, 집세, 임차료
- meeting room 회의실
- interest 관심, 흥미, 관심[흥미]을 끌다
- several 여러 가지의, 몇몇의, 각각[각자]의
- available 구할[이용할] 수 있는, 시간이 있는
- depending on ~에 따라
- accommodate 수용하다, 공간을 제공하다
- reserve 예약하다, 보류하다, 따로 남겨 두다
- confirmation 확인, 확증

02   정답 ③

지문 해석

A: 이 자전거에 대해 어떻게 생각해?
B: 와, 정말 멋져 보이네! 방금 산 거야?
A: 아니, 이건 공유 자전거야. 시에서 자전거 공유 서비스를 시작했어.
B: 정말? 어떻게 작동하는 거야? 내 말은, 그 서비스를 어떻게 이용하는 거야?
A: 쉬워. 자전거 공유 앱을 다운로드하고 온라인으로 결제하면 돼.
B: 복잡하지 않은 것 같네. 아마 이번 주말에 시도해 볼 수 있을 거 같아.
A: 그런데, 이건 전기 자전거야.
B: 응, 딱 보니 알겠어. 멋져 보여.

선지 해석
① 전기 자전거라서 에너지를 절약할 수 있어
② 자전거를 주차할 수 있는 허가증을 신청하기만 하면 돼
③ 자전거 공유 앱을 다운로드하고 온라인으로 결제하면 돼
④ 안전을 위해 항상 헬멧을 착용해야 해

정답 해설
자전거 공유 서비스와 관련된 대화로, 빈칸 앞에 서비스를 어떻게 사용하는 건지 물어보고 있으므로 자전거 공유 서비스의 이용 방법에 대해 대답했음을 짐작할 수 있다. 따라서 밑줄 친 부분에 들어갈 말로 가장 적절한 것은 ③이다.

지문 어휘
- shared 공유의
- launch 시작[착수]하다, 출시[출간]하다, 개시, 출시
- complicated 복잡한
- I can tell 딱 보니 알겠다

03   정답 ④

지문 해석

A: 안녕하세요. 저는 오클랜드에서 오클랜드 항공편을 예약하고 싶습니다.
B: 네. 어떤 특정한 날짜를 원하십니까?
A: 네. 5월 2일에 출발해서 5월 14일에 돌아올 예정입니다.
B: 네. 스케줄에 맞는 것을 발견했습니다. 어떤 좌석을 예약하시겠습니까?
A: 일반석은 저에게 충분합니다.
B: 선호하시는 좌석이 있으신가요?
A: 네, 통로 쪽 좌석을 원합니다.
B: 좋습니다. 항공편이 지금 예약되었습니다.

선지 해석
① 네. 비즈니스 클래스로 업그레이드하고 싶습니다.
② 아니요. 편도 티켓을 구매하고 싶습니다.
③ 아니요. 짐이 없습니다.
④ 네. 통로 쪽 좌석을 원합니다.

정답 해설
항공편 예약과 관련된 대화로, 빈칸 앞에 좌석에 대한 선호도를 물어 보고 있으므로 좌석과 관련하여 대답했음을 짐작할 수 있다. 따라서 밑줄 친 부분에 들어갈 말로 가장 적절한 것은 ④이다.

지문 어휘
- book a flight 항공기를 예약하다
- specific 특정한
- economy class (여객기의) 일반석, 보통석
- aisle 통로, 복도

04   정답 ③

지문 해석

> Kate Anderson: 다음 주 금요일에 워크숍에 오시는 건가요?
> Jim Henson: 글쎄요. 그날은 병원 예약이 되어 있어서요.
> Kate Anderson: 꼭 오셔야 합니다! 워크숍은 우리의 업무 효율성을 향상시킬 수 있는 인공지능 도구에 관한 것입니다.
> Jim Henson: 와, 주제가 정말 흥미롭게 들리네요!
> Kate Anderson: 맞아요. 하지만 워크숍에 참석하려면 자리 예약하는 것을 잊지 마세요.
> Jim Henson: 어떻게 하면 되나요?
> Kate Anderson: <u>게시판에 적힌 설명을 따르세요.</u>

선지 해석
① 자신의 노트북을 가져와야 합니다.
② 이미 예약했습니다.
③ 게시판에 적힌 설명을 따르세요.
④ 진료 예약을 위해 병원에 전화해야 합니다.

정답 해설
워크숍의 참석과 관련된 대화로, 빈칸 앞에 워크숍에 참석하려면 자리를 예약해야 하는데 예약을 어떻게 해야하는지 방법에 대해 물어보고 있다. 따라서 밑줄 친 부분에 들어갈 말로 가장 적절한 것은 ③이다.

지문 어휘
- reserve a seat 좌석을 예약하다
- instruction 설명, 지시
- bulletin board 게시판

진가영 영어
반한다 기출

Vol.2
문법
정답 및 해설

PART 01 문장과 동사
PART 02 준동사
PART 03 조동사와 조동사를 활용한 구문
PART 04 연결어
PART 05 비교 구문

진가영 영어연구소 | cafe.naver.com/easyenglish7

PART 01 문장과 동사

Chapter 01 문장의 이해

ANSWER
01 ③ 02 ④

01

정답 ③

정답 해설

③ [적중 포인트 001] 문장의 구성요소
문장에 동사가 2개 존재하기 위해서는 접속사가 필요하다. 밑줄 친 부분인 be동사와 vary라는 동사가 2개 존재하기 때문에 옳지 않다. 문맥상 be동사를 쓰는 것보다 vary가 더 자연스러우므로 be vary 대신 be를 삭제한 vary로 써야 올바르다.

찐Tip vary는 '다르다, 달라지다'의 뜻의 1형식 자동사로 주로 쓰인다.

오답 해설

① [적중 포인트 054] 분사 판별법[현재분사 VS 과거분사]
& [적중 포인트 039] 현재시제 동사와 be동사의 수 일치
명사 뒤의 현재분사와 과거분사는 명사를 수식하는 형용사적 용법으로서 모두 올 수 있지만 타동사 뒤에 목적어가 있으면 현재분사형으로, 목적어가 없으면 과거분사형으로 쓴다. 따라서 목적어(an earthquake)가 있으므로 현재분사로 올바르게 쓰였다. 또한 주어와 동사 사이에 수식어로 인해 주어와 동사가 멀리 떨어져 있으면 주어 동사 수 일치 확인도 필요하다. 주어는 Fire 단수형이므로 단수동사 is가 올바르게 쓰였다.

찐Tip of + 추상명사(of special interest)는 형용사 역할을 하므로 be동사의 보어자리에 올 수 있다.

② [적중 포인트 049] 5형식 동사의 수동태 구조
consider은 '여기다, 간주하다'의 뜻을 가진 5형식 타동사로, 'consider + 목적어 + (as/to be) 명사/형용사' 구조를 취한다. 밑줄 친 부분은 수동태 형태인 'be considered + (to be) + 명사' 구조로 올바르게 쓰였다.

④ [적중 포인트 045] 능동태와 수동태의 차이
'was created'는 수동태 구조로 타동사 create 뒤에 목적어가 없고 주어인 The world's first digital camera가 '창조되었다'라는 수동의 의미를 나타내고 있으므로 밑줄 친 부분은 올바르게 쓰였다.

선지 해석
① 지진 다음에 발생하는 화재는 보험 산업에 특별한 관심을 불러일으킨다.
② 과거에는 워드 프로세서가 타자 작업자에게 최고의 도구로 여겨졌다.
③ 현금 예측에서 소득의 요소는 회사의 상황에 따라 달라질 것이다.
④ 세계 최초의 디지털 카메라는 1975년에 Eastman Kodak의 Steve Sasson에 의해 만들어졌다.

02

정답 ④

정답 해설

④ [적중 포인트 004] 주절의 주어와 동사가 중요한 부가 의문문
의문사절은 명사절 5가지 중 하나로 주어, 목적어, 보어 자리에 올 수 있다. 'how + 형용사 + 명사 목적어 + 주어 + 동사'의 어순으로 밑줄 친 부분은 올바르게 쓰였다.

오답 해설

① [적중 포인트 092] 비교 대상 일치
비교급 than 뒤에 that이나 those가 나오면 앞에 비교 대상의 명사가 단수인지 복수인지 확인이 반드시 필요하다. 단수면 that, 복수면 those로 받는다. 따라서 비교대상인 traffic은 단수이므로 복수인 those 대신 단수인 that으로 써야 올바르다.

② [적중 포인트 035] 미래를 대신하는 현재시제
시간, 조건 부사절에서는 현재시제가 미래시제를 대신한다. 따라서 I'll be lying on 대신 I am lying on으로 써야 올바르다.

③ [적중 포인트 044] 주어 자리에서 반드시 단수 또는 복수 취급하는 특정 표현
the wealth는 '富(부)'라는 뜻이고, 뒤에 ate라는 동사가 있는 것으로 보아 ate의 주어로 사람이 필요하므로 the wealth 대신 '부유한 사람들'을 뜻하는 the wealthy로 써야 올바르다.

찐Tip 'the 형용사'는 ~(인)한 사람들로 의미로 해석된다.

선지 해석
① 큰 도시의 교통은 작은 도시의 교통보다 더 바쁘다.
② 다음 주에 해변에 누워있을 때, 나는 당신을 생각할 것이다.
③ 과거에는 건포도는 비싼 음식으로, 부유한 사람들만이 그것을 먹었다.
④ 색상의 강도는 해당 색상이 얼마나 많은 회색을 포함하고 있는지와 관련이 있다.

Chapter 02 단어의 이해

ANSWER

01 ② 02 ③ 03 ③ 04 ② 05 ①
06 ④

01
정답 ②

정답 해설
② [적중 포인트 012] 지시대명사 this와 that
비교 표현(라틴어 비교급 superior to)인 뒤에 that이나 those가 나오면 앞에 나온 비교 대상의 수에 따라 단수 명사면 that을 쓰고, 복수 명사면 those를 쓴다. 따라서 단수 명사(the quality)를 받고 있다. 따라서 those 대신 that으로 써야 올바르다.

오답 해설
① [적중 포인트 080] 부사절 접속사의 구분과 특징
접속사 뒤에는 동사를 포함한 절을 이끌고 전치사 뒤에는 명사가 와야 한다. 따라서 뒤에 명사 목적어(the belief)가 있다. 따라서 밑줄 친 부분은 올바르게 쓰였다.
③ [적중 포인트 054] 분사 판별법[현재분사 VS 과거분사]
해당 문장에는 주어, 동사, 주격 보어가 있는 완전 구조이므로 밑줄 친 부분은 분사 자리임을 알 수 있다. 타동사가 목적어를 취하고 있지 않으므로 과거분사를 써야 한다. 따라서 밑줄 친 부분은 올바르게 쓰였다.
④ [적중 포인트 010] 격에 따른 인칭대명사
인칭대명사는 앞에 나온 명사와 성과 수 일치를 확인해야 한다. 따라서 밑줄 친 부분은 복수 명사(most pre-20th century houses)를 받고 있다. 따라서 밑줄 친 부분은 올바르게 쓰였다.

지문 해석
오래된 집들의 품질이 현대 집들보다 우수하다는 믿음에도 불구하고, 20세기 이전의 대부분의 집들의 토대는 현대의 토대에 비해 현저하게 얕으며 그것들의 목재 뼈대의 유연성이나 벽돌과 돌 사이의 모르타르 덕분에 세월의 시험을 견뎌왔을 뿐이다.

02
정답 ③

정답 해설
③ [적중 포인트 015] 주의해야 할 형용사
alive는 서술적 용법으로만 쓰이는 형용사로 보어 자리만 가능하고 뒤에 명사는 올 수 없다. 따라서 뒤에 man이라는 명사가 나오고 있으므로, alive 대신 명사를 앞에서 수식할 수 있는 형용사 live 또는 living으로 써야 올바르다.

오답 해설
① [적중 포인트 067] 주의해야 할 조동사와 조동사 관용 표현
should have p.p.는 '~했어야 했다'라는 의미로, but 다음에 가지못한 이유를 보여주고 있으므로 밑줄 친 부분은 올바르게 쓰였다.

② [적중 포인트 090] 원급 비교 구문
& [적중 포인트 064] to부정사의 관용 구문
'as ~ as' 원급 비교 구문이 쓰인 문장이다. '사람/사물 주어 + used to 동사원형'은 '~하곤 했다'의 의미로 쓰인다. 따라서 밑줄 친 부분은 올바르게 쓰였다.
찐Tip used to 뒤에 앞에 나온 save가 생략된 형태로 쓰였다.
④ [적중 포인트 046] 수동태 불가 동사
look은 자동사로 수동태 구조가 불가능하지만 look at은 '자동사 + 전치사' 구조로, 수동태 구조가 가능하다. 그림(The picture)이 미술 평론가(the art critic)에 의해 '보이는 것'이므로 수동태 was looked at은 올바르게 쓰였다.

선지 해석
① 나는 오늘 아침에 갔어야 했는데, 몸이 좀 안 좋았다.
② 요즘 우리는 예전에 했던 것만큼 많은 돈을 모으지 않는다.
③ 구조대는 살아 있는 남자를 발견해서 기뻐했다.
④ 그 그림은 미술 평론가에 의해 주의 깊게 관찰되었다.

03
정답 ③

정답 해설
③ [적중 포인트 060] to부정사의 명사적 역할
tend는 타동사로 목적어에 형용사를 취할 수 없다. 우리말로 봐도 '환자들과 부상자들'이므로 '~(인)한 사람들'의 표현하기 위해서는 'the 형용사'로 써야 한다. 따라서 sick and wounded 대신 the를 삽입한 the sick and the wounded로 써야 올바르다.

오답 해설
① [적중 포인트 078] 등위접속사와 병치 구조
& [적중 포인트 071] 강조 구문과 강조를 위한 표현
'It ~ that' 강조 구문으로, 'not A but B'가 주어 자리에 위치해 있다. A와 B는 명사형으로 병렬구조도 올바르게 쓰였다.
② [적중 포인트 067] 주의해야 할 조동사와 조동사 관용 표현
'아무리 ~해도 지나치지 않다'의 뜻을 가진 구문으로는 'cannot ~ too 형/부'의 조동사 관용 표현이 있다. 따라서 밑줄 친 부분은 올바르게 쓰였다.
찐Tip 또 다른 표현으로는 'cannot ~ enough = cannot ~ over동사'가 있다.
④ [적중 포인트 043] 혼동하기 쉬운 주어와 동사 수 일치
'there + 동사 + 명사 주어'의 어순과 수 일치 확인을 해야 한다. 주어(a report)가 단수 형태이므로 단수 동사 is는 올바르게 쓰였다.
찐Tip to make matters worse는 '설상가상으로'의 뜻으로 쓰인다.
찐Tip that절은 동격절로 뒤에 완전 구조를 취하고 있으므로 that 또한 올바르게 쓰였다.

선지 해석
① 그를 당황하게 한 것은 그녀의 거절이 아니라 그녀의 무례함이었다.
② 부모는 아이들 앞에서 그들의 말과 행동에 대해 아무리 신중해도 지나치지 않다.
③ 환자들과 부상자들을 돌보기 위해 더 많은 의사가 필요했다.
④ 설상가상으로, 또 다른 태풍이 곧 올 것이라는 보도가 있다.

04

정답 ②

정답 해설

② [적중 포인트 007] 불가산 명사의 종류와 특징
불가산 명사(homework)는 much 또는 little의 수식을 받고 부정관사 a(n)와 복수를 의미하는 -s를 쓰지 않는다. 따라서 many homeworks 대신 much homework로 써야 올바르다.

찐Tip 불가산 명사는 many 또는 few의 수식을 받을 수 없다.

오답 해설

① [적중 포인트 018] 혼동하기 쉬운 부사
부정문에서 '또한'을 의미를 나타내는 not either은 올바르게 쓰였다.

③ [적중 포인트 074] 가정법 과거완료 공식
'if + 주어 + had p.p.'가 나오면 가정법 과거 완료를 의미하고 '주어 + would/should/could/might have p.p.'가 올바르게 쓰였는지 확인해야 한다. 따라서 밑줄 친 부분은 가정법 과거완료 공식으로 올바르게 쓰였다.

④ [적중 포인트 027] 5형식 지각동사의 목적격 보어
'so ~ that' 구조로 that 뒤에 완전 구조를 취해야 한다. 지각동사(hear)는 목적어와 목적보어의 관계가 수동이면 목적보어 자리에는 과거분사를 써야 한다. 따라서 being blown off는 올바르게 쓰였다.

선지 해석

① George는 아직 과제를 완료하지 못했고, Mark도 마찬가지였다.
② 내 여동생은 해야 할 숙제가 너무 많아서 어젯밤에 화가 났다.
③ 만약 그가 은행에서 더 많은 돈을 찾았더라면, 그는 신발을 살 수 있었을텐데.
④ 방 안이 너무 조용해서 나는 밖에서 나뭇잎이 떨어지는 소리도 들을 수 있었다.

05

정답 ①

정답 해설

① [적중 포인트 014] 형용사와 부사의 차이
명사(computers)를 수식할 수 있는 것은 명사가 아닌 형용사이다. 따라서 person 대신 personal로 써야 올바르다.

오답 해설

② [적중 포인트 079] 명사절 접속사의 구분과 특징
& [적중 포인트 055] 감정 분사와 분사형 형용사
what절 뒤에 주어가 없는 불완전 구조로 올바르게 쓰였고, what절은 단수 취급하므로 단수 동사 was도 올바르게 쓰였다. 감정동사는 감정을 유발한다는 의미를 전달하고 사물을 수식할 경우 현재분사형으로 쓴다. '손자에게 일어난 일이 놀라게 하는 것'으로 능동의 의미이므로 현재분사 amazing 또한 올바르게 쓰였다.

③ [적중 포인트 069] 다양한 도치 구문
앞 문장이 긍정문일 경우에는 앞 문장에 대한 긍정 동의는 'and so 조동사 + 주어'를 사용한다. so는 부사이므로 반드시 절과 절을 이어주는 and가 반드시 필요하다. 앞에 be 동사면 so 뒤에도 be 동사를 사용해야 하므로 밑줄 친 부분은 올바르게 쓰였다.

④ [적중 포인트 034] 완료시제와 잘 쓰이는 시간 부사
'since 주어 + 과거시제 동사'의 완료시제를 나타내는 부사는 완료시제 동사를 확인한다. 문맥상 은퇴 이후 지금까지 계속 일을 했다는 의미이므로 현재완료 진행형 have been doing은 올바르게 쓰였다.

선지 해석

① 개인용 컴퓨터를 가장 많이 가지고 있는 나라는 종종 바뀐다.
② 지난 여름 나의 사랑스러운 손자에게 일어난 일은 놀라웠다.
③ 나무 숟가락은 아이들에게 매우 좋은 장난감이고 플라스틱 병 또한 그렇다.
④ 나는 은퇴 후부터 내내 이 일을 해 오고 있다.

06

정답 ④

정답 해설

④ [적중 포인트 015] 주의해야 할 형용사
단위를 나타내는 명사가 수사와 함께 또 다른 명사를 수식하는 형용사 역할을 할 때는 hyphen(-)을 사용하고 항상 단수형을 써야 한다. 따라서 years 대신 year로 써야 올바르다.

찐Tip 명사를 수식하지 않을 때는 복수형으로 쓴다.

찐Tip reach는 대표 3형식 타동사로 전치사 없이 목적어를 취할 수 있다.

오답 해설

① [적중 포인트 030] '말하다' 동사의 구분
& [적중 포인트 084] 관계대명사 주의 사항
'A에게 B에 관해 말하다'의 뜻을 가진 구문으로는 'tell A about B'의 표현이 있다. about의 목적어 역할을 하는 목적격 관계대명사 whom이 teacher과 I told 사이에 생략된 상태로 쓰였다.

② [적중 포인트 005] 단어의 8품사
'shy of + 명사'는 '명사가 부족한, 모자란'의 뜻으로 쓰인다. 따라서 밑줄 친 부분은 올바르게 쓰였다.

찐Tip call은 다양한 형식으로 쓰인다. 'call + 사람'의 3형식일 때는 '사람에게 전화하다'의 뜻으로, 'call + 명사 + 명사'의 5형식일 때는 '~을 ~라고 부르다'의 뜻으로 쓰인다.

③ [적중 포인트 079] 명사절 접속사의 구분과 특징
명사절 접속사 what은 앞에 명사가 없고 뒤에는 불완전 구조를 취한다. what절은 단수 취급하므로 단수동사 was도 올바르게 쓰였다.

선지 해석

① 제가 당신께 말씀드렸던 새로운 선생님은 원래 페루 출신입니다.
② 나는 긴급한 일로 자정이 5분 되기 전에 그에게 전화했다.
③ 상어로 보이는 것이 산호 뒤에 숨어 있었다.
④ 그녀는 일요일에 16세의 친구와 함께 산 정상에 올랐다.

Chapter 03 동사의 유형

ANSWER

01 ②	02 ②	03 ④	04 ①	05 ④
06 ①	07 ①	08 ①	09 ②	10 ④
11 ④	12 ③	13 ③	14 ③	15 ①
16 ③	17 ④	18 ②		

01
정답 ②

정답 해설

② [적중 포인트 046] 수동태 불가 동사
emerge는 '나타나다'의 뜻 1형식 자동사로 수동태 구조로는 쓸 수 없다. 따라서 are emerged 대신 emerge 또는 are emerging으로 써야 올바르다.

오답 해설

① [적중 포인트 019] 주어만 있으면 완전한 1형식 자동사
arrive는 '도착하다'의 뜻 1형식 자동사로 수동태 구조로는 쓸 수 없다. '도시, 나라'와 같은 공간을 목적어로 취할 때는 전치사 in과 결합할 수 있다. 따라서 밑줄 친 부분은 올바르게 쓰였다.

③ [적중 포인트 045] 능동태와 수동태의 차이
'are being shared'는 진행형 수동태로, 주어(cars) 입장에서는 행위를 받는 입장이므로 수동태로 써야 한다. 따라서 밑줄 친 부분은 올바르게 쓰였다.

④ [적중 포인트 054] 분사 판별법[현재분사 VS 과거분사]
주어(entire factories)가 서로 연결 되는 행위를 받는 입장이므로 수동의 과거분사로 써야 한다. 따라서 밑줄 친 부분은 올바르게 쓰였다.

지문 해석

우리는 이미 디지털화된 세상에 도달했다. 디지털화는 전통적인 IT 회사들뿐만 아니라 모든 분야의 회사들에 영향을 미친다. 새로운 및 변화된 비즈니스 모델이 등장하고 있다: 앱을 통해 자동차가 공유되고, 온라인으로 언어를 배우며, 음악이 스트리밍 되고 있다. 하지만 산업도 변하고 있다: 3D 프린터는 기계 부품을 만들고, 로봇이 이를 조립하며, 전체 공장이 서로 지능적으로 연결되고 있다.

02
정답 ②

정답 해설

② [적중 포인트 022] 4형식으로 착각하기 쉬운 3형식 타동사
mention은 '언급하다'의 뜻 4형식으로 착각하기 쉬운 3형식 타동사이다. 따라서 목적어를 두개 취하는 4형식 구조로는 쓸 수 없다. me 대신 to me로 써야 올바르다.

오답 해설

① [적중 포인트 060] to부정사의 명사적 역할
& [적중 포인트 055] 감정 분사와 분사형 형용사
5형식 동사 find는 'find + 가목적어 it + 목적격 보어 + 진목적어 to부정사'의 구조로 쓸 수 있다. 감정을 유발시킨다는 의미이고, 주로 사물을 수식할 경우에는 현재분사 exciting으로 써야 한다. 따라서 밑줄 친 부분은 올바르게 쓰였다.

③ [적중 포인트 025] to부정사를 목적격 보어로 취하는 대표 5형식 타동사
want를 5형식 구조로 쓸 때는 목적격 보어에 to부정사를 써야 한다. 따라서 밑줄 친 부분은 올바르게 쓰였다.

찐Tip want는 3형식 구조로도 쓰이지만, 'want that절'의 구조로는 쓸 수 없다.

④ [적중 포인트 074] 가정법 과거완료 공식
과거 시점에 대한 반대 상황을 가정하고 있으므로 가정법 과거완료를 써야 한다. 가정법 과거 완료 공식인 '주어 + would/should/could/might have p.p.'의 형태로 써야 한다. 따라서 밑줄 친 부분은 올바르게 쓰였다.

선지 해석

① 그는 이곳에서 일하는 것이 흥미롭다는 것을 알았다
② 그녀는 나에게 일찍 떠날 것이라고 언급했다.
③ 나는 그가 오는 것을 원하지 않았다.
④ 좀 더 능숙하고 경험 많은 선생님이었다면 그를 달리 대했을 것이다.

03
정답 ④

정답 해설

④ [적중 포인트 026] 5형식 사역동사의 목적격 보어
사역동사 have는 목적어와 목적보어의 관계가 능동일 경우에는 원형부정사를, 수동일 경우에는 과거분사(p.p.)를 목적보어로 취한다. 여기서 it이 가리키는 것이 the tip of a pencil이고, the tip of a pencil은 '제거되어지는 것'이므로 remove 대신 과거분사 removed로 써야 올바르다.

오답 해설

① [적중 포인트 045] 능동태와 수동태의 차이
사물이 주어 자리에 나오는 경우 수동태 'be p.p.' 구조로 잘 쓰인다. 수동태 구조에서 p.p. 자리에 위치하는 동사가 타동사이고 뒤에 목적어가 없는지도 확인한다. 따라서 밑줄 친 부분인 are expected와 전치사를 수반한 turn in(제출하다)도 be turned in으로 수동태로 올바르게 쓰였다.

② [적중 포인트 038] 시제 관련 표현
'~하자마자 ~했다'라는 의미의 시제관용구문은 'Hardly (Scarcely) + had 주어 p.p. + when(before) + 주어 + 과거동사'로 쓴다. 따라서 밑줄 친 부분은 올바르게 쓰였다.

③ [적중 포인트 066] 조동사 should의 3가지 용법과 생략 구조
주장·요구·명령·제안·충고(recommend)동사 뒤에 that절의 동사는 '(should) 동사원형'으로 쓴다. 따라서 밑줄 친 부분인 buy는 올바르게 쓰였다.

찐Tip 이외 주장·요구·명령·제안·충고동사로는 insist, demand, ask, command, order, suggest 등이 있다.

선지 해석

① 모든 과제는 제시간에 제출될 것으로 예상된다.
② 나는 눈을 감자마자 그녀를 생각하기 시작했다.
③ 중개인은 그녀에게 즉시 주식을 사라고 권했다.
④ 머리에 연필 끝이 꽂힌 여자가 마침내 그것을 제거했다.

04
정답 ①

정답 해설

① [적중 포인트 025] to부정사를 목적격 보어로 취하는 대표 5형식 타동사
'cause + 목적어 + to부정사(동사원형×)'의 구조를 취하므로 slip 대신 to slip으로 써야 올바르다.

찐Tip 콤마(,) + which 뒤에 주어 없는 불완전 구조는 올바르게 쓰였다.

오답 해설

② [적중 포인트 045] 능동태와 수동태의 차이
다음 문장은 'agree on + 목적어'가 수동태 형태인 'be agreed on + 목적어 없음' 구조로 올바르게 쓰였다.

찐Tip '사물 주어 + be p.p.' 구조로 잘 쓰인다.

③ [적중 포인트 027] 5형식 지각동사의 목적격 보어
지각동사(see)의 목적보어 자리에는 to부정사가 아닌 원형부정사, 현재분사를 쓴다. 따라서 밑줄 친 부분인 closing은 올바르게 쓰였다.

찐Tip get은 대표 2형식 자동사로 주격 보어에 형용사가 온다.

④ [적중 포인트 051] 동명사의 명사 역할
전치사 without 뒤에는 명사 또는 동명사를 쓴다. 따라서 밑줄 친 부분인 looking은 올바르게 쓰였다.

찐Tip walk는 '걷다'의 뜻을 가진 1형식 자동사로 쓰이면 수동태 형태(be p.p.)가 아닌 능동태 형태로만 쓸 수 있다.

선지 해석
① 어제 눈이 많이 와서 많은 사람들이 길에서 미끄러졌다.
② 그 협정들은 작년 회의에서 합의된 것이다.
③ 나는 트럭이 가까이 다가오는 것을 보고 겁에 질렸다.
④ 나는 뒤돌아보지 않고 앞문으로 걸어 나갔다.

05
정답 ④

정답 해설
④ [적중 포인트 027] 5형식 지각동사의 목적격 보어
지각동사(see)의 목적보어 자리에는 to부정사가 아닌 원형부정사, 현재분사를 쓴다. 따라서 to yawn 대신 yawn 또는 yawning으로 써야 올바르다.

찐Tip 이 문장에서 see는 동명사 seeing으로 쓰였다.

오답 해설
① [적중 포인트 001] 문장의 구성요소
catching은 '전염성이 있는, 매력적인'의 뜻을 가진 형용사로 역할을 한다. 따라서 밑줄 친 부분은 is의 보어자리에 올바르게 쓰였다.

② [적중 포인트 014] 형용사와 부사의 차이
부사 easily가 과거분사 influenced를 수식하고 있으므로 밑줄 친 부분은 올바르게 쓰였다.

③ [적중 포인트 080] 부사절 접속사의 구분과 특징
부사절 접속사 when이 완전한 절 'humans watch other people yawn'을 이끌고 있으므로 밑줄 친 부분은 올바르게 쓰였다.

지문 해석
하품은 전염성이 있다. 한 사람의 하품이 그룹 전체의 사람들에게 하품을 유발할 수 있다. 공감이 강한 사람들이 다른 사람의 하품에 좀 더 쉽게 영향을 받는 것으로 여겨진다. 뇌 이미징 연구는 인간이 다른 사람들이 하품하는 것을 볼 때 사교적 기능에 연관된 뇌 영역이 활성화되는 것을 보여준다. 심지어 개들도 주인이나 심지어 낯선 사람들이 하품하는 것을 볼 때 하품하는 반응을 보이고 있고, 전염성이 있는 하품은 다른 동물들에서도 관찰되었다.

06
정답 ①

정답 해설
① [적중 포인트 027] 5형식 지각동사의 목적격 보어
heard는 지각동사로 to부정사가 아닌 원형부정사, 현재분사 또는 과거분사를 목적보어로 취한다. 위 문장은 목적어와 목적어보어의 관계가 능동이므로 목적어보어를 원형부정사 또는 현재분사로 써야 한다. 따라서 목적어보어 자리의 sneezeing and coughing은 현재분사 형태로 올바르게 쓰였다.

찐Tip 이외 지각동사로는 see, watch, notice, observe, feel, hear, listen to 등이 있다.

오답 해설
② [적중 포인트 079] 명사절 접속사의 구분과 특징
ask는 4형식 동사로 쓰일 경우 '~을 묻다'라는 의미로 쓰일 때 궁금한 내용을 나타내는 의문의 의미를 갖는 절을 직접목적어로 취한다. 따라서 '내가 무언가 필요한 것이 있는지 없는지를 물어봤다'라는 의미를 나타내기 위해 that 대신 whether 또는 if로 써야 올바르다.

찐Tip 명사절 접속사 if는 타동사 뒤의 목적어 자리에만 쓰인다.

③ [적중 포인트 084] 관계대명사 주의 사항
명사(anything) 뒤에 목적격 관계대명사 that이 생략된 형태로 쓰였다. 목적격 관계대명사 that절은 불완전 구조를 취해야하므로 동사 뒤에 목적어가 없어야 한다. 따라서 he could do it 대신 it을 삭제한 he could do로 써야 올바르다.

찐Tip 계속적 용법에서 쓰인 목적격 관계대명사는 생략될 수 없으므로 주의가 필요하다.

④ [적중 포인트 026] 5형식 사역동사의 목적격 보어
make는 사역동사로 to부정사가 아닌 원형부정사 또는 과거분사를 목적보어로 취한다. 위 문장은 목적어와 목적어보어의 관계가 능동이므로 목적어보어를 원형부정사로 써야 한다. 따라서 to go away 대신 go away로 써야 올바르다.

지문 해석
지난 주에 나는 독감으로 아팠다. 아버지가 내가 재채기와 기침하는 소리를 들었을 때, 내 방 문을 열어서 내가 무언가 필요한 것이 있는지 없는지를 물어봤다. 나는 그의 친절하고 배려심 있는 얼굴을 보게 되어 정말 기뻤지만, 독감을 낫게 하기 위해 그가 할 수 있는 것은 없었다.

07
정답 ①

정답 해설
① [적중 포인트 032] 의미와 구조에 주의해야 할 타동사
found(-founded-founded)는 '~을 설립하다'의 뜻으로, find(-found-found)는 '~을 찾다, 발견하다'의 뜻으로 쓰인다. 문맥상 find가 더 자연스럽다. 또한 사실이 발견되는 것이므로 수동의 형태(be p.p.)로 써야 한다. 따라서 founded 대신 was found로 써야 올바르다.

오답 해설
② [적중 포인트 055] 감정 분사와 분사형 형용사
elected는 명사 officials를 꾸며주고 있으므로 '선출된'을 의미하고 있는 과거분사 형태로 올바르게 쓰였다.

③ [적중 포인트 039] 현재시제 동사와 be동사의 수 일치
host는 명사로 '주인'의 뜻으로 쓰이는데, 주어를 받는 동사가 were로 복수형이므로 주어도 복수 형태로 써야 한다. 따라서 hosts는 올바르게 쓰였다.

④ [적중 포인트 078] 등위접속사와 병치 구조
등위접속사(and) 기준으로 앞의 to pay와 같이 병렬구조로 to say는 올바르게 쓰였다.

찐Tip to부정사로 나열되는 경우는 뒤에 to는 생략이 가능하다.

지문 해석

최근 보고서에 따르면, 뉴욕시의 Airbnb 리스트 중 4분의 3은 불법이었다. 이 보고서는 또한 상업 운영자들이 — 광고 속의 중산층 뉴욕 주민이 아닌 — 독점적으로 Airbnb 손님들에게 공간을 임대해주면서 수백만 달러를 벌고 있다는 것을 발견했다. 지난 주에 당선된 공무원들에게 보내진 편지에서 Airbnb는 그것의 지역 호스트들 중 대부분은 — 87% — "그들의 명세서를 지불하고 그들의 집에 머물기 위해" 그들의 공간을 드물게 대여해주는 거주자들이라고 밝혔다.

08   정답 ①

정답 해설

① [적중 포인트 021] 전치사가 필요 없는 대표 3형식 타동사
ask는 타동사로 전치사 없이 목적어를 바로 취한다. 따라서 to him 대신 him으로 써야 올바르다.

찐Tip ask A about B는 'A에게 B에 관하여 묻다'라는 뜻이다.

오답 해설

② [적중 포인트 088] 전치사와 명사 목적어
but은 전치사로 '~을 제외하고'의 의미로 올바르게 쓰였고, 전치사 뒤에 명사를 쓴 것 또한 올바르게 쓰였다.

③ [적중 포인트 058] 분사를 활용한 표현 및 구문
시간 접속사 while 뒤에 -ing의 형태가 쓰인 분사구문이다. 주어(drinking water)가 단수형태이므로 단수 동사 is 또한 올바르게 쓰였다.

④ [적중 포인트 005] 단어의 8품사
'그렇긴 하지만'의 의미로 쓰일 경우 'that said'로 표현할 수 있다. 따라서 밑줄 친 부분은 올바르게 쓰였다.

선지 해석

① 우리는 그에게 이 일을 하도록 요청했다.
② 그들은 TV 빼고는 모두 훔쳤다.
③ 식사할 때 물 마시는 게 좋니?
④ 그렇긴 하지만, 그것은 여전히 종교적 축제이다.

09   정답 ②

정답 해설

② [적중 포인트 026] 5형식 사역동사의 목적격 보어
사역동사 let은 목적어와 목적보어의 수동의 의미 관계를 갖는 경우에는 반드시 목적보어 자리에 과거분사(p.p.)가 아닌 be p.p.를 써야 한다. 따라서 distracted 대신 be distracted로 써야 올바르다.

오답 해설

① [적중 포인트 026] 5형식 사역동사의 목적격 보어
사역동사 have는 목적어와 목적보어의 관계가 수동일 경우에는 목적보어 자리에 과거분사(p.p.)를 써야 한다. 목적어(the woman)가 체포되는 것이므로 목적보어에 과거분사 arrested는 올바르게 쓰였다.

③ [적중 포인트 026] 5형식 사역동사의 목적격 보어
사역동사 let은 목적어와 목적보어의 관계가 능동일 경우에는 목적보어 자리에 원형부정사를 써야 한다. 따라서 밑줄 친 부분인 know는 올바르게 쓰였다.

④ [적중 포인트 026] 5형식 사역동사의 목적격 보어
사역동사 have는 목적어와 목적보어의 관계가 능동일 경우에는 목적보어 자리에 원형부정사를 써야하므로 밑줄 친 부분인 phone은 올바르게 쓰였고, ask는 5형식 타동사로 목적어와 목적보어의 관계가 능동일 경우에는 목적보어 자리에 to부정사를 써야하므로 to donate 또한 올바르게 쓰였다.

선지 해석

① 경찰 당국은 자신의 이웃을 공격했기 때문에 그 여성을 체포하도록 했다.
② 네가 내는 소음 때문에 내 집중력을 잃게 하지 말아라.
③ 가능한 한 빨리 제가 결과를 알도록 해주세요.
④ 그는 학생들에게 모르는 사람들에게 전화를 걸어 성금을 기부할 것을 부탁하도록 시켰다.

10   정답 ④

정답 해설

④ [적중 포인트 027] 5형식 지각동사의 목적격 보어
지각동사 see는 목적어와 목적보어의 관계가 능동일 경우에는 목적보어 자리에는 to부정사가 아닌 원형부정사, 현재분사를 써야 한다. 주어진 해석에 의하면 목적어인 '한 가족이 이사한다'는 능동의 의미 관계이기 때문에 수동을 의미하는 moved 대신 moving으로 써야 올바르다.

오답 해설

① [적중 포인트 064] to부정사의 관용 구문
hard는 난이형용사로서 주어가 it이 아닌 것이 나오면 to부정사의 목적어가 주어 자리로 상승한 구문으로 난이형용사 다음에 나오는 to부정사 뒤에 목적어가 없어야 한다. 따라서 밑줄 친 부분은 올바르게 쓰였다.

② [적중 포인트 053] 암기해야 할 동명사 표현
'~해도 소용없다'의 의미로 쓰일 경우 'It is no use -ing'로 표현할 수 있다. 따라서 밑줄 친 부분은 올바르게 쓰였다.

③ [적중 포인트 045] 능동태와 수동태의 차이
'사물 주어 + 타동사의 be p.p.'의 구조로 뒤에 목적어가 없으므로 올바르게 쓰였다.

찐Tip every 다음 기수(숫자)가 나오면 복수 명사로 써야하므로 밑줄 친 부분은 올바르게 쓰였다.

찐Tip every 다음 서수(순서)가 나오면 단수 명사로 써야 한다.

선지 해석

① 그의 소설들은 읽기가 어렵다.
② 학생들을 설득하려고 해 봐야 소용없다.
③ 나의 집은 5년마다 페인트칠 된다.
④ 내가 출근할 때 한 가족이 위층에 이사 오는 것을 보았다.

11
정답 ④

정답 해설

④ [적중 포인트 023] 목적어 뒤에 특정 전치사를 수반하는 3형식 타동사
'A가 ~하는 것을 막다'의 뜻을 가진 구문으로 금지, 방해동사 중 'prevent A from -ing'가 있다. 따라서 밑줄 친 부분은 올바르게 쓰였다.

오답 해설

① [적중 포인트 039] 현재시제 동사와 be동사의 수 일치
as는 접속사이며 the old saying은 단수형태 주어이므로 동사도 단수동사로 써야하므로 go 대신 goes로 써야 올바르다.

② [적중 포인트 014] 형용사와 부사의 차이
동사(affect)를 꾸며주는 것은 형용사가 아니라 부사이다. 따라서 형용사 obvious 대신 부사 obviously로 써야 올바르다.

③ [적중 포인트 032] 의미와 구조에 주의해야 할 타동사
help는 5형식으로 쓰일 경우 목적보어 자리에 원형부정사, to부정사를 써야 한다. 따라서 being concentrated 대신 concentrate 또는 to concentrate로 써야 올바르다.

지문 해석

속담에 따르면, 당신은 무엇을 먹느냐에 따라 당신의 모습이 달라진다. 당신이 먹는 음식은 분명히 당신의 신체 수행능력에 영향을 미친다. 그것들은 또한 뇌가 작업을 처리하는 방식에도 영향을 줄 수 있다. 뇌가 그 작업을 잘 처리한다면, 당신은 더 명확하게 생각하고 더 감정적으로 안정된다. 적절한 음식은 집중력을 높이고, 동기 부여를 유지하고, 기억력을 강화하고, 반응 시간을 빠르게 하고, 스트레스를 줄이며, 아마도 심지어 당신의 뇌가 노화되는 것도 막아줄 수도 있다.

12
정답 ③

정답 해설

③ [적중 포인트 023] 목적어 뒤에 특정 전치사를 수반하는 3형식 타동사
'A가 ~하는 것을 막다'의 뜻을 가진 구문으로 금지, 방해동사 중 'prohibit A from -ing'가 있다. 그가 부회장으로 '승진하는 것'을 막는 것이므로 수동형 동명사(being p.p.)형태로 써야한다. 따라서 능동형 동명사 promoting 대신 being promoted로 써야 올바르다.

오답 해설

① [적중 포인트 011] 재귀대명사의 2가지 용법
주어와 동일한 목적어는 인칭대명사가 아니라 재귀대명사로 써야한다. 따라서 밑줄 친 부분은 올바르게 쓰였다.

② [적중 포인트 064] to부정사의 관용 구문
'~하지 않을 수 없다, ~할 수밖에 없다'의 뜻으로 쓰일 경우 'have no choice[option/alternative] but to부정사'로 표현할 수 있다. 따라서 밑줄 친 부분은 올바르게 쓰였다.

④ [적중 포인트 064] to부정사의 관용 구문
난이 형용사(easy) 구문은 'It be동사 + 난이 형용사 + (for 목적어) + to부정사'의 구조로 쓰인다. 따라서 밑줄 친 부분은 올바르게 쓰였다.

선지 해석

① 인간은 환경에 자신을 빨리 적응시킨다.
② 그녀는 그 사고 때문에 그녀의 목표를 포기할 수밖에 없었다.
③ 그 회사는 그가 부회장으로 승진하는 것을 금했다.
④ 그 장난감 자동차를 조립하고 분리하는 것은 쉽다.

13
정답 ③

정답 해설

③ [적중 포인트 020] 주격 보어가 필요한 2형식 자동사
'so 형용사/부사 that 주어 + 동사' 완전 구조로 look은 2형식 동사인 감각동사로 주격보어 자리에 '형용사 또는 like 명사'를 써야 한다. 따라서 밑줄 친 부분은 올바르게 쓰였다.

찐Tip 'as if 주어 + 동사'는 '마치 ~인 것처럼'의 뜻으로 쓰인다.

오답 해설

① [적중 포인트 090] 원급 비교 구문
원급 비교 구문에서 부사 as를 more로 쓰거나 접속사 as를 than으로 쓸 수 없다. 따라서 than 대신 as로 써야 올바르다.

찐Tip 원급 비교 구문 앞의 문장 구조가 완전하면 부사를 쓴다.

② [적중 포인트 001] 문장의 구성요소
목적어인 us 앞에는 명사가 아닌 동사가 필요하다. 따라서 명사 company 대신 동사 accompany로 써야 올바르다.

④ [적중 포인트 007] 불가산 명사의 종류와 특징
sugar는 불가산 명사이므로 the number of 대신 the amount of로 써야 올바르다.

선지 해석

① 벌과 꽃만큼 친밀하게 연결된 생물은 드물다.
② 내 아버지는 그들이 머무는 장소까지 우리를 동반하지는 않았지만, 내가 가야할 것을 주장했다.
③ 이라크의 상황이 매우 심각해 보여서 마치 제3차 세계 대전이 언제든지 발발할 것처럼 보였다.
④ 최근 보고서에 따르면, 미국인들이 섭취하는 설탕의 양은 해마다 크게 변하지 않는다.

14
정답 ③

정답 해설

③ [적중 포인트 021] 전치사가 필요 없는 대표 3형식 타동사
marry는 3형식 타동사이므로 전치사 없이 목적어를 수반해서 'marry + 목적어'로 쓰거나 수동태 구조로 쓸 경우에는 'be married to + 목적어'의 구조로 써야 하므로 has married to 대신 has married 또는 has been married to로 써야 올바르다.

오답 해설

① [적중 포인트 080] 부사절 접속사의 구분과 특징
조건 부사절 접속사인 in case는 '~할 경우에 (대비하여)'라는 의미로 쓰이고 미래시제를 현재시제 동사로 대신하므로 밑줄 친 부분은 올바르게 쓰였다.

② [적중 포인트 053] 암기해야 할 동명사 표현
'~하느라 바쁘다'의 의미로 쓰일 경우 'be busy -ing'로 표현할 수 있다. 따라서 밑줄 친 부분은 올바르게 쓰였다.

④ [적중 포인트 061] to부정사의 형용사적 역할
to부정사는 명사를 수식할 수 있고 to부정사의 의미상 주어는 'for + 명사'의 형태로 쓴다. 따라서 밑줄 친 부분인 for my son to read는 올바르게 쓰였다.

선지 해석

① 혹시 내게 전화하고 싶은 경우에 이게 내 번호야.
② 나는 유럽 여행을 준비하느라 바쁘다.
③ 그녀는 남편과 결혼한 지 20년 이상 되었다.
④ 나는 내 아들이 읽을 책을 한 권 사야 한다.

15 정답 ①

정답 해설

① [적중 포인트 023] 목적어 뒤에 특정 전치사를 수반하는 3형식 타동사
attribute는 3형식 타동사로, 'A를 B의 탓으로 돌리다'의 뜻을 가진 구문으로 'attribute A to B'가 있다. 따라서 for 대신 to로 써야 올바르다.

오답 해설

② [적중 포인트 083] 「전치사＋관계대명사」 완전 구조
'전치사 + 관계대명사'가 나오면 전치사에 유의하고 뒤에 완전 구조인지 확인해야 한다. in which 뒤에 수동태 문장인 완전 구조가 올바르게 쓰였고, 꿈속에서의 내용이므로 전치사 in 또한 올바르게 쓰였다.

③ [적중 포인트 079] 명사절 접속사의 구분과 특징
동사 noticed 뒤에 that은 명사절 접속사로 목적어 역할을 하고 that 뒤에는 항상 완전 구조를 이끈다. 따라서 that 뒤에 완전 구조로 밑줄 친 부분은 올바르게 쓰였다.

찐Tip noticed와 that 사이에 as they danced around him은 부사절로 삽입된 것이다.

④ [적중 포인트 062] to부정사의 부사적 역할
to부정사는 부사 자리에서도 여러 가지 의미로 쓰일 수 있다. 따라서 밑줄 친 부분이 '~하기 위해서'의 뜻을 가진 부사적 용법으로 밑줄 친 부분은 올바르게 쓰였다.

지문 해석

발명가 Elias Howe는 재봉틀의 발견을 식인종에게 붙잡힌 꿈 덕분이라고 말했다. 그는 그들이 그의 주위에서 춤을 출 때 창 끝에 구멍이 있다는 것을 알아차렸고, 그는 이것이 자신의 문제를 해결하는 데 필요한 디자인적 특징이라는 것을 깨달았다.

16 정답 ③

정답 해설

③ [적중 포인트 025] to부정사를 목적격 보어로 취하는 대표 5형식 타동사
believe는 뒤에 목적어(that절)만 쓰거나 'believe + 목적어 + to부정사'의 형태로 써야 한다. 따라서 John believed that Mary would be happy 또는 John believed Mary to be happy로 써야 올바르다.

찐Tip 'believe + 목적어 + that절'의 형태로는 쓸 수 없다.

오답 해설

① [적중 포인트 024] 목적어를 두 개 취하는 4형식 수여동사
promise는 수여동사로 뒤에 that절을 직접목적어로 쓸 수 있다. 따라서 밑줄 친 부분은 올바르게 쓰였다.

② [적중 포인트 024] 목적어를 두 개 취하는 4형식 수여동사
tell은 수여동사로 뒤에 that절을 직접목적어로 쓸 수 있다. 따라서 밑줄 친 부분은 올바르게 쓰였다.

④ [적중 포인트 023] 목적어 뒤에 특정 전치사를 수반하는 3형식 타동사
remind는 통고, 확신동사로 'remind + A(대상) that절'의 구조로 쓸 수 있다. 따라서 밑줄 친 부분은 올바르게 쓰였다.

선지 해석

① John은 Mary에게 그의 방을 청소할 것이라고 약속했다.
② John은 Mary에게 일찍 떠날 것이라고 말했다.
③ John은 Mary가 행복할 것이라고 믿었다.
④ John은 Mary에게 그곳에 일찍 도착해야 한다고 상기시켰다.

17 정답 ④

정답 해설

④ [적중 포인트 021] 전치사가 필요 없는 대표 3형식 타동사
'전치사 + 관계대명사'가 나오면 전치사에 유의하고 뒤에 완전 구조인지 확인해야 한다. affect는 전치사에 주의할 3형식 타동사로 전치사를 쓰지 않고 목적어를 바로 써야하므로 affects on 대신 전치사 on을 삭제한 affects로 써야 올바르다.

오답 해설

① [적중 포인트 054] 분사 판별법[현재분사 VS 과거분사]
명사(a nature documentary) 뒤에 produce는 현재분사인지 과거분사인지 확인해야 한다. 문맥상 명사가 만들어지는 것의 수동의 의미이고 뒤에 목적어도 없으므로 과거분사(p.p.) 형태인 produced는 올바르게 쓰였다.

② [적중 포인트 028] 분사를 목적격 보어로 취하는 5형식 동사
leave는 5형식 동사로 목적보어 자리에 분사나 형용사를 취할 수 있다. 목적어와 목적보어의 관계가 상태를 나타낼 때는 형용사 형태로도 올 수 있다. 따라서 밑줄 친 부분인 heartbroken은 올바르게 쓰였다.

③ [적중 포인트 083] 「전치사＋관계대명사」 완전 구조
which 뒤에 완전 구조로 쓰이고 있으므로 관계대명사는 올 수가 없다. 따라서 관계부사 또는 '전치사 + 관계대명사'로 와야하고, extent는 to와 쓰이므로 전치사 to 또한 올바르게 쓰였다.

지문 해석

BBC에서 제작한 자연 다큐멘터리인 *Blue Planet II*는 플라스틱이 바다에 어느정도의 범위까지 영향을 미치는지 보여준 후 시청자들을 심적으로 깊이 슬프게 만들었다.

18 정답 ②

정답 해설

② [적중 포인트 020] 주격 보어가 필요한 2형식 자동사
감각동사 look은 2형식 동사로 주격 보어 자리에 '형용사 또는 like 명사'가 올 수 있다. 따라서 '명사 + -ly' 형태인 형용사 lovely는 올바르게 쓰였다.

찐Tip 부사는 '형용사 + -ly'형태로 나타내므로 주의가 필요하고 감각동사(look)를 포함한 2형식 동사의 주격 보어로 부사는 절대 올 수 없다.

오답 해설

① [적중 포인트 021] 전치사가 필요 없는 대표 3형식 타동사
approach는 전치사가 필요없는 대표 3형식 타동사이다. 따라서 전치사 to를 삭제해야 올바르다.

③ [적중 포인트 022] 4형식으로 착각하기 쉬운 3형식 타동사
explain은 4형식으로 착각하기 쉬운 3형식 타동사로 4형식 구조인 '간접목적어 + 직접목적어' 목적어 2개를 취할 수 없다. 따라서 us 대신 to us로 써야 올바르다.

④ [적중 포인트 055] 감정 분사와 분사형 형용사
disappoint는 감정동사로 be동사 뒤에 보어로 쓰였다. 감정을 느낀다는 의미로 쓰이고 주로 사람을 수식할 경우에는 과거분사(p.p.) 형태로 써야 한다. 따라서 사람을 수식하고 있으므로 disappointing 대신 disappointed로 써야 올바르다.

지문 해석

- 경찰관은 살인 용의자에게 다가갔다.
- 당신의 아기는 사랑스러워 보인다.
- 그는 우리에게 어떻게 시험을 통과했는지 설명할 것이다.
- 그는 시험 결과에 실망했다.

Chapter 04 동사의 시제

ANSWER

| 01 ④ | 02 ② | 03 ④ | 04 ④ | 05 ② |
| 06 ③ | 07 ② | 08 ① | | |

01

정답 ④

정답 해설

④ [적중 포인트 035] 미래를 대신하는 현재시제
빈칸은 동사의 시제를 물어보는 문제이다. 시간의 부사절에서는 현재시제가 미래를 대신한다. 따라서 밑줄 친 부분에 들어갈 말로 가장 적절한 것은 'finishes'이다.

지문 해석

그녀는 학위를 마치고, 그녀는 공부 분야에서 귀중한 지식을 획득할 것이다.

02

정답 ②

정답 해설

② [적중 포인트 034] 완료시제와 잘 쓰이는 시간 부사
bear는 타동사로 '(아이를) 낳다'라는 뜻으로 쓰이고 뒤에 목적어가 없을 때 'be born'의 형태로 '태어나다'라는 의미로 쓰인다. 따라서 밑줄 친 부분인 was born은 올바르게 쓰였다.

찐Tip 'since 주어 + 과거시제 동사'는 주절에 현재완료 시제 동사와 함께 쓰이므로 주어진 문장에서 have lived 또한 올바르게 쓰였다.

오답 해설

① [적중 포인트 003] 어순이 중요한 간접의문문
간접의문문의 어순은 '의문사 + (주어) + 동사'이므로 밑줄 친 부분인 4형식 동사인 tell의 직접목적어 자리에 쓰인 간접의문문의 어순을 where should you 대신 where you should로 써야 올바르다.

③ [적중 포인트 055] 감정 분사와 분사형 형용사
사물을 수식할 때 감정분사는 현재분사형으로 쓰므로 밑줄 친 부분인 'the novel'을 수식해 주는 감정분사는 excited 대신 exciting으로 써야 올바르다.

④ [적중 포인트 004] 주절의 주어와 동사가 중요한 부가 의문문
부가의문문은 평서문과 반대의 상황으로 만든다. 평서문이 부정문이기 때문에 부가의문문은 긍정으로 만들어야 한다. 또한 평서문의 동사에 맞춰서 부가의문문의 조동사를 써야 하므로 doesn't it 대신 is it으로 써야 올바르다.

선지 해석

① 이 안내서는 홍콩에서 어디를 방문해야 하는지 알려준다.
② 나는 대만에서 태어났지만, 일을 시작한 이후로 한국에 살았다.
③ 그 소설은 너무 재미있어서 시간 가는줄 몰랐고 버스를 놓쳤다.
④ 책 가게들이 더 이상 신문을 취급하지 않는 것은 놀라운 일이 아니야, 그렇지 않니?

03

정답 ④

정답 해설

④ [적중 포인트 033] 과거 시간을 나타내는 부사와 과거시제
'When 주어 과거동사'가 나오면 주절(접속사가 없는 주어 동사 부분)도 과거 관련 시제로 나와야 한다. 따라서 뒤에 현재동사 does 대신 과거동사 did로 써야 올바르다.

찐Tip 부정부사(little)가 문두에 나오면 '조동사 + 주어 ~'인 도치 구조를 취한다.

오답 해설

① [적중 포인트 026] 5형식 사역동사의 목적격 보어
사역동사 have는 목적어와 목적보어의 관계가 수동일 경우에는 목적보어 자리에 과거분사(p.p.)를 써야 한다. 목적어(his political enemies)가 투옥되는 것이므로 목적보어에 과거분사 imprisoned는 올바르게 쓰였다.

② [적중 포인트 081] 주의해야 할 부사절 접속사
조건 부사절 접속사(unless)에서 주어 + 동사 완전 구조로 써야 하고 뒤에 부정어 표현은 나올 수 없다. 따라서 밑줄 친 부분은 올바르게 쓰였다.

③ [적중 포인트 053] 암기해야 할 동명사 표현
'~하기를 기대하다'의 뜻을 가진 구문으로 'look forward to -ing'가 있다. 따라서 밑줄 친 부분은 올바르게 쓰였다.

선지 해석

① 그는 자신의 정적들을 투옥시켰다.
② 경제적 자유가 없다면 진정한 자유가 있을 수 없다.
③ 나는 가능하면 빨리 당신과 거래할 수 있기를 바란다.
④ 30년 전 고향을 떠날 때, 그는 다시는 고향을 못 볼거라고 꿈에도 생각지 않았다.

04

정답 ④

정답 해설

④ [적중 포인트 034] 완료시제와 잘 쓰이는 시간 부사
& [적중 포인트 018] 혼동하기 쉬운 부사
㉠ 'for 기간' 시간부사는 완료시제 동사를 확인한다. 따라서 현재완료시제 형태(have p.p.)인 have brought로 써야 올바르다.
㉡ most는 '대부분'을 뜻하는 형용사이고, almost는 '거의'를 뜻하는 부사이다. 명사(people)를 수식할 수 있는 것은 부사가 아닌 형용사이므로 Most로 써야 올바르다.

지문 해석

지난 50년 동안 화학 분야의 발전은 미국의 생활 방식에 많은 긍정적인 변화를 가져왔다. 대부분의 사람들은 신제품의 안전성을 보장하는 데 정부와 기업을 단순히 신뢰해 왔다.

05
정답 ②

정답 해설
② [적중 포인트 038] 시제 관련 표현
'~하고 나서야 (비로소) ~하다'의 뜻을 가진 구문으로 'It be + not until ~ + that 주어 + 동사'가 있다. 따라서 밑줄 친 부분은 올바르게 쓰였다.

오답 해설
① [적중 포인트 083] 「전치사+관계대명사」 완전 구조
관계대명사 which 뒤에 완전 구조를 취하므로 관계대명사 which 대신 in which 또는 where로 써야 올바르다.

③ [적중 포인트 001] 문장의 구성요소
절과 절을 연결하려면 접속사가 반드시 필요하다. 따라서 주어 동사와 주어 동사 사이 we had 앞에 접속사 so를 넣어야 올바르다.

④ [적중 포인트 064] to부정사의 관용 구문
부사 enough는 형용사나 부사를 후치 수식한다. 따라서 enough fortunate 대신 fortunate enough로 써야 올바르다.

찐Tip ,(콤마) 다음 that절은 올 수 없으므로 ,that 대신 ,which로 써야 올바르다.

선지 해석
① 그들이 10년간 살았던 집이 폭풍에 심하게 손상되었다.
② 수학 시험에 실패했을 때에서야 그는 공부를 열심히 하기로 결심했다.
③ 냉장고에 먹을 것이 하나도 남아있지 않아서, 어젯밤에 우리는 외식을 해야 했다.
④ 우리는 운이 좋게도 그랜드캐년을 방문했는데, 거기에는 경치가 아름다운 곳이 많다.

06
정답 ③

정답 해설
③ [적중 포인트 035] 미래를 대신하는 현재시제
시간, 조건 부사절 접속사 다음에는 미래시제 대신 현재 동사로 쓴다. 또한 arrive는 왕래발착동사인 대표 1형식 자동사이므로 수동태로 쓸 수 없다. 따라서 arrives로 써야 올바르다.

지문 해석
오늘 저녁에 내 비행기가 도착할 때, Maggie는 나를 기다리고 있을 것이다.

07
정답 ②

정답 해설
② [적중 포인트 035] 미래를 대신하는 현재시제
unless와 같은 조건 부사절 접속사 다음에는 미래시제 대신 현재 동사로 쓴다. 따라서 밑줄 친 부분인 leaves가 올바르게 쓰였다.

오답 해설
① [적중 포인트 027] 5형식 지각동사의 목적격 보어
지각동사 watch는 목적어와 목적보어의 관계가 수동일 경우에는 목적보어 자리에 과거분사(p.p.)를 써야 한다. 주어(the game)가 보여지는 것이므로 watching 대신 watched로 써야 올바르다.

찐Tip watch 뒤에 목적어가 없으므로 수동형(be p.p.)으로 쓴다.

③ [적중 포인트 058] 분사를 활용한 표현 및 구문
with 분사구문으로 'with + 목적어' 다음 목적보어 자리에 능동(-ing)인지 수동(p.p.)인지 확인해야 한다. stream은 자동사이므로 수동태 형태로 쓸 수 없다. 따라서 streamed 대신 streaming으로 써야 올바르다.

④ [적중 포인트 082] 관계대명사의 선행사와 문장 구조
& [적중 포인트 019] 주어만 있으면 완전한 1형식 자동사
관계대명사 which는 불완전 구조를 취한다. fall은 '떨어지다'의 의미로 쓰일 때는 1형식 자동사이므로 fell 대신 전치사 into를 삽입한 fell into로 써야 불완전한 구조가 되어 올바르다.

선지 해석
① 경기는 경기장 밖에서 거대한 화면으로 시청되었다.
② 우리는 기차가 5분 안에 떠나지 않으면 회의에 도착하지 못할 것이다.
③ 창문을 통해 햇빛이 들어온 채로, Hugh는 자는 것이 불가능하다고 생각했다.
④ 그녀가 빠졌던 물은 얼음장 같이 차가웠다.

08
정답 ①

정답 해설
① [적중 포인트 033] 과거 시간을 나타내는 부사와 과거시제
'시간 ago'라는 명백한 과거를 나타내는 과거 시간 부사가 나오면 반드시 과거동사(went)를 확인한다. 따라서 밑줄 친 부분은 올바르게 쓰였다.

찐Tip see off는 '~를 배웅하다'의 뜻으로 쓰인다.

오답 해설
② [적중 포인트 059] 원형부정사의 용법과 관용 표현
'~인 체하다'라는 표현은 make believe로 써야 한다. 따라서 made it believe 대신 made believe로 써야 올바르다.

찐Tip 'make it believe'는 없는 표현이다.

③ [적중 포인트 053] 암기해야 할 동명사 표현
'~하기를 기대하다'의 뜻을 가진 구문으로 'look forward to -ing'가 있다. 따라서 to go 대신 to going으로 써야 올바르다.

찐Tip have been to는 '~에 가본 적이 있다'의 뜻으로 쓰인다.

④ [적중 포인트 055] 감정 분사와 분사형 형용사
사물을 수식할 때 감정분사는 현재분사형으로 쓴다. 따라서 밑줄 친 부분인 'anything'을 수식해 주는 감정분사는 interested 대신 interesting으로 써야 올바르다.

선지 해석
① 그는 며칠 전에 친구를 배웅하기 위해 역으로 갔다.
② 버릇없는 그 소년은 아버지가 부르는 것을 못 들은 체했다.
③ 나는 버팔로에 가본 적이 없어서 그곳에 가기를 고대하고 있다.
④ 나는 아직 오늘 신문을 못 읽었어. 뭐 재미있는 것 있니?

Chapter 05 주어와 동사 수 일치

ANSWER

01 ③	02 ①	03 ①	04 ③	05 ②
06 ③	07 ②	08 ①	09 ③	10 ②
11 ②	12 ②	13 ④	14 ④	15 ①
16 ③	17 ③	18 ④	19 ③

01
정답 ③

정답 해설
③ [적중 포인트 043] 혼동하기 쉬운 주어와 동사 수 일치
「There be 동사/1형식 자동사」는 뒤에 나온 명사와 수 일치한다. 문장의 주어가 단수 명사인 'an established process'이므로, 동사도 단수형으로 써야 한다. 따라서 were 대신 was로 써야 올바르다.

오답 해설
① [적중 포인트 060] to부정사의 명사적 역할
동사 tend는 목적어로 to부정사를 취하는 3형식 타동사이다. 따라서 밑줄 친 부분은 올바르게 쓰였다.

② [적중 포인트 088] 전치사와 명사 목적어
장소에 대한 '전치사 + 명사'의 부사구로, 여기서 outside는 '~밖에'라는 의미의 전치사로 사용되었고, 뒤에 명사 목적어가 적절히 따라와 문맥상 자연스럽다. 따라서 밑줄 친 부분은 올바르게 쓰였다.

④ [적중 포인트 049] 5형식 동사의 수동태 구조
'be made + 명사' 형태의 수동태로 '~가 되다'는 뜻을 나타낸다. 따라서 밑줄 친 부분은 올바르게 쓰였다.

지문 해석
우리는 로빈 후드와 일반적인 무법자들을, 왕의 관리들에 맞서고 왕국의 거대한 숲에서 법 밖에서 활동했기 때문에 흔히 도망자처럼 상상하는 경향이 있다. 우리가 잊고 있는 것은, 무법자가 만들어지는 데에는 하나의 정해진 절차가 있었다는 점이다. 대체로, 사람들은 스스로 무법자가 되기를 선택한 것이 아니라, 무법자로 만들어진 것이었다.

02
정답 ①

정답 해설
① [적중 포인트 039] 현재시제 동사와 be동사의 수 일치
동사의 주어가 단수 명사(knowledge)이므로 단수 동사로 수 일치해야 한다. 따라서 are 대신 is로 써야 올바르다.

오답 해설
② [적중 포인트 032] 의미와 구조에 주의해야 할 타동사
help의 목적보어로 원형 부정사와 to부정사가 올 수 있다. 따라서 밑줄 친 부분은 올바르게 쓰였다.

③ [적중 포인트 014] 형용사와 부사의 차이
all은 부사로 조동사 have 뒤에서 쓸 수 있다. 따라서 밑줄 친 부분은 올바르게 쓰였다.

④ [적중 포인트 053] 암기해야 할 동명사 표현
'~하는 데 어려움을 겪다'의 뜻으로 쓰일 때는 'have difficulty[trouble, a hard time] -ing'의 동명사 관용 구문 표현으로 쓸 수 있다. 따라서 밑줄 친 부분을 올바르게 쓰였다.

지문 해석
사운드 시스템, 단어 패턴, 문장 구조는 언어에서 유능한 학생에게 유능한 사람이 될 수 있다는 결론을 내릴 수 있다. 그러나 우리는 모두 영어를 구조적으로 이해하지만 여전히 의사 소통하는 데 어려움을 겪는다.

03
정답 ①

정답 해설
① [적중 포인트 043] 혼동하기 쉬운 주어와 동사 수 일치
the number of는 복수 명사와 단수 동사로 쓰고 '명사의 수'로 해석된다. 따라서 밑줄 친 부분은 올바르게 쓰였다.

오답 해설
② [적중 포인트 033] 과거 시간을 나타내는 부사와 과거시제
시간 ago와 같은 명백한 과거를 나타내는 과거 시간 부사가 나오면 반드시 과거 동사를 확인해야 한다. 따라서 완료시제 have received 대신 과거시제 received로 써야 올바르다.

③ [적중 포인트 083] 「전치사+관계대명사」 완전 구조
관계대명사 뒤의 문장 구조는 불완전 구조이어야 한다. 관계대명사 뒤에 1형식 자동사(slept)가 쓰여 완전한 구조이므로 관계대명사 which 대신 전치사 + 관계대명사인 in which 또는 관계부사 where로 써야 한다.

④ [적중 포인트 002] 구와 절, 문장이 길어지는 이유
해당 문장은 이미 주어, 동사, 목적어로 완전한 구조로 구성되어 있는데 뒤에 대명사(each other)가 나와 있으므로 부사구의 역할을 할 수 있도록 전명구(전치사 + 명사)로 바꿔줘야 한다. 따라서 밑줄 친 부분인 each other 앞에 with을 추가해야 한다.

선지 해석
① 지원자 수가 증가하고 있어서 우리는 기쁘다.
② 나는 2년 전에 그에게서 마지막 이메일을 받았다.
③ 어젯밤에 그가 잔 침대는 꽤 편안했다.
④ 그들은 영상으로 새해 인사를 교환했다.

04
정답 ③

정답 해설
③ [적중 포인트 039] 현재시제 동사와 be동사의 수 일치
주어와 동사 사이에 있는 수식어는 주어와 동사 수 일치에 영향을 미치지 않는다. 따라서 주어는 단수 주어인 the biomedical view이므로 conceal 대신 단수 동사 conceals로 써야 올바르다.

찐Tip 최근에는 주어와 동사 사이에 많은 수식어를 넣어 긴 문장이 출제되므로 주어와 동사를 제대로 찾는 연습이 필요하다.

오답 해설
① [적중 포인트 060] to부정사의 명사적 역할
'5형식 동사(make) + 가목적어 it + 목적보어(형용사/명사) + (for 의미상 주어) + to부정사'의 구조로 to부정사를 받아주기 위한 가목적어 it이 있는지 반드시 확인해야 한다. 따라서 밑줄 친 부분은 올바르게 쓰였다.

찐Tip 이외 5형식 동사로는 believe, consider, find, think가 있다.

② [적중 포인트 047] 다양한 3형식 동사의 수동태 구조
3형식 that절 구조의 수동태로 It be p.p. that절로 가주어 It과 진주어 that절은 올바르게 쓰였고, 명사절 접속사 that은 완전 구조를 수반하므로 뒤에 완전 구조가 온 것 또한 올바르게 쓰였다.
④ [적중 포인트 014] 형용사와 부사의 차이
형용사와 부사를 구분하는 문제이다. 동사 represents를 수식하는 것은 형용사가 아닌 부사이다. 따라서 밑줄 친 부분인 부사 accurately는 올바르게 쓰였다.

지문 해석
이식 기술의 발전으로 장기 질환 말기인 환자들의 수명을 연장하는 것을 가능하게 했지만, 장기이식을 심장이나 신장이 성공적으로 교체되면 끝나는 제한적인 사건으로 보는 생물 의학적 관점이 장기를 이식받는 경험을 더 정확하게 나타내주는 복잡하고 역동적인 과정을 숨긴다는 주장이 제기되고 있다.

05   정답 ②

정답 해설
② [적중 포인트 041] 부분을 나타내는 명사와 수 일치
'most of'는 뒤에 나오는 명사에 수 일치해야 한다. 뒤의 명사(the suggestions)가 복수 형태이므로 단수 동사 was 대신 복수 동사 were로 써야 올바르다.

찐Tip make는 명사(the suggestions)를 후치 수식하는 것으로 뒤에 목적어도 없고 문맥상 제안들이 만들어지는 것이므로 과거분사 made는 올바르게 쓰였다.

오답 해설
① [적중 포인트 067] 주의해야 할 조동사와 조동사 관용 표현
should have p.p.는 '~하지 말았어야 했다'의 뜻으로 과거에 대한 후회나 유감을 나타낸다. 따라서 문맥상 '많이 먹지말아야 했다'의 뜻이 자연스러우므로 밑줄 친 부분은 올바르게 쓰였다.
③ [적중 포인트 080] 부사절 접속사의 구분과 특징
Providing은 부사절 접속사로 S + V와 S + V를 연결해주는 역할을 한다. 따라서 밑줄 친 부분은 올바르게 쓰였다.
④ [적중 포인트 033] 과거 시간을 나타내는 부사와 과거시제
when 주어 + 과거시제 동사로 나왔기 때문에, 주절은 과거보다 앞선 시점을 표현하는 과거완료시제(had p.p.)를 쓸 수 있다. 따라서 밑줄 친 부분은 올바르게 쓰였다.

선지 해석
① 나 몸이 안 좋아. 그렇게 많이 먹지 말았어야 했어.
② 회의에서 제안된 대부분의 의견은 실용적이지 않았다.
③ 방이 깨끗하다면, 나는 어떤 호텔에서 머물러도 상관없다.
④ 우리는 테니스를 30분정도 치고 있었는데 비가 많이 오기 시작했다.

06   정답 ③

정답 해설
③ [적중 포인트 041] 부분을 나타내는 명사와 수 일치
부분을 나타내는 명사가 나오면 of 뒤에 명사를 확인해서 동사와 수 일치한다. 따라서 분수 of 뒤에 명사(the automobiles)가 복수 형태이므로 복수 동사를 써야 하고, 'last year'은 과거 시간 부사로 단순 과거시제 동사와 쓰이므로 were이 가장 적절하다.

지문 해석
작년에 이 지역의 자동차 중 10분의 1이 도난당했다.

07   정답 ③

정답 해설
③ [적중 포인트 039] 현재시제 동사와 be동사의 수 일치
주격 관계대명사가 이끄는 절의 동사는 선행사와 수 일치한다. 선행사(alternative sources)가 복수 형태이므로 단수 동사 is 대신 복수 동사 are로 써야 올바르다.

오답 해설
① [적중 포인트 051] 동명사의 명사 역할
동명사는 문장의 주어로 쓸 수 있다. 따라서 creating은 올바르게 쓰였다.
② [적중 포인트 010] 격에 따른 인칭대명사
대명사 it은 앞 명사 electricity를 지칭하는 것으로 단수 형태이므로 단수 대명사 it은 올바르게 쓰였다.
④ [적중 포인트 054] 분사 판별법[현재분사 VS 과거분사]
현재진행형(am/are/is - ing) 구조로 using은 올바르게 쓰였다.

지문 해석
전기 에너지를 생성하는 것은 환경 문제를 야기한다. 우리는 전기를 포기할 수는 없지만, 우리는 그것을 사용하는 방식을 통제할 수 있다. 우리는 현재 사용하고 있는 것보다 환경에 덜 해로운 대체 에너지원을 사용할 수 있다.

08   정답 ①

정답 해설
① [적중 포인트 043] 혼동하기 쉬운 주어와 동사 수 일치
'many a 단수 명사'는 단수 동사와 수 일치가 올바르게 쓰였고, kill은 타동사로 뒤에 목적어가 없으므로 수동태(be p.p.) 또한 올바르게 쓰였다.

오답 해설
② [적중 포인트 014] 형용사와 부사의 차이
완전한 문장 구조에서 동사를 수식해 주는 부사가 필요하므로 형용사 efficient 대신 부사 efficiently로 써야 올바르다.
③ [적중 포인트 087] 관계대명사 주의 사항
however는 형용사/부사와 쓰일 때는 'however + 형용사/부사 + 주어 + 동사' 구조를 쓴다. 따라서 However you may try hard 대신 However hard you may try로 써야 올바르다.

찐Tip 타동사와 부사로 구성된 이어 동사가 대명사 목적어를 취할 때 어순이 중요한데 '타동사 + 부사 + 대명사'가 아닌 '타동사 + 대명사 + 부사' 순서로 써야 하므로 'carry it out'은 올바르게 쓰였다.

④ [적중 포인트 078] 등위접속사와 병치 구조
밑줄 친 부분인 등위접속사(and)를 기준으로 '형용사, 형용사, and 형용사'의 병렬 구조가 되어야 한다. 따라서 명사 loyalty 대신 형용사 loyal로 써야 올바르다.

선지 해석
① 부주의한 보행자들 중 많은 사람들이 길에서 사망했다.
② 각 관리자는 자신의 업무를 효율적으로 수행해야 한다.
③ 어떻게 노력하든, 그것을 이행할 수 없다.
④ German shepherd 개들은 똑똑하고, 경계심이 강하며, 충성스럽다.

09
정답 ③

정답 해설

③ [적중 포인트 043] 혼동하기 쉬운 주어와 동사 수 일치
team, committee, audience, family와 같은 집합명사는 해석상 집합명사에 관련된 사람들을 지칭하면 복수 동사를 써야한다. 따라서 문맥상 일을 하는 것은 팀의 구성원들, 즉 사람들이기 때문에 복수동사 work는 올바르게 쓰였다.

진Tip team, committee, audience, family와 같은 집합명사는 해석상 집합 전체 개념을 지칭하면 단수 동사를 쓴다.

오답 해설

① [적중 포인트 021] 전치사가 필요 없는 대표 3형식 타동사
leave는 '~을/를 떠나다'라는 뜻의 3형식 타동사로 전치사 없이 바로 목적어를 취할 수 있으므로 전치사에 주의한다. 따라서 leave from 대신 전치사 from을 삭제한 leave로 써야 올바르다.

② [적중 포인트 020] 주격 보어가 필요한 2형식 자동사
& [적중 포인트 078] 등위접속사와 병치 구조
be 동사의 주격 보어로 형용사가 와야 한다. 따라서 등위접속사(and) 기준으로 형용사 weak와 병치구조를 맞춰서 동사 exhaust 대신 형용사 exhausted로 써야 올바르다.

④ [적중 포인트 089] 주의해야 할 전치사
문맥상 '~외에'의 뜻이 자연스러우므로 Beside 대신 Besides로 써야 올바르다.

진Tip beside는 '~옆에'의 뜻으로 쓰인다.

선지 해석

① 먹을 식물이 없다면, 동물들은 서식지를 떠나야 한다.
② 그는 약해지고 지친 Owen과 함께 도착했다.
③ 이 팀은 일반적으로 금요일에 늦게까지 일한다.
④ 문학 외에도, 우리는 역사와 철학을 공부해야 한다.

10
정답 ②

정답 해설

② [적중 포인트 043] 혼동하기 쉬운 주어와 동사 수 일치
'the number of 복수 명사'가 주어 자리에 쓰일 때 단수 동사와 수 일치하므로 복수 동사 continue를 단수 동사 continues로 고쳐야 한다.

오답 해설

① [적중 포인트 045] 능동태와 수동태의 차이
people이 크루즈 타는 것의 주체이므로 능동형 taking은 올바르게 쓰였다.

③ [적중 포인트 069] 다양한 도치 구문
'S + V (긍정) ~, and so + 조동사 + 주어'의 구조는 '~도 그렇다'의 뜻으로 쓰인다. 따라서 밑줄 친 부분은 올바르게 쓰였다.

④ [적중 포인트 007] 불가산 명사의 종류와 특징
information은 대표적인 불가산 명사이므로 단수를 의미하는 a(n) 또는 복수(-s) 표시하지 않는다. 따라서 information은 올바르게 쓰였다.

지문 해석

크루즈를 타는 사람들의 수는 계속해서 증가하고 있으며, 그에 따라 크루즈 경로에 대한 불만의 수도 증가하고 있다. 충분한 정보가 아직 부족하다.

11
정답 ②

정답 해설

② [적중 포인트 044] 주어 자리에서 반드시 단수 또는 복수 취급하는 특정 표현
주어는 명사절인 'whether or not we are likely to get various diseases'이다. 명사절은 단수 취급하므로 복수 동사 depend 대신 단수 동사 depends로 써야 올바르다.

오답 해설

① [적중 포인트 039] 현재시제 동사와 be동사의 수 일치
주어(The immune system)가 단수이므로 단수 동사 fights는 올바르게 쓰였다.

③ [적중 포인트 064] to부정사의 관용 구문
used to는 '~ 하곤 했다'의 뜻으로 used to 뒤에는 동사원형을 써야 한다. 따라서 think는 올바르게 쓰였다.

④ [적중 포인트 034] 완료시제와 잘 쓰이는 시간 부사
recently의 시간 부사는 완료시제 동사와 잘 쓰인다. 따라서 have found는 올바르게 쓰였다.

지문 해석

우리 몸의 면역 체계는 질병을 일으키는 원인인 박테리아와 바이러스랑 싸운다. 따라서 우리가 다양한 질병에 걸릴지 말지는 우리의 면역 체계가 얼마나 잘 작동하는지에 따라 달려있다. 생물학자들은 예전에는 우리의 면역 체계가 우리 몸의 별개이고 독립된 부분인 것으로 생각했지만, 최근에 그들은 우리의 뇌가 우리의 면역 체계에 영향을 줄 수 있다는 것을 발견했다. 이 발견은 감정적 요인과 질병 간에 관계가 있을 수 있음을 보여준다.

12
정답 ②

정답 해설

② [적중 포인트 039] 현재시제 동사와 be동사의 수 일치
문장의 주어(a combination)가 단수 형태이므로 복수 동사 were 대신 단수 동사 was로 써야 올바르다.

오답 해설

① [적중 포인트 083] 「전치사+관계대명사」 완전 구조
during which는 '전치사 + 관계대명사'로 뒤에 주어와 동사 완전 구조를 취한다. which 뒤의 문장이 완전 구조이므로 밑줄 친 부분은 올바르게 쓰였다.

③ [적중 포인트 054] 분사 판별법[현재분사 VS 과거분사]
분사의 수식을 받는 명사가 행동을 당하는 수동의 의미인 경우에는 과거분사로 써야 한다. 따라서 주어(The enhanced design)가 'a Voltaic pile'이라고 불리는 것이므로 과거분사 called는 올바르게 쓰였다.

④ [적중 포인트 080] 부사절 접속사의 구분과 특징
'such 명사 that절'은 '너무 ~해서 …하다'라는 의미로 밑줄 친 부분은 올바르게 쓰였다.

지문 해석

좋은 출발점을 찾기 위해서는, 최초의 현대식 전기 건전지가 개발된 1800년으로 돌아가야 한다. 이탈리아의 알레산드로 볼타(Alessandro Volta)는 은, 구리 및 아연의 조합이 전기 전류를 생성하기에 이상적이라는 것을 발견했다. 개선된 디자인인 "볼타 전지(a Voltaic pile)"는 이러한 금속으로 만든 디스크를 바닷물에 적셔진 골판지 디스크 사이에 쌓음으로써 만들어졌다. 볼타의 연구에 대한 이야기가 많았기 때문에 그는 황제 나폴레옹 앞에서 시연을 하도록 요청받았다.

13
정답 ④

정답 해설
④ [적중 포인트 039] 현재시제 동사와 be동사의 수 일치
동사 explain의 주어는 동격 that절 앞에 The idea이다. 따라서 단수형태 명사와 수 일치해야 하므로 explain 대신 단수 동사 explains로 써야 올바르다.

오답 해설
① [적중 포인트 051] 동명사의 명사 역할
전치사 in 뒤에는 동명사를 써야 한다. 따라서 동명사 allocating은 올바르게 쓰였다.

② [적중 포인트 005] 단어의 8품사
'~와 관련[관계]이 있다'의 뜻으로 쓰일 때는 'have something to do with'의 표현으로 쓸 수 있다. 따라서 밑줄 친 부분은 올바르게 쓰였다.

③ [적중 포인트 084] 관계대명사 주의 사항
& [적중 포인트 014] 형용사와 부사의 차이
관계대명사 that절의 동사 pursue는 명사(universities)와 수 일치해야 하므로 복수 형태로 올바르게 쓰였다. 또한 동사 pursue를 수식하는 부사 properly 또한 올바르게 쓰였다.

지문 해석
대학에 대한 접근을 배분하는 데 있어서 정의(공평)가 대학들이 올바르게 추구하는 가치와 관련이 있다는 생각은 대학 입학증을 판매하는 것이 왜 불공평한지를 설명해 준다.

14
정답 ④

정답 해설
④ [적중 포인트 039] 현재시제 동사와 be동사의 수 일치
문장의 주어(moisture on its surface)가 단수 주어이므로 복수 동사 encourage 대신 단수 동사 encourages로 써야 올바르다.

오답 해설
① [적중 포인트 020] 주격 보어가 필요한 2형식 자동사
stay는 대표 2형식 자동사로 주격 보어 자리에 형용사를 쓴다. 따라서 형용사 fresh는 올바르게 쓰였다.

② [적중 포인트 082] 관계대명사의 선행사와 문장 구조
명사(compartment) 뒤에 which는 관계대명사로 뒤의 문장 구조가 불완전 구조인지 확인해야 한다. 밑줄 친 부분인 which 뒤에 주어가 빠진 불완전 문장으로 올바르게 쓰였다.

③ [적중 포인트 058] 분사를 활용한 표현 및 구문
접속사 before 뒤에 동사 store에 -ing가 붙은 형태로 분사구문이 되었다. 뒤에 목적어(it)가 있는 것으로 보아 능동 형태 storing은 올바르게 쓰였다.

지문 해석
적절하게 보관한다면, 브로콜리는 최대 4일 동안 신선하게 유지될 것이다. 신선한 송이들을 보관하는 가장 좋은 방법은 채소 칸에 개봉된 플라스틱 봉지에 넣어 냉장 보관하는 것이고 이렇게 하면 적절한 습도와 공기 균형을 유지할 수 있으며 비타민 C 함량을 보존하는 데 도움이 된다. 브로콜리를 보관하기 전에 씻지 마라. 왜냐하면 표면에 있는 수분은 곰팡이의 성장을 촉진시킬 수 있기 때문이다.

15
정답 ①

정답 해설
① [적중 포인트 043] 혼동하기 쉬운 주어와 동사 수 일치
the number of는 '명사의 수'라는 뜻으로 뒤에 단수 동사와 수 일치한다. 그러나 문장의 동사는 were인 것으로 보아 '많은 명사'를 뜻하는 a number of로 써야 한다. 따라서 the 대신 a로 써야 올바르다.

오답 해설
② [적중 포인트 088] 전치사와 명사 목적어
'~하도록 억지로 강요받다'의 뜻을 의미하는 구문으로 'be forced into'는 올바르게 쓰였다.

③ [적중 포인트 088] 전치사와 명사 목적어
'~의 조건하에서'의 뜻을 의미하는 구문으로 'under ~ conditions'은 올바르게 쓰였다.

④ [적중 포인트 089] 주의해야 할 전치사
during은 어떤 상황이 발생하고 있는 때를 가리킬 때 쓰이고 for는 어떤 상황이 얼마나 오랜기간 계속되는지를 나타낼 때 쓴다. '1940년대'라는 상황이 발생하고 있는 때를 나타내기 위해 during the 1940's은 올바르게 쓰였다.

지문 해석
그는 1940년대 일부 지역에서 많은 한국인들이 억압적인 조건에서 강제로 일을 하도록 강요받았다는 것을 인정했다.

16
정답 ③

정답 해설
③ [적중 포인트 039] 현재시제 동사와 be동사의 수 일치
주격 관계대명사 that의 선행사가 its skin이 아니고 special cells이므로 special cells와 수 일치해야 한다. 따라서 단수 동사 contains 대신 복수 동사 contain으로 써야 올바르다.

오답 해설
① [적중 포인트 005] 단어의 8품사
all과 함께 복수 형태인 types는 올바르게 쓰였다.

② [적중 포인트 044] 주어 자리에서 반드시 단수 또는 복수 취급하는 특정 표현
'each of 복수 명사'는 단수 동사와 수 일치한다. 따라사 단수 동사 has와 수 일치하는 밑줄 친 부분의 each는 올바르게 쓰였다.

④ [적중 포인트 025] to부정사를 목적격 보어로 취하는 대표 5형식 타동사
allow는 대표 5형식의 타동사로서 목적보어 자리에는 원형부정사가 아닌 to부정사 또는 과거분사를 취해야 한다. 따라서 to change은 올바르게 쓰였다.

지문 해석
오징어, 문어, 갑오징어는 모두 두족류의 유형이다. 이 동물 각각은 피부 아래에 색소를 포함하는 특별한 세포를 가지고 있다. 두족류는 이러한 세포들을 피부로부터 또는 피부로부터 멀어지게 할 수 있다. 이를 통해 그것의 모양과 색상의 패턴을 변화시킬 수 있다.

17 정답 ③

정답 해설

③ [적중 포인트 039] 현재시제 동사와 be동사의 수 일치
'시카고에서 나에게 맞는 옷'이라는 해석이 맥락상 적절하므로 단수 동사 fits의 주어는 복수 명사인 clothes이다. 따라서 단수 동사 fits 대신 복수 동사 fit으로 써야 올바르다.

오답 해설

① [적중 포인트 055] 감정 분사와 분사형 형용사
please는 감정 동사로 주어인 I가 감정을 느낄 때는 과거분사로 써야 한다. 따라서 밑줄 친 pleased는 올바르게 쓰였다.

② [적중 포인트 064] to부정사의 관용 구문
난이 형용사(difiicult) 구문은 'It be동사 + 난이 형용사 + (for 목적어) + to부정사'의 구조로 쓰인다. 따라서 밑줄 친 it's는 올바르게 쓰였다.

④ [적중 포인트 079] 명사절 접속사의 구분과 특징
명사절 접속사 what은 뒤에 불완전 구조를 취한다. 따라서 뒤에 주어가 빠진 불완전 구조가 나오므로 what은 올바르게 쓰였다.

지문 해석

> 나는 내가 충분한 옷을 가지고 있는 것에 만족하고 있다. 미국 남성들은 일반적으로 일본 남성들보다 크기 때문에 시카고에서 나에게 맞는 옷을 찾는 것은 매우 어렵다. 일본에서의 중간 크기는 여기에서는 작은 크기이다.

18 정답 ④

정답 해설

④ [적중 포인트 043] 혼동하기 쉬운 주어와 동사 수 일치
'많은 명사'의 뜻을 가진 구문으로는 'A number of + 복수 명사 + 복수 동사'의 표현이 있다. 따라서 The number of 대신 A number of로 써야 올바르다.

찐Tip 'The number of + 복수 명사 + 단수 동사'는 '명사의 수'의 뜻으로 쓰인다.

오답 해설

① [적중 포인트 093] 원급, 비교급, 최상급 강조 부사
최상급 구문인 the largest와 강조 부사인 by far가 비교급 larger를 수식하고 있다. 따라서 밑줄 친 부분은 올바르게 쓰였다.

② [적중 포인트 098] 비교급을 이용한 표현
'~만큼 ~않다'의 뜻을 가진 구문으로 'not ~ any more than'의 양자부정 표현이 있다. 따라서 밑줄 친 부분은 올바르게 쓰였다.

찐Tip 양자부정 구문 than 뒤에 부정 표현(not)은 금지한다.

③ [적중 포인트 041] 부분을 나타내는 명사와 수 일치
Three-quarters 표현은 분수로 전치사 of를 취하면 뒤에 나오는 명사를 확인해서 동사와 수 일치한다. 따라서 전치사 of 뒤에 나오는 what절은 단수 취급하므로 동사도 단수 형태인 comes가 올바르게 쓰였다.

선지 해석

① 그들은 지구상에서 진화한 가장 큰 동물인데, 공룡보다 훨씬 크다.
② 그녀는 나의 엄마가 그랬던 것만큼이나 아메리카 원주민이라는 용어를 좋아하지 않았다.
③ 우리가 자연에 대해 정보로 받아들이는 것의 4분의 3은 눈을 통해 우리 뇌로 들어온다.
④ 많은 의사들이 의학에서의 모든 최신의 발전에 뒤떨어지지 않기 위해서 열심히 공부한다.

19 정답 ③

정답 해설

③ [적중 포인트 070] 양보 도치 구문과 장소 방향 도치 구문
Among her most prized possessions라는 장소 부사가 나오고 be동사 + 주어가 도치되어 있으므로 be동사와 주어 수 일치를 확인한다. a 1961 bejeweled timepiece가 단수 주어이므로 복수 동사 were 대신 단수 동사 was로 써야 올바르다.

오답 해설

① [적중 포인트 054] 분사 판별법[현재분사 VS 과거분사]
동사 + -ing가 문법 문제에 나오면 동명사 또는 분사 문제인지 먼저 확인한다. 문장에는 이미 동사가 있고 일반적으로 동명사는 콤마를 수반하지 않으므로 declaring은 분사 자리이고 declare 뒤에 목적어가 있으므로 능동형 분사 declaring이 올바르게 쓰였다.

② [적중 포인트 082] 관계대명사의 선행사와 문장 구조
관계대명사는 선행사가 올바르게 쓰였는지 그리고 뒤의 문장 구조가 불완전한지 확인해야 한다. 앞에 나온 명사를 수식하고 있고 뒤에 주어가 없는 불완전 구조로 쓰였기 때문에 관계대명사 that은 올바르게 쓰였다.

④ [적중 포인트 058] 분사를 활용한 표현 및 구문
with 분사구문으로 자동사면 -ing, 타동사 뒤에 목적어가 있으면 -ing, 타동사 뒤에 목적어가 없으면 p.p.로 쓴다. 타동사 cover 뒤에 목적이 없으므로 covered는 올바르게 쓰였다.

지문 해석

> Elizabeth Taylor는 아름다운 보석들에 대한 안목을 가졌으며, 몇 년 동안 놀라운 보석들을 모으다가 한번은 "여자는 항상 더 많은 다이아몬드를 가질 수 있다"고 선언하기도 했다. 2011년에 그녀의 최고급 보석들이 1억 1590만 달러를 벌어들인 저녁 경매에서 Christie's에 의해 팔렸다. 저녁 경매 중 판매된 그녀의 가장 소중한 소유물 중 하나는 Bulgari가 1961년에 보석으로 만든 시계였다. 이 시계는 손목 주위로 감기는 뱀 모양으로 디자인되었으며, 머리와 꼬리가 다이아몬드로 덮여 있고 두 개의 매혹적인 에메랄드 눈이 있고, 정교한 메커니즘으로 사나운 턱을 열어 작은 쿼츠 시계를 드러낸다.

Chapter 06 수동태

ANSWER

01 ③	02 ②	03 ④	04 ③	05 ①
06 ③	07 ②	08 ①	09 ③	10 ②
11 ④	12 ③	13 ②	14 ④	15 ③
16 ①	17 ②	18 ②	19 ②	20 ④

01

정답 ③

정답 해설

③ [적중 포인트 045] 능동태와 수동태의 차이
'contribute to'는 '기여하다'의 의미로, 능동태로 목적어를 취하는 동사이다. 현재 시점 기준에 과거에 사실에 대한 진술을 하고 있으므로 완료부정사로 표현해야 한다. 따라서 밑줄 친 부분에 들어갈 말로 가장 적절한 것은 'have contributed to'이다.

지문 해석

> 인구 과잉이 핵심적인 역할을 했을 수도 있다: 물 부족뿐만 아니라 마야족이 식량을 의존했던 열대 우림 생태계의 과도한 착취가 붕괴에 기여한 것으로 보인다.

02

정답 ②

정답 해설

② [적중 포인트 045] 능동태와 수동태의 차이
목적격 관계대명사절의 수식을 받는 주어(Toys)가 복수이고 '버리는 행위'를 받는 입장이므로 수동태로 표현해야 한다. 따라서 'has recently discarded' 대신 'have recently been discarded'로 써야 올바르다.

오답 해설

① [적중 포인트 003] 어순이 중요한 간접의문문
간접의문문에 대한 문제로, asked가 목적어 두 개를 취하고 있으며, why 다음의 어순이 '주어 동사'의 어순으로 올바르게 쓰였고, 과거시제도 일치하므로 밑줄 친 부분은 올바르게 쓰였다.

③ [적중 포인트 039] 현재시제 동사와 be동사의 수 일치
문장의 주격 보어를 주격 관계대명사절(who is always ready to lend a helping hand)이 수식하는 구조로, 문장의 동사와 주격 관계대명사절의 동사가 각각 단수 명사를 수식하므로 단수 동사 is는 올바르게 쓰였다.

④ [적중 포인트 039] 현재시제 동사와 be동사의 수 일치
전치사 by의 목적어(scents)를 주격 관계대명사절이 수식하는 문장의 구조로, 수식받는 명사가 복수 명사이므로 주격 관계대명사절의 동사는 복수 동사 are로 올바르게 쓰였다.

찐Tip attract는 타동사인데 뒤에 목적어가 없으므로 수동태 구조(be p.p.) 또한 올바르게 쓰였다.

선지 해석

① 그는 나에게 왜 매일 매일 돌아오는지를 물었다.
② 아이들이 일 년 내내 원했던 장난감들이 최근 버려졌다.
③ 그녀는 언제나 도움을 줄 준비가 되어 있는 사람이다.
④ 곤충들은 종종 우리에게 분명하지 않은 냄새에 이끌린다.

03

정답 ④

정답 해설

④ [적중 포인트 045] 능동태와 수동태의 차이
injure은 타동사인데 뒤에 목적어가 없으므로 수동태 구조(be p.p.)로 써야 한다. 따라서 injurig 대신 injured로 써야 올바르다.

오답 해설

① [적중 포인트 039] 현재시제 동사와 be동사의 수 일치
현재 동사는 주어와 수 일치를 해야한다. 문장의 주어(more than 270,000 pedestrians)가 복수이므로 복수 동사 lose는 올바르게 쓰였다.

② [적중 포인트 062] to부정사의 부사적 역할
'결국 ~하지 않게 되다'의 뜻을 가진 구문으로 'never to부정사'가 있다. 따라서 to return은 올바르게 쓰였다.

③ [적중 포인트 090] 원급 비교 구문
'as 원급 as 비교 구문'으로 형용사/부사의 원급이 들어가야 한다. be동사의 보어 자리이므로 형용사 high는 올바르게 쓰였다.

지문 해석

> 매년, 전 세계 도로에서 270,000명 이상의 보행자가 목숨을 잃는다. 많은 사람들은 그들이 어떤 날이든 다시는 돌아오지 않을 것처럼 집을 떠난다. 전 세계적으로, 보행자는 전체 도로 교통 사망사고의 22%를 차지하며, 일부 국가에서는 이 비율이 도로 교통 사망사고의 3분의 2에 달하기도 한다. 수백만 명의 보행자가 치명적이지 않은 부상을 입었고, 일부는 영구적 장애를 가지기도 한다. 이러한 사건들은 경제적 어려움뿐만 아니라 고통과 슬픔을 초래한다.

04

정답 ③

정답 해설

③ [적중 포인트 046] 수동태 불가 동사
result in은 수동태 구조(be p.p.)로 쓰지 않는다. 따라서 'has been resulted in' 대신 'has resulted in'으로 써야 올바르다.

오답 해설

① [적중 포인트 064] to부정사의 관용 구문
난이형용사(difficult) 구문은 'It be + 난이형용사 + to부정사'의 구조로 쓴다. 따라서 to imagine은 올바르게 쓰였다.

② [적중 포인트 058] 분사를 활용한 표현 및 구문
'take 목적어 for granted'는 '목적어를 당연시 여기다'의 뜻으로 쓰인다. 따라서 밑줄 친 부분은 올바르게 쓰였다.

④ [적중 포인트 054] 분사 판별법[현재분사 VS 과거분사]
문장에 이미 주어 동사가 있고 동사원형에 -ing나 ed가 나온다면 분사 문제이고, 이때 타동사 뒤에 목적어가 나오면 능동형인 현재분사를 쓴다. 따라서 affecting은 올바르게 쓰였다.

지문 해석

> 숲의 아름다움과 풍부함이 없는 삶을 상상하는 것은 어려울 것이다. 하지만 과학자들은 우리가 숲을 당연한 것으로 생각해서는 안 된다고 경고한다. 어떤 추정에 따르면, 산림 벌채로 인해 세계의 자연 산림의 80%까지 손실되었다고 한다. 현재 산림 벌채는 태평양의 온대 우림과 같은 야생 지역에 영향을 미치는 전세계적인 문제이다.

05

정답 ①

정답 해설

① [적중 포인트 045] 능동태와 수동태의 차이
feed는 타동사로도 쓰일 수 있는데 뒤에 목적어가 없으므로 수동태 구조(be p.p.)가 올바르게 쓰였다. 또한 its도 앞에 나온 단수 명사(a horse)를 받고 있으므로 올바르게 쓰였다.

오답 해설

② [적중 포인트 058] 분사를 활용한 표현 및 구문
분사구문의 주어가 따로 표시되지 않을 경우 분사구문의 주어는 문장의 주어와 일치한다. 밑줄 친 부분은 문장의 분사 walking의 주어가 따로 표시되어있지 않으므로 분사의 주어는 문장의 주어인 my hat이 되는데 해석상 '모자가 걷는'이라는 어색한 문장이 된다. 따라서 while walking 대신 while I was walking으로 써야 올바르다.

③ [적중 포인트 050] 전치사에 유의해야 할 수동태
know는 '~으로 알려지다'라는 뜻으로 쓰일 경우에는 'be known as'의 수동태 형태로 써야 한다. 따라서 has known 대신 has been known으로 써야 올바르다.

찐Tip 'be known for'은 '~로 알려져 있다'의 뜻으로, 'be known to'는 '~에게 알려져 있다'의 뜻으로 쓰인다. 전치사에 따라 의미가 달라지는 수동태이므로 주의가 필요하다

④ [적중 포인트 014] 형용사와 부사의 차이
형용사인 good은 명사를 수식하거나 보어 자리에 쓰인다. done인 분사를 수식할 경우에는 부사를 써야 한다. 따라서 형용사 good 대신 부사 well로 써야 올바르다.

선지 해석
① 말은 개별적인 욕구와 하는 일의 성질에 따라 먹이가 주어져야 한다.
② 나는 좁은 길을 걷고 있을 때 바람에 내 모자가 날려갔다.
③ 그녀는 자신의 경력 동안 쭉 주로 정치 만화가로 알려져 왔다.
④ 심지어 어린 아이들도 잘한 일에 대해 칭찬받는 것을 좋아한다.

06   정답 ③

정답 해설
③ [적중 포인트 045] 능동태와 수동태의 차이
influence는 3형식 타동사이므로 전치사 없이 목적어를 취한다. 따라서 on food intake에서 on을 삭제해야 한다.

오답 해설
① [적중 포인트 080] 부사절 접속사의 구분과 특징
despite는 전치사로 뒤에 명사 또는 동명사를 목적어로 취할 수 있다. 따라서 밑줄 친 부분은 올바르게 쓰였다.

찐Tip every 다음 단수 명사 또한 올바르게 쓰였다.

② [적중 포인트 061] to부정사의 형용사적 역할
추상 명사를 to부정사가 수식할 때 to부정사는 동격의 의미를 지닌다. 따라서 to find out은 올바르게 쓰였다.

찐Tip if절은 find out의 목적어 역할을 하는 명사절이다.

④ [적중 포인트 061] to부정사의 형용사적 역할
명사인 the right environment를 to부정사의 형용사 용법으로 수식하고 있고, to부정사 앞에 'for + 목적격'은 의미상의 주어로 쓰이고 있다. 따라서 밑줄 친 부분은 올바르게 쓰였다.

선지 해석
① 가능한 모든 일자리를 알아보았음에도 불구하고, 그는 적당한 일자리를 찾지 못했다.
② 당신이 누군가를 믿을 수 있는지 알아보는 최선책은 그 사람을 믿는 것이다.
③ 미각의 민감성은 개인의 음식 섭취와 체중에 크게 영향을 미친다.
④ 부모는 그들의 자녀가 성장하고 학습하는 데 알맞은 환경을 제공할 책임이 있다.

07   정답 ②

정답 해설
② [적중 포인트 045] 능동태와 수동태의 차이
수동태 구조(be p.p.)는 뒤에 목적어가 없어야 한다. 목적어 it이 있는 것으로 보아 수동태 구조로는 올 수 없다. 문맥상 미래완료의 의미이므로 will be finished 대신 will have finished로 써야 올바르다.

오답 해설
① [적중 포인트 035] 미래를 대신하는 현재시제
조건 부사절에서는 의미상 미래일지라도 현재시제가 미래를 대신한다. 따라서 현재시제 stops는 올바르게 쓰였다.

찐Tip 주절에는 미래면 미래시제를 그대로 쓴다.

③ [적중 포인트 034] 완료시제와 잘 쓰이는 시간 부사
그가 나타난 시점은 과거이고 그 전에 내가 기다렸다는 내용이므로 과거시제(appeared)와 과거완료시제(had waited)로 밑줄 친 부분은 올바르게 쓰였다.

④ [적중 포인트 019] 주어만 있으면 완전한 1형식 자동사
'~을 졸업하다'의 뜻으로 쓰일 때는 graduate와 특정 전치사 from과 같이 쓸 수 있다. 따라서 밑줄 친 부분은 올바르게 쓰였다.

찐Tip 전치사 in과 기간 표현이 같이 쓰이면 '기간 후에~'의 뜻으로 쓰여 미래시제와 잘 쓰인다.

선지 해석
① 비가 그치면 나는 외출할 것이다.
② 네가 집에 오면 나는 그것을 이미 끝냈을 것이다.
③ 내가 기다린 지 한 시간 만에 그가 나타났다.
④ 그는 3년 후에 대학을 졸업할 것이다.

08   정답 ①

정답 해설
① [적중 포인트 045] 능동태와 수동태의 차이
주어(innovation)는 발견의 주체가 아닌 객체(대상)이므로 부정사 부분은 수동태로 써야 한다. 따라서 to find 대신 수동 형태인 to be found로 써야 올바르다.

오답 해설
② [적중 포인트 087] 관계대명사 주의 사항
복합관계부사 wherever가 이끄는 양보의 부사절이다. 복합관계부사(wherever) 뒤에 완전 구조를 취하고 있으므로 올바르게 쓰였다.

③ [적중 포인트 039] 현재시제 동사와 be동사의 수 일치
주어(people)가 복수이므로 복수 동사 think는 올바르게 쓰였다.

④ [적중 포인트 010] 격에 따른 인칭대명사
대명사가 나오면 앞명사를 확인해야 한다. they는 앞에 나온 bright and eager people을 가리키고 있다. 따라서 복수 형태 they는 올바르게 쓰였다.

지문 해석
> 기업에서 현재 배우고 있는 혁신은 밝고 열정적인 사람들이 그것을 찾을 수 있다고 생각하는 어디에서든 그것을 발견할 가능성이 높다.

09

정답 ③

정답 해설
③ [적중 포인트 045] 능동태와 수동태의 차이
타동사 damage 뒤에 목적어가 없고 주어(package)가 손상된 것이므로 능동태 damaged 대신 수동태 was damaged로 써야 올바르다.

찐Tip wrong은 부사로도 사용될 수 있으나 형용사나 분사의 앞에서는 wrongly의 형태가 더 흔하게 쓰인다.

오답 해설
① [적중 포인트 034] 완료시제와 잘 쓰이는 시간 부사
그가 담배를 끊은 시점은 과거이고 그 전에 그의 친구들이 이미 담배를 끊었다는 내용이므로 과거시제(stopped)와 과거완료시제(had stopped)로 밑줄 친 부분은 올바르게 쓰였다.

② [적중 포인트 044] 주어 자리에서 반드시 단수 또는 복수 취급하는 특정 표현
that 앞에 명사가 없고 'that + 주어 + 동사'인 완전 구조는 주어, 목적어, 보어 자리에서 명사 역할을 하고, 주어 자리에 that절이 오면 단수 취급한다. 따라서 밑줄 친 부분은 올바르게 쓰였다.

④ [적중 포인트 032] 의미와 구조에 주의해야 할 타동사
want는 to부정사를 목적보어로 취하는 대표 5형식 타동사로 밑줄 친 부분은 올바르게 쓰였다.

찐Tip 구체적인 수는 '수사 + 단수 단위 명사 + 복수 명사'로 표현한다.

선지 해석
① 내가 담배를 끊은 주된 이유는 내 모든 친구들이 이미 담배를 끊은 상태였기 때문이었다.
② 남편이 아내를 이해한다는 것은 반드시 그들이 사이좋게 지낸다는 것을 의미하는 것은 아니다.
③ 잘못된 주소가 붙어있어서 소포가 늦게 도착하고 손상되었다.
④ 그녀는 남편이 집에 오는 길에 달걀 2다스를 사오기를 원한다.

10

정답 ②

정답 해설
② [적중 포인트 045] 능동태와 수동태의 차이
사물이 주어로 나오는 경우 수동태 구조(be p.p.)로 잘 쓰인다. 따라서 held 대신 is held로 써야 올바르다.

찐Tip be held는 '개최되다, 치러지다, 열리다'의 뜻으로 쓰인다.

찐Tip 'every + 기수(숫자) + 복수명사'는 '~마다'의 뜻으로 쓰인다.

오답 해설
① [적중 포인트 034] 완료시제와 잘 쓰이는 시간 부사
'~ 할 리가 없다'의 뜻을 가진 구문으로 'cannot 동사원형'의 표현은 올바르게 쓰였다.

③ [적중 포인트 019] 주어만 있으면 완전한 1형식 자동사
clean은 타동사로 잘 쓰이지만, 자동사로 쓰이면 수동의 의미(닦이다)로 쓰이는 동사이다. 따라서 밑줄 친 부분은 올바르게 쓰였다.

④ [적중 포인트 060] to부정사의 명사적 역할
'think + it + 형용사/명사 + (for 목적어) to부정사'의 구조로 think 동사 뒤에는 it 이라는 가목적어를 쓰고 진목적어를 대신한다. 따라서 밑줄 친 부분은 올바르게 쓰였다.

선지 해석
① 이 가방은 가짜다. 비쌀 리가 없어.
② 한국에서는 대통령 선거가 5년에 한 번씩 치러진다.
③ 이 표면은 쉽게 닦인다.
④ 내일까지 논문을 제출하는 것은 불가능하다고 생각한다.

11

정답 ④

정답 해설
④ [적중 포인트 045] 능동태와 수동태의 차이
promise는 타동사로 뒤에 목적어가 없으면 수동태(be p.p.) 구조로 쓴다. 따라서 밑줄 친 부분은 올바르게 쓰였다.

찐Tip 사물이 주어 자리에 나오는 경우 수동태(be p.p.) 구조로 잘 쓰인다.

오답 해설
① [적중 포인트 060] to부정사의 명사적 역할
'find + 형용사(목적보어) + to부정사(진목적어)'의 구조로는 쓸 수 없으므로 형용사 앞에 가목적어 it을 넣어 가목적어-진목적어 구문으로 써야 한다. 따라서 finding increasingly challenging to stay 대신 it을 넣은 finding it increasingly challenging to stay로 써야 올바르다.

찐Tip increasingly는 형용사(challenging)를 수식하는 역할로 부사로 올바르게 쓰였다.

② [적중 포인트 095] 라틴어 비교 구문과 전치사 to
'be preferable to'의 구조로 써야 한다. to를 than으로 쓰면 안 된다. 따라서 than 대신 to로 써야 올바르다.

③ [적중 포인트 001] 주어만 있으면 완전한 1형식 자동사
destine은 '운명짓다'의 뜻으로 쓰이지만, '~할 운명이다'의 뜻으로 쓰일 때는 수동형인 'be destined to'의 형태로 주로 쓴다. 따라서 destined to 대신 is/was destined to로 써야 올바르다.

선지 해석
① 최고의 소프트웨어 회사들은 앞서 나가기가 점점 더 어려워지고 있다.
② 아이들을 키우기에는 대도시보다 작은 도시가 더 선호되는 것 같다.
③ 그녀는 다른 사람들을 돕는 삶을 살 운명이다.
④ 모든 직장인들에게 일주일의 휴가가 약속되었다.

12

정답 ③

정답 해설
③ [적중 포인트 045] 능동태와 수동태의 차이
to be maintained 뒤에 목적어(the society and its traditions)가 있으므로 수동태가 아닌 능동태로 써야 한다. 따라서 to be maintained 대신 to maintain 또는 to maintaining으로 써야 올바르다.

오답 해설
① [적중 포인트 045] 능동태와 수동태의 차이
& [적중 포인트 014] 형용사와 부사의 차이
identify 뒤에 목적어가 없으므로 수동태 형태로 올바르게 쓰였고, 과거분사(identified)를 수식하고 있으므로 부사(closely) 또한 올바르게 쓰였다.

② [적중 포인트 009] 관사의 종류와 생략
부정관사 a는 people's가 아닌 culture와 연결되므로 올바르게 쓰였다.

④ [적중 포인트 010] 격에 따른 인칭대명사
its는 단수 명사 the society를 받아주고 있으므로 올바르게 쓰였다.

지문 해석
힌두교와 이슬람교처럼 종교가 한 민족의 문화와 밀접하게 연결된 나라들에서 종교 교육은 사회와 그 전통을 유지하는 데 필수적이었다.

13
정답 ②

정답 해설

② [적중 포인트 045] 능동태와 수동태의 차이
현재분사 뒤에 목적어가 없을뿐더러 weekends는 '강조하는 행위의 대상'이 되므로 highlighting 대신 수동의 의미를 전달하는 과거분사 highlighted로 써야 올바르다.

오답 해설

① [적중 포인트 039] 현재시제 동사와 be동사의 수 일치
동사 show의 주어(A graph)는 단수 형태이므로 단수 동사 shows는 올바르게 쓰였다.

③ [적중 포인트 076] if 생략 후 도치된 가정법
'if 주어 should 동사원형'에서 if 생략 후 도치된 가정법으로 'should 주어 동사원형' 형태로 올바르게 쓰였다.

④ [적중 포인트 026] 5형식 사역동사의 목적격 보어
사역동사 have는 목적어와 목적보어의 관계가 수동일 경우에는 과거분사를 목적보어로 취한다. 따라서 목적어(activities)가 계획되어지는 것이고, planned 뒤에 목적어도 없으므로 밑줄 친 부분은 올바르게 쓰였다.

지문 해석

월별 기후학적 데이터의 그래프는 가장 따뜻하고 추운 시기, 가장 비가 많이 오는 시기와 가장 건조한 시기를 보여준다. 또한, 주말은 그 그래프 상에 강조되어 있어 주말에 활동이 계획되어 있다면 빠르게 주말 날씨를 찾을 수 있다.

14
정답 ④

정답 해설

④ [적중 포인트 045] 능동태와 수동태의 차이
melt와 mold의 주어인 they는 wood와 cotton을 가리키는데 해석상 주어와 동사의 관계가 능동이 아닌 수동의 관계이므로 melt and mold 대신 be melted and (be) molded로 써야 올바르다.

오답 해설

① [적중 포인트 039] 현재시제 동사와 be동사의 수 일치
문장의 주어(plastics)가 복수 형태이므로 복수 동사 are은 올바르게 쓰였다.

② [적중 포인트 082] 관계대명사의 선행사와 문장 구조
관계대명사 that 앞에 사물명사(materials)는 올바르게 쓰였고, 뒤에는 주어가 없는 불완전한 구조를 취하고 있으므로 that은 올바르게 쓰였다.

③ [적중 포인트 054] 분사 판별법[현재분사 VS 과거분사]
명사를 수식하는 형용사 역할을 하는 과거분사 made는 뒤에 목적어가 없으므로 올바르게 쓰였다.

지문 해석

플라스틱은 작은 분자들이 연쇄로 결합해서 만들어진 고분자로 구성된 인공적이고 인간이 만든 물질이다. 모든 고분자가 인공적인 것은 아니다 — 나무와 면은 섬유소라는 자연 고분자의 일종이지만, 그것들은 녹이고 주조할 수 없기 때문에 플라스틱으로 간주되지 않는다.

15
정답 ③

정답 해설

③ [적중 포인트 045] 능동태와 수동태의 차이
동사(undergo) 다음에 목적어(unbearable suffering)가 있으므로 수동형태인 must be undergone 대신 능동 형태인 must undergo로 써야 올바르다.

오답 해설

① [적중 포인트 007] 불가산 명사의 종류와 특징
국가명에 -s가 붙더라도 고유명사(불가산 명사)로 본다. 불가산 명사는 단수 취급하고 단수 동사로 일치시켜야 하므로 단수 동사 becomes는 올바르게 쓰였다.

② [적중 포인트 012] 지시대명사 this와 that
those who는 '~하는 사람들'을 뜻하며 those는 복수를 가리키는 대명사로 복수 동사 want는 올바르게 쓰였다.

④ [적중 포인트 009] 관사의 종류와 생략
second 앞에 정관사 the를 붙일 경우 '(순서상으로) 두 번째의[둘째의]'라는 의미로 쓰이고 부정관사 a가 붙을 경우에는 '또 하나의, 다른'이라는 의미로 쓰이므로 밑줄 친 부분은 올바르게 쓰였다.

지문 해석

비록 몇 가지 엄격한 조건이 있긴 하지만 네덜란드는 세계에서 안락사를 허용하는 유일한 국가이다. 죽기 위해 의료 지원을 원하는 사람들은 견딜 수 없는 고통을 겪는 것이 틀림없다. 의사와 환자는 회복에 희망이 없다는 데 동의해야 한다. 그리고 다른 의사와 상담을 해야 한다.

16
정답 ①

정답 해설

① [적중 포인트 046] 수동태 불가 동사
come은 자동사로 능동태로만 표현해야 한다. 따라서 be come 대신 come으로 써야 올바르다.

찐Tip 'come into force'는 '시행되다'의 뜻으로 쓰인다.

오답 해설

② [적중 포인트 005] 단어의 8품사
'~을 중요시 여기다'의 뜻을 가진 구문으로 'think much of'의 표현은 올바르게 쓰였다.

③ [적중 포인트 005] 단어의 8품사
'~을 존경하다, 우러러 보다'의 뜻을 가진 구문으로 'look up to'의 표현은 올바르게 쓰였다.

④ [적중 포인트 005] 단어의 8품사
'~을 만회하다, 보상하다'의 뜻을 가진 구문으로 'make up for'의 표현은 올바르게 쓰였다.

선지 해석

① 이 법률은 6월 1일부터 시행된다.
② 나는 그의 재능을 너무 중요하게 생각하였다.
③ 그들 모두는 그를 그들의 지도자로서 우러러 보았다.
④ 나는 지난 학기의 시험 결과를 만회하기 위해서 더 열심히 공부해야 한다.

17
정답 ②

정답 해설
② [적중 포인트 049] 5형식 동사의 수동태 구조
allow는 to부정사를 목적보어로 취하는 대표 5형식 타동사로 수동태로 쓰일 경우 '목적어 be allowed to 부정사'로 표현한다. 밑줄 친 부분인 allow 뒤에 목적어가 없으므로 수동태로 써야 하고, 주어(people)가 복수 형태이므로 복수 동사로 써야 한다. 따라서 are not allowed to로 써야 올바르다.

오답 해설
① [적중 포인트 049] 5형식 동사의 수동태 구조
allow 뒤에 목적어가 없으므로 능동태 표현은 올바르지 못하다.

③ [적중 포인트 039] 현재시제 동사와 be동사의 수 일치
& ④ [적중 포인트 039] 현재시제 동사와 be동사의 수 일치
빈칸은 동사 자리로 복수 주어인 people과 수 일치하여 복수 동사를 써야 한다. 따라서 단수 동사인 has와 is 표현은 올바르지 못하다.

지문 해석
일반적으로, 입양된 사람들은 그들의 파일[정보]에 접근하도록 허용되지 않는다.

18
정답 ②

정답 해설
② [적중 포인트 048] 4형식 수여동사의 수동태 구조
fine(벌금을 부과하다)은 '주어 + fine + 사람 + 돈'으로 표현하며 수동태로는 '사람 be fined + 돈'의 구조로 표현한다. 따라서 250 dollars was fined to him 대신 He was fined 250 dollars로 써야 올바르다.

오답 해설
① [적중 포인트 048] 4형식 수여동사의 수동태 구조
'award + 간접목적어 + 직접목적어'의 능동태 구조가 수동태 구조로 전환되면 '간접목적어 + be awarded + 직접목적어' 또는 '직접목적어 + be awarded + to 간접목적어'로 쓸 수 있으므로 밑줄 친 부분은 올바르게 쓰였다.

③ [적중 포인트 047] 다양한 3형식 동사의 수동태 구조
사물이 주어 자리에 나오는 경우 수동태(be p.p.) 구조로 잘 쓰인다. 밑줄 친 부분인 사물 주어 English는 가르치는 행동을 하는 주체가 아닌, 행동을 당하는 대상이므로 수동태 구조로 올바르게 쓰였다.

④ [적중 포인트 047] 다양한 3형식 동사의 수동태 구조
사물이 주어 자리에 나오는 경우 수동태(be p.p.) 구조로 잘 쓰인다. 밑줄 친 부분인 사물 주어 our solutions는 설명하는 행동을 하는 주체가 아닌, 행동을 당하는 대상이므로 수동태 구조가 올바르게 쓰였다.

⑤ [적중 포인트 049] 5형식 동사의 수동태 구조
consider는 5형식 타동사이고 타동사 뒤에 목적어가 없으면 수동태(be p.p.) 구조로 쓴다. 따라서 밑줄 친 부분은 올바르게 쓰였다.

선지 해석
① Maria가 1등상을 수상했다.
② 그에게 250달러의 벌금이 부과되었다.
③ 영어는 거기서 가르쳐지지 않았다.
④ 우리의 해결책이 그에게 설명되었다.
⑤ Nash는 천재로 여겨졌다.

19
정답 ②

정답 해설
② [적중 포인트 045] 능동태와 수동태의 차이
동사(repair)의 주어(my car)는 수리되는 것이므로 수동태로 표현해야 한다. 따라서 was repairing 대신 was repaired로 써야 올바르다.

오답 해설
① [적중 포인트 056] 여러 가지 분사구문
분사구문으로 앞에 Being이 생략된 상태로 형용사 주격 보어인 unable이 올바르게 쓰였고, 'be unable to부정사'는 '~을 할 수 없다'라는 의미의 표현이다.

③ [적중 포인트 019] 주어만 있으면 완전한 1형식 자동사
'깨닫게 되다'의 뜻을 가진 구문으로 'come to the realization'의 표현은 올바르게 쓰였다.

④ [적중 포인트 020] 주격 보어가 필요한 2형식 자동사
become은 2형식 동사로 주격 보어에 형용사를 쓴다. 따라서 형용사(dependent)와 형용사를 수식하는 부사(overly)가 올바르게 쓰였다.

지문 해석
자동차가 정비소에서 수리되는 동안 아무것도 할 수 없거나 어디에도 갈 수 없자, 나는 내가 기계와 장비에 지나치게 의존하고 있다는 것을 갑자기 깨닫게 되었다.

20
정답 ④

정답 해설
④ [적중 포인트 047] 다양한 3형식 동사의 수동태 구조
'refer to A as B'는 'A를 B로 언급[지칭]하다'의 뜻으로 쓰인다. the Old and New Testaments는 언급되는 것이고, refer to 뒤에 목적어가 없으므로 수동태 구조(be p.p.)로 써야 한다. 따라서 refer to as 대신 be referred to as로 써야 올바르다.

오답 해설
① [적중 포인트 039] 현재시제 동사와 be동사의 수 일치
& [적중 포인트 032] 의미와 구조에 주의해야 할 타동사
문장의 주어(a narrative)는 단수 형태이므로 단수 동사 helps는 올바르게 쓰였고, help는 to부정사를 목적어로 취할 수 있으므로 to explain 또한 올바르게 쓰였다.

② [적중 포인트 060] to부정사의 명사적 역할
문장의 주어(myths)는 복수 형태이므로 복수 동사 try는 올바르게 쓰였고, 'try to부정사'는 '~ 하려고 노력하다'의 뜻으로 쓰이므로 to make 또한 올바르게 쓰였다.

③ [적중 포인트 082] 관계대명사의 선행사와 문장 구조
관계대명사 that이 나오면 앞에 선행사를 확인하고 뒤는 불완전 구조인지 확인한다. that 뒤에 주어가 빠진 불완전 구조를 취하고 있으므로 밑줄 친 부분은 올바르게 쓰였다.

지문 해석
신화는 어떤 문화의 종교적, 철학적, 도덕적 그리고 정치적 가치를 — 경우에 따라 설명을 돕기 위해 — 담은 이야기다. 신들과 초자연적인 존재에 관한 이야기를 통해 신화는 자연 세계에서의 사건들을 이해하려고 노력한다. 일반적인 관례와는 반대로, 신화는 "거짓"을 의미하지 않는다. 가장 넓은 의미에서, 신화는 보통 진실이거나 부분적으로 진실이거나 거짓이 될 수 있는 이야기들 — 보통 여러 이야기들의 집합체 — 이다. 그러나 그들의 정확성 정도에 관계없이 신화는 종종 어떤 문화의 가장 깊은 신념을 표현한다. 이 정의에 따르면, 일리아드와 오디세이, 코란, 그리고 구약과 신약 성경은 모두 신화로 볼 수 있다.

PART 02 준동사

Chapter 07 동명사

ANSWER
01 ① 02 ② 03 ④ 04 ① 05 ①

01
정답 ①

정답 해설
① [적중 포인트 053] 암기해야 할 동명사 표현
'~에 익숙하다'의 뜻으로 쓰일 때는 'get used to (동)명사'의 전치사 to를 포함한 동명사 표현으로 쓸 수 있다. 따라서 have 대신 having으로 써야 올바르다.

오답 해설
② [적중 포인트 084] 관계대명사 주의 사항
관계사의 계속적 용법으로 쓰인 all of whom은 and all of them과 같은 의미로 '접속사 + 대명사'의 의미인 목적격 관계대명사 whom은 올바르게 쓰였다.

③ [적중 포인트 055] 감정 분사와 분사형 형용사
spread는 과거분사의 형태로 앞 부분의 'only 18 million people'를 수식하고 있으므로 밑줄 친 부분은 올바르게 쓰였다.

④ [적중 포인트 014] 형용사와 부사의 차이
alone은 형용사로 명사, 대명사 바로 뒤에서 그것을 수식하는 형태로 '다만, ~만, ~뿐'의 뜻으로 쓰인다. 따라서 밑줄 친 부분은 올바르게 쓰였다.

지문 해석
자동차와 교통체증을 넘어서, 한 장소에 이렇게 많은 사람들이 모두 빠르게 움직이는 것에 적응하는 데 시간이 걸렸다고 그녀는 말했다. "매사추세츠 주 한 곳에만 600만 명 이상의 사람들과 비교해 보았을 때 호주에는 전체 국가에 퍼져 있는 1800만 명의 사람들만이 있다"라고 그녀는 말했다.

02
정답 ②

정답 해설
② [적중 포인트 051] 동명사의 명사 역할
suggest는 동명사만을 목적어로 취하는 3형식 타동사이다. 따라서 going은 올바르게 쓰였다.

오답 해설
① [적중 포인트 051] 동명사의 명사 역할
& [적중 포인트 079] 명사절 접속사의 구분과 특징
like의 목적어로 '~하기를 좋아한다'를 의미할 때는 동명사를 취한다. 'whether A or B'의 구조로 등위접속사(or)를 기준으로 병치구조를 이뤄야 하므로 to walk 대신 walking으로 써야 올바르다.

③ [적중 포인트 082] 관계대명사의 선행사와 문장 구조
that 앞에 선행사가 있다면 that절은 주어나 목적어가 없는 불완전 구조로 써야 한다. her를 삭제하면 전치사(about) 뒤에 목적어가 없어서 불완전 구조가 되므로 I told you about her is 대신 I told you about is로 써야 올바르다.

④ [적중 포인트 075] 혼합 가정법 공식
if절에 과거 시간 부사와 주절에 현재 시간 부사가 쓰였다면 혼합가정법 공식을 확인해야 한다. 혼합 가정법은 'if 주어 had p.p. 과거시간부사, 주어 + would/should/could/might 동사원형 now(today)'의 공식으로 쓴다. 문장의 last night과 today에 근거하여 혼합 가정법의 형태로 써야 하므로, would have been 대신 would be로 써야 올바르다.

선지 해석
① 그 장소는 당신이 수영을 좋아하든 걷기를 좋아하든 멋진 곳이다.
② 그녀는 회의 후 저녁에 외식하자고 제안했다.
③ 내가 당신에게 말한 그 댄서는 시내로 오고 있는 중이다.
④ 만약 그녀가 어젯밤 약을 먹었더라면, 오늘 더 좋아졌을텐데.

03
정답 ④

정답 해설
④ [적중 포인트 083] 「전치사+관계대명사」 완전 구조
in which(전치사 + 관계대명사) 뒤는 완전 구조를 취해야하므로 주어 자리의 동사는 명사 역할을 할 수 있는 동명사 또는 to부정사로 써야 한다. 따라서 give 대신 giving 또는 to give로 써야 올바르다.

오답 해설
① [적중 포인트 086] 관계부사의 선행사와 완전 구조
where은 선행사(a place)를 수식하는 관계부사로 뒤는 완전 구조를 취하고 있으므로 올바르게 쓰였다.

② [적중 포인트 011] 재귀대명사의 2가지 용법
주어와 동일한 목적어는 인칭대명사가 아니라 재귀대명사로 써야 한다. 따라서 주어가 they이므로 재귀대명사 themselves는 올바르게 쓰였다.

③ [적중 포인트 006] 가산 명사의 종류와 특징
concern은 동사로는 '영향을 미치다, 관련되다'의 뜻으로, 명사로는 '걱정, 염려 / 관심사, 일' 뜻으로 쓰인다. 문맥상 '걱정, 염려'의 뜻이 자연스러우므로 concern은 올바르게 쓰였다.

지문 해석
상호 원조 그룹은 한 개인이 문제를 가져오고 도움을 요청하는 곳이다. 그룹 구성원들이 문제를 가진 개인에게 도움을 제공함으로써 그들 역시 자신들을 돕는 것이다. 각 그룹 구성원은 비슷한 걱정으로 유대감을 형성할 수 있다. 이것은 상호 원조 그룹에서 도움을 주는 것이 일종의 자신을 돕는 형태가 되는 중요한 방법 중 하나이다.

04

정답 ①

정답 해설

① [적중 포인트 051] 동명사의 명사 역할
'고려하다'를 의미하는 cosider은 동명사를 목적어로 취하는 특정 타동사이다. 따라서 동명사 형태인 applying for은 올바르게 쓰였다.

찐Tip apply for은 '~에 지원하다'의 뜻으로 쓰인다.

오답 해설

② [적중 포인트 023] 목적어 뒤에 특정 전치사를 수반하는 3형식 타동사
공급 동사 provide는 'A에게 B를 제공하다'의 뜻으로 쓰일 때는 'provide A with B'로 표현한다. 따라서 '난민들(A)에게 생활필수품(B)을 제공했다'의 뜻으로 쓰이려면 'provided commodities with refugees' 대신 'provided refugees with commodities'로 써야 올바르다.

찐Tip 위와 같은 구문은 A와 B를 바꿔쓰는 것에 주의가 필요하다.

③ [적중 포인트 066] 조동사 should의 3가지 용법과 생략 구조
명령 동사 order 뒤에서 that절의 동사는 (should) 동사원형으로 쓴다. 따라서 was remanded 대신 (should) be remanded로 써야 올바르다.

④ [적중 포인트 018] 혼동하기 쉬운 부사
deeply는 '대단히, 몹시'를 의미하고, deep은 '깊은, 깊게'를 의미한다. 따라서 높낮이를 표현하는 깊이의 뜻으로 쓰이려면 deeply 대신 deep으로 써야 올바르다.

선지 해석

① 유수는 그 회사에 지원하는 것을 고려하고 있다.
② 그 경찰서는 난민들에게 생활필수품을 제공했다.
③ 판사는 죄수가 재구속되어야 한다고 명령했다.
④ 그는 물속으로 깊이 잠수했다.

05

정답 ①

정답 해설

① [적중 포인트 051] 동명사의 명사 역할
need, want, deserve의 목적어가 수동의 의미로 해석될 경우에는 능동형 동명사(-ing)로 쓸 수 있다. 따라서 밑줄 친 부분은 올바르게 쓰였다.

찐Tip need Ring(= to be p.p.)는 수동의 의미를 나타낸다.

오답 해설

② [적중 포인트 046] 수동태 불가 동사
disappear은 대표 1형식 자동사로 수동태 구조인 'be p.p.'로 쓸 수 없다. 따라서 has been disappeared 대신 has disappeared로 써야 올바르다.

③ [적중 포인트 007] 불가산 명사의 종류와 특징
access는 불가산 명사로 부정관사 a(n)와 복수를 의미하는 '-s'를 쓰지 않는다. 따라서 gain an access 대신 an을 삭제한 gain access로 써야 올바르다.

④ [적중 포인트 021] 전치사가 필요 없는 대표 3형식 타동사
accompany는 전치사가 필요 없는 대표 3형식 타동사로 전치사 없이 바로 목적어(her fahter)를 취할 수 있다. 따라서 accompany with 대신 전치사 with을 삭제한 accompany로 써야 올바르다.

지문 해석

① 모든 차량들은 수리될 필요가 있다.
② 즉각적인 보안 위험은 사라졌다.
③ 네트워크에 접근하려면 비밀번호를 입력해야 한다.
④ Seohee는 아버지와 함께 프랑스 여행을 가기로 동의했다.

Chapter 08 분사

ANSWER

01 ④	02 ③	03 ①	04 ②	05 ④
06 ③	07 ④	08 ④	09 ①	10 ②
11 ④	12 ③	13 ④	14 ③	

01

정답 ④

정답 해설

④ [적중 포인트 054] 분사 판별법[현재분사 VS 과거분사]
현재분사 choosing의 수식을 받는 명사(a place)는 '선택하는' 행동을 할 수 없고 사람에 의해서 '선택된' 것이므로 과거분사로 써야 한다. 따라서 choosing을 chosen으로 고쳐야 한다.

오답 해설

① [적중 포인트 051] 동명사의 명사 역할
동명사는 전치사의 목적어로 쓰일 수 있으므로 전치사(besides) 뒤에 동명사 cooking은 올바르게 쓰였다.

② [적중 포인트 051] 동명사의 명사 역할
begin은 동명사를 목적어로 취할 수 있는 타동사이므로 밑줄 친 부분의 rearranging은 올바르게 쓰였다.

③ [적중 포인트 078] 등위접속사와 병렬 구조
문장에서 등위접속사 and를 기준으로 begin의 동명사 목적어들(rearranging, clearing, opening)이 병렬 구조를 이루고 있으므로 밑줄 친 부분의 opening은 올바르게 쓰였다.

지문 해석

불은 요리하는 것 외에도 여러 가지 방식으로 인간에게 유용했다. 불을 이용해 사람들은 자신들에게 맞게 환경을 재구성할 수 있었고, 야생 식품의 성장을 촉진하기 위해 땅을 개간하거나, 식량 동물들이 번식하도록 풍경을 개방한 다음, 불로 몰아 선택된 장소로 유도해 그것들을 수확할 수 있었다.

02

정답 ③

정답 해설

③ [적중 포인트 054] 주의해야 할 조동사와 조동사 관용 표현
빈칸은 주어(some of the clients' money)와 동사(has found) 사이에 위치하며, 이 명사를 꾸며주는 삽입 수식어 역할을 한다. 문맥상 '총 6백만 달러로 추정되는/믿어지는'이라는 의미를 전달해야 하므로, 수동의 의미를 가진 과거분사 believed가 들어가야 한다. 따라서 밑줄 친 부분에 들어갈 말로 가장 적절한 것은 ③이다.

지문 해석

예비 조사는 전부는 아니더라도 일부 고객의 자금, 총 600만 달러로 추정되는 금액이 비상장 기업과 부동산 구매에 흘러 들어갔음을 보여준다.

03

정답 ①

정답 해설
① [적중 포인트 055] 감정 분사와 분사형 형용사
감정동사의 현재분사형은 감정을 유발하는 의미를 전달할 경우에 쓰이고, 과거분사형은 감정을 느끼는 의미를 전달할 경우에 쓰인다. 따라서 주어(We)가 '감동을 받는' 감정을 느끼는 의미이므로 현재분사 touching 대신 과거분사 touched로 써야 올바르다.

찐Tip 앞에 5형식 동사 make가 수동태(be made) 구조로 쓰였다.

오답 해설
② [적중 포인트 088] 전치사와 명사 목적어
전치사(from) 뒤에 명사나 동명사를 목적어로 취할 수 있다. 따라서 밑줄 친 부분인 명사 its cost는 올바르게 쓰였다.

찐Tip 전치사구 apart from이 '~은 차치하고, ~을 제외하고'의 뜻으로 쓰인다.

③ [적중 포인트 058] 분사를 활용한 표현 및 구문
시간 접속사(while)가 이끄는 분사구문인데, 분사구문의 의미상 주어인 They가 '차를 마시는 것'이므로 능동의 현재분사 drinking은 올바르게 쓰였다.

찐Tip while 뒤에 'they were'가 생략되고 분사구문만 남은 형태이다.

④ [적중 포인트 026] 5형식 사역동사의 목적격 보어
사역동사(make)는 목적어와 목적보어의 관계가 능동일 때는 원형부정사를, 수동일 때는 과거분사를 목적보어로 취한다. 그가 그 프로젝트에 적합하게 여겨졌다는 수동의 의미이므로 과거분사 suited는 올바르게 쓰였다.

선지 해석
① 우리는 그의 연설에 감동하게 되었다.
② 비용은 차치하고 그 계획은 훌륭한 것이었다.
③ 그들은 뜨거운 차를 마시는 동안에 일몰을 보았다.
④ 과거 경력 덕분에 그는 그 프로젝트에 적합하였다.

04

정답 ②

정답 해설
② [적중 포인트 054] 분사 판별법[현재분사 VS 과거분사]
문장에 이미 동사가 있고 '동사 + ing'가 나온다면 분사 문제이다. call은 5형식 동사로 뒤에 목적어가 없고 목적보어만 있으므로 수동관계임을 알 수 있다. 따라서 현재분사 calling 대신 과거분사 called로 써야 올바르다.

찐Tip 분사 자리에서 'called + 명사'는 '~라고 불리는'의 뜻으로 쓰인다.

오답 해설
① [적중 포인트 029] 명사나 형용사를 목적격 보어로 취하는 5형식 동사
make는 5형식 동사로 'make + 명사 + 형용사 목적보어'로 쓸 수 있다. 따라서 밑줄 친 부분은 올바르게 쓰였다.

③ [적중 포인트 084] 관계대명사 주의 사항
the body 앞에 목적격 관계대명사(which)가 생략된 구조로 'the body makes'가 앞 명사(the same chemical)를 꾸며주고 있다. 따라서 밑줄 친 부분은 올바르게 쓰였다.

④ [적중 포인트 078] 등위접속사와 병치 구조
등위접속사(or) 기준으로 동명사 eating과 being은 병렬구조로 올바르게 쓰였다.

찐Tip prefer 뒤에서는 명사/동명사/to부정사 모두 쓸 수 있다.

지문 해석
아즈텍인들은 초콜릿이 사람들을 똑똑하게 만든다고 믿었다. 오늘날, 우리는 이것을 믿지 않는다. 그러나 초콜릿에는 페닐에틸아민이라고 불리는 특별한 화학 물질이 포함되어 있다. 이것은 사람이 사랑에 빠져있을 때 체내에서 생성되는 화학 물질과 동일하다. 당신은 어떤 것을 선호하는가 — 초콜릿을 먹는 것 아니면 사랑에 빠지는 것?

05

정답 ④

정답 해설
④ [적중 포인트 058] 분사를 활용한 표현 및 구문
전치사 with는 목적어와 목적보어를 수반하여 동시 동작을 나타내어 '~한 채로, ~하면서'라는 의미로 쓰인다. '다리를 꼰 채로'라는 뜻을 표현할 때는 with the legs crossed로 쓴다. 따라서 crossing 대신 crossed로 써야 올바르다.

오답 해설
① [적중 포인트 052] 동명사의 동사적 성질
having p.p.는 완료형 분사로서 주절보다 더 먼저 발생함을 나타낼 때 쓰고 능동형이므로 타동사인 경우에 뒤에 목적어가 있을 때 사용 가능하다. 따라서 밑줄 친 부분은 올바르게 쓰였다.

② [적중 포인트 056] 여러 가지 분사구문
Being a kind person은 분사 구문이다. 문장의 주어는 she로 그녀가 친절하다는 능동의 의미로 능동형 분사 Being은 올바르게 쓰였다.

찐Tip Being은 생략할 수 있다.

③ [적중 포인트 058] 분사를 활용한 표현 및 구문
'모든 것을 고려해볼 때'라는 의미를 가진 구문으로 'All things considered'의 분사 관용 구문표현이 있다. 따라서 밑줄 친 부분은 올바르게 쓰였다.

선지 해석
① 커피 세 잔을 마셨기 때문에, 그녀는 잠을 이룰 수 없다.
② 친절한 사람이어서, 그녀는 모든 이에게 사랑받는다.
③ 모든 점이 고려된다면, 그녀가 그 직위에 가장 적임인 사람이다.
④ 다리를 꼰 채로 오랫동안 앉아 있는 것은 혈압을 상승시킬 수 있다.

06

정답 ③

정답 해설
③ [적중 포인트 058] 분사를 활용한 표현 및 구문
'with 분사구문'의 목적보어 형태를 물어보는 문제이다. with 뒤에 목적어(the three quarters of the land)와 목적보어(surround)가 수동의 의미 관계이므로 현재분사 surrounding 대신 과거분사 surrounded로 써야 올바르다.

오답 해설
① [적중 포인트 064] to부정사의 관용 구문
'~은 말할 것도 없이'의 뜻을 가진 구문으로 'not to mention = not to speak of = to say nothing of = let alone'의 표현이 있다. 따라서 밑줄 친 부분은 올바르게 쓰였다.

② [적중 포인트 100] 원급과 비교급을 이용한 최상급 대용 표현
비교급 than any other 단수 명사는 최상급 구문의 형태로 단수 명사 girl은 올바르게 쓰였다.

찐Tip 비교급 than all the other 뒤는 복수 명사를 쓴다.

④ [적중 포인트 043] 혼동하기 쉬운 주어와 동사 수 일치
'A number of + 복수 명사 + 복수 동사'로 쓴다. 따라서 밑줄 친 부분은 올바르게 쓰였다.

찐Tip 'The number of + 복수 명사 + 단수 동사'로 쓴다.

선지 해석
① 그녀는 등산은 말할 것도 없고, 야외에 나가는 것을 좋아하지 않는다.
② 그녀는 학급에서 가장 예쁜 소녀이다.
③ 그 나라는 국토의 3/4이 바다로 둘러싸여 있는 소국이다.
④ 많은 학생들이 졸업 후 취직을 위해 열심히 공부한다.

07 정답 ④

정답 해설
④ [적중 포인트 056] 여러 가지 분사구문
분사구문의 주어는 '날씨'이고, 주절의 주어는 'I'이기 때문에 분사구문의 주어와 주절의 주어가 다를 때는 분사구문 앞에 따로 써야 한다. 따라서 날씨를 의미하는 it을 삽입해야 하므로 Being cold outside 대신 It being cold outside로 써야 올바르다.

오답 해설
① [적중 포인트 041] 부분을 나타내는 명사와 수 일치
& [적중 포인트 007] 불가산 명사의 종류와 특징
'all of 명사'는 명사에 수 일치한다. information은 불가산 명사로 항상 단수 취급하고 단수 동사로 일치시킨다. 따라서 단수 동사 was는 올바르게 쓰였다.

찐Tip 대표적인 불가산 명사로 equipment, furniture, evidence, homework, news, advice, money, machinery, clothing, merchandise, jewelry 등이 있다.

② [적중 포인트 067] 주의해야 할 조동사와 조동사 관용 표현
'~했어야 했다'라는 뜻을 가진 구문으로 should have p.p. 또는 ought to have p.p.의 표현이 있다. 따라서 밑줄 친 부분은 올바르게 쓰였다.

③ [적중 포인트 033] 과거 시간을 나타내는 부사와 과거시제
과거 시점을 나타내는 'when 주어 + 과거시제 동사'와 완료시제와 잘 쓰이는 already가 함께 쓰일 때 과거완료시제가 잘 쓰인다. 따라서 밑줄 친 부분은 올바르게 쓰였다.

찐Tip 완료시제의 경우 조동사(have/has/had)와 p.p.가 결합되어 하나의 동사를 이루는데 이때 부사가 위치한다면 조동사와 과거분사(p.p.) 사이에 위치한다.

선지 해석
① 모든 정보는 거짓이었다.
② 토마스는 더 일찍 사과했어야 했다.
③ 우리가 도착했을 때 영화는 이미 시작했었다.
④ 바깥 날씨가 추웠기 때문에 나는 차를 마시려 물을 끓였다.

08 정답 ④

정답 해설
④ [적중 포인트 054] 분사 판별법[현재분사 VS 과거분사]
문장에 이미 '주어 + 동사'가 나와 있고 동사의 p.p.형이 나온다면 분사 문제이다. 타동사 뒤에 목적어(the two dollars)가 있으므로 현재분사로 써야 한다. 따라서 paid back 대신 paying back으로 써야 올바르다.

오답 해설
① [적중 포인트 033] 과거 시간을 나타내는 부사와 과거시제
명백한 과거를 나타내는 과거시간 부사(in 년도)가 나오면 과거시제로 쓴다. 따라서 shoplifted는 올바르게 쓰였다.

② [적중 포인트 034] 완료시제와 잘 쓰이는 시간 부사
guilt-ridden은 '죄의식에 고통받는'의 뜻으로 문맥상 과거시점부터 현재까지 행위가 계속되는 것으로 보아 현재완료시제(have p.p.)는 올바르게 쓰였다. 주어가 'I'이므로 동사 have 또한 올바르게 쓰였다.

③ [적중 포인트 084] 관계대명사 주의 사항
he 앞에 목적격 관계대명사가 생략된 구조로 'he stole'이 앞 명사(the item)를 꾸며주고 있다. shoplifted가 과거시제로 쓰인 것으로 보아 stole 또한 과거시제로 올바르게 쓰였다.

지문 해석
1952년에 Shanton의 Woolworth's 상점에서 도둑질한 남성이 최근 익명의 사과 편지를 상점에 보냈다. 그 편지에서 그는 "나는 요즘 들어 죄책감에 고통받고 있다."라고 말했다. 그가 훔친 물건은 2달러짜리 장난감이었다. 그는 2달러에 이자까지 지불해서 우편을 보냈다.

09 정답 ①

정답 해설
① [적중 포인트 054] 분사 판별법[현재분사 VS 과거분사]
해석상 타인을 혼란에 빠뜨린 것이 아니고 그가 혼란에 빠진 것이고 cover 뒤에 목적어도 없으므로 과거분사로 써야 한다. 따라서 현재분사 covering 대신 과거분사 covered로 써야 올바르다.

오답 해설
② [적중 포인트 054] 분사 판별법[현재분사 VS 과거분사]
해석상 그가 걷는 것으로 능동의 의미인 현재분사를 써야 한다. 따라서 walking은 올바르게 쓰였다.

③ [적중 포인트 058] 분사를 활용한 표현 및 구문
'with 분사구문'으로 'with + 목적어 + 목적보어'의 형태로 목적보어 자리에 분사/형용사/전명구/부사가 올 수 있다. 따라서 형용사 open은 '눈을 뜬 채로'의 의미가 있으므로 올바르게 쓰였다.

찐Tip wide는 부사로 형용사(open)를 수식해주고 있고 wide open은 '크게 뜬'의 뜻으로 쓰인다.

④ [적중 포인트 054] 분사 판별법[현재분사 VS 과거분사]
문맥상 그녀가 직접 손을 흔드는 것으로 능동의 의미인 현재분사를 써야 한다. 따라서 waving은 올바르게 쓰였다.

선지 해석
① 그가 혼란에 빠진 채로 회의실을 떠났다.
② 길을 따라 걷다가 그는 나무뿌리에 걸려 넘어졌다.
③ 눈을 크게 뜬 채로 그녀는 그 남자를 응시했다.
④ 손을 흔들면서 그녀는 기차에 올랐다.

10 정답 ②

정답 해설
② [적중 포인트 054] 분사 판별법[현재분사 VS 과거분사]
문장에 이미 동사(raise)가 있고 '동사 + -ing'가 나오면 분사 문제이다. utilizing은 타동사로 뒤에 목적어가 없으므로 과거분사로 써야 한다. 따라서 Utilizing 대신 Utilized로 써야 올바르다.

오답 해설

① [적중 포인트 014] 형용사와 부사의 차이
'형용사 + 전명구'는 명사(machines)를 후치 수식할 수 있다. 따라서 밑줄 친 부분은 올바르게 쓰였다.

③ [적중 포인트 061] to부정사의 형용사적 역할
'명사 + to부정사'의 구조로 to carry는 앞에 나온 명사(machines)를 수식하는 형용사적 용법으로 올바르게 쓰였다.

④ [적중 포인트 007] 불가산 명사의 종류와 특징
'of + 추상명사'는 형용사로 쓸 수 있다. 'of great benefit'는 be동사의 주격 보어 역할로 올바르게 쓰였다.

지문 해석

가축화된 동물들은 사람이 접근 가능한 가장 오래되고 효과적인 '기계'이다. 이들은 인간의 등과 팔에 긴장을 덜어준다. 다른 기술들과 함께 활용함으로써, 동물들은 인간의 생활 수준을 매우 크게 향상시킬 수 있다. 그것은 보조 식품으로서 (육류와 우유에서 얻는 단백질과 같은) 그리고 짐을 나르거나 물을 들거나 곡물을 갈아내는 기계로서의 역할을 한다. 이들이 아주 분명히 큰 혜택을 제공하기 때문에, 우리는 여러 세기 동안 인간들이 기르는 동물의 수와 질을 증가시킬 것으로 기대할 수 있다. 하지만 놀랍게도, 이것은 일반적으로 그렇지 않았다.

11   정답 ④

정답 해설

④ [적중 포인트 055] 감정 분사와 분사형 형용사
감정 동사는 감정을 유발한다는 의미를 전달하고 사물을 수식할 경우 현재분사로 쓴다. 따라서 excited 대신 exciting으로 써야 올바르다.

오답 해설

① [적중 포인트 091] 비교급 비교 구문
접속사 than과 상응하는 표현은 more이므로 올바르게 쓰였고, 비교급 비교 구문 앞의 문장 구조가 보어가 없는 불완전한 구조이므로 형용사 expensive 또한 올바르게 쓰였다.

② [적중 포인트 039] 현재시제 동사와 be동사의 수 일치
뒤에 show가 복수 동사이므로 명사 또한 복수 형태로 써야 한다. 따라서 commercials는 올바르게 쓰였다.

③ [적중 포인트 078] 등위접속사와 병치 구조
밑줄 기준으로 climbing과 crossing이 병렬 구조로 쓰였다. 따라서 등위접속사 and는 올바르게 쓰였다.

지문 해석

SUV는 대부분의 자동차들보다 더 비싸고 연료도 더 많이 사용한다. 그러나 TV 광고에서는 그들이 돌로 된 산길을 오르고 강을 건너는 것을 보여주며, 이는 많은 사람들에게 흥미로워 보인다.

12   정답 ③

정답 해설

③ [적중 포인트 058] 분사를 활용한 표현 및 구문
consider 뒤에 목적어가 있으므로 현재분사로 써야 한다. 따라서 considered 대신 considering으로 써야 올바르다.

> **찐Tip** '~을 고려[감안]하면'의 뜻을 가진 구문으로 'considering (that)'의 독립 분사 구문 표현이 있다.

오답 해설

① [적중 포인트 053] 암기해야 할 동명사 표현
'look forward to'에서 to는 전치사이므로 뒤에 명사/동명사를 쓴다. 뒤에 명사(this visit)가 있는 것으로 보아 밑줄 친 부분은 올바르게 쓰였다.

② [적중 포인트 065] 조동사 뒤의 동사원형과 조동사의 부정형
would는 추측의 의미로 쓰인 화법 조동사로 뒤에는 동사원형이 나온다. 따라서 밑줄 친 부분은 올바르게 쓰였다.

④ [적중 포인트 055] 감정 분사와 분사형 형용사
dying은 '죽어가는'의 뜻으로 진행의 의미로 쓰였고, 현재분사 형태로 명사를 꾸며 주고 있으므로 올바르게 쓰였다.

지문 해석

죽어가고 있는 남자 옆에 앉아서 7백 마일을 비행기 타고 간 것을 고려한다면, 나는 사람들이 생각하는 것보다 더 많이 이 방문을 기대했다. 그러나 나는 Morrie를 방문할 때 시간의 왜곡에 빠진 것 같았고, 그곳에 있었을 때 나 자신이 더 좋았다.

13   정답 ④

정답 해설

④ [적중 포인트 054] 분사 판별법[현재분사 VS 과거분사]
interested in the arts가 those를 수식하여 '예술에 관심을 갖는 사람들'의 뜻으로 쓰인다. 감정 동사가 감정을 느낀다는 의미를 전달하고 사람을 수식할 경우 과거분사(interested)로 쓴다. 따라서 밑줄 친 부분은 올바르게 쓰였다.

오답 해설

① [적중 포인트 021] 전치사가 필요 없는 대표 3형식 타동사
resemble은 대표 3형식 타동사로 전치사 없이 바로 목적어를 취한다. 따라서 resemble like a book 대신 전치사 like를 삭제한 resemble a book으로 써야 올바르다.

② [적중 포인트 084] 관계대명사 주의 사항
관계대명사 which가 수식하는 선행사(magazines)가 복수 형태이므로 관계대명사의 동사도 복수 형태로 써야 한다. 따라서 단수 동사 reports 대신 복수 동사 report로 써야 올바르다.

③ [적중 포인트 054] 분사 판별법[현재분사 VS 과거분사]
'there be 동사 + 주어'의 구조로 'there are women's magagzines'는 올바르게 쓰였으나, 뒤에 동사(cover)가 접속사 없이 바로 나왔으므로 동사를 앞에 나온 명사를 꾸며줄 수 있는 분사형태로 바꿔야 한다. 뒤에 목적어가 있으므로 cover 대신 covering으로 써야 올바르다.

지문 해석

신문과 비교해서 잡지는 매일이 아닌 주간, 월간, 심지어는 그보다 더 드물게 발행되기 때문에 반드시 최신 정보를 제공하지는 않는다. 잡지는 외부적으로도 주로 책과 비슷한 모습을 가지기 때문에 신문과 다르다. 종이가 두껍고, 사진은 더 다채롭고, 대부분의 기사는 비교적 길다. 독자는 훨씬 더 많은 배경 정보와 상세한 내용들을 경험한다. 다양한 주제에 관해 보도하는 주간 뉴스 잡지도 있지만, 대부분의 잡지는 다양한 소비자들을 유치하기 위해 특화되어 있다. 예를 들어, 유명인사에 관한 젊은이들 잡지뿐만 아니라 패션, 화장품, 레시피를 다루는 여성 잡지들도 있다. 또다른 잡지는 예를 들면 컴퓨터 사용자, 스포츠 팬, 예술에 관심이 있는 사람들과 같은 작은 그룹들을 대상으로 만들기도 한다.

14

정답 ③

정답 해설

③ [적중 포인트 054] 분사 판별법[현재분사 VS 과거분사]
문장에 이미 주어 동사가 있고 '동사 + ing'가 나온다면 분사 문제이다. pay는 타동사로 뒤에 목적어가 없으므로 과거분사로 써야 한다. 따라서 paying 대신 paid로 써야 올바르다.

오답 해설

① [적중 포인트 054] 분사 판별법[현재분사 VS 과거분사]
get은 목적어와 목적보어가 수동의 의미 관계를 갖는 경우에는 과거분사로 써야 한다. 문맥상 stuff가 완성되는 것으로 수동의 의미이므로 과거분사(done)로 쓴다. 따라서 밑줄 친 부분은 올바르게 쓰였다.

찐Tip mean은 동명사를 목적어로 취하는 타동사이다.

② [적중 포인트 084] 관계대명사 주의 사항
관계대명사 that 뒤에 현재동사가 나오면 선행사와 수 일치를 확인해야 한다. 선행사(issues)는 복수이므로 interest와 concern은 복수동사로 올바르게 쓰였다.

④ [적중 포인트 078] 등위접속사와 병치 구조
& [적중 포인트 026] 5형식 사역동사의 목적격 보어
등위접속사(or) 기준으로 to do와 let은 병렬구조로 올바르게 쓰였고, let은 사역동사로 목적어와 목적보어가 능동의 의미 관계를 갖는 경우에는 원형부정사로 써야 한다. 문맥상 life가 스쳐지나가는 것으로 능동의 의미이므로 원형부정사(paas by)로 쓴다. 따라서 밑줄 친 부분은 올바르게 쓰였다.

찐Tip pass by와 같은 이어동사에 부사는 타동사 + 대명사 + 부사(타대부) 순서로 쓴다.

찐Tip 사역동사 let은 목적어와 목적보어가 수동의 의미 관계를 갖는 경우에는 반드시 목적보어를 과거분사가 아닌 be p.p.의 수동태 형태로 쓴다.

지문 해석

집중은 일을 해내는 것을 의미한다. 많은 사람들은 훌륭한 아이디어를 갖고 있지만 그것을 행동하지는 않는다. 예를 들어, 나에게 있어서 기업가의 정의는 혁신과 창의성을 새로운 아이디어를 실행하는 능력과 결합할 수 있는 사람이다. 어떤 사람들은 인생에서 가장 중요한 이분법은 자신이 관심이 있거나 걱정하는 문제에 대해 긍정적인지 부정적인지에 따라 나뉜다고 생각한다. 낙관적인 시각과 비관적인 시각 둘 중 어떤 것을 가지는 게 더 나은지에 대한 이 질문에 많은 관심이 있다. 나는 물어 봐야할 더 나은 질문은 그것에 관한 어떤 것을 할 것인지 아니면 인생이 그냥 흘러가게 할 것인지라고 생각한다.

Chapter 09 부정사

ANSWER

01 ①	02 ①	03 ①	04 ④	05 ③
06 ①	07 ①	08 ②	09 ③	10 ④
11 ①				

01

정답 ①

정답 해설

① [적중 포인트 060] to부정사의 명사적 역할
afford는 to부정사를 목적어로 취하는 특정 3형식 타동사이다. 따라서 wasting 대신 to waste로 써야 올바르다.

오답 해설

② [적중 포인트 019] 주어만 있으면 완전한 1형식 자동사
fade는 '사라지다'의 뜻인 자동사로 능동태로 표현해야 한다. 따라서 밑줄 친 부분은 올바르게 쓰였다.

③ [적중 포인트 053] 암기해야 할 동명사 표현
'~하지 않을 수 없다, ~할 수 밖에 없다'의 뜻을 가진 구문으로는 'have no choice[alternative] but to부정사'의 동명사 관용 표현이 있다. 따라서 밑줄 친 부분은 올바르게 쓰였다.

찐Tip 또 다른 표현으로는 'cannot but 동사원형 = cannot help 동명사'가 있다.

④ [적중 포인트 060] to부정사의 명사적 역할
aim은 타동사로 목적어에 to부정사를 취할 수 있다. 따라서 to start는 올바르게 쓰였다.

찐Tip 동작동사는 진행시제와 잘 쓰인다.

선지 해석

① 나는 단 한 푼의 돈도 낭비할 수 없다.
② 그녀의 얼굴에서 미소가 곧 사라졌다.
③ 그녀는 사임하는 것 외에는 대안이 없었다.
④ 나는 5년 후에 내 사업을 시작할 작정이다.

02

정답 ①

정답 해설

① [적중 포인트 060] to부정사의 명사적 역할
'~을 후회하다'의 뜻을 가진 구문으로는 'regret - ing'의 표현이 있다. 따라서 to tell 대신 telling으로 써야 올바르다.

찐Tip regret to부정사는 '~하게 되어 유감이다'의 뜻으로 쓰인다.

오답 해설

② [적중 포인트 092] 비교 대상 일치
worse는 bad의 비교급으로 '비교급 than'의 비교 표현으로 올바르게 쓰였고, 비교 구문에서 비교 대상이 사물과 사물일 때는 소유대명사(hers)를 써야 한다. 따라서 밑줄 친 부분은 올바르게 쓰였다.

③ [적중 포인트 023] 목적어 뒤에 특정 전치사를 수반하는 3형식 타동사
'통고, 확신' 동사 remind는 특정 전명구로 'A of 명사/A to 동사/A that절'을 쓸 수 있다. 따라서 밑줄 친 부분은 올바르게 쓰였다.

④ [적중 포인트 078] 등위접속사와 병치 구조
관계대명사 who 앞에 사람 선행사이고 뒤에는 주어가 없는 불완전 구조를 취하고 있으므로 밑줄 친 부분은 올바르게 쓰였다.

찐Tip 'look('보다' 동사) + 사람 명사 + in the 신체 일부'의 구문으로 정관사 the는 올바르게 쓰였다.

선지 해석
① 나는 네 열쇠를 잃어버렸다고 네게 말한 것을 후회한다.
② 그 병원에서의 그의 경험은 그녀의 경험보다 더 나빴다.
③ 그것은 내게 지난 24년의 기억을 상기시켜준다.
④ 나는 대화할 때 내 눈을 보는 사람들을 좋아한다.

03 정답 ①

정답 해설
① [적중 포인트 060] to부정사의 명사적 역할
'~할 여유가 있다(없다)'의 뜻을 가진 구문으로는 'can(not) afford to부정사'의 표현이 있다. 따라서 밑줄 친 부분은 올바르게 쓰였다.

오답 해설
② [적중 포인트 064] to부정사의 관용 구문
'~에 익숙하다'의 뜻을 가진 구문으로는 '사람 주어 be used to 명사/동명사'의 표현이 있다. 전치사 to 뒤에는 동명사를 써야 한다. 따라서 to get up 대신 to getting up으로 써야 올바르다.

③ [적중 포인트 043] 혼동하기 쉬운 주어와 동사 수 일치
the number of 복수 명사 뒤에는 단수 동사를 써야 한다. 따라서 복수 동사 are 대신 단수 동사 is로 써야 올바르다.

찐Tip a number of 복수 명사 뒤에는 복수 동사를 쓴다.

④ [적중 포인트 004] 주절의 주어와 동사가 중요한 부가 의문문
부가의문문의 형태를 물어보는 문제이다. 부가의문문의 동사는 평서문(주절)의 동사의 종류와 시제를 맞춘다. 주절의 동사가 일반동사(suppose)이므로 isn't 대신 doesn't로 써야 올바르다.

찐Tip 부가의문문은 평서문이 긍정이면 부정, 평서문이 부정이면 긍정의 부가의문문을 사용한다.

선지 해석
① 가난한 여성은 스마트폰을 살 여유가 없었다.
② 나는 매일 일찍 일어나는 것에 익숙하다.
③ 도시에서 발생하는 화재의 수가 매년 증가하고 있다.
④ 빌은 메리가 결혼했다고 생각하지, 그렇지 않니?

04 정답 ④

정답 해설
④ [적중 포인트 064] to부정사의 관용 구문
'너무 ~해서 ~할 수 없다'의 뜻을 가진 구문으로는 'too 형용사/부사 to 부정사 = so 형용사/부사 that 주어 cannot 동사원형'의 표현이 있다. 따라서 to부정사와 호응되기 위해서는 so distracted 대신 too distracted로 써야 올바르다.

찐Tip know 뒤에 that은 know의 목적어 역할을 하는 명사절 that이다.

오답 해설
① [적중 포인트 069] 다양한 도치 구문
Only 부사(부사구, 부사절)를 포함한 도치구문으로 'only + 전치사 + 명사' 뒤에 '조동사 + 주어 + 동사원형'의 형태로 쓸 수 있다. 따라서 did he recognize는 올바르게 쓰였다.

② [적중 포인트 066] 조동사 should의 3가지 용법과 생략 구조
주장동사(insist)의 that절의 동사는 '(should) 동사원형'으로 쓴다. 따라서 should가 생략된 be constructed는 올바르게 쓰였다.

③ [적중 포인트 070] 양보 도치 구문과 장소 방향 도치 구문
as 양보 도치 구문은 '비록 ~라도'라는 양보의 의미로 쓰인다. as 양보 부사절에는 'As 형용사 a 명사 + as 주어 + 2형식 동사'의 형태로 쓸 수 있다. 따라서 밑줄 친 부분은 올바르게 쓰였다.

선지 해석
① 그 회의 후에야 그는 금융 위기의 심각성을 알아차렸다.
② 장관은 교통문제를 해결하기 위해 강 위에 다리를 건설해야 한다고 주장했다.
③ 비록 그 일이 어려운 것이었지만, Linda는 그것을 끝내기 위해 최선을 다했다.
④ 그는 문자 메시지에 너무 정신이 팔려서 제한속도보다 빠르게 달리고 있다는 것을 몰랐다.

05 정답 ③

정답 해설
③ [적중 포인트 064] to부정사의 관용 구문
to부정사와 같이 쓰여, 강조 부정의 의미를 가지는 부사는 very가 아니라 too를 써야 한다. 따라서 very 대신 too로 써야 올바르다.

오답 해설
① [적중 포인트 078] 등위접속사와 병치 구조
& [적중 포인트 025] to부정사를 목적격 보어로 취하는 대표 5형식 타동사
enable은 to부정사를 목적보어로 취하는 5형식 타동사이다. 등위접속사 (and) 기준으로 to take와 to use는 병렬구조로 올바르게 쓰였다.

찐Tip 'to use'에서 to는 생략된 상태로 쓰였다.

② [적중 포인트 045] 능동태와 수동태의 차이
수동태 구조에서 p.p.자리에 위치하는 동사가 타동사인지 뒤에 목적어가 없는지 확인해야 한다. widow는 타동사로 뒤에 목적어가 없으므로 수동태로 쓴다. 따라서 was widowed는 올바르게 쓰였다.

④ [적중 포인트 062] to부정사의 부사적 역할
to make는 목적(~하기 위해서)에 해당하는 to부정사의 부사적 용법으로 올바르게 쓰였다.

지문 해석
지혜는 우리가 정보와 지식을 받아들여 그것들을 활용하여 좋은 결정을 내릴 수 있게 해준다. 개인적으로, 나의 어머니는 오직 5학년까지만 마쳤고, 우울한 가운데 남편을 잃고 일을 하기에는 너무 어린 6명의 아이들이 있었다. 분명히 그녀는 자식들을 성공적으로 키우기 위해 올바른 결정을 내리기 위한 지식을 활용할 줄 아는 지혜가 필요했다.

06 정답 ①

정답 해설
① [적중 포인트 064] to부정사의 관용 구문
'too 형용사/부사 to부정사' 구문에서 to부정사의 목적어와 그 절의 주어가 같을 때 to부정사 뒤의 목적어는 생략한다. the bag이 주어에 제시되어 있으므로 it을 쓴다면 중복 사용이 된다. 따라서 to lift it 대신 it을 삭제한 to lift로 써야 올바르다.

오답 해설
② [적중 포인트 069] 다양한 도치 구문
문장 처음에 so 형용사로 시작되면 뒤는 도치 구조로 쓰였는지 확인한다. 'so 형용사 + 조동사 + 주어 + that절'의 형태로 쓴다. 따라서 did she look은 올바르게 쓰였다.

③ [적중 포인트 049] 5형식 동사의 수동태 구조
지각동사가 수동태(be p.p.)로 쓰일 때는 목적보어였던 원형부정사는 to 부정사로 전환해야 한다. 따라서 to come은 올바르게 쓰였다.

찐Tip 'be seen + 동사원형'으로는 쓸 수 없다.

④ [적중 포인트 025] to부정사를 목적격 보어로 취하는 대표 5형식 타동사
get은 대표 5형식 타동사로 원형부정사가 아닌 to부정사 또는 과거분사를 목적보어로 취한다. 따라서 to go는 올바르게 쓰였다.

선지 해석
① 그 가방은 너무 무거워서 내가 들어 올릴 수 없었다.
② 그녀가 너무 꼴불견이어서 모든 사람들이 갑자기 웃기 시작했다.
③ 그가 집 밖으로 나오는 것이 목격되었다.
④ 나는 저 아이를 재울 수가 없다.

07 정답 ①

정답 해설
① [적중 포인트 064] to부정사의 관용 구문
Living으로 시작하는 절은 주절과 같은 주어와 접속사가 생략된 분사구문 형태이다. 빈칸 앞은 주어(over 1000 workers)이고 빈칸 뒤는 전치사구가 나왔으므로 빈칸은 동사 자리이다. 문맥상 과거의 반복된 습관을 나타내는 '~하곤 했다'의 뜻이 자연스러우므로 '사람 주어 + used to 동사원형'으로 써야 한다. 따라서 'used to sleep'로 써야 올바르다.

오답 해설
② [적중 포인트 064] to부정사의 관용 구문
'be used to부정사'는 '~하기 위해서 사용되다'의 뜻으로 쓰이고, 사람 주어는 올 수 없으므로 올바르지 못하다.

③ [적중 포인트 001] 문장의 구성요소
& ④ [적중 포인트 001] 문장의 구성요소
빈칸은 동사 자리이므로 동사 형태가 아닌 'to be slepping', 'slepping' 은 올바르지 못하다.

지문 해석
건설 현장의 건물에서 살면서, 1000명 이상의 노동자들이 한 지하실에서 잠을 자곤 했다.

08 정답 ②

정답 해설
② [적중 포인트 064] to부정사의 관용 구문
'~에 익숙하다'의 뜻을 가진 구문으로는 '사람 주어 be used to 명사/동명사'의 표현이 있다. 따라서 전치사 to 뒤에는 동명사를 써야 하고, 등위접속사(and) 기준으로 waiting과 staying은 병렬구조로 올바르게 쓰였다.

오답 해설
① [적중 포인트 064] to부정사의 관용 구문
'~하는 데 시간이 걸리다'의 뜻을 가진 구문으로는 'It takes + (사람) + 시간 + to부정사 = It takes + 시간 + (for사람) + to부정사'의 표현이 있다. 따라서 Time 대신 It으로 써야 올바르다.

찐Tip 가주어(it) 대신에 that이나 time을 주어로 쓰지 않는다.

③ [적중 포인트 064] to부정사의 관용 구문
'too 형용사/부사 to부정사' 구문에서 to부정사의 목적어와 그 절의 주어가 같을 때 to부정사 뒤의 목적어는 생략한다. 따라서 to answer it 대신 it을 삭제한 to answer로 써야 올바르다.

④ [적중 포인트 021] 전치사가 필요 없는 대표 3형식 타동사
tire는 타동사로 전치사 없이 바로 목적어를 취한다. 따라서 tired of me 대신 전치사 of를 삭제한 tired me로 써야 올바르다.

선지 해석
① 어떤 교수의 스타일에 적응하는 데는 항상 시간이 좀 걸린다.
② 나는 마지막 순간까지 기다렸다가 밤을 새우는 데 익숙해있다.
③ 그 수학 문제는 너무 어려워서 그 학생이 답을 할 수 없었다.
④ 나는 너무 많은 시간의 힘든 일로 정말 지쳤다.

09 정답 ③

정답 해설
③ [적중 포인트 064] to부정사의 관용 구문
easy는 난이형용사로서 주어가 it이 아닌 것이 나오면 to부정사의 목적어가 주어 자리로 상승한 구문으로 난이형용사 다음에 나오는 to부정사 뒤에 목적어가 없어야 한다. 따라서 take it for granted 대신 it을 삭제한 take for granted로 써야 올바르다.

오답 해설
① [적중 포인트 064] to부정사의 관용 구문
'~할 사람이 아니다'의 뜻을 가진 구문으로는 'the last man(person) to부정사 = know better than to부정사 = be above -ing = be far from -ing'의 표현이 있다. 따라서 밑줄 친 부분은 올바르게 쓰였다.

② [적중 포인트 067] 주의해야 할 조동사와 조동사 관용 표현
'B하는 것보다 A하는 게 낫다'의 뜻을 가진 구문으로는 'would rather A than B'의 표현이 있다. A, B는 주로 동사원형으로 쓴다. 따라서 make와 fight는 동사원형으로 올바르게 쓰였다.

④ [적중 포인트 080] 부사절 접속사의 구분과 특징
Even though는 양보 부사절 접속사로 뒤에 '주어 + 동사'의 완전 구조를 취한다. 따라서 밑줄 친 부분은 올바르게 쓰였다.

찐Tip very는 원급을 수식하는 부사로 형용사의 원급인 knowledgeable 을 수식하므로 올바르게 쓰였다.

선지 해석
① 그는 결코 당신을 속일 사람이 아니다.
② 그는 주먹다짐을 할 바에야 타협하는 것이 낫다고 생각한다.
③ 프레스코는 이태리 교회의 익숙한 요소이기 때문에 이것을 당연하게 생각하기 쉽다.
④ 그는 대학에 다니지 않았지만 아는 것이 아주 많은 사람이다.

10 정답 ④

정답 해설
④ [적중 포인트 064] to부정사의 관용 구문
'너무 ~해서 ~할 수 없다'의 뜻을 가진 구문으로는 'too 형용사/부사 to 부정사 = so 형/부 that 주어 can't 동사원형'의 표현이 있다. 따라서 too tired of lying 대신 too tired to lie로 써야 올바르다.

> **찐Tip** '분사(p.p.) + be동사 + 명사주어'와 '사람 주어 + who + 동사'의 구조일 때는 주어와 동사 수 일치를 확인해야 한다. 따라서 단수 동사 is는 올바르게 쓰였다.

오답 해설
① [적중 포인트 080] 부사절 접속사의 구분과 특징
접속사(because)는 동사를 포함한 절을 이끈다. 따라서 because 뒤에 '주어 + 동사'로 올바르게 쓰였다.

② [적중 포인트 064] to부정사의 관용 구문
difficult와 같은 난이형용사는 'It(가주어) + be동사 + 난이형용사 + (for 목적어) + to부정사(진주어)'의 구조로 쓴다. 따라서 밑줄 친 부분은 올바르게 쓰였다.

③ [적중 포인트 039] 현재시제 동사와 be동사의 수 일치
주어(people)는 복수명사이므로 복수 동사 have는 올바르게 쓰였다.

선지 해석
① 시간이 부족해서 시험을 끝낼 수 없었다.
② 습관을 깨기란 예상보다 훨씬 어렵다.
③ 대부분의 사람들은 TV에서 지나친 폭력을 매우 싫어한다.
④ 낮에는 너무 바빠 걱정할 틈도 없고, 밤에는 너무 피곤해서 깨어있을 수 없는 사람은 복 받은 사람이다.

11 정답 ①

정답 해설
① [적중 포인트 060] to부정사의 명사적 역할
to는 be동사의 보어 자리로 to부정사의 명사적 용법이다. 따라서 to는 전치사가 아니므로 뒤에 동명사를 쓰면 안 된다. 따라서 proceeding 대신 proceed로 써야 올바르다.

오답 해설
② [적중 포인트 054] 분사 판별법[현재분사 VS 과거분사]
수식받는 명사(evidence) 입장에서 행위를 받는 입장으로 수동의 의미이므로 과거분사 accepted는 올바르게 쓰였다.

③ [적중 포인트 014] 형용사와 부사의 차이
firmly는 과거분사(grounded)를 수식하므로 부사 firmly는 올바르게 쓰였다.

④ [적중 포인트 051] 동명사의 명사 역할
risk는 동명사를 목적어로 취하는 특정 타동사이다. 따라서 confusing은 올바르게 쓰였다.

지문 해석
에세이를 체계화하는 마지막 방법은 비교적 단순한 개념에서 더 복잡한 개념들로 나아가는 것이다. 일반적으로 받아들여지는 증거로 시작함으로써, 독자와의 유대감을 형성하고 에세이가 공유된 경험에 근거를 두고 있음에 확신을 준다. 그에 반해 어려운 자료로 시작하면, 독자를 혼란스럽게 할 위험이 있다.

PART 03 조동사와 조동사를 활용한 구문

Chapter 10 조동사

ANSWER
01 ① 02 ② 03 ③ 04 ④ 05 ②
06 ① 07 ④ 08 ①

01 정답 ①

정답 해설
① [적중 포인트 067] 주의해야 할 조동사와 조동사 관용 표현
& [적중 포인트 033] 과거 시간을 나타내는 부사와 과거시제
& [적중 포인트 045] 능동태와 수동태의 차이
이 문항은 동사의 시제와 태(수동태)를 묻는 문제이다. 시간 부사 'in recent years(최근 몇 년간)'는 현재를 기준으로 한 과거의 기간을 나타내므로, 과거 시제 혹은 현재완료 시제와 함께 쓰인다. 문맥상 직원들은 급여를 받는 입장이므로 수동태가 필요하며, 그 보수를 받지 못했을 가능성을 나타내기 위해서는 'may have been + p.p.' 형태가 적절하다. 즉, 과거에 충분한 급여를 받지 못했을 수도 있다는 의미를 가장 자연스럽게 표현하는 내용이 들어가야 한다. 따라서 밑줄 친 부분에 들어갈 말로 가장 적절한 것은 ①이다.

지문 해석
Whitworths라는 온라인 식료품 쇼핑을 제공하는 소매업체는, 급여를 받는 일부 직원들이 최근 몇 년간 충분한 보수를 받지 못했을 수도 있다는 사실을 발견했다고 말한다.

02 정답 ②

정답 해설
② [적중 포인트 067] 주의해야 할 조동사와 조동사 관용 표현
dare은 본동사와 조동사 기능 둘 다 있으며, 특히 부정문에서 조동사 역할이 가능하다. dare은 일반동사로 쓰일 때는 '부정어(not) + dare + to 부정사'의 형태로, 조동사로 쓰일 때는 'dare[dared] + 부정어(not) + 동사원형'의 형태로 써야 한다. 문맥상 부정문으로 조동사의 쓰임을 묻는 것이므로 dared not이 들어가야 적절하다.

찐Tip not의 위치에 주의해야 하는데 동사원형 앞에 not을 붙여 'dare not 동사원형'의 어순으로 써야 한다.

지문 해석
그 시대에 여성의 남성에 대한 순종의 동양사상이 만연했기 때문에, 그녀는 감히 남성들과 대등하게 만날 수 없었다.

03 정답 ③

정답 해설
③ [적중 포인트 066] 조동사 should의 3가지 용법과 생략 구조
요구(demand)동사의 that절의 동사는 '(should) 동사원형'으로 쓴다. 부정어 not은 동사원형 앞에 써야 하므로 밑줄 친 부분은 올바르게 쓰였다.

오답 해설
① [적중 포인트 093] 원급, 비교급, 최상급 강조 부사
much는 형용사나 부사의 비교급을 강조하고, very는 형용사나 부사의 원급을 수식하므로 much 대신 very로 써야 올바르다.

찐Tip '사람명사 + who + 동사'일 때는 수 일치를 확인해야 한다. 명사(peson)가 단수 형태이므로 단수 동사 makes는 올바르게 쓰였다.

② [적중 포인트 079] 명사절 접속사의 구분과 특징
but은 명사절 접속사 역할을 할 수 없다. 따라서 but 대신 or not과 쓰일 수 있는 명사절 접속사 whether로 써야 올바르다.

④ [적중 포인트 094] 「The 비교급 ~, the 비교급…」 구문
the 비교급 표현은 'the 비교급 주어 + 동사~, the 비교급 주어 + 동사'의 구조로 쓴다. expensiver는 올바른 비교급의 형태가 아니므로 a hotel is expensiver 대신 expensive a hotel is로 써야 올바르다.

선지 해석
① Jessica는 자신의 지식을 향상시키려는 노력을 거의 하지 않는 매우 부주의한 사람이다.
② 그러나 그가 올지 안 올지는 확실하지 않다.
③ 경찰은 그녀가 일시적으로 나라를 떠나지 않도록 요청했다.
④ 호텔이 더 비싸면 비쌀수록 그 서비스는 더 좋을 것이다.

04 정답 ④

정답 해설
④ [적중 포인트 066] 조동사 should의 3가지 용법과 생략 구조
주장(insist)동사의 that절의 동사는 '(should) 동사원형'으로 쓴다. 따라서 밑줄 친 부분은 올바르게 쓰였다.

찐Tip before은 부사절 접속사로 동사를 포함한 절을 이끄므로 뒤에 '주어 + 동사' 형태 또한 올바르게 쓰였다.

오답 해설
① [적중 포인트 090] 원급 비교 구문
원급 비교 구문으로 'as 형용사 a 명사 as~'로 표현할 수 있다. 따라서 she was good swimmer as he was 대신 she was as good a swimmer as he was로 써야 올바르다.

찐Tip as~as 사이 '형용사 + a + 명사'의 어순이 중요하다

② [적중 포인트 045] 능동태와 수동태의 차이
describe는 3형식 타동사이고 뒤에 목적어가 없으므로 수동태(be p.p.)로 써야 한다. 따라서 has described 대신 has been described로 써야 올바르다.

③ [적중 포인트 068] 부정부사와 도치 구문
hardly와 never은 부정부사로 중복해서 쓸 수 없고 단독으로 써야 한다. 문맥상 never(결코 ~않다)이 더 자연스러우므로 hardly never arrived 대신 hardly를 삭제한 never arrived로 써야 올바르다.

찐Tip 명사절 접속사 what은 불완전 구조를 이끌고 주어 자리에 오면 단수 취급해야 하므로 올바르게 쓰였다.

선지 해석
① 더 낫지는 않더라도, 그녀는 그만큼 좋은 수영선수라고 느꼈다.
② 이 현상은 그 주제와 관련해서 부연 설명을 더 하지 않아도 될 정도로 자주 묘사되었다.
③ 우리를 가장 놀라게 한 것은 그가 직장에 결코 지각하지 않았다고 말했다는 사실이다.
④ Mr. Kay가 다른 회사로 이직할 것임을 발표하기도 전에, 매니저는 우리가 새로운 회계사를 뽑기 위한 광고를 해야 한다고 주장했다.

05   정답 ②

정답 해설
② [적중 포인트 066] 조동사 should의 3가지 용법과 생략 구조
명령(command)동사의 that절의 동사는 '(should) 동사원형'으로 쓴다. cease는 자동사와 타동사로 둘 다 쓸 수 있는데 '중단되다'의 뜻으로 쓰일 때는 자동사이다. 따라서 cease는 올바르게 쓰였다.

오답 해설
① [적중 포인트 031] 혼동하기 쉬운 자동사와 타동사
raise는 타동사로 목적어를 취하지 않는 경우에는 수동태 구조로 써야 한다. 따라서 have raised 대신 have been raised로 써야 올바르다. 또는 '생기다'의 뜻인 자동사인 arise는 목적어 없이 능동태로 쓸 수 있다. 따라서 have raised 대신 have arisen으로 써야 올바르다.

찐Tip due to는 이유를 의미하는 전치사로 명사/동명사 목적어를 수반하므로 올바르게 쓰였다.

③ [적중 포인트 037] 시제의 일치와 예외
주절의 동사가 과거(had)이므로 that절의 동사 또한 과거시제로 써야 한다. 따라서 will blow 대신 blew로 써야 올바르다.

④ [적중 포인트 032] 의미와 구조에 주의해야 할 타동사
우리말은 주어는 '거의 모든 식물'이라고 하고 있으므로 most 대신 almost all로 써야 올바르다. 또한 survive는 자동사와 타동사로 둘다 쓸 수 있는데 '~에 살아남다, ~보다 오래 살다'의 뜻으로 쓰일 때는 타동사이다. 따라서 우리말을 보면 '~에도 살아남는다'라고 하고 있으므로 are survived by 대신 survive로 써야 올바르다.

찐Tip 'be survived by'는 '(~을 유족으로 남기고) 먼저 죽다'의 뜻으로 쓰인다.

선지 해석
① 몇 가지 문제가 새로운 회원들 때문에 생겼다.
② 그 위원회는 그 건물의 건설을 중단하라고 명했다.
③ 그들은 한 시간에 40마일이 넘는 바람과 싸워야 했다.
④ 거의 모든 식물의 씨앗은 혹독한 날씨에도 살아남는다.

06   정답 ①

정답 해설
① [적중 포인트 067] 주의해야 할 조동사와 조동사 관용 표현
'B하는 것보다 A하는 게 낫다'의 뜻을 가진 구문으로는 'would rather A than B'의 표현이 있다. A, B는 주로 동사원형으로 쓴다. 따라서 going 대신 go로 써야 올바르다.

오답 해설
② [적중 포인트 006] 가산 명사의 종류와 특징 & [적중 포인트 064] to부정사의 관용 구문
police는 보통 정관사 the와 함께 쓰이고 복수 취급해야 하므로 동사 are은 올바르게 쓰였고, 'be unwilling to부정사'는 '~하기를 꺼리다'의 뜻으로 쓰이고, 여기서 to는 to부정사로 뒤에 동사원형이 와야 한다. 따라서 to interfere은 올바르게 쓰였다.

찐Tip interfere에 전치사 in이 붙으면 '~을 간섭하다, ~에 개입하다'의 뜻으로, 전치사 with이 붙으면 '~을 방해하다'의 뜻으로 쓰인다.

③ [적중 포인트 053] 암기해야 할 동명사 표현
'~해도 소용없다'의 뜻을 가진 구문으로는 'It's no use[good] -ing'의 동명사 관용 표현이 있다. 따라서 밑줄 친 부분은 올바르게 쓰였다.

④ [적중 포인트 021] 전치사가 필요 없는 대표 3형식 타동사
'너무 ~해서 ~하다'의 뜻을 가진 구문으로는 'so + 형용사/부사 + that + 주어 동사'의 표현으로 밑줄 친 부분은 올바르게 쓰였다.

찐Tip one/ones는 앞의 셀 수 있는 명사를 대신 받는데 keys가 복수 형태이므로 ones 또한 올바르게 쓰였다.

선지 해석
① 오늘 밤 나는 영화 보러 가기보다는 집에서 쉬고싶다.
② 경찰은 집안 문제에 대해서는 개입하기를 무척 꺼린다.
③ 네가 통제하지 못하는 과거의 일을 걱정해봐야 소용없다.
④ 내가 자주 열쇠를 엉뚱한 곳에 두어서 내 비서가 나를 위해 여분의 열쇠를 갖고 다닌다.

07   정답 ④

정답 해설
④ [적중 포인트 067] 주의해야 할 조동사와 조동사 관용 표현
문맥상 '~얻지 못했을 것이다'라고 하고 있으므로 'would not have p.p.~'로 써야 자연스럽다. 따라서 should have achieved 대신 wouldn't have achieved로 써야 올바르다.

찐Tip if가 생략된 도치 가정법으로 'Had + 주어 + p.p.~, 주어 + would/should/could/might + have p.p.'의 형태로 올바르게 쓰였다.

오답 해설
① [적중 포인트 035] 미래를 대신하는 현재시제
시간 부사절 접속사(as soon as)에서는 미래시제 대신 현재시제로 써야 한다. 따라서 현재동사 receive는 올바르게 쓰였다.

② [적중 포인트 067] 주의해야 할 조동사와 조동사 관용 표현
문맥상 '~했었야 했다'라고 하고 있으므로 'should(ought to) have p.p.'로 써야 자연스럽다. 따라서 밑줄 친 부분은 올바르게 쓰였다.

③ [적중 포인트 057] 분사의 동사적 성질
분사구문이 발생한 시제는 시간부사 'for 기간'이 있는 것으로 보아 완료시제이고, 문장의 동사 시제는 can speak으로 현재시제이기 때문에 분사구문의 시제와 동사의 시제가 차이가 나므로 완료형 having been으로 올바르게 쓰였다.

선지 해석
① 이 편지를 받는 대로 곧 본사로 와 주십시오.
② 나는 소년 시절에 독서하는 버릇을 길러 놓았어야만 했다.
③ 그는 10년 동안 외국에 있었기 때문에 영어를 매우 유창하게 말할 수 있다.
④ 내가 그때 그 계획을 포기했었다면 이렇게 훌륭한 성과를 얻지 못했을 것이다.

08

정답 ①

정답 해설

① [적중 포인트 066] 조동사 should의 3가지 용법과 생략 구조
주관적 판단 형용사(essential)의 that절의 동사는 '(should) 동사원형'으로 써야 하고, 'It is 주관적 판단 형용사 that 주어 (should) 동사원형'의 구조로 쓴다. 따라서 밑줄 친 부분은 올바르게 쓰였다.

찐Tip 이외 주관적 판단 형용사로는 'important, vital, desirable, imperative, natural, necessary'가 있다.

오답 해설

② [적중 포인트 098] 비교급을 이용한 표현
much[still] more은 '~는 말할 것도 없이'의 뜻으로 앞 문장이 긍정문일 경우에, much[still] less는 같은 뜻으로 앞 문장이 부정문일 경우에 쓰인다. 위 문장은 앞 문장이 부정문(No one~)이기 때문에 much more 대신 much less로 써야 올바르다.

③ [적중 포인트 054] 분사 판별법[현재분사 VS 과거분사]
discuss는 타동사로 영작을 보면 '논의된 바~'의 수동의 의미이고, 뒤에 목적어를 취하고 있지 않으므로 과거분사로 써야 한다. 따라서 discussing 대신 discussed로 써야 올바르다.

④ [적중 포인트 083] 「전치사+관계대명사」 완전 구조
관계대명사 which는 뒤에 불완전 구조를 취한다. 위 문장은 which 뒤에 'S + be p.p.'의 형태인 완전 구조를 취하고 있으므로 관계부사 또는 '전치사 + 관계대명사'를 써야 한다. 따라서 which 대신 in which 또는 where로 써야 올바르다.

선지 해석

① 모든 직원들이 보호 장비를 착용하는 것은 필수적이다.
② 누구도 그에게 늦게까지 일하도록 강요하지 않았고, 그렇게 요청하지도 않을 것이다.
③ 회의에서 논의된 바와 같이, 새로운 정책들은 상당한 이익을 가져다줄 것이다.
④ CEO는 대부분의 회사 제품이 생산되는 공장에 방문했다.

Chapter 11 도치 구문과 강조 구문

ANSWER
01 ① 02 ② 03 ④ 04 ① 05 ④
06 ④ 07 ② 08 ③

01

정답 ①

정답 해설

① [적중 포인트 068] 부정부사와 도치 구문
& [적중 포인트 038] 시제 관련 표현
'~하자마자 ~했다'의 뜻을 가진 구문으로는 'No sooner had + 주어 p.p. + than 주어 + 과거시제 동사'의 도치 표현이 있다. 따라서 No sooner I have finishing 대신 No sooner had I finished로 써야 올바르다.

찐Tip 이와 같은 뜻을 가진 구문으로 '주어 + had no sooner p.p. + than 주어 + 과거시제 동사'의 정치 표현이 있다.

오답 해설

② [적중 포인트 062] to부정사의 부사적 역할
'~해야만 하다'의 뜻을 가진 구문으로는 'will have to부정사'로 표현할 수 있다. 따라서 밑줄 친 부분은 올바르게 쓰였다.

찐Tip 'sooner or later'은 '조만간'의 뜻으로 쓰인다.

③ [적중 포인트 079] 명사절 접속사의 구분과 특징
'A is to B what(as) C is to D'는 'A와 B의 관계는 C와 D의 관계와 같다'의 뜻으로 쓰인다. 따라서 밑줄 친 부분은 올바르게 쓰였다.

④ [적중 포인트 053] 암기해야 할 동명사 표현
'결국 ~하게 되다'의 뜻을 가진 구문으로 'end up -ing'의 표현이 있다. 따라서 밑줄 친 부분은 올바르게 쓰였다.

찐Tip 등위접속사(but)를 기준으로 studied와 ended up은 과거시제가 병렬구조로 올바르게 쓰였다.

선지 해석

① 식사를 마치자마자 나는 다시 배고프기 시작했다.
② 그녀는 조만간 요금을 내야만 할 것이다.
③ 독서와 정신의 관계는 운동과 신체의 관계와 같다.
④ 그는 대학에서 의학을 공부했으나 결국 회계 회사에서 일하게 되었다.

02

정답 ②

정답 해설

② [적중 포인트 068] 부정부사와 도치 구문
부정어 little이 문장 처음에 나오면 뒤에 이어지는 문장의 어순은 '조동사 + 주어'로 도치된다. 일반 동사 dreamed는 바로 주어 앞에 위치하는 것이 아니라 '조동사(do, does, did) + 주어 + 동사원형'의 도치된 형태로 쓰인다. 따라서 Little I dreamed 대신 Little did I dream으로 써야 올바르다.

오답 해설

① [적중 포인트 068] 부정부사와 도치 구문
& [적중 포인트 038] 시제 관련 표현
'~하자마자 ~했다'의 뜻을 가진 구문으로는 'No sooner had 주어 p.p. than 주어 + 과거시제 동사'의 도치 표현이 있다. 따라서 had he seen은 올바르게 쓰였다.

③ [적중 포인트 056] 여러 가지 분사구문
문장 처음에 Written in~은 분사구문으로 의미상의 주어가 주절의 주어 book이다. 책이 쓰여졌다는 것으로 수동의 의미이므로 과거분사 written은 올바르게 쓰였다.

④ [적중 포인트 067] 주의해야 할 조동사와 조동사 관용 표현
'~하지 않을 수 없다'의 뜻을 가진 구문으로는 'cannot help but 동사원형 = cannot help -ing'의 동명사 관용 표현이 있다. 따라서 but 뒤에 동사원형 fall은 올바르게 쓰였다.

선지 해석

① 그가 나를 보자마자 그는 도망갔다.
② 그가 나에게 거짓말을 했다는 것을 나는 꿈도 꾸지 못했다.
③ 간단한 영어로 쓰여져서, 이 책은 많은 사람들에 읽혀졌다.
④ 처음으로 그녀를 만났을 때, 나는 그녀에게 반하지 않을 수 없었다.

03

정답 ④

정답 해설

④ [적중 포인트 069] 다양한 도치 구문
주격 보어(Included)가 문장 처음에 위치하면 '주격 보어 + be동사 + 주어'의 어순이 된다. 주어는 'The Enchanted Horse'는 작품 이름으로 단수 취급을 한다. 따라서 단수 동사 is는 올바르게 쓰였다.

오답 해설

① **[적중 포인트 084] 관계대명사 주의 사항**
문맥상 주격 관계대명사 that에 대한 선행사는 life가 아닌 many forms 로 복수 형태이다. 따라서 단수 동사 has 대신 복수 동사 have로 써야 올바르다.

② **[적중 포인트 064] to부정사의 관용 구문**
'너무 ~해서 ~할 수 없다'의 뜻을 가진 구문으로는 'too 형용사/부사 to 부정사 = so 형용사/부사 that 주어 cannot'의 표현이 있다. so와 to부정사는 호응하지 못하므로 so 대신 too로 써야 올바르다.

③ **[적중 포인트 045] 능동태와 수동태의 차이**
수여동사를 제외하고 수동태(be p.p.) 뒤에 목적어는 올 수 없다. 동사 protect 뒤에 목적어(Egypt)가 있는 것을 보아 능동의 의미로 볼 수 있다. 따라서 has been protected 대신 능동의 현재완료 has protected로 써야 올바르다.

선지 해석

① 바다는 아직 발견되지 않은 많은 종류의 생물을 함유하고 있다.
② 토성의 고리는 지구에서 망원경 없이는 볼 수 없을 만큼 아주 멀리 떨어져 있다.
③ Aswan High Dam은 이집트를 이웃 국가들의 기근으로부터 보호해 왔다.
④ "마법의 말"은 다른 유명한 동화들 중 이 시리즈에 포함되어 있다.

04
정답 ①

정답 해설

① **[적중 포인트 069] 다양한 도치 구문**
neither를 포함한 도치 구문으로 '주어+동사(부정)~, and neither + 조동사 + 주어'의 표현이 있다. 조동사는 앞에 나온 동사의 종류와 시제에 따라 결정되고 뒤에 나온 주어와 수 일치해야 한다. 따라서 앞 동사 believe와 뒤에 주어 I에 맞춰 did로 올바르게 쓰였다.

찐Tip and neither은 nor로 쓸 수 있다.

오답 해설

② **[적중 포인트 083] 「전치사+관계대명사」 완전 구조**
전치사 in은 관계대명사 앞에 올 수 있지만 관계대명사 that 앞에는 올 수 없다. 따라서 관계대명사 that 대신 which로 써야 올바르다.

③ **[적중 포인트 037] 시제의 일치와 예외**
종속절의 내용이 과거에 발생한 역사적 사실(1,2차 세계대전 등등..)이면 항상 과거 시제를 사용한다. 따라서 had broken out 대신 broke out으로 써야 올바르다.

④ **[적중 포인트 060] to부정사의 명사적 역할**
make는 5형식 동사로 to부정사가 목적어 역할을 할 경우 '가목적어(it)-진목적어(to부정사)' 구문으로 쓸 수 있다. 다음 구문으로 '5형식 동사 + 가목적어(it) + 형용사/명사 + (for목적어) + 진목적어(to부정사)'의 형식이 있다. 따라서 made scientists difficult 대신 made it difficult for scientists으로 써야 올바르다.

찐Tip 위 구조로 쓸 수 있는 5형식은 동사는 make, believe, consider, find, think가 있다.

선지 해석

① 그들은 그의 이야기를 믿지 않았고, 나도 마찬가지였다.
② 내가 가장 관심 있는 스포츠는 축구이다.
③ Jamie는 그 책에서 제1차 세계 대전이 1914년에 발발했다는 것을 배웠다.
④ 두 가지 요인으로 인해 과학자들이 지구 상의 종의 수를 결정하는 것을 어렵게 만들었다.

05
정답 ④

정답 해설

④ **[적중 포인트 068] 부정부사와 도치 구문**
부정부사 under no circumstances가 문장 처음에 나오면 뒤에 이어지는 문장의 어순은 '조동사 + 주어'로 도치된다. 따라서 you should 대신 should you로 써야 올바르다. 또한 부정부사는 다른 부정부사와 겹쳐 쓰지 않기 때문에 밑줄 친 부분인 not을 삭제해야 한다.

오답 해설

① **[적중 포인트 060] to부정사의 명사적 역할**
regret은 동명사 목적어를 수반할 때 '~을 후회한다'의 뜻으로 쓰인다. 동명사의 완료형은 본동사의 시제보다 동명사가 발생한 시제가 더 이전에 일어났을 경우를 의미한다. 밑줄 친 부분은 본동사는 현재 시제(regrets)이고, 동명사는 과거(in her youth)에 발생했고, work는 1형식 자동사이므로 능동 완료형 동명사인 having worked는 올바르게 쓰였다.

② **[적중 포인트 078] 등위접속사와 병치 구조**
'both A and B'는 'A와 B 둘 다' 라는 의미의 상관접속사로 A와 B는 병렬구조를 이룬다. 따라서 전치사의 목적어로 명사 experience와 knowledge가 병렬구조로 올바르게 쓰였다.

③ **[적중 포인트 078] 등위접속사와 병치 구조**
등위접속사(and) 기준으로 병렬구조를 이룬다. 밑줄 친 부분인 and를 기준으로 형용사 normal과 healthy가 병렬구조로 올바르게 쓰였다.

선지 해석

① 그녀는 젊었을 때 더 열심히 일하지 않았던 것을 후회한다.
② 그는 경험과 지식을 둘 다 겸비한 사람이다.
③ 분노는 정상적이고 건강한 감정이다.
④ 어떤 상황에서도 너는 이곳을 떠나면 안 된다.

06
정답 ④

정답 해설

④ **[적중 포인트 069] 다양한 도치 구문**
so를 포함한 도치 구문으로 '주어+동사(긍정)~, and so + 조동사 + 주어'의 표현이 있다. 조동사는 앞에 나온 동사의 종류와 시제에 따라 결정되고 뒤에 나온 주어와 수 일치해야 한다. 따라서 앞 동사 loved와 뒤의 주어 her son에 맞춰 did로 올바르게 쓰였다.

찐Tip and neither는 부정문과 호응한다.

오답 해설

① **[적중 포인트 053] 암기해야 할 동명사 표현**
'~을 기대하다'의 뜻을 가진 구문으로는 'look forward to 명사/동명사'의 표현이 있다. 여기서 to는 전치사로 to receive 대신 to receiving으로 써야 올바르다.

② **[적중 포인트 031] 혼동하기 쉬운 자동사와 타동사**
rise는 1형식 자동사로 '일어나다, 떠오르다, 상승하다'의 뜻으로 쓰이고, 명사 목적어를 취할 수 없다. raise는 타동사로 '~을 올리다, ~을 일으키다'의 뜻으로 쓰이고, 목적어(명사)를 취할 수 있다. 따라서 목적어(my salary)가 있으므로 rise 대신 raise로 써야 올바르다.

③ **[적중 포인트 053] 암기해야 할 동명사 표현**
'~할 가치가 있다'의 뜻을 가진 구문으로는 'be worth -ing = be worthy of -ing'의 동명사 관용 표현이 있다. 따라서 considered 대신 considering으로 써야 올바르다.

선지 해석
① 나는 너의 답장을 가능한 한 빨리 받기를 고대한다.
② 그는 내가 일을 열심히 했기 때문에 월급을 올려주겠다고 말했다.
③ 그의 스마트 도시 계획은 고려할 만했다.
④ Cindy는 피아노 치는 것을 매우 좋아했고 그녀의 아들도 그랬다.

07   정답 ②

정답 해설
② [적중 포인트 068] 부정부사와 도치 구문
& [적중 포인트 038] 시제 관련 표현
'~하자마자 ~했다'의 뜻을 가진 구문으로는 'Hardly[Scarcely] + had 주어 p.p. + when[before] 주어 + 과거시제 동사'의 도치 표현이 있다. 따라서 did she enter 대신 had she entered로 써야 올바르다.

오답 해설
① [적중 포인트 054] 분사 판별법[현재분사 VS 과거분사]
문장에서 이미 동사 set이 있는데 동사의 p.p.형인 caught가 나왔으므로 분사 문제이다. 과거분사 caught가 앞에 있는 명사(words)를 꾸며주는데 뒤에 목적어가 없고, words가 붙잡혀진 것이므로 과거분사 caught는 올바르게 쓰였다.

찐Tip 'set + 목적어 -ing'는 '~하게 만들다'의 뜻으로 쓰인다.

③ [적중 포인트 084] 관계대명사 주의 사항
관계대명사 whose는 뒤에 완전 구조를 취한다. whose는 뒤에 나오는 명사 balcony를 수식해주고 있고 여기서 balcony는 전치사 from의 목적어 역할을 하므로 'from whose balcony'는 '전치사 + 명사구'의 형태로 쓰였고, 뒤는 완전 구조로 올바르게 쓰였다.

④ [적중 포인트 044] 주어 자리에서 반드시 단수 또는 복수 취급하는 특정 표현
'the 형용사'가 '~인(한) 사람들'이라는 의미로 해석될 때 복수 취급하고 복수 동사와 수 일치한다. 따라서 복수 동사 have는 올바르게 쓰였다.

찐Tip 'have difficulty -ing'는 '~하는 데 어려움을 겪다'의 뜻으로 쓰인다.

선지 해석
① 지나가면서 들린 몇 마디가 나를 생각하게 만들었다.
② 그녀가 집에 들어가자마자 누군가가 불을 켰다.
③ 우리는 호텔로 차를 타고 갔고, 그 호텔의 발코니에서 마을을 내려다볼 수 있었다.
④ 노숙자들은 보통 일자리를 구하는 데 큰 어려움을 겪으므로 그들은 희망을 잃어가고 있다.

08   정답 ③

정답 해설
③ [적중 포인트 068] 부정부사와 도치 구문
부정부사 not only가 문장 처음에 나오면 '조동사 + 주어' 도치 구조를 확인해야 한다. 'be + 주어 + 명사(동사원형×)'의 도치 구조로는 올바르게 쓰였다. 그러나 도치가 될 때 주어와 동사 수 일치도 확인해야 한다. 따라서 주어(the Palm Beach Post)가 단수 형태이므로 복수 동사 were 대신 단수 동사 was로 써야 올바르다.

오답 해설
① [적중 포인트 028] 분사를 목적격 보어로 취하는 5형식 동사
find의 목적어와 목적보어의 관계가 상태를 나타낼 때는 형용사를 취할 수 있다. 따라서 형용사 empty는 올바르게 쓰였다.

② [적중 포인트 039] 현재시제 동사와 be동사의 수 일치
& [적중 포인트 014] 형용사와 부사의 차이
앞에 단수 동사 was가 있는 것으로 보아 주어도 단수 형태로 올바르게 쓰였고, 형용사(unusual)가 명사(nothing)를 후치 수식해주는 한정적 용법으로도 올바르게 쓰였다.

④ [적중 포인트 054] 분사 판별법[현재분사 VS 과거분사]
compete는 타동사로 뒤에 목적어(paper)를 취하고 있으므로 현재분사로 수식한다. 따라서 현재분사형 competing은 올바르게 쓰였다.

지문 해석
몇 주 전에 나는 동이 튼 직후에 일어나보니 내 옆 침대가 비어 있는 것을 발견했다. 나는 일어나서 우리의 작은 방갈로의 그물망을 쳐 놓은 베란다의 유리 테이블에 목욕가운을 입은 채로 앉아있는 Jenny를 발견했는데 그녀는 신문 위에 숙인 채로 손에 펜을 들고 있었다. 이 장면에는 특별한 점이 없었다. Palm Beach Post는 우리 지역 신문일 뿐만 아니라, 우리 가계 수입의 절반을 이루는 주요한 수입원이었다. 우리는 신문 기자를 하는 커플이었다. Jenny는 "Accent" 섹션에서 특별기사 전문기고가로서 일하고 있으며, 나는 포트로더데일에서 남쪽으로 한 시간 정도 떨어진 곳에 위치해 있는 'South Florida Sun-Sentinel'의 지역 내 경쟁 신문사에서 뉴스 기자로 일하고 있었다.

Chapter 12   가정법

ANSWER
01 ②   02 ④   03 ④   04 ①   05 ④
06 ①   07 ④

01   정답 ②

정답 해설
② [적중 포인트 077] 기타 가정법
'명사가 없다면 ~ 할 것이다'의 뜻을 가진 구문으로는 'Were it not for 명사 + 주어 would/shoud/could/might 동사원형'의 가정법 과거 표현이 있다. 따라서 밑줄 친 부분은 올바르게 쓰였다.

오답 해설
① [적중 포인트 021] 전치사가 필요 없는 대표 3형식 타동사
contact는 3형식 타동사로 전치사 없이 바로 목적어를 취할 수 있다. 따라서 contact to me 대신 전치사 to를 삭제한 contact me로 써야 올바르다.

③ [적중 포인트 039] 현재시제 동사와 be동사의 수 일치
'사람명사 + who + 동사' 구조가 나오면 주어와 동사 수 일치를 확인해야 한다. 선행사가 people로 복수 형태이므로 단수 동사 is 대신 복수 동사 are로 써야 올바르다.

찐Tip allow는 목적어와 목적보어가 능동의 의미관계를 갖는 경우에 목적보어를 to부정사로 써야 한다.

④ [적중 포인트 094] 「The 비교급 ~, the 비교급…」 구문
'~할수록 더 ~하다'라는 뜻의 비교 구문은 'the 비교급 주어 + 동사~, the 비교급 주어 + 동사'의 구조로 쓴다. 따라서 최상급 the worst 대신 비교급 the worse로 써야 올바르다.

선지 해석
① 저번 주에 제가 드렸던 이메일 주소로 저에게 연락해 주세요.
② 물이 없었다면 지구상의 모든 생물은 멸종했을 것이다.
③ 노트북은 사무실 밖에 있는 사람들이 작업을 계속할 수 있게 해준다.
④ 그들이 실수를 설명하려고 노력할수록, 그들의 이야기는 더욱 나쁘게 들렸다.

02
정답 ④

정답 해설
④ [적중 포인트 076] if 생략 후 도치된 가정법
'Had + 주어'로 시작한다면 if가 생략된 가정법이므로 가정법 공식을 확인해야 한다. 'Had + 주어 + p.p. ~, 주어 + would/should/ could/might have p.p.'의 가정법 과거 완료 공식으로 밑줄 친 부분은 올바르게 쓰였다.

오답 해설
① [적중 포인트 053] 암기해야 할 동명사 표현
& [적중 포인트 045] 능동태와 수동태의 차이
object to에서 to는 전치사로 뒤에 동명사를 취한다. ask out 뒤에 목적어가 없으므로 수동태(be p.p.)로 써야 한다. 따라서 objects to be asked 대신 objects to being asked로 써야 올바르다.
② [적중 포인트 003] 어순이 중요한 간접의문문
주어, 목적어, 보어 자리에 where로 시작하면 간접의문문이다. 간접의문문은 '조동사 + 주어'의 도치 구조가 아닌 평서문의 어순인 '주어 + 동사'의 구조로 써야 한다. 따라서 where is the nearest back 대신 where the nearest bank is로 써야 올바르다.
③ [적중 포인트 039] 현재시제 동사와 be동사의 수 일치
문장의 주어(Tom)가 단수 형태이므로 복수 동사 were 대신 단수 동사 was로 써야 올바르다.

선지 해석
① 그녀는 직장 동료들에게 데이트 신청을 받는 것을 반대한다.
② 주변에 가장 가까운 은행이 어디에 있는지 모르겠다.
③ 나의 가장 친한 친구 중 한 명인 Tom은 1985년 4월 4일에 태어났다.
④ 그들이 내 지시를 따랐더라면, 그들은 처벌받지 않았을 것이다.

03
정답 ④

정답 해설
④ [적중 포인트 077] 기타 가정법
'명사가 없었다면, ~했을 것이다'의 뜻을 가진 구문으로는 'if it had not been for 명사 + 주어 + would/should/could/might have p.p.'의 가정법 과거완료 표현이 있다. 따라서 be discovered 대신 have been discovered로 써야 올바르다.

찐Tip 가정법 과거완료는 현재 사실과 반대로 가정해서 현재 결과에 반대로 예측하는 구문이다.

오답 해설
① [적중 포인트 077] 기타 가정법
as if 가정법으로 주절의 동사와 같은 시제의 반대로 가정할 때는 '주어 + 동사(현재, 과거) + as if + 주어 + 과거시제 동사'의 구조로 쓸 수 있다. 따라서 과거 동사 were는 올바르게 쓰였다.

찐Tip 'speak + 언어명'은 '~을 구사하다'의 뜻으로 쓰인다.

② [적중 포인트 072] 가정법 미래 공식
'what if 주어 + should 동사원형'의 형태로 '만일 ~하면 어떻게 하지'의 뜻으로 쓰인다. 따라서 밑줄 친 부분은 올바르게 쓰였다.

③ [적중 포인트 035] 미래를 대신하는 현재시제
시간, 조건 부사절에서는 의미상 미래일지라도 현재시제가 미래를 대신한다. 따라서 현재동사 rains는 올바르게 쓰였다.

찐Tip 주절에는 미래면 미래시제를 그대로 쓴다.

선지 해석
① 그는 마치 자신이 미국 사람인 것처럼 유창하게 영어로 말한다.
② 우리 실패하면 어떻게 하지?
③ 만일 내일 비가 온다면, 나는 그냥 집에 있겠다.
④ 뉴턴이 없었다면 중력 법칙은 발견되지 않았을 것이다.

04
정답 ①

정답 해설
① [적중 포인트 076] if 생략 후 도치된 가정법
if 생략 후 도치된 가정법 미래의 주절에는 '(please) 명령문'을 쓸 수 있다. 'Should + 주어 + 동사원형, (please) 명령문'의 공식으로 밑줄 친 부분은 올바르게 쓰였다.

오답 해설
② [적중 포인트 067] 주의해야 할 조동사와 조동사 관용 표현
'(B보다) A가 낫다'의 뜻을 가진 구문으로는 'would rather A (than B)'의 조동사 관용 표현이 있다. A와 B는 주로 동사원형이 쓰인다. 따라서 to go 대신 go로 써야 올바르다.
③ [적중 포인트 069] 다양한 도치 구문
so와 neither를 이용한 도치 구조로 앞 문장이 부정문일 경우에는 앞 문장에 대한 부정 동의는 'and neither 조동사 + 주어'로 써야 한다. neither은 부사이므로 반드시 절과 절을 이어주는 and가 필요하고, 일반동사는 do/does/did로 써야 한다. 따라서 so 대신 and neither로 써야 올바르다.

찐Tip and neither은 nor로 쓸 수 있다.

④ [적중 포인트 082] 관계대명사의 선행사와 문장 구조
문장과 문장을 연결하는 부분에 접속사가 없으므로 등위접속사(and)를 추가하거나 일반대명사 them을 접속사 기능이 있는 관계대명사(whom)로 써야 한다. 따라서 some of them 대신 and some of them 또는 some of whom으로 써야 올바르다.

선지 해석
① 만약 질문이 있다면 자유롭게 나에게 연락하세요.
② 너는 그녀와 함께 가느니 차라리 집에 머무는 것이 낫겠다.
③ 팀장은 그 계획을 좋아하지 않았고 나머지 직원들도 마찬가지였다.
④ 그는 여행 중에 많은 사람을 만났고 그들 중 일부는 그의 친구가 되었다.

05
정답 ④

정답 해설
④ [적중 포인트 074] 가정법 과거완료 공식
문맥상 과거 사실에 대한 반대를 가정하는 것으로 가정법 과거완료로 써야 한다. 가정법 과거완료는 'If 주어 had p.p. ~, 주어 + would/should/could/might have p.p.'로 would be saved 대신 would have been saved로 써야 올바르다.

찐Tip if wearing safety belts는 if they had been wearing safety belts를 분사구문으로 전환한 표현으로 쓰였다.

06

정답 ①

정답 해설

① [적중 포인트 072] 가정법 미래 공식
'If+주어+should 동사원형'이 나오면 가정법 미래를 의미하므로 주절의 동사가 올바르게 쓰였는지 확인해야 한다. 불확신한 미래를 가정할 경우 'If+주어+should 동사원형~, 주어 + would/should/could/might 동사원형'의 공식으로 밑줄 친 부분은 올바르게 쓰였다.

오답 해설

② [적중 포인트 100] 원급과 비교급을 이용한 최상급 대용 표현
비교급을 이용한 최상급 구문으로 '비교급 than any other' 뒤에는 단수 명사를 쓴다. 따라서 baseball players 대신 baseball player로 써야 올바르다.

찐Tip '비교급 than all the other' 뒤에는 복수 명사를 쓴다.

③ [적중 포인트 038] 시제 관련 표현
'~하자마자 ~했다'의 뜻을 가진 구문으로는 'Hardly[Scarcely] + had 주어 p.p. + when[before] 주어 + 과거시제 동사'의 도치 표현이 있다. 따라서 has 대신 had로 써야 올바르다.

④ [적중 포인트 049] 5형식 동사의 수동태 구조
사역동사 make는 수동태로 쓰일 경우 'be made to부정사/과거분사'로 써야 하고 'be made 동사원형'로는 쓸 수 없다. 따라서 come 대신 to come으로 써야 올바르다.

선지 해석

① 만약 물건이 내일 배송되지 않는다면, 그들은 그것에 대해 불평할 것이다.
② 그는 반에서 다른 어떤 야구 선수보다 더 능숙하다.
③ 바이올리니스트의 연주가 끝나자마자 관객들은 일어서서 박수갈채를 보냈다.
④ 제빵사들이 밀 소비 증진을 요구하면서 밖으로 나오도록 되어 왔다.

오답 해설

① [적중 포인트 034] 완료시제와 잘 쓰이는 시간 부사
과거 어느 시점부터 현재까지 행위와 동작 등의 완료의 의미를 나타내는 현재완료시제(have p.p.)로 쓸 수 있다. 따라서 have shown은 올바르게 쓰였다.

② [적중 포인트 039] 현재시제 동사와 be동사의 수 일치
문장의 주어(accidens)가 복수 형태이므로 복수 동사 occur은 올바르게 쓰였다.

찐Tip occur은 대표 1형식 자동사로 수동태(be p.p) 구조로 쓸 수 없다.

③ [적중 포인트 045] 능동태와 수동태의 차이
cause는 타동사로 사람들에 의해 야기되어지는 것의 수동의 의미로 수동태(be p.p.) 구조로 올바르게 쓰였다.

지문 해석

> 많은 연구들이 안전벨트의 생명을 구하는 가치를 보여줬다. 사고가 발생할 때, 대부분의 부상과 사망은 안전벨트를 하지 않은 사람들에 의해 발생한다. 지난 사고에서 사망한 사람들 중 약 40%가 안전벨트를 착용했었다면, 살았었을 것이다.

07

정답 ④

정답 해설

④ [적중 포인트 073] 가정법 과거 공식
'if + 주어 + 과거 동사'가 나오면 가정법 과거를 의미하고 주절에 '주어 + would/should/could/might 동사원형'이 올바르게 쓰였는지 확인해야 한다. 따라서 주절에 동사원형 be는 올바르게 쓰였다. offend는 타동사로 뒤에 목적어가 없고 수동의 의미이므로 수동태(be p.p.)형태 또한 올바르게 쓰였다.

오답 해설

① [적중 포인트 045] 능동태와 수동태의 차이
suppose는 타동사로 뒤에 목적어 없이 to부정사(to phone)만 있는 것으로 보아 수동태 형태로 되어야 하는 것을 짐작할 수 있다. 따라서 supposed 대신 was supposed로 써야 올바르다.

② [적중 포인트 036] 진행형 불가 동사
know는 인식동사로 진행형(be -ing)으로는 쓸 수 없다. 따라서 have been knowing 대신 have known으로 써야 올바르다.

③ [적중 포인트 065] 조동사 뒤의 동사원형과 조동사의 부정형
had better 뒤에는 동사원형을 써야 한다. 따라서 to go 대신 go로 써야 올바르다.

찐Tip '명령문, or 주어 + 동사'의 구조는 '~해라 그렇지 않으면 주어 + 동사할 것이다'의 뜻으로 쓰인다.

선지 해석

① 그녀가 지난밤에 나에게 전화할 예정이었는데, 하지 않았다.
② 일곱 살 이후로 나는 Jose와 알고 지냈다.
③ 너는 지금 가는 편이 좋겠어, 그렇지 않으면 늦을 거야.
④ 내가 파티에 가지 않으면 Sarah는 화낼텐데.

PART 04 연결어

Chapter 13 접속사

ANSWER

01 ④	02 ④	03 ①	04 ③	05 ③
06 ③	07 ①	08 ②	09 ③	10 ②
11 ④	12 ④	13 ②	14 ②	15 ②
16 ②	17 ④	18 ②		

01

정답 ④

정답 해설

④ [적중 포인트 078] 등위접속사와 병렬 구조
and 뒤에 쓰인 including은 앞에 나온 동사들(features, monitors)과 병렬 구조를 이루어야 하므로 including을 includes로 고쳐야 한다.

오답 해설

① [적중 포인트 054] 분사 판별법[현재분사 VS 과거분사]
밑줄 친 부분의 customized는 명사(programs)를 수식하는 과거분사로 '개인의 요구에 맞춘'이라는 형용사 역할을 하고 있으므로 올바르게 쓰였다.

② [적중 포인트 039] 현재시제 동사와 be동사의 수 일치
문장의 주어가 단수 대명사인 It이므로 동사도 단수 형태로 써야 하므로 밑줄 친 부분은 올바르게 쓰였다.

③ [적중 포인트 078] 등위접속사와 병렬 구조
and를 기준으로 명사(silver aerobics)와 명사(laughter therapy)가 병렬 구조를 이루고 있으므로 밑줄 친 부분의 laughter는 '웃음'이라는 명사로 올바르게 쓰였다.

지문 해석

시는 '스마트 노인복지센터'라는 여가 시설을 개관했으며, 이 시설은 노인들을 위한 맞춤형 프로그램을 제공한다. 이 센터는 실버 에어로빅과 웃음 치료와 같은 가상 활동을 제공하고, 보건소와 협력하여 건강 지표를 관찰하며, 실내 원예 활동도 포함하고 있다.

02

정답 ④

정답 해설

④ [적중 포인트 080] 부사절 접속사의 구분과 특징
전치사 because of 뒤에는 명사가 와야 하는데, 동사를 포함한 절을 이끌고 있다. 따라서 전치사 because of 대신 접속사 because로 써야 올바르다.

오답 해설

① [적중 포인트 006] 가산 명사의 종류와 특징
수 형용사 many는 복수 명사를 수식해 준다. 따라서 밑줄 친 부분은 올바르게 쓰였다.

② [적중 포인트 044] 주어 자리에서 반드시 단수 또는 복수 취급하는 특정 표현
문장의 주어(one)가 단수 형태이므로 동사도 단수 동사로 수 일치해야 한다. 따라서 밑줄 친 부분은 올바르게 쓰였다.

③ [적중 포인트 082] 관계대명사의 선행사와 문장 구조
관계대명사 which는 주어나 목적어가 없는 불완전 구조를 이끈다. 따라서 밑줄 친 부분은 올바르게 쓰였다.

지문 해석

당신이 읽고 있는 책의 많은 미덕 중 하나는, 그 책이 Maps of Meaning이라는 매우 복잡한 작업에 대한 진입점을 제공한다는 것인데, 이 책은 저자가 그 책을 쓰면서 심리학에 대한 접근 방식을 발전시키고 있었기 때문에 매우 복잡한 작품이다.

03

정답 ①

정답 해설

① [적중 포인트 081] 주의해야 할 부사절 접속사
'for fear (that)'은 부사절 접속사로 '~하지 않을까 두려워서, ~할까봐'의 근본적인 의미를 가지고 있으며, '~하지 않도록, ~하지 않기 위해서'로 뜻으로 쓰인다. 그 자체로 부정적인 의미가 포함되어 있으므로 that절에 부정어를 중복하지 않는다. 따라서 'should not be overheard' 대신 not을 삭제한 'should be overheard'로 써야 올바르다.

찐Tip 부정 목적 접속사(lest, for fear)의 that절의 동사는 '(should) 동사원형'으로 쓴다. 여기서 that은 생략이 가능하다.

오답 해설

② [적중 포인트 099] 최상급 구문
'결코 ~할 사람이 아니다'의 뜻을 가진 구문으로는 'be the last man(person) to부정사'의 관용 표현이 있다. 따라서 밑줄 친 부분은 올바르게 쓰였다.

찐Tip 같은 뜻을 가진 구문으로는 'know better than to부정사'의 관용 표현이 있다.

③ [적중 포인트 088] 전치사와 명사 목적어
'be entitled to'에서 to는 전치사로 뒤에 명사 또는 동명사를 쓸 수 있다. 따라서 to의 목적어로 명사(first class travel)는 올바르게 쓰였다.

④ [적중 포인트 013] 부정대명사의 활용
'A와 B는 별개의 것이다'의 뜻을 가진 구문으로는 'A is one thing, and B is another'의 관용 표현이 있다. 따라서 밑줄 친 부분은 올바르게 쓰였다.

선지 해석
① 누가 엿들을까봐 그는 목소리를 낮추었다.
② 그녀는 그 계획을 계속 따라 갈 사람이 결코 아닐 것이다.
③ 고위 간부들은 일등석으로 여행할 자격이 있다.
④ 일하는 것과 돈 버는 것은 별개의 것이다.

04
정답 ③

정답 해설
③ [적중 포인트 079] 명사절 접속사의 구분과 특징
전치사 to의 목적어로 명사절이 쓰였다. 뒤에 목적어가 없는 불완전 구조로 명사절 접속사 what이 와야한다. 따라서 which 대신 what으로 써야 올바르다.

오답 해설
① [적중 포인트 045] 능동태와 수동태의 차이
realize는 타동사로 뒤에 목적어가 없고 문맥상 '실현되는 것'의 수동의 의미로 수동태(be p.p.) 구조로 쓴다. 따라서 밑줄 친 부분은 올바르게 쓰였다.
② [적중 포인트 051] 동명사의 명사 역할
involve는 동명사를 목적어로 취하는 특정 타동사이다. 따라서 creating은 올바르게 쓰였다.
④ [적중 포인트 049] 5형식 동사의 수동태 구조
make는 5형식으로 'make + 목적어 + 명사/형용사'의 형태로 쓸 수 있다. 수동태로 전환되면 'be made + 형용사'의 형태가 된다. 따라서 형용사 productive는 올바르게 쓰였다.

지문 해석
도시 농업(UA)은 오랫동안 도시에서 자리가 없는 변두리 활동이라고 일축되어 왔으나, 그 잠재력이 점차 실현되고 있다. 사실, UA는 식량 자립에 관한 것이다. 이것은 일자리 창출을 포함하며, 특히 가난한 이들을 위한 식량 불안정에 대한 대응이다. 많은 사람들이 믿는 것과는 반대로, UA는 모든 도시에서 발견되며, 때로는 숨어있고 때로는 분명하게 나타난다. 주의 깊게 살펴보면, 대도시는 사용되지 않는 공간이 거의 없다. 가치 있는 빈 땅은 거의 방치되지 않으며, 종종 공식적이든 비공식적이든 점유되어 생산적으로 활용되고 있다.

05
정답 ③

정답 해설
③ [적중 포인트 080] 부사절 접속사의 구분과 특징
시간, 조건 부사절에서는 의미상 미래일지라도 현재시제가 미래를 대신한다. provided는 조건 부사절 접속사이므로 will pay 대신 현재시제 pay로 써야 올바르다.

찐Tip lend는 4형식 수여동사로 목적어 2개(간접목적어 + 직접목적어)를 취할 수 있다. 따라서 목적어 사이에 전치사는 불필요하다.

오답 해설
① [적중 포인트 066] 조동사 should의 3가지 용법과 생략 구조
이성적 판단의 형용사(important)의 that절의 동사는 당위의 의미일 때 '(should) 동사원형'으로 쓴다. 따라서 동사원형 do는 올바르게 쓰였다.

찐Tip 이성적 판단 형용사로는 imperative, vital, natural, necessary 등이 있다.

② [적중 포인트 054] 분사 판별법[현재분사 VS 과거분사]
분사구문이 (,)콤마 사이에 삽입된 형태로 쓰였다. '차는 주차된 것'으로 수동의 의미를 나타내는 과거분사 parked는 올바르게 쓰였다.
④ [적중 포인트 074] 가정법 과거완료 공식
'if + 주어 + had p.p.'가 나오면 가정법 과거 완료를 의미하고 '주어 + would/should/could/might have p.p.'의 형태가 올바르게 쓰였는지 확인해야 한다. 따라서 밑줄 친 부분은 올바르게 쓰였다.

선지 해석
① 남에게 의존하지 말고 너 자신이 직접 그것을 하는 것이 중요하다.
② 은행 앞에 주차된 내 차가 불법 주차로 인해 견인되었다.
③ 토요일까지 돈을 갚을 수 있다면, 돈을 빌려줄게.
④ 만약 태풍이 접근해오지 않았더라면 그 경기가 열렸을 텐데.

06
정답 ③

정답 해설
③ [적중 포인트 080] 부사절 접속사의 구분과 특징
because는 접속사로 동사를 포함한 절을 이끄므로 올바르게 쓰였다.

찐Tip start는 왕래발착동사로 현재진행형(be - ing)으로 쓰이면 미래 시제를 나타낼 수 있다. 따라서 밑줄 친 부분은 올바르게 쓰였다.

오답 해설
① [적중 포인트 016] 수량 형용사와 명사의 수 일치
much는 셀 수 없는 명사를 수식하고 단수 동사를 써야 한다. 뒤에 복수 동사 are이 쓰인 것으로 보아 much 대신 many로 써야 올바르다.

찐Tip many는 셀 수 있는 명사를 수식하고 복수 동사를 쓴다.

② [적중 포인트 055] 감정 분사와 분사형 형용사
감정동사가 감정을 유발한다는 의미를 전달하고 사물을 수식하는 경우에는 현재분사형으로 쓴다. 따라서 크리스마스 파티가 흥미를 유발하는 것의 의미이므로 과거분사 excited 대신 현재분사 exciting으로 써야 올바르다.
④ [적중 포인트 064] to부정사의 관용 구문
'~하곤 했다'의 뜻을 가진 구문으로는 'used to 동사원형'의 표현이 있다. 따라서 문맥상 '과거에 ~하곤 했다'의 의미가 자연스러우므로 to loving 대신 to love로 써야 올바르다.

찐Tip '사물 주어 + be used to부정사'는 '~하기 위해서 사용되다'의 뜻으로, '사람 주어 + be used to -ing'는 '~하는 데 익숙하다'의 뜻으로 쓰인다.

선지 해석
① 은하수 안의 수십억 개의 별 중에서 얼마나 많은 별이 생명을 탄생시킬 수 있을까?
② 크리스마스 파티는 정말 재미있어서, 나는 전혀 시간 가는줄 몰랐다.
③ 나는 오늘 정오에 일을 시작해야하기 때문에 지금 바로 떠나야 한다.
④ 그들은 젊었을 때 책을 훨씬 더 사랑했었다.

07
정답 ①

정답 해설
① [적중 포인트 081] 주의해야 할 부사절 접속사
afterwards는 부사로 '나중에, 이후에'의 뜻으로 쓰인다. 부사는 접속사가 아니므로 주어와 동사를 추가할 수 있는 기능이 없다. 따라서 절과 절을 연결시켜주는 접속사가 필요하다. 따라서 부사 afterwards 대신 접속사 after로 써야 올바르다.

[오답 해설]

② [적중 포인트 036] 진행형 불가 동사
'at the moment'는 '바로 지금(= now)'의 뜻으로 현재와 관련된 시제를 나타낸다. 따라서 현재진행형 시제(be-ing)는 올바르게 쓰였다.

찐Tip 'as + 명사'는 '명사로서'의 뜻으로 쓰인다.

③ [적중 포인트 080] 부사절 접속사의 구분과 특징
until은 접속사와 전치사 모두 가능하다. 뒤에 명사(the marathon)가 나온 것으로 보아 전치사로 쓰였음을 알 수 있다. 따라서 밑줄 친 부분은 올바르게 쓰였다.

찐Tip until과 같은 의미인 by는 전치사로만 가능하므로 동사를 포함한 절을 이끌 수 없다.

④ [적중 포인트 014] 형용사와 부사의 차이
동사, 형용사, 다른 부사 또는 문장 전체를 수식하는 것은 형용사가 아니라 부사이다. 따라서 형용사 married를 수식하는 부사 newly는 올바르게 쓰였다.

찐Tip 'newly-married couple'은 '신혼부부'의 뜻으로 쓰인다.

[선지 해석]

① 우리가 집을 떠난 후에 모든 것이 변했다.
② 현재, 그녀는 서점에서 점원으로 일하고 있다.
③ 나는 마라톤하기 전까지 열심히 훈련하고 그 후에 휴식할 것이다.
④ 이 아름다운 사진 앨범은 신혼 부부들을 위한 완벽한 선물이다.

08   정답 ②

[정답 해설]

② [적중 포인트 078] 등위접속사와 병치 구조
& [적중 포인트 065] 조동사 뒤의 동사원형과 조동사의 부정형
조동사 could에 이어지는 3개의 동사 원형들(build, promote, improve)이 and에 의해서 병치되는 구조가 되어야 한다. 따라서 improving 대신 improve로 써야 올바르다.

[오답 해설]

① [적중 포인트 079] 명사절 접속사의 구분과 특징
& [적중 포인트 044] 주어 자리에서 반드시 단수 또는 복수 취급하는 특정 표현
관계대명사 what 다음에 목적어가 없는 불완전한 구조로 올바르게 쓰였고, 명사절 what절은 단수 취급하므로 단수 동사 is 또한 올바르게 쓰였다. 보어자리의 명사절 접속사 that은 완전 구조를 취하므로 밑줄 친 부분은 올바르게 쓰였다.

③ [적중 포인트 060] to부정사의 명사적 역할
start는 목적어로 to부정사 또는 동명사 모두 가능하다. 따라서 동명사 (buying) 형태로 올바르게 쓰였다.

찐Tip become의 주격 보어의 자리에 형용사(cheaper) 형태 또한 올바르게 쓰였다.

찐Tip 목적어로 to부정사 또는 동명사 모두 가능한 동사로는 begin, like, love, hate 등이 있다.

④ [적중 포인트 039] 현재시제 동사와 be동사의 수 일치
주어(People)가 복수 형태이므로 복수 동사 are는 올바르게 쓰였다.

찐Tip 등위접속사(and)를 기준으로 smart phones와 tablet computers가 명사끼리 병렬구조로 올바르게 쓰였다.

[선지 해석]

① 성격 연구에서 밝혀진 것은 나이가 들면서 변화에 대한 개방성이 감소한다는 것이다.
② 공동 우주 프로그램은 더 큰 이해를 형성하고, 세계 평화를 촉진하며, 과학적 지식을 향상시킬 수 있다.
③ 재사용 가능한 토트백을 더 싸게 한다면 더 많은 사람들이 그 가방을 구입할 가능성이 있다.
④ 오늘날, 더 많은 사람들이 사업상 스마트폰과 태블릿 컴퓨터를 사용하고 있다.

09   정답 ③

[정답 해설]

③ [적중 포인트 079] 명사절 접속사의 구분과 특징
선행사를 포함한 관계대명사 what 뒤에는 불완전 구조가 와야 하는데 밑줄 친 부분인 완전한 구조(주어 + 동사 + 목적어)로 쓰였기 때문에 what 대신 접속사 that을 써야 올바르다.

[오답 해설]

① [적중 포인트 083] 「전치사+관계대명사」 완전 구조
'전치사 + 관계대명사' 뒤에는 완전한 구조와 함께 쓰인다. 밑줄 친 부분인 완전한 구조(주어 + 동사 + 목적어)로 쓰였기 때문에 in(전치사) + which(관계대명사)는 올바르게 쓰였다.

② [적중 포인트 054] 분사 판별법[현재분사 VS 과거분사]
문맥상 동사는 loses가 되어야 하므로 predicted는 the team을 수식하는 분사에 해당한다. 수식받는 명사(the team)가 '행동을 하는' 능동의 의미를 나타낼 경우는 현재분사가 쓰이고, '행동을 당한다' 수동의 의미를 나타낼 경우는 과거분사로 쓰인다. 따라서 수식받는 명사(the team)가 '이길 것으로 예상되는 것'이므로 과거분사 predicted는 올바르게 쓰였다.

④ [적중 포인트 055] 감정 분사와 분사형 형용사
감정동사의 현재분사형은 감정을 유발하는 의미를 전달할 경우에 쓰이고, 과거분사형은 감정을 느끼는 의미를 전달할 경우에 쓰인다. 따라서 수식받는 명사(their opponents)가 '위협적'이라는 감정을 유발하는 의미이므로 현재분사 threatening은 올바르게 쓰였다.

[지문 해석]

> 스포츠에서 이길 것으로 예상되고 추정상 상대방보다 우세한 팀이 뜻밖에 경기에서 지는 역전이 생기는 한 가지 이유는 우세한 팀이 상대방을 그들의 계속된 성공에 위협이 되는 것이라고 인식하지 않았을 수도 있기 때문이다.

10   정답 ②

[정답 해설]

② [적중 포인트 081] 주의해야 할 부사절 접속사
lest는 뒤에 '주어 + (should) 동사원형'을 쓴다. lest는 이미 부정의 의미가 있으므로 중복으로 not을 쓰지 않는다. 그리고 문장의 주어 자리에 쓰인 investigation과 suspicion이 행동하는 것이 아닌 동작을 당하는 대상이고, handle과 arouse는 타동사인데 뒤에 목적어가 없으므로 수동의 의미를 전달하는 수동태 구조인 be handled와 be aroused 또한 올바르게 쓰였다.

찐Tip lest는 'for fear (that)'으로 바꿔쓸 수 있고, '~하지 않도록'의 뜻으로 쓰인다.

11

정답 ④

정답 해설

④ [적중 포인트 080] 부사절 접속사의 구분과 특징
whereas는 부사절 접속사로 완전 구조를 취한다. 완전 구조는 '주어 + 동사'가 필요하므로 whereas is 대신 whereas it is로 써야 올바르다.

찐Tip 난이 형용사 구문은 'It be 난이 형용사 to부정사'로 쓴다.

오답 해설

① [적중 포인트 039] 현재시제 동사와 be동사의 수 일치
문장의 주어(Noise pollution)가 단수 형태이므로 단수 동사 is는 올바르게 쓰였다.

② [적중 포인트 043] 혼동하기 쉬운 주어와 동사 수 일치
'a number of' 뒤에 복수 명사를 써야 한다. 따라서 복수 형태인 ways는 올바르게 쓰였다.

③ [적중 포인트 054] 분사 판별법[현재분사 VS 과거분사]
문장에 이미 주어 동사가 있고 '동사 + ed'가 나온다면 분사 문제이다. introduce 뒤에 목적어가 없고 앞에 수식받는 명사(chemicals)입장에서 행위를 받는 입장이므로 수동의 의미인 과거분사 introduced는 올바르게 쓰였다.

지문 해석

> 소음 공해는 다른 종류의 공해들과는 여러 가지 면에서 다르다. 소음은 일시적이다. 일단 공해가 멈추면 그 환경은 그로부터 자유로워진다. 예를 들어, 대기 오염의 경우에는 이와 같은 상황이 아니다. 우리는 공기에 투입된 화학 물질의 양을 측정할 수 있는 반면에 소음에 대한 누적된 노출을 감시하는 것은 극도로 어렵다.

(상단 좌측 이어지는 내용)

오답 해설

① [적중 포인트 088] 전치사와 명사 목적어
전치사(with) 뒤에는 명사 또는 동명사를 써야 하므로 use 대신 using으로 써야 올바르다.

찐Tip 'charge A with B'는 'A를 B로 비난하다, 고소하다'의 뜻을 가진 구문 표현으로 특정 전치사 with는 올바르게 쓰였다.

③ [적중 포인트 045] 능동태와 수동태 차이
make가 3형식 타동사로 쓰이고 목적어를 취할 때 수동태가 아닌 능동태로 써야 한다. 따라서 be made 대신 be to make로 써야 올바르다.

④ [적중 포인트 055] 감정 분사와 분사형 형용사
lead는 동사로 명사를 수식할 수 없으므로, 동사 lead 대신 명사를 수식할 수 있는 분사인 leading으로 써야 올바르다.

찐Tip 동명사구 주어는 단수 취급하므로 단수 동사 is가 올바르게 쓰였다.

선지 해석

① 그 신문은 자신의 목적을 위해 회사의 돈을 사용한 행위로 그녀를 비난했다.
② 조사는 의심을 불러일으키지 않도록 극도로 주의를 기울여야 했다.
③ 공정을 가속화하는 또 다른 방법은 새로운 시스템으로 전환하는 것이다.
④ 화석 연료를 태우는 것은 기후 변화의 주요 원인들 중 하나이다.

12

정답 ④

정답 해설

④ [적중 포인트 079] 명사절 접속사의 구분과 특징
'네가 여기에 오나 내가 거기에 가나'의 선택적인 의미로 쓰일 때는 주로 접속사 whether을 쓴다. 접속사 that은 확정적인 사실을 전할 때 사용하는 반면에, 불확정적인 사실이나 의심을 표현하는 경우에는 whether를 사용한다. 따라서 that 대신 whether로 써야 올바르다.

찐Tip whether은 or (not)을 수반하여 함께 쓰일 수 있다.

오답 해설

① [적중 포인트 080] 부사절 접속사의 구분과 특징
'~하도록, ~하기 위해서'의 뜻을 가진 부사절 접속사 so that은 올바르게 쓰였다.

② [적중 포인트 026] 5형식 사역동사의 목적격 보어
사역동사 let은 목적어와 목적보어가 능동의 의미 관계를 갖는 경우에는 원형부정사를 쓴다. 따라서 밑줄 친 부분은 올바르게 쓰였다.

찐Tip let은 목적어와 목적보어가 수동의 의미 관계를 갖는 경우에는 반드시 목적보어를 과거분사가 아닌 'be p.p.'의 형태로 쓴다.

찐Tip In case는 조건 부사절 접속사로 조건 부사절에서는 미래시제가 아닌 현재시제로 대신한다.

③ [적중 포인트 058] 분사를 활용한 표현 및 구문
'~에 관해서 말하자면'의 뜻을 가진 구문으로는 'speaking of~'의 분사구문 표현이 있다. 따라서 밑줄 친 부분은 올바르게 쓰였다.

선지 해석

① 당신이 그것을 더 잘 이해할 수 있게 제가 도표를 만들었습니다.
② 제가 사무실에 없을지도 모르니까 제 휴대전화 번호를 알려드릴게요.
③ 선거에 대해서 말하자면 아직까지 누구에게 투표할지 못 정했어.
④ 네가 여기에 오나 내가 거기에 가나 마찬가지다.

13

정답 ②

정답 해설

② [적중 포인트 079] 명사절 접속사의 구분과 특징
명사절 접속사 that은 앞에 명사가 없으면 뒤에 완전 구조를 취한다. 그러나 that 뒤에 주어가 빠진 불완전한 구조이므로 that 대신 명사절 접속사 what으로 써야 올바르다.

찐Tip 'not always'는 부분부정을 나타내고 '항상 ~하는 것은 아니다'의 뜻으로 쓰인다.

오답 해설

① [적중 포인트 028] 분사를 목적격 보어로 취하는 5형식 동사
& [적중 포인트 014] 형용사와 부사의 차이
keep은 목적보어로 분사나 형용사를 취할 수 있다. 따라서 목적보어 자리에 형용사 healthy는 올바르게 쓰였다. 형용사 healthy를 수식해주는 부사 perfectly 또한 올바르게 쓰였다.

③ [적중 포인트 023] 목적어 뒤에 특정 전치사를 수반하는 3형식 타동사
'~하는 것을 막다'의 뜻을 가진 구문으로는 'prevent + 목적어 + from -ing'의 특정 전명구를 수반하는 표현이 있다. 따라서 밑줄 친 부분은 올바르게 쓰였다.

찐Tip 금지, 방해동사로는 keep, stop, prohibit, inhibit, deter, dissuade, discourage, protect 등이 있다.

④ [적중 포인트 025] to부정사를 목적격 보어로 취하는 대표 5형식 타동사
tell은 목적어와 목적보어가 능동의 의미 관계를 갖는 경우에는 to부정사를 목적보어로 취하는 5형식 타동사이다. 따라서 밑줄 친 부분은 올바르게 쓰였다.

찐Tip 'stop -ing'는 '~하는 것을 멈추다'의 뜻으로 쓰인다.

선지 해설
① 당신은 아마도 많은 채소를 먹는 것만으로도 완벽하게 건강을 유지할 수 있다고 생각할지도 모른다.
② 학문적 지식이 항상 올바른 결정을 하도록 이끌어 주는 것은 아니다.
③ 다칠까하는 두려움이 그가 무모한 행동에 가담하는 것을 막지 못했다.
④ Julie의 의사는 그녀에게 가공식품을 많이 먹는 것을 멈추라고 했다.

14 정답 ②

정답 해설
② [적중 포인트 017] 어순에 주의해야 할 형용사와 부사
'너무 ~해서 ~하다'의 뜻을 가진 구문으로는 'such[so] ~ that'의 결과 부사절 접속사 구문 표현이 있다. such는 'such + a + 형용사 + 명사'의 어순으로 밑줄 친 부분은 올바르게 쓰였다.

찐Tip so는 'so + 형용사 + a + 명사'의 어순으로 쓴다.

오답 해설
① [적중 포인트 077] 기타 가정법
as if는 가정법 구문에서 쓰이는 접속사로 쓰이고 형용사 주격 보어를 문장 처음으로 두는 도치 구조를 만들 때는 사용되지 않는다. 따라서 as 양보 도치구문으로 써야 하므로 as if 대신 as로 써야 올바르다.

찐Tip 밑줄 친 부분은 '형용사 + as 주어 + 2형식 동사, 주어 + 동사'의 as 양보 도치 구문으로 쓰였다.

③ [적중 포인트 023] 목적어 뒤에 특정 전치사를 수반하는 3형식 타동사
keep은 '~을 방해하다'라는 의미로 쓰이기 위해서는 'keep + 목적어 + from -ing'의 구조로 쓴다. 따라서 advancing 대신 from advancing으로 써야 올바르다.

④ [적중 포인트 079] 명사절 접속사의 구분과 특징
밑줄 친 부분인 전치사 뒤에 나온 명사절 접속사 자리에는 if와 같은 의미를 지닌 명사절 접속사 whether을 써야 한다. 따라서 if or not 대신 whether or not으로 써야 올바르다.

찐Tip 명사절 if는 타동사 뒤의 목적어 자리에만 쓸 수 있다.

선지 해설
① 당신이 부자일지라도 당신은 진실한 친구들을 살 수는 없다.
② 그것은 너무나 아름다운 유성 폭풍이어서 우리는 밤새 그것을 보았다.
③ 학위가 없는 것이 그녀의 성공을 방해했다.
④ 그는 사형이 폐지되어야 하는지 아닌지에 대한 에세이를 써야 한다.

15 정답 ②

정답 해설
② [적중 포인트 078] 등위접속사와 병치 구조
등위접속사(and)를 기준으로 attempted와 had는 과거동사로 병렬구조는 올바르게 쓰였다.

찐Tip 'needless to say'는 독립부정사로 '말할 필요도 없이'의 뜻으로 쓰인다.

오답 해설
① [적중 포인트 020] 주격 보어가 필요한 2형식 자동사
become은 2형식 동사로 주격 보어 자리에 부사가 아닌 형용사를 써야 한다. 따라서 부사 unpredictably 대신 형용사 unpredictable로 써야 올바르다.

③ [적중 포인트 038] 시제 관련 표현
'~하자마자 ~했다'의 뜻을 가진 구문으로는 'Upon[On] -ing, 주어 + 과거시제 동사'의 동명사 관용 표현이 있다. 따라서 Upon arrived 대신 Upon arriving으로 써야 올바르다.

④ [적중 포인트 017] 어순에 주의해야 할 형용사와 부사
부사 enough는 형용사나 부사를 후치 수식한다. 따라서 부사 enough는 형용사 comfortable을 수식하는 것이므로 enough comfortable 대신 comfortable enough로 써야 올바르다.

찐Tip '형용사/부사 enough to부정사'는 '~하기에 충분히 형용사/부사하다'의 뜻으로 쓰인다.

선지 해설
① 내 상냥한 딸이 갑자기 예측할 수 없이 변했다.
② 그녀는 새로운 방법을 시도했고, 말할 필요도 없이 다른 결과를 얻었다.
③ 도착하자마자, 그는 새로운 환경을 충분히 이용했다.
④ 그는 나에게 뭔가 하고 싶은 일에 대해 얘기할 만큼 충분히 편안함을 느꼈다.

16 정답 ②

정답 해설
② [적중 포인트 078] 등위접속사와 병치 구조
전치사 of의 목적어 3개가 명사 'A, B, and C'의 병렬이 된 구조로 형용사 warm 대신 명사 warmth로 써야 올바르다.

오답 해설
① [적중 포인트 016] 수량 형용사와 명사의 수 일치
both 뒤에 복수 가산 명사를 쓴다. 따라서 sides는 올바르게 쓰였다.

③ [적중 포인트 043] 혼동하기 쉬운 주어와 동사 수 일치
'The number of' 뒤에 복수 명사 + 단수 동사를 쓰고, '명사의 수'의 뜻으로 쓰인다. 따라서 밑줄 친 부분은 올바르게 쓰였다.

찐Tip 'A number of' 뒤에 복수 명사 + 복수 동사를 쓰고, '많은 명사'의 뜻으로 쓰인다.

④ [적중 포인트 076] if 생략 후 도치된 가정법
'Had + 주어'로 시작한다면 if가 생략된 가정법 과거완료이다. 가정법 과거완료는 'Had + 주어 + 과거분사, 주어 + would/should/could/ might + have p.p.'의 공식으로 쓴다. 따라서 밑줄 친 부분은 올바르게 쓰였다.

선지 해설
① 당신은 종이의 양면에 글을 쓸 수 있다.
② 나의 집은 나에게 안정감, 따뜻함, 그리고 사랑의 느낌을 준다.
③ 자동차 사고의 수가 증가하고 있다.
④ 네가 뭘 하려는지 알았더라면, 내가 너를 말렸을 텐데.

17

정답 ④

정답 해설
④ [적중 포인트 078] 등위접속사와 병치 구조
'A가 아니고 B다'의 뜻을 가진 구문으로는 'not A but B'의 표현이 있다. 따라서 not 뒤에 the strongest of the species(가장 강한 생물도), nor 뒤에 the most intelligent(가장 지적인 생물도 아니고), or 뒤에 the one most responsive to change(변화에 가장 잘 반응하는 생물이다)으로 표현하고 있다. 따라서 or 대신 but으로 써야 올바르다.

찐Tip 'not A nor B but C'는 'A도 (아니고) B도 아니고 C이다'의 뜻으로 쓰인다.

오답 해설
① [적중 포인트 060] to부정사의 명사적 역할
remember은 to부정사와 동명사 모두 목적어를 취할 수 있지만 동명사를 쓸 경우에는 '(이미) ~했던 것을 기억하다'의 뜻으로 쓰이므로 밑줄 친 부분은 올바르게 쓰였다.

찐Tip 'remember to부정사'는 '~할 것을 기억하다'의 뜻으로 쓰인다.

② [적중 포인트 064] to부정사의 관용 구문
'~하는 데 시간이 걸리다'의 뜻을 가진 구문으로는 'It takes + (사람) + 시간 + to부정사 = It takes + 시간 + (for 사람) + to부정사'의 표현이 있다. 따라서 밑줄 친 부분은 올바르게 쓰였다.

③ [적중 포인트 080] 부사절 접속사의 구분과 특징
& [적중 포인트 019] 주어만 있으면 완전한 1형식 자동사
as는 부사절 접속사로 '~할 때'의 뜻으로 쓰인다. walk는 1형식 자동사로 뒤에 부사 home도 올바르게 쓰였다.

찐Tip 'inside out'은 '(안팎을) 뒤집어'의 뜻으로 쓰인다.

선지 해설
① 나의 이모는 파티에서 그녀를 만난 것을 기억하지 못했다.
② 나의 첫 책을 쓰는 데 40년이 걸렸다.
③ 학교에서 집으로 걸어오고 있을 때 강풍에 내 우산이 뒤집혔다.
④ 끝까지 생존하는 생물은 가장 강한 생물도, 가장 지적인 생물도 아니고, 변화에 가장 잘 반응하는 생물이다.

18

정답 ②

정답 해설
② [적중 포인트 079] 명사절 접속사의 구분과 특징
how는 의문부사로 완전 구조를 취한다. how 뒤에 전치사 like의 목적어가 없는 불완전 구조이므로 how 대신 의문대명사 what으로 써야 올바르다.

찐Tip 'what 주어 be 동사'는 주어의 인격을 표현할 때 쓸 수 있다.

오답 해설
① [적중 포인트 020] 주격 보어가 필요한 2형식 자동사
seem은 2형식 동사로 주격 보어 자리에 형용사/명사/to부정사를 쓸 수 있다. 따라서 to go는 올바르게 쓰였다.

③ [적중 포인트 080] 부사절 접속사의 구분과 특징
Once는 접속사와 부사 모두 가능하다. 접속사로 쓰일 경우 '만약 (일단) ~하면, ~하자마자'의 뜻으로, 동사를 포함한 절을 이끈다. 따라서 밑줄 친 부분은 올바르게 쓰였다.

④ [적중 포인트 055] 감정 분사와 분사형 형용사
감정동사가 감정을 느낀다는 의미를 전달하고 주로 사람을 수식할 경우 과거분사형으로 쓴다. 내가 당황스러운 감정을 느끼는 것으로 수동의 의미인 과거분사 embarrassed는 올바르게 쓰였다.

지문 해석
어제 수영장에서 모든 것이 잘못되어가는 것처럼 보였다. 내가 도착하자마자 나는 선글라스 위에 앉아서 그것을 부셨다. 하지만 나의 가장 최악의 순간은 전경이 어떤지 보기 위해 높은 다이빙 타워로 올라가기로 결정한 때였다. 내가 그곳에 올라가자마자, 내 친구들이 내가 다이빙을 할 것이라고 생각해서 나를 바라보고 있음을 깨달았다. 나는 그 높이에서 다이빙하기에는 너무 두렵다고 생각했다. 그래서 사다리를 타고 내려왔고, 매우 당황스러웠다.

Chapter 14 관계사

ANSWER
01 ④ 02 ④ 03 ③ 04 ② 05 ③
06 ① 07 ① 08 ② 09 ② 10 ①
11 ④ 12 ③

01

정답 ④

정답 해설
④ [적중 포인트 082] 관계대명사의 선행사와 문장 구조
관계대명사 whom은 목적어 역할을 하기 때문에, 뒤에 나오는 절이 불완전해야 한다. 하지만 여기서는 Athens took its name처럼 완전한 절이 오고 있으므로, '전치사 + 관계대명사'의 형태로 써야 한다. 문맥상 '아테네가 그 여신의 이름을 따서 이름이 지어졌다'는 의미이므로 'take one's name after~'의 구문이 필요하다. 따라서 whom 대신 after whom으로 써야 올바르다.

오답 해설
① [적중 포인트 017] 어순에 주의해야 할 형용사와 부사
such는 'such a + 형용사 + 명사'의 어순으로 쓰이며, 여기서도 such a driving force는 올바른 구조이다. 따라서 밑줄 친 부분은 올바르게 쓰였다.

② [적중 포인트 080] 부사절 접속사의 구분과 특징
'such ~ that'은 결과를 나타내는 구문으로, 여기서 'that it was believed~'는 올리브 나무가 신의 선물로 여겨졌다는 결과절이다. 수동태 was believed도 시제와 의미에 모두 맞기 때문에, 문법적으로 올바른 표현이다. 따라서 밑줄 친 부분은 올바르게 쓰였다.

③ [적중 포인트 063] to부정사의 동사적 성질
to have been은 본동사 시제인 was보다 앞선 시점에서의 동작, 즉 '과거에 선물로 여겨졌던 것'을 나타낸다. 따라서 밑줄 친 부분은 올바르게 쓰였다.

지문 해석
올리브 나무는 고대 그리스 도시 국가들의 경제에서 매우 강력한 원동력이었기 때문에, 신들로부터의 선물, 즉 지혜의 여신 아테나로부터 온 선물로 여겨졌다. 그리고 아테나는 아테네라는 도시 이름의 유래가 된 존재였다.

02 정답 ④

정답 해설

④ [적중 포인트 083] 「전치사+관계대명사」 완전 구조
which는 관계대명사로, 완전한 절 'war is avoided'를 이끌 수 없다. 완전한 절을 이끌 수 있는 것은 '관계부사' 또는 '전치사+관계대명사'이다. 따라서 which 대신 where 또는 in which로 써야 올바르다.

오답 해설

① [적중 포인트 054] 분사 판별법[현재분사 VS 과거분사]
that절 내의 주어 'any international organization'을 수식하는 과거분사구 'designed to keep the peace'는 '평화를 유지하기 위해 설계된'의 뜻으로 쓰였다. 따라서 밑줄 친 부분은 올바르게 쓰였다.

② [적중 포인트 040] 상관접속사와 수 일치
'not merely[only] A but (also) B'의 병렬 구조는 A와 B는 동일한 형태로 써야 한다. 따라서 밑줄 친 부분인 to부정사는 올바르게 쓰였다.

③ [적중 포인트 029] 명사나 형용사를 목적격 보어로 취하는 5형식 동사
see는 5형식 동사로 목적격 보어 자리에 as 명사/형용사를 쓸 수 있다. 따라서 밑줄 친 부분은 올바르게 쓰였다.

지문 해석

> 나에게는 평화를 유지하기 위해 설계된 모든 국제 조직은 단지 말할 뿐만 아니라 행동할 수 있는 권한을 가지고 있는 것처럼 보인다. 사실, 나는 이것을 전쟁을 우연이 아닌 계획적으로 피하는 국제 사회로의 발전을 위한 중심 주제라고 본다.

03 정답 ③

정답 해설

③ [적중 포인트 084] 관계대명사 주의 사항
관계대명사의 격의 일치에 대한 문제이다. 명사(daughter)를 취하면서, 목적어가 없는 불완전 구조를 이끌 수 있는 것은 주격 관계대명사가 아닌 소유격 관계대명사이다. 따라서 who 대신 whose로 써야 올바르다.

오답 해설

① [적중 포인트 060] to부정사의 명사적 역할
'not to spend'는 동사 plan의 목적어로, 'spend A on B'의 구조로 'A를 B에 쓰다'의 뜻으로 쓰였다. 따라서 밑줄 친 부분은 올바르게 쓰였다.

② [적중 포인트 046] 수동태 불가 동사
& [적중 포인트 033] 과거 시간을 나타내는 부사와 과거시제
disappear는 '사라지다'의 뜻인 1형식 자동사로 항상 능동태로 써야 하고, 뒤에 'last month'인 과거 시간 부사가 나오므로 과거 동사로 써야 한다. 따라서 밑줄 친 부분은 올바르게 쓰였다.

④ [적중 포인트 096] 배수 비교 구문에서 배수사의 위치
배수 비교 구문으로 '배수사 + as 형용사/부사 as'의 구조로, 배수사는 항상 원급 비교 앞에 위치해야 하고, 2형식 자동사 was의 주격 보어는 형용사로 써야 한다. 따라서 밑줄 친 부분은 올바르게 쓰였다.

선지 해석

① 당신은 프로젝트에 너무 많은 돈을 쓰지 않도록 계획해야 한다.
② 내 개가 지난달에 사라졌고 그 이후로 계속 보이지 않는다.
③ 내가 돌보는 딸이 있는 사람들이 이사 가게 되어 슬프다.
④ 여행 중에 책을 샀는데, 그 책이 집에서 사는 것보다 두 배 비쌌다.

04 정답 ②

정답 해설

② [적중 포인트 087] 관계대명사 주의 사항
복합관계대명사는 뒤에 불완전 구조를 취한다. whomever 뒤에 주어가 없는 불완전한 구조가 나왔으므로 목적격 whomever 대신 주격 whoever로 써야 올바르다.

찐Tip whomever는 목적어가 없는 불완전한 구조를 이끈다.

오답 해설

① [적중 포인트 034] 완료시제와 잘 쓰이는 시간 부사
& [적중 포인트 046] 수동태 불가 동사
문맥상 보증이 만료된 것이 먼저 일어난 일로 과거완료(had p.p.)로 써야 하고, expire는 자동사로 수동태가 될 수 없으므로 능동형태로 쓴 had expired는 올바르게 쓰였다.

찐Tip free of charge는 '무료로, 무료의'의 뜻으로 쓰인다.

③ [적중 포인트 075] 혼합 가정법 공식
if절에 과거 시간 부사와 주절에 현재 시간 부사가 쓰였다면 혼합 가정법 공식을 확인해야 한다. 혼합 가정법은 'If 주어 had p.p. 과거시간부사, 주어 + would/should/could/might 동사원형 now'의 공식으로 쓴다. 따라서 밑줄 친 부분은 올바르게 쓰였다.

④ [적중 포인트 033] 과거 시간을 나타내는 부사와 과거시제
과거 시간 부사(last year)가 나오면 반드시 과거 동사를 확인한다. 과거 시제 passed away는 올바르게 쓰였다.

찐Tip what is worse는 '설상가상으로, 엎친 데 덮친 격으로'의 뜻으로 쓰인다.

찐Tip become은 2형식 동사로 주격 보어 자리에 형용사를 취하므로 형용사 sick 또한 올바르게 쓰였다.

선지 해석

① 보증이 만료되어서 수리는 무료가 아니었다.
② 설문지를 완성하는 누구에게나 선물카드가 주어질 예정이다.
③ 지난달 내가 휴가를 요청했더라면 지금 하와이에 있을 텐데.
④ 그의 아버지가 갑자기 작년에 돌아가셨고, 설상가상으로 그의 어머니도 병에 걸리셨다.

05 정답 ③

정답 해설

③ [적중 포인트 079] 명사절 접속사의 구분과 특징
관계대명사 which 앞에는 선행사가 있어야 하는데 문장에는 선행사가 없으므로 which 대신 선행사를 포함한 관계대명사 what으로 써야 올바르다.

찐Tip 선행사를 포함한 관계대명사 what은 '~것'의 뜻으로 쓰인다.

오답 해설

① [적중 포인트 084] 관계대명사 주의 사항
관계대명사 who 앞에 선행사(The woman)가 있고 뒤에 주어가 없는 불완전 구조를 취하고 있다. 따라서 밑줄 친 부분은 올바르게 쓰였다.

찐Tip 선행사(The woman)는 단수 형태이므로 단수 동사 lives는 올바르게 쓰였다. woman의 복수형은 women이다.

② [적중 포인트 034] 완료시제와 잘 쓰이는 시간 부사
'have been to 장소'는 '~에 가본 적이 있다'의 뜻으로 쓰인다. 완료시제 동사가 있는 의문문은 'Have/Has/Had S p.p. ~' 어순으로 쓴다. 따라서 밑줄 친 부분은 올바르게 쓰였다.

찐Tip 'have gone to 장소'는 '~에 가버렸다'의 뜻으로 쓰인다.

④ [적중 포인트 084] 관계대명사 주의 사항
The woman 다음에 목적격 관계대명사 whom 또는 that이 생략된 형태로 쓰였고, 동사 fell은 시제, 태 또한 올바르게 쓰였다.

찐Tip 'fall in love with'는 '~와 사랑에 빠지다'의 뜻으로 쓰인다.

선지 해석
① 옆집에 사는 여자는 의사이다.
② 당신은 런던에 가본 적이 있나요?
③ 내가 명령한 것만 하시오.
④ 그가 사랑에 빠졌던 여자는 한 달 뒤에 그를 떠났다.

06   정답 ①

정답 해설
① [적중 포인트 082] 관계대명사의 선행사와 문장 구조
선행사(a Latin American country) 뒤에 주어 없이 동사(was maked)로 불완전 구조를 취하고 있다. 따라서 관계부사 where 대신 주격 관계대명사 which 또는 that으로 써야 올바르다.

찐Tip 관계부사는 선행사에 따라 다르고 뒤에 완전 구조를 취한다.

찐Tip 'throughout most of the twentieth century'는 부사구로 사이에 삽입된 형태로 쓰였다.

오답 해설
② [적중 포인트 039] 현재시제 동사와 be동사의 수 일치
문장의 주어(a Latin American country)가 단수 형태이므로 단수 동사 was는 올바르게 쓰였다.
③ [적중 포인트 082] 관계대명사의 선행사와 문장 구조
사물 선행사가 있고 뒤에 불완전 구조를 취할 수 있는 것은 관계대명사이다. 따라서 관계대명사 which는 올바르게 쓰였다.
④ [적중 포인트 013] 부정대명사의 활용
둘 중에서 하나는 one, 나머지 하나는 the other로 쓴다. 따라서 밑줄 친 부분을 올바르게 쓰였다.

찐Tip 셋 중에서 하나는 one, 다른 하나는 another, 마지막 하나는 the other 또는 the third로 쓴다.

지문 해석
칠레는 20세기 대부분 동안 비교적 진보된 자유 민주주의가 특징이었고 다른 한편으로는 식량을 수입해야 하는 중간정도의 경제 성장을 이룬 남미 국가다.

07   정답 ①

정답 해설
① [적중 포인트 086] 관계부사의 선행사와 완전 구조
관계대명사 which는 뒤에 불완전 구조를 취해야 한다. 그러나 which 뒤에 동사가 수동태(be p.p.) 형태로 쓰여 완전 구조를 취하고 있으므로 관계부사를 써야 한다. 따라서 which 대신 장소 선행사에 맞게 where로 써야 올바르다.

오답 해설
② [적중 포인트 088] 전치사와 명사 목적어
전치사(from) 뒤에 명사 또는 동명사를 취할 수 있다. 목적어(the national dress)를 취할 수 있는 것은 동명사이므로 wearing은 올바르게 쓰였다.

③ [적중 포인트 058] 분사를 활용한 표현 및 구문
시간 접속사(while)가 이끄는 부사절의 주어와 주절의 주어가 같고 부사절의 동사가 be동사인 경우에는 '주어 + be동사'를 생략할 수 있고 생략된 후에는 분사/형용사/전명구가 남게 된다. 따라서 while visiting은 올바르게 쓰였다.

찐Tip 'while -ing'는 '~하는 동안'의 뜻으로 쓰인다.

④ [적중 포인트 088] 전치사와 명사 목적어
명사 ban이 '금지(법)'의 뜻으로 쓰일 때 전치사 on과 함께 쓸 수 있다. 따라서 전치사 on은 올바르게 쓰였다.

지문 해석
오하이오에서 에미리트 관광객이 체포된 사건에 대응하여 UAE 관리자들은 아랍 국가에서 온 여행객들은 "자신들의 안전을 보장하기 위해서" 서양을 방문할 동안 공공장소에서 국가의 옷을 착용하는 것을 자제하는 것이 좋겠다고 일요일에 경고했다. 그리고 두바이 뉴스 보도에 따르면 유럽 국가에서 얼굴 가리는 베일을 착용하는 것을 금지시키는 사항들을 여성들이 준수해야 한다고 말했다.

08   정답 ②

정답 해설
② [적중 포인트 087] 관계대명사 주의 사항
복합관계부사인 however가 형용사와 부사를 수식할 때 'however + 형용사/부사 + 주어 + 동사'의 구조로 쓴다. 따라서 밑줄 친 부분은 올바르게 쓰였다.

오답 해설
① [적중 포인트 058] 분사를 활용한 표현 및 구문
접속사 while이 쓰인 분사구문으로 문장의 주어(she)가 병원에서 일하는 것으로 능동의 의미이므로 현재분사로 써야 한다. 따라서 과거분사 worked 대신 현재분사 working으로 써야 올바르다.

찐Tip work는 1형식 자동사로 항상 능동의 의미이므로 현재분사로 쓴다.

③ [적중 포인트 044] 주어 자리에서 반드시 단수 또는 복수 취급하는 특정 표현
One of 복수 명사는 단수 동사를 쓴다. 따라서 복수 동사 were 대신 단수 동사 was로 써야 올바르다.

찐Tip games와 I saw 사이에 목적격 관계대명사 that이 생략된 상태로 쓰였다.

④ [적중 포인트 083] 「전치사+관계대명사」 완전 구조
전치사(for) 뒤에는 관계대명사 that을 쓸 수 없다. 따라서 선행사가 사물이므로 전치사 뒤에 관계대명사 that 대신 which로 써야 올바르다.

찐Tip '전치사 + 관계대명사'가 나오면 전치사에 유의하고 뒤는 완전 구조인지 확인해야 한다.

선지 해석
① 병원에서 일하면서, 그녀는 처음으로 비행기 공중 곡예를 보았다.
② 아무리 피곤하더라도, 당신은 그 프로젝트를 수행해야 한다.
③ 내가 본 흥미로운 경기들 중 하나는 2010년 월드컵 결승전이었다.
④ 그녀가 찾고 있던 것은 중앙 출입구였다.

09
정답 ②

정답 해설
② [적중 포인트 083] 「전치사＋관계대명사」 완전 구조
전치사(during)와 관계부사(when)가 같이 쓰이는 것은 어색하다는 것을 알 수 있다. 따라서 when 대신 앞의 '2차 세계대전'을 가리키는 것으로 판단하고, 이를 선행사로 하는 관계대명사 which로 써야 올바르다.

찐Tip '전치사 + 관계대명사'는 뒤에 완전 구조를 취한다.

오답 해설
① [적중 포인트 080] 부사절 접속사의 구분과 특징
until은 접속사와 전치사 모두 가능하다. 뒤에 명사(the Second World War)가 쓰인 것으로 보아 전치사임을 알 수 있다. 시간(상태의 지속, 계속)명사와 어울리는 전치사 until은 올바르게 쓰였다.

③ [적중 포인트 089] 주의해야 할 전치사
'from A to B'의 구조로 'A부터 B까지'의 뜻으로 쓰인다. 따라서 전치사 from과 to는 올바르게 쓰였다.

④ [적중 포인트 088] 전치사와 명사 목적어
전치사 in은 월, 년, 계절, 세기 등(길거나 일정한 기간)을 나타내는 명사와 어울린다. 따라서 전치사 in은 올바르게 쓰였다.

지문 해석
미국의 국채는 제2차 세계대전까지만 해도 비교적 적었으나, 제2차 세계대전 동안 단지 5년 만에 430억 달러에서 2590억 달러로 증가했다.

10
정답 ①

정답 해설
① [적중 포인트 084] 관계대명사 주의 사항
관계대명사 which 뒤에는 불완전 구조를 취해야 한다. 그러나 뒤에 완전 구조(주어 + be동사)를 취하고 있기 때문에 which 대신 소유격 관계대명사 whose를 써야 올바르다.

오답 해설
② [적중 포인트 053] 암기해야 할 동명사 표현
'~하는 게 어때'의 뜻을 가진 구문으로는 'what do you say to -ing'의 동명사 관용 표현이 있다. 따라서 밑줄 친 부분은 올바르게 쓰였다.

③ [적중 포인트 088] 전치사와 명사 목적어
전치사(despite) 뒤는 항상 명사(her poor health)를 쓴다. 따라서 밑줄 친 부분은 올바르게 쓰였다.

④ [적중 포인트 075] 혼합 가정법 공식
if절에 과거시간 부사와 주절에 현재시간 부사가 쓰였다면 혼합 가정법 공식을 확인해야 한다. 혼합 가정법은 'If 주어 had p.p. 과거시간부사, 주어 + would/should/could/might 동사원형 now'의 공식으로 쓴다. 따라서 밑줄 친 부분은 올바르게 쓰였다.

선지 해석
① 그들은 창문이 모두 깨진 집을 보았다.
② 일요일 아침에 농구 하는 게 어때?
③ 그녀는 허약한 건상상태에도 불구하고 매일 행복한 삶을 살려고 노력한다.
④ 만약 어젯밤에 비가 오지 않았다면, 지금 도로가 진흙투성이지 않을 텐데.

11
정답 ④

정답 해설
④ [적중 포인트 082] 관계대명사의 선행사와 문장 구조
what은 명사절 접속사로 선행사를 이미 포함하고 있으므로 앞에 선행사를 수식하지 못한다. 선행사(post)를 수식해줄 수 있는 것은 관계대명사이다. 따라서 선행사가 사물이므로 what 대신 which 또는 that으로 써야 올바르다.

찐Tip 관계대명사 which 또는 that 뒤는 불완전 구조를 취한다.

오답 해설
① [적중 포인트 034] 완료시제와 잘 쓰이는 시간 부사
완료시제와 잘 쓰이는 시간 부사는 완료시제 동사를 확인한다. 문장의 동사 시제가 현재완료(has p.p.)로 쓰인 것으로 보아 'for 기간' 시간 부사는 올바르게 쓰였다.

찐Tip 완료 시제를 나타내는 시간 부사가 쓰이면 꼭 완료시제만 써야 하는 것은 아니고, 과거보다 더 과거에 발생한 일은 had p.p.로 쓰니 주의가 필요하다.

② [적중 포인트 054] 분사 판별법[현재분사 VS 과거분사]
문장에 이미 주어 + 동사가 있고 '동사 + ed'가 나온다면 분사 문제이다. mention은 타동사로 뒤에 목적어가 없고, '요구사항이 언급되는 것'으로 수동의 의미인 과거분사 mentioned은 올바르게 쓰였다.

③ [적중 포인트 061] to부정사의 형용사적 역할
추상 명사를 to부정사가 수식할 때 to부정사는 동격의 의미를 지닌다. 따라서 reason to doubt는 '의심할 이유'의 뜻으로 올바르게 쓰였다.

찐Tip 위와 같이 쓰이는 추상 명사로는 chance, plan, attempt, effort, opportunity, way, ability 등이 있다.

지문 해석
저는 Ferrer 부인에 대한 추천서를 요청하신 것에 대한 답변으로 글을 쓰고 있습니다. 그녀는 지난 3년 동안 저의 비서로 일해왔으며, 정말 훌륭한 직원이었습니다. 저는 그녀가 귀하의 채용 공고에 언급된 모든 요구 사항을 충족시키며 실제로 여러 측면에서 그것들을 뛰어넘는다고 생각합니다. 저는 그녀의 완전한 정직성을 의심할 이유를 결코 가져 본 적이 없었습니다. 따라서 저는 당신이 광고한 직책에 Ferrer부인을 추천드립니다.

12
정답 ③

정답 해설
(A) [적중 포인트 082] 관계대명사의 선행사와 문장 구조
앞에 선행사(pictures)가 있는 것으로 보아 선행사를 수식할 수 있는 관계대명사를 써야 한다. 따라서 명사절 접속사 what 대신 관계대명사 that으로 써야 올바르다.

찐Tip 관계대명사 that 뒤는 불완전 구조를 취한다.

(B) [적중 포인트 014] 형용사와 부사의 차이
앞에 과거분사 involved를 수식할 수 있는 것은 형용사가 아닌 부사이다. 따라서 형용사 immediate 대신 부사 immediately로 써야 올바르다.

(C) [적중 포인트 039] 현재시제 동사와 be동사의 수 일치
문장의 주어('A of B'의 형태인 the use of pattern book)는 단수 형태이므로 단수 동사를 써야 한다. 따라서 복수 동사 meet 대신 단수 동사 meets로 써야 올바르다.

찐Tip 'A of B'가 주어일 경우 'of B'는 A를 수식해주는 역할로 동사는 A와 수 일치한다. 단, 부분을 나타내는 명사가 나오면 of 뒤에 명사를 확인해서 수 일치한다.

지문 해석

패턴 책들은 반복되는 구문, 후렴구 및 때로는 운율을 반복적으로 활용한 이야기들을 포함한다. 게다가, 패턴 책은 스토리 이해를 용이하게 해주는 그림들을 종종 포함한다. 예측 가능한 패턴들은 제2언어 독자들이 그들의 제2언어에서 즉각 글을 읽고 쓰는 것을 시작할 수 있게 허용한다. 게다가, 패턴 책의 사용은 읽기 모형을 만들고, 학생들의 현재 언어 능력의 수준을 도전하고, 단순한 문장 패턴의 반복을 통해 이해를 도와주면서, 읽고 쓰는 것의 비계기준을 충족시킨다.

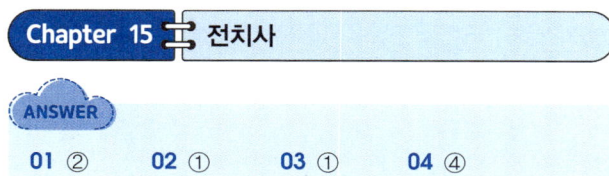

Chapter 15　전치사

ANSWER
01 ②　　02 ①　　03 ①　　04 ④

01　　　　　　　　　　　　　　　　　　　　정답 ②

정답 해설
② [적중 포인트 089] 주의해야 할 전치사
until은 상태의 지속, by는 동작의 완료를 나타내는 동사들과 함께 사용된다. finish는 동작의 완료를 나타내는 동사이므로, until 대신 by로 써야 올바르다.

찐Tip 이외에 by를 써야하는 동사들로는 complete, submit, hand in이 있다.

오답 해설
① [적중 포인트 096] 배수 비교 구문에서 배수사의 위치
'~보다 몇 배 더 …한'의 의미의 배수 비교 구문은 '배수사 + as + 형용사/부사의 원급 + as'로 쓴다. 특히 배수사 다음에 비교 표현이 나와야 하는 어순에 주의가 필요하다. 그리고 비교되는 대상이 'My cat(내 고양이)'과 '그의 고양이'이므로, his cat을 소유대명사로 쓴 his 또한 올바르게 쓰였다.

③ [적중 포인트 037] 시제의 일치와 예외
습관을 나타낼 때는 현재시제를 쓴다. 따라서 밑줄 친 부분인 washes는 올바르게 쓰였다.

찐Tip every other day는 '이틀에 한 번, 하루 걸러'라는 뜻으로 쓰인다.

④ [적중 포인트 065] 조동사 뒤의 동사원형과 조동사의 부정형
had better은 '~하는 편이 낫다'의 의미의 구조동사로 뒤에 to 부정사 대신 동사원형이 와야 한다. 따라서 밑줄 친 부분인 take는 올바르게 쓰였다.

찐Tip in case는 '~할 경우에 (대비하여)'라는 의미의 조건 부사절 접속사로 미래시제를 현재시제 동사로 대신하므로 rains 또한 올바르게 쓰였다.

선지 해석
① 내 고양이 나이는 그의 고양이 나이의 세 배이다.
② 우리는 그 일을 이번 달 말까지 끝내야 한다.
③ 그녀는 이틀에 한 번 머리를 감는다.
④ 너는 비가 올 경우에 대비하여 우산을 갖고 가는 게 낫겠다.

02　　　　　　　　　　　　　　　　　　　　정답 ①

정답 해설
① [적중 포인트 088] 전치사와 명사 목적어
& [적중 포인트 033] 과거 시간을 나타내는 부사와 과거시제
skyrocket는 증가동사로 '~만큼'의 차이를 나타낼 때는 전치사 by와 함께 쓰이므로 올바르게 쓰였다. 과거 시간 부사(in 과거 연도)가 쓰인 것으로 보아 과거시제 skyrocketed 또한 올바르게 쓰였다.

오답 해설
② [적중 포인트 053] 암기해야 할 동명사 표현
tie가 수동태인 be tied to~형태로 쓰였다. to는 to부정사가 아닌 전치사이므로 to 뒤에는 동명사가 와야 한다. 따라서 to improve 대신 to improving으로 써야 올바르다.

③ [적중 포인트 047] 다양한 3형식 동사의 수동태 구조
run over는 타동사이므로 뒤에 목적어가 없으면 being p.p. 구조로 써야 한다. 따라서 running over 대신 being run over로 써야 올바르다.

찐Tip 'escape (from) - ing'는 '~하마터면 (거의) ~할 뻔하다'의 뜻으로 쓰인다.

④ [적중 포인트 054] 분사 판별법[현재분사 VS 과거분사]
문장에 이미 동사가 있고 동사 + ed가 나오면 분사를 물어 보는 문제이다. 분사는 뒤에 목적어가 있는 경우에는 능동형인 -ing로 쓰고, 목적어가 없는 경우에는 수동형인 ed로 쓴다. 따라서 목적어가 있으므로 surrounded 대신 surrounding으로 써야 올바르다.

선지 해석
① 2014년에 중국의 러시아산 석유 수입은 36% 급증했다.
② 잠자는 것은 오랫동안 인간들의 기억력 향상과 연관되어 왔다.
③ 지난 밤, 그녀는 거의 자동차에 치일뻔 했다.
④ 이 실패는 치명적인 우주 셔틀 사고의 원인을 둘러싼 문제들과 연상되는 것이다.

03　　　　　　　　　　　　　　　　　　　　정답 ①

정답 해설
① [적중 포인트 080] 부사절 접속사의 구분과 특징
& [적중 포인트 088] 전치사와 명사 목적어
while은 접속사로 동사를 포함한 절을 이끈다. 그러나 뒤에 명사(this time of year)가 있으므로 앞에 전치사를 써야 한다. 따라서 접속사 while 대신 전치사 during으로 써야 올바르다.

오답 해설
② [적중 포인트 082] 관계대명사의 선행사와 문장 구조
앞에 나온 구, 절, 문장을 대신할 때는 관계대명사 which를 쓴다. 계속적 용법으로 '선행사 + 콤마(,) + 관계대명사'의 형태로 올바르게 쓰였다.

③ [적중 포인트 094] 「The 비교급 ~, the 비교급…」 구문
'the 비교급' 구문을 물어보는 문제이다. '~할수록, 더 ~하다'의 뜻을 가진 구문으로는 'the 비교급 주어 + 동사~, the 비교급 주어 + 동사'의 관용 표현이 있다. 따라서 The colder은 올바르게 쓰였다.

④ [적중 포인트 088] 전치사와 명사 목적어
전치사 with는 외적으로 드러나는 '도구, 원인, 이유'의 부사구를 이끈다. 따라서 전치사 with은 올바르게 쓰였다.

지문 해석

> 해마다 이 시기동안 뉴욕의 크리스마스는 많은 영화들에 등장하는데, 이는 이 휴일이 뉴욕시(the Big Apple)에서 가장 로맨틱하고 특별한 것을 의미한다. 날씨가 더 추워질수록 도시는 다채로운 조명과 장식으로 더욱 밝아진다.

04

정답 ④

정답 해설

④ [적중 포인트 088] 전치사와 명사 목적어
'벽돌로 유리창을 깼다'에서 벽돌이라는 도구, 수단을 나타낼 때는 전치사 by 대신 with으로 써야 올바르다.

오답 해설

① [적중 포인트 061] to부정사의 형용사적 역할
to부정사의 수식을 받는 명사가 to부정사의 의미상의 목적어일 때 to부정사 뒤의 목적어는 생략한다. 따라서 밑줄 친 부분은 올바르게 쓰였다.

찐Tip '너무 ~해서 ~하다'의 뜻을 가진 부사절 접속사 so that은 보통 '~, so that'으로 '콤마'표시가 필요하다. 그러나 구어체에서는 '콤마'표시 없이 so that을 결과적인 의미의 부사절 접속사로 사용하기도 한다.

② [적중 포인트 055] 감정 분사와 분사형 형용사
감정동사가 감정을 유발하는 의미를 전달하고 사물을 수식할 경우 현재분사형으로 쓴다. film이 지루함을 유발하는 것으로 능동의 의미로 현재분사 boring은 올바르게 쓰였다.

③ [적중 포인트 063] to부정사의 동사적 성질
인성 형용사(thoughtful)는 to부정사 앞에 의미상의 주어를 따로 표시할 때 'of 목적격'으로 표시하고, 'It be + 인성 형용사 + of 목적격 + to부정사'의 구조로 쓴다. 따라서 밑줄 친 부분은 올바르게 쓰였다.

찐Tip 인성 형용사로는 kind, wise, good, considerate, prudent, foolish, stupid, cruel, sensible, careful, generous 등이 있다.

선지 해석

① 예산이 빡빡해서 나는 15달러밖에 쓸 수가 없다.
② 그의 최근 영화는 이전 작품들보다 훨씬 더 지루하다.
③ 우리 회사 모든 구성원의 이름을 기억하다니 그는 생각이 깊군요.
④ 현관 열쇠를 잃어버려서 안으로 들어가기 위해 나는 벽돌로 유리창을 깼다.

PART 05 비교

Chapter 16 비교 구문

ANSWER

01 ①	02 ②	03 ②	04 ④	05 ④
06 ②	07 ④	08 ④	09 ③	10 ④
11 ①	12 ③			

01
정답 ①

정답 해설

① [적중 포인트 098] 비교급을 이용한 표현
비교급을 이용한 표현으로 긍정문에는 much[still] more을 써야 하고, 부정문에는 much[still] less를 써야 한다. 따라서 해당 문장은 not을 포함한 부정문이므로 still more 대신 still less로 써야 올바르다.

오답 해설

② [적중 포인트 058] 분사를 활용한 표현 및 구문
접속사 다음에는 분사구문이 사용되므로 분사 판별법에 따라서 올바른 분사의 형태를 확인한다. 분사구문의 주어인 주문(the order)이 확인된다는 수동의 의미이고 타동사 confirm 뒤에 목적어가 없으므로 과거분사를 쓴다. 따라서 밑줄 친 부분은 올바르게 쓰였다.

③ [적중 포인트 035] 미래를 대신하는 현재시제
조건 부사절에는 미래의 내용을 현재시제로 써야 한다. 따라서 조건 부사절 접속사 Provided that 뒤에 현재시제(leaves)가 쓰였다. 따라서 밑줄 친 부분은 올바르게 쓰였다.

④ [적중 포인트 007] 불가산 명사의 종류와 특징
news는 불가산 명사로 much 또는 little의 수식을 받을 수 있다. 따라서 밑줄 친 부분은 올바르게 쓰였다.

선지 해석

① 그들은 시를 읽는 것에 흥미를 느끼지 않으며, 더욱이 쓰는 것에는 더 흥미를 느끼지 않는다.
② 일단 확인되면, 주문이 당신의 주소로 배송될 예정이다.
③ 여객선이 정각에 떠난다면, 우리는 아침에 항구에 도착할 것이다.
④ 외국 기자들은 수도에서의 짧은 체류 중에 최대한 많은 뉴스를 다루기를 희망한다.

02
정답 ②

정답 해설

② [적중 포인트 100] 원급과 비교급을 이용한 최상급 대용 표현
부정 주어(nothing) + 비교급 비교 구문에서 more를 as로 쓰거나 than을 as로 쓰면 안된다. 따라서 as 대신 than으로 써야 올바르다.

찐Tip 비교급 비교 구문 앞의 문장 구조가 보어가 없는 불완전 구조면 형용사를 쓴다.

오답 해설

① [적중 포인트 064] to부정사의 관용 구문
easy와 같은 난이형용사는 'It(가주어) + be동사 + 난이형용사 + (for 목적어) + to부정사(진주어)'의 구조로 쓴다. 따라서 밑줄 친 부분은 올바르게 쓰였다.

찐Tip 'by no means'는 '결코 ~이 아닌'의 뜻으로 쓰인다.

③ [적중 포인트 067] 주의해야 할 조동사와 조동사 관용 표현
'아무리 ~해도 지나치지 않다'의 뜻을 가진 구문으로는 'cannot ~ 형용사/부사'의 조동사 관용 표현이 있다. 따라서 밑줄 친 부분은 올바르게 쓰였다.

찐Tip 같은 뜻을 가진 구문으로는 'cannot ~ enough = cannot ~ over동사'의 조동사 관용 표현이 있다.

④ [적중 포인트 079] 명사절 접속사의 구분과 특징
명사절 접속사 what은 불완전 구조를 취하고, 문장 안에서 주어, 목적어, 보어 역할을 한다. 따라서 밑줄 친 부분인 believe의 목적어로 what은 올바르게 쓰였다.

선지 해석

① 우리가 영어를 단시간에 배우는 것은 결코 쉬운 일이 아니다.
② 우리 인생에서 시간보다 더 소중한 것은 없다.
③ 아이들은 길을 건널 때 아무리 조심해도 지나치지 않다.
④ 그녀는 남들이 말하는 것을 쉽게 믿는다.

03
정답 ②

정답 해설

② [적중 포인트 095] 라틴어 비교 구문과 전치사 to
'prefer A to B'의 비교 구문에서 A와 B는 비교대상이 일치가 되어야 한다. 따라서 명사(Michelangelo's painting)와 명사(his sculpture)가 비교되어야 하므로 to viewing his sculpture 대신 viewing을 삭제한 to his sculpture로 써야 올바르다.

오답 해설

① [적중 포인트 039] 현재시제 동사와 be동사의 수 일치
복수 동사 prefer와 수 일치를 하기 위해서는 복수 주어가 필요하므로 art history professors는 올바르게 쓰였다.

③ [적중 포인트 011] 재귀대명사의 2가지 용법
주어(Michelangelo) 바로 다음에 재귀대명사를 사용하여 강조하는 용법으로 쓸 수 있으므로 재귀대명사 himself는 올바르게 쓰였다.

④ [적중 포인트 091] 비교급 비교 구문
형용사나 부사 앞에 more을 써서 비교급을 나타내므로 올바르게 쓰였다.

⑤ [적중 포인트 012] 지시대명사 this와 that
'the latter'은 '후자'의 뜻으로, 문맥상 his sculpture를 가리키는 것으로 올바르게 쓰였다.

지문 해석

미켈란젤로 자신은 후자(자신의 조각품)를 더 자랑스러워했지만, 나의 미술 역사 교수들은 그의 조각품보다 미켈란젤로의 그림을 더 좋아한다.

04
정답 ④

정답 해설

④ [적중 포인트 098] 비교급을 이용한 표현
'~은 말할 것도 없이'의 뜻을 가진 구문으로는 'still[much] more, still[much] less'의 비교급을 이용한 표현이 있다. 두 표현은 의미상의 차이가 없지만 부정문과 어울리는 표현은 'still[much] less'이다. 따라서 still more 대신 still less로 써야 올바르다.

찐Tip 긍정문과 어울리는 표현은 'still[much] more'이다.

오답 해설

① [적중 포인트 058] 분사를 활용한 표현 및 구문
with 분사구문으로 'with + 명사 목적어 + 형용사'의 구조로 '목적어가 형용사할 때/하면서'의 뜻으로 쓰인다. 따라서 밑줄 친 부분은 올바르게 쓰였다.

② [적중 포인트 017] 어순에 주의해야 할 형용사와 부사
so는 어순에 주의해야 할 부사이다. 'so + 형용사 + a + 명사'의 어순으로 써야 한다. 따라서 밑줄 친 부분은 올바르게 쓰였다.

찐Tip 원급 비교 구문 'as ~ as'에서 부정문일때는 앞 부사 as를 so로 대신 쓸 수 있다.

③ [적중 포인트 006] 가산 명사의 종류와 특징
'How many 명사 + 동사 + 주어~'의 어순으로 밑줄 친 부분은 올바르게 쓰였다.

찐Tip 인칭대명사는 앞에 나온 명사와 성과 수 일치를 확인하고 격에 따라 올바른 형태를 써야 한다.

찐Tip 가산명사(bags)는 How many로 시작하는 의문문을 만들 수 있다.

선지 해석

① 많은 사람들이 아파서 회의가 취소되었다.
② 이것은 우리가 예상했던 것만큼 그렇게 간단한 문제는 아니다.
③ 학생들이 몇 개의 가방을 가지고 탑승할 건가요?
④ 아무런 해명도 없었다. 사과는 말할 것도 없고.

05
정답 ④

정답 해설

④ [적중 포인트 095] 라틴어 비교 구문과 전치사 to
'~보다 ~를 더 좋아하다'의 뜻을 가진 구문으로는 'prefer to부정사 (rather) than to부정사'의 비교 표현이 있다. 따라서 to going 대신 to go로 써야 올바르다.

찐Tip 이와 같은 뜻을 가진 구문으로는 'prefer (동)명사 to (동)명사'의 비교 표현이 있다.

오답 해설

① [적중 포인트 053] 암기해야 할 동명사 표현
'~하는 것을 규칙으로 삼다'의 뜻을 가진 구문으로는 'make it a rule to 부정사 = make a point of -ing = be in the habit of -ing'의 동명사 관용 표현이 있다. 따라서 밑줄 친 부분은 올바르게 쓰였다.

② [적중 포인트 089] 주의해야 할 전치사
'붙잡다(grab)동사 + 사람명사 + by the 신체 일부'의 특정 구문으로 정관사 the는 올바르게 쓰였다.

③ [적중 포인트 088] 전치사와 명사 목적어
'owing to'는 전치사로 명사구(the heavy rain)는 올바르게 쓰였다.

찐Tip 차이를 의미하는 전치사 by 또한 올바르게 쓰였다.

선지 해석

① 나는 매달 두세 번 그에게 전화하기로 규칙을 세웠다.
② 그는 나의 팔을 붙잡고 도움을 요청했다.
③ 폭우로 인해 그 강은 120cm 상승했다.
④ 나는 눈 오는 날 밖에 나가는 것보다 집에 있는 것을 더 좋아한다.

06
정답 ②

정답 해설

② [적중 포인트 098] 비교급을 이용한 표현
'C가 D가 아니듯 A도 B가 아니다'의 뜻을 가진 구문으로는 'A is no more B than C is D'의 양자 부정 표현이 있다. 양자 부정에서 than 뒤에는 부정의 의미지만 부정어 not을 쓰지 않는다. 따라서 you don't 대신 you do로 써야 올바르다.

오답 해설

① [적중 포인트 030] '말하다' 동사의 구분
'A가 B를 단념하게 하다'의 뜻을 가진 구문으로는 'talk A out of B'의 표현이 있다. 따라서 밑줄 친 부분은 올바르게 쓰였다.

찐Tip 'talk A into B'는 'A를 설득하여 B시키다, A에게 이야기하여 B하게 하다'의 뜻으로 쓰인다.

③ [적중 포인트 045] 능동태와 수동태의 차이
outnumber는 완전 타동사로 수동태 형태인 'be outnumbered'로 쓰여 '~보다 열세이다'의 뜻으로 쓰인다. 따라서 밑줄 친 부분은 올바르게 쓰였다.

④ [적중 포인트 018] 혼동하기 쉬운 부사
'not always'는 부분 부정으로 '항상 ~하는 것은 아니다'의 뜻으로 쓰인다. 따라서 밑줄 친 부분은 올바르게 쓰였다.

찐Tip of 뒤에 a(n)는 'the same(같은)'의 의미로 사용될 수 있다.

선지 해석

① 그녀가 어리석은 계획을 포기하도록 설득해 줄래요?
② 그녀의 어머니에 대해서는 나도 너만큼 아는 것이 없다.
③ 그의 군대는 거의 2대 1로 수적 열세였다.
④ 같은 나이의 두 소녀라고 해서 반드시 생각이 같은 것은 아니다.

07
정답 ④

정답 해설

④ [적중 포인트 092] 비교 대상 일치
비교 접속사(than)를 기준으로 비교대상을 일치시켜야 한다. 따라서 to stay(to부정사)와의 형태를 맞춰야 하므로 getting 대신 to get으로 써야 올바르다.

오답 해설

① [적중 포인트 091] 비교급 비교 구문
비교 접속사(than) 뒤에 비교대상을 동명사(maintaining) 형태로 쓰고 앞 명사(more serious problem)와 비교하고 있으므로 올바르게 쓰였다.

② [적중 포인트 091] 비교급 비교 구문
형용사 social의 비교급으로 앞에 '~더 적은[덜한]'을 뜻하는 less는 올바르게 쓰였다.

③ [적중 포인트 092] 비교 대상 일치
접속사 than은 비교급과 함께 쓰이므로 easy의 비교급인 easier는 올바르게 쓰였다.

지문 해석

도시를 유지하는 것보다 더 심각한 문제가 있다. 사람들이 혼자서 일하는 것이 더 편해질수록, 그들은 덜 사교적이 될 수도 있다. 또 다른 비즈니스 미팅을 위해 옷을 차려입는 것보다 편안한 운동복이나 목욕 가운으로 집에 머무르는 것이 더 쉽다!

08   정답 ④

정답 해설
④ [적중 포인트 092] 비교 대상 일치
비교하는 두 대상이 Your son's hair와 your hair가 되어야 하므로 주격대명사 you 대신 소유대명사 yours로 써야 올바르다.

오답 해설
① [적중 포인트 090] 원급 비교 구문
'as 형용사/부사 원급 as'의 원급 비교 구문에서 원급 비교 구문 앞의 문장 구조가 보어가 없는 불완전한 구조면 형용사를 쓴다. 따라서 밑줄 친 부분은 올바르게 쓰였다.

② [적중 포인트 064] to부정사의 관용 구문
& [적중 포인트 092] 비교 대상 일치
easy와 같은 난이 형용사는 'It(가주어) + be동사 + 난이형용사 + (for 목적어) + to부정사(진주어)'의 구조로 밑줄 친 부분은 올바르게 쓰였고, 비교급 than 뒤에 to부정사가 나오면 다른 비교대상도 to 부정사로 나와야 하므로 to write 또한 올바르게 쓰였다.

③ [적중 포인트 091] 비교급 비교 구문
'more 형용사/부사 than'의 비교급 비교 구문에서 비교급 비교 구문 앞의 문장 구조가 보어가 없는 불완전한 구조면 형용사를 쓴다. 따라서 밑줄 친 부분은 올바르게 쓰였다.

찐Tip 'You have more money than I have much money'에서 주절과 중복된 형태인 have much money가 생략된 구조로 쓰였다.

찐Tip money는 불가산명사로 부정관사 a(n)와 복수를 의미하는 −s를 쓰지 않고, many나 few의 수식을 받을 수 없다.

선지 해석
① 제인은 보기만큼 젊지 않다.
② 전화하는 것이 편지 쓰는 것보다 더 쉽다.
③ 너는 나보다 돈이 많다.
④ 당신 아들 머리는 당신 머리와 같은 색깔이다.

09   정답 ③

정답 해설
③ [적중 포인트 090] 원급 비교 구문
원급 비교 구문 'as 형용사/부사 원급 as'에 형용사를 쓸지 부사를 쓸지는 문장 구조를 통해 확인한다. 비교 구문 앞에 문장 구조(주어 + 동사 + 목적어)가 완전하면 부사를 써야 하므로 형용사 efficient 대신 부사 efficiently로 써야 올바르다.

오답 해설
① [적중 포인트 081] 주의해야 할 부사절 접속사
부정 부사절 접속사 lest는 '주어 + (should) 동사원형'을 수반한다. 따라서 밑줄 친 부분은 올바르게 쓰였다.

찐Tip lest 뒤에 부정어 not을 중복하여 쓰지 않는다.

② [적중 포인트 054] 분사 판별법[현재분사 VS 과거분사]
밑줄 친 부분은 분사구문이다. convinced의 주어는 (,)콤마 다음의 주어(he)로 그가 확신을 느낀다(당한다)는 수동의 의미이므로 과거분사 convinced는 올바르게 쓰였다.

④ [적중 포인트 043] 혼동하기 쉬운 주어와 동사 수 일치
Statistics는 '통계학'의 뜻으로 쓰일 때는 단수 취급하고, '통계자료/수치'의 뜻으로 쓰일 때는 복수 취급한다. 문맥상 '통계자료/수치'의 뜻이 자연스러우므로 복수 동사 show도 올바르게 쓰였다.

찐Tip 부분을 나타내는 명사가 나오면 of 뒤에 명사를 확인해서 동사와 수 일치해야 하므로 복수 동사 fail은 올바르게 쓰였다.

선지 해석
① 그녀는 아기를 깨우지 않기 위해 불을 켜지 않았다.
② 그가 실수를 저질렀다고 확신하고, 그는 고객들에게 사과했다.
③ 우리는 Mr. Park이 그가 할 수 있는 만큼 부서를 최대한 효율적으로 운영할 것을 바란다.
④ 통계자료에 따르면 새로운 사업의 약 50%가 첫 해에 실패한다는 것을 보여준다.

10   정답 ④

정답 해설
④ [적중 포인트 090] 원급 비교 구문
원급 비교 구문인 'as 원급 as' 구문은 부정문에서는 'so 원급 as'로 쓸 수도 있다. 다만, 'so 원급 as' 구문에서 원급을 비교급으로 쓸 수 없다. 따라서 stingier 대신 stingy로 써야 올바르다.

오답 해설
① [적중 포인트 088] 전치사와 명사 목적어
동사가 전치사(at)의 목적어 역할을 하기 위해서는 동명사로 써야 한다. 따라서 at 뒤에 동명사 getting은 올바르게 쓰였다.

찐Tip 'be good at'는 '~을 잘하다, 능숙하다'의 뜻으로 쓰인다.

② [적중 포인트 092] 비교 대상 일치
비교급 than 뒤에 that과 those가 나온다면 앞에 나온 명사와 수 일치가 중요하다. 주어(traffic jams)가 복수 형태이므로 those는 올바르게 쓰였다.

찐Tip '비교급 than any other + 단수 명사'는 최상급을 나타내는 표현이다.

③ [적중 포인트 084] 관계대명사 주의 사항
동명사가 주어로 쓰일 때는 단수 취급하므로 단수 동사 is는 올바르게 쓰였고, 앞에 사람 선행사(person)가 있고 뒤에 전치사 to의 목적어가 없는 불완전 구조를 취하고 있으므로 목적격 관계대명사 whom을 쓸 수 있다.

찐Tip the person과 you are speaking to 사이에 목적격 관계대명사 whom이 생략된 상태로 쓰였다.

선지 해석
① 그 연사는 자기 생각을 청중에게 전달하는 데 능숙하지 않았다.
② 서울의 교통 체증은 세계 어느 도시보다 심각하다.
③ 네가 말하고 있는 사람과 시선을 마주치는 것은 서양 국가에서 중요하다.
④ 그는 사람들이 생각했던 만큼 인색하지 않았다는 것이 드러났다.

11

정답 ①

정답 해설
① [적중 포인트 092] 비교 대상 일치
비교 표현(비교급 than) 기준으로 비교대상 일치 여부를 확인하는 문제이다. 처음 기대했던 예산과 지금 25% 더 높은 예산을 서로 비교하는 것으로 than 뒤에 주어(The budget)가 생략된 상태로 쓰였다. 주어(The budget)가 기대되는 것으로 수동의 의미이므로 과거분사로 써야 한다. 따라서 expecting 대신 expected로 써야 올바르다.

오답 해설
② [적중 포인트 061] to부정사의 형용사적 역할
to부정사가 work를 수식하고 있는 형태로 to부정사의 형용사적 용법으로 쓰이고 있다. 주어(work)가 '해야 될 일'의 뜻으로 수동태 형태인 'to be done'은 올바르게 쓰였다.

③ [적중 포인트 064] to부정사의 관용 구문
'~하는 데 ~시간이 걸리다'의 뜻으로 쓰일 때는 'It take + 시간 + (for 사람) + to부정사'의 구문 표현이 있다. 따라서 밑줄 친 부분은 올바르게 쓰였다.

찐Tip 'at least'는 '적어도, 최소한'의 뜻으로 쓰인다.

④ [적중 포인트 082] 관계대명사의 선행사와 문장 구조
& [적중 포인트 039] 현재시제 동사와 be동사의 수 일치
관계대명사 who는 앞에 나온 The head(부서장)를 선행사로 받고 뒤에 주어가 없는 불완전 구조를 취하고 있으므로 올바르게 쓰였고, who 뒤에 동사도 동작을 하는 주체(The head)가 단수 형태이므로 단수 동사 receives 또한 올바르게 쓰였다.

선지 해석
① 예산은 처음 기대했던 것보다 약 25퍼센트 더 높다.
② 시스템 업그레이드를 위해 해야 될 많은 일이 있다.
③ 그 프로젝트를 완성하는데 최소 한 달, 어쩌면 더 긴 시간이 걸릴 것이다.
④ 월급을 두 배 받는 그 부서장이 책임을 져야 한다.

12

정답 ③

정답 해설
③ [적중 포인트 097] 원급을 이용한 표현
'not so much as 동사'의 원급을 활용한 구문으로 '~조차 없다[않다]'의 뜻으로 쓰인다. 이때 동사의 형태인 mention은 대표 3형식 타동사로 전치사 없이 바로 목적어를 취할 수 있다. 따라서 밑줄 친 부분은 올바르게 쓰였다.

오답 해설
① [적중 포인트 088] 전치사와 명사 목적어
전치사 during은 뒤에 특정한 기간을 명사로 취할 수 있고, 전치사 for은 뒤에 막연한 기간(숫자 + 명사)를 명사로 취할 수 있다. 따라서 during 대신 for로 써야 올바르다.

② [적중 포인트 046] 수동태 불가 동사
suffer from은 '자동사 + 전치사'의 형태로 수동태(be p.p) 형태로는 쓸 수 없다. 따라서 수동 형태 is suffered from 대신 능동 형태 suffered form으로 써야 올바르다.

④ [적중 포인트 014] 형용사와 부사의 차이
financial은 형용사(independent)를 수식하고 있는 형태로, 형용사를 수식 할 수 있는 것은 형용사가 아닌 부사이다. 따라서 형용사 financial 대신 부사 financially로 써야 올바르다.

찐Tip 부사는 동사, 형용사, 다른 부사 또는 문장 전체를 수식하는 역할로 쓸 수 있고, 형용사는 명사를 수식하거나 보어 역할로 쓸 수 있다.

선지 해석
① 내 아버지는 6주 동안 병원에 있었다
② 가족 모두가 독감으로 고통받고 있다.
③ 그녀는 그것을 언급조차 하지 않았다.
④ 그녀는 재정적으로 독립하고 싶어한다.

진가영 영어
반한다 기출

Vol. 3

독해
정답 및 해설

PART 01 홈페이지 게시글 유형
PART 02 전자메일 유형
PART 03 안내문 유형
PART 04 중심 내용 파악 유형
PART 05 문장 제거 유형
PART 06 문장 삽입 유형
PART 07 순서 배열 유형
PART 08 빈칸 추론 유형

진가영 영어연구소 | cafe.naver.com/easyenglish7

PART 01 홈페이지 게시글 유형

ANSWER

01 ②	02 ④	03 ④	04 ④	05 ①
06 ③	07 ①	08 ④	09 ④	10 ④
11 ④				

01
정답 ②

정답 해설
이 글은 플라스틱 사용을 줄이기 위한 전 세계적인 캠페인을 소개하고, 사람들이 이에 동참할 수 있도록 유도하는 내용을 담고 있다. 특히, 일회용품 대신 재사용 가능한 용기를 사용하자는 제안과 함께, 구체적인 실천 항목과 참여 기간을 선택하도록 안내하고 있는 점에서 '플라스틱 없는 도전(Plastic-Free Challenge)'에 참여하자는 취지가 분명히 드러난다. 따라서 글의 제목으로 가장 적절한 것은 ②이다.

선지 해석
① 일회용품의 개발
② 플라스틱 없는 도전에 참여하세요
③ 플라스틱 제품을 처리하는 방법
④ 에너지를 절약하는 간단한 방법들

02
정답 ④

정답 해설
본문의 열두 번째 문장에서 참여 기간을 선택하는 부분 중 '지금부터 계속 참여하기' 항목이 언급되고 있다. 따라서 글의 내용과 일치하지 않는 것은 ④이다.

오답 해설
① 본문의 네 번째 문장에서 언급하고 있으므로 일치한다.
② 본문의 네 번째 문장에서 언급하고 있으므로 일치한다.
③ 본문의 여덟 번째 문장에서 활동을 선택하는 내용이 언급되고 있으므로 일치한다.

지문 해석

> **플라스틱 없는 도전에 참여하세요**
>
> 매년 7월, 전 세계 사람들은 일상생활에서 흔한 플라스틱 폐기물을 제외하려고 노력하고 대신 재사용 가능한 용기나 생분해성 재료로 만든 제품을 사용하려고 합니다. 우리는 이것이 훌륭한 생각이라고 생각하며, 집이나 직장에서 1년 내내 실천하는 것도 좋은 방법이라고 생각합니다.
>
> 이 운동은 2011년 서호주에서 시작되어, 이후 전 세계로 퍼져나갔고, 우리의 편리한 생활 방식의 일부인 플라스틱 재료들로 지구가 포화되는 것을 막고, 비전을 홍보하는 데 도움을 주고 있습니다.
>
> 많은 제품들은 한 번 사용하고 버리도록 설계되어 있습니다. 이러한 제품들은 전 세계의 집, 학교, 직장, 거리에서 쓰레기통을 가득 채우고 있습니다.
>
> 여러분은 플라스틱 폐기물이 없는 세상을 만드는 목표를 성취하는 데 도움이 될 수 있습니다.
>
> **당신이 할 일을 선택하세요**
> ☐ 일회용 플라스틱 포장을 피하기
> ☐ 바다에 버려질 수 있는 테이크아웃 용품 겨냥하기
> ☐ 플라스틱을 완전히 끊기
>
> **참여 기간을 선택하세요**
> ☐ 1일 동안 참여하기
> ☐ 1주일 동안 참여하기
> ☐ 1개월 동안 참여하기
> ☐ 지금부터 계속 참여하기

지문 어휘
☐ exclude 제외하다, 배제하다
☐ common 흔한
☐ plastic waste 플라스틱 폐기물
☐ reusable 재사용할 수 있는
☐ biodegradable 생분해성의
☐ material 재료
☐ promote 홍보하다, 촉진하다
☐ saturated 포화된, 흠뻑 젖은
☐ convenience 편의, 편리
☐ dispose of 버리다, 처리하다
☐ fill up ~을 가득 채우다
☐ bin 쓰레기통
☐ across the world 전 세계에
☐ single-use 일회용의
☐ from now on 지금부터 계속

03
정답 ④

정답 해설
이 글은 '연체된 주차 위반 딱지 과태료를 납부하라'는 문자 메시지를 통해 사람들을 속이려는 사기 사건에 대해 시민들에게 경고하고 주의를 당부하고 있다. 주요 내용은 이러한 메시지가 공식 기관이 보낸 것이 아님을 알리고, 링크 클릭이나 지급 내역 제공을 금지하며, 시에서 승인한 주차 위반 딱지 고지 방법에 대해서도 설명하고 있다. 따라서 글의 제목으로 가장 적절한 것은 ④이다.

선지 해석
① 시에서 주차 위반 딱지를 납부하는 방법
② 주차위반 딱지를 받지 않는 방법
③ 시간과 돈을 아끼세요! 유용한 주차 팁
④ 경고! 가짜 주차위반 딱지 결제 문자 메시지

04

정답 ④

정답 해설
본문의 여덟 번째 문장에서 '등록된 차량 소유자에게 딱지가 우편으로 발송된다'라고 언급하고 있다. 따라서 글의 내용과 일치하는 것은 ④이다.

오답 해설
① 본문의 세 번째 문장에서 '링크를 클릭하거나 결제 세부 정보를 제공하지 마십시오'라고 언급하고 있으므로 일치하지 않는다.
② 본문의 네 번째 문장에서 '해당 메시지는 휴대폰 서비스 제공업체에 신고한 후 삭제하십시오'라고 언급하고 있으므로 일치하지 않는다.
③ 본문의 다섯 번째 문장에서 '저희는 문자, 미디어, 또는 소셜 미디어를 통해 과태료를 고지하지 않는다'라고 언급하고 있으므로 일치하지 않는다.

지문 해석

> **경고! 가짜 주차 위반 딱지 결제 문자 메시지**
>
> 우리는 연체된 주차 위반 딱지 과태료를 납부하라는 문자 메시지를 통해 사람들을 노리는 사기 사건에 대해 통지받았습니다.
> - 이러한 문자 메시지는 저희가 보낸 것이 아닙니다.
> - 링크를 클릭하거나 결제 세부 정보를 제공하지 마십시오.
> - 해당 메시지는 휴대폰 서비스 제공 기관에 신고한 후 삭제하십시오.
> - 저희는 문자, 미디어, 또는 소셜 미디어를 통해 과태료를 고지하지 않습니다.
>
> 시에서 승인된 주차 위반 딱지 고지 방법:
> - 차량에 직접 딱지를 부착합니다
> - 등록된 차량 소유자에게 딱지가 우편으로 발송됩니다

지문 어휘
☐ notify 통지하다, 알리다
☐ overdue (지불·반납 등의) 기한이 지난, 연체된
☐ parking ticket 주차 위반 딱지
☐ report 신고하다, 발표하다, 보도하다
☐ delete 삭제하다
☐ fine 과태료, 벌금
☐ approved 승인된, 공인된, 입증된
☐ vehicle 차량, 탈것, 운송 수단
☐ post 발송하다, 우편(물)
☐ registered 등록[등기]한, 기명의

05

정답 ①

정답 해설
밑줄 친 critical은 '중요한, 중대한, 비판적인, 비난하는'이라는 뜻으로, 문맥상 이와 의미가 가장 가까운 것은 ① 'pivotal(중요한, 중심이 되는, 추축의)'이다.

오답 해설
② perilous 위험한, 모험적인
③ analytical 분석적인
④ judgmental 도덕적 판단의, 재판의[에 관한]

06

정답 ③

정답 해설
이 글은 NHC Foundation이라는 기관이 무엇을 하는 곳이며, NHC를 어떻게 지원하고 있는지를 독자에게 알리고 있다. 초반부에서는 건강이 인권의 중요한 요소이며, 사회적 안녕과 경제 성장, 평화에 기여한다고 설명하면서 건강의 중요성을 강조하고 있다. 그러나 건강에 대한 접근이 공평하지 않다는 문제점을 지적하며, 이 문제 해결을 위한 기관으로 NHC와 NHC Foundation을 소개하고 있다. 따라서 글의 목적으로 가장 적절한 것은 ③이다.

지문 해석

> **사람들을 위한 건강**
>
> 사람들은 행복하고, 건강하며, 번영하는 삶을 살 수 있어야 합니다. 건강은 인권의 본질적인 요소이며, 사회적 복지, 경제 성장, 그리고 평화에 중요한 기여를 합니다.
>
> 하지만 건강에 대한 접근은 공평하지 않습니다.
>
> 국립보건센터 재단(NHC 재단)은 국립보건센터(NHC)가 모든 사람들이 최고 수준의 건강을 누리는 나라를 실현하겠다는 비전을 달성할 수 있도록 지원하기 위해 존재합니다. NHC는 건강을 증진하고 취약 계층을 지원하는 것을 목표로 합니다. NHC 재단은 기업, 자선가, 일반 대중 등 다양한 주체들과 협력함으로써 NHC를 돕는 데 전념하고 있습니다.

지문 어휘
☐ prosperous 번영한, 번창한
☐ substantial 본질적인, 실체의, 상당한
☐ contribution 기여, 기부금
☐ equitable 공평한, 공정한
☐ foundation 재단, 설립, 토대
☐ attain 달성하다, 이루다
☐ promote 증진[촉진]하다, 홍보하다, 승진시키다
☐ vulnerable 취약한, 연약한
☐ philanthropist 자선가

07

정답 ①

정답 해설
본문의 세 번째 문장에서 언급하고 있다. 따라서 글의 내용과 일치하는 것은 ①이다.

선지 해석
① 이곳은 국내 생산자들에게 마케팅 기회를 창출한다.
② 이곳은 전 세계적으로 건강한 식품 소비를 제한한다.
③ 이곳은 생산자보다 소비자에게 이익을 주는 데 전념하고 있다.
④ 이곳은 결정을 내리기 전에 다른 기관들로부터 지시를 받는다.

오답 해설
② 본문의 네 번째 문장에서 '우리는 농업 산업에 가치 있는 서비스를 제공하여 국내외 소비자에게 건강에 좋은 식품의 품질과 가용성을 보장한다'라고 언급하고 있으므로 일치하지 않는다.
③ 본문의 여섯 번째 문장에서 '생산자, 거래자 및 소비자에게 이익이 되는 경쟁력 있고 효율적인 시장을 촉진한다'라고 언급하고 있으므로 일치하지 않는다.

④ 본문의 아홉 번째 문장에서 '우리는 프로그램과 서비스에 대한 신뢰를 형성하기 위해 독립적이고 객관적으로 행동한다'라고 언급하고 있으므로 일치하지 않는다.

08

정답 ④

정답 해설
밑줄 친 fair는 '공정한, 타당한'이라는 뜻으로, 문맥상 이와 의미가 가장 가까운 것은 ④ 'impartial(공정한, 공평한)'이다.

오답 해설
① free 자유로운, 무료의, ~이 없는
② mutual 상호 간의, 서로의, 공동[공통]의
③ profitable 수익성이 있는, 유익한

지문 해석

> **농업 마케팅 사무소**
>
> **사명**
> 우리는 식품, 섬유 및 특수 작물의 국내 생산자를 위한 국내외 마케팅 기회를 창출하는 프로그램을 운영합니다. 또한, 우리는 농업 산업에 가치 있는 서비스를 제공하여 국내외 소비자에게 건강에 좋은 식품의 품질과 가용성을 보장합니다.
>
> **비전**
> 우리는 국내외 시장에서 국산 농산물의 전략적 마케팅을 촉진하며, 공정한 거래 관행을 보장하고 생산자, 거래자 및 소비자에게 이익이 되는 경쟁적이고 효율적인 시장을 촉진합니다.
>
> **핵심 가치**
> • 정직성과 진정성: 우리는 우리가 하는 모든 일에서 완전한 정직성과 진정성을 기대하고 요구합니다.
> • 독립성과 객관성: 우리는 프로그램과 서비스에 대한 신뢰를 형성하기 위해 독립적이고 객관적으로 행동합니다.

지문 어휘
☐ administer 운영하다, 관리하다
☐ domestic 국내의, 가정의
☐ international 국외의, 국제적인
☐ fiber 섬유
☐ specialty crop 특수 작물
☐ agriculture 농업
☐ availability 가용성, 이용 가능성
☐ wholesome 건강에 좋은, 건전한
☐ facilitate 촉진하다, 용이하게 하다
☐ practice 관행, 관례, 실행, 실천
☐ integrity 진정(성), 진실(성)
☐ expect 기대하다, 예상하다
☐ independence 독립, 자립
☐ objectivity 객관성

09

정답 ④

정답 해설
본문의 여덟 번째 문장에서 '방문객들에게 국가 역사와 문화에 대한 통찰력을 제공하기 위해 정기적인 문화 행사가 열린다'라고 언급하고 있다. 따라서 글의 내용과 일치하는 것은 ④이다.

오답 해설
① 본문의 세 번째 문장에서 '우리는 경치가 좋은 시골에서 이 유산을 체험하고 평화를 향한 지속적인 외침을 들어보도록 여러분을 초대한다'라고 언급하고 있으므로 일치하지 않는다.
② 본문의 다섯 번째 문장에서 '총 15만 점의 독립운동 관련 유물이 8개의 전시관에 전시되어 있다'라고 언급하고 있으므로 일치하지 않는다.
③ 본문의 여섯 번째 문장에서 '독립운동에 대한 연구에 전념하는 이 박물관은 관련 역사 주제에 대해 학술 활동을 지원한다'라고 언급하고 있으므로 일치하지 않는다.

지문 해석

> **국립독립기념관**
>
> 국립독립기념관은 전시, 연구, 교육 프로그램을 통해 국가의 역사를 보존하며, 국민의 자긍심을 고취시키고 있습니다. 우리는 경치가 좋은 시골에서 이 유산을 체험하고 평화를 향한 지속적인 외침을 들어보도록 여러분을 초대합니다.
>
> **주요 프로젝트**
> • **전시 및 소장품 관리**: 총 15만 점의 독립운동 관련 유물이 8개의 전시관에 전시되어 있습니다.
> • **연구**: 독립운동에 대한 연구에 전념하는 이 박물관은 관련 역사 주제에 대해 학술 활동을 지원합니다.
> • **교육**: 교육 프로그램을 통해 국가 정체성을 고취하고, 시민들의 역사에 대한 이해를 심화시킵니다.
> • **문화 행사**: 방문객들에게 국가 역사와 문화에 대한 통찰력을 제공하기 위해 정기적인 문화 행사가 열립니다.

선지 해석
① 이곳은 많은 고층 건물들로 둘러싸인 도시 환경에 위치해 있다.
② 이곳은 독립운동과 관련된 100만 개 이상의 유물을 전시하고 있다.
③ 이곳은 학술 프로젝트 대신 교육 활동을 지원한다.
④ 이곳은 방문객들에게 정기적으로 문화 행사를 제공한다.

지문 어휘
☐ exhibition 전시, 표현
☐ enduring 지속적인, 오래가는
☐ scenic 경치가 좋은
☐ relic 유물, 유적
☐ movement 운동, 이동, 움직임
☐ dedicated 전념하는, 헌신적인
☐ scholarly 학술적인, 학문적인
☐ identity 정체성, 독자성, 유사성
☐ deepen 심화시키다, 깊게 하다, 악화되다
☐ insight 통찰력, 이해
☐ skyscraper 고층 건물

10

정답 ④

정답 해설
본문의 여섯 번째 문장에서 '모바일 기기 사용이 불편한 사람들을 위한 웹 버전의 앱 또한 있다'라고 언급하고 있다. 따라서 글의 내용과 일치하지 않는 것은 ④이다.

오답 해설
① 본문의 세 번째 문장에서 언급하고 있으므로 일치한다.
② 본문의 네 번째 문장에서 언급하고 있으므로 일치한다.
③ 본문의 다섯 번째 문장에서 언급하고 있으므로 일치한다.

지문 해석

> 당신의 세관 신고를 위해 새로운 Enter-K 앱을 사용하세요.
>
> 공항에 당신이 도착하자마자 새로운 Enter-K 앱을 사용하세요. Enter-K에 의해 제공되는 한 가지 주목할 만한 특징은 Advance Declaration(사전 신고)인데, 이것은 여행자들에게 미리 그들의 세관 신고서를 제출할 수 있는 옵션을 허용하고 그들이 우리의 모든 국제 공항에서 시간을 절약할 수 있게 합니다. Enter-K는 계속 진행 중인 Traveller Modernization(여행자 현대화) 계획의 일환으로 미래에 국경 관련 추가 기능을 계속 도입하여 전체적인 국경 경험을 더욱 향상시킬 것입니다. 당신이 도착하기 전에 온라인 스토어에서 최신 버전의 앱을 간단히 다운로드 하세요. 모바일 기기 사용이 불편한 사람들을 위한 웹 버전의 앱 또한 있습니다.

선지 해석
① 이것은 여행자들이 사전에 세관 신고를 할 수 있게 한다.
② 추후 더 많은 기능이 추가될 예정이다.
③ 여행자들은 온라인 스토어에서 그것을 다운로드 할 수 있다.
④ 이것은 개인 모바일 기기에서만 작동한다.

지문 어휘
- [ ] customs 세관, 관세
- [ ] declaration (세관·세무서에의) 신고(서), 선언, 발표
- [ ] notable 주목할 만한, 눈에 띄는, 중요한, 유명한
- [ ] allow 허용하다, 허락하다, 용납하다
- [ ] submit 제출하다, 항복[굴복]하다
- [ ] enable ~할 수 있게 하다, 가능하게 하다
- [ ] international 국제적인, 국제의
- [ ] ongoing 계속 진행 중인
- [ ] introduce 도입하다, 소개하다, 안내하다
- [ ] border 국경, 경계, 가장자리, 접하다, 경계를 이루다
- [ ] related 관련된, 친척의, 동족의
- [ ] latest 최신의, 최근의

11

정답 ④

정답 해설
본문의 일곱 번째 문장에서 언급하고 있다. 따라서 글의 내용과 일치하는 것은 ④이다.

오답 해설
① 본문의 세 번째 문장에서 'OLC는 최저 임금, 적정 임금, 그리고 초과 근무 수당 등이 종업원에게 지급되고 종업원의 휴식 및 점심시간이 제공되도록 보장하는 것에 책임이 있다'라고 언급되어 있을 뿐, 세금 납부에 대한 내용은 언급되지 않았으므로 일치하지 않는다.
② 본문의 네 번째 문장에서 '게다가, OLC는 미성년자 고용에 관한 권한을 가지고 있다'라고 언급하고 있으므로 일치하지 않는다.
③ 본문의 다섯 번째 문장에서 '노동과 관련된 문제들을 효율적이고 전문적이며 효과적인 방법으로 해결하는 것이 본 사무소의 비전이자 임무다'라고 언급되어 있을 뿐, 고용주의 사업 기회들을 촉진한다는 내용은 언급되지 않았으므로 일치하지 않는다.

지문 해석

> 노동위원회(OLC) 사무소의 책임
>
> OLC는 국가의 주요 노동 규제 기관입니다. OLC는 최저 임금, 적정 임금, 그리고 초과 근무 수당 등이 종업원에게 지급되고 종업원의 휴식 및 점심시간이 제공되도록 보장하는 것에 책임이 있습니다. 게다가, OLC는 미성년자 고용에 관한 권한을 가지고 있습니다. 노동과 관련된 문제들을 효율적이고 전문적이며 효과적인 방법으로 해결하는 것이 본 사무소의 비전이자 임무입니다. 이것은 고용주와 종업원에게 법에 따른 그들의 권리와 책임에 대해 교육하는 것을 포함합니다. OLC는 근로자가 공정하게 대우받고 모든 근무 시간에 대해 보상을 받는 것을 보장할 수 있도록 필요할 때 집행 조치를 취합니다.

선지 해석
① 이것은 직원들이 세금을 제대로 납부하도록 보장한다.
② 이것은 성인 근로자의 고용에만 권한을 가지고 있다.
③ 이것은 고용주의 사업 기회들을 촉진한다.
④ 이것은 직원들이 불공정하게 대우 받을 때 조치를 취한다.

지문 어휘
- [ ] commissioner 위원, 장관
- [ ] principal 주요한, 주된, 학장, 총장
- [ ] regulatory 규제의, 규정의, 조절의
- [ ] ensure 보장하다, 확실하게 하다, 안전하게 하다
- [ ] minimum wage 최저 임금
- [ ] prevailing wage 적정 임금
- [ ] overtime 초과[시간 외] 근무, 잔업, 야근
- [ ] minor 미성년자, 부전공, 작은, 가벼운
- [ ] resolve 해결하다, 결심하다, 분해[용해]하다
- [ ] enforcement 집행, 시행, 실시
- [ ] treat 대우하다, 취급하다, 다루다
- [ ] fairly 공정하게, 공평하게, 상당히, 꽤
- [ ] compensate for 보상하다, 보충하다

01 홈페이지 게시글 유형 기출 독해 어휘 복습 TEST

1	exclude	제외하다, 배제하다	21	approved	승인된, 공인된, 입증된
2	common	흔한	22	vehicle	차량, 탈것, 운송 수단
3	plastic waste	플라스틱 폐기물	23	post	발송하다, 우편(물)
4	reusable	재사용할 수 있는	24	registered	등록[등기]한, 기명의
5	biodegradable	생분해성의	25	prosperous	번영한, 번창한
6	material	재료	26	substantial	본질적인, 실체의, 상당한
7	promote	증진[촉진]하다, 홍보하다, 승진시키다	27	contribution	기여, 기부금
8	saturated	포화된, 흠뻑 젖은	28	equitable	공평한, 공정한
9	convenience	편의, 편리	29	foundation	재단, 설립, 토대
10	dispose of	버리다, 처리하다	30	attain	달성하다, 이루다
11	fill up	~을 가득 채우다	31	vulnerable	취약한, 연약한
12	bin	쓰레기통	32	philanthropist	자선가
13	across the world	전 세계에	33	administer	운영하다, 관리하다
14	single-use	일회용의	34	domestic	국내의, 가정의
15	from now on	지금부터 계속	35	international	국외의, 국제적인
16	notify	통지하다, 알리다	36	fiber	섬유
17	overdue	(지불·반납 등의) 기한이 지난, 연체된	37	specialty crop	특수 작물
18	report	신고하다, 발표하다, 보도하다	38	agriculture	농업
19	delete	삭제하다	39	availability	가용성, 이용 가능성
20	fine	과태료, 벌금	40	wholesome	건강에 좋은, 건전한

#	단어	뜻	#	단어	뜻
41	facilitate	촉진하다, 용이하게 하다	61	submit	제출하다, 항복[굴복]하다
42	practice	관행, 관례, 실행, 실천	62	enable	~할 수 있게 하다, 가능하게 하다
43	integrity	진정(성), 진실(성)	63	ongoing	계속 진행 중인
44	expect	기대하다, 예상하다	64	introduce	도입하다, 소개하다, 안내하다
45	independence	독립, 자립	65	border	국경, 경계, 가장자리, 접하다, 경계를 이루다
46	objectivity	객관성	66	related	관련된, 친척의, 동족의
47	exhibition	전시, 표현	67	latest	최신의, 최근의
48	enduring	지속적인, 오래가는	68	commissioner	위원, 장관
49	relic	유물, 유적	69	principal	주요한, 주된, 학장, 총장
50	movement	운동, 이동, 움직임	70	regulatory	규제의, 규정의, 조절의
51	dedicated	전념하는, 헌신적인	71	ensure	보장하다, 확실하게 하다, 안전하게 하다
52	scholarly	학술적인, 학문적인	72	minimum wage	최저 임금
53	identity	정체성, 독자성, 유사성	73	prevailing wage	적정 임금
54	deepen	심화시키다, 깊게 하다, 악화되다	74	overtime	초과[시간 외] 근무, 잔업, 야근
55	insight	통찰력, 이해	75	minor	미성년자, 부전공, 작은, 가벼운
56	skyscraper	고층 건물	76	resolve	해결하다, 결심하다, 분해[용해]하다
57	customs	세관, 관세	77	enforcement	집행, 시행, 실시
58	declaration	(세관·세무서에의) 신고(서), 선언, 발표	78	treat	대우하다, 취급하다, 다루다
59	notable	주목할 만한, 눈에 띄는, 중요한, 유명한	79	fairly	공정하게, 공평하게, 상당히, 꽤
60	allow	허용하다, 허락하다, 용납하다	80	compensate for	보상하다, 보충하다

PART 02 전자메일 유형

ANSWER
01 ③   02 ②   03 ③   04 ③   05 ①

01 정답 ③

정답 해설
이 전자메일은 새로 생긴 스포츠 시설에서 발생하는 소음(응원, 외침, 휘슬, 공 소리 등)으로 인해 삶의 질이 떨어졌다고 호소하며, 이 문제에 대해 적절한 조치를 요청하고 있다. 따라서 글의 목적으로 가장 적절한 것은 ③이다.

02 정답 ②

정답 해설
밑줄 친 step은 '조치, 걸음, 단계, 계단'이라는 뜻으로, 문맥상 이와 의미가 가장 가까운 것은 ② 'actions(조치, 움직임, 작용)'이다.

오답 해설
① movements 움직임, 이동, 운동, 진전
③ levels 정도, 수준, 단계, 관점
④ stairs 계단, 층계

지문 해석

수신인: 클리프턴 구청
발신인: Rachael Beasly
날짜: 6월 7일
제목: 인근의 과도한 소음

담당자분께,
이 이메일이 당신에게 잘 도착하기를 바랍니다. 저는 특히 새로운 스포츠 경기장에서 발생하는 우리 동네의 과도한 소음 수준에 대하여 우려와 불만을 표현하기 위해 글을 씁니다.

클리프턴 지역 주민으로서, 저는 항상 우리 지역 사회의 평화를 높이 평가해왔습니다. 그러나, 계속되는 소음으로 인한 방해는 우리 가족의 안녕과 우리 삶의 전반적인 질에 상당히 영향을 미치고 있습니다. 그 소음의 원인은 관중들의 환호, 선수들의 외침, 휘슬 소리, 그리고 공이 부딪히는 소리를 포함합니다.

저는 당신이 이 문제를 조사하여 소음으로 인한 방해를 해결하기 위한 적절한 조치를 취해 주시기를 부탁드립니다. 이 문제에 관한 당신의 관심에 감사드리며, 우리 인근의 평온을 회복하는 데 도움이 될 수 있는 신속한 대응에 감사드립니다.

진심을 담아,
Rachael Beasly

지문 어휘
□ concern 관계하다, 관련되다, 걱정시키다, 염려[우려]하게 만들다, 일, 관계, 관심, 걱정, 우려
□ regarding ~에 대하여, ~에 관하여
□ excessive 과도한, 지나친
□ district 지역, 지방
□ look into ~을 조사하다, ~을 들여다 보다, 주의 깊게 살피다
□ matter 문제, 물질, 재료, 중요하다, 문제가 되다
□ take steps 조치를 취하다
□ address 해결하다, 다루다, 처리하다, 주소를 쓰다, 연설하다
□ tranquility 평온, 고요, 차분함

03 정답 ③

정답 해설
이 전자메일은 Woodville 시의회에 지역 주민이 겪고 있는 엘름 스트리트의 도로 문제와 센트럴 파크의 가로등 문제를 해결해 달라고 요청하고 있다. 따라서 글의 목적으로 가장 적절한 것은 ③이다.

지문 해석

수신인: citycouncil@woodville.gov
발신인: headcouncil@woodville.gov
날짜: 2025년 4월 3일
제목: 시의회에 알림

Woodville 시의회 의원 여러분께,

저는 우리 지역 사회에서 주의를 기울여야 할 몇 가지 문제를 알리기 위해 이 글을 씁니다. 엘름 스트리트 123번지에 거주하는 주민 John Smith가 엘름 스트리트, 특히 메이플 애비뉴와 오크 스트리트 사이 구간의 도로 상태 문제를 보고했습니다. 최근의 폭우 이후 악화된 많은 움푹 패인 곳과 균열이 있으며, 이는 교통 혼란과 안전 문제를 초래하고 있습니다. 임시 보수가 이루어졌음에도 불구하고, 문제는 계속되고 있습니다.

이 주민은 센트럴 파크, 특히 파크 레인 주변의 조명이 불량한 것에 대해서도 우려를 표했는데, 이는 고장 나거나 사라진 가로등 때문에 경미한 사고가 발생했고, 부동산 가치도 하락했기 때문입니다. 그는 시의회에 엘름 스트리트를 수리하고 공원의 조명을 개선해 줄 것을 요청합니다.

저는 시의회가 우리 지역 사회의 안전과 복지를 위해 이러한 문제를 해결해 줄 것을 요청합니다. 이 문제들에 관심을 가져주셔서 감사합니다. 저는 이러한 문제들을 효과적으로 해결하기 위해 우리가 함께 협력할 것이라고 믿습니다.

진심을 담아,
Stephen James
Woodville 시의회 의장

선지 해석
① 시의회의 노력에 대해 감사를 표현하려고
② 시의회 위원들을 센트럴 파크에 방문하도록 초대하려고
③ 시의회에 지역 사회 문제를 해결해 달라고 요청하려고
④ 해당 지역에서 이루어진 최근 보수 작업에 대해 시의회에 알리려고

지문 어휘
- council 의회, 자문 위원회
- inform 알리다, 통지하다
- issue 문제, 주제, 쟁점, 사안
- pothole (도로에) 움푹 패인 곳
- crack 균열, 금
- worsen 악화되다, 악화시키다
- heavy rain 폭우, 호우
- disruption 혼잡, 혼란, 분열, 붕괴
- temporary 일시적인, 임시의
- streetlight 가로등
- minor 경미한, 가벼운, 작은
- property 부동산, 재산, 소유물, 건물 (구내)
- request 요청[요구/신청]하다
- address 해결하다, 고심하다
- resolve 해결하다, 다짐하다

04
정답 ③

정답 해설
이 전자메일은 작성자가 지난주 면접 이후, 자신의 지원이 현재 어떤 단계에 있는지, 즉 채용 결정 일정이나 향후 절차에 대한 정보를 공유해 줄 것을 요청하고 있다. 먼저 면접에 대한 감사의 인사를 전하며 예의를 갖춘 뒤, 본격적으로 지원의 진행 상황에 대해 문의하고 있다. 따라서 글의 목적으로 가장 적절한 것은 ③이다.

지문 해석
수신인: chlsbrown@cbsys.com
발신인: tomsmith@boogle.com
날짜: 2025년 6월 21일
제목: 면접에 대해 감사드립니다

Charles Brown 씨께,

저는 지난주 면접에 대해 감사의 인사를 드리기 위해 이 글을 씁니다. 저희의 대화는 매우 유익했습니다. 귀하께서 공유해 주신 새로운 계정 관리 시스템에 대한 정보는 매우 유익했습니다.

저는 지금 제 지원의 진행 상황에 대해 어떤 최신 정보가 있는지 확인하고자 합니다.

이 직책은 저와 제 경력 목표와 매우 잘 맞는 것 같습니다. 결정 일정이나 다음 절차에 대해 공유해 주실 수 있는 부분이 있다면 정말 감사하겠습니다.

필요하다면 추가 정보도 기꺼이 제공하겠습니다. 다시 한번 감사드립니다.

진심을 담아,

Tom Smith

선지 해석
① 지원서를 제출하려고
② 면접 약속을 잡으려고
③ 결정 과정에 대한 최신 정보를 문의하려고
④ 회사의 사업에 대한 더 많은 정보를 요청하려고

지문 어휘
- conversation 대화
- valuable 매우 유익한, 소중한
- follow up 더 알아보다, ~을 덧붙이다, 후속 조치하다
- status 상황, 신분, 지위
- application 지원, 신청
- timeline 일정, 연대표
- additional 추가의

05
정답 ①

정답 해설
이 전자메일은 고객들에게 사이버 범죄로부터 자신을 보호하는 방법에 대한 정보를 제공하고 있다. 강력한 비밀번호 사용, 소프트웨어 업데이트, 의심스러운 이메일이나 전화에 대한 주의, OTP 활용, 데이터 백업 등 다양한 보안 수칙을 안내함으로써, 전반적으로 사이버 위협에 대한 경각심을 일깨우는 것이 이 글의 핵심 목적이다. 따라서 글의 목적으로 가장 적절한 것은 ①이다.

지문 해석
수신인: cbsclients@calbank.com
발신인: calbanks@calmail.com
날짜: 2024년 5월 7일
제목: 중요 공지

친애하는 고객님들께,

오늘날 사이버 범죄는 여러분의 보안에 심각한 위협을 가하고 있습니다. 신뢰받는 파트너로서, 우리는 여러분의 개인 및 비즈니스 정보를 보호하는 데 도움을 드리고자 합니다. 사이버 위협으로부터 자신을 보호하는 다섯 가지 간단한 방법은 다음과 같습니다:

1. 강력한 비밀번호를 사용하고 자주 변경하세요.
2. 소프트웨어와 장비를 최신 상태로 유지하세요.
3. 빠르게 행동하거나 민감한 정보를 제공하라는 압박을 가하는 의심스러운 전자 우편, 링크, 전화에 조심하세요.
4. 이중 인증을 활성화하고 가능한 경우 항상 사용하세요. 캘리포니아 은행 및 저축에 연락할 때, 신원을 확인하기 위해 일회용 비밀번호(OTP)를 사용해야 합니다.
5. 데이터를 정기적으로 백업하세요.
온라인에서 안전을 유지하는 방법에 대해 더 알아보려면 보안 센터를 방문하세요. 사이버 보안은 팀의 노력입니다. 함께 협력하여 우리와 전 세계를 위한 더 안전한 온라인 환경을 만들어 나가도록 합시다.

진심을 담아,

California Bank & Savings

선지 해석

① 고객들에게 사이버 위협으로부터 자신을 어떻게 보호할 수 있는지 알리려고
② 고객들에게 소프트웨어와 기기를 어떻게 업데이트하는지 알리려고
③ 고객들에게 비밀번호를 어떻게 더 강하게 만드는지 알리려고
④ 고객들에게 OTP(일회용 비밀번호)를 어떻게 안전하게 지키는지 알리려고

지문 어휘

☐ cybercrime 사이버 범죄
☐ protect 보호하다, 지키다
☐ personal 개인의, 사적인
☐ threat 위협, 협박
☐ frequently 자주, 흔히
☐ up to date 최신의, 최근의
☐ wary of ~을 조심하는
☐ suspicious 의심스러운, 수상쩍은
☐ sensitive 민감한, 예민한
☐ authentication 인증, 증명
☐ verify 확인하다, 입증하다
☐ back up (파일·프로그램 등을) 백업하다
☐ regularly 정기[규칙]적으로

02 전자메일 유형 기출 독해 어휘 복습 TEST 정답

#	단어	뜻	#	단어	뜻
1	concern	관계하다, 관련되다, 걱정시키다, 염려[우려]하게 만들다, 일, 관계, 관심, 걱정, 우려	21	address	해결하다, 고심하다
2	regarding	~에 대하여, ~에 관하여	22	resolve	해결하다, 다짐하다
3	excessive	과도한, 지나친	23	conversation	대화
4	district	지역, 지방	24	valuable	매우 유익한, 소중한
5	look into	~을 조사하다, ~을 들여다 보다, 주의 깊게 살피다	25	follow up	더 알아보다, ~을 덧붙이다, 후속 조치하다
6	matter	문제, 물질, 재료, 중요하다, 문제가 되다	26	status	상황, 신분, 지위
7	take steps	조치를 취하다	27	timeline	일정, 연대표
8	address	해결하다, 다루다, 처리하다, 주소를 쓰다, 연설하다	28	additional	추가의
9	tranquility	평온, 고요, 차분함	29	protect	보호하다, 지키다
10	council	의회, 자문 위원회	30	personal	개인의, 사적인
11	inform	알리다, 통지하다	31	threat	위협, 협박
12	issue	문제, 주제, 쟁점, 사안	32	frequently	자주, 흔히
13	pothole	(도로에) 움푹 패인 곳	33	up to date	최신의, 최근의
14	crack	균열, 금	34	wary of	~을 조심하는
15	worsen	악화되다, 악화시키다	35	suspicious	의심스러운, 수상쩍은
16	disruption	혼잡, 혼란, 분열, 붕괴	36	sensitive	민감한, 예민한
17	temporary	일시적인, 임시의	37	authentication	인증, 증명
18	minor	경미한, 가벼운, 작은	38	verify	확인하다, 입증하다
19	property	부동산, 재산, 소유물, 건물 (구내)	39	back up	(파일·프로그램 등을) 백업하다
20	request	요청[요구/신청]하다	40	regularly	정기[규칙]적으로

PART 03 안내문 유형

ANSWER

01 ③ 02 ② 03 ② 04 ③ 05 ①
06 ③ 07 ④ 08 ② 09 ② 10 ③

01   정답 ③

정답 해설

밑줄 친 assess는 '평가하다, 재다'라는 뜻으로, 문맥상 이와 의미가 가장 가까운 것은 ③ 'evaluate(평가하다, 감정하다)'이다.

오답 해설

① upgrade 개선하다, 향상시키다, 승진시키다
② prolong 연장시키다, 연장하다
④ render 제공하다, 주다, 만들다, 제시[제출]하다

02   정답 ②

정답 해설

이 글은 영사 서비스를 이용한 후, 피드백을 제공하거나 불만 사항이 있을 경우 이를 어떻게 제기할 수 있는지를 안내하고 있다. 특히 문제가 있었던 경우 이를 알려주는 것이 서비스 평가와 개선에 도움이 된다는 점을 강조하며, 피드백을 적극적으로 환영하고 있다. 또한 불만 제기의 절차에 대해서도 구체적으로 설명하고 있다. 따라서 글의 목적으로 가장 적절한 것은 ②이다.

선지 해석

① 영사관으로 가는 길을 안내하려고
② 불만을 제기하는 방법을 설명하려고
③ 채용 절차를 설명하려고
④ 영업[운영] 시간을 알리려고

지문 해석

> **영사 서비스**
>
> 그것이 영국 내에서 받은 것이든, 해외 대사관, 고등판무관 사무실 또는 영사관에서 받은 것이든 상관없이 저희는 당사의 영사 서비스에 대한 모든 피드백을 환영합니다. 서비스를 <u>평가하고</u> 개선하는 데 도움이 되도록 우리가 실수했을 때 우리에게 말씀해주세요.
>
> <u>여러분이 받은 영사 서비스에 대해 불만을 제기하고자 하는 경우, 우리는 가능한 한 신속하게 해결할 수 있도록 도와드리기를 원합니다.</u> 다른 사람을 대신해 불만을 제기하는 경우, 저희가 답변을 드리기 전에 그 사람으로부터 서명된 서면 동의를 받아야 하며, 이 동의서는 저희가 해당 개인 정보를 귀하와 공유하는 것을 허락하는 내용이어야 합니다.
>
> <u>불만 사항의 세부 내용을 저희 피드백 연락 양식으로 보내주시기 바랍니다.</u> 귀하의 불만 사항을 기록하고 검토하며, 귀하가 제공한 정보를 활용하여 우리가 고객에게 최상의 도움과 지원을 제공하는 것을 보장하는 데 도움이 되도록 하겠습니다. 해당 대사관, 고등판무관 사무실, 영사관이 당신에게 회신할 것입니다.

지문 어휘

☐ consular 영사의, 영사관의
☐ receive 받다, 받아들이다
☐ embassy 대사관
☐ high commission 고등판무관 사무실
☐ consulate 영사관
☐ abroad 해외에(서), 해외로
☐ make a complaint 불만을 제기하다
☐ resolve 해결하다, 다짐하다
☐ on behalf of ~을 대신하여, 대표하여
☐ consent 동의(서), 승낙, 합의
☐ reply 답장을 보내다, 대답하다
☐ record 기록하다, 녹음하다
☐ examine 검토하다, 조사하다
☐ form 양식, 형식, 종류, 모습

03   정답 ②

정답 해설

이 글은 City Harbour Festival이라는 지역 축제를 소개하는 안내문으로, 이 축제는 지역 사회의 다양한 문화를 함께 즐기고, 공동체의 유산과 재능을 기념하는 것을 목적으로 하고 있다. 축제에는 여러 무대에서 펼쳐지는 라이브 공연, 다양한 음식을 제공하는 푸드 트럭, 그리고 공동체 구성원들이 함께 참여할 수 있는 다양한 행사들이 포함되어 있어, 단순한 이벤트를 넘어 지역 사회의 다양성과 활기를 잘 보여주는 문화 축제임을 강조하고 있다. 따라서 글의 제목으로 가장 적절한 것은 ②이다.

선지 해석

① 당신의 지역 사회를 위한 안전 규정을 만드세요
② 우리의 활기찬 지역 사회 행사를 축하하세요
③ 당신의 신나는 해양 체험을 계획하세요
④ 우리의 도시 유산을 재현하세요

04   정답 ③

정답 해설

본문의 열세 번째 문장에서 '무료 시식뿐만 아니라 다양하고 맛있는 요리를 제공하는 다양한 푸드 트럭과 함께 축제를 즐기세요'라고 언급하고 있을 뿐, 무료 요리 강습에 대한 내용은 언급되지 않았으므로 글의 내용과 일치하지 않는 것은 ③이다.

오답 해설

① 본문의 두 번째 문장에서 언급하고 있으므로 일치한다.
② 본문의 일곱 번째 문장에서 언급하고 있으므로 일치한다.
④ 본문의 열네 번째 문장에서 언급하고 있으므로 일치한다.

지문 해석

우리의 활기찬 지역사회 행사를 축하하세요

우리는 우리의 공유된 유산, 문화, 그리고 지역 재능을 기념하기 위해 우리의 다양한 지역 사회를 화합하게 하는 연례행사인 곧 있을 City Harbour Festival을 발표하게 되어 기쁩니다. 여러분의 달력에 표시하고 신나는 주말에 우리와 함께 하세요!

세부 사항
- 날짜: 6월 16일, 금요일 − 6월 18일, 일요일
- 시간: 오전 10:00 − 오후 8:00 (금, 토)
  오전 10:00 − 오후 6:00 (일)
- 장소: City Harbour 공원, 시내 중심가, 주변 지역

하이라이트
- 라이브 공연
  축제장 곳곳에 다수의 무대에서 다양한 라이브 음악, 춤, 그리고 연극 공연을 즐기세요.
- 푸드 트럭
  무료 시식뿐만 아니라 다양하고 맛있는 요리를 제공하는 다양한 푸드 트럭과 함께 축제를 즐기세요.

행사 및 활동의 전체 일정은 당사 웹사이트 www.cityharbourfestival.org를 방문하거나 축제사무소인 (552) 234-5678로 연락주세요.

지문 어휘

- vibrant 활기찬, 생기가 넘치는, 강렬한, 선명한
- upcoming 곧 있을, 다가오는
- bring together 화합하게 하다, 모으다, 화해시키다
- heritage 유산, 전승, 전통
- a variety of 다양한, 여러 가지의
- throughout 곳곳에, 도처에, ~동안, ~내내
- feast 잔치, 연회, 축제일, 포식하다
- cuisine 요리, 요리법
- form 양식, 형식, 종류, 모습

05   정답 ①

정답 해설

이 글은 딤즈데일 호수가 현재 심각한 위기에 처해 있으며, 아직 완전히 죽지는 않았지만 상태가 점차 악화되고 있음을 주민들에게 알리고 있다. 주민들이 호수의 중요성을 인식하고 보호 활동에 동참할 수 있도록 특별 모임에 초대하여, 문제의 심각성을 공유하고 구체적인 대응 방안과 참여 방법을 안내하는 내용을 담고 있다. 따라서 글의 제목으로 가장 적절한 것은 ①이다.

선지 해석

① 딤즈데일 호수가 죽어가고 있다
② 호수의 아름다움에 대한 찬사
③ 딤즈데일 호수의 문화적 가치
④ 대학에 대한 호수의 중요성

06   정답 ③

정답 해설

본문의 열두 번째 문장에서 '비 오는 경우: 대학 도서관 203호'라고 언급하고 있다. 따라서 글의 내용과 일치하지 않는 것은 ③이다.

오답 해설

① 본문의 다섯 번째 문장에서 언급하고 있으므로 일치한다.
② 본문의 여덟 번째 문장에서 언급하고 있으므로 일치한다.
④ 본문의 열다섯 번째 문장에서 언급하고 있으므로 일치한다.

지문 해석

딤즈데일 호수가 죽어가고 있다

가까운 이웃으로서, 여러분은 호수를 구하는 방법을 알아야 할 것입니다.

아직 죽은 것은 아니지만, 딤즈데일 호수는 이런 결말을 향해 가고 있습니다. 그러니 아직 살아 있을 때 이 아름다운 호수에게 경의를 표해 주세요.

지금 몇몇 헌신적인 사람들이 호수를 구하기 위해 노력하고 있습니다. 그들은 이에 대해 여러분에게 알리기 위해 특별 회의를 개최할 예정입니다. 무엇이 이루어지고 있으며, 어떻게 도움을 줄 수 있는지 배워보세요. 이것은 여러분의 재산 가치에도 영향을 미칩니다.
누가 죽어가는 호수 근처에 살고 싶겠어요?

중앙주 지역 계획 위원회에서 주최합니다

- 장소: 그린 시티 공원, 서던 주립 대학 맞은편
  (비 오는 경우: 대학 도서관 203호)
- 날짜: 2024년 7월 6일 토요일
- 시간: 오후 2시

회의에 관한 질문은 저희 웹사이트 www.planningcouncilsavelake.org을 방문하시거나 사무실(432) 345-6789로 연락해 주시기 바랍니다.

지문 어휘

- lake 호수
- die 죽다, 없어지다
- close 가까운
- head toward ~을 향해 가다
- pay respect to ~에 경의를 표하다
- dedicated 헌신적인, 전념하는
- affect 영향을 미치다
- property 재산, 소유물, 부동산, 건물 (구내)
- sponsor 주관[주최]하다, 후원하다
- opposite 맞은 편의, 건너편의
- in case of ~의 경우에

07

정답 ④

정답 해설
본문의 열네 번째 문장에서 '6월 30일 주에는 캠프가 없습니다'라고 언급하고 있다. 따라서 글의 내용과 일치하지 않는 것은 ④이다.

오답 해설
① 본문의 세 번째 문장에서 언급하고 있으므로 일치한다.
② 본문의 다섯 번째 문장 그리고 여섯 번째 문장에서 언급하고 있으므로 일치한다.
③ 본문의 아홉 번째 문장에서 언급하고 있으므로 일치한다.

지문 해석

> **2025 어린이 여름 미술 캠프**
>
> 스탠 호세 미술관(SJAM)과 함께 신나는 한 주를 보내세요! 캠프 참가자들은 전시회의 비하인드 스토리를 접하고, 예술 창작 과정을 실험해 보며, 학생 전시회에서 자신의 작품을 자랑할 수 있습니다.
>
> **대상**
> 6세부터 14세까지의 어린이
> 각 참가자는 자신의 학습 스타일과 실력에 맞는 개인별 예술 지원과 격려, 창의적인 도전을 받게 됩니다.
>
> **내용**
> 경력이 있는 갤러리 교사들과 스튜디오 미술 교육자들이 이끄는, 미술 재료와 과정에 대한 창의적인 탐구가 결합된 SJAM의 여름 미술 캠프와 함께하세요. 또한, 캠프 참가자들은 STEM(과학·기술·공학·수학) 컨설턴트 Eddie Brown이 개발한 해석 중심의 미술 및 과학 수업에도 참여하게 됩니다.
>
> **아트 캠프 전시회**
> 각 참가자의 예술적 성취를 기념하기 위해, 가족과 보호자를 매주 열리는 캠프 참가자들의 작품 전시회 환영 연회에 초대합니다.
>
> **일정**
> 모든 캠프는 월요일부터 금요일까지 오전 9시부터 오후 3시까지 진행됩니다.
> 6월 9일(월)부터 7월 25일(금)까지 (6월 30일 주에는 캠프가 없습니다)

선지 해석
① 캠프 참가자들은 학생 전시회에서 자신의 작품을 전시할 기회를 갖게 된다.
② 이 캠프는 6세에서 14세 아동을 위한 개별적인 예술 지원을 포함하고 있다.
③ STEM(과학·기술·공학·수학) 전문가가 해석 중심의 미술 및 과학 수업을 개발했다.
④ 이 캠프는 6월 9일부터 7월 25일까지 휴식 없이 운영된다.

지문 어휘
☐ behind-the-scenes 무대 뒤에서
☐ access 접근하다, 들어가다, 이용하다
☐ experiment 실험하다, 시험 삼아 해 보다
☐ show off 자랑하다, 과시하다
☐ exhibition 전시회
☐ encouragement 격려, 고무
☐ exploration 탐구, 탐사
☐ material (물건의) 재료
☐ process 과정, 절차
☐ experienced 경험[경력]이 있는, 능숙한
☐ interpretive 해석 중심의, 해석을 제공하는
☐ invite 초대하다, 초청하다
☐ caregiver 보호자, 돌보는 사람
☐ reception 환영[축하] 연회, 접수처[프런트]
☐ celebrate 기념하다, 축하하다
☐ achievement 성취, 달성, 업적
☐ participant 참가자

08

정답 ②

정답 해설
본문의 여섯 번째 문장에서 '보건복지부의 프로그램은 공중보건국 산하 8개 기관과 복지 분야 3개 기관을 포함한 11개 운영 부서가 관리한다'라고 언급하고 있다. 따라서 글의 내용과 일치하는 것은 ②이다.

오답 해설
① 본문의 세 번째 문장에서 '보건복지부의 사명은 모든 국민의 건강과 복지를 증진하는 것이다'라고 언급하고 있으므로 일치하지 않는다.
③ 본문의 일곱 번째 문장에서 '세계가 상호 연결되어 있기 때문에 그 사명을 완수하기 위해 전 세계적으로도 활동에 참여하고 있다'라고 언급하고 있으므로 일치하지 않는다.
④ 본문의 열 번째 문장에서 'HHS는 공통 주제들에 대해 다른 연방 부처 및 기관들과 긴밀히 협력하고 있다'라고 언급하고 있으므로 일치하지 않는다

지문 해석

> **보건복지부**
>
> **강령**
> 보건복지부(HHS)의 사명은 효과적인 보건 및 복지 서비스를 제공하고, 의학, 공중보건, 사회복지의 기초가 되는 과학 분야에서 건전하고 지속적인 발전을 촉진함으로써, 모든 국민의 건강과 복지를 높이는 것입니다.
>
> **조직 구조**
> HHS는 다양한 활동 영역을 포괄하는 프로그램과 계획을 통해 사명을 달성합니다. 보건복지부의 프로그램은 공중보건국 산하 8개 기관과 복지 분야 3개 기관을 포함한 11개 운영 부서가 관리합니다. HHS는 미국 국민의 건강과 복지를 보호하고 증진하는 국내 기관이지만, 세계가 상호 연결되어 있기 때문에 그 사명을 완수하기 위해 전 세계적으로도 활동에 참여하고 있습니다.
>
> **부처 간 협력**
> 건강 및 복지 서비스 성과 향상은 보건복지부 단독으로는 달성할 수 없으며, 목표와 과제를 이루기 위해 협력이 필수적입니다.
> HHS는 공통 주제들에 대해 다른 연방 부처 및 기관들과 긴밀히 협력하고 있습니다.

선지 해석
① HHS는 오직 저소득 가정의 건강과 복지 향상만을 목표로 한다.
② HHS의 프로그램들은 11개의 운영 부서에 의해 관리된다.
③ HHS는 그 임무를 완수하기 위해 외국과 협력하지 않는다.
④ HHS는 목표를 달성하기 위해 다른 연방 부서나 기관들과는 독립적으로 활동한다.

지문 어휘

- mission statement (기업·조직의) 강령
- enhance 높이다, 향상시키다
- foster 촉진하다, 조성하다
- sustained 지속된, 일관된
- underlying 기초가 되는, 근본적인
- medicine 의학, 의료, 약
- accomplish 달성하다, 성취하다, 해내다
- division 부서, 분과
- domestic 국내의, 가정(용)의
- interconnectedness 상호 연결됨
- fulfill 완수하다, 성취하다
- outcome 성과, 결과
- objective 목표, 목적
- department 부처, 부서, 학과
- cross-cutting 공통의

09   정답 ②

정답 해설
본문의 동그라미 부분에서 '12세 미만 어린이가 무료인 것은 입장료'라고 언급하고 있고, 상품 추첨은 매시간 진행되는 입장과는 별개의 것임을 알 수 있다. 따라서 글의 내용과 일치하지 않는 것은 ②이다.

오답 해설
① 본문의 세 번째 문장에서 언급하고 있으므로 일치한다.
③ 본문의 여섯 번째 문장에서 언급하고 있으므로 일치한다.
④ 본문의 일곱 번째 문장에서 언급하고 있으므로 일치한다.

지문 해석

미 동부 해안 최대 규모의 항공 수집품 전시회

일시
2025년 9월 6일 토요일,
오전 10시 – 오후 6시

장소
그랜드 박람회 센터 에어포트가 160번지

- 10달러 입장료
- 12세 미만 어린이 무료
- 매시간 상품 추첨

구하기 힘든 항공 및 교통 수집품을 전시한 테이블이 90개 이상!

다음과 같은 아주 멋진 국내 및 외국 항공사 수집품을 만나보고 구매하세요:

항공사 및 여행 포스터, 다이캐스트 모형(정교한 축소 모형), 수천 개의 기타 역사적인 항공 및 교통 관련 유물과 훨씬 더 많은 것들!

선지 해석
① 미 동부 최대 규모의 항공 수집품 전시회가 9월에 열릴 예정이다.
② 상품 추첨은 12세 미만 어린이에게만 제공된다.
③ 희귀한 항공 및 교통 수집품이 전시회에 전시될 예정이다.
④ 방문객들은 국내외 수집품을 모두 볼 수 있다.

지문 어휘
- avenue 가, 거리
- admission 입장료
- free 무료의
- door prize 참가자에게 추첨으로 주는 상품
- collectible 수집품
- sensational 아주 멋진, 선풍적인
- domestic 국내의, 가정의
- foreign 외국의, 대외의

10   정답 ③

본문의 여덟 번째 문장에서 '휴무: 추수감사절, 크리스마스, 새해 첫날'이라고 언급하고 있다. 따라서 글의 내용과 일치하지 않는 것은 ③이다.

오답 해설
① 본문의 첫 번째 문장에서 언급하고 있으므로 일치한다.
② 본문의 일곱 번째 문장에서 언급하고 있으므로 일치한다.
④ 본문의 아홉 번째 문장에서 언급하고 있으므로 일치한다.

지문 해석

David Williams 도서관 및 박물관은 매주 7일 운영되며, 11월부터 3월까지는 오전 9시부터 오후 5시까지, 4월부터 10월까지는 오전 9시부터 오후 6시까지 열려 있습니다. 온라인 티켓은 아래 링크에서 구매할 수 있습니다. 구매 후 이메일로 확인서를 받게 됩니다 (스팸 폴더도 확인해 주세요). 이 확인서를 인쇄하여 지참하거나 스마트 기기에서 제시하여 구매 증빙자료로 지참하세요.

- 온라인 티켓: buy.davidwilliams.com/events

David Williams 도서관 및 박물관과 David Williams의 집(국립 유산 서비스 운영)은 성인 입장료를 각각 $10.00에 판매하고 있습니다. 집 투어 티켓은 정상 업무 시간 중 현장에서 구매할 수 있습니다.

- 휴무: 추수감사절, 크리스마스, 새해 첫날

David Williams 도서관 연구실에서 연구를 진행하는 데는 비용이 들지 않습니다.

추가 정보는 1 (800) 333-7777로 문의해 주세요.

선지 해석
① 도서관과 박물관은 12월에 오후 5시에 문을 닫는다.
② 방문객들은 그 집에 대한 투어 티켓을 현장에서 구매할 수 있다.
③ David Williams의 집은 연중 내내 개방되어 있다.
④ 누구나 도서관의 자료 조사실에서 무료로 연구할 수 있다.

지문 어휘
- purchase 구매하다, 구입하다
- below 아래에
- confirmation 확인(서)
- proof 증명(서), 증거(물)
- separate 각각의, 별개의, 분리된
- admission 입장료
- on-site 현장의
- charge 비용, 요금

03 안내문 유형 기출 독해 어휘 복습 TEST

1	consular	영사의, 영사관의	21	feast	잔치, 연회, 축제일, 포식하다
2	receive	받다, 받아들이다	22	cuisine	요리, 요리법
3	embassy	대사관	23	form	양식, 형식, 종류, 모습
4	high commission	고등판무관 사무실	24	lake	호수
5	consulate	영사관	25	close	가까운
6	abroad	해외에(서), 해외로	26	head toward	~을 향해 가다
7	make a complaint	불만을 제기하다	27	pay respect to	~에 경의를 표하다
8	resolve	해결하다, 다짐하다	28	dedicated	헌신적인, 전념하는
9	on behalf of	~을 대신하여, 대표하여	29	affect	영향을 미치다
10	consent	동의(서), 승낙, 합의	30	property	재산, 소유물, 부동산, 건물 (구내)
11	reply	답장을 보내다, 대답하다	31	sponsor	주관[주최]하다, 후원하다
12	record	기록하다, 녹음하다	32	opposite	맞은 편의, 건너편의
13	examine	검토하다, 조사하다	33	in case of	~의 경우에
14	form	양식, 형식, 종류, 모습	34	access	접근하다, 들어가다, 이용하다
15	vibrant	활기찬, 생기가 넘치는, 강렬한, 선명한	35	experiment	실험하다, 시험 삼아 해 보다
16	upcoming	곧 있을, 다가오는	36	show off	자랑하다, 과시하다
17	bring together	화합하게 하다, 모으다, 화해시키다	37	exhibition	전시회
18	heritage	유산, 전승, 전통	38	artistic	예술의
19	a variety of	다양한, 여러 가지의	39	encouragement	격려, 고무
20	throughout	곳곳에, 도처에, ~동안, ~내내	40	exploration	탐구, 탐사

41	material	(물건의) 재료	61	fulfill	완수하다, 성취하다
42	process	과정, 절차	62	outcome	성과, 결과
43	experienced	경험[경력]이 있는, 능숙한	63	objective	목표, 목적
44	interpretive	해석 중심의, 해석을 제공하는	64	department	부처, 부서, 학과
45	invite	초대하다, 초청하다	65	cross-cutting	공통의
46	caregiver	보호자, 돌보는 사람	66	avenue	~가, 거리
47	reception	환영[축하] 연회, 접수처[프런트]	67	admission	입장료
48	celebrate	기념하다, 축하하다	68	free	무료의
49	achievement	성취, 달성, 업적	69	door prize	참가자에게 추첨으로 주는 상품
50	participant	참가자	70	collectible	수집품
51	mission statement	(기업·조직의) 강령	71	sensational	아주 멋진, 선풍적인
52	enhance	높이다, 향상시키다	72	domestic	국내의, 가정의
53	foster	촉진하다, 조성하다	73	foreign	외국의, 대외의
54	sustained	지속된, 일관된	74	purchase	구매하다, 구입하다
55	underlying	기초가 되는, 근본적인	75	below	아래에
56	medicine	의학, 의료, 약	76	confirmation	확인(서)
57	accomplish	달성하다, 성취하다, 해내다	77	proof	증명(서), 증거(물)
58	division	부서, 분과	78	separate	각각의, 별개의, 분리된
59	domestic	국내의, 가정(용)의	79	on-site	현장의
60	interconnectedness	상호 연결됨	80	charge	비용, 요금

PART 04 중심 내용 파악 유형

ANSWER

01 ③	02 ①	03 ④	04 ②	05 ④
06 ①	07 ④	08 ①	09 ③	10 ③
11 ③	12 ①	13 ②	14 ②	15 ②
16 ④	17 ②	18 ③	19 ①	20 ③
21 ①	22 ④	23 ①	24 ②	25 ③
26 ④	27 ④	28 ①	29 ③	30 ②
31 ①	32 ③	33 ③	34 ④	35 ①
36 ④	37 ③	38 ③	39 ②	

01
정답 ③

정답 해설

이 글 초반부에는 젊은이들의 잠재력을 강조하면서, 특히 농업 분야에서 젊은 농부들이 수행하는 중요한 역할을 이야기하고 중반부 이후부터는 그들이 겪는 어려움(토지 소유 문제, 대출 접근성, 기후 리스크 등)에 대해 설명하고 있다. 따라서 글의 주제로 가장 적절한 것은 ③이다.

지문 해석

젊은 사람들은 학습 속도가 빠르다. 그들은 에너지가 넘치고, 활동적이며, '할 수 있다'는 사고방식을 가지고 있다. 지원과 적절한 기회가 주어지면, 그들은 자신의 성장뿐 아니라 지역 사회 발전에서도 주도적인 역할을 할 수 있다. 많은 개발 도상국에서 농업은 여전히 가장 큰 고용 사업체이며, 젊은 농부들은 미래 세대의 식량 안보를 책임지는 데 중요한 역할을 한다. 하지만 그들은 많은 어려움에 직면해 있다. 예를 들어, 집이 없으면 토지를 소유하거나 대출을 받기가 매우 어렵다. 그런데 젊은 사람들은 경력을 시작하는 단계이기 때문에 집이 없는 경우가 많다. 농업에 종사하는 것은 많은 장기적인 투자를 필요로 한다. 그것은 또한 상당히 위험하고 불확실한데, 왜냐하면 그것이 기후에 크게 의존하기 때문이다. 홍수, 가뭄, 폭풍은 농부들의 농작물을 손상시키거나 파괴할 수 있으며, 가축에도 영향을 줄 수 있다.

선지 해석

① 농업 분야에서 일하는 것의 경제적 이점
② 현대 농업 방식에서 기술의 중요성
③ 젊은 농부들의 역할과 그들이 직면한 도전들
④ 도시 개발을 위한 젊은이들의 노력

지문 어휘

☐ fast 빠른
☐ mentality 사고방식
☐ developing country 개발 도상국
☐ agriculture 농업
☐ employer 고용 사업체, 고용주
☐ security 안보, 보안, 경비
☐ face 직면하다
☐ challenge 어려움, 도전
☐ loan 대출하다, 빌려주다
☐ long-term 장기적인
☐ investment 투자
☐ risky 위험한
☐ uncertain 불확실한, 불안정한
☐ rely on 의존하다
☐ climate 기후
☐ flooding 홍수, 범람
☐ drought 가뭄
☐ storm 폭풍(우)
☐ livestock 가축

02
정답 ①

정답 해설

이 글은 글 초반부에 인공 청색광이 저녁에 해로운 이유를 설명하고, 글 중반부에는 햇빛에서 받는 자연 청색광은 오히려 건강에 이로운 반대 효과를 보인다고 언급한다. 이후에는 낮 동안 햇빛에 충분히 노출되면 저녁에 인공 청색광으로 인한 해로운 영향을 완화할 수 있다는 점을 설명하며 햇빛이 인공 청색광의 부작용을 줄이는 데 도움이 된다고 이야기하고 있다. 따라서 글의 주제로 가장 적절한 것은 ①이다.

지문 해석

기기에서 나오는 인공 청색광이 저녁에 매우 해로울 수도 있는 이유는, 그것이 태양의 자연 청색광을 흉내 내기 때문인데, 이것이 신체의 생체 시계를 혼란스럽게 만든다. 한 연구에 따르면, 저녁 시간에 인공 청색광을 보면, 수면을 유도하는 멜라토닌 호르몬의 분비가 급격히 감소하여, 취침 시간에 지장을 주고 낮 동안의 행동에도 영향을 미친다고 한다. 하지만 같은 청색광일지라도 햇빛에서 받는 자연 청색광은 그와 반대 효과를 보이는데, 햇빛은 건강을 증진시키는 광범위한 스펙트럼의 빛을 포함하고 있기 때문이다. 연구에 따르면, 낮 동안 청색광을 많이 받을수록, 저녁에 화면에서 나오는 인공 청색광의 해로운 영향을 방어할 수 있는 능력이 커진다고 한다. 따라서 하루를 햇빛으로 채우는 것은 청색광의 축적을 만들어내어 밤에 그 인공 청색광이 주는 영향을 상쇄하는 데 도움이 된다. 다시 말해서, 아이들이 낮에 햇빛에 많이 노출될수록, 나중에 인공 청색광의 해로움으로부터 그들의 뇌가 방어벽을 더 잘 구축할 수 있다.

선지 해석

① 인공 청색광의 영향에 대항하는 데 있어 햇빛의 도움
② 낮 동안 기기를 사용하는 것의 위험성
③ 화면이 아이들의 수면 주기에 영향을 미치는 방식
④ 저녁에 멜라토닌 수치가 떨어지는 이유

지문 어휘

☐ artificial 인공의, 인조의
☐ blue light 청색광
☐ mimic 흉내내다, 모방하다
☐ circadian clock 생체 시계

- drastically 급격히
- disrupt 방해하다, 지장을 주다
- opposite 반대의
- counteract 상쇄하다, 대응하다
- consequence 영향, 결과
- exposure 노출, 폭로
- harm 해로움, 피해

03

정답 ④

정답 해설

우주 정거장에서의 혁신적인 야생 동물 모니터링에 대한 글로, 국제 우주 정거장이 새로운 장비를 통해 야생 동물 모니터링을 혁신하고, 동물의 위치와 생리학적 데이터, 환경 정보를 수집하여 생태계 건강을 분석함을 설명하고 있다. 따라서 글의 주제로 가장 적절한 것은 ④이다.

지문 해석

> 국제 우주 정거장이 지구에서 약 240마일 상공을 돌며 세계의 야생 동물을 모니터링하고 동물 추적 과학에 혁신을 일으킬 준비를 하고 있다. 2018년 우주 유영을 한 러시아 우주인들이 설치한 대형 안테나와 기타 장비가 테스트 중이며, 올 여름에는 완전히 운영될 예정이다. 이 시스템은 이전 추적 기술보다 훨씬 넓은 범위의 데이터를 전달하며, 동물의 위치뿐만 아니라 생리학과 환경까지 기록할 수 있다. 이는 야생 동물의 이동을 밀접하게 모니터링을 해야 하는 과학자, 환경 보호 활동가 및 기타 연구자들에게 도움을 주며, 세계 생태계의 건강에 대한 보다 자세한 정보를 제공할 것이다.

선지 해석

① 지구 생태계의 지속 가능성 평가
② 러시아 우주비행사들의 성공적인 훈련 프로젝트
③ 궤도 전초기지에서 행해진 동물 실험
④ 우주 정거장에서 혁신적인 야생 동물 모니터링

지문 어휘

- space station 우주 정거장
- orbit 궤도를 돌다, 궤도, 영향권
- revolutionize 혁신을 일으키다
- install 설치하다, 설비하다
- spacewalk 우주 유영
- relay 전달하다, 중계하다
- previous 이전의, 바로 앞의
- physiology 생리학
- conservationist 환경 보호 활동가

04

정답 ②

정답 해설

글의 주된 내용은 동물 질병 발생에 대한 준비와 대응의 중요성을 강조하고 있다. BOAH는 동물 질병 발생에 대비하는 것을 최우선 과제로 삼고 있으며, 이는 동물 질병 전염이 경제적 피해와 공공 건강에 미치는 영향을 고려한 것이다. 따라서 글의 요지로 가장 적절한 것은 ②이다.

지문 해석

> **동물 건강 비상 사태**
> 동물 질병 발생에 대한 준비는 수십 년 동안 동물 건강 위원회(BOAH)의 최우선 과제가 되어 왔습니다. 전염성이 매우 높은 동물 질병 사건은 공중 보건이나 식품 안전 및 보안 결과뿐만 아니라 경제적으로 파괴적인 영향을 미칠 수 있습니다.
>
> **외국 동물 질병**
> 외국 동물 질병(FAD)은 현재 해당 국가에서 발견되지 않는 질병으로, 동물에게 심각한 질병이나 사망을 초래할 수 있으며, 다른 국가 및 주와의 무역 기회를 없애 경제적으로 큰 피해를 줄 수 있습니다.
>
> FAD 진단 교육을 받은 여러 BOAH 수의사들이 24시간 대기 중이며, FAD 의심 사례를 조사합니다. 조사는 FAD를 나타내는 임상 징후가 있는 동물에 대한 보고가 접수되거나 진단 실험실에서 의심스러운 검사 결과를 확인할 때 시작됩니다.

선지 해석

① BOAH는 FAD를 위한 수의사 교육에 중점을 둔다.
② BOAH의 주요 목표는 동물 질병 전염에 대응하는 것이다.
③ BOAH는 국제 무역 기회를 적극적으로 추진한다.
④ BOAH는 FAD의 원인에 대한 연구를 주도하는 것을 목표로 한다.

지문 어휘

- preparedness 준비, 각오
- outbreak 발생, 발발
- top priority 최우선(과제)
- contagious 전염되는, 전염성의
- devastating 파괴적인, 충격적인
- consequence 결과, 중요함
- currently 현재, 지금
- extensive 아주 넓은, 대규모의, 광범위한
- eliminate 없애다, 제거하다
- veterinarian 수의사
- diagnose 진단하다
- investigate 조사하다, 수사하다
- clinical 임상의
- indicative ~을 나타내는[보여주는], 직설법의

05

정답 ④

정답 해설
살모넬라에 의한 식중독의 예방을 위한 글로, 식약처는 식중독 증가 사례를 경고하며, 계란을 만질 때 손을 씻지 않아 음식이나 도구를 준비할 때 식품 중독이 발생할 수 있다고 경고했다. 특히, 살모넬라 박테리아에 의한 식중독이 증가하고 있으며, 식품 안전을 위해 계란을 냉장하고 완전히 익혀야 함을 강조하고 있다. 따라서 글의 주제로 적절한 것은 ④이다.

지문 해석
식품의약품안전처는 음식을 준비하거나 도구를 사용하기 전에 사람들이 달걀을 만지고 손을 씻는 것에 소홀하는 교차 오염의 결과로 식중독 사례가 발생했다고 경고했다. 이러한 위험을 완화시키기 위해 식약처는 달걀을 냉장 보관하고 노른자와 흰자가 모두 단단해질 때까지 그것들을 완전히 익힐 것을 권고했다. 지난 5년간, 놀랍게도 7,400명의 사람들이 살모넬라균에 의해 야기된 식중독을 경험했다. 살모넬라균은 따뜻한 온도에서 번성하며, 대략 섭씨 37도가 최적의 성장 조건이다. 날달걀 또는 설익은 달걀을 먹고 날음식과 익힌 음식을 분리하지 못하는 것이 살모넬라균 감염의 가장 흔한 원인으로 확인되었다. 살모넬라균과 관련된 질병의 위험을 최소화하기 위해 식품 안전 조치를 우선시하고 적절한 조리 관행을 지키는 것이 중요하다.

선지 해석
① 면역 체계에 계란 섭취가 미치는 이점들
② 살모넬라 감염에 대한 다양한 치료법들
③ 따뜻한 온도에서 살모넬라 박테리아의 수명
④ 살모넬라 감염 예방을 위한 계란의 안전한 취급 방법

지문 어휘
- ministry (정부의 각) 부처, 목사, 성직자
- food poisoning 식중독
- utensil 도구, 기구, 가정용품
- advise 권고하다, 충고하다, 조언하다
- yolk (달걀 등의) 노른자(위)
- firm 단단한, 확고한, 회사
- staggering 놀랍게도, 충격적인, 믿기 어려운, 비틀거리는
- thrive 번성하다, 번영하다, 성장하다, 잘 자라다
- temperature 온도, 기온, 체온
- degree (온도 단위인) 도, 정도, 학위, 등급
- optimal 최적의, 최선의
- raw 날것의, 익히지 않은, 가공되지 않은
- undercooked (음식이) 설익은
- common 흔한, 공동의, 공통의
- infection 감염, 전염병
- prioritize 우선시하다, 우선순위를 매기다, 우선적으로 처리하다
- adhere to 지키다, ~을 고수하다
- minimize 최소화하다, 축소하다
- illness 질병, 질환, 아픔

06

정답 ①

정답 해설
교육격차 해소를 위한 노력과 과제에 대한 글로, 전문가들이 격차를 줄이기 위해 효과적인 개입, 공정한 자원 할당, 포용적인 정책이 필요하고 강조하고 있다. 따라서 글의 요지로 적절한 것은 ①이다.

지문 해석
교육 격차를 해결하기 위한 지속적인 노력에도 불구하고, 학생들 간의 끊임없이 지속되는 성취 격차는 교육 체제의 상당한 불평등을 계속해서 강조하고 있다. 최근 자료들은 저소득층 배경과 취약 계층을 포함한 소외된 학생들이 학업 성적에서 동료들보다 계속 뒤처지고 있음을 보여준다. 격차는 교육 형평성과 사회 이동성을 달성하는 데 어려움을 제기한다. 전문가들은 이러한 격차를 해소하고 사회경제적 지위나 배경에 관계없이 모든 학생들에게 균등한 기회를 보장하기 위해 표적적 개입, 공평한 자원 배분, 포용적 정책의 필요성을 강조한다. 지속적인 교육 격차의 문제는 교육 체제의 모든 수준에서 해결책을 찾기 위한 노력으로 해결되어야 한다.

선지 해석
① 우리는 지속적인 교육 불평등을 해결해야 한다.
② 교육 전문가들은 새로운 학교 정책에 초점을 맞출 필요가 있다.
③ 성취 격차를 해소하기 위해 새로운 교수 방법이 필요하다.
④ 교육 논의에서 가정 소득은 고려되지 않아야 한다.

지문 어휘
- despite ~에도 불구하고
- ongoing 지속적인, 계속 진행 중인
- disparity 격차, 차이
- persistent 끊임없이 지속되는, 끈질긴, 집요한
- highlight 강조하다, 돋보이게 하다
- inequity 불공평, 불공정
- reveal 드러내다, 나타내다, 밝히다
- marginalize ~을 소외되게 하다, 사회적으로 무시하다
- low-income 저소득의
- background 배경, 배후 사정
- vulnerable 취약한, 연약한
- lag behind ~보다 뒤(처)지다, 뒤떨어지다
- pose 제기하다, 두다, 놓다, 자세[태도]를 취하다, ~인 체하다
- challenge 어려움, 도전, 이의를 제기하다
- mobility 이동성, 기동성, 유동성
- emphasize 강조하다
- intervention 개입, 간섭
- equitable 공평한, 공정한
- allocation 배분, 할당
- inclusive 포용적인, 포괄적인, 포함된
- bridge the gap 격차를 해소하다
- status 지위, 신분, 자격
- address 해결하다, 다루다, 연설하다, 주소, 연설

07

정답 ④

정답 해설
Arthur Evans는 크레타 섬의 크노소스 궁전 발굴을 통해 미노아 문화를 실제로 확인했다는 것을 설명하는 글로, 이 글이 강조하는 것은 이것이 신화적 이야기가 아닌 실제 유물과 벽화를 통해 기원전 1900년부터 1450년까지의 미노아 문명이었다는 것이다. 따라서 글의 주제로 가장 적절한 것은 ④이다.

지문 해석
한 사람이 하나의 전체 문화에 우리의 눈을 뜨게 하는 데 책임을 질 수 있다는 것은 믿기 힘든 것 같지만, 영국의 고고학자 Arthur Evans가 크레타섬에 있는 크노소스 궁전의 유적을 성공적으로 발굴하기 전까지 지중해의 위대한 미노스 문화는 사실보다 더 전설에 가까웠다. 실제로 그곳의 가장 유명한 거주자는 신화의 한 생명체 였는데, 반인 반우 미노타우로스였고, 신화 속에 나오는 미노스 왕의 궁전 아래에서 살았다고 전해진다. 그러나 Evans가 증명했듯이 이 왕국은 신화가 아니었다. 20세기 초의 일련의 발굴에서 Evans는 보석류, 조각품, 도자기, 황소의 뿔 모양을 한 제단, 그리고 미노아의 삶을 보여주는 벽화 등 기원전 1900년부터 1450년까지 절정에 달했던 미노스 시대의 귀중한 인공물을 발견했다.

선지 해석
① 미노스 왕의 성공적인 발굴
② 미노아 시대의 유물을 감상하기
③ 크레타섬에 있는 궁전의 웅장함
④ 미노아 문화를 현실의 영역으로 가져오기

지문 어휘
☐ incredible 믿기 어려운, 놀라운
☐ excavate 발굴하다
☐ famed 유명한, 명성이 있는
☐ resident 거주자
☐ mythology 신화학, 신화
☐ excavation 발굴 작업, 발굴 지역
☐ jewelry 보석류
☐ carving 조각품, 새긴 무늬
☐ pottery 도기, 도자기
☐ altar 제단

08

정답 ①

정답 해설
나쁜 화폐의 높은 비율의 귀금속 동전으로 인해 좋은 화폐의 품위가 저하되었다. 좋은 동전은 퇴출되고 나쁜 동전이 유통되며, 왕들은 재발행으로 자금을 보충함을 설명하는 글이다. 따라서 글의 제목으로 가장 적절한 것은 ①이다.

지문 해석
나쁜 화폐 형태에 의한 좋은 화폐의 통화 가치 저하는 더 낮은 가치의 금속으로 희석된 더 낮은 비율의 금이나 은으로 재발행된 귀금속의 비율이 높은 동전을 통해 발생했다. 이러한 품질의 조악화는 나쁜 동전으로 좋은 동전을 몰아냈다. 아무도 그들이 보유하고 있던 좋은 동전을 쓰지 않았고 이런 이유로 좋은 동전이 유통에서 사라지게 되었으며 그 비축되었다. 한편, 보통 끊이지 않는 전쟁과 그 밖의 방탕한 생활로 보물을 잃은 왕이었던 발행인이 이러한 조치의 배후였다. 그들은 할 수 있는 모든 좋은 옛 동전을 모아 녹여서 낮은 순도로 재발행하고, 차액을 착복했다. 옛 물건을 다시 보관하는 것은 종종 불법이었지만, 왕이 국고를 보충하는 동안, 적어도 한동안은 사람들은 그렇게 했다.

선지 해석
① 나쁜 화폐가 좋은 화폐를 대체하는 방법
② 좋은 동전의 요소들
③ 왜 동전을 녹이지 말아야 하는가?
④ 나쁜 화폐란 무엇인가?

지문 어휘
☐ currency debasement 통화 훼손, 화폐 가치 하락
☐ occur 발생하다, 일어나다
☐ precious 귀중한, 소중한
☐ dilute 희석하다, 약화시키다
☐ adulteration 불순물 첨가, 오염
☐ out of circulation 순환에서 제외된, 유통에서 제외된
☐ hoard 비축하다, 저장하다
☐ treasure 보물, 귀중품
☐ dissolute 방탕한, 타락한
☐ melt 녹다, 용해되다
☐ illegal 불법적인, 불법의
☐ replenish 보충하다, 채우다
☐ treasury 국고, 재무부
☐ at least 최소한, 적어도

09

정답 ③

정답 해설
라틴 아메리카의 재생 에너지 확대와 그에 따른 석유 의존도 감소에 대한 글이다. 첫 번째 문장에서의 라틴아메리카의 재생 가능한 에너지의 큰 발전에 대한 진술을 바탕으로 석유 의존도가 감소함의 구체적인 사례를 들고 있다. 따라서 글의 주제로 적절한 것은 ③이다.

지문 해석
최근 몇 년 동안 라틴 아메리카는 풍력, 태양력, 지열 및 바이오연료 등 놀라운 재생 에너지 자원을 적극적으로 활용하는 데 큰 진전을 이루었다. 라틴 아메리카의 전력 부문은 이미 석유에 대한 의존도를 점차적으로 줄이기 시작했다. 2015년에서 2040년 사이에 라틴 아메리카의 전력 생산량은 거의 두 배로 늘어날 것으로 예상된다. 라틴 아메리카의 새로운 대규모 발전소 중 사실상 석유를 연료로 사용하는 곳은 없어질 것이며, 이는 다양한 기술의 발전을 가져올 것이다. 전통적으로 석유를 수입해 왔던 중앙아메리카와 카리브해 국가들이 이 세기 초반 10년 동안 높고 불안정한 가격에 시달리다가 가장 먼저 석유 기반 발전소에서 벗어나기 시작했다.

선지 해석
① 라틴 아메리카의 호황을 누리는 석유 산업
② 라틴 아메리카의 쇠퇴하는 전력 사업
③ 라틴 아메리카의 재생 가능 에너지 발전
④ 라틴 아메리카의 석유 기반 자원의 공격적인 개발

지문 어휘
☐ stride 큰 발전, 큰 걸음, 성큼성큼 걷다
☐ exploit 이용하다, 착취하다
☐ geothermal 지열의

- biofuel 바이오 연료
- large-scale 대규모의, 광범한
- import 수입하다, 수입(품)
- volatile 변동성이 큰, 불안한, 휘발성의

10

정답 ③

정답 해설
조직 리더로서 자원 관리의 중요성을 강조하는 글로, 두 번째 그리고 세 번째 문장에서 '조직의 리더로서 그러한 자원의 사용을 더 효율적 그리고 효과적으로 만들어야 한다'고 진술하고 있다. 따라서 글의 제목으로 적절한 것은 ③이다.

지문 해석
모든 조직은 자신의 목표를 달성하기 위해 사용할 수 있는 자원을 가지고 있다. 당신의 조직이 얼마나 잘 수행하는지는 부분적으로 보유한 자원의 양에 달려있지만, 대부분은 사람과 돈과 같은 자원을 얼마나 잘 활용하는지에 달려있다. 당신이 조직의 리더로서 조직의 인력과 의제를 통제할 수 있다면, 언제든 그 자원의 활용을 더 효율적이고 효과적으로 만들 수 있다. 이는 자동적으로 일어나는 것은 아니다. 사람과 자금을 신중하게 관리하고, 가장 중요한 것을 가장 중요한 것으로 여기며, 좋은 결정을 내리고, 마주하는 문제를 해결함으로써, 당신이 가진 것을 최대한 활용할 수 있다.

선지 해석
① 조직 내 자원 교환하기
② 외부 통제를 설정하는 리더의 능력
③ 자원을 최대한 활용하기: 리더의 방식
④ 조직의 기술적 역량: 성공의 장애물

지문 어휘
- organization 조직, 단체, 준비, 구성
- function 기능, 행사, 기능하다
- efficient 효율적인, 능률적인, 유능한
- effective 효과적인, 실질적인
- control 통제, 지배, 지배하다, 제한하다
- personnel 인원, 직원들, 인사과
- agenda 의제, 안건
- encounter 만나다, 직면하다
- available 이용할[구할] 수 있는

11

정답 ③

정답 해설
사랑과 안전감을 만드는 비언어적인 신호의 힘을 주제로 하는 글로, 비언어적인 신호는 우리에게 사랑받는 느낌을 줄 뿐 아니라 안전하고 스트레스를 완화하는 효과가 있다는 것을 강조하는 글이다. 첫 번째 문장이 이 글의 주제문으로 '사랑받는 느낌과 그것이 유발하는 생물학적 반응은 언어적인 요소가 아닌 비언어적인 신호에 의해 유발된다'고 진술한 다음 동물에서의 구체적인 예를 들어 설명하고 있다. 따라서 글의 제목으로 가장 알맞은 것은 ③이다.

지문 해석
사랑받는 느낌과 그것이 자극하는 생물학적 반응은 목소리의 톤, 얼굴 표정, 적절한 감촉 같은 비언어적인 신호에 의해 유발된다. 비언어적인 신호는 발화되는 말보다 우리가 함께 있는 사람이 우리에게 관심이 있고, 우리를 이해하며 소중하게 여기고 있다고 느끼게 해준다. 우리가 그들과 함께 있을 때, 우리는 안전하다고 느낀다. 우리는 심지어 야생에서 비언어적인 신호의 힘을 본다. 포식자들의 추적을 피한 후에, 동물들은 종종 스트레스 해소의 수단으로 서로 코를 비빈다. 이러한 신체 접촉은 안전에 대한 확신을 제공하고 스트레스를 완화한다.

선지 해석
① 야생 동물은 어떻게 생각하고 느끼는가?
② 효과적인 의사소통이 성공의 비결이다
③ 비언어적인 의사소통은 말보다 더 크게 말한다
④ 언어적인 신호: 감정을 표현하는 주요 수단

지문 어휘
- biological 생물학의
- trigger 촉발시키다, 일으키다, 방아쇠
- nonverbal 비언어적인
- evade 피하다, 회피하다
- chase 뒤쫓다, 추적하다
- predator 포식자
- nuzzle 코를 비벼대다, 코로 구멍을 파다
- means 수단, 방법, 수입
- reassurance 안심, 안도, 확신
- relieve 완화하다, 줄이다

12

정답 ①

정답 해설
장난감을 통해 아이에게 건강한 비의존성을 가르치는 방법을 주제로 하는 글로, 장난감과 선물이 많이 모일 때, 건강한 비의존성을 가르치기 위해 아이를 장난감으로 둘러싸지 않고, 바구니에 정리하고, 회전시키며, 애착 없는 태도를 모델로 삼도록 하라는 제안을 하는 글이다. 특히 2번째 문장의 '당신은 이 시간들을 사물에 대한 건강한 비의존성을 가르치기 위해 사용할 수 있다'의 내용을 바탕으로 글의 주제로 가장 알맞은 것은 ①이다.

지문 해석
명절이나 생일처럼 아이의 삶에서 장난감과 선물이 모이는 시기가 있다. 당신은 이러한 시기들을 물건에 대한 건강한 비의존성을 가르치는 데 사용할 수 있다. 당신의 아이를 장난감들로 둘러싸지 마라. 대신에, 그것들을 바구니에 정리하고, 한 번에 한 바구니씩 꺼내 놓고, 가끔 바구니를 교체해라. 소중히 간직한 물건을 잠시 치워두면, 그것을 꺼내는 것이 즐거운 기억과 관점의 새로움을 만든다. 당신의 아이가 잠시 치워둔 장난감을 요구한다고 가정해 보자. 당신은 이미 주변 환경에 있는 물건 혹은 경험으로 주의를 돌릴 수 있다. 만약 당신이 소유물을 잃어버리거나 깨뜨린다면, 당신의 아이가 무집착의 태도를 발달시키기 시작할 수 있도록 좋은 태도("나는 그것을 가지고 있는 동안 감사했어!")를 만들도록 노력해라. 만약 그녀의 장난감이 망가지거나 잃어버린다면, "나는 그것으로 즐거운 시간을 보냈어."라고 말할 수 있도록 도와줘라.

선지 해석

① 소유물에 대한 건강한 태도를 형성하는 것
② 다른 사람들과 장난감을 공유하는 것의 가치를 배우는 것
③ 장난감을 질서정연하게 정리하는 방법을 가르치는 것
④ 좋지 않은 방식으로 행동한 책임을 받아들이는 것

지문 어휘

- accumulate 모으다, 축적하다
- nondependency 비의존성
- surround 둘러싸다, 에워싸다
- rotate 회전시키다
- cherish 소중히 여기다, 아끼다, 간직하다
- put away 넣다, 치우다
- delightful 즐거운, 매우 기쁜
- freshness 새로움, 신선함
- outlook 관점, 전망, 시야
- possession 소유물, 소지품
- nonattachment 무집착, 집착없음
- direct ~로 돌리다, 향하다, 겨냥하다
- broken 깨진, 부서진, 고장난

13

정답 ②

정답 해설

자녀 칭찬 방법이 자녀들의 발달에 영향을 미치는 중요성을 주제로 하는 글로, 부모들이 자녀의 자존감을 높이기 위해 자녀의 지능을 칭찬하는 것은 자녀들이 실패했을 때 능력 부족의 탓으로 보고 미래의 성취노력에서 성과가 좋지 않음을 지적하고 있다. 따라서 글의 요지로 가장 알맞은 것은 '자녀의 칭찬하는 방법'의 핵심어가 있고, '지능에 대한 칭찬의 부정적인 진술'이 있는 ②이다.

지문 해석

많은 부모들은 "자존감 운동"에 의해 잘못 인도되었는데, 이 운동은 그들의 아이들의 자존감을 높이는 방법이 자녀들에게 그들이 일을 얼마나 잘 하는지 알려주는 것이라고 말해왔다. 불행하게도, 자녀에게 그들의 능력에 대해 확신시키려는 시도는 실패할 가능성이 높은데, 왜냐하면 인생은 성공과 실패를 통해 그들이 실제로 얼마나 능력이 있고 능력이 없는지를 분명하게 말해주기 때문이다. 연구는 자녀를 어떻게 칭찬하는지가 자녀의 발달에 강력한 영향을 미친다는 것을 보여준다. 몇몇 연구원들은 그들의 노력에 비해 그들의 지능으로 칭찬받은 아이들이 결과에 지나치게 집중하게 되었다는 것을 발견했다. 실패 후에 이러한 아이들은 덜 지속했고, 적은 즐거움을 보여주며, 실패를 능력 부족의 탓으로 여기고, 미래의 성취 노력에서도 저조한 성과를 보였다. 아이들의 지능을 칭찬하는 것은 그들이 실패를 어리석음과 동일시하기 시작했기 때문에 어려움을 두려워하게 만들었다.

선지 해석

① 빈번한 칭찬이 아이들의 자존감을 높인다.
② 지능에 대한 칭찬은 부정적인 효과를 초래한다.
③ 아이는 성공을 통해 실패에 대한 두려움을 극복해야 한다.
④ 부모는 과정보다 결과에 집중해야 한다.

지문 어휘

- misguide 잘못 이끌다, 그릇되게 지도하다, 잘못 인식시키다
- self-esteem 자부심, 자존감
- movement 움직임, 행동
- competence 능력, 능숙함
- fail 실패하다
- unequivocally 명백하게, 분명하게
- influence 영향
- development 발달
- praise 칭찬, 칭찬하다
- intelligence 지능
- focused 집중한, 집중적인
- persist 지속하다, 집요하게[끈질기게] 계속하다
- attribute ~의 탓으로 보다, 속성, 특성, 특질
- equate 동일시하다
- stupidity 어리석음, 우둔함

14

정답 ②

정답 해설

인간의 뇌의 사교적인 기능을 주제로 하는 글로, Daniel Goleman의 연구 결과를 인용하면서 자신의 주장을 펼치고 있다. 우리의 뇌는 상대방과의 관계에 끌리며, 의미 있는 연결성이 필요하지만 우리는 점점 외로움을 느끼고 외로워지고 있다고 믿는다고 말한다. 그럼에도 불구하고 우리의 뇌는 인간과의 상호작용을 갈망한다고 진술하고 있다. 따라서 글의 제목으로 가장 적절한 것은 ②이다.

지문 해석

유명한 작가인 Daniel Goleman은 인간관계의 과학에 평생을 바쳐왔다. 그의 책 '사회적 지능'에서는 우리의 뇌가 얼마나 사교적인지 설명하기 위해 신경 사회학의 결과들을 논한다. Goleman에 따르면, 우리는 다른 사람과 관계를 맺을 때마다 다른 사람의 뇌에 끌린다. 우리의 관계를 깊게 하기 위해 다른 사람들과 의미 있는 연결성을 가지고자 하는 인간의 욕구는 우리가 갈망하는 것이지만 우리가 어느 때보다 더 외롭고, 외로움은 전 세계적인 건강 유행병이라는 것을 시사하는 수많은 기사와 연구들이 있다. 특히 호주에서 실시된 국립 Lifeline 조사에 따르면 조사대상자들의 80% 이상이 우리 사회가 더 외로운 곳이 되어가고 있다고 믿고 있다. 하지만 우리의 뇌는 인간과의 상호 작용을 갈망한다.

선지 해석

① 외로운 사람들
② 사교적인 두뇌
③ 정신 건강 조사의 필요성
④ 인간과의 연결성의 위험성

지문 어휘

- well-known 유명한, 잘 알려진
- author 작가
- dedicate 바치다, 전념하다
- discuss 논의하다, 상의하다
- neuro-sociology 신경 사회학
- sociable 사교적인, 붙임성 있는
- engage 관여하다
- connectivity 연결성
- be drawn (마음이) 끌리다
- crave 갈망하다, 열망하다
- countless 무수한
- lonely 외로운
- article 글, 기사
- epidemic 유행성의, 전염성의, 유행병

15

정답 ②

정답 해설
잠재된 재능을 성공으로 이끌기 위한 방법을 주제로 하는 글로, 장점을 타고난 사람들도 수년간의 신중한 연습으로 그 장점을 재능으로 발전시킬 수 있고, 장점이 없는 사람들 또한 의도적인 연습을 통해 멀리 놓은 재능을 개발할 수 있음을 강조하고 있다. 따라서 글의 주제로 가장 적절한 것은 ②이다.

지문 해석
확실히 일부 사람들은 장점을 가지고 태어난다 (예를 들어, 기수에 적합한 신체 크기, 농구 선수에 적합한 키, 음악가에 적합한 "귀"). 그러나 수년간의 의식하고 의도적인 연습에 대한 전념만이 그러한 장점들을 재능으로 그리고 그 재능을 성공으로 바꿀 수 있다. 동일한 종류의 헌신적인 연습을 통해, 그러한 장점을 타고나지 않은 사람들도 천성이 그들이 닿기 어려운 곳에 조금 더 멀리 놓은 재능을 개발할 수 있다. 예를 들어, 당신은 수학에 재능이 없다고 느낄지라도, 의식하고 의도적인 연습을 통해 수학적 능력을 상당히 향상시킬 수 있다. 또는 자기 자신이 "본래" 수줍음이 많다고 생각한다면, 시간과 노력을 들여 사교적 기술을 개발함으로써 사회적인 행사에서 활기 있게, 우아하게, 그리고 쉽게 사람들과 상호작용할 수 있다.

선지 해석
① 어떤 사람들이 다른 사람들에 비해 가지고 있는 장점들
② 재능을 기르기 위한 끊임없는 노력의 중요성
③ 수줍은 사람들이 사회적 상호작용에서 겪는 어려움들
④ 자신의 강점과 약점을 이해할 필요성

지문 어휘
☐ jockey (경마에서 특히 직업적으로 말을 타는) 기수
☐ height 키, 신장
☐ dedication 헌신, 전념
☐ deliberate 고의의, 의도적인, 신중한, 사려 깊은
☐ shy 수줍음을 타는
☐ put in 쏟다, 들이다
☐ grace 우아함
☐ ease 쉬움, 용이함

16

정답 ④

정답 해설
바이러스와 식물의 상호작용을 주제로 하는 글로, Roossinck 박사와 동료들은 우연히 바이러스가 가뭄에 대한 내성을 증가시키는 것을 발견하고, 추가 실험을 통해 이것이 여러 식물에도 적용된다는 것을 확인했음을 보여주는 글이다. 따라서 글의 요지로 가장 적절한 것은 ④이다.

지문 해석
Roossinck 박사와 그녀의 동료들은 우연히 한 바이러스가 식물 실험에서 널리 사용되는 식물에서 가뭄에 대한 저항성을 증가시키는 것을 발견했다. 관련된 바이러스로 진행된 추가 실험은 그것이 15개의 다른 식물 종에도 사실이라는 것을 보여줬다. Roossinck 박사는 지금 다양한 식물의 내열성을 증가시키는 다른 유형의 바이러스를 연구하기 위한 실험을 진행하고 있다. 그녀는 다양한 종류의 바이러스가 숙주에게 제공하는 이점들에 대한 더 깊은 이해를 하기 위해 자신의 연구를 확장하기를 희망한다. 이는 점점 더 많은 생물학자들이 가지고 있는 견해인 많은 생물들이 자립이 아닌 공생에 의존한다는 것을 뒷받침하는 데 도움이 될 것이다.

선지 해석
① 바이러스는 생물학적 존재의 자급자족을 보여준다.
② 생물학자들은 식물들을 바이러스가 없는 상태로 유지하기 위해 모든 것을 해야 한다.
③ 공생의 원리는 감염된 식물에 적용될 수 없다.
④ 바이러스는 때때로 숙주에게 해를 끼치기보다는 이롭다.

지문 어휘
☐ colleague 동료
☐ resistance 저항력, 내성
☐ drought 가뭄
☐ botanical 식물(학)의
☐ further 더 이상의, 추가의
☐ related 관련된
☐ heat tolerance 내열성
☐ a range of 다양한
☐ extend 확장하다, 연장하다
☐ host 숙주
☐ biologist 생물학자
☐ rely on 의지하다
☐ symbiosis 공생
☐ do good (~에게) 이롭다, 도움이 되다

17

정답 ②

정답 해설
성공적인 앵커가 되기 위한 자격들을 설명하는 글로, 앵커로서의 역할과 필요한 능력에 대한 가이드라인을 제시하고 있다. 2번째 문장부터 앵커로서 가져야 할 능력들을 나열하고 있다. 따라서 글의 주제로 가장 적절한 것은 ②이다.

지문 해석
당신은 성공적인 앵커가 되고 싶은가? 그렇다면 이 점을 명심해라. 앵커로서, 개인은 뉴스 방송, 특별 보도 및 기타 유형의 뉴스 프로그램 동안 시청자에게 뉴스와 정보를 전달하도록 요청받을 것이다. 이것은 뉴스 사건을 해석하는 것, 즉흥적으로 이야기하는 것, 그리고 대본을 사용할 수 없을 때 효과적으로 뉴스 속보를 전달하는 것을 포함할 것이다. 앵커 업무는 또한 이야기를 모으고 쓰는 것을 포함한다. 앵커는 대본을 명확하고 효과적으로 전달할 수 있어야 한다. 강력한 글쓰기 능력, 믿을 수 있는 뉴스 판단력, 그리고 시각적 스토리텔링의 강한 감각은 필수적인 기술이다. 이 사람은 정보원을 양성하고 새로운 정보를 직업의 정기적인 부분으로 찾는 자발적으로 행동하는 사람이어야 한다. 발생하는 대로 뉴스 속보를 즉흥적으로 하고 설명할 수 있는 능력뿐만 아니라 생방송 보도 기술도 중요하다.

선지 해석
① 생방송 뉴스 제작의 어려움들
② 뉴스 앵커가 되기 위한 자격들
③ 저널리스트의 사회적 역할의 중요성
④ 올바른 여론 형성의 중요성

지문 어휘
☐ anchor 앵커
☐ call upon 요청하다
☐ communicate 전달하다, 의사소통을 하다
☐ script 원고, 대본
☐ interpret 해석하다, 이해하다

- [ ] adlib 각본에 없는 대사를 말하다, 즉흥적으로 하다
- [ ] breaking news 뉴스 속보
- [ ] gathering 수집, 모임
- [ ] solid 믿을 수 있는, 견고한, 고체의, 단단한
- [ ] self-starter 자발적으로 행동하는 사람
- [ ] cultivate 양성하다, 경작하다, 재배하다
- [ ] journalist 저널리스트, 기자, 언론인

18 정답 ③

정답 해설

화장품과 초상화 사진의 상호작용에 대한 글로, 화장품이 초상화와 어떻게 상호작용하며 미적 가치를 높였는지에 대해 설명하고 있다. 특히, 자신의 초상화 사진의 피부를 더 밝게 보이게 원하는 사람들의 요청으로, 초상화 사진에 화장품을 사용한다는 진술과 이러한 사진들을 바탕으로 화장품 광고를 한다는 진술이 '3번째, 4번째' 문장을 통해서 설명하고 있다. 따라서 글의 주제로 가장 적절한 것은 ③이다.

지문 해석

화장품은 인물 사진 기법과 매우 밀접하게 연관되어 있어서 일부 사진술 입문서들은 그것들을 위한 비법이 포함되어 있었다. 미국의 사진작가들도, 때때로, 원판과 인화사진을 수정하기 위해 화장품을 사용했고, 약간의 루즈로 여성들의 얼굴에 활기를 띠게 했다. 어두운 피부를 가진 몇몇 고객들은 그들을 더 밝아 보일 수 있는 사진을 요청했다. 1935년 아프리카계 미국인 신문에 등장한 피부 미백 광고는 잡티가 없는 더 밝은 피부를 만들 수 있는 그것의 제품이 사진작가들이 만들어낸 것과 같은 모습을 이룰 수 있다고 약속함으로써 이 관행을 언급했다. 얼굴에 관심을 끌고 화장품 사용을 장려함으로써, 인물 사진은 매끄럽고 종종 밝은 색의 피부에 대한 미적 가치를 높였다.

선지 해설

① 화장품의 과도한 사용의 부작용
② 사진작가들에 의해 조장된 화장품의 남용
③ 얼굴을 더 좋게 만들기 위한 화장품의 적극적인 사용
④ 사진술의 발달로 인한 줄어든 화장품의 사용

지문 어휘

- [ ] cosmetic 화장품
- [ ] photography 사진술, 사진 찍기
- [ ] portraiture 인물 사진 기법, 초상화, 초상화법
- [ ] handbook 입문서, 안내서
- [ ] recipe 비결, 비법, 요리법
- [ ] retouch 수정하다, 손질하다
- [ ] negative 원판, 음화, 부정적인
- [ ] trace 약간, 조금, 자취, 흔적, 추척하다
- [ ] enliven 생기를 주다, 활기를 띠게 하다
- [ ] skin lightener 피부 미백제
- [ ] aesthetic 미적인
- [ ] excessive 과도한, 지나친
- [ ] overuse 남용, 남용하다
- [ ] decreased 줄어든

19 정답 ①

정답 해설

전자와 빛의 상호작용하는 방식으로 레이저 발생 원리를 설명하는 글이다. 따라서 글의 제목으로 가장 적절한 것은 ①이다.

지문 해석

레이저는 빛이 전자와 상호작용하는 방식 때문에 가능하다. 전자는 그 특정한 원자나 분자의 특정한 에너지 준위 또는 상태에서 존재한다. 에너지 준위는 고리 또는 핵 주위의 궤도로 생각될 수 있다. 외부 고리의 전자는 내부 고리에 있는 전자들보다 더 높은 에너지 준위에 있다. 전자는 예를 들어, 빛의 섬광과 같은 에너지 주입에 의해 더 높은 에너지 준위로 상승할 수 있다. 전자가 외부에서 내부로 떨어질 때, "과잉" 에너지는 빛으로 방출된다. 방출된 빛의 파장 또는 색상은 방출되는 에너지의 양과 정확하게 관련이 있다. 사용되는 특정 레이저 물질에 따라, 특정 파장의 빛이 흡수되고 (전자를 활성화하거나 촉발시키기 위해) 특정 파장이 방출된다 (전자가 초기의 준위로 떨어질 때).

선지 해석

① 레이저는 어떻게 만들어지는가?
② 레이저는 언제 발명되었는가?
③ 레이저는 어떤 전자를 방출하는가?
④ 전자는 왜 빛을 반사하나?

지문 어휘

- [ ] electron 전자
- [ ] atom 원자
- [ ] molecule 분자
- [ ] particular 특정한, 특별한, 개별적인
- [ ] orbit 궤도, 궤도를 돌다
- [ ] nucleus (원자)핵, 중심
- [ ] injection 주입
- [ ] bump up ~을 올리다
- [ ] give off (냄새·열·빛 등을) 내다[발하다]
- [ ] emit 방출하다, 내뿜다
- [ ] wavelength 파장 길이
- [ ] energize 활성화시키다, 활기를 돋우다
- [ ] excite 흥분시키다, 자극하다, 불러일으키다, 촉발시키다

20 정답 ③

정답 해설

일본과 미국 학생들을 예로 들면서, 문화마다 다른 시각을 가지고 있음을 설명하는 글이다. 실험의 결과로 중심의 물고기에 대해서는 동일한 수를 언급했지만, 일본 학생들은 미국 학생들에 비해 비활성화된 것들에 대해서는 60% 이상 혹은 두 배 이상 언급을 했음을 밝히고 있다. 따라서 글의 제목으로 가장 적절한 것은 ③이다.

지문 해석

다른 문화권의 사람들은 세상을 다르게 보는가? 한 심리학자가 일본과 미국 학생들에게 물고기와 다른 수중 물체의 사실적인 동영상으로 된 장면을 보여주고 그들이 본 것을 보고하도록 요청했다. 미국인들과 일본인들은 중심의 물고기에 대해서는 거의 같은 수로 언급했지만, 일본인들은 물, 바위, 거품, 그리고 비활성 동식물을 포함한 배경 요소에 대해 60% 이상 더 많은 언급을 했다. 게다가, 일본인과 미국인 참가자들이 활동적인 동물들과 관련된 움직임에 대해 거의 같은 수의 언급을 한 반면, 일본인 참가자들은 비활성적이고 배경적인 물체들과 관련된 관계에 대해 거의 두 배나 더 많은 언급을 했다. 아마도 가장 강력하게, 일본 참가자들의 맨 처음 문장은 환경을 언급하는 반면, 미국인들의 첫 번째 문장은 초점 물고기를 언급하는 것일 가능성이 세 배 더 높았다.

선지 해석
① 일본인과 미국인 사이의 언어 장벽
② 뇌에서 물체와 배경의 연관성
③ 인식에 있어서의 문화적 차이
④ 세부적인 것에 더 집중하는 사람들의 우월성

지문 어휘
- view 보다, 여기다
- psychologist 심리학자
- animated 동영상으로 된, 만화 영화로 된, 활기찬
- scene 장면
- make (a) reference 언급하다
- focal 중심의, 초점의
- element 요소
- including ~을 포함하여
- inert 움직이지 않는, 비활성의
- participant 참가자
- tellingly 강력하게
- sentence 문장, 판결, 선고
- refer to ~을 언급[지칭]하다
- the very first 맨 처음
- perception 인지, 자각

21
정답 ①

정답 해설
누군가 제안을 했을 때 그 제안과 관련된 변경사항들을 어떻게 제안해야 하는지 설명하는 글이다. 여러 가지의 사항들이 있더라도 한 번에 제안해야 하는 이유와 그 예시들을 상세히 설명하고 있다. 따라서 글의 요지로 가장 적절한 것은 ①이다.

지문 해석
만약 누군가가 당신에게 제안을 하고 당신이 정당하게 그것의 일부를 걱정한다면, 당신은 보통 당신의 모든 변경사항을 한 번에 제안하는 것이 더 낫다. "월급이 좀 적습니다. 그것에 대해 어떻게 해주실 수 있나요?"라고 말하지 말고, 그러고 나서 그녀가 그것에 노력을 들이자마자, "감사합니다. 이제 제가 원하는 것이 두 가지 더 있습니다..."라고 되돌아가지도 마라. 처음에 한 가지만 요구한다면, 그녀는 그것을 얻는 것이 당신이 그 제안을 받아들일 (또는 최소한의 결정을 내릴) 준비가 될 것으로 생각할지도 모른다. 만약 당신이 계속해서 "그리고 한 가지 더..."라고 말한다면, 그녀는 관대하거나 이해심 있는 기분을 유지할 것 같지 않다. 게다가, 만약 당신이 한 가지 이상의 요청이 있다면, 당신이 원하는 ― A, B, C, 그리고 D ― 모든 것을 단순하게 언급하지 말아라; 또한 당신에게 있어 각각의 상대적인 중요성을 신호로 보내라. 그렇지 않으면, 그녀는 가장 중요하게 생각하지 않는 두 가지를 선택할 수도 있는데, 왜냐하면 그것들은 당신에게 주기 매우 쉽기 때문이고, 그녀는 당신과 타협했다고 느낄지도 모른다.

선지 해석
① 여러 문제를 연속적으로 하지 말고, 동시에 협상하라.
② 성공적인 협상을 위해 민감한 주제를 피하라.
③ 당신의 협상에 적절한 시간을 선택하라.
④ 급여를 협상할 때 너무 직접적이지 않도록 해라.

지문 어휘
- legitimately 정당하게, 합법적으로
- concerned 걱정하는, 관심이 있는
- work on ~에 노력을 들이다, 착수하다
- once ~하자마자, ~할 때
- assume 추정하다, 알다, 띠다
- generous 관대한
- understanding 이해심 있는
- request 요청
- mention 언급하다
- relative 상대적인
- meet halfway 타협하다, 절충하다
- multiple 다수의, 다양한, 복잡한

22
정답 ④

정답 해설
인력 생산성 향상을 위한 다중 작업 방지를 주장하는 글이다. 이 글 곳곳에서 생산성을 향상시키기 위해 에너지 낭비인 다중 작업을 끝내도록 장려해야 한다고 주장하며 글 마지막에 전문가의 견해를 인용하여 하나의 일에 집중하라고 이야기하고 있다. 따라서 글의 제목으로 가장 적절한 것은 ④이다.

지문 해석
직원이 주어진 시간 내에 처리하는 작업(생산된 제품들, 응대받은 고객들)의 양으로 정의되는 ― 개인 생산성 향상을 통한 효율성을 최적화할 수 있는 영역 중 하나는 인력이다. 최적의 성과를 보장하기 위해 당신이 올바른 장비, 환경 및 교육에 투자했는지 확인하는 것뿐만 아니라, 현재의 에너지 낭비인 다중 작업을 끝내도록 장려하여 생산성을 높일 수 있다. 연구들은 당신이 동시에 다른 프로젝트들을 수행하려고 할 때 작업을 완료하는 데 25%에서 40% 더 오래 걸린다는 것을 보여준다. 컨설팅 회사인 The Energy Project의 사업 개발 부사장인 Andrew Deutsher는 생산성을 높이기 위해 "지속적인 기간 동안 중단 없이 한 가지 일을 수행하라."라고 말한다.

선지 해석
① 인생에서 더 많은 선택지를 만드는 방법
② 일상의 신체적 기능을 향상시키는 방법
③ 다중 작업은 더 나은 효율성을 위한 답이다
④ 더 큰 효율성을 위해 하나의 일에 집중하라

지문 어휘
- efficiency 효율성
- optimize 최적화하다
- customer 손님, 고객
- employee 직원, 고용인, 종업원
- equipment 장비
- encourage 장려하다, 격려하다
- multitasking 다중 작업, 멀티태스킹
- energy drain 에너지 낭비
- simultaneously 동시에
- vice president 부사장
- uninterrupted 중단 없는, 방해받지 않는
- sustain 유지하다, 지속시키다

23

정답 ①

정답 해설
사람들이 자신과 비슷하게 옷을 입은 사람들에게 더 많은 도움을 주는 이유에 대한 글이다. 다른 옷을 입은 경우보다 비슷한 옷을 입은 사람들끼리는 상호작용에서 더 긍정적으로 대한다는 것을 보여주는 실험 결과를 설명하고 있다. 따라서 글의 요지로 가장 적절한 것은 ①이다.

지문 해석
젊은이들이 '히피' 또는 '스트레이트' 패션으로 옷을 입는 경향이 있었던 때인 1970년대 초에 행해진 한 연구에서, 실험자들은 히피나 스트레이트 복장을 하고 대학생들에게 전화를 걸어 10센트를 달라고 요청했다. 실험자가 학생과 같은 방식으로 옷을 입었을 때, 그 요청은 사례 중 3분의 2 이상이 받아들여졌고, 학생과 요청자가 다르게 옷을 입었을 때, 10센트짜리 동전은 절반 미만으로 제공되었다. 또 다른 실험은 비슷한 다른 사람에 대한 우리의 긍정적인 반응이 얼마나 자동적일 수 있는지를 보여줬다. 반전 시위에 참가한 시위자들은 비슷한 복장을 한 요청자의 탄원서에 서명할 가능성이 더 높았으며, 그것을 우선 읽어보려고 애를 쓰지 않고도 그렇게 할 가능성이 더 높은 것으로 밝혀졌다.

선지 해석
① 사람들은 자신과 비슷하게 옷을 입은 사람들을 도와줄 가능성이 더 높다.
② 옷을 갖춰 입는 것은 청원서에 서명할 확률을 높인다.
③ 전화를 거는 것은 다른 학생들과 어울리는 효율적인 방법이다.
④ 1970년대 초반에는 일부 대학생이 독특한 패션으로 인해 동경받았다.

지문 어휘
☐ experimenter 실험자
☐ attire 복장, 의복
☐ dime 10센트
☐ requester 요청자
☐ dissimilarly 닮지 않게, 다르게
☐ automatic 자동의, 무의식적인, 반사적인
☐ marcher 시위자, 가두 행진 참가자
☐ antiwar 반전의, 전쟁 반대의
☐ petition 청원(서), 탄원(서), 신청서, 청원하다, 탄원하다
☐ dress up 옷을 갖춰[격식을 차려] 입다
☐ socialize 어울리다, 교제하다, 사귀다
☐ admire 동경하다, 존경하다, 칭찬하다

24

정답 ②

정답 해설
영양과 스포츠 훈련의 관계에 대한 글로, 스포츠 훈련을 위해서는 올바른 영양 섭취와 규칙적인 식사 계획이 필요하며, 이를 소홀히 하면 훈련 성과가 손상될 수 있음을 설명하고 있다. 따라서 글의 주제로 가장 적절한 것은 ②이다.

지문 해석
매일의 훈련은 운동선수, 특히 훈련에 전념하는 것이 거의 전업인 엘리트 운동선수에게 특별한 영양적 필요를 만들어 낸다. 하지만 레크리에이션 스포츠조차도 영양상의 문제를 만들어낼 것이다. 그리고 스포츠에 당신의 관여 수준이 어떻든 간에, 만약 당신이 훈련으로부터 최대의 이득을 달성하려면 이러한 문제들에 대응해야 한다. 건강한 식사 없이는, 당신의 훈련 목적의 많은 부분이 손실될 수 있다. 최악의 경우, 식사 문제와 결핍은 직접적으로 훈련 성과를 손상시킬 수 있다. 다른 상황에서는, 당신은 향상될 수 있지만, 당신의 잠재력에 미치지 못하거나 당신의 경쟁자들보다 느린 속도로 향상될 수 있다. 그러나 긍정적인 측면에서는, 매일 올바른 식사 계획으로, 훈련에 대한 당신의 헌신은 완전히 보상받을 것이다.

선지 해석
① 신체의 유연성을 향상시키는 방법
② 운동에서 잘 먹는 것의 중요성
③ 과도한 다이어트로 인한 건강 문제점들
④ 지속적인 훈련을 통해 기술들을 향상시키기

지문 어휘
☐ nutritional 영양적인, 영양상의
☐ athlete 운동선수
☐ commitment 전념, 헌신, 약속
☐ recreational 레크리에이션, 오락의
☐ involvement 관련, 관여, 몰두
☐ return 이득, 수익, 돌아옴, 반납
☐ sound 건강한, 철저한, 타당한
☐ dietary 식사의, 식이요법의
☐ deficiency 결핍, 부족
☐ flexibility 유연성, 신축성
☐ continuous 지속적인, 계속되는

25

정답 ③

정답 해설
따뜻해지는 기온과 바다의 산소 감소로 인하여 다양한 어종들과 해양 생물들이 줄어들고 있음을 설명하는 글이다. 이에 대해 과학자와 작가 William Cheung의 주장을 추가적으로 부연 설명하고 있다. 따라서 글의 제목으로 가장 적절한 것은 ③이다.

지문 해석
따뜻해지는 기온과 바다의 산소 감소가 — 참다랑어와 농어부터 연어, 진환도 상어, 해덕 그리고 대구까지 — 수백 어종을 이전에 생각했던 것보다 훨씬 더 줄어들게 할 것이라고 새로운 연구는 결론을 내린다. 더 따뜻해진 바다가 그것들의 신진대사를 촉진하기 때문에, 물고기, 오징어 그리고 다른 수중에서 호흡하는 생물들이 바다에서 더 많은 산소를 들이마셔야 할 것이다. 동시에, 따뜻해지고 있는 바다는 이미 바다의 많은 부분에서 산소의 이용 가능성을 줄이고 있다. British Columbia 대학교의 한 쌍의 과학자들은 물고기의 몸이 그것들의 아가미보다 더 빠르게 자라고 있기 때문에, 이러한 동물들은 결국 정상적인 성장을 지속하는 데 충분한 산소를 얻지 못하는 지점에 이를 것이라고 주장한다. "우리가 발견한 것은 물의 온도가 섭씨 1도 높아질 때 물고기의 크기가 20~30퍼센트씩 줄어든다는 것이었다,"라고 저자 William Cheung은 말한다.

선지 해석
① 지금은 물고기가 예전보다 더 빠르게 자란다
② 바다의 온도에 대한 산소의 영향
③ 기후 변화가 세계 어종을 줄어들게 할 수 있다
④ 바다 생물들이 낮은 신진대사로 어떻게 생존하는가

지문 어휘
- oxygen 산소
- shrink 줄어들게 하다, 감소하다
- tuna 참치, 참다랑어
- grouper 농어
- salmon 연어
- thresher shark 진환도 상어
- haddock 해덕
- cod 대구
- metabolism 신진대사
- squid 오징어
- availability 이용 가능성
- gill 아가미
- eventually 결국
- sustain 유지하다, 지속시키다
- Celsius 섭씨의

26
정답 ④

정답 해설
세계화 시대의 비판과 급진주의자들의 새로운 움직임을 주제로 하는 글이다. 사회주의가 후퇴하고 시장 자본주의가 도입되면서 자본주의가 발달하게 되었지만 자본주의의 발달에 따른 문제점들로 인하여 서구 사회에서 자발적인 기구와 자선단체, 비정부기구들에 참여하고 환경운동에 관한 연합이 생겨났다는 내용이다. 따라서 글의 주제로 가장 적절한 것은 ④이다.

지문 해석
20세기 후반 동안 사회주의는 서구와 개발도상국의 많은 지역에서 후퇴하는 중이었다. 시장 자본주의의 진화의 이 새로운 단계 동안, 세계 무역 양식은 점점 더 상호 연결되게 되었고, 정보 기술의 발전은 규제가 완화된 금융 시장이 국경을 넘어 거대한 자본의 흐름을 몇 초 안에 이동할 수 있다는 것을 의미했다. '세계화'는 무역을 증가시키고, 생산성 향상을 장려하며, 가격을 낮추었지만, 비평가들은 그것이 저임금층을 착취하고, 환경 문제에 무관심하며, 제3세계가 독점적인 형태의 자본주의의 지배를 받게 했다고 주장했다. 이 과정에 항의하기를 원했던 서구 사회 내의 많은 급진주의자들은 좌파의 소외된 정당보다는 자발적인 단체, 자선 단체 그리고 다른 비정부 조직에 가입했다. 환경 운동 자체는 세계가 서로 상호 연결되어 있다는 인식에서 시작되었고, 흩어져 있지만, 분노한 국제적인 이해관계의 연합이 등장했다.

선지 해석
① 과거 개발도상국에서의 세계화의 긍정적인 현상
② 20세기 사회주의의 쇠퇴와 자본주의의 출현
③ 세계 자본시장과 좌파 정치 조직 사이의 갈등
④ 세계 자본주의의 착취적 특성과 다양한 사회적 반응들

지문 어휘
- socialism 사회주의
- retreat 퇴각, 후퇴, 후퇴하다, 쇠퇴하다
- capitalism 자본주의
- interlink 연결하다
- deregulate 규제를 철폐하다
- developing world 개발도상국
- national boundary 국경
- boost 촉진시키다
- allege 혐의를 제기하다
- exploit 착취하다, 이용하다
- low-paid 저임금의
- subject 지배하에 두다, 종속시키다
- monopolistic 독점적인
- capitalism 자본주의
- radical 급진주의자
- marginalized 소외된
- voluntary 자발적인, 임의적인
- charity 자선, 자선 단체
- non-governmental organization 비정부 단체
- political party 정당
- diffuse 분산되다, 확산되다
- international coalition 국제 연합
- interest 이해관계, 이익, 관심, 흥미
- affirmative 긍정적인, 확언적인

27
정답 ④

정답 해설
디지털 전환(디지털화에 초점을 맞춘 분석적 전략)이 사회적으로 어떠한 의미를 가지는지에 대해 이야기 하는 글이다. 디지털화에 대한 개념의 설명이 5번째 줄의 '소셜미디어'를 예를 들면서 구체적으로 이해가 되는 글이다. 따라서 글의 제목으로 가장 적절한 것은 ④이다.

지문 해석
'전환'의 정의는 우리가 사회적 현실 내에서 디지털화의 역할에 집중할 수 있도록 하는 분석적 전략으로서 디지털 전환을 제시한다. 분석적인 관점으로서 디지털 전환은 디지털화의 사회적 의미를 분석하고 논의할 수 있게 한다. 따라서 '디지털 전환'이라는 용어는 한 사회 내에서 디지털화의 역할에 초점을 맞춘 분석적 접근 방식을 의미한다. 만약 언어적 전환이 언어를 통해 현실이 구성된다는 인식론적 가정에 의해 정의된다면, 디지털 전환은 사회적 현실이 디지털화에 의해 점점 더 정의된다는 가정에 기초한다. 소셜미디어는 사회적 관계의 디지털화를 상징한다. 개인들은 소셜 네트워킹 사이트(SNS)에서 정체성 관리에 점점 더 참여하고 있다. SNS는 다방향성인데, 이것은 사용자들이 서로 연결하여 정보를 공유할 수 있다는 것을 의미한다.

선지 해석
① SNS에서 정체성 재창조하기
② 언어학적 전환 대 디지털 전환
③ 디지털 시대에서 정보 공유하는 방법
④ 사회적 현실 안에서의 디지털화

지문 어휘
- definition 정의
- cast A as B A를 B로 제시하다, 묘사하다, 간주하다
- digitalization 디지털화
- perspective 관점, 시각
- societal 사회의, 사회적인
- term 용어
- signify 의미하다
- linguistic 언어적
- assumption 가정, 추정
- construct 구성하다, 건설하다
- symbolize 상징하다
- engage in ~에 참여하다, 종사하다
- identity 정체성, 신원
- polydirectional 다방향적인

28

정답 ①

정답 해설
이 글은 유대교의 철학인 "tikkun olam"에 대해 이야기 하면서, 이것은 '세상을 고치기'라는 뜻임을 밝히고 있다. 그리고, 인간으로서 우리의 일은 망가진 것을 고치는 것이 이 철학의 핵심임을 강조하면서, 우리가 세상을 개선하는 데 노력해야 한다고 주장한다. 그리고 '치료' 등의 표현이 반복적으로 나타나고 있다. 따라서 글의 요지로 가장 적절한 것은 ①이다.

지문 해석
"유대교에서, 우리는 주로 우리의 행동에 의해 정의된다,"라고 몬트리올에 있는 Emanu-El-Beth Sholom 사원 선임 랍비 Lisa Grushcow는 말한다. "당신은 절대 관념적인 개혁가가 되어서는 안 된다." 이 개념은 유대인의 틱쿤 올람의 개념과 관련이 있는데, 이것은 "세상을 고치기"라고 번역이 된다. 인간으로서 우리의 일은 "망가진 것을 고치는 것이다. 우리 자신과 서로를 돌볼 뿐만 아니라 우리 주위에 더 나은 세상을 만드는 것이 우리의 의무이다."라고 그녀는 말했다. 이 철학은 선함을 서비스에 기반을 둔 것으로 개념화한다. "나는 좋은 사람인가?"라고 묻는 대신에, "내가 세상에서 무슨 도움이 되는가?"라고 묻고 싶을지도 모른다. Grushcow의 사원은 이러한 믿음들을 그들의 공동체 안팎에서 실천한다. 예를 들어, 그들은 1970년대에 두 명의 난민 가족을 베트남에서 캐나다로 오도록 지원했다.

선지 해석
① 우리는 세상을 치유하기 위해 노력해야 한다.
② 공동체는 피난처로서 기능해야 한다.
③ 우리는 선량함을 믿음으로 개념화해야 한다.
④ 사원은 지역사회에 기여해야 한다.

지문 어휘
- Judaism 유대교
- rabbi (유대교의 지도자·교사인) 라비, 선생님
- armchair 안락의자
- do-gooder 공상적 박애주의자[개혁가]
- translate 번역하다, 해석하다
- repair 수리하다, 바로잡다
- mend 고치다, 수리하다
- incumbent 의무적인, 재임 중인
- take care of ~을 돌보다
- conceptualize 개념화하다, 개념적으로 설명하다
- goodness 선량함, 착함
- put A into action A를 행동으로 옮기다
- sponsor 후원하다
- refugee 난민

29

정답 ③

정답 해설
아이들 간의 비디오 게임 중 분쟁을 해결하는 방법에 대한 글로, 아이들이 비디오 게임 중에 싸울 때, 부모는 가까이 있어서 상황을 모니터하고, 대화와 문제 해결 능력을 통해 해결책을 찾도록 도와야 함을 3번째 문장 "아이들을 비난하거나 비난하지 않고 앉아서 그 문제에 대해 토론하도록 노력하세요"의 진술을 통해서 강조하고 있다. 따라서 글의 요지로 가장 알맞은 것은 ③이다.

지문 해석
만약 당신의 아이들이 비디오 게임을 할 때마다 싸운다면, 그들이 게임을 하기 위해 앉을 때 그들의 말을 들을 수 있을 만큼 충분히 가까이에 있는지 확인해라. 그들이 사용하고 있는 공격적인 단어나 목소리의 톤을 듣고, 그것이 발전하기 전에 개입하려고 노력해라. 일단 화가 풀리면, 아이들을 탓하거나 비난하지 않고 앉아서 그 문제에 대해 토론하도록 노력해라. 각각의 아이들에게 말할 기회를 주고, 중단하지 않고, 그들 스스로 문제에 대한 해결책을 생각해 내도록 해라. 아이들이 초등학생이 될 때까지, 그들은 어떤 해결책들이 원원의 솔루션이고 어떤 것들이 시간이 지남에 따라 서로 작용하고 만족시킬 수 있는지를 평가할 수 있다. 그들은 또한 해결책이 더 이상 효과가 없을 때 문제를 다시 논의하는 법을 배워야 한다.

선지 해석
① 당신의 아이들에게 그들의 시험을 평가하도록 요청하라.
② 당신의 아이들이 서로 경쟁하도록 하라.
③ 아이들이 갈등을 해결하는 법을 배울 수 있도록 도와줘라.
④ 아이들에게 논쟁에서 이기는 법을 가르쳐줘라.

지문 어휘
- close 가까이, 가까운
- aggressive 공격적인
- intervene 개입하다, 간섭하다
- temper 화, 기질, 분노
- discuss 토론하다, 상의하다
- uninterrupted 중단되지 않는, 연속된
- come up with ~을 제시하다, 생각해내다
- resolve 해결하다, 결심하다
- revisit 다시 논의하다, 다시 방문하다

30

정답 ②

정답 해설
다른 이들의 아이디어를 듣는 것의 중요성을 대화의 의미 있는 전제조건으로 설명하는 글이다. 글의 초반부에 다른 사람의 아이디어를 듣는 것은 당신이 믿는 세상과 당신 자신과 그 안에서 당신의 위치에 대한 이야기가 그대로 남아 있는지 알 수 있는 한 가지 방법이라고 하였고 중간 부분에서 그러나 듣지 않고 목소리를 높이는 것은 냄비와 냄비를 함께 두드리는 것과 같다고 진술하고 있다. 따라서 글의 요지로 가장 적절한 것은 ②이다.

지문 해석
다른 사람의 생각들을 듣는 것은 당신 자신과 그 안에서 당신의 위치에 대한 이야기뿐만 아니라 세상에 대해 당신이 믿는 이야기가 여전히 그대로 남아 있는지 아는 한 가지 방법이다. 우리 모두는 우리의 신념을 조사하고, 그것들을 환기시키고, 그것들이 숨을 쉬게 할 필요가 있다. 다른 사람들이, 특히 우리가 기본적이라고 여기는 개념에 대해 말해야 하는 것을 듣는 것은 우리 머리와 마음의 창문을 여는 것과 같다. 목소리를 높이는 것은 중요하다. 그러나 듣지 않고 목소리를 높이는 것은 냄비와 팬을 함께 세게 치는 것과 같다: 비록 그것이 당신이 주목받게 할지라도 존중받도록 하지는 않을 것이다. 대화를 의미 있게 하기 위한 세 가지 전제 조건이 있다: 1. 당신은 당신이 무슨 말을 하고 있는지 알아야 하고, 이는 당신이 독창적인 의견을 가지고 있고 진부하거나, 독창성이 없거나, 이미 만들어진 주장을 되풀이하지 않는다는 것을 의미한다; 2. 당신은 상대방을 존중하고 비록 당신이 그들의

입장에 동의하지 않더라도 진정으로 그들을 예의 바르게 대한다; 3. 당신은 연속된 좋은 유머와 통찰력으로 주제에 대한 자신의 관점을 다루면서 상대방의 말을 경청할 수 있을 만큼 똑똑하고 충분한 정보를 가지고 있어야 한다.

선지 해석
① 우리는 다른 사람들을 설득하기 위해 더 단호해야 한다.
② 우리는 원활하게 의사소통하기 위해 듣고 목소리를 높일 필요가 있다.
③ 우리는 우리가 보는 세상에 대한 믿음을 바꾸는 것을 꺼린다.
④ 우리는 선택한 것만 듣고 다른 의견들을 애써 무시한다.

지문 어휘
- intact 그대로의, 온전한, 손상되지 않은
- foundational 기본적인, 근본적인
- speak up 큰소리로 말하다, 거리낌 없이 말하다
- pot 냄비, 항아리
- pan (손잡이가 달린 얕은) 팬, 냄비
- bang 세게 치다, 쾅 하고 치다
- attention 주목, 주의
- worn-out 진부한, 써서 낡은, 지친
- hand-me-down 독창성이 없는, 만들어 놓은, 헌 옷의
- pre-fab 미리 만들어진
- authentically 확실히, 진정하게
- willing 기꺼이 하는, 꺼리지 않는
- courteously 정중히, 공손하게
- informed 알고 있는
- opposition 상대방, 반대
- uninterrupted 중단되지 않은, 연속된
- discernment 통찰력, 식별, 인식

31   정답 ①

정답 해설
예술이 미래에서 가질 목적과 역할을 예술가들이 직면할 미래 인간의 문제들, 즉 예술에서 보이는 정체성 정치학과 환경 운동 등을 설명하는 글이다. 3번째 문장에서 미래에 예술이 어떤 역할을 하고 어떤 모습을 띠게 될 것인가에 대해 생각해 볼만하다고 제시하고 있고 이후의 내용에서 변화하는 미래에 예술이 어떤 모습을 띠게 될지 반복적으로 진술하고 있다. 따라서 글의 제목으로 가장 적절한 것은 ①이다.

지문 해석
미래는 불확실할 수 있지만, 기후 변화, 변화하는 인구 통계, 지정학과 같은 어떤 것들은 확실하다. 유일한 보장은 변화가 있을 것이라는 거고, 그 중에는 멋진 것과 끔찍한 것이 모두 있을 것이다. 예술이 현재와 미래에 어떤 도움이 될 뿐만 아니라, 예술가들이 이러한 변화에 어떻게 반응할 것인지는 고려할 가치가 있다. 보고서는 2040년까지 인간이 초래한 기후 변화의 영향을 피할 수 없게 될 것이며, 20년 후에는 예술과 삶의 중심에서 그것이 큰 이슈가 될 것을 시사한다. 미래의 예술가들은 미래 인간과 인공지능, 우주 공간의 인류 식민지 그리고 잠재적인 파멸과 같은 포스트 휴먼과 포스트 인류세의 가능성과 씨름할 것이다. 미투 운동과 흑인 민권 운동(흑인의 생명은 소중하다)과 관련된 예술에서 보이는 정체성 정치는 환경 보호주의, 경계 정치학 그리고 이주가 훨씬 더 뚜렷하게 집중을 받으면서 더 성장할 것이다. 예술은 점점 다양해지고 우리가 기대하는 것처럼 '예술처럼' 보이지 않을 수도 있다. 미래에는, 모두가 볼 수 있는 온라인에 우리의 삶이 보이는 것에 싫증나게 되고 우리의 사생활이 거의 없어지면, 익명성이 명성보다 더 바람직할 수도 있다. 수천, 혹은 수백만 개의 좋아요와 팔로워들 대신, 우리는 진실성과 관계에 굶주릴 것이다. 예술은, 결국, 개인적이기 보다는, 더 집단적이고 경험적이 된다.

선지 해석
① 미래의 예술은 어떤 모습일까?
② 지구 온난화가 우리의 삶에 어떤 영향을 미칠까?
③ 인공지능이 환경에 어떤 영향을 미칠까?
④ 정치적 운동 때문에 어떤 변화가 일어날까?

지문 어휘
- demographics 인구 통계학
- geopolitics 지정학
- wrestle with ~과 씨름하다
- post-human 포스트휴먼
  (인간과 로봇 및 기술의 경계가 사라져 현존하는 인간을 넘어선 신인류)
- Anthropocene 인류세(人類世)
  (인류가 지질학과 생태계에 상당한 영향력을 미치기 시작한 이후의 시대)
- doom 파멸, 죽음
- identity politics 정체성 정치
  (인종·성·종교·계급 등 여러 기준으로 분화된 집단이 각 집단의 권리를 주장하는 데 주력하는 정치)
- environmentalism 환경 보호주의, 환경 결정론
- migration 이주, 이동
- diverse 다양한
- anonymity 익명성
- fame 명성
- authenticity 진실성
- collective 집단적인

32   정답 ③

정답 해설
일을 강박적으로 느끼는 젊은 근로자들의 업무 환경 변화를 요구한다는 내용의 글이다. 글의 첫 부분에 많은 사람들이 일에 강박을 느낀다고 하며 일을 하면서 개인 시간을 보내기 위해 많은 노력을 하며 생기는 여러 부작용을 제시하고 있다. 그러나 점점 더 많은 젊은 근로자들이 이에 대해 반발하며 유연성을 요구하고 있다고 진술하고 있다. 따라서 글의 주제로 가장 적절한 것은 ③이다.

지문 해석
많은 사람들에게 일은 강박이 되었다. 그것은 사람들이 급여를 위해 하는 일 이외에 아이, 열정, 애완동물, 또는 어떤 종류의 삶을 위한 시간을 찾기 위해 애쓰면서 극도의 피로, 불행, 그리고 성 불평등을 야기했다. 그러나 점점 더 젊은 근로자들이 반발하고 있다. 그들 중 더 많은 이들이 원격 근무를 할 수 있고 늦게 출근하거나 일찍 퇴근할 수 있는 혹은 운동 혹은 명상을 위한 시간을 낼 수 있는 능력과 같은 일상적인 것들과 함께, 이를테면, 새로 태어난 아기를 위한 유급휴가와 넉넉한 휴가 시간과 같은 유연성을 기대하고 요구한다. 그들 삶의 나머지는 특정 장소와 시간에 묶여 있지 않고 그들의 전화에서 일어나는데, — 일은 왜 달라야 하는가?

선지 해석
① 급여를 늘리는 방법들
② 불평등 해소에 대한 강박관념
③ 일에서 유연성 증대에 대한 요구 증가
④ 긴 휴가가 주는 이점들

지문 어휘
- obsession 강박, 집착, 사로잡힘
- burnout 업무 스트레스로 인한 심리적, 육체적 지침
- inequity 불공평
- paycheck 급여
- flexibility 유연성
- paid leave 유급 휴가
- generous 넉넉한, 관대한, 너그러운
- work remotely 원격 근무
- meditation 명상

33   정답 ③

정답 해설
태블릿 컴퓨터에서 사용되는 터치스크린 기술에 관해 설명하는 글이다. 터치스크린 기술의 작동 원리를 열거하고 터치스크린의 유형에 대해서 소거하고 있다. 따라서 글의 주제로 가장 적절한 것은 ③이다.

지문 해석
태블릿 컴퓨터에서 사용할 수 있는 전자책 애플리케이션은 터치스크린 기술을 사용한다. 몇몇 터치스크린들은 마주 보도록 놓인 두 개의 금속 표면들을 덮고 있는 유리판을 특징으로 한다. 스크린이 만져지면, 두 개의 금속 표면들은 압력을 느끼고 접촉한다. 이 압력은 전기 신호를 컴퓨터로 보내고, 이것은 그 접촉을 명령어로 전환한다. 이 버전의 터치스크린은 손가락의 압력에 반응하기 때문에 저항식 스크린으로 알려져 있다. 다른 태블릿 컴퓨터들은 유리판 아래에 하나의 전기가 흐르는 금속 막을 특징으로 한다. 사용자가 스크린을 터치하면 전류 중 일부가 유리를 통해 사용자의 손가락으로 지나간다. 전하가 이동되면 컴퓨터는 전력 손실을 명령으로 해석해 사용자가 원하는 기능을 수행한다. 이러한 유형의 화면을 정전식 화면으로 알려져 있다.

선지 해석
① 사용자가 새로운 기술을 배우는 방법
② 태블릿 컴퓨터에서 전자책이 작동하는 방법
③ 터치스크린 기술이 작동하는 방법
④ 터치스크린의 발전 과정

지문 어휘
- e-book 전자책
- glass panel 유리판
- electronically-charged 전자적으로 충전된
- metallic 금속의, 금속으로 만든
- translate 전환하다, 바꾸다, 번역하다
- command (컴퓨터에 대한) 명령어, 명령, 명령하다
- version 버전, 형태
- pressure 압력, 압박
- resistive screen 저항식 스크린
- pass through 지나가다, 거쳐가다
- charge 전하, 충전, 책임, 요금
- transfer 이동하다, 옮기다
- capacitive screen 정전식 스크린

34   정답 ④

정답 해설
루이 14세가 '베르사유 궁전'을 건설하는 과정(기원)에 대한 이야기이다. 베르사유의 보잘것없는 오두막에서 엄청난 궁전으로 변하는 과정을 설명하고 있다. 따라서 글의 제목으로 가장 적절한 것은 ④이다.

지문 해석
루이 14세는 그의 위대함에 걸맞은 궁전이 필요해서, 그는 베르사유에 거대한 새 집을 짓기로 결정했는데, 그곳에는 작은 사냥꾼 오두막 집이 있었다. 거의 50년의 노동 끝에, 이 작은 사냥꾼 오두막은 4분의 1마일 길이의 거대한 궁전으로 바뀌었다. 강에서 물을 끌어오고 습지대의 물을 빼내기 위해 운하를 팠다. 베르사유는 유명한 거울의 방 같은 정교한 방들로 가득 차 있었는데, 그곳에는 17개의 거울들이 17개의 커다란 창문 맞은편에 있었고, 아폴론 방에는 순 은빛 왕좌가 있었다. Apollo와 Jupiter, Neptune과 같은 그리스 신들 수백 개의 동상들이 정원들에 서 있었다; 각각의 신은 루이의 얼굴을 하고 있었다!

선지 해석
① 그리스 신들의 진면목
② 거울의 방 vs. 아폴로의 살롱
③ 운하가 베르사유에 물 이상의 것을 가져다 주었나?
④ 베르사유: 초라한 오두막에서 엄청난 궁전으로

지문 어휘
- palace 궁전, 왕궁
- lodge 오두막
- canal 운하
- statue 조각상
- drain 물을 빼내다, 배수하다, 고갈시키다
- marshland 습지대
- throne 왕좌
- humble 변변치 않은, 초라한, 겸손한

35   정답 ①

정답 해설
노인들의 중요성과 현대 사회에서의 역할을 강조하는 글이다. 글의 초반부에서는 노인들이 공동체에서 배제되는 것이 합리적이라는 내용으로 제시하였으나 3번째 문장에서 역접 표현인 But 이하의 내용으로 노인들이 공동체 내에서 흔들리지 않는 중심점을 제공함으로써 가족들에게 물질적인 것에 대한 보상을 제공한다고 설명하고 있다. 따라서 글의 요지로 가장 적절한 것은 ①이다.

지문 해석
진화론적으로, 살아남기를 원하는 모든 종들은 그것의 자원을 신중하게 관리해야 한다. 이것은 음식과 다른 맛있는 것들이 우선적으로 사육가들, 전사들, 사냥꾼들, 농부들, 건설가들 그리고 분명히, 아이들에게 우선적으로 가야하고, 그들이 기여하는 것보다 소비하는 것으로 여겨질 수 있는 노인들을 위해 남겨지는 것은 많이 없다는 것을 의미한다. 그러나, 심지어 현대의학이 기대수명들을 늘리기 전에도, 보통 가정들은 조부모들과 심지어 증조부모들을 포함하고 있었다. 그것은 가족들 주변에 종종 몰아치는 혼란에 침착하고 논리적인 사유를 하는 중심을 제공하면서, 나이든 사람들이 소비하는 것을 행동적으로 되돌려 주기 때문이다 ― 즉, 노인들은 종종 그들 주변에서 소용돌이치는 소동에 평준화, 합리적인 중심을 제공한다.

선지 해석
① 노인들은 가족에게 기여해왔다.
② 현대 의학은 노인들의 역할에 초점을 두었다.
③ 한 가정에 자원을 잘 배분하는 것이 그것의 번영을 결정한다.
④ 대가족은 한정된 자원의 희생으로 이루어진다.

지문 어휘
- evolutionarily 진화론적으로
- species 종
- breeder 사육사, 양성자
- contribute 기여하다
- extend 확장하다, 연장하다
- life expectancy 기대 수명, 평균 수명
- old folk 노인들
- great-grandparent 증조부모
- materially 물질적으로
- leveling 평준화, 평등화, 단순화
- tumult 소란, 소동
- swirl 소용돌이치다, 빙빙 돌다, 소용돌이
- prosperity 번영, 번성, 번창
- extended family 대가족

36
정답 ④

정답 해설
다양한 분야에서 활용되는 현대 지도 기술의 다양한 응용에 대한 글로, 생물학, 지구 물리학, 컴퓨터 게임, 가상 현실, 개념도 등 다양한 분야에서 활용되는 현대 지도 기술의 응용 형태와 그 중요성에 대한 설명하고 있다. 따라서 글의 제목으로 가장 적절한 것은 ④이다.

지문 해석
> 지도 제작 기술은 많은 새로운 응용 프로그램들에서 사용되고 있다. 생물학 연구원들은 DNA의 분자 구조("게놈의 지도화")를 탐색하고 있고, 지구 물리학자들은 지구의 중심핵의 구조를 지도화하고 있고, 해양학자들은 해저를 지도화하고 있다. 컴퓨터 게임들은 규칙들, 위험들, 보상들이 변화하는 다양한 가상의 "땅" 혹은 단계들을 가지고 있다. 컴퓨터화는 이제 훈련과 오락에 유용할 수 있는 특별한 상황을 가장하는 인공적인 환경인 "가상 현실"로 현실에 도전한다. 지도 제작 기술은 관념 영역에서도 사용되고 있다. 예를 들어, 생각들 사이의 관계는 개념도라고 불리는 것을 사용하여 보일 수 있다. 일반적인 또는 "중심적인" 생각에서 시작하여, 관련된 생각들이 연결되고, 주요 개념 주위에 망을 구축할 수 있다. 이것은 전통적인 정의에 의한 지도는 아니지만 지도 제작의 도구나 기술이 사용되었고, 어떤 면에서는 지도와 유사하다.

선지 해석
① 컴퓨터화된 지도 vs. 전통적인 지도
② 지도 제작법은 어디에서 시작되었는가?
③ DNA의 비밀에 대한 방법들을 찾기
④ 새로운 영역을 지도로 표현하기

지문 어휘
- mapping technology 지도제작 기술
- map 지도, 지도를 만들다
- application 응용 프로그램, 응용, 적용, 지원, 신청
- genome 게놈(유전자 총체)
- molecular 분자
- geophysicist 지구 물리학자
- Earth's core 지구의 중심핵
- oceanographer 해양학자
- ocean floor 해저
- reward 보상, 보상하다
- virtual reality 가상 현실
- artificial 인공의, 인위적인
- realm 영역, 범위
- concept map 개념도
- central 중심적인
- cartography 지도 제작(법)

37
정답 ③

정답 해설
성과 피드백의 적절한 설계와 전략에 대한 글로, 성과 피드백을 제공할 때 고려해야 할 요소와 다양한 성과 수준에 따른 효과적인 피드백 전략에 대한 설명하고 있다. 첫 문장에서 주제를 제시하고 2번째에서 4번째 문장의 예시를 통해서 개별적인 피드백의 방법을 제시하고 있으므로 글의 요지로 가장 적절한 것은 ③이다.

지문 해석
> 성과에 대한 피드백을 줄 때, 당신은 받는 사람의 과거의 성과와 그것의 빈도, 양 그리고 내용을 설계하는 데 있어서 그 또는 그녀의 미래 잠재력에 대한 당신의 추정치를 고려해야 한다. 성장 가능성이 있는 고성과자들에게는, 피드백은 그들이 교정적인 행동을 하게끔 촉구하기에 충분할 정도로 자주 있어야 하지만, 너무 자주 이루어져 그것이 통제하는 것으로서 여겨지고 그들의 주도권을 약화시킬 정도로 자주 있어서는 안 된다. 그들의 일에 정착하고 발전에 제한된 가능성을 가진 적합한 성과를 내는 수행자들에게는 거의 피드백이 필요하지 않은데, 왜냐하면 그들이 믿을 수 있고 꾸준한 행동을 과거에 보여주었고 과거에 그들에 업무를 알고, 무엇이 완료될 필요가 있는지 알아차리고 있기 때문이다. 그들의 직장에서 내보내질 필요가 있을 좋지 못한 성과를 내는 사람들에게는, 그들의 성과가 향상되지 않으면 피드백은 자주 있어야 하고 매우 구체적이어야 하며, 피드백에 근거하여 행동하는 것과 일시적으로 해고되거나 해고되는 것과 같은 부정적인 제재 사이의 연관성이 분명하게 만들어져야 한다.

선지 해석
① 당신의 피드백의 시기를 잘 맞춰라.
② 부정적인 피드백을 사용자의 사정에 맞춰서 하라.
③ 피드백을 그 사람에 맞춰라.
④ 목표 지향적인 피드백을 피하라.

지문 어휘
- performance 성과, 수행
- recipient 받는 사람, 수령인, 수취인
- potential 잠재력, 잠재적인
- frequency 빈도
- amount 양

- □ prod 촉구하다, 자극하다
- □ corrective 바로잡는, 교정의
- □ sap 수액, 원기, 약화시키다
- □ initiative 진취성, 결단력, 주도권
- □ adequate 적합한, 충분한
- □ sanction 제재, 허가, 제재를 가하다, 허가하다
- □ lay off 해고하다
- □ fire 해고하다
- □ explicit 분명한, 명백한, 노골적인
- □ customize 사용자의 사정[희망]에 맞추다, 주문에 응하여 만들다
- □ tailor (특정한 목적·사람 등에) 맞추다[조정하다], 재단사
- □ goal-oriented 목표 지향적인

38   정답 ③

정답 해설
단순한 이름이 커리어에 미치는 영향에 대한 글로, 이름의 단순성이 커리어 성과에 영향을 미치는 것을 조사한 결과, 더 단순한 이름을 가진 사람들이 더 빨리 진급하고 파트너십을 획득하는 경향이 있다는 연구결과를 근거로 설명하고 있다. 따라서 글의 주제로 가장 적절한 것은 ③이다.

지문 해석
두 사람이 같은 날에 법률 사무소에서 일하기 시작한다고 상상해보자. 한 사람은 매우 단순한 이름을 가지고 있다. 다른 사람은 매우 복잡한 이름을 가지고 있다. 우리는 이후 16년간의 그들의 경력에 있어 더 간단한 이름을 가지고 있는 사람이 더 빨리 법조계 서열이 올라갈 것이라는 꽤나 타당한 증거를 가지고 있다. 그들은 그들의 경력의 중반부에 파트너십을 더 빨리 획득할 것이다. 그리고 로스쿨에서 졸업하고 8년 또는 9년차 정도가 되었을 때 더 단순한 이름을 가진 사람들은 파트너(이사)가 될 가능성이 대략 7에서 10퍼센트 더 높은데, 이것은 인상적인 결과이다. 우리는 여기에서 모든 종류의 다른 대안적인 설명들을 제거하고자 한다. 예를 들어, 외국 이름이 발음하기 더 어려운 경향이 있기 때문에, 우리는 그것이 외래성에 관한 것이 아님을 보여주려 한다. 그러나 당신이 그렇게 정말 진정한 내집단에 속한 영국계 미국인 이름들을 가지고 있는 백인 남성들을 본다고 하더라도, 당신은 영국계 미국 이름들을 가진 그러한 백인 남성들 중에서 그들의 이름들이 더 단순하다면 그들은 위로 올라갈 가능성이 더 높다는 것을 알게 된다. 그러므로 간단함은 다양한 결과들을 결정하는 이름에 있어서의 하나의 핵심적인 특징이다.

선지 해석
① 법적 이름의 발달
② 매력적인 이름의 개념
③ 간단한 이름의 이점
④ 외국 이름의 뿌리

지문 어휘
- □ hierarchy 계층, 계급
- □ attain 이루다, 달성하다
- □ striking 인상적인, 현저한, 두드러진
- □ eliminate 제거하다
- □ alternative 대안적인
- □ foreignness 외래성, 이질성
- □ pronounce 발음하다
- □ in-group 내집단
- □ outcome 결과

39   정답 ②

정답 해설
디지털 혁명과 뉴스룸의 변화에 따르는 기자들에게 주는 조언을 주제로 하는 글로, 디지털 혁명으로 인해 뉴스룸에서의 변화와 기자들에게 필요한 새로운 접근 방식을 설명하고 있다. 따라서 글의 주제로 가장 적절한 것은 ②이다.

지문 해석
디지털 혁명이 전국의 뉴스룸에 근본적인 변화를 일으키게 됨에 따라 여기에 모든 기자들을 위한 내 조언이 있다. 나는 25년 동안 기자였기 때문에 여섯 번의 기술적 라이프 사이클을 겪었다. 가장 극적인 변화들은 마지막의 6년간에 왔다. 이는 내가 더욱 잦은 빈도로 진행하면서 원가를 만들어가고 있음을 의미한다. 뉴스 업계에 있어 많은 시간 동안 우리는 우리가 하고 있는 것에 관해 모른다. 우리는 아침에 출근을 하고, 누군가는 '세금 정책, 이민, 기후 변화에 관해 글을 써주실래요?'라고 말한다. 기자들이 하루에 한 번씩 마감이 있었을 때, 우리는 기자들은 아침에는 배우고 밤에는 가르쳐야 한다고 말을 했다 ― 그 기자가 24시간 전에는 알지 못했던 주제에 관해 내일의 독자들에게 알려주는 기사를 쓰는 것 말이다. 이제 이것은 마치 정시에는 배우고 30분에는 가르치는 것과 같다. 예를 들면 나는 또한 정치 팟캐스트를 운영 중인데 우리는 실시간 인터뷰를 하기 위해 어디에서든 그것을 이용할 수 있어야만 한다. 나는 점점 더 대본 없이 일하고 있다.

선지 해석
① 선생님으로서의 기자
② 기자와 즉석에서 하기
③ 정치학에서의 기술
④ 저널리즘과 기술의 영역들

지문 어휘
- □ upend 철저한[근본적인] 영향을 주다, 거꾸로 세우다, 엎어놓다
- □ dramatic 극적인
- □ transformation 변화, 변신
- □ make up 만들어 내다, 꾸미다, 구성하다, 화장하다
- □ once-a-day 하루에 한 번의
- □ deadline 마감 기한
- □ inform 알리다, 통지하다
- □ real-time 실시간
- □ script 대본, 원고
- □ improvisation 즉석에서 하기

04 중심 내용 파악 유형 기출 독해 어휘 복습 TEST

1	mentality	사고방식	21	organization	조직, 단체, 준비, 구성
2	employer	고용 사업체, 고용주	22	means	수단, 방법, 수입
3	face	직면하다	23	relieve	완화하다, 줄이다
4	loan	대출하다, 빌려주다	24	cherish	소중히 여기다, 아끼다, 간직하다
5	artificial	인공의, 인조의	25	competence	능력, 능숙함
6	mimic	흉내내다, 모방하다	26	attribute	~의 탓으로 보다, 속성, 특성, 자질
7	drastically	급격히	27	equate	동일시하다
8	disrupt	방해하다, 지장을 주다	28	dedicate	바치다, 전념하다
9	counteract	상쇄하다, 대응하다	29	discuss	논의하다, 상의하다
10	contagious	전염되는, 전염성의	30	crave	갈망하다, 열망하다
11	eliminate	없애다, 제거하다	31	countless	무수한
12	ministry	(정부의 각) 부처, 목사, 성직자	32	deliberate	고의의, 의도적인, 신중한, 사려 깊은
13	infection	감염, 전염병	33	resistance	저항력, 내성
14	install	설치하다, 설비하다	34	extend	확장하다, 연장하다
15	disparity	격차, 차이	35	solid	믿을 수 있는, 견고한, 고체의, 단단한
16	emphasize	강조하다, 두드러지게 하다	36	cultivate	양성하다, 경작하다, 재배하다
17	excavate	발굴하다	37	negative	원판, 음화, 부정적인
18	exploit	이용하다, 착취하다	38	excessive	과도한, 지나친
19	dilute	희석하다, 약화시키다	39	overuse	남용, 남용하다
20	replenish	보충하다, 채우다	40	give off	(냄새·열·빛 등을) 내다[발하다]

41	emit	방출하다, 내뿜다	61	incumbent	의무적인, 재임 중인
42	excite	흥분시키다, 자극하다, 불러일으키다, 촉발시키다	62	intervene	개입하다, 간섭하다
43	focal	중심의, 초점의	63	uninterrupted	중단되지 않는, 연속된
44	inert	움직이지 않는, 비활성의	64	intact	그대로의, 온전한, 손상되지 않은
45	concerned	걱정하는, 관심이 있는	65	courteously	정중히, 공손하게
46	meet halfway	타협하다, 절충하다	66	discernment	통찰력, 식별, 인식
47	optimize	최적화하다	67	migration	이주, 이동
48	simultaneously	동시에	68	anonymity	익명성
49	sustain	유지하다, 지속시키다	69	obsession	강박, 집착, 사로잡힘
50	petition	청원(서), 탄원(서), 신청서, 청원하다, 탄원하다	70	generous	넉넉한, 관대한, 너그러운
51	flexibility	유연성, 신축성	71	meditation	명상
52	shrink	줄어들게 하다, 감소하다	72	pressure	압력, 압박
53	allege	혐의를 제기하다	73	leveling	평준화, 평등화, 단순화
54	subject	지배하에 두다, 종속시키다	74	tumult	소란, 소동
55	diffuse	분산되다, 확산되다	75	prosperity	번영, 번성, 번창
56	merit	받을 만하다[자격/가치가 있다], 가치, 장점	76	frequency	빈도
57	assumption	가정, 추정	77	sanction	제재, 허가, 제재를 가하다, 허가하다
58	construct	구성하다, 건설하다	78	striking	인상적인, 현저한, 두드러진
59	signify	의미하다	79	transformation	변화, 변신
60	mend	고치다, 수리하다	80	inform	알리다, 통지하다

PART 05 문장 제거 유형

ANSWER

01 ④	02 ④	03 ②	04 ③	05 ④
06 ③	07 ③	08 ④	09 ②	10 ①
11 ③	12 ④	13 ②	14 ②	15 ②
16 ④	17 ③	18 ②	19 ④	20 ③
21 ③	22 ④	23 ②	24 ④	25 ③
26 ③	27 ④	28 ③	29 ④	30 ②

01 정답 ④

정답 해설

이 글은 AI 시대의 고용 변화에 대한 현실적인 대응 방안을 중심으로 전개되고 있다. 교육과 직업 재훈련, 사회적 보호, 노동자의 권리 보장, 포용적인 노동시장 조성, 사회적 대화의 중요성 등이 강조되며, AI 혁명에 따른 고용 구조 변화에 적극적으로 대응하자는 메시지를 담고 있다. ①, ②, ③ 문장은 모두 이러한 취지를 바탕으로 노동자 보호와 고용시장 안정을 위한 구체적인 방안을 제시하고 있다. 반면, ④번 문장은 "AI가 향후 10년 안에 인간의 모든 일을 완전히 대체할 것"이라는 극단적이고 비현실적인 전망을 담고 있어, 글 전체의 균형 잡힌 문제 인식과 해결 중심의 주제와 무관하다. 따라서 글의 흐름상 어색한 문장은 ④이다.

지문 해석

OECD 국가들이 생성형 AI의 급속한 발전과 AI 기술을 갖춘 인재의 증가로 강조되는 AI 혁명에 대비하면서, 고용 환경은 큰 변화의 태세를 취하고 있다. ① 이 변화에 대응하기 위해, 현재와 미래의 노동자 모두에게 필요한 기술을 갖추도록 훈련과 교육을 우선시하고 이직자들을 충분한 사회 보호로 지원하는 것이 중요하다. ② 또한 노동자의 권리를 보호하고, AI 통합에 직면하여 포용적인 노동시장을 보장하는 것이 가장 중요해진다. ③ 사회적 대화도 이 새로운 시대의 성공에 핵심이 될 것이다. (④ 많은 전문가들은 AI가 향후 10년 이내에 인간의 모든 직업을 완전히 대체할 것이라고 믿는다.) 종합적으로 이러한 조치들은 AI 혁명이 모두에게 혜택을 주고, 잠재적 위험을 성장과 혁신의 기회로 바꾸는 것을 보장할 것이다.

지문 어휘

- prepare 준비하다, 대비하다
- revolution 혁명
- underscore 강조하다, 밑줄을 긋다
- rapid 빠른
- advancement 발전, 진보
- landscape 전망, 풍경
- employment 고용, 취업, 직장
- poise 태세를 취하다, 유지하다, 균형을 잡다
- shift 변화
- current 현재의, 지금의
- displaced worker 이직자, 해직자
- adequate 적절한, 충분한
- safeguard 보호하다
- inclusive 폭넓은, 포괄적인
- paramount 가장 중요한
- dialogue 대화
- era 시대
- replace 대체하다, 대신하다
- decade 10년
- transform 바꾸다, 변형시키다

02 정답 ④

정답 해설

이 글은 영국 과학자들이 비타민 D가 풍부한 특별한 토마토를 재배한 연구에 대해 설명하고 있다. 글 초반에서는 비타민 D의 중요성과 결핍이 전 세계적으로 심각하다는 문제의식을 제시하고 있다. 이어서 ①, ②, ③ 문장은 토마토에 비타민 D를 강화하기 위한 구체적인 연구 과정과 결과를 단계별로 설명한다. 반면, ④번 문장은 토마토의 섭취 방식(샐러드나 요리로 먹는다는 점)을 일반적인 식문화 측면에서 언급할 뿐, 연구의 목적과 과정, 비타민 D 강화라는 핵심 내용과 직접적인 관련성이 약하다. 따라서 글의 흐름상 어색한 문장은 ④이다.

지문 해석

영국의 과학자들은 사람들의 건강에 중요한 비타민 D가 추가된 특별한 토마토를 재배했다. 전 세계적으로 약 10억 명이 비타민 D 결핍을 겪고 있다. ① 토마토에는 자연적으로 비타민 D로 전환되는 물질이 들어 있다. ② 연구팀은 토마토 식물의 유전자를 변형해, 이 물질이 보통보다 더 많이 생성되도록 품종을 재배했다. ③ 그 결과, 토마토 한 개에는 중간 크기 달걀 두 개 분량의 비타민 D가 들어 있게 되었다. (④ 게다가 토마토는 보통 샐러드에 생으로 먹거나 익힌 채소로 제공된다.) 과학자들은 이 기술이 다른 식품에도 적용될 수 있을 것이라고 보고 있다.

지문 어휘

- extra 추가의
- deficiency 결핍, 부족
- billion 10억
- worldwide 전 세계적인
- substance 물질, 실체
- convert 전환되다, 개조되다
- alter 변경하다, 바꾸다
- breed 재배하다, 사육하다
- usual 보통의, 평상시의
- raw 날것의, 익히지 않은
- cooked 익힌

03

정답 ②

정답 해설

반응 에세이의 개념과 작성 방법에 대한 글로, 반응 에세이는 주어진 자극에 대한 개인의 감정과 의견을 표현하는 글쓰기 과제로, 글쓴이는 자극을 요약하고 자신의 반응을 제시해야 함을 설명하고 있다. 반응 에세이에서 중요한 것은 주어진 자극에 대한 개인의 감정이나 의견을 표현하는 것이며, 사실을 수집하여 주장을 방어하는 것이 아니다. 따라서 글의 흐름상 어색한 문장은 사실수집의 중요성을 말하는 ②이다.

지문 해석

매우 일반적인 종류의 글쓰기 과제는 모든 학문 분야에서 나타나는 반응 또는 응답이다. ① 반응 에세이에서는 보통 "프롬프터" — 시각적이거나 서면 자극 — 가 제공되어 이에 대해 생각하고 응답하는 방식이다. (② 당신의 주장을 효과적으로 방어하기 위해 신뢰할 수 있는 사실을 모으는 것이 매우 중요하다.) ③ 이 유형의 글쓰기를 위한 일반적인 프롬프트나 자극에는 인용문, 문학 작품, 사진, 그림, 멀티미디어 프레젠테이션, 뉴스 사건 등이 포함된다. ④ 반응은 특정 프롬프트에 대한 작가의 감정, 의견 및 개인적인 관찰에 중점을 둔다. 반응 에세이를 작성할 때의 작업은 두 가지이다: 프롬프트를 간결하게 요약하고 이에 대한 개인적인 반응을 제시하는 것이다.

지문 어휘

- [ ] discipline 분야, 훈육, 규율, 훈육하다, 징계하다
- [ ] prompt 프롬프터의, 즉각적인, 신속한, 촉발하다, 유도하다
- [ ] reliable 신뢰할[믿을] 수 있는
- [ ] argument 주장, 논쟁, 언쟁
- [ ] quote 인용문, 인용하다
- [ ] literature 문학, 문헌
- [ ] focus on 중점을 두다, 초점을 맞추다
- [ ] opinion 의견, 견해
- [ ] briefly 간결하게, 간단히, 잠시
- [ ] summarize 요약하다

04

정답 ③

정답 해설

어린이들의 성장에서 중요한 '자연'을 강조하는 글이다. 어린이와 함께 도시 공원을 방문하는 것은 단순히 스트레스 해소뿐만 아니라 학업 성과 향상, 기분 및 집중력 향상과 같은 거대한 이점을 가져올 수 있음을 설명하고 있다. 그러나 ③번의 진술은 '자연에서의 활동의 단점'을 언급하고 있으므로 글의 일관성에서 위배가 된다. 따라서 글의 흐름상 어색한 문장은 ③이다.

지문 해석

어린 아이들의 모든 부모나 보호자는 집에서 나가고 싶은 필사적인 충동과 심지어 지역 공원으로의 짧은 여행의 마법 같은 회복 효과를 경험했을 것이다. ① 여기서 아마도 단지 기분을 푸는 것 이상의 일이 일어나고 있을 것이다. ② 더 나은 학업 성취로부터 향상된 기분과 집중에 이르기까지, 아이들에게 자연에 들어가는 것의 이점들은 엄청나다. (③ 야외 활동들은 그들이 가족과 양질의 시간을 보내는 것을 어렵게 만든다.) ④ 자연에 대한 어린 시절의 경험들은 성인기에 환경 보호주의를 신장시킬 수도 있다. 도시의 녹지 공간에 접근하는 것은 아이들의 사회적 관계망과 우정에 역할을 할 수 있다.

지문 어휘

- [ ] guardian 보호자, 후견인
- [ ] desperate 필사적인, 절망적인
- [ ] urge 충동, 욕구, 충고하다, 권고하다
- [ ] get out of ~에서 나오다, 도망치다
- [ ] restorative 회복하는, 복원하는
- [ ] probably 아마
- [ ] going on (일이) 일어나고 있는
- [ ] let off steam 기분을 풀다, 울분[열기 등]을 발산하다
- [ ] get into ~에 들어가다, ~에 도착하다

05

정답 ④

정답 해설

일부 사람들은 NASA의 아폴로 프로그램이 달 착륙을 가짜로 만들었다고 주장하며, 미국의 우주 경쟁에서의 패배와 방사선에 대한 우려를 근거로 한다. ④번의 진술이 사실이라면, 달 착륙에 대한 근거가 되므로, 다음 글에서 제거가 되어야 한다. 따라서 글의 흐름상 어색한 문장은 ④이다.

지문 해석

반대되는 모든 증거들에도 불구하고, NASA의 아폴로 우주 프로그램이 실제로 달에 사람을 착륙시킨 적이 없다고 진지하게 믿는 사람들이 있다. 이 사람들은 달 착륙이 러시아와 필사적으로 경쟁하며 체면을 잃을까봐 두려워하는 정부에 의해 영구화된 거대한 음모에 불과하다고 주장한다. ① 이 음모론자들은 미국이 우주 개발 경쟁에서 러시아와 경쟁할 수 없다는 것을 알았고 따라서 하는 수 없이 일련의 성공적인 달 착륙을 조작했다고 주장한다. ② 음모론 옹호자들은 그들이 증거라고 간주하는 것 중에 몇 가지를 인용한다. ③ 그들의 논거에 결정적인 것은 우주 비행사들이 지구의 자기장에 갇힌 방사선의 지역인 밴 앨런 벨트를 결코 안전하게 통과할 수 없었을 것이라는 주장이다. (④ 그들은 또한 우주선의 금속 덮개가 방사선을 차단하도록 설계되었다는 사실을 지적한다.) 만약 우주 비행사들이 진정으로 벨트를 통과했다면, 그들은 죽었을 것이라고 음모론자들은 말한다.

지문 어휘

- [ ] land 상륙시키다, 상륙하다
- [ ] landing 착륙
- [ ] conspiracy 음모
- [ ] perpetuate 계속되게 하다, 영속시키다
- [ ] competition 경쟁
- [ ] therefore 그러므로, 따라서
- [ ] advocate 옹호하다, 지지하다
- [ ] radiation 방사선
- [ ] trapped 갇힌, 가두어진

06

정답 ③

정답 해설

비판적 사고와 감정과 관계가 있고, 감정 관리의 중요성을 강조하는 글이다. 글의 전개가 '감정이 관련됨의 여부'의 비교의 논리로 이어지고 있는데, '동일한 정보를 여러 관점에서 보는 것이 중요하지 않다'는 ③번이 '감정과 관련됨의 여부'와는 관련이 없는 진술로, 일관성에서 위반된다. 따라서 글의 흐름상 어색한 문장은 ③이다.

지문 해석

비판적 사고는 감정 없는 과정처럼 들릴 수 있지만, 감정과 열정적인 반응을 불러일으킬 수 있다. 특히 우리는 자신의 의견이나 신념에 반하는 증거를 좋아하지 않을 수 있다. ① 만약 증거가 도전적인 방향을 가리킨다면, 그것은 예상치 못한 분노, 좌절, 불안의 감정을 불러일으킬 수 있다. ② 학계는 전통적으로 자신을 논리적이고 감정 없는 것으로 간주하려 하지만, 만약 감정이 드러나면 이는 특히 어려운 일이 될 수 있다. (③ 예를 들어, 같은 정보를 여러 관점에서 바라보는 것은 중요하지 않다.) ④ 이러한 상황에서 자신의 감정을 관리할 수 있는 능력은 유용한 기술이다. 당신이 침착하게 행동하고 논리적으로 자신의 이유를 제시할 수 있다면, 설득력 있게 자신의 관점을 주장할 수 있을 것이다.

지문 어휘

- critical thinking 비판적 사고
- unemotional 감정 없는, 감정을 드러내지 않는
- process 과정, 절차, 처리하다
- passionate 열정적인, 열렬한
- contradict 모순되다, 부정하다
- challenging 도전적인, 저항하는
- rouse 불러일으키다, 깨우다
- frustration 좌절감, 불만
- anxiety 불안, 염려, 걱정거리, 열망
- convincing 설득력 있는, 확실한

07   정답 ③

정답 해설

하이브리드 근무로의 전환과 사무실 밀도에 미치는 영향을 주제로, 미국인 근로자와 고용주를 대상으로 한 조사 결과, 하이브리드 업무로의 변화가 명확하게 드러나고 있으며, 이로 인한 사무실에서 일하는 시간이 줄어들었지만, 사무실 공간 수요는 크게 감소하지 않았고, 밀도 문제는 여전히 존재한다는 것을 설명하는 글이다. ③ 문장의 '대부분의 직원들은 월요일과 금요일에 집에서 일하기를 원한다'는 진술은 글의 주제인 '하이브리드 업무'의 주제와 벗어나는 진술이다. 따라서 글의 흐름상 어색한 문장은 ③이다.

지문 해석

5,000명의 미국 근로자와 500개의 미국 기업을 대상으로 실시한 우리의 월간조사에서, 사무직 및 지식노동자들 사이에서 하이브리드 근무로의 큰 변화가 명확하게 드러나고 있다. ① 최근에 생긴 표준은 사무실에서 주 3일, 집에서 주 2일로 현장 근무 일수를 30% 이상 단축하는 것이다. 당신은 이러한 삭감이 사무실 공간에 대한 수요를 크게 감소시킬 것이라고 생각할지도 모른다. ② 그러나 우리의 설문조사 데이터는 사무실 공간이 평균 1%에서 2% 감소하는 것을 시사하고, 이는 공간이 아닌 밀도에서의 큰 감소를 의미한다.. 우리는 그 이유를 이해할 수 있다. 사무실의 고밀도는 불편하고 많은 직원들은 그들 책상 주위에 사람들이 붐비는 것을 싫어한다. (③ 대부분의 직원들은 월요일과 금요일에 집에서 일하기를 원한다.) 밀도에 대한 불편함은 로비, 주방, 특히 엘리베이터까지 확대된다. ④ 밀도를 줄일 수 있는 유일한 확실한 방법은 평방 피트를 크게 줄이지 않고 현장에서의 근무일을 줄이는 것이다. 우리의 조사 증거에 따르면 밀도에 대한 불편함은 계속 남아 있다.

지문 어휘

- shift 전환, 전환하다
- hybrid work 하이브리드 업무
  (온라인과 오프라인의 작업 방식을 조합한 새로운 업무 방식)
- emerging 최근 생겨난
- norm 기준
- density 밀도, 농도
- uncomfortable 불편한
- sure-fire 확실한, 틀림없는, 실패하지 않는
- reduce 줄이다, 축소하다, 감소시키다
- square footage 평방 피트
- here to stay 계속 유지될

08   정답 ④

정답 해설

단편 소설 작가의 성공 비결로서의 인간에 대한 관심을 주제로 하는 글로, 작가로서 사람들을 좋아하는 태도는 작품을 좋아하게 만들며, 사람들에게 관심을 가져야 작가로서 성공할 수 있다는 편집장의 말을 강조하는 글이다. ④는 '자기 자신에게 긍정적인 말을 하는 마술사의 예'이므로 글의 맥락과 맞지 않다. 따라서 글의 흐름상 어색한 문장은 ④이다.

지문 해석

나는 한때 단편 소설 쓰기 수업을 들었고, 그 과정 중에 일류의 잡지의 저명한 편집장이 우리 수업에서 강연했다. ① 그는 매일 자신의 책상에 온 수십 편의 이야기 중 아무거나 골라서 몇 단락을 읽은 후에 저자가 사람들을 좋아하는지 아닌지를 느낄 수 있다고 말했다. ② "만약 저자가 사람들을 좋아하지 않는다면, 사람들도 그의 이야기를 좋아하지 않을 것입니다."라고 그는 말했다. ③ 그 편집장은 소설 작성에 관한 강연 중에 계속해서 사람들에 관심을 가져야 하는 중요성을 강조했다. (④ 위대한 마술사인 Thurston은 무대에 올라갈 때마다 자신에게 "나는 성공해서 감사하다"라고 말했다고 한다.) 강연의 끝에서 그는 "다시 말하지만, 성공한 소설 작가가 되길 원한다면 사람들에게 관심을 가져야 합니다."라고 끝마쳤다.

지문 어휘

- short-story 단편 소설
- renowned 유명한, 명성 있는
- editor 편집장, 편집자
- leading 주요한
- pick up 고르다
- paragraph 문단, 단락, 절
- stress 강조하다
- conclude 결론을 내리다, 끝내다

09   정답 ②

정답 해설

해파리의 형광 단백질을 활용하여 태양 에너지를 생성하는 새로운 방법을 소개하는 글이며, 이것이 지속 가능한 에너지의 중요한 대안임을 강조하고 있다. ②는 '태양광 발전의 폐해'에 대한 진술로, 해파리의 형광 단백질을 이용한, 미래 깨끗한 에너지의 대안이라는 글의 주제와 관계가 없다. 따라서 전체 흐름과 가장 관계없는 문장은 ②이다.

지문 해석

지속 가능한 에너지의 새로운 원천 분야에서 가장 흥미로운 발견 중 하나는 해파리의 바이오 태양 에너지이다. 과학자들은 이 동물의 형광 단백질이 현재의 광전 에너지보다 더 지속 가능한 방법으로 태양 에너지를 생성하는 데 사용될 수 있다는 것을 발견했다. 이 에너지는 어떻게 생성될까? ① 그 과정은 해파리의 형광 단백질을 에너지를 생성하고 작은 장치로 전달할 수 있는 태양 전지로 변환하는 것을 포함한다. (② 무분별한 태양광 발전으로 인해 자연환경이 훼손되고 있다는 지적이 끊이지 않고 있다.) ③ 이 생명체들을 자연적인 에너지원으로 사용하는 것의 주요 이점은 화석 연료를 사용하지 않거나 제한된 자원의 사용을 요구하는 깨끗한 대안이라는 것이다. ④ 비록 이 프로젝트가 아직 시험 단계에 있지만, 이 에너지원은 점점 더 보편화되고 있는 소형 전자 장치 유형에 전력을 공급하기 위한 친환경 대안이 될 수 있을 것으로 기대된다.

지문 어휘

- jellyfish 해파리
- fluorescent 형광성의, 선명한
- reckless 무분별한, 무모한, 신중하지 못한
- fossil fuel 화석 연료
- limited 제한된, 한정된
- trial phase 시험 단계
- expand 확대시키다, 팽창하다
- green 환경보호의, 친환경적인
- device 장치, 기구

10 정답 ①

정답 해설

패스트 패션과 그로 인한 일회용 문화에 대한 문제를 제기하고, 이를 해결하기 위한 지속 가능한 패션의 중요성을 강조하고 있다. 작가가 강조하는 문장은 마지막 문장인 '일회용 문화와 빠른 패션 위기를 해결하기 위해 패션의 지속 가능성이라는 개념이 주목받고 있다'를 통해 '지속 가능한 패션'을 강조하고 있다. 그러나 ① 문장은 '소비자들이 패스트 패션의 품질에 만족한다'는 패스트 패션에 대한 긍정적인 진술로 글의 흐름과 관계가 없다. 따라서 전체 흐름과 가장 관계없는 문장은 ①이다.

지문 해석

패스트 패션은 최신 패션 트렌드에 대응하기 위해 빠른 속도로 저렴한 의류를 생산하는 방법이다. 패스트 패션 시대에 쇼핑이 오락 형태로 진화하면서 고객들은 지속 가능성 전문가들이 말하는 일회용 문화에 기여하고 있다. 이것은 고객들이 제품을 재활용하거나 기부하는 것이 아니라 쓸모없는 것으로 간주되면 그냥 폐기한다는 것을 의미한다. (① 소비자들은 일반적으로 패스트 패션 브랜드 의류의 품질에 만족한다.) ② 결과적으로, 이러한 버려진 물건들은 환경에 큰 부담을 더한다. ③ 일회용 문화와 패스트 패션 위기를 해결하기 위해 패션의 지속 가능성이라는 개념이 주목받고 있다. ④ 지속 가능한 패션은 사회경제적, 환경적 관심사를 고려하여 가능한 지속 가능하게 생산, 유통 및 활용되는 의류, 신발 및 액세서리를 포함한다.

지문 어휘

- sustainability 지속 가능성
- throwaway 일회용
- socio-economic 사회 경제적인
- environmental 환경적인
- concern 관심사, 중요한 것, 걱정, 염려, 영향을 미치다

11 정답 ③

정답 해설

어떻게 아이들이 논쟁 능력을 배울 수 있는지와 논쟁의 중요성을 강조하는 글로, 논쟁과 긴장된 환경이 창의력에 기여할 수 있다는 것을 강조하고 있다. ③은 '평화로운 환경이 창의력에 기여한다'고 진술하고 있으므로 글의 일관성에서 벗어난다. 따라서 글의 흐름상 가장 어색한 문장은 ③이다.

지문 해석

좋은 논쟁을 하는 기술은 인생에서 매우 중요하다. 하지만 그것은 소수의 부모들이 그들의 아이들에게 가르치는 것이다. ① 우리는 아이들에게 안정적인 가정을 제공해 주고 싶어서 우리는 형제자매들이 싸우는 것을 막고 우리만의 논쟁을 비공개로 한다. ② 하지만 아이들이 의견 차이에 절대 노출되지 않는다면, 우리는 결국 그들의 창의력을 제한할 수도 있다. (③ 아이들은 평화로운 환경에서 많은 칭찬과 격려를 받으며 자유롭게 브레인스토밍을 할 때 가장 창의적이다.) ④ 대단히 창의력이 뛰어난 사람들은 종종 긴장감이 가득한 가정에서 성장하는 것으로 나타났다. 그들은 주먹다짐이나 개인적인 모욕에 둘러싸여 있는 것이 아니라, 진정한 의견 차이로 둘러싸여 있다. 30대 초반의 성인들에게 상상력이 풍부한 이야기를 쓰라고 했을 때, 가장 창의적인 이야기들은 25년 전에 가장 갈등이 많았던 부모님들에게서 나왔다.

지문 어휘

- argument 논쟁, 주장
- stable 안정적인
- quarrel 말다툼, 언쟁
- disagreement 불일치, 의견 차이
- creativity 창의성
- brainstorm 아이디어 회의
- encouragement 격려
- peaceful 평화로운
- tension 긴장, 긴장감
- fistfight 주먹싸움
- insult 모욕, 모욕하다
- imaginative 상상력이 풍부한
- conflict 갈등, 충돌
- quarter-century 25년, 1/4세기
- exposure 노출, 폭로
- limit 제한하다

12 정답 ④

정답 해설

일상 업무 스트레스로 인한 지침의 만성적인 질환인 번아웃을 주제로 하는 글이다. 본문의 내용은 번아웃이라는 개념과 유형에 대해서 나열하고 있는데 ④는 감정노동자들은 그들의 직업에 매우 의욕적으로 들어간다고 진술하고 있으므로 글의 일관성에서 벗어난다. 따라서 글의 흐름상 가장 어색한 문장은 ④이다.

지문 해석

번아웃이라는 용어는 업무 압박으로 인한 "지치는 것"을 의미한다. 번아웃은 일상의 업무 스트레스 요인이 직원들에게 피해를 입히면서 발생하는 만성적인 질환이다. ① 번아웃에 대한 가장 널리 채택된 개념화는 Maslach와 그녀의 동료들이 인간 서비스 노동자에 대한 연구에서 발전되어 왔다. Maslach는 번아웃이 서로 연관된 3개의 차원으로 이루어져 있다고 본다. 첫 번째 요소인 감정적인 소모는 실제로 번아웃 현상의 핵심이다. ② 근로자들은 피곤하거나, 좌절하거나, 지치거나, 직장에서 다른 날을 맞이할 수 없을 때 감정적인 피로로 고통 받는다. 번아웃 현상의 두 번째 요소는 개인적인 성취의 결여이다. ③ 이러한 번아웃 현상의 차원은 자신을 실패자로 간주하고, 업무 요건을 효과적으로 이행할 수 없는 근로자를 나타낸다. (④ 감정노동자들은 육체적으로 지쳤음에도 불구하고 매우 의욕적으로 그들의 직업에 들어간다.) 번아웃의 세 번째 요소는 비인격화이다. 이 요소는 직무의 일부로 다른 사람들(예를 들어, 고객들, 환자들, 학생들)과 대인 관계에서 의사소통해야 하는 노동자들과만 관련된다.

지문 어휘

- burnout 번아웃, 극도의 피로
- chronic 만성적인, 장기적인
- stressor 스트레스를 유발하는 요인
- toll 대가, 비용, 통행료
- conceptualization 개념화, 개념적인 해석
- interrelated 상호 관련된, 연결된
- dimension 요소, 차원
- exhaustion 탈진, 피로
- core 핵심
- phenomenon 현상
- fatigued 피로한, 지친
- frustrated 좌절한, 좌절감을 느끼는
- used up 다 쓴, 지친
- incapable 무능한, ~을 할 수 없는
- effectively 효과적으로
- requirement 요구사항
- depersonalization 비인격화, 몰개성화, 객관화
- interpersonally 대인 관계에서

13   정답 ②

정답 해설

아리스토텔레스의 작품과 자연 철학의 발전에 대한 글로, 체계적인 자연 세계와의 인류의 관계적인 측면에서 아리스토텔레스의 역할을 강조하고 있다. 본문의 내용은 아리스토텔레스 철학이 현재 학문들에 영향을 미쳤다는 내용의 글인데, '그들의 지식을 전파하는 인쇄기의 힘을 강조하는' ②는 아리스토텔레스의 철학에 벗어나는 내용이다. 따라서 글의 흐름상 적절하지 않은 문장은 ②이다.

지문 해석

15세기에는 과학, 철학, 마술 사이에 어떤 구분도 없었다. 이 세 가지 모두 '자연 철학'이라는 일반적인 주제에 포함되었다. ① 고전 작가들의 재발견이 자연 철학의 발전에 중요했는데, 가장 중요하게는 아리스토텔레스의 작품들이었다. (② 인문주의자들은 그들의 지식을 전파하는 인쇄기의 힘을 빠르게 깨달았다.) ③ 15세기 초에 아리스토텔레스는 스콜라 학파 철학과 과학의 논쟁에 기초가 되었다. ④ 아랍어 번역 작품들과 Averroes와 Avicenna의 논평 안에서 살아있는, 아리스토텔레스는 자연세계와의 인류의 관계에 대한 체계적인 관점을 제공했다. 그의 물리학, 형이상학, 그리고 기상학과 같은 살아남은 문헌들은 학자들에게 자연계를 창조한 힘을 이해할 수 있는 논리적 도구를 제공했다.

지문 어휘

- natural philosophy 자연 철학
- recovery 회복
- humanist 인문주의자
- printing press 인쇄기
- scholastic 스콜라 철학의, 학문적인
- speculation 추측, 사색
- systematic 체계적인
- perspective 시각, 관점
- physics 물리학
- metaphysics 형이상학
- meteorology 기상학
- logical 논리적인
- force 힘, 역력

14   정답 ②

정답 해설

산문 소설을 통해 상상력을 발휘하고 다른 세계를 탐험하며 공감을 형성하는 경험을 강조하는 글이다. 그러나 ②의 내용은 '실제 세계에서의 장소'를 언급하고 있으므로, '소설과 상상력을 통한 세계'라는 주제와 거리가 있다. 따라서 글의 흐름상 가장 어색한 문장은 ②이다.

지문 해석

소설은 많은 용도를 가지고 있고 그것들 중 하나는 공감을 형성하는 것이다. 당신이 TV를 보거나 영화를 볼 때, 당신은 다른 사람들에게 일어나는 일들을 보고 있다. 산문 소설은 26개의 글자[알파벳]와 몇 개의 구두점을 통해 쌓아올린 것이다. 그리고 당신과 당신만이 상상력을 발휘하여 세상을 창조하고 그곳에서 살고 다른 눈을 통해 관찰한다. ① 당신은 무언가를 느끼고, 그렇지 않다면 당신이 결코 알지 못할 장소와 세상들을 방문한다. (② 다행히도, 지난 10년 동안, 세계에서 가장 아름답고 알려지지 않은 많은 장소들이 주목을 받았다.) ③ 저 밖에 있는 다른 사람들도 모두 나라는 것을 알게 된다. ④ 당신은 다른 사람이 되고 있고, 당신이 당신의 세상으로 돌아가면, 당신은 약간 달라질 것이다.

지문 어휘

- empathy 감정 이입, 공감
- prose 산문(체)
- punctuation mark 구두점
- imagination 상상력
- spotlight 주목을 받다
- slightly 약간, 조금

15

정답 ②

정답 해설

의학 인류학자들이 질병 전염 패턴과 인간의 적응에 대한 연구를 통해 어떻게 의료 서비스를 개선하는 데 기여하는지를 다루고 있는 글이다. ②는 '인도주의적인 동기에서의 전망과 지위와 보상의 고려'에 대한 진술로, '인류 인류학자들의 의료에 대한 기여'와는 관계가 없는 문장이다. 따라서 전체 흐름과 관계없는 문장은 ②이다.

지문 해석

인간 생물학 및 생리학에 대한 폭넓은 교육을 받은 의학 인류학자들은 질병 전염 패턴과 말라리아나 수면병과 같은 질병의 존재에 어떻게 적응하는지를 연구한다. ① 바이러스와 박테리아의 전염은 사람들의 식생활, 위생, 다른 행동의 영향을 많이 받기 때문에 많은 의학 인류학자들은 전염병학자와 팀을 이루어 질병의 확산에 영향을 미치는 문화적 관행을 파악한다. (② 비록 대부분의 학생들이 성공적인 의학 경력의 금전적 보상보다는 인도주의적 이유로 의학을 입학한다는 것이 일반적인 믿음일 수 있지만, 선진국에서는 지위와 보상에 대한 전망이 아마도 하나의 동기일 것이다.) ③ 질병의 원인과 증상, 어떻게 질병을 가장 잘 치료하는지, 전통 치료사와 의사의 능력, 치유 과정에 지역사회가 참여하는 중요성에 대해 서로 다른 문화들은 다른 생각을 갖고 있다. ④ 의료 인류학자는 인간 공동체가 이러한 것들을 어떻게 인식하는지 연구함으로써 병원 및 다른 기관이 보다 효과적으로 의료 서비스를 제공할 수 있도록 지원한다.

지문 어휘

- transmission 전염, 전파, 전달
- practice 관행, 관례, 실행, 실천
- cause 원인, 이유
- symptom 증상, 징후
- traditional healer 전통 치료사
- involvement 참여, 개입, 몰두, 열중
- perception 인식, 지각

16

정답 ④

정답 해설

위협 감지 시 신체 반응을 할 때의 호르몬의 역할에 대한 설명을 하는 글이다. ④ 문장은 인간이 의식적으로 호르몬을 분비한다는 내용으로 글의 일관성에서 벗어난다. 따라서 글의 흐름상 가장 어색한 문장은 ④이다.

지문 해석

두뇌가 인접한 환경에서 위협을 감지할 때, 그것은 신체에서 복잡한 일련의 사건들을 일으킨다. 그것은 화학 호르몬을 혈류로 방출하는 기관인 다양한 분비샘에 전기적 신호를 보낸다. 혈액은 이 호르몬들을 그 다음에 다양한 일을 하도록 유도되는 다른 기관으로 빠르게 운반한다. ① 예를 들어, 신장 위의 부신은 신체의 스트레스 호르몬인 아드레날린을 배출한다. ② 아드레날린은 위험의 징후를 경계하기 위해 눈을 크게 뜨고, 혈액과 여분의 호르몬이 계속 흐르게 하기 위해 심장을 더 빠르게 펌프질하고, 골격 근육을 긴장시켜서 그들이 위협에 맞서거나 도망칠 준비를 하는 것과 같은 일들을 하면서 몸 전체를 돌아다닌다. ③ 그 전체 과정은 몸을 자신의 생명을 위해 싸우거나 뛸 수 있도록 준비시키기 때문에 투쟁 — 도피 반응이라고 불린다. (④ 인간은 의식적으로 다양한 호르몬의 분비를 통제하기 위해 그들의 분비샘을 조절한다.) 일단 그 반응이 시작되면, 호르몬은 논리적으로 설득할 수 없기 때문에 그것을 무시하는 것은 불가능하다.

지문 어휘

- threat 위협
- initiate 시작하다, 착수시키다
- complex 복잡한
- a string of 일련의, 연속적인
- electrical 전기적인
- gland (내분비)샘
- chemical 화학적인
- hormone 호르몬
- bloodstream 혈류
- pump out 내보내다
- widen 넓히다, 커지다
- be on the lookout 주의를 기울이다, 세심히 살피다
- skeletal muscle 골격근
- lash out 공격하다, 싸우다, 혹평하다, 비난하다
- fight-or-flight response 투쟁 혹은 도피 반응
- consciously 의식적으로

17

정답 ③

정답 해설

이 글의 주제는 '철학자들은 인류학자의 연구에 관심이 없다'이다. ③은 '훌륭한 철학자들이 인류학과 같은 분야에서 영감을 얻는다'는 내용이므로 주제와 반대가 되는 진술이다. 따라서 글의 흐름상 가장 어색한 문장은 ③이다.

지문 해석

철학자들은 인류학자들이 철학에 관심을 갖는 것만큼 인류학에 관심을 갖지 않았다. ① 영향력 있는 현대의 철학자들 중 그들의 연구에 인류학적 연구를 고려한 사람은 거의 없었다. ② 사회과학 철학을 전공하는 사람들은 인류학 연구의 사례를 고려하거나 분석할 수 있지만, 대부분 개념적 요점이나 인식론적 차이를 설명하거나 인식론적 또는 윤리적 영향을 비판하기 위해서였다. (③ 사실, 우리 시대의 위대한 철학자들은 종종 인류학과 심리학 같은 다른 분야로부터 영감을 얻는다.) ④ 철학과 학생들은 인류학에 대해 공부하거나 진지한 관심을 보이지 않는다. 그들은 과학에서 실험적인 방법에 대해 배울 수는 있지만, 인류학적 현장 연구에 대해서는 거의 배우지 않는다.

지문 어휘

- anthropology 인류학
- influential 영향력 있는
- contemporary 현대의, 동시대의
- specialize in 전공하다
- analyze 분석하다
- research 연구
- illustrate 설명하다, 실증하다
- conceptual 개념적인
- epistemological 인식론의
- distinction 구분
- ethical 윤리적인
- implication 함축, 암시, 영향, 결과
- inspiration 영감
- fieldwork 현장 연구

18

정답 ②

정답 해설

금융 위기와 금융 체계 안정화의 발전에 대한 글로, 2007년의 금융 위기를 겪은 후, 금융 체계 안정화를 위해 은행들의 자본화와 규제 강화 등의 발전이 이루어지고 있음을 보여주고 있다. 이 글은 문제점으로 '너무 커진 월스트리트의 은행들'을 언급하고, 글의 전개방향은 이의 해결책이 진술되어야 하는데, ②에서 언급한 '가상화폐'는 이 글의 주제와 상관없다. 따라서 글의 흐름상 가장 어색한 것은 ②이다.

지문 해석

2007년, 우리의 가장 큰 걱정은 "파산하기에는 너무 크다"는 것이었다. Wall Street의 은행들은 그렇게 어마어마한 크기로 성장했고, 금융 체계의 안정에 있어 너무도 중심이 되어 합리적인 정부라면 그들을 파산하도록 내버려둘 수가 없었다. ① 그들이 보호 받는 상태임을 알고 있기 때문에, 은행들은 과도하게 위험한 투자를 주택 시장에 하고 훨씬 복잡한 금융파생상품들을 고안해 냈다. (② 비트코인과 이더리움과 같은 새로운 가상 화폐들은 어떻게 돈이 작용 할 수 있고 작용해야 하는지에 대한 우리의 이해를 급진적으로 변화시켰다.) ③ 그 결과는 1929년 우리 경제의 붕괴 이후 최악의 금융 위기였다. ④ 2007년 이래로 파산하기에는 너무 큰 것에 대한 딜레마를 해결하는 데 있어서 큰 발전을 해오고 있다. 우리의 은행들은 그 어느 때보다 더 잘 투자를 받는다. 우리의 단속 기관들은 대형 기관들의 규칙적인 스트레스 테스트를 시행한다.

지문 어휘

- concern 걱정, 염려
- staggering 충격적인, 믿기 어려운
- financial 금융의
- rational 합리적인
- excessively 과도하게, 지나치게
- complicated 복잡한
- derivative 파생상품
- virtual currency 가상 화폐
- financial crisis 금융 위기
- breakdown 붕괴
- progress 진전, 진척, 진행하다, 나아가다
- address 다루다, 연설하다
- capitalize 투자하다, 자본화하다
- institution 기관

19

정답 ④

정답 해설

아이들의 놀이터와 변화된 환경에 대한 글로, 역사 속 아이들의 놀이터가 자연적인 장소에서 현대의 디지털 환경으로 변화하면서 아이들의 놀이 습관과 활동이 변화되어 전통적인 놀이터에서 아이들이 보이지 않음을 강조하는 글이다. 아이들의 자연의 놀이터가 점점 역할을 못하고 있다는 진술의 글인데, ④는 아이들이 '자연에서의 놀이터'에서 놀고 있다는 진술이므로 글의 일관성에서 벗어난다. 따라서 글의 흐름상 가장 어색한 문장은 ④이다.

지문 해석

역사를 통틀어 아이들의 놀이터는 황야, 들판, 개울, 그리고 도시의 언덕과 도로, 거리, 마을, 시내, 도시의 공터였다. ① 놀이터라는 용어는 아이들이 자유롭고 자발적인 게임을 하기 위해 모인 모든 장소들을 나타낸다. ② 불과 지난 몇십 년 사이에 아이들은 비디오 게임, 문자, 그리고 사회 연결망과의 사랑이 커짐에 따라 이런 자연적 놀이터를 떠나왔다. ③ 심지어 미국의 시골에서도 조금밖에 없는 아이들이 어른들과 동반되지 않은 채 여전히 자유롭게 돌아다니는 방식으로 한다. (④ 학교 밖에 있을 때, 그들은 모래를 파거나, 요새를 짓거나, 전통 게임을 하거나, 등산하거나, 혹은 공놀이를 하면서 흔히 동네에서 발견된다.) 그들은 계곡, 언덕 그리고 들판의 자연적 지역으로부터 빠르게 사라지고 있고 도시 거주자처럼 오락을 위해 실내에서 앉아 하는 사이버 장난감으로 눈을 돌리고 있다.

지문 어휘

- playground 놀이터
- wilderness 황야, 황무지
- spontaneous 자발적인, 즉흥적인
- free-ranging 자유롭게 돌아다니는
- unaccompanied 동반되지 않은
- terrain 지역, 지형
- sedentary 정적인, 주로 앉아서 하는

20

정답 ③

정답 해설

다양한 독서 형식의 분류와 목적에 대한 글로, 다양한 독서 형식 중 정보 획득을 위한 독서, 실용서나 설명서의 읽기, 그리고 속독 수업을 통한 빠른 훑어보기의 필요성에 대해 설명하고 있다. 즉, '정보를 목적으로 한 독서'가 주제인데, ③의 '일련의 감정과 은유와 단어들의 결합'은 정보를 목적으로 한 독서가 아니기 때문에 글의 일관성에서 벗어난다. 따라서 글의 흐름상 가장 적절하지 않은 문장은 ③이다.

지문 해석

내가 보기에는 각각 독특한 방식과 목적을 가진 네 종류의 독서를 이름 짓는 것은 가능할 것 같다. 첫 번째는 정보를 얻기 위한 독서 — 무역, 정치, 또는 무언가를 성취하는 방법에 관해 배우기 위해 읽는 것이다. ① 우리는 이런 식으로 신문을 읽거나, 대부분의 교과서 또는 자전거를 조립하는 방법에 대한 설명서를 읽는다. ② 이러한 자료의 대부분을 가지고 독자는 페이지를 빨리 훑어보는 법을 배울 수 있고, 필요한 것을 찾아내고, 문장의 운율이나 은유 구사와 같은 자신과 무관한 것을 무시한다. (③ 우리는 또한 은유와 단어들의 연관성을 통해 감정의 궤적을 나타낸다.) ④ 속독 수업은 페이지 전체에 걸쳐 빠르게 움직이도록 눈을 훈련시키면서 우리가 이러한 목적을 위해 책을 읽는 데 도움을 줄 수 있다.

지문 어휘

- accomplish 성취하다, 달성하다
- direction 안내, 지시사항, 방향
- assemble 조립하다, 모으다
- scan 빠르게 훑어보다
- irrelevant 무관한, 관련 없는
- metaphor 은유, 비유
- register 나타내다, 기록하다, 등록하다
- association 연관, 연상

21
정답 ③

정답 해설
프레디 머큐리와 그가 이끈 밴드 Queen의 음악과 스타일에 대한 이야기를 다루고 있는 글이며, ②에서 'Queen의 음악과 스타일'이 뚜렷해 졌음을 강조하고 있다. 그러나 ③은 'Freddie의 유년시절'에 대한 진술로, 글의 주제인 'Freddie의 음악스타일'과는 거리가 있다. 따라서 글의 흐름과 가장 관계없는 문장은 ③이다.

지문 해석
Queen에 의한 불멸의 오페라 풍으로 스타일된 싱글 보헤미안 랩소디는 1975년에 발표되어 9주 동안 영국 차트의 정상에 올랐다. ① 길이와 독특한 스타일 때문에 거의 발매되지 않을 뻔했지만, Freddie가 들려지게 될 것이라고 강력히 주장했던 노래는 즉시 눈에 띄는 히트를 쳤다. ② 이때쯤에 Freddie의 독특한 재능들은 분명해지고 있었는데, 그것들은 놀랄 만한 음역대의 목소리, 그리고 Queen에게 그것의 다채롭고 예측할 수 없으며 이색적인 개성을 주었던 무대에서의 존재감이었다. (③ Bomi와 Jer Bulsara의 아들인 Freddie는 어린 시절의 대부분을 인도에서 보냈고 그곳에서 St. Peter의 기숙학교에 다녔다.) ④ 곧 그들이 유럽, 일본과 Freddie의 노래 Crazy Little thing Called Love로 1979년 차트에서 1위를 차지했던 미국에서까지 성공하면서, Queen의 인기는 영국의 해안을 넘어 뻗어나갔다.

지문 어휘
- nearly 거의
- release 발매하다, 풀어주다
- remarkable 놀라운, 주목할 만한
- range 음역대
- presence 있음, 존재, 참석
- flamboyant 이색적인, 화려한
- boarding school 기숙학교
- extend 뻗다, 연장하다, 확장하다
- triumph 성공하다, 승리를 거두다

22
정답 ④

정답 해설
입냄새와 잇몸 질환 사이의 관계에 대해 다루며 조기 발견의 중요성을 강조하고 있는 글이다. 특히 강조하고 있는 것은 '박테리아로 말미암은 문제'인데, ④는 '흡연으로 말미암은 잇몸 조직의 손상'에 대한 내용으로 글의 일관성에서 벗어난다. 따라서 글의 흐름과 관계없는 문장은 ④이다.

지문 해석
잇몸 질환은 종종 입 냄새의 원인으로 지목된다. 사실, 입냄새는 잇몸 질환의 경고 신호다. ① 이 문제는 치아에 플라크가 축적된 결과로 처음 발생한다. ② 치석 속의 박테리아는 잇몸을 자극하여 잇몸이 연해지고 부어오르고 출혈이 일어나기 쉽다. ③ 박테리아가 내뿜는 냄새가 역겨운 가스도 입냄새를 유발할 수 있다. (④ 흡연은 당신의 치아에 뼈와 부드러운 조직의 부착에 영향을 미침으로써 당신의 잇몸 조직을 손상시킨다.) 하지만 박테리아가 유발하는 입냄새를 알아차릴 때 주의를 기울인다면, 더 발전된 단계에 이르기 전에 잇몸 질환을 발견할 수 있을 것이다.

지문 어휘
- gum disease 잇몸 질환
- plaque 치석
- irritate 자극하다, 짜증나게 하다
- tender 부드러운, 연한
- swollen 부어오른, 불어난
- prone to ~하기 쉬운
- advanced 진행된
- attachment 부착

23
정답 ④

정답 해설
벼의 유전자 발견으로 홍수에 강한 농작물 생산 가능성 증대에 대한 글로, 생물학자들은 벼의 유전자를 통해 1주일 이상의 물에 잠기는 환경에서 생존할 수 있는 능력을 이끌었고, 이러한 발견은 홍수 위험 지역에서의 농작물 수확 증가를 희망하며, 풍년을 이끌어내고 경제적 손실을 감소시키기 위한 가능성을 열어 놓았음을 설명하고 있다. '벼를 생존하게 하는 유전자를 발견한 것'은 좋은 소식인데, 이것을 '무서운 소식'이라고 진술한 ④ 문장의 내용이 글의 일관성에 벗어난다. 따라서 글의 흐름상 가장 어색한 문장은 ④이다.

지문 해석
생물학자들은 벼가 현재보다 일주일 이상 더 긴 2주까지 물속에 잠긴 채로 생존하게 할 수 있는 유전자를 찾아냈다. 일주일 이상 물속에 있는 식물들은 산소를 빼앗기고 시들어 죽는다. ① 과학자들은 그들의 발견이 홍수에 취약한 지역에서의 작물 수확을 연장시킬 것을 희망한다. ② 이러한 범람하기 쉬운 아시아 지역의 벼 재배자들은 과도하게 물에 잠긴 논 때문에 매년 10억 달러로 추정되는 돈을 잃는다. ③ 그들은 새로운 유전자가 태풍과 장마철에 발생하는 재정적 피해를 줄이고 풍작을 가져오고 더 강인한 벼 품종을 가져오기를 희망한다. (④ 이것은 이러한 취약한 지역의 사람들에게 끔찍한 소식이고, 그들은 도시화의 피해자이며 작물 부족을 겪는다.) 쌀 생산량은 다음 20년에 걸쳐 10억 명의 사람들이 그들의 주식을 얻을 수 있는 것을 확실하게 하기 위해 30퍼센트만큼 증가해야 한다.

지문 어휘
- submerge 물속에 잠기다, 잠수하다
- deprive of 빼앗다, 박탈하다
- perish 죽다, 사라지다, 소멸되다
- prolong 연장시키다, 늘이다
- susceptible 취약한, 민감한, 영향을 받기 쉬운
- water logged 물에 잠긴
- rice paddy 쌀, 벼
- lead to 가져오다, 이끌다
- incur 발생시키다, 초래하다
- bumper 풍작의, 대단히 큰
- vulnerable 취약한
- urbanization 도시화

24
정답 ④

정답 해설
듣는 능력과 사랑받음의 관계에 대한 글로, 대부분의 사람들은 말하기를 좋아하며, 듣는 능력은 귀하게 여겨지는 흔하지 않은 재능임을 강조하는 글이다. 문제에서 요구하는 것은 문맥에서 바르지 않은 단어를 고르는 것으로, 듣는 것이 더 적은 적들을 만든다는 일반론의 예외적인 사항을 예시를 통해 이야기를 하는 ④는 부정적인 진술이 되어야 한다. 따라서 '그럼에도 불구하고, 그의 듣기의 결과는 그를 인기 있게 만들지 않았다'의 의미가 되어야 한다. 따라서 '인기 없는(unpopular)' 대신에 인기 있는(popular)'이 들어가야 한다.

지문 해석

대부분의 사람들은 말하는 것을 좋아하나 듣는 것을 좋아하는 사람들은 거의 없다, 하지만 잘 듣는 것은 모든 사람들이 귀하게 여겨야하는 ① 흔하지 않은 재능이다. 그들은 더 많이 듣기 때문에, 주변사람들에게 일어나는 일에 대하여 대부분의 사람들보다 더 많이 알고 더 민감한 경향이 있다. 게다가 좋은 청자들은 받아들이거나 견뎌내는 것을, 판단하거나 비판하는 것보다 더 잘하게 된다. 그러므로 그들은 대부분의 사람들보다 ② 더 적은 적을 가지고 있다. 사실, 그들이 아마도 가장 사랑받는 사람일 것이다. 그러나 그러한 일반론에도 ③ 예외는 있다. 예를 들어 John Steinback은 훌륭한 청자였다고 알려졌지만 그는 그가 글을 썼던 일부 사람들에게 미움을 받았다. 경청하는 그의 능력이 그의 쓰기 능력에 기여한 것은 틀림없다. 그럼에도 불구하고, 그의 경청의 결과는 그를 ④ 인기 없게(→ 인기 있게) 만들지 않았다.

지문 어휘

☐ treasure 보물, 귀하게 여기다
☐ go on 시작하다
☐ inclined ~을 하고 싶은, ~할 것 같은
☐ tolerate 용인하다, 참다, 견디다
☐ beloved 인기 많은, 사랑받는
☐ generality 일반론
☐ no doubt 틀림없는, 아마
☐ contribute 기여하다, 헌신하다, ~의 원인이 되다
☐ capacity 능력, 수용력

25 정답 ③

정답 해설

르네상스 시대 주방과 식당의 계층과 역할에 대한 글로, 르네상스 시대 주방과 식당 내에서 각 역할의 분명한 계층이 있음과, 주방에서 만찬을 준비하기 위해 협력하는 다양한 사람들의 역할과 책임을 설명하고 하고 있다. 르네상스 시대의 주방에서 일하는 사람들의 위계질서를 주제로 한 글로, ③ '이러한 공들인 장식들과 음식을 전달하는 것은 "the front of the house"라고 식당에서 불리는 것이다'의 진술은 사람들의 위계와는 상관없는 내용이다. 따라서 글의 흐름상 가장 어색한 문장은 ③이다.

지문 해석

르네상스 시대 주방에는 정성을 들인 만찬을 만들기 위해 함께 일하는 도움을 주는 사람들의 분명한 계급이 있었다. ① 최고의 위치에는, 우리가 보았던 것처럼, 집사라는 scalco가 있었는데, 그 사람은 주방을 책임졌을 뿐만 아니라 식당도 책임을 지고 있었다. ② 식당은 집사에 의해 감독이 되었는데, 이 사람은 은식기와 식탁용 리넨제품들을 책임을 졌고 만찬을 시작하고 끝내는 요리들을 제공했다 — 식사를 시작할 때의 차가운 요리, 샐러드, 치즈 그리고 과일과 식사의 끝에는 디저트들과 과자들이 있었다. (③ 이러한 공들인 장식들과 음식을 전달하는 것은 "the front of the house"라고 식당에서 불리는 것이다.) ④ 주방은 주방장들에 의해 감독되었고, 그는 요리사의 조수들, 페이스트리 요리사들과 주방 보조들을 지휘했다.

지문 어휘

☐ hierarchy 계급, 계층
☐ elaborate 정성을 들인, 정교한
☐ banquet 연회, 만찬
☐ scalco (식당의) 집사
☐ steward 지배인, 집사
☐ supervise 감독하다, 지휘하다
☐ butler 집사, 하인 우두머리
☐ silverware 은제품, 은식기류
☐ serve 섬기다, 제공하다, 주다
☐ head cook 주방장

26 정답 ③

정답 해설

아동문학상의 증가와 그것의 의미를 주제로 하는 글로, 최근 아동문학상의 급증과 다양성에 대해 설명하며, 이러한 상들이 어린이들과 어른들의 선택을 통해 아동문학의 영향력을 인정받고, 좋은 독서 경험을 위한 출발점을 제공한다는 내용을 다루고 있다. 아동 문학상에 대한 전반적으로 설명하고 있는데 ③은 출판 산업에 대한 기여에 대한 시상식에 대해 진술하고 있다. 따라서 글의 흐름상 가장 어색한 문장은 ③이다.

지문 해석

최근에 아동문학상이 급증하고 있다; 오늘날 다양한 기관에서 수여하는 100여개가 넘는 다양한 상이 있다. ① 이 상들은 특정한 장르의 책이나 단순히 일정 기간 안에 출간된 모든 아동문학 중 최고의 도서에 주어질 수 있다. 상은 특정한 책이나 아동 문학 세계에 공헌한 작가의 일생에 줄 수도 있다. ② 대부분의 아동문학상은 어른들에 의해 선택되나 현재는 더욱 많은 어린이들이 선정한 도서상이 존재한다. 대부분의 국가에서 주어지는 더 큰 국가적인 상은 가장 영향력이 있으며, 어린 독자를 위해 출간되는 훌륭한 책들이라는 대중적인 인식을 높이는 데 상당히 기여한다. (③ 출판 산업에 대한 뛰어난 기여에 대한 한 시상식이 보류되었다.) ④ 물론 독자들은 수상한 책에 대해 너무 많은 신뢰를 주지 않을 정도로 현명하다. 상이 필연적으로 좋은 독서 경험을 의미하지는 않으나, 책을 선정할 때 좋은 출발점을 제공한다.

지문 어휘

☐ proliferate 급증하다, 확산되다
☐ a variety of 다양한
☐ publish 출간하다, 발표하다
☐ lifetime 일생, 생애
☐ contribution 기여, 공헌
☐ influential 영향력 있는
☐ awareness 인식, 의식
☐ outstanding 뛰어난, 두드러진
☐ put on hold 보류하다, 연기하다
☐ faith 믿음, 신뢰, 신앙

27
정답 ④

정답 해설
북대서양 참고래 개체 수 감소의 심각성과 구조적 문제에 대한 새로운 모델 분석에 대한 글로, 첫 문장에서 참고래의 개체 수 조사내용이 좋지 않다고 설명했다. 2번째 문장부터는 참고래의 개체 수의 부정적인 결과를 나열하고 있는데, ④는 고래가 온전한 상태로 남아있다는 긍정적인 내용으로 글의 주제문에 맞지 않고 새로운 내용이 추가될 수 있는 연결사도 없다. 그리고 고래의 수컷과 암컷의 개체 수의 비교도 이 글하고는 상관없는 내용이다. 따라서 글의 흐름상 가장 어색한 문장은 ④이다.

지문 해석
연구원들은 북방긴수염고래 개체 수에 대해 더 나은 추정치를 제공할 수 있을 것이라고 말한 새로운 모델을 개발했지만 그 소식은 좋지 않다. ① 그 모델은 멸종 위기에 처한 종들을 살리기 위한 노력의 일환으로 멸종 위기에 처한 동물을 구하는 데 결정적으로 중요할 수 있다고 Peter Corken 국립해양 과학 연구소장은 말했다. ② 그 기관은 이 분석이 2010년 이래로 개체 수가 거의 100퍼센트 감소했다고 말하고 있다. ③ "한 가지 문제는 개체 수가 정말로 줄어들고 있는가? 아니면 단지 우리가 그걸 보지 못하고 있는 것인가? 이것이 문제였다. 개체 수는 정말로 줄어들고 있으며, 그게 요점이다."라고 Corkeron이 말했다. (④ 그 새로운 조사 모델은 수많은 긴수염고래들이 온전한 상태로 남아 있다는 것이 성공적으로 입증되었으며 그런 걱정에도 불구하고, 고래 수컷과 암컷 사이의 개체 수 격차가 커지고 있다.)

지문 어휘
- North Atlantic right whale 북방긴수염고래
- critically 결정적으로, 중대하게
- endangered 멸종 위기에 처한
- species 종, 종류
- mortality 사망률, 사망
- agency 기관, 단체
- decline 감소하다, 줄어들다
- bottom line 핵심, 요점
- intact 온전한, 전혀 다치지 않은
- worrisome 걱정스러운, 귀찮은
- widen 커지다, 확대되다
- gap 격차, 간격, 차이

28
정답 ③

정답 해설
체육관을 벗어난(운동하지 않은) 14일간의 영향과 회복에 대한 글이다. 당신이 14일 동안 운동을 하지 않으면(체육관으로 돌아오지 않으면) 당신의 근육뿐만 아니라 당신의 수행능력, 뇌, 잠 등에도 영향을 미친다는 주제를 바탕으로 글이 이어진다. 하지만 ③은 단백질(먹는 것)에 대한 내용으로 운동과 관련된 글의 일관성에서 벗어난다. 따라서 글의 흐름상 가장 어색한 문장은 ③이다.

지문 해석
당신이 여행을 하는 중이거나, 당신의 가족에 집중을 하거나, 혹은 직장에서의 바쁜 시즌을 경험하는 것과는 상관없이, 체육관을 벗어난 14일은 이것의 대가를 치를 것이다 — 이것은 단지 당신의 근육뿐만 아니라, 당신의 수행능력, 뇌, 그리고 수면에 대해서 역시 대가를 치를 것이다. ① 대부분의 전문가들은 2주후에 당신이 체육관으로 돌아오지 않는다면, 당신은 어려움에 처할 것이라는 것에 동의한다. "운동을 하지 않은 2주의 시점에, 건강한 상태의 감소를 자연적으로 나타내는 수많은 생리학적인 표식들이 있다"고 엘리트 운동선수들과 일을 하는 뉴욕에 있는 운동 생리학자이자 트레이너인 Scott Weiss가 말한다. ② 결국, 모든 사람의 인체의 능력에도 불구하고, 인체(심지어 건강한 인체)는 매우 민감한 시스템이며, 훈련을 통해 발생하는 생리적 변화(근육의 힘 또는 더 큰 호기성 기저)는 훈련 부담이 줄어들면 간단히 사라질 것이라고 그는 언급한다. 훈련의 요구가 현재에 있지 않기 때문에 당신의 몸은 단순히 기준선을 향하여 갈 것이다. (③ 더 많은 단백질이 더 많은 근육들을 당신의 몸에서 빠른 속도로 만드는 데 요구되어진다.) ④ 물론, 얼마나 많이 그리고 얼마나 빨리 건강을 손상시킬 것인지는 당신이 얼마나 건강한지, 나이가 몇 살인지, 그리고 얼마나 오랜 기간 동안 땀을 흘리는 습관을 가지고 있었는지와 같은 많은 요소들에 따라 달라진다. Weiss는 "2~8개월 동안 운동을 전혀 하지 않으면 마치 전에 운동을 하지 않은 것처럼 체력 수준이 떨어질 것"이라고 언급한다.

지문 어휘
- toll 대가, 영향
- physiological 생리적인
- marker 지표, 표시
- fitness 신체 단련, 건강
- physiologist 생리학자
- aerobic 호기성의, 유산소의
- load 부담, 짐
- dwindle 줄어들다, 감소하다
- note 언급하다, 주목하다
- baseline 기준선
- protein 단백질
- decondition 건강을 손상시키다
- a slew of 많은

29
정답 ④

정답 해설
과식의 장기적 영향 연구와 세대 간 건강에 대한 글로, 19세기 스웨덴에서 시작된 연구에서 수확 변동에 따른 과식과 영양 부족이 세대 간 건강에 미치는 영향이 밝혀져, 과식의 부정적인 영향이 지속됨을 발견하게 되었음을 설명하고 있다. 그런데 ④는 '자손들(소년과 소녀 모두)이 좋은 수확으로 이익을 보았다'는 긍정적인 진술의 내용으로 글의 일관성에서 벗어난다. 따라서 글의 흐름상 가장 어색한 것은 ④이다.

지문 해석
최첨단 현대 과학의 한 이야기는 19세기 북부 스웨덴의 고립된 지역에서 시작되었다. ① 그 국가의 이 지역은 그 세기 전반에 걸쳐 예측할 수 없는 수확을 하였다. 수확이 실패했던 수년 동안, 주민들은 굶주렸다. 그러나, 수확이 좋았던 해에는 상황이 매우 좋았다. ② 수확이 안 좋았던 시기 동안에 굶주렸던 사람들이, 수확이 좋았던 시기에는 상당히 과식을 하게 되었다. 한 스웨덴 과학자가 이러한 식습관의 장기적인 영향에 대해 의문을 가졌다. 그는 그 지역의 건강기록과 수확과의 관계를 연구하였다. 그는 그가 발견한 것에 놀랐다. ③ 수확이 좋았던 시기에 과식을 했던 소년들은 거의 먹지 못했던 소년들의 자녀들과 손주들보다 약 6년 정도 더 일찍 죽는 후손들을 낳았다. 다른 과학자들도 소녀들에게 똑같은 결과를 발견하였다. (④ 소년들과 소녀들 모두 풍년이었던 수확기로부터 상당히 혜택을 받았다.) 과학자들은 과식의 단 한 가지 이유가 수 세대에 걸쳐 계속되는 부정적인 영향을 가질 수 있다는 결론을 내릴 수밖에 없었다.

지문 어휘

- cutting edge 최첨단
- isolated 고립된, 외딴
- unpredictable 예측할 수 없는, 불확실한
- harvest 수확, 수확하다, 거둬들이다
- overeat 과식하다, 지나치게 먹다
- astonish 깜짝 놀라게 하다
- effect 영향, 결과, 효과
- conclude 끝내다, 결론을 내리다

30

정답 ②

정답 해설

라틴 아메리카와 히스패닉 문화에서의 어린 소녀의 성인의식인 La Quinceanera를 설명하고 있는 글이다. 하지만 ②는 이 문화와 다른 문화 사이의 성인의식을 비교하여 계급적 차이를 알아낼 수 있다는 내용으로 글의 일관성에서 벗어난다. 따라서 글의 흐름상 가장 어색한 문장은 ②이다.

지문 해석

> 어린 소녀들이 여성으로 인정받는 통과의례의 가장 큰 축하행사 중 하나가 라틴 아메리카와 히스패닉 문화에 있다. 이 행사는 La Quinceanera 또는 15번째 생일이라고 불린다. ① 이것은 어린 여성이 이제 결혼할 나이가 되었음을 알려주는 것이다. 이날은 보통 감사의 미사로 시작한다. (② 한 문화에서의 통과 의식을 다른 문화의 그것과 비교함으로써, 우리는 계급의 지위에서의 차이를 가늠할 수 있다.) 어린 여성은 완전한 길이의 흰색 또는 파스텔 색의 드레스를 입고 들러리와 남성 호위자로 봉사하는 14명의 친구들과 친척들에 의해 수행된다. ③ 그녀의 부모와 대부모는 제단의 발치에서 그녀를 둘러싼다. 미사가 끝날 때, 주인공인 어린 여성 자신은 처녀의 제단에 꽃다발을 바치는 동안 다른 어린 친척들은 참석한 사람들에게 작은 선물을 준다. ④ 미사에 이어 춤과 케익과 토스트 등이 있는 화려한 파티가 있게 된다. 마지막으로 저녁을 마치기 위해 이 어린 여성은 자신이 가장 좋아하는 호위자와 왈츠를 춘다.

지문 어휘

- passage 통행, 통과
- Mass (특히 로마 가톨릭교에서) 미사
- rite 의식, 의례
- assess 가늠하다, 재다, 평가하다
- status 신분, 지위
- surround 둘러싸다, 포위하다
- relative 친척, 동족, 상대적인, 비교상의
- altar 제단

05 문장 제거 파악 유형 기출 독해 어휘 복습 TEST

1	rapid	빠른	21	reduce	줄이다, 축소하다, 감소시키다
2	poise	태세를 취하다, 유지하다, 균형을 잡다	22	renowned	유명한, 명성 있는
3	inclusive	폭넓은, 포괄적인	23	paragraph	문단, 단락, 절
4	paramount	가장 중요한	24	conclude	끝내다, 결론을 내리다
5	replace	대체하다, 대신하다	25	reckless	무분별한, 무모한, 신중하지 못한
6	discipline	분야, 훈육, 규율, 훈육하다, 징계하다	26	limited	제한된, 한정된
7	quote	인용문, 인용하다	27	argument	논쟁, 주장
8	summarize	요약하다	28	quarrel	말다툼, 언쟁
9	extra	추가의	29	insult	모욕, 모욕하다
10	deficiency	결핍, 부족	30	exposure	노출, 폭로
11	desperate	필사적인, 절망적인	31	toll	대가, 비용, 통행료
12	urge	충동, 욕구, 충고하다, 권고하다	32	fatigued	피로한, 지친
13	get out of	~에서 나오다, 도망치다	33	incapable	무능한, ~을 할 수 없는
14	let off steam	기분을 풀다, 울분[열기 등]을 발산하다	34	depersonalization	비인격화, 몰개성화, 객관화
15	conspiracy	음모	35	speculation	추측, 사색
16	advocate	옹호하다, 지지하다	36	empathy	감정 이입, 공감
17	contradict	모순되다, 부정하다	37	slightly	약간, 조금
18	rouse	불러일으키다, 깨우다	38	transmission	전염, 전파, 전달
19	anxiety	불안, 염려, 걱정거리, 열망	39	practice	관행, 관례, 실행, 실천
20	density	밀도, 농도	40	involvement	참여, 개입, 몰두, 열중

41	initiate	시작하다, 착수시키다	61	triumph	성공하다, 승리를 거두다
42	a string of	일련의, 연속적인	62	irritate	자극하다, 짜증나게 하다
43	chemical	화학적인	63	tender	부드러운, 연한
44	widen	넓히다, 커지다	64	submerge	물속에 잠기다, 잠수하다
45	lash out	공격하다, 싸우다, 혹평하다, 비난하다	65	deprive of	빼앗다, 박탈하다
46	anthropology	인류학	66	prolong	연장시키다, 늘이다
47	contemporary	현대의, 동시대의	67	incur	발생시키다, 초래하다
48	illustrate	설명하다, 실증하다	68	urbanization	도시화
49	implication	함축, 암시, 영향, 결과	69	inclined	~을 하고 싶은, ~할 것 같은
50	progress	진전, 진척, 진행하다, 나아가다	70	tolerate	용인하다, 참다, 견디다
51	spontaneous	자발적인, 즉흥적인	71	no doubt	틀림없는, 아마
52	sedentary	정적인, 주로 앉아서 하는	72	hierarchy	계급, 계층
53	direction	안내, 지시사항, 방향	73	supervise	감독하다, 지휘하다
54	irrelevant	무관한, 관련 없는	74	proliferate	급증하다, 확산되다
55	metaphor	은유, 비유	75	outstanding	뛰어난, 두드러진
56	register	나타내다, 기록하다, 등록하다	76	put on hold	보류하다, 연기하다
57	association	연관, 연상	77	intact	온전한, 전혀 다치지 않은
58	remarkable	놀라운, 주목할 만한	78	dwindle	줄어들다, 감소하다
59	presence	있음, 존재, 참석	79	isolated	고립된, 외딴
60	flamboyant	이색적인, 화려한	80	astonish	깜짝 놀라게 하다

PART 06 문장 삽입 유형

ANSWER

01 ④	02 ②	03 ②	04 ③	05 ③
06 ④	07 ③	08 ②	09 ③	10 ②
11 ③	12 ④	13 ③	14 ②	15 ③
16 ④	17 ②	18 ④	19 ④	20 ④
21 ④	22 ④	23 ③	24 ②	25 ④
26 ④	27 ④	28 ③	29 ③	30 ②

01

정답 ④

정답 해설

이 글은 정보 소비를 효율적으로 관리하는 방법에 대해 다루고 있다. 주의가 산만해지는 활동을 줄이기 위해, 정보 소비를 정해진 시간에 계획적으로 하도록 권장하며, 상황 인식은 유지하되 불필요한 정보는 피하는 방법을 알려주고 있다. 주어진 문장은 "뉴스나 소셜 미디어처럼 산만하게 만드는 활동은 정해진 시간에만 하도록 시간 계획을 세워야 한다"는 내용을 담고 있다. 이 진술에 대한 구체적인 예시로 등장하는 것이 ④번 다음 문장인데, 여기서는 "아침에 30분 동안 뉴스를 읽고, 하루가 끝날 때 30분 동안 소셜 미디어를 이용하는 것"과 같은 시간 배분의 예를 제시하고 있다. 따라서 주어진 문장이 들어갈 위치로 가장 적절한 것은 ④이다.

지문 해석

운전하는 법을 배울 때, 당신은 문제를 미리 예상할 수 있도록 충분히 넓게 유지하되, 당신이 주의가 산만해질 정도로 너무 넓지는 않은 상황 인식의 수준을 유지하도록 배운다. 당신의 프로젝트도 마찬가지이다. (①) 당신은 인생과 일에 영향을 미칠 수 있는 당신의 주변의 상황은 알아야 할 필요가 있지만, 그런 것들과 무관한 일까지 알 필요는 없다. (②) 나는 외부 세계를 완전히 무시하는 '완전 현실도피주의자' 모델을 옹호하는 것은 아니다. (③) 오히려, 나는 불필요한 것들이 주의를 빼앗지 않도록 정보를 받아들이는 방식을 정리하라고 권하고 싶다. (④ <u>뉴스 소비나 소셜 미디어 훑어보기 같은 산만하게 하는 활동은 미리 정해진 시간에만 하도록 시간 계획을 짜라.</u>) 아마 아침에는 30분 동안 뉴스를 읽고, 하루가 끝날 때는 30분 동안 소셜 미디어를 하며 하는 일 없이 지내는 식으로 결정해볼 수도 있을 것이다.

지문 어휘

- [ ] schedule 시간 계획을 짜다
- [ ] relegate (덜 중요한 위치로) 밀쳐 버리다
- [ ] distracting 산만하게 하는
- [ ] consumption 소비, 소모
- [ ] prescribed 미리 정해진, 규정된
- [ ] maintain 유지하다, 지키다
- [ ] awareness 인식, 의식
- [ ] anticipate 예상하다, 기대하다
- [ ] irrelevant 무관한, 상관없는
- [ ] advocate 옹호하다, 지지하다
- [ ] ostrich 현실도피주의자
- [ ] recommend 권하다, 추천하다
- [ ] intake 받아[끌어]들임, 섭취
- [ ] extraneous 관련 없는
- [ ] decide 결정하다

02

정답 ②

정답 해설

주어진 문장은 'However'로 시작해 앞의 내용을 반박하며, 'this'는 체온을 낮추는 가장 빠른 방법과는 거리가 있다고 말한다. 따라서 이 문장 앞에는 사람들이 일반적으로 시도하지만 실제로는 효과적이지 않은 냉각 방법이 먼저 나와야 한다. ②번 문장 앞에서는 더울 때 대부분 얼굴을 식히려 한다는 행동이 소개되므로, 'this'는 이 행동을 가리킨다. 또한 ②번 문장 뒤에는 'Certainly'로 그 방법의 장점이 언급되지만, 'But actually'를 통해 다시 비효율적임을 강조하고 있다. 따라서 주어진 문장이 들어갈 위치로 가장 적절한 것은 ②이다.

지문 해석

과학적으로 입증된 간단한 방법들이 많이 있어서 더위를 이겨내는 데 도움이 된다. (①) 더위를 느끼고 누군가가 선풍기를 건네준다면, 대부분 얼굴을 먼저 식히려 할 것이다. (② <u>하지만 포츠머스 대학교의 Mike Tipton 교수에 따르면, 이것은 체온을 낮추는 가장 빠른 방법과는 거리가 있다.</u>) 분명히, 얼굴에 바람을 쐬면 그 부위의 냉각 수용체가 자극되어 강한 시원함을 느낄 수 있다. 하지만 실제로 그것은 당신의 신체에서 열을 빼내지는 못할 것이다. 그보다는 더 나은 방법으로, 손을 15~20분 동안 찬물에 담그는 것이 있다. (③) 당신의 손은 표면적 대비 질량 비율이 높아서, 당신이 더울 때는 그 속에서 많은 혈액이 흐른다. (④) 만약 당신의 심부 체온이 높다면, 열은 내리기 위해 신체는 혈액을 손발로 보낼 것이다.

지문 어휘

- [ ] lower 낮추다, 내리다
- [ ] temperature 체온, 온도
- [ ] handle 다루다, 처리하다
- [ ] fan 선풍기, 부채질을 하다
- [ ] stimulate 자극하다, 활성화시키다
- [ ] receptor (인체의) 수용체
- [ ] extract 빼다, 뽑다, 추출하다
- [ ] immerse (액체 속에) 담그다
- [ ] surface 표면, 지면
- [ ] flow 흐르다, 이동하다
- [ ] extremity 손발

03

정답 ②

정답 해설

행동주의의 정의와 특성에 대한 글로, 행동주의는 목표 달성을 위한 의도적이고 에너지가 넘치는 행동으로 정의되며, 때로는 대립적이고 논란이 많은 활동으로 나타남을 설명하고 있다. 주어진 문장은 활동주의의 특성을 설명하는 내용으로, 활동주의가 대립적이고 혼란스러운 성격을 가지고 있음을 강조한다. 따라서 주어진 문장이 들어갈 위치로 가장 적절한 것은 ②이다.

지문 해석

행동주의는 종종 개인과 집단이 원하는 목표를 달성하기 위해 연습하는 의도적이고, 격렬하거나 에너지가 넘치는 행동으로 정의된다. (①) 어떤 사람들에게 행동주의는 정치적 또는 사회적 변화에 대한 인식된 필요에 영향을 미치기 위한 이론적 또는 이념적으로 집중된 프로젝트이다. (② 다른 사람들에게 행동주의는 논란이 많고 파괴적이다; 결국에는, 그것은 종종 사물의 질서에 직접적으로 도전하는 대립적인 활동으로 나타난다.) 행동주의는 불편하고, 때로는 지저분하며, 거의 항상 격렬하다. (③) 게다가, 행동주의자들, 즉 실행 가능한 전략을 개발하고, 특정 문제에 집단적인 스포트라이트를 집중하고, 궁극적으로 사람들을 행동으로 옮기는 사람들의 존재와 헌신 없이는 발생하지 않는다. (④) 저명한 학자가 시사하듯이, 효과적인 활동가들은 또한 때때로 큰 소리로 소음을 낸다.

지문 어휘

- [ ] activism 행동주의, 능동주의
- [ ] controversial 논란이 많은
- [ ] disruptive 파괴적인, 분열시키는, 지장을 주는
- [ ] after all 결국에는, 어쨌든
- [ ] confrontational 대립의, 모순되는
- [ ] define 정의하다, 규정하다
- [ ] vigorous 격렬한, 활발한, 건강한
- [ ] theoretically 이론적으로
- [ ] ideologically 이념적으로, 사상적으로
- [ ] messy 지저분한, 엉망인, 골치 아픈
- [ ] strenuous 격렬한, 몹시 힘든, 완강한, 불굴의
- [ ] presence 존재, 참석, 있음
- [ ] commitment 헌신, 약속, 전념
- [ ] scholar 학자, 장학생

04

정답 ③

정답 해설

Clean Air Act(1970년) 후, Chay와 Greenstone의 경제학적 평가에 따르면, 미 연방 정부의 공기 오염 규제는 공장 및 도시에서의 대기 질을 개선하고, 경제적 가치를 창출했음을 과거의 상황과 대비시킨 글이다. 주어진 제시문은 과거의 문제점을 강조하고 있으므로 ②번의 '그 결과 오염에 대한 규제 없이 가동을 허용했고, 오염이 매우 높은 수준에 도달함'의 진술 다음에 위치해야 한다. 따라서 주어진 문장이 들어갈 위치로 가장 적절한 것은 ③이다.

지문 해석

경제학자 Chay와 Greenstone은 1970년 청정대기법 이후 대기오염 정화의 가치를 평가했다. (①) 1970년 이전에는 대기오염에 대한 연방 정부의 규제가 거의 없었고, 주 의원들의 의제에서 그 문제가 중요하지 않았다. (②) 결과적으로, 많은 주들이 오염에 대한 규제 없이 공장들이 가동하는 것을 허용했고, 몇몇 고도로 산업화된 주들에서는 오염이 매우 높은 수준에 도달했다. (③ 특히 많은 도시의 주들에서는 총 부유입자의 양으로 측정되는 대기오염이 위험 수준에 도달했다.) (④) 청정대기법은 무엇이 5가지 특히 위험한 오염물질의 과도하게 높은 수준을 구성하는 지에 대한 지침을 제정했다. 1970년 이 법령과 1977년 개정에 이후에, 대기의 질에 개선이 있었다.

지문 어휘

- [ ] act 법령, 행동, 행동하다
- [ ] federal 연방 정부의, 연방제의
- [ ] agenda 의제, 안건
- [ ] legislator 입법자, 법률 제정자, 의회[국회]의원
- [ ] county (자치)주, 군
- [ ] operate 가동[작동]하다, 작용하다, 수술하다
- [ ] suspend 부유시키다, 매달다, 중지하다, 연기하다
- [ ] particle 입자, 조각, 미립자
- [ ] constitute ~을 구성하다, 이루다, 설립하다
- [ ] excessively 과도하게, 지나치게
- [ ] pollutant 오염 물질, 오염원
- [ ] amendment 개정, 수정

05

정답 ③

정답 해설

고래 사냥과 무역을 중심으로 한 마카 부족의 중요한 거점인 워싱턴 올림픽 반도의 Ozette 마을이 진흙 사태로 인해 그들의 생활과 유물이 보존되었고, 최근의 폭풍으로 인한 침식으로 인해 그들의 생활과 유물이 밝혀졌음을 설명하는 글이다. 주어진 제시문은 진흙이 집들을 덮쳐, 그들의 생활상을 알 수 있게 봉인했다는 것이고 이와 관련된 부가 설명을 ③번이 하고 있으므로, 주어진 문장이 들어갈 위치로 가장 적절한 것은 ③이다.

지문 해석

워싱턴주 올림픽 반도의 최서단에 있는 Ozette 마을에서 Makah 부족 구성원들은 고래를 사냥했다. (①) 그들은 선반과 훈제장 안에서 그들의 어획물을 훈제했으며, 퓨젓 사운드와 인근 밴쿠버섬 주변의 이웃 그룹들과 거래했다. (②) Ozette는 그 지역에 수천 년 동안 기반을 두고 살아온 원주민인 Makah 부족에 의해 거주된 다섯 개의 주요 마을 중 하나였다. (③ 부족의 구전 역사와 고고학적 증거는 1500년에서 1700년 사이 어느 때에 이류가 마을의 일부를 파괴하였고 여러 개의 전통가옥들을 덮어 내용물을 봉인했다는 것을 시사한다.) 그렇지 않았다면 살아남지 못했을 바구니, 옷, 수면 요, 포경 도구를 포함한 수천 개의 인공물들이 진흙 속에 보존되었다. (④) 1970년, 한 폭풍은 이러한 전통가옥들의 잔해와 인공물들을 드러내는 해안의 침식을 야기했다.

지문 어휘

- [ ] westernmost 서쪽 최고의
- [ ] peninsula 반도
- [ ] rack 선반, 벽걸이
- [ ] smokehouses 훈연 공장

- inhabit 거주하다, 살다
- archaeological 고고학적인
- mudslide 산사태
- longhouse 길게 붙은 공동 주택, 일잣(一字)집
- artifact 유물, 유적
- preserve 보존하다, 지키다, 전유물
- reveal 드러내다, 밝히다

06

정답 ④

정답 해설
인어공주의 왕자의 생일 파티를 몰래 구경한 경험에 대한 글로, '인어가 빠르게 그녀의 머리를 밖으로 다시 드러냈다'는 부분 전에는 '물에 들어갔다'는 진술이 나와야 하며, 이 진술 다음에는 머리를 드러내고 보았다는 진술이 나와야 한다. 따라서 주어진 문장이 들어갈 위치로 적절한 것은 ④이다.

지문 해석
작은 인어공주는 선실 작은 창문까지 곧장 헤엄쳐 갔고, 파도가 그녀를 들어 올릴 때마다 투명한 유리를 통해 잘 차려입은 사람들의 무리를 볼 수 있었다. 그들 중에는 젊은 왕자가 있었는데, 그는 그 자리에서 가장 잘생긴 사람이었고 큰 검은 눈을 가지고 있었다. (①) 그날은 그의 생일이었기 때문에 그렇게 많은 흥분이 있었다. (②) 젊은 왕자가 선원들이 춤추고 있는 갑판으로 나왔을 때, 100개가 넘는 로켓이 하늘로 쏘아 올라가 반짝이며 터졌고, 하늘을 낮처럼 밝게 만들었다. (③) 작은 인어공주는 너무 놀라서 물속으로 잠수했다. (④ 그러나 그녀는 곧 다시 머리를 내밀었다.) 그리고 보라! 마치 하늘에 있는 모든 별들이 그녀 쪽으로 떨어지는 것 같았다. 그녀는 이런 불꽃놀이를 본 적이 없었다.

지문 어휘
- cabin 선실, 오두막
- prince 왕자
- mermaid 인어
- startle 깜짝 놀라게 하다

07

정답 ③

정답 해설
텍사스 보안관들의 인터넷을 활용한 국경 감시를 주제로 하는 글로, 텍사스 보안관들이 인터넷을 이용해 불법 횡단을 감시하는 '가상 텍사스 의원' 시스템을 도입했다는 것을 소개하는 글이다. 주어진 문장에서 '그들 (They)'은 ② 다음 문장에서 언급되고 있는 '텍사스 보안관들 (Texas sheriffs)'을 의미한다. 따라서 주어진 문장이 들어갈 위치로 알맞은 것은 ③이다.

지문 해석
이민 개혁은 정치적 지뢰밭이다. (①) 광범위한 정치적 지지를 받는 이민 정책의 유일한 측면은 불법 이민자들의 유입을 제한하기 위해 멕시코와의 미국 국경을 확보하겠다는 결의이다. (②) 텍사스 보안관들은 최근 국경을 감시하는 것을 돕기 위해 인터넷의 새로운 사용법을 개발했다. (③ 그들은 불법 횡단으로 알려진 장소에 비디오 카메라를 설치했고, 카메라의 라이브 비디오 자료를 웹 사이트에 게시했다.) (④) 국경 감시를 돕고자 하는 시민들은 온라인에 접속해 "가상 텍사스 보안관" 역할을 할 수 있다. 국경을 넘으려는 사람을 보면 보안관 사무실로 보고서를 보내고, 때때로 미국 국경 순찰대의 도움을 받아 더 알아보기도 한다.

지문 어휘
- install 설치하다
- known for ~로 알려진
- feed 먹이다, 먹이, 자료, 원료
- immigration 이주, 이민, 출입국 관리소
- reform 개혁, 개선, 개혁하다, 개선하다
- minefield 지뢰밭
- policy 정책
- command 명령하다, 지시하다, 지휘하다
- resolve 결의, 결심, 결심하다, 해결하다
- sheriff 대리인, 의원, 보안관
- novel 소설, 새로운, 기발한
- monitor 감시하다
- virtual 가상의
- deputy 대리인, 의원, 보안관
- border 국경, 경계, 가장자리
- follow up 더 알아보다, ~을 덧붙이다
- Border Patrol 국경 순찰대

08

정답 ②

정답 해설
자기 평가의 중요성을 강조하는 글로, 자기 평가 요청은 자신의 성과를 주관적으로 설명하는 것으로, 자기 홍보는 채용과 승진 등에 유리한 기회를 제공할 수 있으므로 더 많은 자기 홍보를 하는 사람들이 더 좋은 결과를 얻을 수 있음을 강조하고 있다. 주어진 문장은 글의 주제문에 해당하며, 그 다음에 구체적인 예시가 이어져야 한다. 그 구체적인 예시의 시작이 ② 다음의 '학교 지원서, 취업 지원서, 면접, 성과 평가, 회의' 등이 구체적인 예시가 된다. 따라서 주어진 문장이 들어갈 위치로 알맞은 것은 ②이다.

지문 해석
회계 분기가 막 끝났다. 상사가 당신에게 이번 분기의 판매 성과에 대해 얼마나 잘 수행했는지 묻기 위해서 왔다. 당신은 어떻게 자신의 성과를 설명할까? 훌륭하다고? 좋다고? 형편없다고? (①) 객관적인 성과 지표(예를 들어 이번 분기에 얼마나 매출을 올렸는지)에 관해 묻는 경우와 달리, 주관적으로 성과를 설명하는 것은 종종 명확하지 않다. 정답이 없다. (② 그러나 이러한 자기 평가 요청은 경력 전반에 걸쳐 만연하다). 당신은 학교 지원서, 취업 지원서, 면접, 업무 평가, 회의 그리고 계속되는 목록에서 자신의 성과를 주관적으로 설명하라는 요청을 받는다. (③) 당신이 성과를 어떻게 설명하는지가 우리가 자기 홍보의 수준이라고 부르는 것이다. (④) 자기 홍보는 업무의 만연한 부분이기 때문에, 자기 홍보를 더 많이 하는 사람들은 채용되는 기회, 승진, 급여 인상 또는 보너스를 받을 가능성이 더 높을 수 있다.

지문 어휘
- pervasive 만연하는, 스며드는
- fiscal quarter 회계 분기, 재무 분기
- come by 잠깐 들르다, 얻다
- describe 말로 설명하다, 묘사하다
- objective 목적, 목표, 객관적인
- bring in 벌다, 이익을 가져오다
- subjectively 주관적으로
- self-promotion 자기 홍보
- pervasive 만연하는, 스며드는

09

정답 ③

정답 해설

헬스케어 챗봇의 역할과 중요성에 대한 글로, 헬스케어 챗봇이 진단과 조언을 제공하여 사람들이 질병에 대한 정보를 얻고 집에서 편안하게 사용할 수 있도록 도와주는 중요성을 강조하고 있다. 주어진 문장에서 '이 문제 (this problem)'를 해결한다고 한 것으로 보아 앞에 문제점의 내용이 나와야 한다. 따라서 주어진 문장이 들어가기에 가장 적절한 곳은 ③이다.

지문 해석

질병에 걸리는 것에 대한 두려움 혹은 막대한 진료비 때문에 병원이나 보건소에 가는 것을 망설이는 사람들이 많아졌다. (①) 이것은 그들로 하여금 인터넷상에서 검증되지 않은 정보원에 근거하여 스스로 자가 진단하게 한다. (②) 이것은 종종 오진되고 부적절한 약을 먹을 경우 사람의 정신적, 신체적 건강에 해로운 영향을 미친다는 것을 증명한다. (③ 건강 관리 챗봇은 이 문제를 해결하고 집에서 편안하게 사용할 수 있는 사람들을 위한 적절한 진단과 조언을 보장하는 것을 목적으로 한다.) 챗봇은 진단의 심각도에 따라 처방전 없이 살 수 있는 약을 처방하거나 검증된 의료 전문가에게의 진단을 확대한다. (④) 광범위하고 다양한 증상, 위험 요인 및 치료에 대해 교육을 받은 대화형 챗봇은 특히 COVID-19의 경우 사용자 건강 문의를 쉽게 처리할 수 있다.

지문 어휘

☐ ensure 보장하다, 반드시 ~하게 하다
☐ comfort 위로하다, 위안하다, 편하게 하다
☐ contract (병에) 걸리다
☐ consultation fee 진료비, 진찰료
☐ unverified 검증되지 않은
☐ misdiagnosed 오진을 받은
☐ over the counter 처방전 없이 살 수 있는
☐ escalate 확대하다, 증가되다
☐ symptom 증상, 징후
☐ risk factor 위험 인자, 위험 요인

10

정답 ②

정답 해설

이 글은 COVID-19로 인한 원격 근무의 증가와 함께 미래의 일자리와 작업 환경이 어떻게 형성될 수 있는지를 탐구하며, 하이브리드 작업 모델의 중요성을 강조하고 있다. 주어진 문장은 역접(But)으로 시작하고 '원격 근무의 기회가 없다'는 부정적 진술로, 앞에 원격 근무의 긍정적인 진술이 나와야 한다. 따라서 주어진 문장이 들어가기에 가장 적절한 곳은 ②이다.

지문 해석

COVID-19의 확산은 원격 근무에 방해가 되는 문화적 및 기술적 장벽을 깨부수었다. 원격 근무가 지속될 가능성에 대한 분석에서 선진국의 노동력의 20~25%가 일주일에 3~5일 범위에서 재택 근무를 할 수 있는 것으로 나타났다. (①) 이는 COVID-19 이전보다 원격 근무가 4~5배 더 많은 것이다. (② 그러나 여기서 주목할 점은 노동자의 절반 이상이 원격 근무의 기회가 거의 없거나 아예 없다는 것이다.) 게다가 원격으로 할 수 있는 모든 일이 되어서는 안 된다; 예를 들어 협상, 브레인스토밍 및 민감한 피드백 제공은 원격으로 했을 때 덜 효과적일 수 있는 활동이다. (③) 원격 근무의 전망은 작업 환경, 직무 및 당면한 작업에 따라 달라지므로 일부 작업은 현장에서 발생하고 일부는 원격에서 발생하는 혼합체 근무 상황은 지속될 가능성이 높다. (④) 혼합체 세계에서 지속 가능한 성과와 행복을 실현하려면 성과와 생산성의 주요 동력은 보상이 아니라 직원에게 제공되는 목적 의식이어야 한다.

지문 어휘

☐ workforce 노동자, 노동력
☐ flatten 깨부수다, 납작하게 만들다
☐ negotiation 협상, 절충
☐ effective 효과적인
☐ outlook 전망, 관점
☐ persist 지속되다, 끝까지 하다
☐ sustainable 지속 가능한
☐ productivity 생산성
☐ compensation 보상

11

정답 ③

정답 해설

이 글은 기후 변화와 식량 안보 문제를 다루며, 이 도전적인 과제들이 동시에 기회를 제공한다는 관점을 강조하고 있다. 주어진 문장의 '이것들 (These)'은 앞 문장에서 언급한 '생물적 및 비생물적 스트레스, 적응 전략 개발, 품종 개발, 유전적 잠재력 발현'을 지칭하는 지시대명사이다. 따라서 ② 문장의 다음에 위치해야 한다. 따라서 주어진 문장이 들어가기에 가장 적절한 곳은 ③이다.

지문 해석

지구 온난화는 인간이 함께 살아가야 하는 현실이다. (①) 이것은 지구에 있는 인간의 존재에 영향을 미치는 모든 매개 변수들 중에서 지구상의 생명체에게 가장 중요하고 지구 온난화로 인해 가장 위협을 받는 것은 식량 안전 보장이기 때문에 인지해야 할 매우 중요한 문제이다. (②) 미래의 식량 안전보장은 기후 변화로 인해 야기되는 생물적 및 비생물적인 스트레스의 결합, 성장기의 날씨 변동성, 다양한 주변 조건에 더 적합한 품종의 개발, 그리고 이러한 품종들이 변화하는 기후 조건하에서 유전적 잠재력을 발현할 수 있도록 하는 효과적인 적응 전략을 개발하는 능력에 의존한다. (③ 이것들은 미래의 기후를 예측하는 우리의 능력의 불확실성 때문에 해결하기 불가능한 난제로 보일 수 있다.) 하지만, 이러한 난제들은 또한 우리에게 토양과 식물, 대기의 상호 작용에 대한 이해를 높일 수 있는 기회를 제공하며, 이러한 지식을 어떻게 활용하여 전 세계 모든 지역에 걸쳐 식량 안전보장을 향상시키는 궁극적인 목표를 달성할 수 있도록 할 수 있는지를 보여준다. (④)

지문 어휘

☐ predict 예측하다, 예견하다
☐ global warming 지구 온난화
☐ food security 식량 안전보장
☐ be dependent on ~에 의존하다
☐ variability 변동성, 가변성
☐ adaptation 적응, 각색
☐ interaction 상호 작용
☐ enhanced 향상된, 높아진
☐ ultimate 궁극적인, 최후의

12

정답 ④

정답 해설

중력에 대한 신체적 영향(반응)과 대처법에 대한 글이다. 혈액이 다리에 강제로 들어가 신체의 나머지 산소를 빼앗을 때 치명적일 수 있다는 진술을 ② 다음 문장에서 진술하고 있고, 그 ③ 다음 문장에서 그 해결책으로 몸을 수평으로 유지하는 것을 제시하고 있다. 그리고 그 결과로 주어진 문장에서 이야기하는 '혈액과 생명을 유지하는 산소는 심장이 뇌로 순환하기가 더 쉽다'고 진술하고 있다. 따라서 주어진 문장의 들어갈 위치로 가장 적절한 곳은 ④이다.

지문 해석

사람들은 다양한 방식으로 중력, 또는 g-force에 노출될 수 있다. 등을 때리는 것과 같이 신체의 일부에만 영향을 미치는 국부적일 수 있다. 그것은 또한 자동차 충돌에서 겪게 되는 강력한 힘과 같이 순간적일 수 있다. 세 번째 유형의 중력은 지속되거나 적어도 몇 초 동안 지속된다. (①) 지속적이고 신체적인 중력은 사람들에게 가장 위험하다. (②) 신체는 일반적으로 지속적인 중력보다 국부적이거나 순간적인 중력을 더 잘 견디는데, 이는 혈액이 다리에 강제로 들어가 신체의 나머지 산소를 빼앗기 때문에 치명적일 수 있다. (③) 앉거나 서 있는 대신에 몸이 수평이거나 눕는 동안 지속적인 중력을 가하는 것은 다리가 아닌 등에 피가 고이기 때문에 사람들이 더 견딜 수 있는 경향이 있다. (④ 따라서 혈액과, 생명을 유지하는 산소는 심장이 뇌로 순환하기가 더 쉽다.) 우주비행사와 전투기 조종사와 같은 어떤 사람들은 그들의 신체의 중력에 대한 저항력을 높이기 위해 특별한 훈련을 받는다.

지문 어휘

- [ ] circulate 순환하다, 유포하다
- [ ] be exposed to ~에 노출되다
- [ ] gravitational force 중력
- [ ] localized 국부적인, 국지적인
- [ ] affect 영향을 미치다
- [ ] slap 때리다
- [ ] momentary 순간적인, 잠깐의
- [ ] endure 견디다
- [ ] sustained 지속된, 한결같은, 일관된
- [ ] lasting 영속적인, 지속적인
- [ ] deadly 치명적인
- [ ] deprive 빼앗다
- [ ] horizontal 수평의, 가로의
- [ ] lie down 눕다
- [ ] tolerable 견딜 수 있는
- [ ] astronaut 우주 비행사
- [ ] resistance 저항, 저항력

13 정답 ③

정답 해설

비유와 유사성의 본질적인 특징들을 주제로 하는 글이다. 주어진 문장은 심장을 펌프에 비교하는 것이 진정한 비유라고 진술하고 있으며, 심장과 펌프에 대한 설명이 ③ 다음 문장부터 이어지고 있다. 따라서 주어진 문장이 들어갈 위치로 가장 적절한 곳은 ③이다.

지문 해석

비유는 두 가지가 상당히 근본적인 많은 점에서 유사하다고 가정되는 비유적 표현이다. 그 두개는 크게 다르지만, 그것들의 구조, 그것들 일부의 관계들 혹은 그것들이 제공하는 핵심적인 목적들은 유사하다. 장미와 카네이션은 유사하지 않다. (①) 그들은 둘 다 줄기와 잎을 가지고 있고 둘 다 빨간색일 수 있다. (②) 하지만 그들은 같은 방식으로 이러한 특성들을 보여준다; 그들은 같은 속에 속한다. (③ 그러나, 심장을 펌프에 비유하는 것은 진정한 비유이다.) 이것들은 서로 전혀 다른 것들이지만, 그것들은 중요한 특성들을 공유한다: 기계 장치, 밸브의 보유, 압력을 증가시키고 감소시키는 능력, 그리고 유체를 이동시키는 능력. (④) 그리고 심장과 펌프는 이러한 특성들을 다른 방식과 다른 맥락에서 보여준다.

지문 어휘

- [ ] comparison 비유, 비교
- [ ] analogy 비유, 유추
- [ ] alike 비슷한, 유사한
- [ ] fundamental 근본적인, 기본적인
- [ ] structure 구조, 체계
- [ ] relationship 관계, 연결
- [ ] essential 필수적인, 본질적인
- [ ] dissimilar 같지 않은, 다른
- [ ] genus (생물 분류상의) 속
- [ ] disparate 서로 전혀 다른, 이질적인
- [ ] apparatus 기구, 장치
- [ ] possession 소유, 소지, 보유
- [ ] capacity 능력
- [ ] fluid 유체, 유동체

14 정답 ②

정답 해설

직장에서의 복장이 어떻게 변화하고 그에 따른 걱정거리가 생겨났는지에 대해 다룬 글이며, 직장 캐주얼의 의미와 영향에 대해 설명하고 있다. 주어진 문장에 '그러나 (however)'로 문장의 앞뒤에 대조적인 내용이 진술되어야 한다. ② 이전에는 "dress-down day"와 "casual day" 관행의 의도를 진술하고 있고, ② 다음에 원래의 긍정적인 의도와 다른 부작용에 대한 내용을 진술하고 있다. 따라서 주어진 문장이 들어가기에 가장 적절한 곳은 ②이다.

지문 해석

우리가 직장에서 어떻게 옷을 입는 지는 새로운 선택 요소가 되었으며, 그것과 함께 새로운 걱정거리가 되었다. (①) "약식 복장으로 근무하는 날" 또는 "평상복 출근일"이 가지는 관행은, 10년 전 쯤에 나타나기 시작했는데, 직원들에게 생활이 더 편안해지도록, 그들이 돈을 절약하고 사무실에서 더 편안함을 느낄 수 있게 하도록 의도되었다. (② 그러나, 그 효과는 정반대였다.) 평범한 직장 옷 외에도, 직원들은 "직장 캐주얼" 옷을 만들어내야 했다. (③) 그것은 정말, 당신이 주말에 집에서 입는 운동복과 티셔츠일 수는 없었다. (④) 그것은 특정한 이미지를 — 느긋하지만 또한 진지한 이미지를 — 유지하는 엄선된 옷이어야 했다.

지문 어휘

- [ ] reverse (정)반대, 뒤바꾸다
- [ ] dress-down day 약식 복장으로 근무하는 날
- [ ] casual day 평상복 출근일
- [ ] workplace 직장
- [ ] relaxed 편안한, 여유 있는

15 정답 ③

정답 해설

농업 분야에서 자유 시장 시스템이 어떻게 작동하지 않고 농부와 가족 농장에 미치는 영향을 탐구하며, 시장에서의 가격 변동이 농업에 미치는 영향을 논의하는 글이다. 기업 경제에서는 '공급과 수요 사이의 균형'을 찾을 수 있음을 ①과 ② 다음 문장에서 진술하고 있고, 농업 경제에서는 그 균형을 찾기 어려움을 ③과 ④ 다음 문장에서 진술하고 있다. 주어진 문장은 '농업경제의 상황'에 대한 설명으로 시작하고 있다. 따라서 주어진 문장이 들어가기에 가장 적절한 곳은 ③이다.

지문 해석

자유 시장은 농업에서 잘된 적이 없고 앞으로도 그럴 것이다. (①) 가족 농장의 경제학은 기업의 경제학과 매우 다르다; 가격이 하락하면, 그 기업은 사람들을 해고하고 공장을 놀릴 수 있다. (②) 결국 시장은 공급과 수요 사이에서 새로운 균형을 찾는다. (③ 하지만 음식에 대한 수요는 탄력적이지 않다; 사람들은 단지 음식이 싸다고 더 많이 먹지 않는다.) 그리고 농부를 해고하는 것은 공급을 줄이는 데 도움이 되지 않는다. (④) 당신은 나를 해고할 수는 있지만 나의 땅을 해고할 수는 없는 것은 현금 유동성이 더 필요하거나 내가 그러한 것보다 더 효율적이라고 생각하는 다른 농부가 와서 농사를 지을 것이기 때문이다.

지문 어휘

☐ agriculture 농업
☐ lay off 해고하다
☐ idle (특히 일시적으로 공장·일꾼 등을) 놀리다, 빈둥거리다
☐ cash flow 현금 유동성

16 정답 ④

정답 해설

역사 탐정을 위한 필수 자료의 보고인 기록 보관소에 대한 글이다. 주어진 문장에서 '예를 들어 (for example)'로 시작하면서 구체적인 사례로 뉴저지의 주 기록 보관소에서 보유하는 자료에 대한 내용을 설명하고 있으므로 ④ 이전에 'many state and local archives~'로 시작하는 부분의 예시로 볼 수 있다. 따라서 주어진 문장이 들어갈 위치로 가장 적절한 것은 ④이다.

지문 해석

기록 보관소는 자료의 귀중한 발굴물이다: 오디오에서 비디오, 신문, 잡지, 인쇄물에 이르기까지 — 이것은 어떠한 역사 탐정 수사에 있어서 그것들이 없어서는 안 되게 만든다. 도서관과 기록 보관소는 동일하게 보일 수 있지만 차이점은 중요하다. (①) 기록 보관소 소장품은 거의 항상 1차 자료로 구성되는 반면, 도서관은 2차 자료로 구성된다. (②) 한국 전쟁에 대해 더 배우기 위해, 여러분은 역사책을 찾기 위해 도서관에 갈 것이다. (③) 만약 여러분이 정부 문서나 한국 전쟁 군인들이 쓴 편지를 읽고 싶다면, 여러분은 기록 보관소로 갈 것이다. 만약 여러분이 정보를 찾고 있다면, 여러분을 위한 기록 보관소가 있을 것이다. 많은 주 및 지역 기록 보관소는 놀랍고 다양한 자료인 공공 기록을 저장한다. (④ 예를 들어, 뉴저지의 기록 보관소는 30,000입방피트 이상의 종이와 25,000릴의 마이크로필름을 보관하고 있다.) 당신의 주의 기록 보관소를 온라인으로 검색하면 의회 회의록뿐만 아니라 더 많은 자료를 포함하고 있음을 당신에게 빠르게 보여줄 것이다 — 자세한 토지 보조금 정보가 발견될 수 있으며, 오래된 도시 지도, 범죄 기록 그리고 행상인 면허 신청서와 같은 특이한 것들이 있다.

지문 어휘

☐ archive 기록 보관소
☐ material 재료, 자료
☐ indispensable 없어서는 안 될, 필수적인
☐ investigation 수사, 조사, 연구
☐ primary source 1차 자료
☐ secondary source 2차 자료
☐ minutes 회의록
☐ legislature 입법부, 의회
☐ oddity 이상한 것, 특이한 것
☐ peddler 행상인
☐ application 지원서, 신청서, 응용, 적용

17 정답 ②

정답 해설

일 중독의 긍정적인 측면과 그 이유와 이점을 일 중독자의 심리적 요인을 중심으로 설명하고 있는 글이다. 일이 사람들에게 제공하는 것을 '급여, 자신감, 정체성, 사회적 관계'를 열거하고 있다. 따라서 주어진 문장은 급여 다음의 내용에 이어져야 한다. 따라서 주어진 문장이 들어갈 위치로 가장 적절한 것은 ②이다.

지문 해석

왜 일 중독자들은 그들의 일을 그렇게 즐기는가? 주로 일하는 것이 몇 가지 중요한 이점을 제공하기 때문이다. (①) 그것은 사람들에게 생계를 유지하는 방법인 급여를 제공한다. (② 그리고 일하는 것은 재정적인 안정보다 더 많은 것을 제공한다.) 그것은 사람들에게 자신감을 준다; 그들은 도전적인 작품을 만들고 "내가 그것을 만들었다"고 말할 수 있을 때 만족감을 느낀다. (③) 심리학자들은 일이 사람들에게 주체성을 준다고 주장한다; 그들은 그들이 자아와 개성을 얻을 수 있도록 일을 한다. (④) 게다가, 대부분의 직업은 사람들에게 다른 사람들을 만날 수 있는 사회적으로 용인되는 방법을 제공한다. 일하는 것은 긍정적인 중독이라고 말할 수 있다; 아마도 일 중독자들은 그들의 일에 대해 강박적일 수 있지만, 그들의 중독은 안전하고 심지어 이로운 것처럼 보인다.

지문 어휘

☐ workaholic 직장 중독자
☐ financial 재정의, 금융의
☐ paycheck 급여 수표
☐ self-confidence 자신감
☐ satisfaction 만족감, 충족
☐ challenging 힘든, 도전적인
☐ psychologist 심리학자
☐ identity 정체성, 신원
☐ individualism 개인주의
☐ acceptable 수용 가능한
☐ addiction 중독
☐ compulsive 강박적인, 강제적인
☐ advantageous 유리한, 이로운

18 정답 ④

정답 해설

프랑스의 화학자 Edouard Benedictus가 안전유리를 만든 과정을 설명하는 글이다. 주어진 문장에서 'It was then he remembered his experience~' 부분에서 바로 그때에 경험을 떠올렸다고 했으므로 이전까지는 기억하지 못했음을 알 수 있다. ③ 다음 문장에서 그는 유리 플라스크의 내용을 기록했지만 잊어버렸다고 했고, ④ 다음 문장에서 그가 안전유리를 만드는 데 성공했다고 진술하고 있으므로, 주어진 문장이 들어갈 위치로 가장 적절한 것은 ④이다.

지문 해석

1903년 Edouard Benedictus라는 프랑스 화학자가 어느 날 유리 플라스크를 딱딱한 바닥에 떨어뜨려 그것을 깨뜨렸다. (①) 그러나 그 화학자가 놀랍게도, 플라스크는 산산조각이 나지 않았고, 여전히 원래의 모양을 유지하고 있었다. (②) 그가 플라스크를 조사했을 때, 그는 플라스크에 담겨있던 콜로디온 용액에서 남아 있는 잔여물인 필름 코팅이 내부에 들어 있었다는 것을 발견했다. (③) 그는 이 특이한 현상을

노트에 적었지만, 몇 주 뒤에 자동차 사고에서 날아오는 자동차 앞 유리에 의해 심하게 다친 사람들에 대한 기사를 신문에서 읽었을 때까지만 해도 더 이상 그것에 대해 생각하지 않았다. (④ 그때 그는 유리 플라스크에 대한 그의 경험을 기억했고, 그는 그렇게 빠르게 그것이 산산조각이 나지 않도록 차량 앞 유리에 특수한 코팅이 적용될지도 모른다고 생각했다.) 그 후로 얼마 지나지 않아, 그는 세계 최초의 안전 유리를 만드는 데 성공했다.

지문 어휘

- special 특수한, 특별한
- apply to 적용되다
- shatter 산산이 부서지다, 산산조각 나다
- retain 유지하다, 보유하다
- original 원래의, 본래의, 원본
- residue 나머지, 잔여물
- solution 용액
- collodion 콜로디온(활성화된 셀룰로오스를 주성분으로 하는 약품)
- unusual 특이한, 드문, 색다른
- phenomenon 현상
- windshield (자동차의) 앞 유리
- thereafter 그 후에

19　　　　　　　　　　　　　　　　정답 ④

정답 해설

밀레니얼 세대를 주제로 한 글로, 주어진 문장은 밀레니얼 세대의 긍정적인 측면이다. 따라서 긍정적인 내용으로 이어지는 진술 앞에 위치해야 한다. 그 긍정적인 진술은 '그리고 그것은 그들이 많은 이들이 추정하는 것보다 더 나은 재정적 상태에 놓일 수 있다'는 내용의 앞에 나와야 한다. 따라서 주어진 문장이 들어갈 위치로 가장 적절한 것은 ④이다.

지문 해석

밀레니얼 세대는 종종 현대에서 가장 가난하고 경제적으로 부담이 큰 세대로 분류된다. 그들 중 다수가 대학을 졸업하여 학자금 대출이라는 해결해야 할 충격적인 짐을 진 채, 미국이 지금까지 목격해 왔던 것들 중에서 최악의 노동 시장 중 하나에 진입했다. (①) 당연히, 밀레니얼 세대는 삶의 비슷한 단계에서 X세대보다 적은 자산을 축적했는데, 주로 그들 중 더 적은 수가 집을 소유하지 못했기 때문이다. (②) 그러나 서로 다른 세대의 미국인들이 무엇을 아끼는지에 대한 가장 상세한 그림을 제공하는 새로운 데이터는 그러한 평가를 더 복잡하게 만든다. (③) 그렇다, 1965년에서 1980년 사이에 태어난 X세대는 순자산이 더 높다. (④ 그러나 1981년과 1996년 사이에 태어난 밀레니얼 세대가 같은 나이인 22~37세대에 비해 X세대들이 했던 것보다 은퇴를 위해 더 적극적으로 저축하고 있다는 명백한 증거도 있다.) 그리고 그것은 많은 사람들이 추정하는 것보다 그들을 더 나은 재정적 상태에 이르게 할 수도 있다.

지문 어휘

- evidence 증거
- aggressively 적극적으로, 공격적으로
- retirement 은퇴, 퇴직
- label 분류하다, 라벨을 붙이다
- staggering 충격적인, 믿기 어려운
- accumulate 모으다, 축적하다
- detailed 상세한
- complicate 복잡하게 하다, 복잡한
- assessment 평가, 판단
- net worth 순자산
- financial 금융의, 재정의

20　　　　　　　　　　　　　　　　정답 ④

정답 해설

(자면서 꾸는) 꿈의 중요성을 강조하며, 꿈이 우리에게 영감, 연결, 정보, 그리고 희망을 제공함을 설명하고 있는 글이다. 주어진 문장의 'this'가 지칭하는 것은 ③ 다음 문장의 '꿈은 건강한 삶의 필수적인 부분이다'의 내용이다. 그리고 글쓴이가 강조하는 부분이며, 이에 대한 부연설명을 하고 있는 ④ 다음 문장과 자연스럽게 연결된다. 따라서 아래 문장이 들어가기에 가장 적절한 곳은 ④이다.

지문 해석

어떤 사람들은 꿈이 가치가 없다고 믿지만, 밤에 일어나는 이러한 드라마들을 무관하다고 치부하는 것은 잘못된 것이다. 기억하는 것에서 얻을 수 있는 것이 있다. (①) 우리는 더 연결되고, 더 완전하고, 더 제대로 진행되고 있다고 느낄 수 있다. 우리는 영감, 정보, 그리고 편안함을 받을 수 있다. Albert Einstein은 그의 상대성 이론이 꿈에 의해 영감을 받았다고 말했다. (②) 사실, 그는 꿈들이 그의 많은 발견의 원인이 되었다고 주장했다. (③) 꿈을 꾸는 이유를 묻는 것은 우리가 왜 숨을 쉬는지 의문을 제기하는 것만큼 타당한 질문이다. 꿈을 꾸는 것은 건강한 삶의 필수적인 부분이다. (④ 좋은 소식은 우리가 꿈을 기억하든 안하든 이것이 사실이라는 것이다.) 많은 사람들이 구체적인 꿈을 기억하지 못할지라도, 깨어났을 때 어떤 문제에 대한 새로운 접근법에 영감을 얻는다고 말한다.

지문 어휘

- nocturnal 밤에 일어나는, 야행성의
- irrelevant 무관한, 상관없는
- on track 제대로 진행되고 있는
- inspiration 영감
- make sense 이해하다, 타당하다
- questioning 질문, 의문, 심문
- integral 필수적인, 완전한
- discovery 발견

21　　　　　　　　　　　　　　　　정답 ④

정답 해설

우주여행과 인간의 생리적 영향을 주제로, 연구된 우주여행의 역사와, 지구 대기권 너머의 환경과 우주여행이 인간의 몸에 미치는 생리적 영향에 관한 내용을 다루는 글이다. 주어진 문장에서의 '이러한 질병들(these ailments)'에 대한 내용이 ③ 다음 문장에서 언급되고, 구체적인 예시가 ④ 다음 문장에서 이어지고 있다. 따라서 주어진 문장이 들어갈 위치로 가장 적절한 것은 ④이다.

지문 해석

수세기 동안, 인간은 하늘을 쳐다보았고 우리 행성의 영역 너머에 무엇이 존재하는지 궁금해했다. (①) 고대 천문학자들은 우주에 대해 더 많은 것을 배우기를 바라며 밤하늘을 조사했다. 더 최근에는, 몇몇 영화들은 우주 공간에서 인간의 생명을 유지할 수 있는 가능성을 탐구했고, 반면에 다른 영화들은 외계 생명체가 우리 행성을 방문했을지에 대해 의문을 가졌다. (②) 1961년 우주 비행사 Yuri Gagarin이 우주여행을 한 최초의 인간이 된 이후로, 과학자들은 지구 대기권 너머의 상태가 어떤지, 우주여행이 인체에 어떤 영향을 미치는지 연구해 왔다. (③) 대부분의 우주 비행사들이 우주에서 몇 달 이상을 보내지는 않지만, 그들이 지구로 돌아올 때 많은 사람들이 생리적, 심리적 문제를 겪는다. (④) 이러한 질병들 중 일부는 일시적이지만, 다른 것들은 장기적일 수 있다. 우주 비행사들의 3분의 2 이상이 우주여행을 하는 동안 멀미로 고통받는다. 무중력 환경에서, 신체는 위와 아래를 구별할 수 없다. 신체의 내부 균형 시스템은 혼란스러운 신호를 뇌에 보내며, 이것은 며칠 동안 오래 지속되는 메스꺼움을 초래할 수 있다.

지문 어휘
- ailment 질병
- realm 영역, 범위, 왕국
- astronomer 천문학자
- explore 탐구하다, 분석하다
- extraterrestrial 외계의
- astronaut 우주 비행사
- effect 영향, 결과, 효과
- physiological 생리적인
- psychological 심리적인, 정신적인
- gravity-free 무중력
- differentiate 구별하다, 구분 짓다
- result in 결과를 초래하다
- nausea 메스꺼움
- lasting 영속적인, 지속적인

22 정답 ④

정답 해설
단기목표 설정의 중요성과 행복한 뇌의 집중력에 대한 글로, 긍정적인 뇌의 특성을 기반으로, 단기 목표를 통한 집중과 성취를 통해 장기적인 목표를 이루는 방법에 대해 설명하고 있다. 주어진 문장에 'the same thing'이라는 대명사가 있으며, 본문의 내용은 '예시 → 예시 → 결론'으로 이어지고 있으며, 그 예시는 '살을 빼는 것'으로 ②와 ③ 다음 문장에서 설명하고 있으므로 주어진 문장이 들어갈 위치로 가장 적절한 것은 ④이다.

지문 해석
행복한 뇌는 단기간에 집중하는 경향이 있다. (①) 그것이 사실이라면, 궁극적으로 장기 목표를 달성하는 데에 어떤 단기 목표를 달성할 수 있을 지를 생각해 보는 것이 좋다. (②) 예를 들어, 만약 여러분이 6개월 안에 30파운드를 빼기를 원한다면, 여러분은 어떤 단기 목표를 여러분을 거기에 도달하게 할 더 작은 무게의 증가량을 빼는 것과 연관 지을 수 있는가? (③) 아마 2파운드를 빼는 걸 매주 스스로에게 보람 있는 것만큼 간단한 일일 것이다. (④ 그 동일한 생각은 업무에서 성과 향상하는 것과 같은 다양한 목표에도 적용될 수 있다.) 전체적인 목표를 더 작고 단기적인 부분으로 나눔으로써, 우리는 직업에서 목표의 엄청남에 압도되는 대신에 우리는 점진적인 성취에 초점을 맞출 수 있다.

지문 어휘
- apply to ~에 적용되다
- improve 나아지다, 향상시키다
- performance 성과
- short term 단기
- accomplish 완수하다, 달성하다
- associate 연상하다, 연관짓다
- increment 증가, 임금 인상
- weight 체중
- rewarding 보람 있는
- incremental 점진적인, 증가하는
- accomplishment 성취, 업적
- overwhelm 압도하다
- enormity 엄청남, 막대함, 심각함
- profession 직업, 직종

23 정답 ③

정답 해설
문화적 다양성과 직업 이동에 대한 글로, 직업에 관한 인식이 문화에 따라 어떻게 달라질 수 있는지를 설명하는 글로, '미국의 문화', '집단주의적 문화', 그리고 '개인주의적 문화'라는 세 가지 범주에서 차이점을 설명하고 있다. 이때, 보기의 문장에서 언급하는 '이러한 상황에서 (In this situation)'는 어떠한 문화를 가리키고 있는지를 찾은 것이 문제 풀이의 핵심이 된다. 보기의 문장에서 직장 조직과 그 조직 내 사람들에 대한 책임을 강조하고 있으므로 '집단적인 문화'에 대해 진술하고 있으므로 ② 다음 문장 뒤에 오는 것이 자연스럽고, ③ 다음 문장에는 '개인적인 문화'에 대한 내용이 진술되고 있다. 따라서 보기의 문장이 들어갈 위치로 가장 적절한 것은 ③이다.

지문 해석
직업의 의미에서의 문화적 다양성은 또한 다른 면에서도 그것들 자체를 드러나게 된다. (①) 예를 들어 미국 문화에서는 직업을 단순히 돈을 모으고 생계를 꾸리기 위한 수단으로 쉽게 생각한다. (②) 다른 문화에서는, 특히 집단주의적 문화의 경우 직업은 오히려 더 큰 집단에 대한 의무를 이행하는 것으로 여겨질 수 있다. (③ 이러한 상황에서 우리는 그 또는 그녀가 속한 직장 조직에 대한, 그리고 그 조직을 구성하고 있는 사람들에 대한 개인의 사회적 책임으로 인하여 개개인이 하나의 직업에서 또 다른 직업으로 더 적게 이동할 것임을 기대하게 된다.) 개인주의적 문화의 경우, 한 직업을 떠나 다른 직업으로 이동하는 것이 더 쉽게 여겨질 수 있는데 왜냐하면 직업을 개인으로부터 더욱 쉽게 분리할 수 있기 때문이다. (④) 다른 직업도 그만큼 쉽게 동일한 목표를 달성할 수 있을 것이다.

지문 어휘
- obligation 의무, 책임, 책무
- comprise 구성하다
- accumulate 모으다, 축적하다
- make a living 생계를 꾸리다
- collectivistic 집단주의의
- fulfill 이행하다, 달성하다
- accomplish 완수하다, 달성하다

24 정답 ③

정답 해설
'하드 파워'에 상대가 되는 '소프트 파워'의 개념을 소개하고, 이것이 권력과 정치에 새로운 시각을 제공하는 방식을 다루고 있는 글이다. ② 다음 문장에서 '하드 파워'에 대한 설명을 하고 있고, ③ 다음 문장부터는 '소프트 파워'에 대한 설명을 하고 있다. 주어진 문장은 접속부사 '반대로 (on the contrary)'로 시작하여 '소프트 파워'에 대한 진술을 시작하고 있다. 따라서 주어진 문장이 들어가기에 가장 적절한 곳은 ③이다.

지문 해석

"소프트 파워"의 개념은 1990년대 초에 클린턴 행정부의 부대변인인 미국의 정치학자 Joseph Nye, Jr에 의해 형성되었다. 미국의 J. Nye 교수의 아이디어는 "파워"의 개념에 대한 해석을 새롭게 보도록 했고, 과학적 논쟁을 불러일으켰고, 국제정치의 실용적인 측면을 자극했다. (①) 그의 연구에서 그는 "하드 파워"와 "소프트 파워"라는 두 가지 힘의 유형을 발견한다. (②) 그는 "하드 파워"를 "다른 사람들이 그들의 초기 선호와 전략에 모순되는 방식으로 행동하도록 하는 능력"이라고 정의한다. (③ "소프트 파워"는 반대로 "강요나 수수료가 아닌 유인과 설득을 통해 목표를 달성하는 능력"이다.) 국가의 "소프트 파워"는 세계 정치 과정에서 다른 참가자들을 "매혹시키고", 자국 문화의 매력을 (다른 사람들에게 매력적인) 보여주고, 정치적 가치와 외교 정책(합법적이고 도덕적으로 정당하다고 여겨진다면)의 보여주는 능력이다. (④) "소프트 파워"의 주요 구성요소는 문화, 정치적 가치와 외교 정책이다.

지문 어휘

- on the contrary 그와는 반대로
- persuasion 설득, 신념
- coercion 강제, 강압, 강요
- administration 집행, 행정직, 행정부
- interpretation 해석, 이해, 설명
- strategy 전략, 작전
- charm 매력
- demonstrate 입증하다, 설명하다, 보여주다
- attractiveness 매력, 매혹
- context 맥락, 상황
- legitimate 합법적인, 정당한, 타당한
- component 구성 요소
- morally 도덕적으로
- justified 정당한, 당연한

25

정답 ④

정답 해설

언어와 인식의 변화에 대한 글로, 시간이 지나면서 우리의 인식과 언어 생산은 변화하는데, 특히 새로운 환경에 적응하며 언어 습관과 방언이 변화하며, 이는 논란의 여지가 있으나 의식적이든 아니든 변화가 일어날 수 있음을 보여주는 글이다. 주어진 문장에서 'some'과 'others'는 세부사항의 대조의 관계를 나타낸다. 따라서 일반적인 진술이 끝난 다음에 나와야 한다. ③ 다음 문장에 '모든 사람들이 같은 정도로 이렇게 하는 것은 아니다'는 일반적인 진술 다음에 오는 것이 자연스럽다. 따라서 주어진 문장이 들어갈 위치로 가장 적절한 것은 ④이다.

지문 해석

말투에 대한 우리의 인식과 생산은 시간이 지나면서 변한다. (①) 만약 우리가 장기간 동안 우리의 고향을 떠나게 된다면 우리 주변의 새로운 억양이 이상하다는 우리의 인식은 단지 일시적일 뿐이다. (②) 서서히 우리는 다른 사람들이 억양을 가지고 있다는 느낌을 잃을 것이고 우리는 새로운 기준에 우리의 말하는 패턴을 맞추기 위해 적응하기 시작할 것이다. (③) 모든 사람들이 같은 정도로 이렇게 하는 것은 아니다. (④ 어떤 사람들은 원래의 억양과 방언 어휘, 구절들과 몸짓들에 대해 몹시 자랑스러워하는 반면, 다른 사람들은 그들이 더 이상 "군중에서 두드러지지" 않도록 말하기 습관을 바꿈으로써 새로운 환경에 빠르게 적응한다.) 그들이 의식적으로 이것을 하는지 아닌지는 논쟁의 여지가 있고 개개인에 따라 다를 수 있지만, 언어와 관련된 대부분의 과정들처럼, 변화는 아마도 우리가 그것들을 인식하기 전에 일어날 것이고, 아마도 우리가 인식한다면 아마 일어나지 못할 것이다.

지문 어휘

- accent 억양, 말씨, 악센트, 강세
- dialect 방언, 사투리
- phrase 표현, 어구
- accommodate 적응하다, 조정하다, 수용하다
- stand out 두드러지다
- perception 지각, 인식
- with time 시간이 흐름에 따라, 마침내
- temporary 일시적인, 임시의
- fit in 적응하다, 어울리다
- norm 규범, 표준
- consciously 의식적으로
- be open to ~의 여지가 있다
- debate 논쟁, 논란, 토론

26

정답 ④

정답 해설

고대 올림픽과 그 안의 극한 스포츠에 대한 글로, 올림픽의 성격과 그 안에서 벌어진 극한 스포츠 활동을 설명하고 있다. '만약 둘 다 항복하지 않는다면, 그 둘은 한 사람이 쓰러질 때까지 주먹을 교환할 것이다'는 진술은, 주어진 문장에서 언급된 '그 두 사람(the two)'에 대한 언급이 된 다음 문장에 와야 자연스럽다. ③ 다음 문장에 두 사람이 언급되어 있다. 따라서 주어진 문장이 들어갈 위치로 가장 적절한 것은 ④이다.

지문 해석

고대 올림픽은 우리의 현대 경기와 같이, 운동선수들에게 그들의 건강과 우월성을 증명하는 기회를 제공했다. (①) 고대 올림픽 경기들은 약자를 없애고 강자를 미화하기 위해 고안되었다. 승자들은 벼랑 끝으로 내몰렸다. (②) 현대와 같이, 사람들은 익스트림 스포츠를 사랑했다. 가장 좋아하는 경기들 중 하나가 33번째 올림픽에서 추가되었다. 이것은 판크라티온, 즉 레슬링과 복싱의 극단적인 혼합이었다. 그리스어의 판크라티온은 "총력"을 의미한다. 그 남자들은 상대방을 엉망으로 만들 수 있는 금속 징이 달린 가죽 끈을 착용했다. (③) 그 위험한 형태의 레슬링은 시간이나 무게 제한이 없었다. 이 경기에서는, 단지 두 가지 규칙이 적용되었다. 첫 번째로, 레슬링 선수들은 그들의 엄지 손가락으로 눈을 찌르는 것이 허용되지 않았다. 두 번째로, 그들은 물수 없었다. 그 외의 다른 것은 정당한 행위로 여겨졌다. 그 경기는 복싱 경기와 같은 방식으로 결정되었다. <u>경쟁자들은 그 둘 중 한 명이 쓰러질 때까지 계속되었다.</u> (④ <u>만약 둘 다 항복하지 않는다면, 그 둘은 한 사람이 쓰러질 때까지 주먹을 교환할 것이다.</u>) 오직 가장 강하고 굳게 결심한 운동선수들만 이 경기를 시도했다. 경쟁자의 손가락을 부러뜨려서 그의 별명을 얻은 레슬링 "Mr. Fingertips"를 상상해 보라!

지문 어휘

- surrender 항복하다, 굴복하다
- superiority 우월성
- glorify 미화하다, 칭찬하다
- gouge 찌르다
- contender 경쟁자, 도전자
- determined 굳게 결심한, 단호한

27

정답 ④

정답 해설

사냥을 통한 동물 분배와 사회적 상호작용의 원칙에 대한 글로, 사냥을 통해 얻은 동물의 분배를 예로 들어, 사회적인 상호작용과 도덕성을 강조하는 방식으로 사냥꾼들 간의 자원 분배와 친족 의무에 대한 원칙을 설명하고 있다. ④ 앞 문장에 이런 불균형의 예시가 나오고 ④ 다음 문장에 불균형을 수정함으로써 그에 대한 결과를 진술하고 있다. 따라서 주어진 문장이 들어갈 위치로 가장 적절한 곳은 ④이다.

지문 해석

사냥을 통해 동물을 죽였을 때, 발생하는 이런 단순한 분배 상황을 검토해 보자. 사람들은 그 동물을 얻는 데 각 사냥꾼들의 행해진 일의 양에 따라 그 동물이 분배될 것으로 기대할지 모른다. (①) 어느 정도까지는 이 원칙이 따라지나, 다른 사람들 역시 그들의 권리를 갖는다. (②) 그 진영의 각각의 사람은 자기와 사냥꾼들과의 관계에 따라 몫을 받는다. (③) 예를 들어 한 마리의 캥거루가 사냥되었을 때, 사냥꾼들은 그들의 친척들에게 그것의 주요 부분을 줘야 하고 심지어 최악의 부분을 사냥꾼들 자신이 가질 수 있다. (④ 이런 불평등은 그들이 다른 사람들의 사냥감으로부터 더 좋은 몫을 자신들의 차례에서 받음으로써 수정될 수 있다.) 각 사람들에게 장기적으로 순수한 결과는 실질적으로는 똑같으나, 이런 시스템을 통해서 친족의 의무라는 원칙과 음식을 공유하는 도덕성이 강조되어져 왔다.

지문 어휘

- inequality 불균형, 불평등
- kill 죽이다, 사냥감
- distribution 분배, 분포, 유통
- portion 분배하다, 나누다
- kinfolk 친척, 친족
- substantially 상당히, 실질적으로
- principle 원리, 원칙
- kinship 친족, 연대감
- obligation 의무
- morality 도덕성
- emphasize 강조하다, 두드러지게 하다

28

정답 ③

정답 해설

새로운 대륙이 있다는 주장과 그 대륙의 특징에 대한 이 글은 뉴질랜드 아래에 숨겨져 있는 Zealandia라는 미확인 대륙에 대한 지질학자들의 주장과 관련된 내용을 다루고 있으며, 대륙의 크기, 바다 아래의 비중, 그리고 대양의 없음에 따른 특징 등을 설명하고 있다. 주어진 문장에서 언급한 '뉴질랜드, 뉴칼레도니아 및 일부 작은 섬(New Zealand, New Caledonia and a few small islands)'을 ③ 다음 문장의 '이러한 소수 지역들(Except those tiny areas)을 제외하고'와 연결되고 있다. 따라서 주어진 문장이 들어갈 위치로 가장 적절한 곳은 ③이다.

지문 해석

뉴질랜드 아래에 길고 숨겨져 있는 Zealandis라고 불리는 대륙이 있다고 지질학자들은 말한다. 그러나 어떠한 사람도 공식적으로 새로운 대륙을 지정하지 않았기 때문에 개인적인 지질학자들은 궁극적으로 스스로 판단을 해야 할 것이다. (①) 지질학자 팀이 Zealndia가 약 490만 평방 킬로미터를 덮는 대륙지각의 연속적인 확장이라고 주장하면서 신대륙에 대한 과학적 주장을 했다. (②) 그것은 대략 인도의 아대륙의 크기이다. 다른 대부분의 건조한 대륙과는 달리, 뉴질랜드의 약 94%가 바다 밑에 숨어 있다. (③ 오로지 뉴질랜드, 뉴칼레도니아 및 일부 작은 섬만이 파도 위에 보인다.) 이러한 소수 지역들만 제외하고, 모든 Zealandia의 부분들은 물속에 잠겨있다. "우리가 세계의 바다를 모두 제거할 수 있다면, Zealandia가 대양 지각에서 3000미터 가량 위로 튀어나온 것이 분명히 보일 것이다." 라고 지질학자는 말한다. (④) "만약 해수면이 없었다면, 우리는 오래 전에 Zealandia를 그것의 원래 존재인 대륙으로 인식했을 것이다."

지문 어휘

- beneath 아래에, 밑에
- continent 대륙
- geologist 지질학자
- designate 지정하다, 지명하다
- pitch 던지다, 제시하다
- case 경우, 사건, 사실, 주장
- subcontinent 아(亞)대륙
- pull the plug on 제거하다, 생명 유지 장치를 떼어 내다
- stand out 튀어나오다, 두드러지다

29

정답 ③

정답 해설

바쁜 일상에서의 여러 가지 일들에 대한 글로, 여러 가지 해야 할 일들로 인해 바쁜 일상을 겪으면서 주인공의 경험과 감정을 풍부하게 묘사하고 있다. 그녀가 먹은 많은 식사가 그녀를 피곤하게 해서 잠에 빠지게 할 준비가 되게 하였다는 주어진 문장이 원인이 되고, 그 결과 그녀는 코를 골고 있었다(잠을 자고 있었다)가 원인의 결과가 된다. 따라서 주어진 문장이 들어갈 위치로 가장 적절한 것은 ③이다.

지문 해석

내가 도착하자마자 다양한 의무들이 나를 기다리고 있었다. 나는 소녀들이 공부하는 시간에 함께 앉아 있어야 했다. (①) 그때가 내가 기도문을 읽을 차례였고 나는 그들이 잠자리에 드는 것을 보았다. 그 이후에 나는 다른 선생님들과 식사를 했다. (②) 우리가 드디어 잠을 자기 위해 물러났을 때조차도 Miss Gryce는 변함없이 여전히 나의 벗이었다. 촛대의 초가 아주 조금 밖에 남지 않아서 그것이 모두 타버릴 때까지 그녀가 말을 걸지 않을까 나는 두려웠다. (③ 그러나 다행히 그녀가 먹은 많은 양의 저녁식사가 그녀를 피곤하게 하여 잠에 빠질 준비가 되게 하였다.) 그녀는 내가 옷을 벗기도 전에 이미 코를 골고 있었다. 단지 일 인치의 초가 남아 있었다. (④) 나는 그때 나의 편지를 꺼냈고, 인장은 이니셜 F였다. 나는 그 봉인을 부수어 편지를 뜯었고, 그 내용은 간결했다.

지문 어휘

- supper 저녁식사
- see to bed 잠자리로 보내다
- afterward 나중에
- inevitable 피할 수 없는
- companion 동반자, 동행
- dread 두려워하다
- lest ~하지 않기 위해서
- snoring 코를 고는
- take out 꺼내다
- seal 인장
- brief 간단한, 간결한, 짧은

30

정답 ②

정답 해설

사전 활용의 중요성과 장애요소에 대한 글로, 사전은 신뢰할 수 있는 단어 학습 출처이지만 사용 습관을 개발하는 것이 중요하며, 단어 찾기가 번거로워서 학습에 방해가 될 수 있음을 설명하고 있다. 주어진 문장은 단어 학습에 대한 부정적인 진술이며, 이것을 보충 설명하는 문장이 ② 다음 문장에 진술되고 있다. 따라서 주어진 문장이 들어갈 위치로 가장 적절한 곳은 ②이다.

지문 해석

> 사전은 단어 연구를 위한 당신의 가장 신뢰할 수 있는 자원이다. 그러나 그것들을 사용하는 습관은 길러질 필요가 있다. 물론, 읽기를 멈추고 단어를 찾아보는 것은 성가신 방해처럼 느껴질 수 있다. 당신은 계속하면 결국 맥락에서 그것을 이해하게 될 것이라고 스스로에게 말할 수 있다. (①) 사실, 학습지도서에서도 종종 그것을 조언을 한다. (② <u>그러나, 이해를 하는 것이 발생하지 않는다면, 당신은 당신 자신이 졸고 있는 것을 발견하게 될 것이다.</u>) 종종 이것은 잠을 필요로 하는 것이 아니라 점진적으로 의식을 잃어가는 것이다. (③) 여기에서 요령은 노곤함이 발생하기 전에 단어 공부를 위해 사전을 잡는 충분한 의지를 발휘하는 것이 쉬울 때를 인지하는 것이다. (④) 이러한 특별한 노력이 필요함에도 불구하고, 의미가 명확해지면 인지할 수 있는 안도감이 그 노력을 가치 있게 만들 것이다.

지문 어휘

- [ ] drowsy 졸리는, 나른하게 만드는
- [ ] reliable 신뢰할 수 있는
- [ ] cultivate 기르다, 경작하다
- [ ] annoying 짜증나는
- [ ] interruption 방해
- [ ] look up 찾아보다
- [ ] gradual 점진적인
- [ ] consciousness 의식
- [ ] knack 요령
- [ ] confusion 혼란
- [ ] exert 발휘하다, 가하다, 힘쓰다
- [ ] sufficient 충분한
- [ ] willpower 의지
- [ ] clarified 명확해진
- [ ] perceptible 인지할 수 있는
- [ ] relief 안도감
- [ ] worthwhile 가치 있는

06 문장 삽입 파악 유형 기출 독해 어휘 복습 TEST

1	distracting	산만하게 하는	21	come by	잠깐 들르다, 얻다
2	prescribed	미리 정해진, 규정된	22	subjectively	주관적으로
3	recommend	권하다, 추천하다	23	unverified	검증되지 않은
4	extraneous	관련없는	24	escalate	확대되다, 증가되다
5	handle	다루다, 처리하다	25	negotiation	협상, 절충
6	extract	빼다, 뽑다, 추출하다	26	outlook	전망, 관점
7	controversial	논란이 많은	27	variability	변동성, 가변성
8	messy	지저분한, 엉망인, 골치 아픈	28	ultimate	궁극적인, 최후의
9	strenuous	격렬한, 몹시 힘든, 완강한, 불굴의	29	circulate	순환하다, 유포하다
10	commitment	헌신, 약속, 전념	30	localized	국부적인, 국지적인
11	federal	연방 정부의, 연방제의	31	momentary	순간적인, 잠깐의
12	suspend	부유시키다, 매달다, 중지하다, 연기하다	32	horizontal	수평의, 가로의
13	inhabit	거주하다, 살다	33	analogy	비유, 유추
14	preserve	보존하다, 지키다, 전유물	34	structure	구조, 체계
15	reveal	드러내다, 밝히다	35	dissimilar	같지 않은, 다른
16	cabin	선실, 오두막	36	reverse	(정)반대, 뒤바꾸다
17	startle	깜짝 놀라게 하다	37	relaxed	편안한, 여유 있는
18	reform	개혁, 개선, 개혁하다, 개선하다	38	lay off	해고하다
19	resolve	결의, 결심, 결심하다, 해결하다	39	application	지원서, 신청서, 응용, 적용
20	deputy	대리인, 의원, 보안관	40	indispensable	없어서는 안 될, 필수적인

#	단어	뜻	#	단어	뜻
41	financial	재정의, 금융의	61	coercion	강제, 강압, 강요
42	satisfaction	만족감, 충족	62	dialect	방언, 사투리
43	addiction	중독	63	fit in	적응하다, 어울리다
44	compulsive	강박적인, 강제적인	64	be open to	~의 여지가 있다
45	advantageous	이로운, 유리한	65	debate	논쟁, 논란, 토론
46	shatter	산산이 부서지다, 산산조각 나다	66	superiority	우월성
47	retain	유지하다, 보유하다	67	glorify	미화하다, 칭찬하다
48	residue	나머지, 잔여물	68	contender	경쟁자, 도전자
49	retirement	은퇴, 퇴직	69	distribution	분배, 분포, 유통
50	staggering	충격적인, 믿기 어려운	70	portion	분배하다, 나누다
51	inspiration	영감	71	kinfolk	친척, 친족
52	integral	필수적인, 완전한	72	beneath	아래에, 밑에
53	realm	영역, 범위, 왕국	73	continent	대륙
54	astronomer	천문학자	74	stand out	튀어나오다, 두드러지다
55	result in	결과를 초래하다	75	afterward	나중에
56	lasting	영속적인, 지속적인	76	companion	동반자, 동행
57	incremental	점진적인, 증가하는	77	brief	간단한, 간결한, 짧은
58	obligation	의무, 책임, 책무	78	drowsy	졸리는, 나른하게 만드는
59	on the contrary	그와는 반대로	79	willpower	의지
60	persuasion	설득, 신념	80	worthwhile	가치 있는

PART 07 순서 배열 유형

ANSWER

01 ③	02 ②	03 ③	04 ②	05 ②
06 ③	07 ③	08 ②	09 ②	10 ④
11 ②	12 ③	13 ③	14 ③	15 ④
16 ①	17 ③	18 ①	19 ②	20 ②
21 ③	22 ②	23 ③	24 ③	25 ①
26 ①	27 ③	28 ③	29 ④	30 ②
31 ③	32 ②	33 ②	34 ②	35 ④
36 ③				

01
정답 ③

정답 해설

이 글은 능력 기반 보상의 필요성을 강조하고 있다. 사회는 경제적 보상과 책임 있는 자리를 능력에 따라 분배해야 하며, 이는 효율성과 공정성을 통해 생산성을 높이고, 차별 없는 보상을 가능하게 한다고 주장한다. 주어진 문장은 '사회가 보상과 책임을 능력에 따라 배분해야 한다는 생각'이 여러 이유로 매력적이라는 점을 설명하고 있으며, 이러한 이유를 구체적으로 보충하는 (C)로 자연스럽게 이어진다. (C)에서는 그 이유 중 두 가지가 효율성과 공정성임을 밝히고, 이후 (A)에서 '효율성', (B)에서 '공정성' 각각을 구체적으로 설명하고 있다. 따라서 글의 순서로 가장 적절한 것은 ③이다.

지문 해석

사회가 경제적 보상과 책임 있는 자리를 능력에 따라 배분해야 한다는 생각은 여러 가지 이유로 매력적이다.
(C) 이러한 이유들 중 두 가지는 채용 시 능력을 기준으로 삼아야 한다는 주장에 대한 일반화된 형태이며, 그것은 효율성과 공정성이다.
(A) 노력과 진취성, 재능을 보상하는 경제 시스템은 기여도와 상관없이 모두에게 동일한 보수를 지급하거나, 편애에 따라 사회적 지위를 분배하는 시스템보다 생산성이 더 높을 가능성이 크다.
(B) 사람들을 오직 그들의 능력에 따라 보상하는 것 또한 공정성이라는 미덕을 지니는데, 이는 성취 이외의 어떤 기준에 의해서도 차별하지 않기 때문이다.

지문 어휘

☐ allocate 배분하다, 할당하다
☐ reward 보상
☐ position 위치, 자리
☐ responsibility 책임
☐ merit 능력, 장점, 가치
☐ appeal 매력적이다, 관심[흥미]을 끌다
☐ reason 이유, 근거
☐ initiative 진취성, 결단력, 계획
☐ be likely to ~할 가능성이 있다
☐ regardless of ~에 상관없이
☐ contribution 기여도, 기부금
☐ favoritism 편애, 편파
☐ virtue 장점, 미덕, 선
☐ fairness 공정성
☐ discriminate 차별하다, 식별하다
☐ generalized 일반화된
☐ efficiency 효율(성), 능률

02
정답 ②

정답 해설

주어진 문장은 보통 아기가 땅에서 무언가를 줍는 일이 골칫거리라는 일반적인 인식을 말하고 있다. 이에 반해, (B)는 세 살배기 Ziv Nitzan이 땅에서 우연히 4,000년 된 이집트 유물을 발견한 사례를 'But'을 통해 자연스럽게 소개한다. 이어서 (A)는 'the find'를 받아 유물청이 이것이 중기 청동기 시대의 인장임을 밝혀낸 과정을 설명한다. 마지막으로 (C)는 'the seal'을 다시 언급하며, 장관이 이 발견의 의미를 강조하는 말로 마무리하는 것이 자연스럽다. 따라서 글의 순서로 가장 적절한 것은 ②이다.

지문 해석

보통 아기들이 땅에서 뭔가를 주워 올리는 것은 골칫거리를 의미한다.
(B) 하지만 이스라엘의 세 살배기 Ziv Nitzan이 바위처럼 보이는 것에 묻은 모래를 솔로 털어내던 중, 그녀는 거의 4,000년 된 이집트 유물을 발견했다.
(A) 가족은 이 발견을 이스라엘 문화재 관리국에 신고했고, 당국은 이것이 중기 청동기 시대의 딱정벌레 모양 인장임을 확인했다.
(C) Ziv는 훌륭한 시민상 증서를 받았고, 이스라엘 문화재 장관은 이 인장이 "우리에게 큰 이야기를 연결해준다"며, "아이들도 역사를 발견하는 데 참여할 수 있다"고 말했다.

지문 어휘

☐ toddler 아기, 유아
☐ trouble 골칫거리, 곤란
☐ brush away 솔로 털다
☐ artifact 유물
☐ beetle 딱정벌레
☐ seal 인장, 도장
☐ bronze age 청동기 시대
☐ certificate 증서, 자격증

03

정답 ③

정답 해설

Nick이 캠핑을 할 때 요리하는 장면을 묘사하는 글이다. 소나무 조각으로 불을 피우고, 철망 그릴을 설치했다는 제시문 다음에는 Nick이 그릴 위에 프라이팬을 올리고 음식을 데우는 과정이 자연스럽게 이어진다. 먼저 (C)에서 프라이팬을 그릴 위에 올리고, (A)에서는 기포가 생기는 모습을 설명하며, 마지막으로 (B)에서 작은 기포들이 더 빨리 올라오고 있는 모습과 함께 글이 마무리된다. 따라서 글의 순서로 가장 적절한 것은 ③이다.

지문 해석

Nick은 그루터기에서 도끼로 얻은 소나무 조각으로 불을 피우기 시작했다. 그는 불 위에 철망 그릴을 얹고, 네 개의 다리를 부츠로 땅에 눌러 고정했다.
(C) Nick은 불꽃 위에 그릴에 프라이팬을 올렸다. 그는 더 배가 고팠다. 콩과 스파게티가 데워졌다. 그는 그것들을 저어 섞었다.
(A) 그것들은 기포가 생기기 시작했고, 작은 기포들이 힘겹게 표면으로 올라왔다. 좋은 냄새가 났다. Nick은 토마토케첩 병을 꺼내고 빵 네 조각을 잘랐다.
(B) 작은 기포들이 이제 더 빨리 올라오고 있었다. Nick은 불 옆에 앉아 프라이팬을 들어 올렸다.

지문 어휘

- pine 소나무, 솔
- stump (나무의) 그루터기, 남은 부분
- surface 표면, 지면
- beside 옆에, ~에 비해
- lift 들어 올리다, 올라가다
- flame 불꽃, 불길, 활활 타오르다
- warm 데워지다, 따뜻해지다, 따뜻한
- stir 섞다, 젓다, 흔들리다, 동요, 충격, 젓기

04

정답 ②

정답 해설

어려운 상황에서 빵을 집에 가져가 필사적으로 노력하는 가족들과 함께 식사를 즐기고 있는 내용의 이야기이다. 첫 문장에서 주인공이 빵을 몰래 가져가는 상황이 기술되어 있다. 그 후에 이어질 글에서는 그 빵을 가지고 어떻게 행동했는지에 관한 내용이 나와야 하므로 빵을 가지고 집으로 돌아가는 동안의 상황을 묘사한 (B)가 먼저 나오고, 여동생과 어머니를 식탁에 앉게 하는 (A)의 내용이 이어진 다음, 빵을 같이 먹는 (C)의 상황으로 글이 마무리가 되어야 한다. 따라서 글의 순서로 적절한 것은 ②이다.

지문 해석

누군가가 무슨 일이 일어났는지 목격하기 전에 나는 빵 덩어리들을 내 셔츠 아래로 아무렇게나 넣고 헌팅 재킷을 몸에 꽉 감싸 입고 신속하게 걸어 나갔다.
(B) 빵의 열기가 내 피부 안을 태웠지만, 나는 그것을 더 단단히 꽉 움켜잡고 삶에 매달렸다. 집에 도착할 때쯤, 빵 덩어리들은 약간 식었지만 속은 여전히 따뜻했다.
(A) 내가 그것들을 식탁에 떨어뜨릴 때, 내 누나의 손이 다가와 한 덩어리를 찢으려고 했지만 나는 그녀를 앉히고 식탁에 어머니께서 우리와 함께 하도록 했고, 따뜻한 차를 따랐다.
(C) 나는 빵을 잘랐다. 우리는 한 조각 한 조각씩, 빵 한 덩이 전체를 먹었다. 그것은 건포도와 견과류로 가득찬 좋은 푸짐한 빵이었다.

지문 어휘

- witness 목격하다, 목격자, 증인
- shove 아무렇게나 넣다, 밀치다
- tightly 꽉, 단단히, 빽빽이
- swiftly 신속하게, 재빠르게
- burn 태우다, 불에 타다, 화상을 입히다
- clutch (꽉) 움켜잡다
- cling to 매달리다, 고수하다
- by the time ~할 때쯤, ~할 때까지
- tear off 찢어내다, 떼어내다, ~을 벗기다
- chunk 덩어리
- pour (음료를) 따르다[따라 주다], 붓다
- slice 자르다, 썰다, 조각, 부분
- entire 전체의, 전부의
- hearty 푸짐한, 원기 왕성한, 애정어린, 친절한
- filled with ~으로 가득찬
- raisin 건포도
- nut 견과

05

정답 ②

정답 해설

영화배우와 스포츠 스타에 대한 관심은 그들의 활약을 넘어 개인적인 측면까지 이어진다. 양쪽 모두 이러한 관심을 촉진하지만, 그들의 진정성과 일하는 방식에 근본적인 차이가 있음을 설명하는 글이다. 영화와 스포츠 스타에 대한 관심에 대한 언급을 한 제시문 다음에 '영화스타'에 대한 언급을 하는 (B)로 연결되며, '스포츠스타'에 대한 언급을 하는 (A)로 이어져야 하며, 마지막으로 '영화스타'와 '스포츠스타'에 차이에 대한 설명을 하는 (C)로 이어져야 한다. 따라서 글의 순서로 적절한 것은 ②이다.

지문 해석

영화와 스포츠 스타에 대한 관심은 화면과 경기장에서의 활약을 넘어선다.
(B) 신문 칼럼, 전문 잡지, 텔레비전 프로그램, 웹사이트는 유명한 할리우드 배우들의 사생활들을 때로는 정확하게 기록한다.
(A) 유니폼에서 벗어난 숙련된 야구, 축구, 농구 선수들의 행동들은 마찬가지로 비슷하게 대중의 관심을 끈다.
(C) 두 산업 모두 이러한 관심을 적극적으로 장려하는데 이것은 관객을 확대하고 따라서 수입을 증가시킨다. 그러나 근본적인 차이가 그들을 나눈다: 스포츠 스타들이 생계를 위해 하는 것은 영화 스타들이 하는 것과는 다른 방식으로 진정성이 있다는 것이다.

지문 어휘

- arena 경기장, 투기장
- celebrated 유명한, 축하받는
- accurately 정확하게
- promote 촉진하다, 홍보하다
- expand 확장하다, 넓히다
- fundamental 기본적인, 근본적인
- authentic 진정한, 진짜의

06

정답 ③

정답 해설

컴퓨터 보조 언어 학습(CALL)의 특성에 대한 글이다. 컴퓨터 보조 언어 학습(CALL)의 장점과 단점에 대한 제시문 다음에 이러한 장점과 단점의 이유에 대한 진술인 (B)로 이어져야 하며, 기술에 대한 진술인 나머지 문장들은 강조의 역할을 하는 접속부사(Yet)를 기준으로 '새로운 지식과 기술을 요한다'는 내용의 (C) 다음에, 기술들이 너무 빠르게 변해서 그 분야에서 더 나아가기 위해서는 끊임없이 갱신되어야 한다는 결론의 (A)가 이어져야 한다. 따라서 글의 순서로 적절한 것은 ③이다.

지문 해석

컴퓨터 보조 언어 학습(CALL)은 연구와 실행의 분야로서 흥미롭지만 좌절감을 주기도 한다.
(B) 그것은 복잡하고 역동적이며 빠르게 변화하기 때문에 흥미롭지만, 같은 이유로 인해 좌절감을 준다.
(C) 기술은 언어 학습 영역에 새로운 차원을 더하며, 이를 전문적인 실행에 적용하려는 사람들에게 새로운 지식과 기술을 요구한다.
(A) 그러나 기술이 너무 빠르게 변화하기 때문에, CALL 지식과 기술은 그 분야에서 더 나아가기 위해 끊임없이 갱신되어야 한다.

지문 어휘

- practice 실행, 실천, 관행, 관례
- renew 갱신하다, 재개하다
- rapidly 빠르게
- complex 복잡한, (건물) 단지
- dynamic 역동적인, 활발한, 역학
- dimension 차원, 관점, 규모, 크기
- domain 영역, 범위, 소유지[영토]
- professional 전문적인, 전문가의

07

정답 ③

정답 해설

고대 로마를 예로 들면서 정부 행정의 중요성을 강조하는 글로, 고대 로마는 라틴어에 기초한 효과적인 행정 체계를 가지고 있었고, 그들은 대영제국에서 흑해에 이르는 광대한 영토를 통치할 수 있었음을 설명하고 있는 글이다.
제시문에서 언급한 문명에 대한 추가적인 설명을 (B)에서, 'civilization'이 'citizen'이라는 라틴어 단어에서 비롯됨을 언급하고, 이어서 (C)에서는 로마의 지리적 범위와 로마어의 중요성에 대해 언급하며, 마지막 (A)에서는 로마가 광범위한 지역을 효과적으로 통치하기 위해 행정시스템 필요함을 이야기 한다. 따라서 글의 순서로 알맞은 것은 ③이다.

지문 해석

모든 문명은 정부의 행정에 의존한다. 아마도 고대 로마보다 이것의 전형적인 예가 되는 문명은 없을 것이다.
(B) 실제로, "문명"이라는 단어 자체는 "시민"을 의미하는 라틴어 civis 에서 왔다.
(C) 라틴어는 고대 로마의 언어인데, 로마의 영토는 지중해 분지에서 북쪽의 그레이트브리튼섬 일부와 동쪽의 흑해까지 뻗어 있었다.
(A) 이처럼 넓은 지역을 통치하기 위해서는 현재 이탈리아 중부에 기반을 둔 로마인들은 효과적인 행정 체계가 필요했다.

지문 어휘

- administration 행정, 관리, 집행
- civilization 문명
- exemplify 전형적인 예가 되다, 예를 들다
- rule 통치하다, 지배하다
- effective 효과적인
- territory 영토, 지역, 영역
- Mediterranean 지중해
- basin 분지, 유역
- the Black Sea 흑해

08

정답 ②

정답 해설

인공지능의 변화를 주제로 하는 글로, AI에 대한 예전의 종말론적인 대화와 달리, 최근에는 AI가 더 이상 무서운 존재가 아니라 다양한 용도로 활용될 수 있는 기술로 변화하고 있으며, 이는 산업에서 큰 관심을 받고 있기 때문임을 보여주는 글이다. 부정적인 제시문에서 또 다른 부정적인 '인류의 종말'을 언급하는 (B)의 진술로 이어져야 하며, 긍정적인 AI에 대한 인식에 대해 진술이 '그러나 (however)' 다음에 이어져야 하며, 그리고 긍정적인 진술로서의 '이러한 변화(This shift)'가 이어져야 한다. 따라서 글의 순서로 알맞은 것은 ②이다.

지문 해석

몇 년 전만 해도, 인공지능(AI)에 관한 모든 대화가 종말론적인 예측으로 끝나는 것처럼 보였다.
(B) 2014년에는 해당 분야의 전문가가 AI로 인해 우리가 악마를 소환하고 있다고 말했고, 노벨상 수상자인 한 물리학자는 AI가 인류의 종말을 가져올 수 있다고 말했다.
(A) 최근에는 그러나 상황이 변하기 시작했다. AI는 무서운 블랙박스에서 사람들이 다양한 경우에 활용할 수 있는 것으로 변해갔다.
(C) 이러한 변화는 이러한 기술들이 마침내 산업에서, 특히 시장 기회에 충분한 양으로 연구되고 있기 때문이다.

지문 어휘

- artificial intelligence (AI) 인공지능
- apocalyptic 종말론적, 세상에 종말이 온 듯한
- prediction 예측, 예견
- summon 소환하다, 부르다
- physicist 물리학자
- demon 악마, 악령
- spell 가져오다, 의미하다
- human race 인류
- scale 규모, 범위, 등급
- explore 탐구하다, 분석하다

09

정답 ②

정답 해설

스포츠팬들의 우울증에 대한 글로, 이 글은 스포츠팬들이 스포츠에서의 패배나 실망으로 인해 경험하는 우울증에 대해 다루고 있으며, 이 현상이 정신 건강과 신체 건강에 미치는 부정적인 영향과 해결책을 제시하는 글이다. 제시문에서 스포츠팬들의 우울증에 대해 언급 후, '스포츠팬 우울증의 원인과 영향'에 대한 진술인 (B)로 연결되며, '스포츠팬 우울증의 기타 원인들'에 대한 (A)로 연결된 다음, '스포츠 우울증의 해결책'을 제시하는 (C)로 연결되어야 한다. 따라서 글의 순서로 적절한 것은 ②이다.

지문 해석

스포츠 팬의 우울증은 많은 열렬한 스포츠팬들에게 영향을 미치는 실제 현상으로, 특히 실망이나 패배의 시기에 더욱 그렇다.
(B) 많은 팬들에게 그들이 가장 좋아하는 팀이나 운동선수들에 대한 그들의 감정적 투자는 너무 강렬해서 기대를 잃거나 충족시키지 못하는 것은 슬픔, 좌절감 그리고 심지어 우울증으로 이어질 수 있다. 연구에 따르면 스포츠팬의 우울증은 정신적 그리고 신체적 건강 모두에 다양한 부정적인 영향을 미칠 수 있다.
(A) 팬들은 스트레스 수준의 증가와 불안 또는 우울증에 걸릴 위험성의 증가뿐만 아니라 기분, 식욕, 그리고 수면의 질의 감소를 경험할 수 있다. 한 팀의 성공에 대한 개인적인 투자, 특정한 팀을 지원하라는 사회적인 압력, 그리고 종종 세간의 이목을 끄는 스포츠 경기에 수반되는 강력한 언론 보도와 정밀 조사를 포함하여, 스포츠 팬 우울증을 유발할 수 있는 많은 요인들이 있다.
(C) 스포츠 팬의 우울증의 부정적인 영향을 완화하기 위해서는 팬들이 스포츠에 대한 건강한 관점을 유지하고 궁극적으로 단순한 게임이라는 것을 기억하는 것이 중요하다. 운동과 같은 자기 관리 활동에 참여하고, 사랑하는 사람들과 시간을 보내고, 정신 건강 전문가에게 지원을 구하는 것도 도움이 될 수 있다.

지문 어휘

- [ ] defeat 패배
- [ ] mood 기분, 분위기
- [ ] appetite 식욕
- [ ] stress level 스트레스 수준
- [ ] anxiety 불안, 염려, 걱정거리
- [ ] depression 우울증, 불경기
- [ ] scrutiny 정밀 조사, 철저한 검토
- [ ] sadness 슬픔, 슬픈 일
- [ ] frustration 좌절, 불안
- [ ] mitigate 완화시키다, 경감시키다
- [ ] perspective 시각, 관점
- [ ] engage in 참여하다, 관여하다

10

정답 ④

정답 해설

소와 우유 생산의 복잡성에 대해 다루고 있으며, 이것이 인간 눈에는 단순해 보이지만 미시적인 차원에서는 굉장히 복잡하다는 점을 강조하고 있는 글이다. 첫 번째 문장으로 우유로 만드는 과정이 '단순하다'는 (C)로 이어져야 하는데, 그 이유는 그 과정이 '복잡하다'는 진술의 (B)와 대조를 이루기 때문이다. 마지막으로 '그 복잡성이 더 커진다'는 (A)로 이어져야 한다. 따라서 글의 순서로 가장 적절한 것은 ④이다.

지문 해석

인간의 수준에서, 소는 단순해 보인다. 당신이 풀을 먹이면 당신에게 소는 우유로 보답한다. 그것은 비밀이 소와 몇몇 다른 포유동물(대부분은 풀을 소화할 수 없음)에 국한된 특징이다.
(C) 당신은 그 과정을 이용하기 위해 세부적인 것들을 이해할 필요가 없다. 이것은 풀에서 우유로의 변환으로, 생물학보다는 화학이나 연금술과 더 닮은 간단한 변화이다. 그것은, 나름대로 마술이지만, 확실하게 작동하는 것은 이성적인 마술이다. 필요한 것은 잔디와 소 한 마리, 그리고 몇 세대에 걸친 실용적인 노하우뿐이다.
(B) 하지만 현미경으로 보면, 모든 것이 더 복잡해진다. 자세히 들여다보면 볼수록 더 복잡해진다. 우유는 하나의 물질이 아니라 많은 물질의 혼합물이다. 잔디는 너무 복잡해서 우리는 아직도 풀을 완전히 이해하지 못한다.
(A) 소의 복잡성은 훨씬 더 크다. 특히, 암소 (또한 황소도)는 새로운 세대의 젖소를 만들 수 있다. 이것은 인간적인 차원에서는 단순하지만, 미시적인 차원에서는 표현할 수 없을 정도로 복잡하다.

지문 어휘

- [ ] trick 특징, 묘기, 재주, 속임수
- [ ] complexity 복잡성
- [ ] mammal 포유류
- [ ] digest 소화하다
- [ ] microscopic 미시적인, 미세한
- [ ] mixture 혼합물
- [ ] exploit 이용하다, 착취하다
- [ ] transformation 변화, 변신
- [ ] rational 합리적인, 이성적인
- [ ] reliably 확실하게, 믿을 수 있게
- [ ] practical 실용적인, 현실적인

11

정답 ②

정답 해설

주어진 문장에서 입법 수준에서는 기술 대기업들이 기술 자원들과 혁신에 대해 그렇게 변경할 수 없는 통제를 가져야 할 이유는 없다고 언급하고 있다. (B)에서 사적이고 개인적인 차원에서도 그들이 당신의 삶을 통제해야 할 이유가 없다고 언급하고 있다. 이어서 (C)에서 우리는 우리가 소비하는 디지털 제품들의 종류들과 양에 대해 절대적인 통제권을 행사할 자격이 있으며 특히 부모는 자녀에게 제공되는 기술 제품을 통제해야 한다고 이야기하고 있다. 뒤이어 (A)에서 그 예시로, 당신이 자녀에게 스마트폰을 사주지 않으면 그는 스마트폰을 갖지 못할 것이라고 설명하고 있다. 따라서 글의 순서로 가장 적절한 것은 ②이다.

지문 해석

입법 수준에서, 기술 대기업들이 기술 자원들과 혁신에 대해 그렇게 변경할 수 없는 통제를 가져야 할 이유는 없다.
(B) 사적이며 개인적인 수준에서도, 그들이 당신들의 삶을 통제해야 할 이유 또한 없다. 정책, 정치, 그리고 우리의 사생활에서 우리의 데이터가 최고 응찰자에게 팔릴 것이고, 우리의 아이들이 온라인 게임에 중독될 것이며, 우리의 삶들이 메타버스에서 살 것이라는 것을 "불가피한" 것으로 받아들여서는 안 된다.
(C) 자유로운 국민으로서, 우리는 우리가 소비하는 디지털 제품들의 종류들과 양들에 대해 절대적인 통제권을 행사할 권리가 있다. 특히, 부모들은 어떤 기술 제품들이 자녀에게 가는지 통제해야 한다.
(A) Daily Wire의 Matt Walsh가 지적했듯이, 예를 들어, 만약 당신의 아이에게 스마트폰을 사주지 않으면 그는 그것을 가질 수 없다. 관리없이 그의 모든 충동을 충족시킬 있게 하는 장치를 그의 손에 넣어줄 필요는 없다.

지문 어휘

- [ ] lawmaking 입법
- [ ] ironclad 변경할 수 없는, 이의를 제기할 수 없는
- [ ] grip 통제, 지배, 꽉 붙잡음, 움켜쥠
- [ ] innovation 혁신, 쇄신
- [ ] point 지적하다, 지시하다, 가리키다

- ☐ indulge 충족시키다, 채우다
- ☐ supervision 관리, 감독, 지도, 지휘
- ☐ inevitable 불가피한, 필연적인
- ☐ bidder 응찰자, 가격 제시자
- ☐ entitle 권리[자격]를 주다
- ☐ addict 중독되게 하다, 중독자
- ☐ exert 행사하다, 가하다, 분투하다
- ☐ absolute 절대적인, 완전한, 확실한

12

정답 ③

정답 해설

Lamarck의 후천적 특성 이론과 진화론에 대한 오해에 대해 설명하는 글이다. 첫 번째 문장에서 특정한 형질들(특징들)을 발전시킨다고 언급하고 있고, 이 형질들(특징들)에 대한 설명을 (B)에서 하고 있다. 이 특징들을 '획득형질의 유전'이라고 칭하고 나서 그에 따른 구체적인 예시로 (C)가 이어져야 한다. (C)에서는 특정한 형질이 유전되기 위해서는 DNA를 변형시켜야 한다고 말하고 있다. 마지막 문장 (A)에서는 이러한 유전적 변형이 이루어져 있다는 증거가 없다고 진술하고 있다. 따라서 글의 순서로 가장 적절한 것은 ③이다.

지문 해석

> 오늘날, Lamarck는 적응이 어떻게 진화하는지에 대한 잘못된 설명으로 인해 불공평하게 기억되고 있다. 그는 특정 신체 부위를 사용하거나 사용하지 않음으로써 유기체가 특정한 특징들을 발달시킬 것이라고 제안했다.
> (B) Lamarck는 이러한 특징들이 자손들에게 전달될 것이라고 생각했다. Lamarck는 이 생각을 후천적 특징의 계승이라고 불렀다.
> (C) 예를 들어, Lamarck는 캥거루의 강력한 뒷다리가 선조들이 점프를 해서 다리를 튼튼하게 하고 그 후에 다리의 힘을 자손들에게 물려준 결과라고 설명할 수도 있다. 그러나 후천적 특징이 기 위해서는 특정 유전자의 DNA를 어떻게든 수정해야 할 것이다.
> (A) 이런 일이 일어난다는 증거는 없다. 그럼에도 불구하고, Lamarck는 유기체가 그들의 환경에 적응할 때 진화가 일어난다고 제안했다는 것에 주목해야 한다. 이 생각은 Darwin의 기초를 닦을 수 있도록 도움이 되었다.

지문 어휘

- ☐ adaptation 적응, 적응력
- ☐ evolve 진화하다, 발달하다
- ☐ organism 생물체
- ☐ characteristic 특징, 특성
- ☐ inheritance 유전, 상속
- ☐ offspring 자손, 자식
- ☐ mistaken 잘못된, 틀린
- ☐ proposal 제안
- ☐ environment 환경
- ☐ ancestor 조상
- ☐ strengthen 강화하다, 강력해지다
- ☐ hind leg 뒷다리
- ☐ modify 수정하다, 변경하다
- ☐ gene 유전자

13

정답 ③

정답 해설

시각 장애인을 위한 새로운 서비스 'Aira'에 대한 글이다. 시각 장애인들이 일상생활에서 마주하는 어려움에 대한 언급 다음에 문제의 해결책을 제시하는 (B)가 이어져야 하며, (A)에서는 이러한 문제를 해결하기 위한 새로운 서비스 'Aira'에 대해 언급한 다음 마지막으로 (C)에서 이 서비스에 대한 추가적인 설명이 이어져야 한다. 따라서 글의 순서로 가장 적절한 것은 ③이다.

지문 해석

> 시각 장애인들에게, 우편물을 분류하거나 세탁을 많이 하는 것과 같은 일상적인 일들은 어려움을 안겨준다.
> (B) 하지만 그들이 볼 수 있는 누군가의 눈을 "빌릴" 수 있다면 어떨까?
> (A) 그것은 수천 명의 사용자들이 스마트폰 또는 Aira의 전용 안경을 사용하면서, 그들의 주변 환경의 생중계 비디오를 온-디맨드 에이전트에게 스트리밍할 수 있게 해주는 새로운 서비스인 Aira의 기반이 되는 생각이다.
> (C) 1년 내내 이용할 수 있는 Aira 에이전트들은 질문에 답변하고, 물체를 설명하거나, 사용자에게 위치를 안내할 수 있다.

지문 어휘

- ☐ blind 시각 장애인
- ☐ task 일, 과업, 과제
- ☐ sort 종류, 유형, 분류하다, 구분하다
- ☐ laundry 세탁
- ☐ challenge 도전, 어려움
- ☐ borrow 빌리다, 대여하다
- ☐ surroundings 주변 환경
- ☐ proprietary 전용의, 사유의, 독점의
- ☐ 24/7 1년 내내, 언제나

14

정답 ③

정답 해설

영장류의 먹이 선택과 사회적 행동에 대한 글로, 영장류가 새로운 먹이를 선택할 때 샘플링 하는 방법을 통해 음식안정성을 확인한다는 것을 원숭이의 예를 통해 설명하고 있는 글이다. 첫 번째 문장은 음식을 안정성을 확인하는 '샘플링'에 대해 설명하는 (C)가 나와야 하며, 그 샘플링의 부정적인 상황의 (B)의 경우와 그 샘플링이 긍정적인 상황인 (A)로 이어져야 한다. 따라서 글의 순서로 가장 적절한 것은 ③이다.

지문 해석

> 일단 그들이 자신의 어미를 떠나면, 영장류들은 그들이 마주치는 새로운 먹이가 안전한지 그리고 모을 가치가 있는지에 관해 계속 결정을 내려야 한다.
> (C) 그들 자신을 실험 도구로 사용하는 것은 하나의 선택이지만, 사회적 영장류들은 더 나은 방법을 발견했다. Kenneth Glander는 그것을 "샘플링"이라고 부른다. 짖는원숭이들은 새로운 서식지로 이동할 때, 그 무리의 한 구성원이 한 나무에 가서, 몇 개의 잎들을 먹고, 그리고 나서 하루를 기다린다.
> (B) 만약 그 식물이 특히 강한 독소를 숨기고 있다면, 시식자의 몸은 그것을 분해하려고 할 것이며, 대개 그 과정에서 그 원숭이를 병이 들게 만든다. "나는 이런 일이 일어나는 것을 본 적이 있습니다,"라고 Glander는 말한다. "그 무리의 다른 구성원들은 큰 관심을 갖고 지켜보고 있어요 — 만약 그 동물이 병이 들게 된다면, 다른 어떠한 동물도 그 나무에 들어가지 않을 것입니다. 주어지고 있는 신호 즉 사회적 신호가 있습니다."

(A) 같은 이유로, 만약 시식자가 괜찮으면, 그 시식자는 며칠 뒤에 그 나무에 다시 들어갈 것이고, 조금 더 먹고, 그러고 나서 다시 기다리며, 천천히 많은 분량으로 커진다. 마침내 만약 그 원숭이가 건강을 유지한다면, 다른 구성원들은 이것이 괜찮다고 생각하고, 그들은 그 새로운 먹이를 채택한다.

지문 어휘
- primate 영장류
- encounter 마주치다
- reenter 다시 들어가다
- toxin 독소
- breakdown 분해, 고장, 붕괴
- adopt 채택하다, 입양하다
- harbor 숨기다, 숨겨 주다
- process 과정, 절차, 처리하다
- experiment 실험
- habitat 서식지
- troop 무리, 부대

15 정답 ④

정답 해설
갈등 해결의 진화에 대해 다루며, 새로운 아이디어와 전문분야의 선구자들에 대한 연구와 이와 반대의 상황에 대해 설명하고 있는 글이다. 글의 소재인 '갈등 해결의 역사적 진화'에 대한 '갈등연구의 가치'를 아는 선구자들의 설명을 하는 (C)가 첫 번째 문장이 되어야 하고, '갈등연구의 가치'를 인정하지 않는 (B)로 이어지고, 마지막으로 이에 대한 이유를 설명하는 (A)로 이어져야 한다. 따라서 글의 순서로 가장 적절한 것은 ④이다.

지문 해석
갈등 해결의 역사적 진화는 냉전의 최고조였던 1950년대와 1960년대에 활기를 찾았는데, 그 당시 초강대국들 사이에 핵무기의 개발과 갈등이 인류의 생존을 위협하는 것처럼 보였다.
(C) 서로 다른 지식 분야에서 온 한 그룹의 선구자들은, 갈등이 국제 관계에서 발생하든, 국내 정치에서, 산업 관계에서, 지역사회에서 또는 개인들 간에 발생하든, 비슷한 특성을 가진 일반적인 현상으로서 갈등을 연구하는 그 가치를 알았다.
(B) 하지만 그들은 일부 사람들에게는 진지하게 받아들여지지 않았다. 국제 관계 종사자들은 국제 갈등에 대해 자신만의 이해를 가지고 있었고, 제안된 바와 같은 새로운 접근법에서 가치를 보지 않았다.
(A) 새로운 아이디어에 내포된 분석과 실행의 결합은, 전통적인 학술 기관이나 외교관과 정치인 같은 전문직 종사자들의 관례와 조화를 이루기가 쉽지 않았다.

지문 어휘
- conflict 갈등, 충돌, 분쟁
- resolution 해결
- gain momentum 활기를 찾다, 번성하다
- the Cold War 냉전
- superpower 초강대국
- threaten 위협하다, 협박하다
- combination 결합, 조합
- reconcile 조화시키다, 받아들이다
- traditional 전통적인
- scholarly 학문적인, 학술적인
- institution 기관, 단체, 협회
- practitioner 실무자
- diplomat 외교관
- approach 접근법
- pioneer 개척자
- discipline 규율, 훈육, 지식 분야
- property 재산, 자산, 토지, 특성, 속성
- domestic 국내의, 가정의

16 정답 ①

정답 해설
애매모호함에 대한 부정적인 면을 복통을 호소하는 환자의 예를 통해서 설명하고 있는 글이다. 주어진 글 다음에 첫 번째 문장인 검사실로 보낸 결과가 일주일 뒤에 나온다는 내용인 (B)가 나와야 하며, 검사의 결과를 듣고 안도감이 불안감 대체된다는 내용인 (A)로 이어지고, 정확한 원인을 몰라 좌절감을 느낀다는 (C)로 이어져야 한다. 따라서 글의 순서로 가장 적절한 것은 ①이다.

지문 해석
애매모호함은 너무나 불편해서 그것은 심지어 좋은 소식을 나쁜 것으로 바꿀 수 있다. 당신이 지속되는 복통으로 의사에게 간다. 당신의 의사는 그 이유가 무엇인지 알아내지 못하고, 그래서 그녀는 테스트를 위해 당신을 검사실로 보낸다.
(B) 일주일 후에 당신은 결과를 듣도록 다시 호출된다. 당신이 마침내 그녀의 진료실에 도착할 때, 당신의 의사는 웃으면서, 당신에게 테스트가 모든 음성이라고 말해준다.
(A) 그리고 무슨 일이 일어나는가? 당신의 즉각적인 안도는 이상한 불안감으로 대체될 수 있다. 당신은 여전히 그 통증이 무엇이었는지 알지 못한다. 틀림없이 어딘가에 설명이 있을 것이다.
(C) 아마 그것이 암이고 그들이 그것을 놓쳤을지도 모른다. 아마 더 나쁠지도 모른다. 분명히 그들은 원인을 찾을 수 있어야 한다. 당신은 확실한 대답의 부족으로 좌절감을 느낀다.

지문 어휘
- ambiguity 애매모호함
- uncomfortable 불편한
- stomachache 복통
- figure out 파악하다
- lab 실험실
- immediate 즉각적인, 즉시의
- relief 안도, 안심, 경감
- weird 이상한, 기이한, 기괴한
- discomfort 불편, 불안
- negative 부정적인, 소극적인
- frustrated 좌절감을 느끼는, 불만스러워 하는
- definitive 확실한, 최종적인

17

정답 ③

정답 해설

영장류의 의사소통과 언어와의 비교를 하면서 언어와 특징과 영장류들의 의사소통에 대해서 설명하는 글이다. 주어진 글은 인간의 언어가 다른 동물들보다 뛰어나다는 내용이며 (C) 앞부분 역시 인간 언어가 더 뛰어나다는 내용이므로 다음에 이어질 내용으로 가장 적절하고 (A) 앞부분은 (C) 내용과 같은 내용이지만, nevertheless를 통해 동물들의 복잡한 의사소통 시스템의 내용으로 바뀌었다. (B)는 (A)의 복잡한 의사소통 다음 내용으로 연결된다. 따라서 글의 순서로 가장 적절한 것은 ③이다.

지문 해석

확실히, 인간의 언어는 원숭이와 유인원의 분명히 제한된 발성으로부터 눈에 띄게 차이가 난다. 게다가, 그것은 어떤 다른 형태의 동물적 의사소통을 훨씬 능가하는 정교화의 정도를 보여준다.
(C) 심지어 우리의 가장 가까운 영장류 종자들조차도 몇 년 동안 집중적인 훈련을 받은 후에도 기본적인 의사소통 시스템 이상의 것을 습득할 수 없는 것처럼 보인다. 언어라는 복잡성은 확실히 종의 특유한 특성이다.
(A) 그렇긴 하지만, 많은 종들은 인간의 언어에는 크게 미치지 못하더라도, 자연 환경에서 인상적인 복잡한 의사소통 체계를 보여준다.
(B) 그리고 그들은 인간과 함께 자랐을 때처럼 인공적인 맥락에서 훨씬 더 복잡한 시스템을 배울 수 있다.

지문 어휘

- to be sure 분명히, 확실히
- that said 그렇긴 하지만
- stand out 눈에 띄다, 뚜렷하게 나타나다
- decidedly 확실히, 분명히
- restricted 제한된
- vocalization 발성
- ape 유인원
- sophistication 정교화
- fall short 부족해지다
- nevertheless 그럼에도 불구하고
- setting 환경, 배경
- alongside 함께, 동시에
- primate 영장류
- cousin 사촌, 친척, 종자
- incapable of ~할 수 없는
- acquire 습득하다, 획득하다
- rudimentary 기본적인, 기초적인
- intensive 집중적인

18

정답 ①

정답 해설

지속 가능한 에너지 공급을 위한 지역공동체 조직들의 활동들을 여러 회사들의 예를 통해서 설명하는 글이다. 주어진 글의 마지막 부분에 신재생 에너지를 지지하는 캠페인에 대한 내용이 더 강조되고 있다는 것을 알 수 있고 이후의 이어지는 내용은 신재생 에너지를 지지하는 캠페인의 구체적인 예의 내용이 나와야한다. (C)에서 영국의 신재생 에너지 운동을 소개하는 예시가 나오고 (A)에서 태양 발전 회사에 대한 설명을 하고 나서, (B)에서 비슷한 미국의 신재생 에너지 단체까지 소개하는 것이 올바르다. 따라서 글의 순서로 가장 적절한 것은 ①이다.

지문 해석

지구 기후 변화에 대한 증가하는 걱정은 화석 연료 추출 소비에 대한 캠페인뿐만 아니라 신재생 에너지를 지지할 수 있는 캠페인을 조직하는 활동에도 동기를 부여해왔다.
(C) 영국 정부가 재생 에너지 산업의 성장을 빠르게 가속화하지 못하는 것에 좌절한 환경 운동가들은 2500개 가정에 의해 사용되는 연간 전력만큼을 생산하는 걸로 추정되는 내륙의 풍력 발전 단지를 소유한, 2000명 이상의 지역공동체가 소유하는 조직인 Westmill Wind Farm 주식회사를 설립했다. Westmill Wind Farm 주식회사는 지역의 시민들이 Westmill Solar 주식회사를 설립하도록 영감을 주었다.
(A) 이 태양 발전 협동조합은 1,400가구에 전력을 공급할 수 있는 충분한 에너지를 생산하는 국내 최초의 대규모 태양 발전 회사이며, 구성원들의 말로 볼 때, 태양 발전이 "그들의 지붕 위에뿐 아니라 공익 시설의 규모로 평범한 사람들이 청정에너지를 생산할 수 있도록 하는 지속 가능하고 '민주적인' 에너지 공급의 새로운 시대"를 대표한다는 것을 가시적으로 상기시키는 것이다.
(B) 이와 비슷하게 미국의 재생에너지 지지자들은 "참여 전력회사 고객이 집단적으로 소유한 중규모 설비를 통해 청정발전을 전달하는 모델"을 개척한 기업 Clean Energy Collecive를 설립했다.

지문 어휘

- fossil fuel 화석 연료
- renewable 재생 가능한
- solar 태양의
- cooperative 협동조합
- sustainable 지속 가능한
- democratic 민주적인
- utility 유용, 공익 시설
- medium 중간의
- onshore 육지의, 내륙의
- wind farm 풍력 발전소
- organization 조직
- electricity 전기

19

정답 ②

정답 해설

종교와 긍정적인 역할에 대한 글로, 종교가 인내와 성장을 촉진하고 어려움을 극복하는 데 어떤 역할을 하는지를 강조하는 글이다. 종교외에도 사람에게 영향을 미치는 '아이를 갖는 것, 전쟁, 자연재해'들에 대한 언급을 한 (B) 다음에는 다시 '종교가 평생 동안의 준비에 가장 큰 영향을 미친다'는 (C)가 이어져야 하며, 종교가 없다면 '자기만족하거나, 천박하거나, 조잡하거나, 단순히 포기하는 사람들'이 '자랑스러워 할 어려운 결정'을 돕는 역할을 종교가 한다는 (A)로 이어져야 한다. 따라서 글의 순서로 가장 적절한 것은 ②이다.

지문 해석

종교는 확실히 사람에게서 최고를 이끌어낼 수 있지만, 그 속성이 가진 유일한 현상은 아니다.
(B) 아이를 갖는 것은 종종 사람에게 놀랄 만큼 성숙한 영향을 미친다. 유명한 말이지만, 전쟁은 홍수나 허리케인과 같은 자연 재해와 마찬가지로 사람들에게 일어날 수 있는 많은 기회를 준다.

(C) 그러나 하루하루 빠짐없이 평생 동안의 준비에는 아마도 종교만큼 효과적인 것이 없을 것이다. 그것은 강력하고 재능 있는 사람들을 더 겸손하고 인내심 있게 만들고, 보통 사람들을 그들 자신보다 성장하게 하며, 음주 또는 마약이나 범죄로부터 벗어나는데 필사적으로 도움을 필요로 하는 많은 사람들에게 견고한 지원을 제공한다.
(A) 그렇지 않으면 자기 만족적이거나, 천박하거나, 조잡하거나, 단순히 그만두는 사람이 될 수도 있는 사람들은 우리 모두가 자랑스러워 할 어려운 결정을 내리는 데 도움을 주는 삶에 대한 관점을 고려한다면, 그들의 종교에 의해 종종 기품 있게 된다.

지문 어휘
- ennoble 품위를 높이다, 기품 있게 하다
- perspective 관점, 시각
- maturing 성장, 성숙
- abundance 풍부, 충만, 다수, 대량
- lifelong 일생일대의
- bracing 격렬한, 힘찬
- humble 겸손한, 낮은
- patient 인내심 있는, 환자
- sturdy 튼튼한, 강인한
- desperately 필사적으로, 절박하게

20   정답 ②

정답 해설
인구 증가와 자원 고갈 사이의 관계를 다루며, 이로 인해 발생하는 환경 문제들을 나열하는 글이다. 자원고갈에 대한 결과에 대한 진술을 하는 (B)가 먼저 나와야 하며, 인구증가로 인한 이산화 탄소배출에 대한 (A)로 이어지고, 마지막으로 '장기적인 기후변화'에 대한 (C)로 이어져야 한다. 따라서 글의 순서로 가장 적절한 것은 ②이다.

지문 해석
더 많은 사람들이 더 많은 자원을 필요로 하는데, 이는 인구가 증가함에 따라 지구의 자원이 더 빠르게 고갈된다는 것을 의미한다.
(B) 이 고갈의 결과는 인간이 증가하는 인구수를 수용하기 위해 자원을 지구에서 제거함에 따라 삼림 벌채와 생물 다양성의 손실이다.
(A) 인구 증가 또한 대부분 이산화탄소 배출로 인한 온실가스를 증가시킨다. 시각화해보면, 4배의 인구 증가를 보인 20세기 동안 이산화탄소 배출량은 12배 증가했다.
(C) 온실가스가 증가함에 따라 기후 패턴도 증가하여 궁극적으로 기후 변화라고 불리는 장기적인 패턴을 초래한다.

지문 어휘
- emission 배출, 방출
- deforestation 산림 파괴
- biodiversity 생물 다양성
- accommodate 수용하다, 공간을 제공하다
- greenhouse gas 온실 가스
- long term 장기적인

21   정답 ③

정답 해설
Sequoya와 체로키 자모가 어떻게 체로키 문화와 전통을 보존하는 데 기여했는지를 시간순으로 설명하고 있는 글이다. 글쓰기를 배웠다는 (C)가 Sequoya의 탄생 내용의 다음으로 이어져야 하고, 체로키 자모를 발명했다는 (A) 다음에 '출판 산업이 발전하도록 도왔다'는 (B)로 이어져야 한다. 따라서 글의 순서로 가장 적절한 것은 ③이다.

지문 해석
Sequoya(1760?-1843)는 테네시 주 동부에서 태어났고, 체로키 인디언 부족의 전통과 종교에 대한 지식으로 높이 평가받는 명성 있는 가문에서 태어났다.
(C) 어렸을 때, Sequoya는 체로키 인디언의 구전을 배웠고, 어른이 되면서 그는 유럽계 미국인 문화를 접하게 되었다. 그의 편지에서 Sequoya는 어떻게 유럽계 미국인들이 의사소통을 하기 위해 사용했던 글쓰기 방법에 매료되었는지 언급한다.
(A) 그의 백성들을 위해 글쓰기가 가진 가능성을 인식한 Sequoya는 1821년에 체로키 자모를 발명했다. 이 글쓰기 체계로, Sequoya는 고대 부족의 관습을 기록할 수 있었다.
(B) 더욱 중요한 것은, 그의 알파벳이 체로키 국가가 신문과 책을 인쇄할 수 있도록 출판 산업을 발전시킬 수 있도록 도왔다는 것이다. 취학 연령의 아이들은 그들의 언어로 체로키 문화와 전통에 대해 배울 수 있었다.

지문 어휘
- prestigious 훌륭한, 명성 있는
- tribal 부족의, 종족의
- religion 종교
- custom 관습, 풍습
- publishing industry 출판 산업
- oral tradition 구전
- mention 언급하다, 말하다

22   정답 ②

정답 해설
캘리포니아 만 지역의 주유소 밀집 현상과 주유소 위치 결정에 대해 다룬 글이다. 주어진 글에는 주유소가 지역 주민들에게 서비스를 제공하기 위한 것이라고 생각한다고 통념을 제시하고 있다. (B)에 이러한 통념은 모순이라며 잘못되었음을 말하고 주유소가 일반적으로 밀집도가 높다고 하고 있고, (A)에 밀집도가 높은 이유를 보여주고 있고, 마지막으로 (C)에 이유를 추가적으로 진술하고 있다. 따라서 글의 순서로 가장 적절한 것은 ②이다.

지문 해석
캘리포니아 만 지역의 샌프란시스코 주변에는 수백 개의 주유소가 있다. 누군가는 주유소가 지역 주민들에게 서비스를 제공하기 위해 퍼져 나갈 것이라고 생각할지도 모른다.
(B) 그러나 이 생각은 일반적인 관찰에 의해 모순된다. 당신이 주유소를 방문할 때마다, 거의 항상 근처에 다른 주유소가 있는데, 종종 바로 길 건너편에 있다. 일반적으로 주유소는 밀집도가 높다.
(A) 이러한 현상은 부분적으로 인구 집단에 기인한다. 주유소는 옥수수 밭처럼 인구가 적은 지역보다는 도시처럼 수요가 많은 곳에서 더 흔할 것이다.
(C) 게다가 여러 가지 요인이 작용하고 있다. 주유소의 입지는 수요, 부동산 가격, 인구 증가 추정, 주유의 용이성 등의 공급 고려 등이 수반되는 최적화 문제이다.

지문 어휘

- phenomenon 현상
- population 인구
- cluster 집단, 무리
- demand 수요
- sparsely 드문드문, 성기게
- cornfield 옥수수밭
- contradict 반박하다, 부정하다
- vicinity 주변, 근처
- clustered 집결한, 모여 있는
- optimization 최적화
- real estate 부동산

23   정답 ③

정답 해설

스트레스가 심혈관 질환의 중요한 위험이 될 수 있다고 설명하는 글이다. (C)에서 스트레스의 한 원인으로 운전을 예로 들며, 이 내용을 (A)의 this로 이어 받아서 운전의 스트레스를 줄일 수 있는 방법이 있는 것인지 묻고 있다. 그리고 (B)에서 새로운 연구에 따르면 운전 중 음악을 듣는 방법이 효과적이라고 진술하고 있다. 따라서 글의 순서로 가장 적절한 것은 ③이다.

지문 해석

과거의 연구는 빈번한 심리적 스트레스를 경험하는 것이 심혈관 질환의 중대한 위험 요인이 될 수 있다는 것을 보여 주는데, 이것은 미국에서 20세 이상인 사람들의 거의 절반에게 발생하는 질환이다.
(C) 빈번한 스트레스의 한 가지 원인은 운전인데, 이는 교통 체증과 관련된 스트레스 요인이나 미숙한 운전자들에게 종종 동반하는 불안감 때문이다.
(A) 하지만, 이것은 매일 운전하는 사람들이 심장 질환이 생기도록 되어 있다는 것을 의미하는가, 아니면 운전의 스트레스를 완화시킬 수 있는 간단한 방법이 있는가?
(B) 새로운 연구에 따르면, 그것은 있다. 연구원들은 운전하는 동안에 음악을 듣는 것이 심장 건강에 영향을 미치는 스트레스를 완화하는 데 도움이 된다고 언급했다.

지문 어휘

- psychological 심리적인, 정신의
- cardiovascular 심혈관의
- risk factor 위험 요소
- note 언급하다, 말하다
- heavy traffic 교통체증
- anxiety 불안, 염려, 걱정거리
- relieve 완화시키다, 줄이다

24   정답 ③

정답 해설

시간을 말하기 위해 해와 달을 사용했었던 산업화 이전의 시기에 말하고 있는 글이다. 주어진 문장의 산업화 이전의 시기는 (B)에서 When mechanical clocks first appeared로 이어질 수 있고, 시계가 처음 생겨서 시계를 갖는 것이 fashionable하게 여겨졌다는 내용은 (C) these clocks were decorative로 이어진다. (C)에서 마을마다 different ways to tell the time을 가지고 있었기 때문에 문제점이 생겼다고 설명하고 이에 대한 예로 (A)의 첫 부분에서 이러한 서로 다른 표준시간대가 혼란을 야기한다는 내용이 나오고 있다. 특히 '시계'에 대한 설명은 these라는 지시형용사를 통해 (B)에서 (C)로 이어짐을 알 수 있고, 'time zone'에 대한 설명이 (C)에서 (A)로 이어지므로 있음을 알 수 있다. 따라서 글의 순서로 가장 적절한 것은 ③이다.

지문 해석

오늘날 시계는 우리의 삶을 너무 많이 지배하고 있어서 시계가 없는 삶은 상상하기 어렵다. 산업화 이전에, 대부분의 사회는 태양이나 달을 사용하여 시간을 알 수 있었다.
(B) 기계식 시계가 처음 등장했을 때, 그것들은 즉시 인기가 있었다. 시계나 손목시계를 갖는 것은 유행이었다. 사람들은 "시계의" 또는 "시계"라는 표현을 이 새로운 시간 측정 방법을 언급하기 위해 발명하기도 했다.
(C) 이 시계들은 장식적이었지만, 항상 유용하지는 않았다. 마을, 지방, 심지어 이웃 마을에서도 시간을 알 수 있는 방법이 달랐기 때문이다. 여행자들은 한 장소에서 다른 장소로 이동할 때 반복적으로 시계를 다시 맞춰야 했다. 미국에는 1860년대에 약 70개의 다른 시간대가 있었다.
(A) 철도망이 발달하면서 시간 기준이 없다는 사실이 재앙이었다. 종종, 단지 몇 마일 떨어져 있는 역들은 그들의 시계를 다른 시간에 맞춘다. 여행자들에게 많은 혼란이 있었다.

지문 어휘

- dominate 지배하다
- railroad 철로
- confusion 혼란, 혼돈, 당혹
- mechanical clock 기계식 시계
- fashionable 유행인
- refer to 언급하다, 참고하다
- province 주, 지방, 분야
- reset 재설정하다

25   정답 ①

정답 해설

자동차 공유와 단기 임대 프로그램이 증가함에 따라 자동차 제품 사용 및 환경에 어떤 변화가 일어날 수 있는지 다루고 있는 글이다. 자동차의 의존도가 낮아지면서 나타나는 변화들에 언급하고 있는 제시문 다음에 미래에 대한 전망을 하는 (A)가 나와야 하며, 자동차가 개인화와 자아정체성에 대한 것으로서 보다는 브랜드 홍보와 광고 및 홍보채널로 역할을 한다는 (C)가 이어져야 하며, 그로 인한 결과에 대한 설명을 하는 (B)로 이어져야 한다. 따라서 글의 순서로 가장 적절한 것은 ①이다.

지문 해석

자동차가 사람에 대한 의존도가 낮아지고 있는 만큼 자동차 공유와 단기 임대 프로그램 참여율이 높아지는 등 소비자가 제품을 사용하는 수단과 상황도 큰 변화를 겪을 가능성이 높다.
(A) 멀지 않은 미래에 운전자가 없는 자동차가 당신이 필요할 때 당신에게 올 수 있고, 그것을 끝냈을 때, 그것은 주차 공간 없이 운전해서 갈 수 있다. 자동차 공유의 증가와 단기 임대 또한 상응하는 외장 자동차 디자인의 중요성 감소와 관련이 있을 것으로 보인다.
(C) 자동차 외부는 개인화와 자아 정체성을 위한 매개체 역할을 하기보다는 점점 더 자유로운 자동차 미디어가 제공하는 것과 같은 브랜드 홍보 프로그램을 포함한 광고 및 기타 홍보 활동을 위한 채널을 제시하게 될 것이다.
(B) 그 결과, 자동차에서 파생되는 상징적 의미와 소비자의 자아 정체성 및 지위와의 관계가 차례로 변화할 가능성이 높다.

지문 어휘

- dependent 의존적인
- significant 중요한, 상당한
- participation 참여
- short term 단기
- leasing 임대, 대여
- driverless car 무인 자동차
- exterior 외부, 겉
- symbolic 상징적
- meaning 의미
- self identity 자아 정체성
- status 지위, 상태
- represent 제시하다, 보여주다, 나타내다, 대표하다
- advertising 광고
- promotional 홍보의

26   정답 ①

정답 해설

일본의 자동차 조립 라인에서의 접근 방식을 미국에서의 상황과 비교하는 글이다. 이 글에서의 핵심적인 질문은 '왜 문이 꼭 맞는 것을 확인하지 않는지'이다. 제시문 다음에 처음 나와야 할 것은 '미국과 일본에서의 차이점'을 언급하고 있는 (A)의 '뭔가 빠져 있었다'이다. 그리고 그러한 이유를 물어보는 (B)로 이어져야 하며, 추가적인 설명을 하는 (C)로 이어져야 한다. 따라서 글의 순서로 가장 적절한 것은 ①이다.

지문 해석

일본 조립라인을 보러 일본에 간 미국 자동차 임원들의 멋진 사연이 있다. 줄의 끝에는 미국처럼 문짝에 경첩에 달았다
(A) 그런데 뭔가 빠져 있었다. 미국에서는 라인 노동자가 고무망치를 가지고 문 가장자리를 두드려서 그것이 완벽하게 맞는지 확인하곤 했다. 일본에서는 그런 일이 존재하지 않는 것 같았다
(B) 당황한 미국 자동차 임원들은 어느 시점에 문이 꼭 맞는 것을 확인하는지 물었다. 그들의 일본인 안내원이 그들을 바라보며 열없게 웃었다. "애초에 디자인할 때 꼭 맞도록 한다"고 말했다
(C) 일본 자동차 공장에서 그들은 문제를 조사하지 않고 데이터를 축적하여 최상의 해결책을 찾아내지 않았다 ─ 그들은 처음부터 그들이 원하는 결과를 설계했다. 만약 그들이 원하는 결과를 얻지 못했다면, 그들은 그것이 그 과정의 시작에서 내린 결정 때문이라고 이해했다.

지문 어휘

- executive 경영진, 임원
- assembly 조립, 집회, 의회
- hinge 경첩, 경첩을 달다
- tap 가볍게 치다
- ensure 확실히 하다
- confused 당황한, 혼란스러운
- outcome 결과

27   정답 ③

정답 해설

히로시마와 나가사키에 떨어진 원자 폭탄의 파괴적인 영향과 일본의 항복에 대해 다루고 있는 글이다. 강조하는 문장은 "1945년 8월 6일 오전 8시 15분, 미군 전투기는 일본, 히로시마에 원자 폭탄을 떨어트렸다. 즉시 8만 명의 사람이 죽었다."이다. 이 문장을 바탕으로 사건의 시간의 흐름과, 제시문에서 제시하는 '두개의 전선'에 대한 설명을 바탕으로 올바른 순서를 정할 수 있다. 첫 번째 문장은 두개의 최전선을 언급하는 (B)가 나와야 하며, 히로시마에 원자 폭탄을 투하한 (C)로 이어져야 하며, 삼일 후에 일본이 항복했다는 (A)로 이어져야 한다. 따라서 글의 순서로 가장 적절한 것은 ③이다.

지문 해석

세계 2차 대전에서 일본은 독일과 이탈리아와 함께 참전했다. 그래서 지금 유럽 전쟁 지대와 태평양에 있는 두 개의 전선이 있었다.
(B) 1941년 후반에, 미국과 영국, 프랑스는 독일과 일본에 대항하는 전쟁에 참여했다. 미국 군대는 두 최선으로 보내졌다.
(C) 1945년 8월 6일 오전 8시 15분, 미군 전투기는 일본, 히로시마에 원자 폭탄을 떨어트렸다. 즉시 8만 명의 사람이 죽었다. 히로시마는 바로 사라졌다. 그 폭발의 중심부에 있던 사람들은 사라졌다. 남은 것이라곤 건물의 벽에 까맣게 그을린 그림자가 전부였다.
(A) 3일 후에 미국은 나가사키의 또 다른 도시에 폭탄을 떨어뜨렸다. 일본은 바로 항복하였고, 세계 2차 대전은 마침내 끝이 났다.

지문 어휘

- drop 떨어뜨리다
- surrender 항복하다, 포기하다
- participate 참가하다
- instant 순간, 즉각적인
- cease 그치다, 중단되다
- evaporate 증발하다, 사라지다
- remain 남다
- charred 타버린, 탄 색의

28   정답 ③

정답 해설

상사가 직원의 생산성과 일의 질에 어떤 영향을 미치는지에 대해 설명하고 있는 글로, '상사가 대하기 어려운 사람의 부류라는 것은 비밀이 아니다'가 글의 주제이다. 주어진 글에 대한 언급을 하는 (B)로 시작해야 하며, 이러한 상사의 부정적인 언급을 하는 (C)로 이어져야 하고, '동시에 즐거운 상사'에 대해 언급을 하는 (A)로 이어져야 한다. 따라서 글의 순서로 가장 적절한 것은 ③이다.

지문 해석

많은 다른 요소들뿐만 아니라 에어컨과 신선한 물이 있는 냉장고, 유연한 일정과 동료들과의 좋은 관계와 같은 사소한 것들은 직원들의 생산성과 일(노동)의 질에 영향을 미친다.
(B) 이와 관련하여 가장 중요한 요소 중의 하나는 일의 처리 과정을 지시하는 관리자 또는 상사이다.

(C) 상사가 대하기 어려운 사람의 부류라는 것은 비밀이 아니다. 그들의 다수는 부당하게 많은 것을 요구하고, 그들의 책임을 다른 직원들에게 돌리는 등의 경향이 있다.
(A) 동시에 그들의 직원의 생산성을 높이도록 관리할 뿐만 아니라 직원들을 친절하게 대하고 함께 일하는 것이 즐거운 상사들도 많이 있다.

지문 어휘

- flexible 유명한, 융통성 있는
- impact 영향을 미치다
- maintain 유지하다
- treat 대하다, 처우하다
- pleasant 즐거운, 기분좋은
- direct 지시하다, 관리하다
- demanding 요구가 많은, 힘든
- prone to ~하는 경향이 있는, ~하기 쉬운
- shift 옮기다, 전환하다

29   정답 ④

정답 해설

한국의 인터넷 문제와 중독 현상에 대한 글로, 한국의 뛰어난 인터넷 접속 환경은 중독과 학교 결석과 같은 부정적 영향을 가져오며, 이에 대한 문제가 국가적으로 논의되고 있는 상황을 다루고 있다. 주어진 글에 대한 재진술로 어떤 다른 국가도 인터넷을 포용하지 못한다는 (B)가 와야하고, 그러한 포용에는 상당한 대가를 치른다는 역접의 내용으로 (C)가 오고, 상당한 대가를 (A)의 이러한 중독 이라고 받는 것이 자연스럽다. 따라서 글의 순서로 가장 적절한 것은 ④이다.

지문 해석

한국은 지구상에서 가장 인터넷 연결이 잘 되어 있는 나라라고 자랑한다.
(B) 사실, 아마도 어떤 다른 나라도 그렇게 완전히 인터넷을 수용하고 있지 않다.
(C) 그러나 웹에 대한 그런 재빠른 접근은 다수의 집착하는 사용자들이 그들의 컴퓨터 화면으로부터 그들이 자기 자신을 떼어 놓을 수 없다는 것을 알게 되면서 대가가 따랐다.
(A) 이 중독은 최근 몇 년 동안 한국에서 국가적 문제가 되고 있는데, 사용자들이 여러 날 동안 계속해서 온라인 게임을 한 후 피로로 급사하기 시작했기 때문이다. 점점 더 많은 학생들이 온라인에 접속해 있기 위해 학교를 빼먹고 있고, 이것은 몹시 경쟁적인 사회에서 충격적일 정도로 자멸적인 행동이다.

지문 어휘

- boast 자랑하다
- wired nation 인터넷에 연결된 국가
- addiction 중독
- national 국가의, 전국적인
- exhaustion 피로, 고갈
- days on end 연속으로 며칠 동안
- intensely 극심한, 강렬한
- competitive 경쟁을 하는, 경쟁력 있는
- embrace 받아들이다
- obsessed 빠져있는, 집착하는

30   정답 ②

정답 해설

사회 세계의 복잡성과 이해에 대한 글로, 글은 사회 현상의 복잡성과 이해에 대한 고민과 경제학자들의 접근 방식을 다루고 있다. 주어진 문장의 make sense of the social world를 받아 (A)에서 make sense of it을 위한 방법에 대한 내용을 다루고 있다. 이어 stripped down 이라는 말을 처음으로 언급한 후, When I say "stripped down," 이라는 말로 풀어 설명하는 것으로 (C)가 뒤따름을 알 수 있다. (B)에서 경제학자의 말을 인용해 이런 현상에 대한 설명을 마무리 짓는 것을 thus를 통해 알 수 있다. 따라서 글의 순서로 가장 적절한 것은 ②이다.

지문 해석

우리를 괴롭힐 수 있는 생각이 하나 있다: 아마 모든 것이 다른 모든 것에 영향을 미치므로, 어떻게 우리가 사회 세계를 이해할 수 있을까? 하지만 우리가 그 걱정에 짓눌린다면, 우리는 결코 나아갈 수 없을 것이다.
(A) 내가 익숙한 모든 규율은 그것을 이해하기 위해 세상에 대한 캐리커처를 그린다. 현대 경제학자는 의도적으로 저 밖에서 일어난 현상들의 묘사를 벗겨내려고 하는 '모형'을 만듦으로써 이런 일을 한다.
(C) 내가 "벗겨졌다"라고 하면 정말로 벗겨졌다는 걸 의미한다. 이것이 현실의 그런 측면들이 어떻게 작용하고 상호 작용하는지 이해할 수 있게 해주기를 바라면서 우리 사이에서 경제학자들이 한두 가지 인과적 요인들에 초점을 맞추고 다른 모든 것은 배제하는 것이 흔한 일은 아니다.
(B) 경제학자인 John Maynard Keynes는 우리 주제를 이렇게 묘사했다: "경제학은 현 시대와 관련된 모형을 고르는 예술에 결합된 모형들의 관점에서 생각하는 과학이다."

지문 어휘

- haunt 출몰하다, 나타나다
- make sense of 이해하다, 의미를 파악하다
- weigh down 무겁게 누르다, 짓누르다
- discipline 규율, 훈육, 지식 분야
- stripped down 불필요한 것을 모두 뺀, 가장 기본적인 것만 남긴
- representation 표현, 묘사
- phenomena 현상, 사건
- relevant 관련된, 적절한
- contemporary 동시대의, 현대의
- causal 인과의
- exclude 제외하다
- aspect 측면, 관점

31

정답 ③

정답 해설
'생체 자기 제어' 기술과 자발적인 통제력을 주제로 하는 글로, '생체 자기 제어' 기술에 대한 설명으로, 전자센서를 이용해 몸의 심박 수, 혈압, 피부 온도 등의 변수를 측정하고 시각·청각적인 디스플레이로 해당 변수를 피드백하며 개인이 몸의 기능을 통제할 수 있음을 설명하고 있다. (A)의 그러한 변수는 (B)의 심박수, 혈압, 그리고 피부 온도와 같은 변수들에서 나온 것이고, 추가적으로 (C)에 생체 자기 제어에 대한 추가 설명이 이어져야 한다. 따라서 글의 순서로 가장 적절한 것은 ③이다.

지문 해석
> 개인이 자동적, 또는 무의식적인 몸의 기능에 대한 일부 자발적인 통제력을, 그러한 기능들을 전자적으로 측정한 것들을 관찰함으로써 일부 자발적인 통제력을 얻을 수 있도록 하는 기술은 생체 자기 제어로 알려져 있다.
> (B) 전자센서가 심박 수, 혈압, 피부 온도 등의 변수를 측정하기 위해 몸의 다양한 부분에 부착된다.
> (A) 그러한 변수들이 바라는 방향으로 움직일 때 (예를 들면, 혈압이 내려간다), 이것은 시각적이고 청각적인 디스플레이 피드백을 텔레비전세트나, 장치들 혹은 빛과 같은 기기들에 나타나게 한다.
> (C) 생체 자기 제어 훈련은 사람이 그 디스플레이를 촉발시켰던 생각 패턴 또는 행동들을 재생하여 원하는 반응을 얻어낼 수 있도록 가르친다.

지문 어휘
- gain 얻다, 획득하다
- biofeedback 생체 자기 제어
- sensor 센서, 감지기
- blood pressure 혈압
- trigger 촉발시키다, 일으키다, 방아쇠
- equipment 장비, 기기
- attach 붙이다, 첨부하다
- variable 변수, 변동이 심한
- reproduce 재생하다, 복사[복제]하다

32

정답 ②

정답 해설
건강 추적 기술의 중요성과 노인들을 위한 생명 보호를 주제로 하는 글로, 건강 추적 기술의 인기 상승과 노인들을 위한 생명 보호를 위한 기술의 중요성을 설명하고 있다. 노인들과 특별한 환경에서 살아가는 사람들을 위한 기술의 중요성에 대해 소개하는 (B)부터 시작해야 하고, (A)의 'a popular gerotechnology'에서 (C)의 'this technology'로 이어진다. 따라서 글의 순서로 가장 적절한 것은 ②이다.

지문 해석
> 당신의 건강을 감시하고 추적하는 장비들이 모든 연령층에서 인기를 얻어가고 있다.
> (B) 그러나, 노인들, 특히 집에 돌보는 사람들이 없는 사람들에게는, 이러한 기술들은 생명을 살릴 수 있다.
> (A) 예를 들어, 낙상은 65세 이상의 성인들의 주요한 죽음의 원인이다. 낙상 경보는 대중적인 노인을 위한 양로 기술로 수년간 우리 주변에 있었지만, 최근에 개선되었다.
> (C) 이러한 단순한 기술들은 노인이 쓰러지는 그 순간 자동적으로 가까운 가족 구성원의 911에 경보를 울린다.

지문 어휘
- device 기기, 장치
- monitor 모니터하다, 감시하다
- track 추적하다
- fall 낙상, 떨어짐, 넘어지다, 떨어지다
- leading 주요한, 선도적인
- cause 원인
- improve 개선하다
- senior 노인
- caretaker 간병인
- lifesaving 생명을 구하는

33

정답 ②

정답 해설
주어진 글에서는 집단요법의 혁신적 접근법인 Jacob L. Moreno의 심리 드라마에 대한 내용이 소개되고 있고, 그 다음에는 'Moreno의 이론적인 관점과 영향력'에 설명하는 (B)로 이어져야 하며, 그가 사회적 상호작용을 통해 창의성을 발현하도록 돕기 위해 연극적 기법을 사용했음을 언급하는 (A)로 이어져야 하고, 마지막으로 그가 가장 중요하게 여겼던 연극적 도구 중 하나인 '역할 바꾸기'에 진술인 (C)로 이어져야 한다. 따라서 글의 순서로 가장 적절한 것은 ②이다.

지문 해석
> 가장 혁신적인 집단 치료 접근법은 Jacob L. Moreno의 독창적인 생각인 사이코드라마 집단 치료의 한 형태로써 사이코드라마는 정신병은 본질적으로 정신 또는 마음 안에서 발생한다는 프로이드의 세계관과는 상당히 다른 전제 조건으로 시작되었다.
> (B) 주류 관점과는 다른 그의 이론적 차이에도 불구하고, 20세기에 정신적 의식을 형성하는 데 있어 Moreno의 영향력은 상당했다. 그는 인간의 본질은 창조하는 것이고, 창조적인 생활이 인간의 건강과 행복의 핵심이라고 믿었다.
> (A) 그러나 그는 창조성이 거의 유일한 과정이 아니라 사회적인 상호관계에 의해 발생된 무엇이라고 또한 믿었다. 그는 창조성과 일반적인 사회적 신뢰를 증대하는 수단으로서 역할극과 즉흥극을 포함한 연극적 기법에 상당히 의존했다.
> (C) 그의 가장 중요한 연극적 도구는 그가 역할 바꾸기라고 부르는 즉, 참가자들에게 다른 사람의 모습을 하도록 요구하는 것이었다. 마치 한 사람이 다른 사람의 가죽을 쓴 것인 양 하는 행동은 동정적 충동을 이끌어내는 데 도움을 주고 그것을 더 높은 수준의 표현으로 발전시키기 위해 고안되었다.

지문 어휘
- innovative 혁신적인
- group therapy 집단 치료
- psychodrama 사이코드라마, 심리극
- brainchild 독창적인 생각, 창작품
- premise 전제
- alien 다른, 이질적인, 외국의
- psyche 정신, 마음
- solitary 유일한, 고독한
- bring out ~을 꺼내다, 이끌다
- improvisation 즉흥(극)
- means 수단, 수입
- consciousness 의식
- considerable 상당한

- reversal 전환
- persona 모습
- pretend ~인 체하다, 가장하다
- empathic 감정이입의
- impulse 자극, 욕망

34

정답 ②

정답 해설

컴퓨터 기술과 교육의 현대적인 발전에 대한 글이다. 제시문에서 언급하고 있는 '현대까지 이르는 발명품' 다음에 '컴퓨터'를 언급하는 (B)로 이어져야 하며, 컴퓨터 네트워크에 대한 진술의 (C)로 이어져야 하며, 그 다음에는 강의 접근성에 대한 진술의 (A)로 이어져야 한다. 따라서 글의 순서로 가장 적절한 것은 ②이다.

지문 해석

세대를 통해, 근면한 개인들은 삶을 더 쉽게 만들기 위해 계속적으로 편리한 것들을 만들어 왔다. 바퀴의 발명부터 전구에 이르기까지 발명품들은 사회를 더욱 앞으로 나아가게 했다.
(B) 하나의 최근의 현대식 발명품은 컴퓨터다. 그리고 그것은 사람들의 삶의 많은 측면을 향상 시켜왔다. 이것은 교육의 분야에서 더욱이 사실이다. 고등교육에서 컴퓨터 기술의 하나의 중요한 영향은 강의 이용성이다.
(C) 컴퓨터 네트워크의 발전의 결과로써, 학생들은 많은 대학들에서 실시간으로 강의를 받을 수 있다. 그들은 이제 디지털화면 앞에 앉아, 또 다른 대학에서 강의되어지는 강의를 듣는 것이 가능하다.
(A) 게다가, 상호작용적인 매체들은 강의에 대해 질문하거나, 또는 e-mail을 통해 다른 학생들과 의견을 교환하기 위해 사용되어질 수 있다. 그러한 컴퓨터화 된 강의들은 학생들에게 전에는 사용할 수 없었던 지식에 대한 접근성을 주었다.

지문 어휘

- interactive 상호작용하는
- access 접근, 입장, 접근하다, 이용하다
- previously 이전에
- unavailable 이용 불가능한
- availability 이용 가능성
- lecture 강의, 강연, 강의하다
- via 경유하여, 거쳐, 통하여
- obtain 얻다, 구하다
- real time 실시간

35

정답 ④

정답 해설

미지의 폭포를 발견하는 경험에 대한 글로, 필자가 Lewis와 함께한 여정에서 폭포 발견과 송어 낚시의 특별한 순간을 회상하는 글이다. 과거의 하나의 일화를 바탕으로 한 글이다. 따라서 사건의 시간의 흐름을 찾아야 한다. 제시문의 시점은 '새벽'이고, 폭포 소리와 관련된 표현은 멀리서 들리는 소리 (C)와 그 소리 (B)이다. 그리고 마지막에 오후에 있었던 진술인 (A)로 이어져야 한다. 따라서 글의 순서로 가장 적절한 것은 ④이다.

지문 해석

나는 Lewis가 그 폭포들을 발견했던 그 날을 기억한다. 그들은 그들의 야영지를 해가 뜰 때 떠났고 몇 시간 후에 그들은 아름다운 평야를 만났으며, 그 평야에 그들이 전에 한 장소에서 본 것보다 더 많은 들소들이 있었다.
(C) 그들은 멀리서 들리는 폭포의 소리를 들을 때까지 계속해 갔고 멀리서 솟아났다가 사라지는 물보라의 기둥을 발견했다. 그들은 그 소리가 점점 더 커질 때까지 그 소리를 따라갔다.
(B) 잠시 후에 그 소리는 엄청났다. 그리고 그들은 Missouri강의 거대한 폭포들에 있었다. 그들이 거기에 도착한 것은 정오 즈음이었다.
(A) 그날 오후에 한 기분 좋은 일이 일어났다. 그들은 폭포 아래로 낚시하러 갔다가 송어 여섯 마리를 잡았는데, 좋은 송어들이였고, 16인치에서 23인치 길이였다.

지문 어휘

- plain 평야
- tremendous 엄청난, 대단한
- fall 폭포
- distant 먼
- column 기둥
- camp 야영지, 캠프장
- faraway 멀리 떨어진
- trout 송어

36

정답 ③

정답 해설

주어진 제시문에 마지막 문장에서 질문을 던지고 있다. 이 경우 이에 대한 대답이 와야 할 것이다. (B)는 이에 대한 대답으로 제일 먼저 와야 한다. (A)와 (C)의 경우, (C)의 마지막에서 언급한 perception, memory, and emotion이 (A)의 three of the key aspects와 연결되므로 (C)가 오고 (A)로 이어져야 한다. 따라서 주어진 글의 순서로 가장 적절한 것은 ③이다.

지문 해석

모든 동물들은 수면시간 동안 인간과 동일한 두뇌 활동을 보여준다. 그들이 꿈을 꾸느냐, 마느냐, 다음의 질문을 제기함에 의해서만이 대답할 수 있는 또 다른 문제이다: 동물들은 지각능력이 있는가?
(B) 오늘날 많은 과학자들은 동물들은 아마도 제한된 형태의 지각능력을, 즉 언어, 그리고 명제적이거나 상징적인 사고에 대한 능력이 부재한다는 점에서 우리 인간의 것과는 다른 지각능력을 가지고 있다고 생각한다.
(C) 동물들은 분명 비록 그들이 꿈을 꾸더라도 꿈에 대해 이야기해 줄 수 없다. 그러나 대체 어떤 애완동물 주인이 그, 혹은 그녀가 사랑하는 동물 친구가 지각력과 기억, 그리고 감정을 갖고 있다는 것을 의심하겠는가?
(A) 이것이 바로 지각능력의 세 가지 중요한 요소이다. 그리고 동물들이 우리와 같은 음성언어를 가지고 있는지 없는지와 상관없이 이러한 것들은 경험되어질 수 있는 것이다. 동물의 두뇌가 수면시간 동안 활동한다면, 동물들이 어떤 인식적이고 감정적인, 그리고 기억과 관련된 종류의 활동을 한다고 가정하지 않을 이유가 무엇이겠는가?

지문 어휘

- activation 활동, 활성화
- pose (질문을) 제기하다
- aspect 요소, 면
- consciousness 의식
- perceptual 인식의
- lack 부족하다
- capacity 공간, 능력
- propositional 명제적인
- even if ~일지라도
- perception 지각, 자각, 인식, 의식

07 순서 배열 파악 유형 기출 독해 어휘 복습 TEST

1	reward	보상	21	scrutiny	정밀 조사, 철저한 검토
2	appeal	매력적이다, 관심[흥미]을 끌다	22	mitigate	완화시키다, 경감시키다
3	regardless of	~에 상관없이	23	mammal	포유류
4	favoritism	편애, 편파	24	rational	합리적인, 이성적인
5	discriminate	차별하다, 식별하다	25	practical	실용적인, 현실적인
6	certificate	증서, 자격증	26	indulge	충족시키다, 채우다
7	surface	표면, 지면	27	exert	행사하다, 가하다, 분투하다
8	beside	옆에, ~에 비해	28	evolve	진화하다, 발달하다
9	stir	섞다, 젓다, 흔들리다, 동요, 충격, 젓기	29	inheritance	유전, 상속
10	witness	목격하다, 목격자, 증인	30	offspring	자손, 자식
11	tear off	찢어내다, 떼어내다, ~을 벗기다	31	mistaken	잘못된, 틀린
12	hearty	푸짐한, 원기 왕성한, 애정어린, 친절한	32	surroundings	주변 환경
13	expand	확장하다, 넓히다	33	proprietary	전용의, 사유의, 독점의
14	authentic	진정한, 진짜의	34	breakdown	분해, 고장, 붕괴
15	renew	갱신하다, 재개하다	35	adopt	채택하다, 입양하다
16	dimension	차원, 관점, 규모, 크기	36	harbor	숨기다, 숨겨 주다
17	exemplify	전형적인 예가 되다, 예를 들다	37	reconcile	조화시키다, 받아들이다
18	prediction	예측, 예견	38	institution	기관, 단체, 협회
19	summon	불러내다, 소환하다	39	diplomat	외교관
20	depression	우울증, 불경기	40	property	특성, 속성

41	immediate	즉각적인	61	represent	제시하다, 보여주다, 나타내다, 대표하다
42	weird	이상한, 기이한, 기괴한	62	promotional	홍보의
43	definitive	확실한, 최종적인	63	executive	경영진, 임원
44	fall short	부족해지다	64	assembly	조립, 집회, 의회
45	rudimentary	기본적인, 기초적인	65	surrender	항복하다, 포기하다
46	intensive	집중적인	66	cease	그치다, 중단되다
47	utility	유용, 공익 시설	67	evaporate	증발하다, 사라지다
48	medium	중간의	68	flexible	유연한, 융통성 있는
49	abundance	풍부, 충만, 다수, 대량	69	demanding	요구가 많은, 힘든
50	humble	겸손한, 낮은	70	prone to	~하는 경향이 있는, ~하기 쉬운
51	sturdy	튼튼한, 강인한	71	exhaustion	피로, 고갈
52	deplete	고갈시키다, 대폭 감소시키다	72	days on end	연속으로 며칠 동안
53	accommodate	수용하다, 공간을 제공하다	73	obsessed	빠져있는, 집착하는
54	prestigious	훌륭한, 명성 있는	74	make sense of	이해하다, 의미를 파악하다
55	sparsely	드문드문, 성기게	75	representation	표현, 묘사
56	cardiovascular	심혈관의	76	attach	붙이다, 첨부하다
57	confusion	혼란, 혼동, 당혹	77	variable	변수, 변동이 심한
58	refer to	언급하다, 참고하다	78	solitary	유일한, 고독한
59	province	주, 지방, 분야	79	pretend	~인 체하다, 가장하다
60	exterior	외부, 겉	80	tremendous	엄청난, 대단한

PART 08 빈칸 추론

ANSWER

01 ③	02 ④	03 ②	04 ①	05 ④
06 ③	07 ①	08 ③	09 ②	10 ①
11 ①	12 ①	12 ②	14 ①	15 ①
16 ③	17 ①	18 ③	19 ④	20 ②
21 ②	22 ④	23 ③	24 ①	25 ②
26 ④	27 ①	28 ①	29 ①	30 ②
31 ③	32 ①	33 ②	34 ③	35 ③
36 ①	37 ②	38 ④	39 ②	40 ②
41 ①	42 ②	43 ①	44 ①	45 ②
46 ①	47 ②	48 ④	49 ①	50 ③
51 ②	52 ③			

지문 어휘

- [ ] active 적극적인, 능동적인
- [ ] listening 경청, 청취
- [ ] discipline 수양, 훈련, 규율
- [ ] involve 포함하다, 관련시키다
- [ ] communication 의사소통, 연락
- [ ] quietly 조용히, 침착하게
- [ ] immediately 즉시, 즉각
- [ ] process 처리하다, 가공하다
- [ ] inflection 억양, 어조
- [ ] perceived 인식된, 인지된
- [ ] meaning 의미, 뜻
- [ ] noise 소리, 잡음
- [ ] unless ~하지 않는 한
- [ ] vigilant 주의를 기울이는, 경계하는
- [ ] pay attention to 주의를 기울이다, 주목하다
- [ ] come into 작용하다
- [ ] closely 면밀하게, 가까이

01   정답 ③

정답 해설

이 글은 적극적 경청(active listening)의 중요성과 그 기술을 익히는 데 필요한 노력과 훈련에 대한 이야기를 하고 있으며 빈칸에서는 적극적 경청에 꼭 필요한 요소를 묻고 있다. 빈칸 뒷부분에서 경청이 단순히 듣는 것이 아니라, 자신의 욕구를 억제하고 상대방에게 집중하는 과정임을 강조한다. 또한 마지막 문장에서, 단순히 듣는 것과 달리 진정한 경청은 상대의 말을 주의 깊게 따라가야 한다고 말하고 있다. 이런 내용은 경청이 높은 수준의 자기 통제를 요구한다는 점을 분명히 보여준다. 따라서 밑줄 친 부분에 들어갈 말로 가장 적절한 것은 ③이다.

지문 해석

적극적 경청은 높은 수준의 자기 통제력이 필요한 예술이자, 기술이며, 수양이다. 좋은 듣기 기술을 개발하려면, 당신은 효과적인 의사소통에 무엇이 포함되는지를 이해하고 조용히 앉아 듣는 기술을 길러야 한다. 이것은 자신의 필요를 무시하고 말을 하고 있는 사람에게 집중하는 것을 포함하는데, 이는 인간 두뇌의 작동 방식 때문에 더 어려워진 하나의 과제이다. 누군가가 당신에게 말을 걸 때, 당신의 뇌는 즉시 단어, 몸짓, 어조, 억양, 그리고 상대방으로부터 나오는 인식되는 의미를 처리하기 시작한다. 한 개의 소리를 듣는 대신, 당신은 두 개의 소리를 듣는다 — 즉 하나는 상대방이 내는 소리이고, 다른 하나는 당신 머릿속의 소리이다. 당신이 스스로 주의를 기울이도록 훈련하지 않으면, 뇌는 보통 당신 머릿속 소리에 주의를 기울이게 된다. 그것이 바로 적극적 경청 기법들이 작용하기 시작하는 지점이다. 듣는다는 것은, 당신이 상대방이 말하는 것에 주의를 기울이고 그것을 매우 면밀하게 따라갈 때 비로소 경청이 된다.

선지 해석

① 자율성 감각
② 창의적인 사고방식
③ 높은 수준의 자기 통제력
④ 외향적인 성격

02   정답 ④

정답 해설

이 글은 휴일 기간에 사람들이 선천적 소비 성향과 사회적 압박 때문에 과도하게 지출하게 된다고 이야기하고 있다. 또한 빈칸 앞부분에서는 장기 목표는 훨씬 더 추상적이어서, 즉각적 만족을 미루려면 더 많은 인지적 노력이 필요하기 때문에 우리는 과소비한다고 강조하고 있다. 빈칸을 포함한 문장에서도 "인색해 보이고 싶지 않아서"라는 표현이 나오는데, 이는 개인적 욕구를 넘어서 타인에게 어떻게 보일지에 대한 사회적 압박이 과소비로 이어진다는 점을 보여준다. 따라서 밑줄 친 부분에 들어갈 말로 가장 적절한 것은 ④이다.

지문 해석

휴가 시즌은 감사의 마음을 전하고, 지난 한 해를 깊이 생각해보며, 가족 그리고 친구들과 시간을 보내는 시기이다. 그러나 조심하지 않으면, 휴가 구매에 과소비를 하게 되는 시기가 될 수도 있다. 전문가들은 사람들이 과소비를 하려는 선천적인 충동을 가지고 있다고 말한다. 사람들은 소비자가 되도록 "설계"되어 있다. 사랑하는 이들에게 선물을 주는 데서 오는 단기적인 만족감이, 돈을 잘 다루기 위해 필요한 장기적인 집중을 가릴 수 있다. 그것이 많은 사람들이 부족한 부분이다. 우리는 장기적인 목표가 훨씬 더 추상적이기 때문에 과소비를 할 수 있으며, 즉각적인 만족을 미루기 위해서는 추가적인 인지 처리가 필요하다. 게다가 소비자들은 "인색해" 보이고 싶지 않아서 자신이 원하는 것보다 더 많이 소비하도록 하는 사회적 압박을 느낄 수도 있다. 많은 기업들도 휴가 기간 동안 사람들이 평소보다 더 많이 소비하도록 부추기는 정책들을 조장하기도 한다.

선지 해석
① 해외 기업에서 일하고 싶은 욕구
② 장기 목표를 세우는 데 책임감
③ 연휴 시즌 동안 소비를 줄이고 싶은 느낌
④ 자신이 원하는 것보다 더 많이 소비하도록 하는 사회적 압박

지문 어휘
- holiday 휴가, 방학
- reflect 깊이 생각하다, 심사숙고하다
- past 지난, 과거의
- careful 조심하는, 주의 깊은
- overspend 과소비하다, 초과 지출하다
- innate 선천적인, 타고난
- impulse 충동, 자극
- gratification 만족(감)
- eclipse 가리다, 어둡게 하다
- fall short 부족하다, 모자라다
- abstract 추상적인
- extra 추가의
- cognitive 인지의, 인식의
- delay 미루다, 연기하다
- instant 즉각적인
- cheap 값싼, 싸구려의, 인색한
- usual 평상시의, 흔히 하는[있는]

03   정답 ②

정답 해설
이 글 초반에서는 인간이 과거보다 더 많이 알고 있다고 생각하지만, 실제로는 개개인의 지식이 매우 한정적이며 다른 사람의 전문 지식에 크게 의존하고 있다는 점을 중요하게 다루고 있다. 특히, 글 후반부에서는 "지식의 착각(knowledge illusion)"이라는 개념을 제시하면서, 우리가 실제로는 잘 알지 못하는 것을 자주 사용하는 것만으로 잘 안다고 착각한다고 설명한다. 빈칸이 포함된 문장에서도 "마치 그것이 우리 자신의 지식인 것처럼(as if it were our own)"이라는 표현을 통해 타인의 지식을 자신의 지식으로 착각하는 현상을 강조하고 있다. 따라서 밑줄 친 부분에 들어갈 말로 가장 적절한 것은 ②이다.

지문 해석
석기 시대의 수렵·채집인은 자신의 옷을 만드는 법, 불을 피우는 법, 토끼를 사냥하는 법, 그리고 사자를 피하는 법을 알고 있었다. 오늘날 우리는 훨씬 더 많은 것을 안다고 생각하지만, 개인적으로는 실제로 훨씬 적게 알고 있다. 우리는 거의 모든 필요를 위해 다른 사람들의 전문 지식에 의존한다. 한 가지 겸손하게 만드는 실험에서, 사람들은 일반적인 지퍼의 작동 원리를 얼마나 잘 이해하고 있는지 평가하도록 요청받았다. 대부분의 사람들은 자신이 지퍼를 아주 잘 이해하고 있다고 자신 있게 말했다—어쨌든 지퍼를 늘 사용하기 때문이다. 그 후 지퍼 작동 과정의 모든 단계를 가능한 한 자세히 설명해 달라고 했을 때, 대부분의 사람들은 전혀 알지 못했다. 이것을 Steven Sloman과 Philip Fernbach는 '지식의 착각'이라고 칭했다. 우리는 개인적으로는 거의 알지 못하면서도 많은 것을 안다고 생각하는데, 그 이유는 다른 사람들의 머릿속에 있는 지식을 마치 자신의 것인 양 여기기 때문이다.

선지 해석
① 직접적인 경험을 통한
② 다른 사람들의 머릿속에 있는
③ 교육받는 동안 얻어진
④ 시행착오를 통해 배운

지문 어휘
- hunter-gatherer 수렵·채집인
- escape 피하다, 달아나다
- rely on 의존하다, 기대다
- expertise 전문 지식
- humble 겸손한
- evaluate 평가하다
- ordinary 일반적인, 보통의, 평범한
- confidently 자신 있게, 확신을 갖고
- describe 말하다, 묘사하다
- operation 작동, 활동
- term 칭하다, 부르다
- knowledge 지식

04   정답 ①

정답 해설
이 글은 인간의 지능이 단순히 생존을 위한 실용적 문제를 해결하기 위해 발달한 것이 아니라, 서로를 이기고 속이고 이해하며 경쟁하기 위해 진화했다는 점을 강조하고 있다. 글 초반부에서 가젤이 치타보다 빠를 필요는 없고 다른 가젤보다 빠르면 된다는 비유를 들어, 경쟁에서 상대보다 우위에 서는 것이 중요하다는 점을 설명한다. 후반부에서도 인간의 지능은 실용적 문제 해결이 아니라 다른 사람을 이기는 데 쓰인다고 반복해서 언급하며, 결국 중요한 것은 절대적인 지적 능력이 아니라 상대적인 우월성임을 말하고 있다. 따라서 밑줄 친 부분에 들어갈 말로 가장 적절한 것은 ①이다.

지문 해석
아프리카 사바나에 사는 가젤은 치타에게 잡아먹히지 않으려고 애쓰지만, 치타가 공격할 때 다른 가젤보다 더 빨리 도망치려는 노력도 한다. 가젤에게 중요한 것은 치타보다 빠른 것이 아니라 다른 가젤보다 빠른 것이다. 이와 마찬가지로, 심리학자들은 사람들이 햄릿의 대사를 외우거나 미적분을 이해하는 능력을 부여받았는지 궁금해하는데, 이러한 능력들은 인간의 지능이 형성된 원시 환경에서는 별로 쓸모가 없었기 때문이다. 아인슈타인조차도 털코뿔소를 잡는 방법을 알아내는 데는 다른 사람들만큼이나 속수무책이었을 것이다. 이 퍼즐에 대해 명확한 해답을 처음 제시한 사람은 케임브리지 대학교의 심리학자 Nicholas Humphrey였다. 우리는 지능을 실용적인 문제를 해결하기 위해서가 아니라 서로보다 한 수 앞서기 위해 사용한다. 다른 사람을 속이고, 속임수를 간파하고, 사람들의 동기를 이해하고, 조종하는 것 — 이런 것들이야말로 지능이 쓰이는 분야이다. 그래서 중요한 것은 당신이 얼마나 똑똑하고 교활한가가 아니라, 다른 사람들보다 얼마나 더 똑똑하고 교활한가이다.

선지 해석
① 당신이 얼마나 똑똑하고 교활한가가 아니라, 다른 사람들보다 얼마나 더 똑똑하고 교활한가
② 자신의 이익보다 집단의 이익에 따라 행동하는 것
③ 구성원들이 협력하여 자신들에게 이로운 최적의 해결책을 찾는 사회를 설계하는 것
④ 주어진 조건에서 실용적인 문제에 대한 최선의 해결책을 찾아내는 것

지문 어휘

- outrun ~보다 더 빨리[멀리] 달리다
- psychologist 심리학자
- wonder 궁금해하다
- endow 부여하다, 기부하다
- mankind 사람들, 인간
- rhinoceros 코뿔소
- intellect 지능
- practical 실용적인, 현실적인
- outwit ~보다 한 수 앞서다
- deceive 속이다, 기만하다
- deceit 속임수, 사기
- manipulate 조종하다, 다루다
- clever 똑똑한, 영리한
- crafty 교활한

05   정답 ④

정답 해설

'기술 발전과 고용과의 관계'에 대한 글로, 기술 발전은 특정 산업의 일자리를 파괴할 수 있지만, 역사적 증거는 오히려 경제의 생산성과 소득을 증가시켜 노동 수요를 높일 수 있음을 강조하는 글이다. 따라서 상품에 대한 수요 증가로 인해 노동에 대한 수요도 증가하게 되어, 이로 인해 실직한 노동자들이 다른 산업에서 일자리를 찾을 수 있는 가능성이 높아진다. 따라서 밑줄 친 부분에 들어갈 말로 가장 적절한 것은 ④이다.

지문 해석

기술 발달은 섬유와 같은 특정 산업에서 일자리를 파괴할 수 있다. 그러나 역사적 증거는 기술 발전이 국가 전체에서 실업을 초래하지 않는다는 것을 보여준다. 기술 발전은 전체 경제의 생산성과 소득을 증가시키며, 높은 소득은 상품에 대한 수요를 증가시키고, 따라서 노동력에 대한 높은 수요도 증가한다. 결과적으로 한 산업에서 일자리를 잃은 근로자들은 다른 산업에서 일자리를 찾을 수 있을 거지만, 그들 중 많은 사람들은 이것이 시간이 걸릴 수 있고, 러다이트(the Luddites)와 같은 그들 중 일부는 그들의 새로운 일자리에서 결국 더 낮은 임금을 받게 될 것이다.

선지 해설

① 증가하는 실직
② 직장에서의 승진 지연
③ 직장의 만족도 향상
④ 노동력에 대한 높은 수요

지문 어휘

- progress 발달, 진보, 전진, 진행. 나아가다, 진행하다
- textile 섬유 산업, 직물, 옷감
- unemployment 실업(률)
- overall 전체의, 종합[전반]적인
- income 소득, 수입
- be able to ~할 수 있다, ~이 가능하다
- end up 결국 ~하게 되다
- wage 임금, 급료

06   정답 ③

정답 해설

석유의 경제적 영향과 대체 에너지의 한계에 대한 글로, 석유는 세계 경제에 큰 영향을 미치며, 가격 변동이 경제 성장과 생산자에 미치는 부정적인 영향이 큼을 세 번째 문장을 중심으로 설명하고 있다. 따라서 밑줄 친 부분에 들어갈 말로 가장 적절한 것은 ③이다.

지문 해석

석유를 대체할 수 있는 것은 없으며, 이것은 큰 호황과 깊은 불황에 빠지기 쉬운 이유 중 하나로, 그로 인해 세계 경제도 영향을 받는다. 우리는 석탄이나 천연가스, 원자력 또는 신재생 에너지를 통해 전기를 생성할 수 있지만, 가격에 따라 에너지원에서 에너지원으로 전환하더라도 석유는 여전히 운송을 위한 가장 주요한 연료이다. 세계 경제가 활기를 띨 때, 석유에 대한 수요가 증가하고, 가격이 상승하며 생산자들이 더 많은 석유를 퍼내도록 자극한다. 필연적으로 이러한 높은 가격은 경제 성장을 저해하고 공급자들이 과잉 생산을 하고 있을 때 수요를 줄인다. 가격이 급락하면 사이클이 다시 시작된다. 이는 가격이 급락할 때 빈손이 될 수 있는 생산자들에게 나쁘며, 미래의 에너지 가격이 불확실한 소비자와 산업에도 피해를 준다. 1990년대의 낮은 석유 가격은 미국 자동차 회사들을 안심시켜 처참한 안일함에 빠지게 했다. 석유가 비싸졌을 때 사용할 수 있는 효율적인 모델이 거의 없었기 때문이다.

선지 해설

① 자동차 산업이 번창하는
② 이것은 국경 간의 혼란을 초래하는
③ 이것은 큰 호황과 깊은 불황에 빠지기 쉬운
④ 재생 에너지에 대한 연구가 제한적인

지문 어휘

- substitute 대체하다, 대신하다, 대체물, 대리자
- generate 생성하다, 만들어 내다, 발생시키다
- coal 석탄
- renewables 재생 가능 에너지, 신재생 에너지
- bust 불황, 실패, 파산
- predominant 주요한, 우세한, 지배적인, 두드러진, 뚜렷한
- inevitably 필연적으로, 불가피하게
- supplier 공급자, 공급 회사
- overproduce 과잉 생산하다
- plummet 급락하다, 곤두박질치다
- lull into ~를 안심시켜 ~하게 만들다
- disastrous 처참한, 재앙의, 불길한
- complacency 안주, 안일

07   정답 ①

정답 해설

21세기 말까지 거의 모든 국가에서 낮아지는 출산율은 인구 감소로 이어지며, 이 변화로 인해 고령화가 급증하며 미래의 과제로 세금, 노인 건강 관리, 양육 책임, 퇴직 등이 우려되고 있음을 설명하고 있다. 빈칸의 내용은 '세금, 노인 건강 관리, 돌봄 책임 및 은퇴를 포함한 문제들'을 포괄하는 '인구 감소로 말미암은 문제점'에 대해 나와야 한다. 따라서 밑줄 친 부분에 들어갈 말로 적절한 것은 ①이다.

지문 해석

떨어지는 출산율이 세기말까지 거의 모든 국가의 인구 감소를 야기할 것으로 예상된다. 세계 출산율은 1950년에 4.7명이었지만 2017년에는 거의 절반인 2.4명으로 감소했다. 2100년에는 1.7명 아래로 떨어질 것으로 예상된다. 결과적으로, 일부 연구원들은 지구상의 사람들의 수가 세기말에는 88억 명으로 떨어지기 전에 2064년에 97억 명으로 절정에 달할 것으로 예측한다. 이 전환은 태어나는 수만큼 많은 사람들이 80세에 도달하며 또한 인구의 상당한 고령화로 이어질 것이다. 이러한 인구학적 변화는 세금, 노인 건강관리, 돌봄 책임 및 은퇴를 포함한 미래의 문제에 대한 우려를 제기한다. 새로운 인구의 지형으로의 "부드러운 착륙"을 보장하기 위해 연구원들은 전환의 신중한 관리의 필요성을 강조한다.

선지 해석
① 미래의 문제에 대한 우려를 제기한다
② 뒤집힌 연령 구조 현상을 완화한다
③ 감소한 결혼율 문제를 보상한다
④ 문제 해결을 위한 즉각적인 해결책을 제공한다

지문 어휘
☐ fertility rate 출산율, 출생률
☐ project 예상하다, 추정하다, 계획하다, 계획, 과제
☐ shrink 줄어들다, 오그라들다
☐ population 인구, 주민
☐ nearly 거의, 대략
☐ lead to ~로 이어지다
☐ aging 고령화, 노령화, 노화
☐ demographic 인구 통계학적인, 인구학의, 인구의
☐ taxation 조세
☐ elderly 노인, 어르신들, 나이가 지긋한
☐ caregiving 돌봄, 부양
☐ management 관리, 경영, 운영
☐ mitigate 완화하다, 진정시키다

08
정답 ③

정답 해설
청취자의 역할과 책임을 강조하는 글로, 이 글은 나쁜 청취자와 좋은 청취자 간의 차이를 강조하며, 좋은 청취자는 발표자의 외모나 말하는 방식이 아닌 정보에 집중하며, 우리가 듣는 것을 이해하기 위한 확실한 방법은 우리에게 내재된 책임을 떠맡는 것이라 설명하고 있다. 추론의 근거로 다섯 번째 문장의 진술을 통해서 '우리의 책임'을 표현하는 선택지를 고르면 된다. 따라서 밑줄 친 부분에 들어갈 말로 적절한 것은 ③이다.

지문 해석
많은 청자들은 "누가 그런 등장인물의 말을 들을 수 있을까? 그가 그의 메모들로부터 읽는 것을 언제 멈출 수 있을까?"라고 혼자 생각함으로써 그들의 부주의에 대해 화자를 비난한다. 좋은 청자는 다르게 반응한다. 그는 화자를 보고 "이 남자는 무능하다. 거의 누구나 그것보다 더 잘 말할 수 있을 것 같다"고 생각할 것이다. 그러나 이러한 초기의 유사성으로부터 그는 다른 결론으로 넘어가면서 생각한다. "하지만 잠시만. 나는 그의 성격이나 전달력에 관심이 없어. 나는 그가 무엇을 알고 있는지 알고 싶어. 이 남자는 내가 알아야 할 것들을 알고 있나?" 근본적으로, 우리는 "우리 자신의 경험으로 듣는다." 우리가 그의 메시지를 이해할 수 있는 능력이 잘못 갖추어져 있기 때문에 화자에게 책임이 있는가? 우리가 듣는 모든 것을 이해할 수는 없지만, 우리의 이해 수준을 높일 수 있는 한 가지 확실한 방법은 본질적으로 우리의 것인 책임을 지는 것이다.

선지 해석
① 화자가 알고 있는 것을 무시하는
② 화자의 성격을 분석하는
③ 본질적으로 우리의 것인 책임을 지는
④ 화자의 말 전달 능력에 집중하는

지문 어휘
☐ blame 비난하다, ~을 탓하다, 비난, 책임
☐ inattention 부주의, 태만, 무관심
☐ initial 초기의, 처음의
☐ personality 성격, 인격, 개성
☐ find out ~을 알아내다, 알게 되다
☐ speaker 화자, 발표자, 연설가
☐ responsible ~에 대해 책임이 있는, ~의 원인이 되는
☐ equip 갖추다, 차려입게 하다
☐ comprehend 이해하다, 파악하다, 포함하다, 의미하다
☐ assume (책임을) 지다, (권력을) 쥐다, (역할을) 맡다, 추정하다
☐ inherently 본질적으로, 선천적으로

09
정답 ②

정답 해설
정치인, 기업, 사회 활동가, 직장 등의 모든 분야에서 설득이 중요한 역할을 함을 강조하는 글이다. 첫 번째 문장이 글의 주제문으로 두 번째 문장 이하의 '주요 정치인', '주요 산업과 특별 이익 집단', '거의 모든 지역 단체의 운동가', '직장인들'의 구체적인 사례를 통해서 '설득'을 하려한다는 것을 설명하고 있다. 추가적으로 의사소통의 시간 80 퍼센트가 설득을 목적으로 사용된다는 구체적인 연구결과를 통해서 밑줄 친 부분에 들어갈 말로 가장 적절한 것은 ②이다.

지문 해석
설득은 인생의 거의 모든 분야에서 나타난다. 거의 모든 주요 정치인들은 대중에게 호소할 방법에 대한 조언을 제공할 미디어 컨설턴트와 정치 전문가들을 고용한다. 사실상 모든 주요 기업과 특수 이익 단체들은 그것의 우려들을 의회나 주 정부 또는 지방 정부에 전달하기 위해 로비스트를 고용한다. 거의 모든 지역사회에서 활동가들은 중요한 정책 문제에 대해 동료 시민들을 설득하려고 노력한다. 직장 역시 항상 사무실 정치와 설득을 위한 비옥한 장소였다. 한 연구는 일반 관리자들이 그들의 시간의 80% 이상을 언어적 의사소통에-그 중 대부분은 동료 직원들을 설득하기 위한 목적으로 소비한다고 추정한다. 복사기의 등장으로, 사무실 내 설득을 위한 완전히 새로운 매체인 복사된 메모가 발명되었다. 미 국방부에서만 하루에 평균 35만 페이지를 복사하는데, 이는 소설 1,000권에 상당하는 것이다.

선지 해석
① 사업가들은 좋은 설득 능력들을 가져야 한다
② 설득은 인생의 거의 모든 분야에서 나타난다
③ 당신은 수많은 광고판과 포스터를 접하게 될 것이다
④ 대중 매체 캠페인들은 정부에 유용하다

지문 어휘
- appeal 매력, 호소
- virtually 사실상, 거의
- special-interest group 이해관계 단체
- lobbyist 로비스트, 목회가
- persuasion 설득, 강요
- verbal 말로 된, 언어의
- equivalent 동등한, 상당한

10
정답 ①

정답 해설
성인은 주로 언어를 통해 사회적 상호 작용을 하지만, 어린이는 언어 없이도 쉽게 상호 작용할 수 있음을 강조하는 글이다. 따라서 밑줄 친 부분에 들어갈 말로 가장 적절한 것은 ①이다.

지문 해석
성인에게 사회적 상호 작용은 주로 언어라는 수단을 통해 발생한다는 점에 주목하는 것이 중요하다. 모국어를 사용하는 성인들은 그 언어를 사용하지 않는 누군가와 상호 작용하는 것에 시간을 거의 바치지 않고, 그 결과 성인 외국인은 의미 있고 확장된 언어 교환에 참여할 기회를 거의 갖지 못할 것이다. 그에 반해 어린아이는 종종 다른 아이들, 심지어 성인에게도 쉽게 받아들여진다. 어린아이들에게 언어는 사회적 상호 작용에 있어서는 필수적이지 않다. 예를 들어, 이른바 '병행 놀이'는 어린아이들 사이에서 흔하다. 그들은 단지 서로 함께 있는 사람들과 앉아서 가끔씩만 말을 하고 혼자서 노는 것만으로도 만족할 수 있다. 어른들은 사회적 상호 작용에서 언어가 중요한 역할을 하지 않는 상황에 있는 그들 자신을 거의 발견하지 못한다.

선지 해석
① 사회적 상호 작용에서 언어가 중요한 역할을 하지 않는
② 그들의 의견은 동료들에게 쉽게 받아들여지는
③ 그들은 다른 언어를 사용하라고 요청받는
④ 의사소통 능력이 매우 요구되는

지문 어휘
- medium 매체, 수단
- devote 헌신하다, 전념하다
- readily 즉시, 기꺼이
- parallel play 병렬 놀이 (어린이들이 함께 있으면서 각자의 활동을 하는 것)
- occasionally 가끔, 때때로

11
정답 ①

정답 해설
밀레니얼 세대들의 문화적 재정적 차이를 주제로 하는 글이다. 특히 여섯 번째 문장의 진술을 통해서 '1세대'와 '2세대'의 문화적, 재정적인 차이가 있음을 나타내고 있으므로, 마지막 문장에서 'Gen Y.1'과 'Gen Y.2'의 우선순위들과 필요성에 있어서의 '차이'를 나타내는 단어가 정답이 된다. 따라서 밑줄 친 부분에 들어갈 말로 적절한 것은 ①이다.

지문 해석
Javelin Research는 모든 밀레니얼 세대가 현재 동일한 생애 단계에 있지 않다는 것을 알아냈다. 모든 밀레니얼은 모두 세기가 바뀌는 시기쯤에 태어났지만, 그들 중 일부는 여전히 초기 성인기에 있어 새로운 직업에 대응하고 자리 잡는 중이다. 반면에, 더 나이가 많은 밀레니얼 세대는 이미 집을 가지고 가족을 이루고 있다. 자녀를 가지는 것이 어떻게 여러분의 관심사와 우선순위를 바꿀 수 있는지 상상해 볼 수 있다. 그래서 마케팅 목적으로 이 세대를 Gen Y.1과 Gen Y.2로 나누는 것이 유용하다. 이 두 그룹은 문화적으로 다를 뿐만 아니라 금융 생활의 단계에서도 매우 다르다. 젊은 그룹은 금융 초보자로서 구매력을 보이기 시작한 것입니다. 반면에 후자 그룹은 신용 기록이 있고 첫 대출을 가진 사람들이자 어린 자녀를 기르고 있습니다. Gen Y.1과 Gen Y.2 사이의 우선순위와 요구 사항의 대조는 광범위하다.

선지 해석
① 대조
② 감소
③ 반복
④ 능력

지문 어휘
- Millennials 밀레니얼 세대
- century 세기, 100년
- adulthood 성인, 성년
- settle down 안정을 찾다
- priority 우선 사항, 우선 순위
- financial 금융의, 재정의
- mortgage 대출(금), 융자(금), 저당 잡히다

12
정답 ①

정답 해설
단기적인 이윤을 추구하는 자유화된 시장에서의 수력발전 가치에 대한 글이다. 수력발전에 있어서의 자본시장에서의 '비용 압박(Cost Pressures)'으로 말미암아, 투자가에게 '단기적인 과정이 아닌(not a short-term process)' 것이 인기가 있는 투자 (a popular investment)가 되지 못함을 빈칸 앞에서 진술하고 있으므로 대부분의 개인 투자자들이 선호하는 것은 '더 단기적인 것'이 되어야 한다. 따라서 밑줄 친 부분에 들어갈 말로 적절한 것은 ①이다.

지문 해석
자유화된 시장에서의 비용 압박은 기존과 미래의 수력발전 계획에 서로 다른 영향을 미친다. 비용 구조 때문에 기존의 수력발전소는 항상 수익을 낼 수 있다. 그러나 미래의 수력발전 계획의 기획과 건설은 단기적인 과정이 아니기 때문에, 전력 생산 비용이 낮더라도 인기가 있는 투자 대상은 아니다. 대부분의 민간 투자자들은 더 단기적인 기술들에 자금을 지원하기를 선호하여, 기존의 수력 발전소는 고수익 사업으로 보이지만 새로운 수력 발전소에는 아무도 투자하고 싶어하지 않는 역설적인 상황이 발생한다. 공공 주주/소유주(국가, 도시, 지방 자치 단체)가 관련된 경우에는 그들은 공급 안정성의 중요성을 알 수 있고 장기적인 투자도 높이 평가하기 때문에 상황이 매우 다르게 나타난다.

선지 해석
① 더 단기적인 기술들
② 모든 첨단 기술 산업들
③ 공익 증진
④ 전기 공급 강화

지문 어휘
- liberalize 자유화하다, 완화하다
- existing 기존의, 현재 사용되는
- scheme 계획, 방안, 책략을 꾸미다
- hydropower plant 수력 발전소
- paradoxical 역설적인
- cash cow 고수익 사업[상품]
- shareholder 주주
- municipality 지방 자치제
- supply 공급, 공급[제공]하다

13
정답 ②

정답 해설
글로벌 브랜드 광고의 표준화 필요성 증대를 주제로 하는 글로, 글로벌 브랜드들은 온라인 마케팅과 소셜 미디어의 인기 상승으로 인해 '광고 표준화'를 필요로 하며, 국경을 넘나들기 쉬운 소비자들을 위해 캠페인을 전개하기 어렵기 때문에 전 세계적으로 디지털 사이트를 조정하고 있음을 설명하고 있다. 첫 번째 문장이 이 글의 주제문으로 '표준화(standardization)'를 한다는 것은 '획일적'으로 한다는 것을 의미한다. 따라서 밑줄 친 부분에 들어갈 말로 알맞은 것은 ②이다.

지문 해석
최근 몇 년 동안 온라인 마케팅과 소셜 미디어 공유의 인기 상승으로 인해 글로벌 브랜드들의 광고 표준화에 대한 필요성이 증가하고 있다. 대부분의 대형 마케팅 및 광고 캠페인에는 대규모의 온라인 참여가 포함된다. 연결된 소비자들은 이제 인터넷과 소셜 미디어를 통해 쉽게 국경을 넘나들 수 있으며, 이로 인해 광고주들이 통제되고 정돈된 방식으로 적합한 캠페인을 시작하는 것이 어려워지고 있다. 그 결과, 대부분의 글로벌 소비자 브랜드들은 국제적으로 디지털 사이트를 동일하게 한다. 예를 들어, 전 세계적으로 호주와 아르헨티나부터 프랑스, 루마니아, 러시아에 이르기까지 코카-콜라 웹과 소셜 미디어 사이트들은 놀라우리만큼 획일적이다. 전부 친숙한 빨간색 코카콜라의 튀기는 소리, 상징적인 코카콜라 병 모양과 코카콜라 음악과 "Taste the Feeling" 테마를 특징으로 한다.

선지 해석
① 실험적인
② 획일적인
③ 국지적인
④ 다양한

지문 어휘
- popularity 인기
- standardization 표준화, 규격화, 통일, 획일
- presence 있음, 존재, 실재, 참석
- roll out 출시하다, 시작하다, 밀어서 펴다
- orderly 정돈된, 질서 있는
- coordinate 조정[조화]하다, 동등하게 하다
- feature 특징, 특징을 가지다
- splash 튀기는 소리, 얼룩
- iconic 대표적인, 상징적인
- uniform 획일적인, 균일한
- feature ~의 특징을 이루다

14
정답 ①

정답 해설
과학심리학의 발전과 분야 간 협력의 중요성을 강조하는 글로, 심리학이 과학적으로 성숙하고 발전하려면, 이질적인 부분이 완전해지고 다시 통합되어야 한다는 것을 강조하는 글이다. 문제점에 대한 해결책을 제시하고 그 근거를 제시하는 구조를 가진 글로, 두 번째 문장에서 "심리학 분야가 과학적으로 성숙하고 발전하려면, 그것의 이질적인 부분(예를 들어, 신경과학, 발달, 인지, 성격, 그리고 사회)이 완전해지고 다시 통합되어야 한다"는 진술을 통해서 밑줄 친 부분에 들어갈 말로 알맞은 것은 ①이다.

지문 해석
지난 50년 동안, 훈련이 점점 더 전문화되고 초점이 좁혀짐에 따라 심리학의 모든 주요 하위 학문들은 서로 점점 더 고립되어 왔다. 일부 심리학자들이 오랫동안 주장해 온 것처럼, 심리학 분야가 과학적으로 성숙하고 발전하려면, 그것의 이질적인 부분(예를 들어, 신경과학, 발달, 인지, 성격, 그리고 사회)이 완전해지고 다시 통합되어야 한다. 과학은 서로 다른 주제가 이론적, 경험적으로 단순화된 이론적 틀 아래 통합될 때 발전한다. 과학 심리학은 다양한 하위 영역의 심리학자들 간의 협업을 장려하여 지속적인 분열이 아닌 일관성을 달성하는 데 도움이 될 것이다. 이렇게 함으로써, 과학 심리학은 분야 내의 모든 주요 파벌을 하나의 학문으로 통합함으로써 심리학 전체에 대한 본보기로 역할을 할지도 모른다. 과학 심리학이 어떻게 자원을 결합하고 통일된 관점에서 과학을 공부할 것인가에 대한 모 학문의 모델이 될 수 있다면 그것은 작지 않은 위업이자 작지 않은 중요성이 될 것이다.

선지 해석
① 통일된 관점에서
② 역동적인 측면에서
③ 역사 전반에 걸쳐서
④ 정확한 증거와 함께

지문 어휘
- subdiscipline 학문 분야의 하위 구분
- mature 성숙하다, 성숙한, 다 자란
- disparate 서로 전혀 다른, 이질적인
- neuroscience 신경 과학
- cognitive 인지의
- integrate 통합하다
- empirical 경험에 의거한, 실증적인
- simplify 간소화하다
- coherence 일관성
- fragmentation 분열
- fraction 파벌, 분할, 분수
- parent discipline 모 학문
- unified 통합된, 통일된

15
정답 ①

정답 해설
불안을 피하기 위한 전략의 역설에 대한 글로, 우리는 불안한 시대에 살며 불안을 줄이기 위해 다양한 전략을 사용하지만, 이러한 회피 전략은 장기적으로 불안을 더 심해지게 한다는 것을 강조하고 있다. 빈칸 문장에서 문제 해결을 위해 불안 회피 전략이 결국 도움이 되지 않는다고 진술하고 있다. 따라서 밑줄 친 부분에 들어갈 말로 가장 적절한 것은 ①이다.

지문 해석

우리는 불안의 시대에 살고 있다. 불안한 것은 불편하고 무서운 경험이 될 수 있기 때문에, 우리는 순간의 불안을 줄이는 데 도움이 되는 의식적이거나 무의식적인 전략들에 의지한다 — 영화나 TV 쇼 시청하기, 먹기, 비디오 게임 플레이하기, 과로하기, 게다가 스마트폰은 낮이나 밤이든 언제든지 주의 산만을 만든다. 심리학적 연구에 따르면, 주의 산만은 흔한 불안 회피 전략으로 역할한다. 그러나 역설적으로, 이러한 회피 전략은 장기적으로 불안을 더 악화시킨다. 불안한 것은 유사에 빠지는 것과 같은 것이다 — 더 많이 그것과 싸우수록 더 깊이 가라앉는다. 실제로, 연구는 잘 알려진 구절인 "당신이 저항하는 것은 지속된다"를 강력하게 지지한다.

선지 해석
① 역설적으로
② 다행히도
③ 중립적으로
④ 창조적으로

지문 어휘
☐ anxiety 불안
☐ uncomfortable 불편한, 불안한
☐ resort to 의지하다, 의존하다
☐ conscious 의식적인
☐ unconscious 무의식적인
☐ strategy 전략, 방법
☐ overwork 과로하다, 혹사하다
☐ distraction 주의 산만, 방해
☐ quicksand 유사(바람이나 물에 의해 아래로 흘러내리는 모래), 헤어나기 힘든 상황
☐ sink 가라앉다
☐ phase 단계
☐ resist 저항하다
☐ persist 지속되다, 집요하게 계속하다

16 정답 ③

정답 해설
효율적인 정보 관리를 주제로 하는 글로, 효율적인 정보 관리를 위해 미결 서류함의 수를 최소화하여 스트레스를 줄이고 생산적으로 일할 수 있다. 미결 서류함은 모든 메시지와 수신 정보를 처리해야 할 장소로, 미결 서류함의 수가 적을수록 관리가 용이해짐을 마지막 문장에서 강조하고 있다. 따라서 밑줄 친 부분에 들어갈 말로 가장 적절한 것은 ③이다.

지문 해석
당신은 얼마나 다양한 방식으로 정보를 받아들이는가? 어떤 사람들은 답장해야 할 여섯 가지 종류의 커뮤니케이션을 가지고 있을 수도 있다 — 텍스트 메시지, 음성 메일, 종이 문서, 일반 우편, 블로그 글, 다른 온라인 서비스의 메시지 등. 각각은 하나의 인박스 유형이며, 지속적으로 처리되어야 한다. 이는 끝없는 프로세스지만, 지치거나 스트레스 받을 필요는 없다. 정보 관리를 더 관리하기 쉬운 수준으로 낮추고 생산적인 영역으로 이동시키기 위해서는 당신이 가지고 있는 미결 서류함의 수를 최소화함으로써 시작해야 한다. 메시지를 확인하거나 수신 정보를 읽기 위해 가야 할 모든 장소는 미결 서류함이며, 가지고 있는 미결 서류함이 많을수록 모든 것을 관리하기가 더 어려워진다. 필요한 방식으로 여전히 기능을 수행할 수 있도록 당신이 가진 미결 서류함의 수를 최소한으로 줄여라.

선지 해석
① 동시에 여러 목표를 설정함으로써
② 들어오는 정보에 몰두함으로써
③ 당신이 가지고 있는 미결 서류함의 수를 최소화함으로써
④ 당신이 열정적인 정보를 선택함으로써

지문 어휘
☐ in-box 미결 서류함, 받은 편지함
☐ process 처리하다
☐ continuous 연속적인
☐ exhausting 지치게 하는, 소모적인
☐ management 관리
☐ immerse 담그다, 몰두하다, 몰두하게 만들다
☐ minimize 최소화하다, 축소하다
☐ at once 즉시, 동시에[한꺼번에]

17 정답 ①

정답 해설
해수면 상승 대비를 위한 굴의 역할에 대한 글로, 굴과 같은 작은 생물체도 환경을 보호하고 생태계 균형을 유지하는데 중요한 역할을 할 수 있으며, 굴이 여러 가지 환경적 이점을 제공하고 있다고 설명한다. 4번째 문장에서 "성체 굴 한 마리가 하루에 최대 50갤런의 물을 여과할 수 있어서 수로가 더 깨끗해진다"는 진술을 통해서 빈칸에 들어갈 말로 가장 적절한 것은 ①이다.

지문 해석
지구 기온이 상승함에 따라 해수면도 상승하여 전 세계 연안 지역 공동체를 위협하고 있다. 놀랍게도, 굴과 같은 작은 유기체들도 우리의 방어물이 될 수 있다. 굴은 생태계와 주민들의 건강에 파급효과를 미치는 핵심종이다. 성체 굴 한 마리가 하루에 최대 50갤런의 물을 여과할 수 있어서 수로가 더 깨끗해진다. 건강한 굴 암초는 또한 생물 다양성과 생태계 균형을 촉진하면서 수백 개의 다른 해양 생물들에게 집을 제공한다. 해수면 상승으로 인해 홍수가 만연하게 발생하면 굴 암초는 폭풍을 완화시키고 더 많은 해안 침식으로부터 보호하는 벽 역할을 한다.

선지 해석
① 우리의 방어물이 될 수 있다
② 비상식량이 될 수 있다
③ 미세 플라스틱에 의해 오염될지도 모른다
④ 지역 주민들의 수입을 증가시킬 수 있다

지문 어휘
☐ sea level 해수면
☐ coastal community 연안 지역 공동체
☐ organism 유기체, 생물체
☐ oyster 굴
☐ keystone 핵심, 쐐기돌
☐ reef 암초
☐ biodiversity 생물 다양성
☐ ecosystem 생태계
☐ pervasive 만연하는
☐ buffer 완화하다, 보호하다, 완충제
☐ come to ~이 되다, 의식을 회복하다
☐ defence 방어[물], 수비, 옹호

18

정답 ③

정답 해설
기후 변화와 오염으로부터 세계의 바다와 수로를 보호하기 위한 긴급한 필요성을 강조하기 위해 차가운 열린 물에서의 장거리 수영을 하는 Lewis Pugh에 대한 글이다. 빈칸이 들어갈 문장은 5번째 문장과 6번째 문장의 "그는 보통 수영을 할 때 매우 공격적입니다. 왜냐하면 그는 빨리 끝내고 차가운 물에서 벗어나고 싶기 때문입니다"의 진술과는 반대가 되는 진술이 나와야 한다. 따라서 빈칸에 들어갈 말로 가장 적절한 것은 ③이다.

지문 해설
Lewis Pugh는 영국의 지구력 수영 선수로, 차갑고 탁 트인 바다에서 장거리 수영을 하는 것으로 가장 잘 알려져 있다. 그는 기후 변화와 오염의 영향으로부터 세계의 바다와 수로를 보호해야 하는 긴급한 필요성에 관심을 끌기 위한 방법으로 추운 곳에서 수영을 한다. 2019년에 Pugh는 에베레스트 산 근처의 네팔 Khumbu 지역에 위치한 Imja 호수에서 수영하기로 결정했다. 첫 번째 시도가 실패한 후, Lewis는 해발 5,300 미터에서 수영하는 가장 좋은 방법에 대해 논의하기 위한 평가 회의를 가졌다. 그는 보통 수영을 할 때 매우 공격적이다. 왜냐하면 그는 빨리 끝내고 차가운 물에서 벗어나고 싶기 때문이다. 하지만 이번에 그는 겸손을 보여주었고 천천히 수영했다.

선지 해석
① 비통
② 분노
③ 겸손
④ 자신감

지문 어휘
- endurance 지구력, 내구성, 인내
- long-distance 장거리
- urgent 긴급한, 시급한
- waterway 수로, 항로
- pollution 오염
- aggressive 공격적인

19

정답 ④

정답 해설
물속에서 위협이 되는 그린란드의 거대 빙하에 대한 글이다. 주제문에 해당되는 2번째 문장에서 아래에서부터의 공격으로 인해 빙산이 녹는다고 진술하고 있다. 그리고 마지막 문장을 통해서도 많은 양의 열은 빙하가 녹는 것을 가속화하는 논리가 타당함을 알 수 있다. 따라서 밑줄 친 부분에 들어갈 말로 가장 적절한 것은 ④이다.

지문 해설
과학자들은 더 높은 대기 온도가 그린란드의 빙상 표면을 녹이는 원인이 되고 있다는 것을 오랫동안 알고 있었다. 그러나 새로운 연구는 얼음을 아래에서부터 공격하기 시작한 또 다른 위협을 발견했다: 거대한 빙하 아래로 이동하는 따뜻한 바닷물이 빙하를 훨씬 더 빨리 녹게 하고 있다. 이 연구 결과는 그린란드 북동부에 있는 Nioghalvfjerdsfjorden 빙하의 많은 "빙설" 중 하나를 연구한 연구원들에 의해 학술지 Nature Geoscience에 발표되었다. 빙설은 육지의 얼음과 분리되지 않고 물 위에 떠 있는 얼음 조각이다. 이 과학자들이 연구한 거대한 것은 길이가 거의 50마일이다. 이 조사는 대서양의 따뜻한 물이 빙하를 향해 직접 흐를 수 있는 폭이 1마일 이상인 수중 해류가 많은 양의 열을 얼음과 접촉시켜서 빙하가 녹는 것을 가속화하는 것을 밝혀냈다.

① 분리시키는 것
② 지연시키는 것
③ 막는 것
④ 가속화하는 것

지문 어휘
- contribute ~한 원인이 되다
- ice sheet 빙산
- underneath 아래에, 밑면에
- glacier 빙하
- journal 저널, 학술지
- ice tongue 빙설
- northeast 북동쪽의
- float 떠다니다
- break off 분리되다, 떨어지다
- massive 거대한, 심각한
- reveal 드러내다, 밝히다
- underwater current 수중 해류
- Atlantic Ocean 대서양
- accelerate 가속화하다, 촉진하다

20

정답 ②

정답 해설
이 글은 노동 지도자들, 사업가들, 장관들, 교육자들, 그리고 광고주들 같은 유명인들이 대중의 신뢰를 얻기 위한 선전 기법을 주제로 하는 글이다. 구체적인 예시들을 통해서 청중에게 자신도 평범한 사람 중 하나라는 인상을 주기 위해 노력한다는 내용이 이어지고 있다. 따라서 밑줄 친 부분에 들어갈 말로 가장 적절한 것은 ②이다.

지문 해설
가장 자주 사용되는 선전 기법 중 하나는 대중들에게 선전가의 견해가 일반인의 견해를 반영하고 있으며 그들의 최선의 이익을 위해 일하고 있다고 확신시키는 것이다. 육체노동자 청중에게 말하는 정치인은 소매를 걷어붙이고, 넥타이를 풀고, 군중의 특정 관용구를 사용하려고 시도할 수 있다. 그는 심지어 자신이 "그냥 사람들 중 한 명"이라는 인상을 주기 위해 의도적으로 언어를 잘못 사용할 수도 있다. 이 기법은 일반적으로 정치인의 견해가 연설되는 군중의 견해와 같다는 인상을 주기 위해 화려한 추상어를 사용하기도 한다. 노동 지도자들, 사업가들, 장관들, 교육자들, 그리고 광고주들은 우리와 같은 그저 평범한 사람들처럼 보임으로써 우리의 신뢰를 얻기 위해 이 기술을 사용해왔다.

선지 해석
① 화려한 추상어를 뛰어 넘는
② 우리와 같은 그저 평범한 사람들
③ 다른 사람들과 다른 무언가
④ 대중보다 더 잘 교육받은

지문 어휘
- propaganda 선전
- interest 이해관계, 이익, 관심, 흥미
- blue-collar 육체노동자의
- undo 풀다, 원상태로 돌리다
- idiom 관용구, 숙어
- incorrectly 부적절하게
- on purpose 의도적으로, 고의로
- glittering generality 화려한 추상어, 미사여구

- [ ] businesspeople 사업가들
- [ ] minister 장관, 성직자, 목사
- [ ] confidence 신뢰, 자신, 확신
- [ ] plain 평범한, 보통의, 평원, 평지
- [ ] folk 사람들

21 　　　　　　　　　　　　　　　　　정답 ②

정답 해설

에너지 보존의 법칙을 롤러코스터를 통해 보여주는 글이다. 롤러코스터의 상하의 움직임과 에너지 변환에 대한 설명을 하면서, 위치 에너지와 운동 에너지를 설명하고 하고, 마지막에는 브레이크를 통해 운동 에너지가 열 에너지로 변환되는 것을 언급하고 있다. 따라서 열 에너지를 유발시키는 것은 브레이크와 선로의 마찰임을 쉽게 추론할 수 있다. 따라서 밑줄 친 부분에 들어갈 말로 가장 적절한 것은 ②이다.

지문 해석

롤러코스터가 트랙의 최초의 리프트 언덕을 오르면서, 이 롤러코스터는 위치 에너지를 만들어 내고 있다 — 더 높이 이것이 지구 위로 올라가면 올라갈수록, 그만큼 중력의 당기는 힘이 더 강해질 것이다. 롤러코스터가 리프트 언덕을 넘어 하강하기 시작할 때, 그것의 위치 에너지는 운동 에너지, 즉 이동 에너지가 된다. 일반적인 오해는 롤러코스터가 트랙을 따라 에너지를 잃는다는 것이다. 그러나, 에너지 보존의 법칙이라고 불리는 물리학의 중요한 법칙은 에너지가 결코 생성되거나 파괴될 수 없다는 것이다. 그것은 단순히 한 형태에서 다른 형태로 변할 뿐이다. 트랙이 다시 오르막길로 올라갈 때마다 그 차량들의 가속도 — 자신의 운동 에너지 — 는 그것들을 위로 옮기고 그것은 위치 에너지를 만들어 롤러코스터는 반복적으로 잠재 에너지를 운동 에너지로 전환하였다 다시 되돌아온다. 놀이기구가 끝날 때, 롤러코스터 자동차는 두 표면 사이에 마찰을 일으키는 브레이크 장치에 의해 속도를 늦춘다. 이 운동은 그것들을 뜨겁게 만들며, 이는 제동 중에 운동 에너지가 열 에너지로 바뀐다는 것을 의미한다. 탑승자들은 트랙의 끝에서 에너지를 잃는다고 잘못 생각할 수 있다, 그러나 그 에너지는 단지 다른 형태로 혹은 다른 형태에서 바뀔 뿐이다.

선지 해석

① 중력
② 마찰
③ 진공
④ 가속

지문 어휘

- [ ] lift hill 리프트 언덕
- [ ] potential energy 위치 에너지
- [ ] gravity 중력
- [ ] kinetic energy 운동 에너지
- [ ] misperception 오해
- [ ] law of conservation of energy 에너지 보존의 법칙
- [ ] momentum 탄력, 가속도, 운동량
- [ ] rider 승객

22 　　　　　　　　　　　　　　　　　정답 ④

정답 해설

이 글은 특정 직업에서 수화가 어떻게 사용되고 있으며, 앞으로 더 발전될 필요성이 있음을 설명하고 있다. 4번째 문장에서 '서로 좀 떨어져서 일하는 사람들은, 만약 그들이 소통하기를 원한다면, 특별한 신호를 고안해야 한다'의 진술을 통해서 빈칸에 들어갈 말로 가장 적절한 것은 ④이다.

지문 해석

사람들이 그들의 손짓 언어를 조금 더 완전하게 발전시켜야 하는 몇몇 직업들이 있다. 우리는 심판들과 심판들이 선수들에게 지시를 전달하기 위해 팔과 손을 사용하는 것을 본다 — 크리켓처럼 손가락 하나를 위로 향하게 하면 타자가 아웃되어 삼주문을 떠나야 한다는 것을 의미한다. 오케스트라 지휘자는 자신의 움직임을 통해 음악가들을 통제한다. 서로 좀 떨어져서 일하는 사람들은, 만약 그들이 소통하기를 원한다면, 특별한 신호를 고안해야 한다. 기계들이 매우 큰 소리를 내는 공장과 같은 시끄러운 환경에서 일하는 사람들이나, 초등학생들로 가득 찬 수영장 주변의 인명 구조원들도 마찬가지이다.

선지 해석

① 그들의 부모들과 아이들을 지지하는
② 완전히 새로운 업무 방식에 적응하는
③ 기본적인 인권을 위해 법정에서 싸우는
④ 그들의 손짓 언어를 조금 더 완전하게 발전시켜야 하는

지문 어휘

- [ ] referee 심판
- [ ] umpire 심판
- [ ] cricket 크리켓(스포츠)
- [ ] conductor 지휘자
- [ ] noisy 시끄러운, 떠들썩한
- [ ] lifeguard 인명 구조원, 안전 요원
- [ ] entirely 전적으로, 완전히
- [ ] fully 완전히, 충분히
- [ ] signing 손짓 언어, 수화

23 　　　　　　　　　　　　　　　　　정답 ③

정답 해설

수력학의 문명과 물의 관계에 대한 글로, 6번째 문장에서 '로마 제국은 그들이 지배했던 땅 전체에 걸쳐 광대한 송수로 망을 건설했기 때문에, 로마인들은 물과 권력 사이의 관련성을 이해했는데, 그것들 중 많은 것들이 손상되지 않은 채 있다'의 진술을 통해서 빈칸에 들어갈 말로 가장 적절한 것은 ③이다.

지문 해석

물과 문명은 밀접한 관련이 있다. "수력학의 문명"이라는 아이디어는, 물이 역사를 통틀어 많은 대규모 문명에 대한 통합적 배경과 타당한 이유라고, 주장한다. 예컨대, 여러 세기 동안 존속된 다양한 중국 제국들은 부분적으로 황허 강을 따라 홍수를 통제함으로써 그들이 그랬던 만큼 오랫동안 살아남았다. 수력 이론의 한 가지 해석은, 인구를 대도시로 모은 타당한 이유가 물을 관리하기 위한 것이라는 점이다. 또 다른 해석은 대규모 치수 사업이 대도시의 출현을 가능하게 한다고 말한다. 로마 제국은 그들이 지배했던 땅 전체에 걸쳐 광대한 송수로 망을 건설했기 때문에, 로마인들은 물과 권력 사이의 관련성을 이해했는데,

> 그것들 중 많은 것들이 손상되지 않은 채 있다. 예컨대, 프랑스 남부에 있는 Pont du Gard는 오늘날 수력 공공 기반 시설에 대한 인류의 투자의 증거로서 세워져 있다. 로마 통치자들은 <u>그들의 권한을 집중하고 강화하는</u> 방법으로 도로, 다리 그리고 수계(水系)를 건설했다.

선지 해석
① 젊은이들을 교육하는 것에 집중하는
② 지역 시장에서 자유로운 거래를 금지하는
③ 그들의 권한을 집중하고 강화하는
④ 그들의 토지를 다른 나라에 넘겨주는

지문 어휘
- civilization 문명
- go hand in hand 밀접한 관련이 있다
- justification 정당화
- Yellow River 황하
- interpretation 해석
- intact 손상되지 않은, 온전한, 그대로의
- infrastructure 기반 시설
- testament 증거
- governor 통치자, 지배자
- authority 권위, 권한
- property 재산, 자산, 토지, 특성, 속성
- give up to (~에게) ~을 넘겨주다

24 정답 ①

정답 해설
영국인들의 과소비로 인한 사회와 환경의 문제를 주제로 하는 글이다. 본문의 마지막 문장에서 연간 30만 톤의 옷을 버리고 있다고 언급하고 2번째 문장에서는 한두 번 입고 버릴 만큼 많은 옷을 사고 있다고 언급하고 있으므로 빈칸에는 필요하지 않은 옷을 구입하는 데 돈을 쓰고 있다는 내용이 들어가야 올바르다. 따라서 밑줄 친 부분에 들어갈 말로 가장 적절한 것은 ①이다.

지문 해석
> 소셜 미디어, 잡지, 상품 진열장은 매일 사람들에게 살 것을 쏟아 붓고, 영국 소비자들은 그 어느 때 보다 더 많은 옷과 신발을 사고 있다. 온라인 쇼핑은 고객들이 아무 생각 없이 사는 것이 쉽고, 한편, 주요 브랜드들은 그들이 두세 번 입고 버려지는 일회용품처럼 취급될 정도로 그렇게 싼 옷을 제공하는 것을 의미한다. 영국에서 보통 사람들은 1년에 새 옷에 1,000파운드 이상을 소비하는데, 이것은 그들의 수입의 약 4%에 해당한다. 그것은 별것 아닌 것처럼 들릴 수도 있지만, 그 수치는 사회와 환경을 위해 훨씬 더 걱정스러운 두 가지 추세를 숨기고 있다. 첫째, 소비자 지출의 상당 부분은 신용카드를 통해 이루어진다. 영국인들은 현재 신용카드 회사에 성인 1인당 약 670파운드를 빚지고 있다. 이는 평균 의상 예산의 66%에 해당하는 금액이다. 또한, 사람들은 그들이 가지고 있지 않은 돈을 쓸 뿐만 아니라, <u>그들이 필요하지 않은</u> 것을 사기 위해 그것을 사용하고 있다. 영국은 매년 30만 톤의 옷을 버리며, 그 중 대부분은 매립지로 들어간다.

선지 해석
① 그들은 필요하지 않은
② 일상 필수품인
③ 곧 재활용될
④ 다른 사람들에게 건네줄 수 있는

지문 어휘
- bombard 쏟아 붓다, 퍼붓다
- disposable item 일회용품
- throw away 버리다, 없애다
- figure 수치, 인물, 모양
- spending 지출
- wardrobe 옷장, 옷
- budget 예산, 비용
- via 경유하여, 거쳐, 통하여
- landfill 매립지
- necessity 필수품
- hand down ~을 물려주다

25 정답 ②

정답 해설
고급 식당의 고객들은 식당의 우수성을 기대하고 기꺼이 높은 가격을 지불하려고 한다는 내용을 설명하는 글이다. 빈칸의 앞 내용은 레스토랑의 서비스 향상에 대한 내용이고 빈칸의 뒤에서 비용을 기꺼이 지불한다고 하였으므로 밑줄 친 부분에 들어갈 말로 가장 적절한 것은 ②이다.

지문 해석
> 우수성은 고급 식사에서 절대적인 전제조건인데, 그 이유는 부과된 요금이 매우 비싸기 때문이다. 운영자는 식당을 효율적으로 만들기 위해 가능한 모든 것을 할 수 있지만, 손님들은 여전히 신중하고 개인적인 서비스, 즉 매우 숙련된 요리사가 주문하도록 준비되고 능숙한 종업원에 의해 전달되는 음식을 기대한다. 이 서비스는 말 그대로 육체노동이기 때문에 생산성에 있어 약간 개선만이 가능하다. 예를 들어, 요리사, 서빙하는 사람 또는 바텐더가 인간 수행의 한계에 도달하기 전에는 훨씬 더 빨리 움직일 수 있다. 따라서 효율성 향상을 통한 오직 보통의 절약만 가능하므로 가격 상승은 <u>불가피하다</u>. (가격이 오르면 소비자들이 더 안목이 있다는 것은 경제학의 공리이다.) 따라서 이 고급 레스토랑의 손님은 우수성을 기대하고, 요구하며, 기꺼이 비용을 지불한다.

선지 해석
① 터무니없는, 우스꽝스러운
② 불가피한
③ 말도 안 되는, 터무니없는
④ 상상할 수 없는

지문 어휘
- excellence 뛰어남, 우수함
- absolute 절대적인
- prerequisite 전제 조건
- fine dining 고급 식당
- operator 경영자, 운영자
- efficient 효율적인
- manual labor 육체노동, 수작업
- marginal 미미한, 중요하지 않은, 주변적인
- productivity 생산성
- moderate 보통의, 적당한
- escalation 상승
- axiom of economic 경제학의 공리
- discriminate 구별하다, 식별하다, 차별하다
- discriminating 안목 있는
- clientele 손님, 고객

26
정답 ④

정답 해설
멀리 떨어진 팀과의 협업을 위한 신뢰와 자율성의 중요성을 강조하는 글이다. 3번째 문장과 4번째 문장에서 '권한을 부여받는', '신뢰할 수 있는 사람에게 책임을 넘기는 것'은 자율성을 주는 것을 의미한다. 따라서 밑줄 친 부분에 들어갈 말로 가장 적절한 것은 ④이다.

지문 해석
점점 더 많은 지도자들이 컨설턴트나 프리랜서뿐만 아니라 국내나 전 세계에 흩어져 있는 팀들과 함께 멀리서 작업하고 있기 때문에 당신은 그들에게 더 많은 자율성을 부여해야 할 것이다. 당신이 더 많은 신뢰를 줄수록, 다른 사람들은 당신을 더 신뢰한다. 나는 직무 만족도와 사람들이 매 순간마다 자신들을 따라다니는 사람 없이 일을 완벽히 수행하기 위해 얼마나 권한을 부여 받는지 사이에는 직접적인 상관관계가 있다고 확신한다. 신뢰할 수 있는 사람에게 책임을 넘기는 것은 조직이 보다 원활하게 운영되도록 할 뿐만 아니라 당신이 더 중요한 사안들에 집중하도록 더 많은 시간을 마련해 줄 수도 있다.

선지 해설
① 일
② 보상들
③ 제한들
④ 자율성

지문 어휘
- remotely 원격으로
- scattered 산발적인, 흩어져 있는, 드문드문 있는
- autonomy 자율성, 자주성
- correlation 상관관계, 연관성
- job satisfaction 직무 만족도
- empower 권한을 부여하다
- execute 실행하다, 수행하다
- give away 나누어주다, 내주다
- smoothly 원활하게
- organization 조직, 단체

27
정답 ①

정답 해설
이 글은 가을의 나뭇잎이 자연의 순환과 새로운 성장을 위한 과정에서 어떤 역할을 하는지를 설명하고 있다. 이 문제를 해결하기 위해서는 글 전체의 맥락을 파악해야한다. 자작나무, 참나무, 전나무, 소나무 등은 항상 새로운 성장을 하며 오래된 것을 제거해야 하며, 이것은 가을마다 잎이 떨어지는 것을 통해 나타냄을 파악해야 한다. 즉 나무가 폐기물을 제거하고 오래된 잎을 떨어뜨리는 이러한 역할을 하는 것을 비유적인 표현으로 빈칸에 들어갈 말로 가장 적절한 것은 ①이다.

지문 해석
너도밤나무, 떡갈나무, 가문비나무, 소나무는 항상 새로운 성장을 하고, 오래된 것을 없애야 한다. 가장 분명한 변화는 매년 가을에 일어난다. 잎은 그들의 목적에 부합해 왔다. 잎들은 이제 닳아서 곤충들의 손상으로 가득 차 있다. 나무들이 그들에게 작별을 고하기 전에, 그들[나무]은 폐기물들을 그들[나뭇잎]에게 퍼 붓는다. 당신은 그들이 스스로를 구제하기 위해 이 기회를 잡고 있다고 말할 수 있다. 그리고 나서, 그들은 그것이 자라고 있는 나뭇가지로부터 각각의 잎을 분리하기 위해 약한 조직의 층을 기른다. 그리고 잎들은 다음번 산들 바람에 땅으로 굴러 떨어진다. 이제 땅을 덮고 당신이 그것들[낙엽들] 사이로 애써 나아갈 때 그렇게 만족스러운 소리를 내는 바스락거리는 나뭇잎들은 기본적으로 나무 화장지이다.

선지 해설
① 나무 화장지
② 식물 부엌
③ 나무의 폐
④ 곤충의 부모

지문 어휘
- beech 너도밤나무
- oak 떡갈나무
- spruce 가문비나무
- autumn 가을
- pine 소나무
- get rid of ~을 제거하다
- obvious 분명한, 명백한
- waste product 폐기물
- separate 분리되다, 갈라지다
- twig 잔가지
- tumble 굴러 떨어지다, 크게 추락하다
- breeze 산들바람
- rustling 바스락거리는 소리

28
정답 ①

정답 해설
작은 씨앗의 생존과 그 조건에 대한 글로 작은 씨앗들이 어떻게 역경을 극복하며 생존하는지를 설명하며, 어떤 환경에서 씨앗의 생명이 위협받는지도 설명하고 있다. 6번째 문장에서 '만약 이런 솜털 같은 작은 씨앗 꾸러미가 가문비나무나 너도밤나무 숲에 떨어진다면, 씨앗의 삶은 시작하기 전에 끝난다'의 진술을 통해서 빈칸에는 이러한 작은 씨앗들이 생존하기 위해서는 다른 개체들이 없는 곳이 필요함을 알 수 있다. 따라서 빈칸에 들어갈 말로 가장 적절한 것은 ①이다.

지문 해석
버드나무와 미루나무의 씨앗은 너무 작아서 솜털에서 두 개의 작고 어두운 점을 발견할 수 있다. 이 씨앗들 중 하나는 무게가 0.0001 그램밖에 나가지 않는다. 이렇게 약한 에너지를 비축하면, 묘목은 수증기가 다 떨어지기 전에 겨우 1~2 밀리미터만 자랄 수 있고 어린 잎을 이용해 스스로 만든 음식에 의존해야 한다. 하지만 그것은 작은 새싹을 위협할 경쟁이 없는 곳에서만 효과가 있다. 그것에 그늘을 드리우는 다른 식물들은 새로운 생명을 즉시 소멸시킬 것이다. 그래서, 만약 이런 솜 털 같은 작은 씨앗 꾸러미가 가문비나무나 너도밤나무 숲에 떨어진다면, 씨앗의 삶은 시작도 하기 전에 끝난다. 그래서 버드나무와 미루나무들은 빈 지역에 정착하기를 선호한다.

선지 해설
① 빈 지역에 정착하기를 선호한다
② 초식동물의 먹이로 선정되다
③ 인간의 개입을 피하도록 진화해왔다
④ 먼 겨울까지 그들의 죽은 잎을 달다

지문 어휘
- willow 버드나무
- poplar 미루나무
- make out ~을 알아보다
- fluffy 부드러운, 솜털의
- seedling 묘목
- run out of ~을 다 써버리다
- sprout 싹
- shade 그늘, 그늘지게 하다
- beech 너도밤나무
- unoccupied 비어있는, 점령되지 않은

29 정답 ①

정답 해설
'탄소-14 연대 측정법'을 주제로 하는 글이다. 이 측정법은 유기체가 사망한 후 탄소-14가 질량을 잃으며 붕괴하는 방식으로 연대를 측정하는 탄소-14 방식이다. (A)는 탄소-14가 사망한 후 시간이 지남에 따라 감소한다는 것을 나타내야 하므로 '감소하다(decreases)'가 들어가야 적절하고, (B)는 유기체가 살아있을 때 탄소-14의 방사선이 감지될 수 있으며, 탄소-14 농도는 유기체가 얼마나 오래 살아있었는지를 측정하는 것이라는 것을 나타내므로 '죽은(dead)'이 들어가야 적절하다.

지문 해석
유기체가 살아있을 때, 그것은 주변의 공기에서 이산화탄소를 흡수한다. 이산화탄소의 대부분은 탄소-12로 이루어져 있지만, 일부는 탄소-14로 이루어져 있다. 그래서 살아있는 유기체는 항상 아주 적은 양의 방사성 탄소인 탄소-14를 포함하고 있다. 살아있는 유기체 옆에 있는 검출기는 유기체에서 탄소-14에 의해 방출된 방사선을 기록할 것이다. 그 유기체가 죽으면 더 이상 이산화탄소를 흡수하지 않는다. 어떤 새로운 탄소-14도 추가되지 않고, 오래된 탄소-14는 천천히 질소로 분해된다. 탄소-14의 양은 시간이 지날수록 서서히 (A) 감소한다. 시간이 지남에 따라 탄소-14로부터의 방사선이 점점 더 적게 만들어진다. 그러므로 유기체에 대해 검출된 탄소-14 방사선의 양은 유기체가 (B) 죽은 지 얼마나 됐는지에 대한 측정법이다. 유기체의 연대를 결정하는 이 방법은 탄소-14 연대 측정이라고 불린다. 탄소-14의 부패는 고고학자들이 한 때 살았던 물질의 연대를 알아낼 수 있게 해준다. 남아있는 방사선량을 측정하는 것은 대략적인 연대를 나타낸다.

선지 해석
  (A)   (B)
① 감소한다 …… 죽은
② 증가한다 …… 살아있는
③ 감소한다 …… 생산적인
④ 증가한다 …… 소극적인

지문 어휘
- organism 생물체
- carbon dioxide 이산화탄소
- radioactive 방사성의
- radiation 방사선
- nitrogen 질소
- determine 결정하다, 알아내다, 밝히다
- decay 부패, 부식, 부패하다, 썩다
- measure 측정하다, 재다
- archaeologist 고고학자
- remaining 남은, 남아 있는
- approximate 대략적인, 근사치인

30 정답 ②

정답 해설
생명체의 멸종과 진화를 주제로 하는 글로, 빈칸이 있는 문장 다음에 150만 종과 천만 종의 생물들을 진술하고 있다. 따라서 밑줄 친 부분에 들어갈 말로 가장 적절한 것은 ②이다.

지문 해석
과거와 현재의 모든 생명체는 사라졌거나 혹은 멸종될 것이다. 그러나, 각 종들이 지난 38억 년의 지구 생명의 역사 동안 사라지면서, 새로운 종들이 그것들을 대체하기 위해 혹은 신생의 자원들을 이용하기 위해 필연적으로 나타났다. 소수의 아주 단순한 유기체로부터 다수의 복잡한 다세포 형태가 이 거대한 기간에 걸쳐 진화했다. 19세기 영국 박물학자 Charles Darwin이 "미스터리 중의 미스터리"라고 한때 언급했던 새로운 종의 기원은 인간이 지구를 함께 공유하는 이 놀라운 생물체들의 다양성을 만들어내는 데 책임이 있는 자연적인 종분화 과정이다. 비록 분류학자들은 현재 약 150만 개의 살아있는 종을 인정하지만, 실제 숫자는 아마도 천만 종에 가까울 것이다. 이 다수의 생물학적 지위를 인정하는 것은 무엇이 하나의 종을 구성하고 있는지에 대한 명확한 이해를 요구하며, 이것은 진화 생물학자들이 아직 보편적으로 받아들여지는 정의에 합의하지 못했다는 점을 고려하면 쉬운 일이 아니다.

선지 해석
① 생물학자들의 기술
② 생물체들의 다양성
③ 멸종된 유기체들의 목록
④ 멸종 위기 종의 수집

지문 어휘
- vanish 사라지다
- creature 생물
- extinct 멸종된, 사라진
- species 종
- multicellular 다세포의
- evolve 진화하다
- speciation 종 분화
- taxonomist 분류학자
- constitute 구성하다, 이루다
- universally 보편적으로
- diversity 다양성
- inventory 목록

31 정답 ③

정답 해설
'우리가 완전히 알지 못하는 것, 우리의 날마다의 일을 하는 것, 특정한 문제를 해결하는 것, 도덕적인 문제들, 생각들' 등이 빈칸에 대한 예시들로 예시들을 일반화할 수 있는 표현으로 밑줄 친 부분에 들어갈 말로 가장 적절한 것은 ③이다.

지문 해석

우리 모두는 어떤 것을 물려받는다. 어떤 경우에는, 그것은 돈, 재산 또는 할머니의 웨딩드레스나 아버지의 도구 세트와 같은 가족의 가보와 같은 어떤 물건일 수 있다. 하지만 그 외에도, 우리 모두는 다른 것을 물려받는다, 훨씬 덜 구체적이고 유형적인 것, 심지어 우리가 완전히 알지 못할 수도 있는 것도 말이다. 그것은 일상적인 일을 하는 방법일 수도 있고, 우리가 특정한 문제를 해결하거나 우리 자신을 위한 도덕적 문제를 결정하는 방법일 수도 있다. 그것은 휴일이나 특정한 날짜에 소풍을 가는 전통을 지키는 특별한 방식일 수도 있다. 그것은 우리의 사고에 중요하거나 중심적인 것일 수도 있고, 우리가 오랫동안 무심코 받아들인 사소한 것일 수도 있다.

선지 해석

① 우리 일상생활과 관련이 거의 없는
② 우리 도덕적 기준에 반하는
③ 훨씬 덜 구체적이고 유형적인
④ 거대한 큰 금전적 가치를 가진

지문 어휘

☐ inherit 물려받다
☐ property 재산, 자산, 토지, 특성, 속성
☐ heirloom 가보, 세습자산
☐ daily task 일상적인 일
☐ particular 특정한
☐ moral 도덕적인
☐ minor 중요하지 않은
☐ casually 일상적으로, 무의식적으로
☐ concrete 구체적인, 사실에 의거한
☐ tangible 유형의, 만질[감지할] 수 있는
☐ monetary 금전의, 통화의

32   정답 ①

정답 해설

외부 영향과 동료압박에 대한 글로, 외부 압박과 경쟁에 대한 생각을 통해 사람들이 어떻게 영향을 받고 반응하는지를 구체적인 사례를 통해 설명하고 있다. 3번째 문장부터 6번째 문장까지가 구체적인 문장이고, 마지막 두개의 문장을 통해서 '압박'에 대한 목표에 대해 설명하고 있다. 따라서 빈칸에는 이들 일반화할 수 있는 표현으로 빈칸에 들어갈 말로 가장 적절한 것은 ①이다.

지문 해석

감수성이 예민한 젊은이들만 동료 압박에 영향을 받기 쉬운 것은 아니다. 우리 대부분은 아마도 판매원에게 압력을 받은 경험이 있을 것이다. 당신은 지금까지 판매 대표가 당신에게 70%의 경쟁자들이 그들의 서비스를 사용하고 있으니, 당신은 왜 사용하지 않는가라고 말함으로써 당신에게 '사무실용 서비스(office solution)'을 판매하려고 시도한 적이 있지 않은가? 하지만 경쟁자들 중 70%가 바보라면 어떻게 할 것인가? 아니면 그 70%에게 너무 많은 부가가치가 주어지거나 기회를 거절할 수 없을 정도로 낮은 가격을 제시한다면 어떻게 할 것인가? 이 관행은 오직 한 가지만 하기 위해 고안되었다. 당신이 무언가를 놓치고 있거나 다른 사람들이 당신만 알고 있다는 것을 느끼게 하기 위해서.

선지 해석

① 동료 압박
② 충동구매
③ 괴롭히기 직전
④ 치열한 경쟁

지문 어휘

☐ impressionable 감수성이 예민한, 쉽게 외부의 영향을 받는
☐ youth 젊은이
☐ subject to 영향을 받기 쉬운
☐ salesman 판매원, 영업 사원
☐ competitor 경쟁자, 참가자
☐ idiot 바보
☐ value added 부가 가치
☐ keen 치열한, 열렬한, 예리한
☐ miss out 놓치다, ~을 빠뜨리다

33   정답 ②

정답 해설

자연적 위험에 대한 이해와 대처하는 사람들의 방식대한 글로, 사람들이 항상 이성적으로 대처하는 것은 아님을 강조하고 있다. 빈칸에는 3번째 문장의 '그러나, 인간이 항상 이성적인 것은 아니다'의 진술과 맥락을 같이 하는 '항상 적절하게 행동하지는 않는다'가 들어가야 한다. 특히 첫 번째 문장의 '이러한 것을 잘 아는 과학자조차도 늘 피할 수 있는 것은 아니다'의 진술을 통해서 사람들이 항상 이성적인 것은 아니라는 것을 강조하고 있다. 따라서 빈칸에 들어갈 말로 가장 적절한 것은 ②이다.

지문 해석

현재 자연적인 위험 요소들과 그것들이 사람들과 그것들의 재산에 미치는 부정적인 영향들에 대해 많은 것이 알려져 있다. 어떤 논리적인 사람이 그러한 잠재적인 영향을 피하거나 최소한 그러한 영향을 최소화하기 위해 그들의 행동이나 재산을 수정하는 것은 명백해 보일 것이다. 그러나, 인간이 항상 이성적인 것은 아니다. 누군가가 개인적인 경험을 하거나 그러한 경험을 가진 누군가를 알기 전까지, 대부분의 사람들은 무의식적으로 "여기서는 그런 일이 일어나지 않을 것이다" 또는 "나에게는 그런 일이 일어나지 않을 것이다"라고 믿는다. 위험 요소들, 그것들이 발생할 확률들, 그리고 사건의 비용에 대해 아는 것이 있는 과학자들조차 항상 적절하게 행동하지는 않는다.

선지 해석

① 침묵을 지키는 것을 거부하다
② 항상 적절하게 행동하지는 않는다
③ 유전적 요인을 가장 높은 목표로 둔다
④ 자연의 위험 요소를 정의하는 데 어려움을 겪다

지문 어휘

☐ hazard 위험 요소
☐ negative 부정적인
☐ obvious 분명한, 명백한
☐ at least 적어도
☐ rational 합리적인
☐ modify 수정하다, 변경하다
☐ subconscious 잠재의식적인, 무의식적인
☐ occurrence 발생
☐ appropriately 적절하게
☐ property 재산, 자산, 토지, 특성, 속성
☐ odds 가능성, 역경, 곤란

34

정답 ③

정답 해설

지식의 단편화와 의미의 상실을 주제로 하는 글로, 현대 교육은 단편적인 지식으로 가득한 세계를 형성하며, 이로 인한 의미의 상실과 아노미에 대한 우려를 나타내는 글이다. 4번째 문장에서 '그리하여 당신은 부분적인 견해를 갖게 된다'의 진술을 통해서 밑줄 친 부분에 들어갈 말로 가장 적절한 것은 ③이다.

지문 해석

왜 모든 것의 역사에 신경쓰는가? 오늘날 우리는 단편적으로 우리의 세계에 대해 가르치고 배운다. 문학 수업에서는 유전자에 대해 배우지 않고; 물리학 수업에서는 인간의 진화에 대해 배우지 않는다. 그래서 당신은 부분적인 세계관을 가진다. 그것은 교육에서 의미를 찾는 것을 어렵게 만든다. 프랑스 사회학자 Emile Durkheim은 이 혼미감과 무의미감을 아노미라고 불렀고 그는 그것이 절망과 심지어 자살로 이어질 수 있다고 주장했다. 독일 사회학자 Max Weber는 세계의 "각성"에 관해 이야기했다. 과거에, 사람들은 그들의 세계에 대한 통일된 시각 즉, 보통 그들 자신의 종교적 전통의 기원 이야기들에 의해 제공된 시각을 가지고 있었다. 그 통일된 시각은 목적감, 의미감, 심지어 세상과 삶에 대한 황홀감을 주었다. 하지만, 오늘날, 많은 작가들은 과학과 합리성의 세계에서 무의미감은 불가피하다고 주장했다. 현대성은 무의미함을 의미하는 것 같다.

선지 해석

① 과거에 역사 연구는 과학으로부터의 각성을 필요로 했다
② 최근에 과학은 우리에게 많은 기발한 묘책과 의의를 주었다
③ 오늘날 우리는 우리 세계에 대해 단편적으로 가르치고 배운다
④ 최근에 역사는 몇 가지 분야로 나누어졌다

지문 어휘

☐ bother 신경 쓰다, 귀찮게 하다
☐ gene 유전자
☐ evolution 진화
☐ partial view 부분적인 세계관
☐ disorientation 혼미, 방향 감각 상실
☐ meaninglessness 무의미함
☐ anomie 무질서, 사회적 불안
☐ despair 절망, 절망하다
☐ suicide 자살
☐ disenchantment 각성, 눈뜸, 환멸감
☐ unified 통일된, 통합된, 하나로 된
☐ inevitable 불가피한
☐ rationality 합리성
☐ modernity 현대성
☐ in fragments 단편적으로
☐ delve into 조사하다

35

정답 ③

정답 해설

1840년대 아일랜드 기근과 인구 변화에 대한 글로, 아일랜드의 기근으로 인해 약 백만 명의 사망과 약 4백만 명의 인구 변화가 발생했던 역사를 다루고 있다. (A) 뒤 문장에서 앞 문장을 보충 설명하는 구조인데, '그들은 살아남을 정도로 충분히 먹지 않았다'의 진술을 통해 '기아(starvation)'가 가장 적절하고, (B) 뒤 문장에서 '고향 섬에서 미국으로 떠났다'의 진술을 통해 '이주하다(emigrate)'가 가장 적절하다.

지문 해석

1840년대에 아일랜드의 섬은 기근에 시달렸다. 아일랜드는 인구를 먹일 충분한 식량을 생산할 수 없었기 때문에, 약 백만 명의 사람들이 (A) 기아로 죽었다; 그들은 단지 살아남기 위해 먹기에 충분하지 않았다. 이 기근은 또 다른 125만 명의 사람들이 (B) 이주하도록 야기했다; 많은 사람들은 그들의 고향 섬에서 미국으로 떠났다; 나머지는 캐나다, 호주, 칠레, 그리고 다른 나라들로 갔다. 기근 전에 아일랜드의 인구는 약 6백만 명이었다. 그 엄청난 식량 부족 후에 그것은 약 4백만이었다.

선지 해석

	(A)	(B)
①	탈수	추방당하다
②	정신적 외상	이주해 오다
③	기아, 굶주림	이주하다
④	피로	구금되다

지문 어휘

☐ suffer 시달리다, 고통을 받다
☐ famine 기근
☐ emigrate 이주하다
☐ leave for ~로 떠나다
☐ feed 먹이를 주다
☐ approximately 대략적으로
☐ shortage 부족

36

정답 ①

정답 해설

언어의 이중성과 소리의 복잡성에 대한 글로, 언어와 소리는 중복되는 연결고리를 통해 의미를 전달하며, 인간과 새 모두에게 특화된 음성 체계가 뇌의 절반을 통해 학습되며 사용됨을 설명하고 있다. 빈칸 뒤에 이어지는 내용은 빈칸의 내용과 같은 재진술로 '배열순서가 중요하다'의 의미이므로 빈칸에 들어갈 말로 가장 적절한 것은 ①이다.

지문 해석

엄밀한 의미의 언어는 그 자체로 두 개의 층을 이루고 있다. 개별적 소음들은 단지 가끔씩만 의미가 있다. 대부분의 경우 다채로운 말의 소리가 중복되는 연결고리를 통해 결합되었을 때에만 일관성 있는 메시지를 전달하게 되는데 이는 마치 다양한 색깔의 아이스크림이 녹아 서로 섞이는 것과 같다. 새소리에 있어서도 또한 개별적인 음들은 종종 거의 의미가 없다: 배열순서가 중요하다. 인간과 새 둘 다에게 있어 이러한 특화된 음성 체계를 조절하는 것은 뇌의 절반, 주로 왼쪽 절반에 의해 행하여지며 그 체계는 상대적으로 삶의 초기에 학습된다. 그리고 많은 인간의 언어가 방언을 가지고 있듯이 몇몇 종의 새들 역시 그러하다: 캘리포니아에서 흰줄무늬 참새는 지역마다 다른 노랫소리를 갖고 있어서 캘리포니아 사람들은 아마도 이러한 참새 소리를 들음으로써 자신이 그 주의 어디에 있는지를 구별할 수 있을 것이다.

선지 해석

① 개별적인 음들은 종종 거의 의미가 없다
② 주기적인 소리가 중요하다
③ 방언이 중요한 역할을 하다
④ 어떤 소리 체계도 존재하지 않다

지문 어휘
- layered 층이 있는, 층을 이룬
- occasionally 가끔
- meaningful 의미 있는
- convey 전달하다
- coherent 일관성 있는, 논리 정연한
- overlapping 겹쳐진
- sequence 순서, 차례
- dialect 방언, 사투리
- white-crowned sparrow 흰줄무늬 참새
- area 지역
- note 음, 음표, 메모, 주목[주의]하다
- rhythmic 주기적인

37
정답 ②

정답 해설
심리학자 Daniel Kahneman으로 말미암은 의사결정과 경제학의 패러다임 변화에 대한 글로, '인간은 이성적 의사결정자들이다'의 '통념'을 바탕으로, 이것을 논박하는 단락구조를 가지고 있다. 빈칸 앞에서 진술한 '하나의 선택이 다수의 개별적 요소들에 의해 설명될 때까지 배짱에 의거한 의사결정을 지연시키는 것이다'의 진술을 통해서 밑줄 친 부분에 들어갈 말로 가장 적절한 것은 ②이다.

지문 해석
노벨상 수상자인 심리학자 Daniel Kahneman은 인간이 이성적 의사결정자라는 개념을 뒤집으며 경제학에 관한 세계의 사고방식을 변화시켰다. 그 과정에서 그의 학문 전체에 걸친 영향력은 의사들이 의학적 결정을 내리는 방식, 그리고 투자가들이 월 스트리트에서의 위험을 평가하는 방식을 변화시켰다. 한 논문에서 Kahneman과 그의 동료들은 큰 전략적 결정을 내리기 위한 과정에 대한 개요를 제시했다. '조정 평가 프로토콜', 혹은 MAP라고 부르는 그들이 제시한 접근법은 한 가지 간단한 목표를 갖는다: 하나의 선택이 다수의 개별적 요소들에 의해 설명될 때까지 직감에 의거한 의사결정을 연기하는 것이다. "MAP의 가장 중요한 목표 중에 하나는 기본적으로 직감을 미루는 것이다"라고 Kahneman은 최근 '포스트'와의 인터뷰에서 말했다. 이러한 구조화된 과정은 이전에 선택된 여섯 개에서 일곱 개의 요소들에 의거하여 하나의 결정을 분해하고 각각을 개별적으로 논의한 후, 이들에게 상대적인 백분점수를 부여하고 마지막으로 총체적 판단을 위해 그 점수를 사용할 것을 요구한다.

선지 해석
① 개선시키는
② 미루는
③ 소유하는
④ 촉진하는

지문 어휘
- psychologist 심리학자
- upend 철저한[근본적인] 영향을 주다, 거꾸로 세우다, 엎어놓다
- rational 합리적인, 이성적인
- discipline 훈육, 훈련, 학과
- alter 변경하다, 바꾸다
- evaluate 평가하다
- outline 개요를 제시하다, 윤곽을 보여주다
- label ~라고 부르다, 분류하다
- gut 직감, 창자, 배짱
- intuition 직감, 직관
- call for 요구하다
- attribute 특성, 탓으로 돌리다
- holistic 전체적인, 종합적인

38
정답 ④

정답 해설
양심, 생활위생 그리고 성공과의 관계를 주제로 하는 글로, 일반적으로 성실한 사람들은 생활을 잘 정돈하며 일을 효율적으로 처리함으로써 성공을 이루는 경향이 있다는 심리학적 연구 결과를 보여주는 글이다. 결국 성실하면 불성실과 무질서로 인해 초래되는 스트레스를 겪지 않아도 된다는 표현이 들어가야 한다. 따라서 빈칸에 들어갈 말로 가장 적절한 것은 ④이다.

지문 해석
"매우 성실한 직원들은 나머지 우리들보다 일련의 업무를 더 잘한다."고 Illinois 대학 심리학자 Brent Roberts는 말하는데, 그는 성실함을 연구했다. Roberts는 그들의 성공을 "위생" 요인들에 돌렸다. 성실한 사람들은 그들의 생활을 잘 정돈하는 경향이 있다. 무질서한, 불성실한 사람은 그들의 파일들 사이에서 올바른 서류를 뽑아내기 위해 20분이나 30분을 허비할지도 모르는데, 이는 성실한 사람이라면 피하는 경향이 있는 비효율적인 경험이다. 기본적으로, 사람들은 성실함으로써, 자신들이 그렇지 않으면 만들어낼 스트레스를 회피한다.

선지 해석
① 방해들을 처리한다
② 철저히 일한다
③ 규범을 따른다
④ 스트레스를 회피한다

지문 어휘
- conscientious 양심적인, 성실한
- a series of 일련의
- psychologist 심리학자
- hygiene 위생
- tendency 경향, 동향, 성향
- organize 조직하다, 정리하다
- inefficient 비효율적인
- otherwise 그렇지 않으면, 다른 방식으로
- deal with 처리하다
- setback 방해, 차질
- thorough 철저한, 빈틈없는
- norm 규범, 규준, 기준
- sidestep 회피하다, 피하다

39
정답 ②

정답 해설
환경 파괴와 불평등의 시대를 주제로 하는 글로, 이 글은 기후 변화, 환경 파괴, 대량 멸종 등의 위기로 인한 현재의 지구 상황과 이로 인한 불평등을 강조하며, 'Capitalocene'이라는 용어를 제안하여 자본주의와 환경 파괴의 관련성을 강조하는 글이다. 빈칸 앞 문장에 세계에서 가장 부유한 40여 명이 최빈층 37억 명의 재산을 합한 만큼을 소유하며 환경에도 더 지대한 영향을 미치고 있다는 내용을 다루고 있다. 따라서 빈칸에 들어갈 말로 가장 적절한 것은 ②이다.

지문 해석

기후 변화, 산림파괴, 널리 퍼진 오염, 그리고 생물의 다양성의 여섯 번째 대량 멸종 모두 오늘날 우리 세계에서의 모든 삶을 정의한다 — (즉) "인류세"로 알려지게 된 시대로 정의한다. 이러한 위기들은 세계적인 환경적인 한계들을 매우 초과하는 생산과 소비들에 의해 만들어졌으나, 그러나 비난은 공평하게 공유되지 않는다. 세상의 42명의 가장 부자들이 가난한 37억 명의 부만큼을 가지고 있으며, 그들은 더 큰 환경적인 충격들을 만들어 낸다. 그래서, 몇몇 사람들은 끝없는 성장의 자본주의의 논리와 소수의 주머니로의 부의 축적이라는 자본주의의 논리를 반영하면서, 생태계의 파괴의 시대와 점점 커져가는 불평등을 묘사하기 위해서 "Capitalocene"이라는 용어를 사용하는 것을 제안해 왔다.

선지 해석

① 여전히 우리가 도달할 수 있는 더 좋은 세상
② 소수의 주머니로의 부의 축적
③ 기후변화에의 효과적인 대응
④ 더욱 성공할 수 있는 미래를 향한 불타는 욕망

지문 어휘

- deforestation 산림 파괴, 산림 벌채
- mass 대규모의
- widespread 널리 퍼진, 보편적인
- extinction 멸종
- biodiversity 생물 다양성
- Anthropocene 인류세
- underpin 뒷받침하다, 근거를 대다
- ecological 생태계의
- far from 전혀 ~이 아닌
- generate 발생시키다, 만들어내다
- impact 영향, 충격
- evenly 균등하게
- devastation 황폐화, 대대적인 파괴
- inequality 불평등
- reflect 반영하다
- viable 성공[실행] 가능한

40 정답 ②

정답 해설

도시 공간의 활용의 일환으로 오피스 빌딩을 주거용으로 재개발하는 것을 주제로 하는 글로, 현재 사무용 건물 공석과 주택 부족 문제를 해결하기 위해 오피스 빌딩을 주거용으로 재개발해야 하는 필요성을 강조하고 있다. 따라서 빈칸에 들어갈 말로 가장 적절한 것은 ②이다.

지문 해석

현재 사무실용 건물의 수요 시장이 폭락하여 많은 비어있는 건물이 발생함에 따라, 우리는 주거용과 상업용 또는 사무용 기능의 교환이 가능한 계획을 개발할 필요가 있다. 이 빈자리는 역사적인 수준에 도달했다. 현재 네덜란드의 주요 도시들은 약 5백만 평방미터의 사무실 공간을 가지고 있는 반면 16만 채의 집이 부족하다. 네덜란드 부동산 개발 협회에 따르면 이 평방미터 중 적어도 100만미터가 공석이 될 것으로 예상된다고 한다. 주요 도시 주변에는 빈 사무실용 건물들로 이루어진 '유령 도시'의 위험이 현실화되고 있다. 이러한 전망에도 불구하고, 사무실용 건물 활동은 고수익의 기간 동안 계획되었던 것처럼 완전히 기울어져 계속되고 있다. 그러므로, 사무실용 건물에 대한 많은 계획이 주택을 위한 것으로 재개발되어야 하는 것이 필수적이다.

선지 해석

① 건물의 유지관리 비용을 줄이기 위해 새로운 디자인이 채택되어야 하는
② 사무실용 건물에 대한 많은 계획이 주택을 위한 것으로 재개발되어야 하는
③ 주거용 건물 상업용 건물로 전환되어야 하는
④ 우리는 가능한 한 많은 가게를 설계하고 전달하는

지문 어휘

- plummet 급락하다, 곤두박질치다
- vacant 비어 있는
- property 재산, 자산, 토지, 특성, 속성
- exchange 교환, 교환하다
- unoccupied 비어있는, 점령되지 않은
- shortage 부족
- ghost town 유령 도시
- high return 고소득, 고수익
- convert 개조하다, 전환시키다

41 정답 ①

정답 해설

언어와 지각의 관계를 에스키모어와 아즈텍어의 비교를 통해서 설명하는 글로, 언어학자의 가설에 따르면, 언어에 따라 우리의 지각도 달라진다는 것이다. 빈칸에는 에스키모어는 눈에 대해 32가지 다른 단어를 가지고 있는 것과 대조를 이루는 내용이 나와야 하며, 아즈텍어는 눈, 추위, 얼음을 하나의 단어로 구분하지 않아서 '하나의 같은 현상'으로 인식함을 표현해야 한다. 따라서 빈칸에 들어갈 말로 가장 적절한 것은 ①이다.

지문 해석

비록 우리 모두는 보는 눈, 듣는 귀, 냄새 맡는 코, 느끼는 피부, 맛보는 입과 같은 세상을 감지하는 동일한 신체적 기관을 가지고 있지만 언어학자 Edward Sapir와 Benjamin Lee Whorf에 의해 제안된 유명한 가설에 따르면, 세상에 대한 우리의 인식은 우리가 말하는 언어에 상당 부분 의존한다. 그들은 언어는 우리가 특정한 방식으로 세상을 "보는" 안경과 같다고 가설을 세웠다. 언어와 인식 사이의 관계에 대한 대표적인 예는 눈이라는 단어이다. 에스키모 언어들은 눈에 대한 32개의 다른 단어들을 가지고 있다. 예를 들어, 에스키모어들은 내리는 눈, 땅 위의 눈, 얼음처럼 단단하게 쌓인 눈, 미끄러운 눈, 바람이 불면 움직이는 눈, 그리고 우리가 "옥수수 가루"라고 부르는 눈에 대한 다른 단어들을 가지고 있다. 대조적으로, 멕시코의 고대 아즈텍 언어들은 눈, 추위, 그리고 얼음을 의미하는 단 하나의 단어만을 사용했다. 그러므로, 만일 Sapir-Whorf 가설이 맞고 우리가 단어를 가지고 있는 것들만 인식할 수 있다면, 아즈텍 사람들은 눈, 추위, 그리고 얼음을 하나의 같은 현상으로 인식했다.

선지 해석

① 하나의 같은 현상
② 서로 구별되는 것
③ 독특한 특징을 가진 별개의 것들
④ 특정한 신체 기관에 의해 감지되는 어떤 것

지문 어휘

☐ perception 지각, 자각, 통찰력
☐ language 언어
☐ hypothesis 가설, 추정, 추측
☐ linguist 언어학자
☐ classic 전형적인, 대표적인
☐ perceive 감지하다, 인지하다, 인식하다
☐ phenomenon 현상
☐ separate 별개의, 구분된, 분리된, 서로 다른

42
정답 ②

정답 해설

인도의 교육 혁신을 이끄는 Everonn Education의 역할을 소재로 하는 글로, Everonn Education의 설립자 Kisha Padbhan은 인도의 대규모 교육 시스템을 향상시키기 위해 가상 교실과 강의를 활용하는 방법을 제시하며, 이를 통해 교사 부족과 교육 격차를 해소하려는 노력하고 있음을 진술하고 있다. 빈칸은 앞 문장에 제시한 'Everonn의 해결책'이 나와야 하며, 8번째 문장부터는 그 해결책으로 제시된 사례들을 진술하고 있다. 따라서 밑줄 친 부분에 들어갈 말로 가장 적절한 것은 ②이다.

지문 해석

Mumbai시에 있는 Everonn Education의 설립자인 Kisha Padbhan는 그의 사업을 국가 건설로 본다. 인도의 2억 3천만 명(유치원부터 대학까지)의 학생 연령 인구는 세계에서 가장 큰 규모 중 하나이다. 정부는 8백 3십억 달러를 교육에 쓰지만, 심각한 격차가 존재한다. "교사와 교사 교육 기관이 충분하지 않다"라고 Kisha는 말한다. "인도 외딴 지역의 아이들에게 부족한 것은 좋은 교사와 양질의 내용에 대한 노출이다." Everonn의 해결책은 무엇인가? 가상 교실을 통해 그 격차를 메우기 위해 이 회사는 양방향 비디오와 오디오를 활용한 위성 네트워크를 사용한다. 이것은 인도 28개 주 중 24개 주의 1800개 대학과 7800개 학교에 연결된다. 또한 이것은 디지털화된 수업부터 장차 엔지니어가 되기 위한 입학 시험 준비과정에 이르기까지 모든 것을 제공하고 구직자를 위한 훈련 과정도 있다.

선지 해석

① 교사 교육 시설의 질을 향상시키기 위해
② 가상교실을 통해 그 격차를 메우기 위해
③ 학생들을 디지털 기술에 익숙하게 하기 위해
④ 자질을 갖춘 교육자를 전국에 배치하기 위해

지문 어휘

☐ founder 창립자, 설립자
☐ kindergarten 유치원
☐ instruction 교육, 가르침, 명령, 지시
☐ institute 기관, 단체, 협회
☐ access 접근, 접근하다
☐ exposure 노출, 경험
☐ content 내용
☐ satellite 위성
☐ entrance 입장, 등장
☐ prep 예습, 준비
☐ aspiring 장차 ~가 되려는, 포부가 있는
☐ job-seeker 구직자
☐ familiarize 익숙하게 하다
☐ two-way 양방향의

43
정답 ①

정답 해설

과학과 기술의 발전에서 나타나는 지배력과 강제성에 대한 글로, 과학과 기술의 발전으로 인해 현대 사회에서 인간을 지배하고 강제하는 현상에 대해 설명하고 있다. 이 글은 세부적인 사항을 열거한 다음 주제문을 의문문과 그것에 대한 답변으로 제시하고 있다. 문제점의 원인을 '목적과 목표가 없고, 인간을 비인간화 시키는 것'으로 보고 있다. 따라서 밑줄 친 부분에 들어갈 말로 가장 적절한 것은 ①이다.

지문 해석

우리의 시대에 자신의 생명력을 가지고 사람들을 지배하는 것은 시장 법칙뿐만 아니라 과학과 기술의 발전 또한 그러하다. 수많은 이유들 때문에, 과학의 문제들과 조직은 오늘날 그러해서 과학자는 그의 문제를 선택하지 않다; 문제들이 그 과학자들을 강제한다. 그는 하나의 문제를 풀고, 그 결과는 그가 더 안전하고 확신하는 것이 아니라, 열 개의 다른 새로운 문제들이 하나의 문제가 있었던 곳에 열려 있다. 그 문제들은 과학자가 그것들을 해결하게 강제한다; 그는 지금까지 보다 더 빠른 속도로 앞서 나가야 한다. 산업의 기술에게도 마찬가지이다. 과학의 속도는 기술의 속도를 강제한다. 이론 물리학은 우리에게 원자 에너지를 강제하고, 원자 폭탄의 성공적인 생산은 우리에게 수소 폭탄의 제조를 강제한다. 우리는 우리의 문제들을 선택하지 않고, 우리는 우리의 제품들을 선택하지 않는다; 우리는 강제 된다 — 무엇에 의해서 일까? 그것을 초월하는 목적과 목표가 없고, 인간을 그것의 부속물로 만드는 시스템에 의해서다.

선지 해석

① 인간을 그것의 부속물로 만드는
② 안전성의 잘못된 인식을 만드는
③ 창의적인 도전들로 사람에게 영감을 주는
④ 과학자들이 시장법을 통제하도록 권한을 부여하는

지문 어휘

☐ rule over 지배하다
☐ fission bomb 원자 폭탄
☐ manufacture 제조, 생산, 제조하다
☐ hydrogen bomb 수소 폭탄
☐ transcend 초월하다, 능가하다
☐ appendix 부속물, 부록
☐ empower 권한을 부여하다
☐ secure 안전한, 확고한

44
정답 ④

정답 해설

성공한 사람들의 비밀인 집중의 힘에 대한 글로, 성공한 사람들이 하나에 집중하고 우선 순위를 설정하여 내적 질서로 이끌어내야함을 강조하고 있다. 빈칸에는 우선 순위를 의미하는 표현이 나와야 한다. 따라서 밑줄 친 부분에 들어갈 말로 가장 적절한 것은 ④이다.

지문 해석

성공한 사람들의 비밀은 보통 그들이 한 가지 일에 완전히 집중할 수 있다는 것이다. 비록 그들의 머릿속에 많은 것이 있다 하더라도, 그들은 많은 약속들이 서로를 방해하지 않고, 대신 좋은 내적 순서로 이끌어내는 방법을 발견했다. 그리고 이 순서는 꽤 간단하다: 가장 중요한 일이 먼저다. 이론적으로, 그것은 꽤 명확해 보이지만, 일상생활에서

그것은 오히려 다르게 보인다. 당신은 우선순위를 결정하려고 노력했을지 모르지만, 매일의 사소한 문제들과 예측하지 못한 모든 방해들 때문에 실패했다. 예를 들어, 다른 사무실로 도망치고, 어떠한 방해도 받지 않도록 함으로써, 방해를 분리하라. 당신이 우선순위의 한 가지 일에 집중할 때, 당신은 당신이 가지고 있었는지도 몰랐던 에너지를 가지고 있다는 것을 발견할 것이다.

선지 해석
① 빠를수록 더 좋다
② 전혀 하지 않는 것보다 늦은 것이 더 낫다
③ 눈에서 멀어지면, 마음에서 멀어진다
④ 가장 중요한 일이 먼저다

지문 어휘
☐ concentrate 집중하다, 전념하다
☐ commitment 약속, 전념, 헌신, 책무
☐ impede 방해하다, 지연시키다
☐ priority 우선순위
☐ trivial 사소한, 하찮은
☐ unforeseen 예측하지 못한, 뜻밖의
☐ distraction 방해, 주의 산만
☐ disturbance 방해, 소란, 장애
☐ escape 도망하다, 달아나다
☐ get in the way 방해되다

45

정답 ②

정답 해설
광고 성공의 보이지 않는 부분에 대한 글로, 광고의 성공에 있어 시각적인 표면 뒤의 숨겨진 요소 사이의 관계를 강조하는 글이다. 2번째 문장에서 '당신이 볼 수 없는 부분이 당신이 볼 수 있는 부분보다 광고의 성공과 더 관련이 있다'의 진술을 통해서 빈칸은 겉으로 드러나지 않는 부분을 의미하는 표현이 나와야 한다. 따라서 빈칸에 들어갈 말로 가장 적절한 것은 ②이다.

지문 해석
훌륭한 광고는 멋진 것이다; 그래서 당신이 광고를 좋아하는 것이다. 하지만 당신이 보고 있는 것은 거기에 있는 것의 절반에 불과하고, 당신이 볼 수 없는 부분은 당신이 볼 수 있는 부분보다 그 광고의 성공과 더 많은 관련이 있다. 표면의 특징들(멋진 표제, 시각적인 것, 줄거리, 등장인물들, 해설 소리 또는 무엇이든)이 놀라운 효과를 발휘하기 전에, 광고는 중요한 할 말이 있어야 한다. 그것은 실제 소비자 동기나 실제 소비자 문제를 다루거나, 아무에게도 말하지 않는다. 그렇다면, 훌륭한 광고를 만들기 위해서는 광고가 시작하는 곳에서 시작해야 한다: 보이지 않는 부분에서 말이다.

선지 해석
① 효과적인 도구
② 보이지 않는 부분
③ 기업의 요구 사항들
④ 표면의 특징들

지문 어휘
☐ advertising 광고
☐ surface 표면, 겉, 표면의, 피상적인
☐ feature 특징, 특성
☐ headline 표제, 주요 제목
☐ visual 시각적인
☐ voiceover (TV따위의 화면 밖의) 해설 소리
☐ matter 문제, 상황, 중요하다, 문제되다
☐ address 다루다, 연설하다
☐ consumer 소비자
☐ motive 동기, 이유
☐ invisible 보이지 않는, 무형의
☐ corporate 기업의, 회사의

46

정답 ①

정답 해설
눈과 귀의 정보 수집과 정보 처리의 차이를 주제로 하는 글로, 눈과 귀의 상대적인 복잡성과 신경 크기를 통해 정보 전달의 효율성을 서로 비교하고 있다.
(A) 4번째 문장에서 '시신경은 달팽이관 신경보다 약 18배 많다'는 진술을 통해서, '눈과 귀를 뇌의 중심에 연결하는 신경들의 크기'를 '추가하는(adding)' 것보다는 '비교하는(comparing)' 것이 가장 적절하다.
(B) '눈이 귀보다 정보를 무엇하는데 수천 배 더 효율적이다'라는 진술을 통해서, 눈으로 수집하는 정보의 양에 대한 글이므로 '모으다 (sweeping up)'가 가장 적절하다.

지문 해석
눈에 의해 수집된 정보의 양은 귀와는 대조적으로 정확하게 계산되지 않았다. 그러한 계산은 번역 과정을 포함할 뿐만 아니라 과학자들은 무엇이 중요한지에 대한 지식 부족으로 인해 장애를 겪어 왔다. 그러나 두 체계의 상대적 복잡성에 대한 일반적인 개념은 눈과 귀 사이를 연결하는 신경들의 크기를 뇌의 중심과 (A) 비교함으로써 얻을 수 있다. 시신경은 달팽이관 신경보다 약 18배 많은 뉴런을 포함하고 있기 때문에 훨씬 더 많은 정보를 전달한다고 가정한다. 사실, 정상적으로 위험을 알리는 대상들에 있어서, 아마도 정보를 (B) 쓸어 모으는 데 있어 눈이 귀의 수천 배 더 효율적일 지도 모른다.

선지 해석
　　　(A)　　　　　　(B)
① 비교하는 …… 쓸어 모으는 데
② 비교하는 …… 줄이는 데
③ 추가하는 …… 전파하는 데
④ 추가하는 …… 정리하는 데

지문 어휘
☐ contrast with ~와 대조를 이루다
☐ precisely 정확하게, 신중하게
☐ calculate 계산하다, 산출하다
☐ translation 번역
☐ handicap 장애, 불리한 조건
☐ count 중요하다, 세다
☐ notion 개념, 생각
☐ complexity 복잡성
☐ optic nerve 시신경
☐ roughly 대략, 거의
☐ assume 가정하다, 추측하다
☐ transmit 전송하다, 보내다
☐ alert 기민한, 경계하는, (위험 등을)알리다

- sweep up 쓸다, 쓸어 담다
- disseminate 퍼뜨리다, 전파하다

47

정답 ②

정답 해설

빈곤선 근처에 있는 사람들이 왜 동료들을 더 도와주는지에 대한 이유를 설명하는 글이다. 첫 번째 문장(의문문)의 대답으로 가난한 사람들이 그들의 동료들을 더 잘 도와주는 경향이 있는 이유로 적절한 것을 선택해야 한다. 따라서 빈칸은 '고통이 있는 사람이 그 고통을 더 잘 알기에 고통이 있는 사람에 공감을 느끼고 도와주고 더 주의를 기울인다'는 진술로 이어져야 한다. 따라서 밑줄 친 부분에 들어갈 말로 가장 적절한 것은 ②이다.

지문 해석

왜 빈곤선 근처에 맴도는 사람들이(가난에 가까운 사람들이) 동료들을 더 도와줄 가능성이 높은가? Keltner는 부분적으로는 가난한 사람들의 경우 힘든 시기들을 견뎌내기 위해 자주 함께 뭉쳐야만 한다고 생각한다 — 이것은 아마 그들을 좀 더 사회적으로 기민하게 만드는 과정이다. 그는 "만약 여러분이 불확실성에 직면한다면, 그것이 여러분으로 하여금 좀 더 다른 사람에게 적응시키도록 만들어 준다. 당신은 이와 같은 강력한 사회적 관계망을 형성하게 될 것이다"라고 말한다. 예를 들어, 만약 가난한 젊은 엄마에게 갓 태어난 아기가 있다면 그녀는 음식과 생필품, 그리고 육아를 확보하기 위한 도움이 필요할 수도 있을 것이고, 만약 그녀가 건강한 사회생활을 하고 있다면 그녀의 공동체 멤버들은 협력할 것이다. 그러나 제한된 수입은 이러한 공감과 사회적 반응성을 개발하는데 있어 거의 필수적인 조건은 아니다. 우리의 은행 계좌의 크기(잔액)와는 상관없이, 우리 자신의 고통이 다른 사람들의 필요에 더 주의를 기울이도록 강제하고 우리가 잘 알고 있는 그런 고통에 빠진 사람을 보고 개입할 때, 고통은 이타주의 혹은 영웅주의에 전달자가 된다.

선지 해설

① 더 무관심하도록
② 더 주의를 기울이도록
③ 덜 사로잡혀 있도록
④ 덜 관련되도록

지문 어휘

- hover 맴돌다
- poverty line 빈곤선(최저한도의 생활을 유지하는 데 필요한 수입 수준)
- band together 함께 뭉치다, 무리를 이루다
- tough 힘든, 어려운
- astute 교활한, 약삭빠른
- uncertainty 불확실성
- orient to ~에 적응시키다
- secure 안심하는, 안전한, 획득하다, 확보하다
- pitch in 협력하다
- prerequisite 전제 조건
- empathy 감정이입, 공감
- regardless of ~에 상관없이
- conduit 전달자
- altruism 이타주의, 이타심
- intervene 개입하다, 끼어들다
- in the clutches 괴로운 상황에, 위기에 처해서

48

정답 ④

정답 해설

상하이 Soleil 백화점 아웃렛의 독특한 시도에 대한 글로, 상하이의 Soleil 백화점 아웃렛이 고객 유치를 위한 창의적인 방법으로 대담한 미끄럼틀 도입을 시도하며, 오프라인 쇼핑의 어려움을 극복하고자 함을 설명하고 있다. 따라서 빈칸에는 이 글의 주제인 창의적인 방법의 하나의 사례인 5층의 미끄럼틀의 내용이 반드시 들어가야 한다. 따라서 밑줄 친 부분에 들어갈 말로 가장 적절한 것은 ④이다.

지문 해석

상하이에 있는 Soleil 백화점 아웃렛은 고급 브랜드와 독점적인 위치 등 현대식 중국 소매업계에서 성공하기 위해 필요한 모든 편의 시설을 갖추고 있는 것으로 보인다. 그러나 이러한 장점에도 불구하고 매장 관리자들은 고객 유치를 위한 뭔가가 여전히 놓치고 생각했다. 그래서 다음 주에 그들은 쇼핑객들이 5층 럭셔리 부티크에서 1층 럭셔리 부티크까지 아슬아슬한 속도로 타고 내려올 수 있는 엄청나게 크고, 비틀린, 용 모양의 미끄럼틀을 발표한다. 소셜 미디어 사용자들은 농담 반 진담 반으로 그 미끄럼틀이 누군가를 죽이지 않을지 궁금해 한다. 그러나 Soleil은 중국 쇼핑몰이 완전히 사라질 우려가 있다는 다른 걱정을 하고 있다. 한때 겉보기에는 끝없는 공급을 이루어 오던 중국 구매자는 온라인 쇼핑이 증가함에 따라 더 이상 오프라인 매장에 나타나고 있지 않으며, 여전히 고급 상품들을 사러 해외로 나가고 있다. 따라서 그들의 시간과 돈을 쓰는 다른 방식을 가진 고객들을 위해 이 거대한 공간을 다른 목적으로 사용하도록 하는 것은 많은 창의성이 필요할 것이다. 5층짜리 용 미끄럼틀이 나쁜 시작은 아닐지도 모른다.

선지 해설

① 명품 브랜드들이 Soleil에서 번창하고 있다
② Soleil는 대담한 조치에 반대하기로 결정했다
③ 온라인 고객 기반을 증가하는 것이 마지막 희망일지도 모른다
④ 5층짜리 용 미끄럼틀이 나쁜 시작은 아닐지도 모른다

지문 어휘

- amenity 생활 편의 시설
- retail 소매, 유통, 소매하다
- exclusive 독점적인, 배타적인
- attract 끌어들이다
- unveil 덮개를 벗기다, 발표하다
- death-defying 아슬아슬한, 죽음에 도전하는
- half-jokingly 농담 반 진담 반으로
- concern 우려, 걱정
- seemingly 겉보기에는, 외견상으로
- turn up 나타나다
- brick-and-mortar 소매의, 오프라인 거래의
- repurpose 다른 목적에 맞게 만들다
- massive 거대한, 엄청나게 큰
- thrive 번창하다, 성장하다
- bold 대담한, 용감한

49

정답 ①

정답 해설

이 글은 미래에 대한 다양한 시나리오를 만드는 것의 중요성과 예측의 어려움을 강조하며, 불확실한 미래에 대비하기 위해 합리적인 시나리오를 고려하는 중요성을 다루고 있다. 이 미래 계획에 대한 의견은 빈칸 다음에 나오는데, 그 내용으로 'the 비교급' 구문으로 '우리가 이러한 문제들을 예측하려 노력하면 노력할수록, 우리는 그것들을 더 잘 통제할 수 있다'라는 진술을 통해, 미래 계획의 필요성에 대해서 이야기를 하고 있다. 따라서 밑줄 친 부분에 들어갈 말로 가장 적절한 것은 ①이다.

지문 해석

미래발전에 대한 많은 가능한 시나리오들을 만드는 것은 쉽고, 각각의 시나리오는 외관상 동일하게 가능성이 있다. 어려운 일은 실제로 어떤 일이 발생할 것인지를 아는 것이다. 시간이 지나고 나서 보니까, 이것은 보통 명백하게 보인다. 시간이 지남에 따라 우리가 과거를 돌아볼 때, 각 사건은 명확하며 논리적으로 선행 사건으로부터 뒤따라 나온 것으로 보인다. 그러나 사건이 일어나기 전에 가능성의 수는 끝이 없는 것처럼 보인다. 특히 복잡한 사회 및 기술 변화를 포함하는 분야에서 성공적인 예측을 위한 방법은 없으며, 많은 결정 요인이 알려지지 않았으며, 어떤 경우에도 확실히 단일 그룹의 통제 하에 있지 않다. 그럼에도 불구하고 미래를 위한 합리적인 시나리오를 만드는 것이 중요하다. 우리는 새로운 기술들이 이익들과 문제들 둘 다 가져올 것이라는 것을 알고 있고, 특별히 인간적이고 사회적인 문제들에서 그러하다. 더 많이 우리가 이러한 문제들을 예측하려 노력하면 노력할수록, 우리는 그것들을 더 잘 통제할 수 있다.

선지 해석

① 미래를 위한 합리적인 시나리오를 만드는
② 미래의 변화로 인해 가능한 이익 배당금을 정당화하는
③ 기술적 문제의 다양한 측면을 빠뜨리는
④ 현재에 초점을 맞추는 것이 어떤 것인지를 고려해보는

지문 어휘

- devise 고안하다, 마련하다
- numerous 수많은, 다양한
- task 과제, 임무
- take place 발생하다
- in hindsight 지나고 나서 보니까
- prediction 예측, 예견
- involve 수반하다, 포함하다, 관련시키다
- dividend 이익, 배당금
- anticipate 기대하다, 예상하다
- legitimize 정당화하다, 합법화하다
- leave out 생략하다, 빼다, 무시하다

50

정답 ③

정답 해설

확증편향과 이것이 결정에 미치는 영향을 주제로 하는 글로, 확증편향으로부터 결정을 보호하고 상상력 약한 부분과 새로운 정보에 대한 질문의 중요성을 이해하는 것이 필요함을 강조하고 있다. 확증편향이라는 문제를 해결을 어떻게 하는지에 대한 해결책이 빈칸에 들어가야 한다. 따라서 밑줄 친 부분에 들어갈 말로 가장 적절한 것은 ③이다.

지문 해석

우리의 마음이 하는 속임수들 중 하나는 우리가 이미 믿고 있는 것들을 확인하는 증거들을 강조하는 것이다. 만약 우리가 경쟁자에 대한 소문을 듣는다면, 우리는 "그 녀석이 형편없는 사람인줄 알고 있었어"라고 생각하는 경향이 있다. 우리가 제일 친한 친구에 관한 똑같은 소문을 듣는다면 우리는 "그건 단지 뜬소문이야"라고 말할 가능성이 높다. 일단 당신이 이러한 마음의 습관—확증 편향이라 불리는—을 알게 되면 당신은 이것을 여러 곳에서 목격하기 시작할 것이다. 이것은 우리가 좀 더 훌륭한 결정을 내리기를 원할 때 중요하다. 우리가 생각하는 바가 맞는 한 확증 편향은 문제가 없다. 그러나 너무 자주 우리는 틀리며, 너무 늦게야 결정을 내려주는 증거들에 주목하게 된다. 어떻게 우리가 확증 편향으로부터 우리의 결정을 보호할지는 어떤 이유에서 확증 편향이 심리적으로 발생하는지를 인지하는 것에 달려있다. 이에는 두 개의 가능성 있는 이유가 있다. 하나는 우리는 맹점을 가지고 있으며, 또 다른 하나는 우리가 새로운 정보에 대해 질문하는 것에 실패한다는 점이다.

선지 해석

① 우리의 경쟁자들이 우리를 믿게 만드는지
② 우리의 맹점이 우리로 하여금 더 나은 결정을 하도록 도와주는지
③ 우리가 확증 편향으로부터 우리의 결정들을 보호할지
④ 우리는 정확히 같은 편견을 형성하는지

지문 어휘

- trick 속임수, 장난
- highlight 강조하다
- evidence 증거
- confirm 확인해주다, 확정하다
- gossip 풍문, 소문
- nasty 끔찍한, 형편없는, 못된
- confirmation bias 확증 편향
- psychologically 심리적으로, 정신적으로
- blind spot 맹점, 약점

51

정답 ②

정답 해설

소비재 기업의 글로벌 전략과 도전에 대한 글로, 도전에 대한 해결책으로 수출 혹은 현지생산을 제시하고 있다. 빈칸에는 Sweets Co.가 겪는 문제에 대한 원인이 들어가야 한다. 글의 주제가 외국에서 생산과 판매(수출)하는 것이다. 스위스 회사가 성장하지 못한 이유는 외국에서 생산을 하지 않을 뿐만 아니라 수출도 하지 않기 때문이다. 따라서 밑줄 친 부분에 들어갈 말로 가장 적절한 것은 ②이다.

지문 해석

소비재 제품 브랜드에서의 큰 회사들에게 있어, 외국으로 수출하는 것과 지역 노동력과 함께 지역의 취향을 목적으로 외국에서 생산하는 것은 해야 할 올바른 것이다. 그렇게 하는데 있어서, 기업들은 그들의 비용구조를 향상시키면서 신흥 국가들에의 빠르게 확장되는 소비자 시장에 있어 성장할 수 있는 방법을 찾았다. 그러나 Sweets Co.는 국내 시장에 머물러 있다. 회사의 제품들이 방부제들로 충분히 있어서 먼 시장으로의 긴 여행을 견딜 수 있다는 것을 의미하지만, Sweets Co. 회사는 해외에서의 생산은 말할 것도 없이 수출을 거의 하지 않는다. 변화하는 세계를 목표로 하는 사업전략과 제품들을 업데이트하지 않는 꺼림과 무능력은 그 회사에게 분명히 타격을 주고 있다.

선지 해석

① 수입에 열중한다
② 수출을 거의 하지 않는다
③ 운영을 능률화하기로 결정하고 있다
④ 신흥 시장으로 확장하고 있는 중이다

지문 어휘

☐ be loaded with 충분히 있다
☐ preservative 방부제
☐ endure 견디다
☐ let alone 말할 것도 없이, ~은 커녕
☐ unwillingness 본의 아님, 자발적이 아님
☐ inability 무능, 불능
☐ import 수입, 수입하다
☐ export 수출, 수출하다
☐ streamline 간소화하다, 능률화하다

52

정답 ③

정답 해설

택시 운전기사들의 지식과 숙련도에 관한 연구를 주제로 하는 글로, 한 연구는 런던의 택시 운전기사들이 특별한 훈련을 통해 쌓은 지식과 숙련도가 새로운 길을 찾아내는 능력에 어떤 영향을 미치는지를 설명하고 있다. 연구의 실험결과로 택시 운전기사들이 새롭고 알지 못하는 환경에서도 잘 해 낸다고 진술하고 있다. 따라서 밑줄 친 부분에 들어갈 말로 가장 적절한 것은 ③이다.

지문 해석

런던의 택시 운전기사들은 자신들의 운행 허가를 얻기 위해 그 도시의 이만오천개가 넘는 길에 대한 배치도를 배우는 것을 포함하여 "지식"으로 알려진 강렬한 훈련을 몇 년간 받아야 할 의무를 진다. 한 연구자와 그녀의 팀은 택시 운전기사들과 일반인을 조사했다. 이 두 그룹은 아일랜드의 어떤 마을을 통과하는 그들에게 익숙하지 않은 길들의 비디오를 보도록 요청되었다. 그리고 나서 그들은 길을 그려내고, 주요 지형지물을 구별하고, 장소 사이의 거리를 추정하는 것이 포함된 테스트를 받도록 요청받았다. 이 두 그룹은 테스트의 대부분에서 잘 했으나, 택시 운전기사들은 새로운 길을 찾아내는 데 있어서는 상당히 더 잘 했다. 이 결과는 택시 운전기사들의 숙련도가 새롭고 알지 못하는 지역에도 일반화되는 것을 보여준다. 그들의 의도된 연습을 통한 수년 간의 훈련과 학습이 그들이 유사한 도전들을 심지어 그들이 잘 알지 못하거나 전혀 알지 못하는 장소에서 조차 잘 수행할 수 있도록 준비시킨다.

선지 해석

① 한정되는
② 헌신하는
③ 일반화되는
④ 공헌하는

지문 어휘

☐ undertake 착수하다, 떠맡다, ~할 의무를 지다
☐ intense 강렬한
☐ operating license 운행 허가
☐ route 길, 경로
☐ layout 배치
☐ investigate 조사하다
☐ landmark 주요 지형지물
☐ mastery 숙련도
☐ deliberate 의도적인, 고의의, 사려 깊은

08 빈칸 추론 유형 기출 독해 어휘 복습 TEST 정답

1	involve	포함하다, 관련시키다	21	elderly	노인, 어르신들, 나이가 지긋한
2	perceived	인식된, 인지된	22	inattention	부주의, 태만, 무관심
3	vigilant	주의를 기울이는, 경계하는	23	comprehend	이해하다, 파악하다, 포함하다, 의미하다
4	reflect	깊이 생각하다, 심사숙고하다	24	persuasion	설득, 강요
5	innate	선천적인, 타고난	25	devote	헌신하다, 전념하다
6	eclipse	가리다, 어둡게 하다	26	settle down	안정을 찾다, 정착하다
7	fall short	부족하다, 모자라다	27	mortgage	대출(금), 융자(금), 저당 잡히다
8	escape	피하다, 달아나다	28	existing	기존의, 현재 사용되는
9	ordinary	일반적인, 보통의, 평범한	29	paradoxical	역설적인
10	wonder	궁금해하다	30	standardization	표준화, 규격화, 통일, 획일
11	unemployment	실업(률)	31	roll out	출시하다, 시작하다, 밀어서 펴다
12	income	소득, 수입	32	uniform	획일적인, 균일한
13	substitute	대체하다, 대신하다, 대체물, 대리자	33	disparate	서로 전혀 다른, 이질적인
14	predominant	주요한, 우세한, 지배적인, 두드러진, 뚜렷한	34	empirical	경험에 의거한, 실증적인
15	inevitably	필연적으로, 불가피하게	35	distraction	주의 산만, 방해
16	disastrous	처참한, 재앙의, 불길한	36	persist	지속되다, 집요하게 계속 하다
17	project	예상하다, 추정하다, 계획하다, 계획, 과제	37	immerse	담그다, 몰두하다, 몰두하게 만들다
18	population	인구, 주민	38	buffer	완화하다, 보호하다, 완충제
19	aging	고령화, 노령화, 노화	39	break off	분리되다, 떨어지다
20	demographic	인구 통계학적인, 인구학의, 인구의	40	massive	거대한, 심각한

41	plain	평범한, 보통의, 평원, 평지	61	coherent	일관성 있는, 논리 정연한
42	misperception	오해	62	sequence	순서, 차례
43	interpretation	해석, 이해, 설명	63	outline	개요를 제시하다, 윤곽을 보여주다
44	throw away	버리다, 없애다	64	intuition	직감, 직관
45	budget	예산, 비용	65	conscientious	양심적인, 성실한
46	hand down	~을 물려주다	66	setback	방해, 차질
47	prerequisite	전제 조건	67	underpin	뒷받침하다, 근거를 대다
48	unoccupied	비어있는, 점령되지 않은	68	plummet	급락하다, 곤두박질치다
49	determine	결정하다, 알아내다, 밝히다	69	hypothesis	가설, 추정, 추측
50	decay	부패, 부식, 부패하다, 썩다	70	entrance	입장, 등장
51	measure	측정하다, 재다	71	manufacture	제조, 생산, 제조하다
52	approximate	대략적인, 근사치인	72	transcend	초월하다, 능가하다
53	extinct	멸종된, 사라진	73	impede	방해하다, 지연시키다
54	concrete	구체적인, 사실에 의거한	74	trivial	사소한, 하찮은
55	subject to	영향을 받기 쉬운	75	alert	기민한, 경계하는, (위험 등을) 알리다
56	keen	치열한, 열렬한, 예리한	76	astute	교활한, 약삭빠른
57	modify	수정하다, 변경하다	77	altruism	이타주의, 이타심
58	subconscious	잠재의식적인, 무의식적인	78	legitimize	정당화하다, 합법화하다
59	odds	가능성, 역경, 곤란	79	nasty	끔찍한, 형편없는, 못된
60	bother	신경 쓰다, 귀찮게 하다	80	streamline	간소화하다, 능률화하다

진가영 영어

New Trend 단기합격 길라잡이

기본서

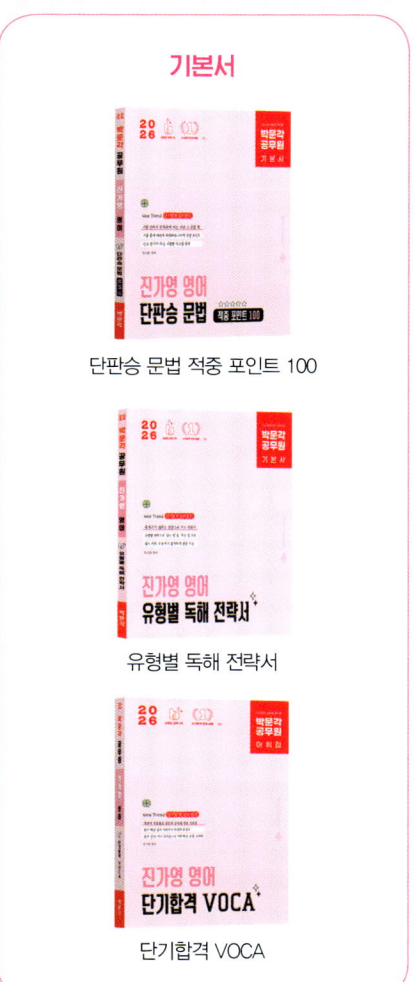

단판승 문법 적중 포인트 100

유형별 독해 전략서

단기합격 VOCA

기출문제집

반한다 기출

진가영 영어 정답 및 해설
반드시 한번에 다 잡는다 기출

 박문각 공무원
진가영 영어 온라인강의
www.pmg.co.kr

 박문각 북스파
박문각 공식
온라인 서점

 박문각 공무원
진가영 영어 연구소
cafe.naver.com/easyenglish7

 박문각 공무원
진가영 영어
오픈채팅방

2025년 국가직 9급 일반행정 합격 수강생 김**

교재와 커리 구성만으로도 탄탄하게 이루어져 있지만 마지막으로 가영쌤만의 장점! 왜 가영쌤이어야 했는지, 그 이유를 꼽자면 바로 진심을 다해 수강생을 도와주시려고 한다는 점입니다! 저의 경우에는 처음 공시를 시작했을 때 어려움을 겪었던 문법 파트와, 공부 기간이 늘어남에도 불구하고 마땅한 해결책을 찾구 못해 힘들어했던 독해 순서 맞추기 유형과 문장 삽입 유형에 대한 고민이 깊을 때마다 가영쌤께 찾아가서 질문을 드리고 도움을 요청하였습니다. 그럴 때마다 항상 진심을 다해 도와주려 하시고, 구체적으로 어떻게 문제인지 정확하게 진단해 주시면서 명확한 솔루션을 주신 덕에 단점을 보완하고 무려 100점이라는 성적으로 합격할 수 있었습니다~!! 항상 너무 감사드립니다 교수님~!!~!!
Thank you for everything you've done for me!!

2025년 국가직 9급 교정직 합격 수강생 한**

제가 공시하러 처음 왔을 때 2024년 4월 월간 모의고사 영어점수가 30점이었어요. 그러다 5월부터 수업을 들어가기 시작했는데 그때 임신 중인 선생님께서 저희를 위해 일요일에도 보강하시는 모습 보고 저는 이 선생님 밑에서 최고득점하고 싶은 마음이 들었습니다. 선생님 커리큘럼 상담 모든 게 다 반영돼서 95점이 나온 거 같아요. 인생에 목표가 있어 행복한 시간이었고 좋은 친구 옆에서 공부한 거에 감사하고 최고의 선생님의 가르침을 받아서 인생에서 가장 기억에 남을 순간일 것 같습니다. 앞으로 저는 더 많은 걸 도전할 거 같아요. 저는 꺾이지 않고 계속 노력하는 선생님이 너무 좋았습니다. 가끔 올라가서 인사 올리겠습니다. 존경하는 선생님.

2025년 검찰직 합격 수강생 대**

2024년 1월부터 박문각 인강으로 공부해서 1년 3개월 동안 공부했고 검찰직 합격했습니다. 인강 들으면서 전화 상담까지 해주셨던 교수님은 진가영 교수님뿐이셔서, 게다가 영어가 심리적으로 오랫동안 힘든 과목이었기 때문에 감사한 마음뿐입니다. 워낙 영어가 취약 과목이었고 꽤 오랫동안 독해 때문에 힘든 시간을 보냈지만 임신, 출산하시면서도 강의에 영향 없이 최선을 다해 주시는 모습에 감동을 받았고 그만큼 교수님께서 이 일을 얼마나 소중히 하고 계시는지 느껴졌습니다. 교수님이 안보이는 곳에서 얼마나 노력하고 계시는지 너무 잘 알 것 같아서 그저 리스펙이라고 밖에는 표현할 길이 없습니다. 마지막 문법 특강 끝에 기도하시듯 손 모으고 말씀하시는 모습에 뭉클했고 나는 교수님처럼 내 일에 최선을 다한 적이 있었는지 스스로 반성도 하게 되었습니다. 간절한 시간을 보낸 만큼 앞으로 최선을 다해서 공직 생활하도록 하겠습니다.

2025년 국가직 9급 우정직 합격 수강생 경**

제가 생각하는 가영쌤만의 장점은 첫째로, 미친 반복입니다. 공부가 하기 싫어도, 저절로 하게 되고, 강의를 듣지 않아도 떠오르는 경지가 될 때까지 정말 열심히 가르쳐주십니다. 동형 문제를 풀 때 알아서 개념이 뽑아져 나올 정도로 들었고, 단어강의는 최소 20회독을 했을 정도로 많이 복습하니 이젠 툭 치면 알아서 가영쌤이 가르쳐주신 내용이 나옵니다. 둘째로, 가영쌤의 친절하고 꼼꼼한 학생관리입니다. 현강에서는 학생들 하나하나 잘 챙겨주시고, 질문은 시간이 오래 걸려도 자세하게 받아주시며, 상담 신청했을 때 누구보다 열정적인 자세로 상담을 받아주십니다. 카페에서도 학생들 질문을 잘 받아주시기도 하니, 현강생 뿐 아니라 인강생도 가영쌤의 정성을 느끼실 수 있습니다. 셋째로, 자신의 실력을 점검하고 보완할 수 있는 다양한 커리큘럼입니다. 구문이 부족하면 구문 강의로, 문법이 부족하면 단판승으로, 독해가 부족하면 독해 끝판왕으로, 신경향이 낯설면 신경향 독해 마스터로 보완할 수 있도록 세분화되어 있습니다. 꼭 모든 강의를 강제로 들을 필요는 없지만, 부족한 부분이 있다면 발췌하시는 것도 좋은 선택입니다.

 2024 고객선호브랜드지수 1위
교육(교육서비스)부문

 2023 고객선호브랜드지수 1위
교육(교육서비스)부문

 2022 한국 브랜드 만족지수 1위
교육(교육서비스)부문 1위

 2021 조선일보 국가브랜드 대상
에듀테크 부문 수상

 2021 대한민국 소비자 선호도 1위
교육부문 1위

 2020 한국 산업의 1등
브랜드 대상 수상

 2019 한국 우수브랜드
평가대상 수상

 2018 대한민국 교육산업 대상
교육서비스 부문 수상

2년 연속 수석 합격자 배출 2023~2024년 박문각 공무원 온/오프 수강생 기준

정가 32,000원

ISBN 979-11-7519-114-3

박문각 www.pmg.co.kr   교재문의 02-6466-7202   동영상강의 문의 02-6466-7201

데일리 학습 [루틴 형성]

단기합격 VOCA

- 객관적 적중률로 검증된 공무원 전용 어휘 학습
- 필수어휘·핵심어휘·실무어휘까지 한번에 총정리!

굿모닝 '기출 문장' 구문독해

- 양질의 기출 문장으로 꾸준한 30분 트레이닝
- 독해를 감이 아닌 구조로 읽어, 빠르고 정확한 해석 실력 완성!

진가영 영어

매일합격[일일] 모의고사

- 하루 10문제로 가볍게 시작하는 영어 루틴
- 영어가 익숙해지고 실력이 쌓이는 가장 확실한 방법!

올타임 레전드 하프 모의고사

- 수업 시간에 배운 핵심 개념들을 문제로 복습
- 중간 실력 점검으로 부족한 부분을 파악하고 보완!

가영쌤과 점수 수직 상승을 만들어 낸 "생생한" 후기

★★★★★ 2025년 국가직 9급 일반행정 합격   김**

교재와 커리 구성만으로도 탄탄하게 이루어져 있지만 마지막으로 가영쌤만의 장점! 왜 가영쌤이어야 했는지, 그 이유를 꼽자면 바로 진심을 다해 수강생을 도와주시려고 한다는 점입니다! 저의 경우에는 처음 공시를 시작했을 때 어려움을 겪었던 문법 파트와, 공부 기간이 늘어남에도 불구하고 마땅한 해결책을 찾지 못해 힘들어했던 독해 순서 맞추기 유형과 문장 삽입 유형에 대한 고민이 깊을 때마다 가영쌤께 찾아가서 질문을 드리고 도움을 요청하였었습니다. 그럴 때마다 항상 진심을 다해 도와주려 하시고, 구체적으로 어떻게 문제인지 정확하게 진단해 주시면서 명확한 솔루션을 주신 덕에 단점을 보완하고 무려 100점이라는 성적으로 합격할 수 있었습니다~!!! 항상 너무 감사드립니다 교수님~!!~!! Thank you for everything you've done for me!!

★★★★★ 2025년 국가직 9급 교정직 합격   한**

제가 공시하러 처음 왔을 때 2024년 4월 월간 모의고사 영어점수가 30점이었어요. 그러다 5월부터 수업을 들어가기 시작했는데 그때 임신 중인 선생님께서 저희를 위해 일요일에도 보강하시는 모습 보고 저는 이 선생님 밑에서 최고득점하고 싶은 마음이 들었습니다. 선생님 커리큘럼 상담 모든 게 다 반영돼서 95점이 나온 거 같아요. 인생에 목표가 있어 행복한 시간이었고 좋은 친구 옆에서 공부한 거에 감사하고 최고의 선생님의 가르침을 받아서 인생에서 가장 기억에 남을 순간일 것 같습니다. 앞으로 저는 더 많은 걸 도전할 거 같아요. 저는 꺾이지 않고 계속 노력하는 선생님이 너무 좋았습니다. 가끔 올라가서 인사 올리겠습니다. 존경하는 선생님.

★★★★★ 2025년 국가직 9급 우정직 합격   경**

제가 생각하는 가영쌤만의 장점은 첫째로, 미친 반복입니다. 공부가 하기 싫어도, 저절로 하게 되고, 강의를 듣지 않아도 떠오르는 경지가 될 때까지 정말 열심히 가르쳐주십니다. 동형 문제를 풀 때 알아서 개념이 뽑아져 나올 정도로 들었고, 단어강의는 최소 20회독을 했을 정도로 많이 복습하니 이젠 툭 치면 알아서 가영쌤이 가르쳐주신 내용이 나옵니다. 둘째로, 가영쌤의 친절하고 꼼꼼한 학생관리입니다. 현강에서는 학생들 하나하나 잘 챙겨주시고, 질문은 시간이 오래 걸려도 자세하게 받아주시며, 상담 신청했을 때 누구보다도 열정적인 자세로 상담을 받아주십니다. 카페에서도 학생들 질문을 잘 받아주시기도 하니, 현강생 뿐 아니라 인강생도 가영쌤의 정성을 느끼실 수 있습니다. 셋째로, 자신의 실력을 점검하고 보완할 수 있는 다양한 커리큘럼입니다. 구문이 부족하면 구문 강의로, 문법이 부족하면 단판승으로, 독해가 부족하면 독해 끝판왕으로, 신경향이 낯설면 신경향 독해 마스터로 보완할 수 있도록 세분화되어 있습니다. 꼭 모든 강의를 강제로 들을 필요는 없지만, 부족한 부분이 있다면 발췌하시는 것도 좋은 선택입니다.

★★★★★ 2025년 검찰직 합격   대**

2024년 1월부터 박문각 인강으로 공부해서 1년 3개월 동안 공부했고 검찰직 합격했습니다. 인강 들으면서 전화 상담까지 해주셨던 교수님은 진가영 교수님뿐이셔서, 게다가 영어가 심리적으로 오랫동안 힘든 과목이었기 때문에 감사한 마음뿐입니다. 워낙 영어가 취약 과목이었고 꽤 오랫동안 독해 때문에 힘든 시간을 보냈지만 임신, 출산하시면서도 강의에 영향 없이 최선을 다해 주시는 모습에 감동을 받았고 그만큼 교수님께서 이 일을 얼마나 소중히 하고 계시는지 느껴졌습니다. 교수님이 안보이는 곳에서 얼마나 노력하고 계시는지 너무 잘 알 것 같아서 그저 리스펙이라고 밖에는 표현할 길이 없습니다. 마지막 문법 특강 끝에 기도하시듯 손 모으고 말씀하시는 모습에 뭉클했고 나는 교수님처럼 내 일에 최선을 다한 적이 있었는지 스스로 반성도 하게 되었습니다. 간절한 시간을 보낸 만큼 앞으로 최선을 다해서 공직 생활하도록 하겠습니다.